HC4539 .P57 1987

W9-CHB-056

3 204 014 933 600

The Political Economy of Japan

Volume 1

The Political Economy of Japan
is a three-volume work under the
general editorship of Yasusuke
Murakami and Hugh T. Patrick.
Volumes 2 and 3, currently in
preparation, are: Vol. 2, *The
Changing International Context*,
edited by Takashi Inoguchi and
Daniel I. Okimoto; Vol. 3, *Cultural
and Social Dynamics*, edited by
Shumpei Kumon and Henry
Rosovsky.

Edited by Kozo Yamamura and Yasukichi Yasuba

The Political Economy of Japan

Volume 1

The Domestic Transformation

 Stanford University Press, Stanford, California 1987

HC
462.9
.P57
1987
V.1

ADB 7319 - 0/3
Soc 270

Stanford University Press
Stanford, California
© 1987 by the Board of Trustees of the
Leland Stanford Junior University
Printed in the United States of America

Japanese language rights assigned to
the National Institute for Research Advancement
37F Shinjuku Mitsui Building, 2-1-1 Nishi-Shinjuku,
Shinjuku-ku, Tokyo, Japan

CIP data appear at the end of the book

Published with the
assistance of the Japan Foundation

RECEIVED

JAN 2 1 1988

KENNEDY SCHOOL OF
GOVERNMENT LIBRARY

The Japan Political Economy Research Committee
acknowledges with deep appreciation the support
provided by the two core funding institutions for the project,
the National Institute for Research Advancement, Tokyo,
and the East-West Center, Honolulu.

Contents

Tables

Sato: Saving and Investment

Noguchi: Public Finance

Hamada and Horiuchi: Political Economy

Aoki: The Japanese Firm

Koike: Human Resource Development

Figures

Hamada and Horiuchi: Political Economy

Aoki: The Japanese Firm

Koike: Human Resource Development

Okimoto and Saxonhouse: Technology

Uekusa: Industrial Organization

Muramatsu and Krauss: Patterned Pluralism

Contributors

Masahiko Aoki, Professor, Department of Economics, Stanford University

Martin Bronfenbrenner, Professor, Department of Economics, Aoyama Gakuin University

George C. Eads, Vice President and Chief Economist, General Motors Corporation; formerly Dean, School of Public Affairs, University of Maryland, College Park

Koichi Hamada, Professor, Department of Economics, Yale University

Akiyoshi Horiuchi, Professor, Faculty of Economics, University of Tokyo

Kazuo Koike, Professor, Institute of Economics, Kyoto University

Yutaka Kosai, Professor, Tokyo Institute of Technology

Ellis S. Krauss, Professor, Department of Political Science, University of Pittsburgh

Yasusuke Murakami, Professor, Department of Social Sciences, University of Tokyo

Michio Muramatsu, Professor, Faculty of Law, Kyoto University

Yukio Noguchi, Professor, Faculty of Economics, Hitotsubashi University

Daniel I. Okimoto, Associate Professor, Department of Political Science, Stanford University

Hugh T. Patrick, Professor, Graduate School of Business, Columbia University

Thomas P. Rohlen, Professor of Anthropology and the International Strategic Institute at Stanford University

Kazuo Sato, Professor, Department of Economics, Rutgers University

Gary R. Saxonhouse, Professor, Department of Economics, University of Michigan

Masu Uekusa, Professor, Faculty of Economics, University of Tokyo

Kozo Yamamura, Professor, Henry M. Jackson School of International Studies, University of Washington

Yasukichi Yasuba, Professor, Faculty of Economics, Osaka University

The genesis of the three volumes that make up *The Political Economy of Japan* lies in the profound transformation of both Japan and the global political-economic system since World War II. Japan's sustained surge of rapid economic growth has brought it to the forefront of nations. The implications continue to be far-reaching and deep—within Japan in terms of societal and cultural as well as economic and political change, and internationally in terms of the mutual accommodation between the global system and Japan at a time of Japanese resurgence on the one hand and a decline in the capacity of the United States to serve as world leader on the other.

A new era is emerging—for Japan and the world as a whole. Since the early 1970s, Japan's political economy, and the international system as well, have undergone a sea change. In historical perspective—by economic criteria at least, such as living standards, levels of technology, and growth rates—the changes were so great that by 1980 the postwar era could be said to have come to an end. Japan is now in a transition to a new era, the major features of which can only be sensed imperfectly. Yet even with its economic transformation Japan is a remarkably stable democracy and society, seemingly without major political, economic, or social problems. Nor are there ideological or social schisms so pervasive or profound as to threaten that stability. Embedded in Japanese culture are great historical continuities that endure and yet are unusually susceptible to pragmatic adaptation as conditions change. These characteristics are well reflected in the ongoing evolution of economic, political, and social institutions.

The major purpose of these volumes is to evaluate the political economy of Japan as it approaches the 1990s. Explaining where Japan is today requires some explanation of how it arrived at that point; our intention, however, is not a history of the evolution of Japan's postwar political economy. The papers in these volumes are in principle future-oriented —they raise questions about where Japan is going as it approaches the twenty-first century and offer insights, albeit speculative, about future tendencies, prospects, and problems. The analysis of Japan's political economy is important in its own right. In addition, it will help us better understand the present and future of all industrial democracies; they face similar problems, and their futures will be inextricably linked.

Japan's economic performance and behavior over the long run, and particularly in transition periods, cannot be explained by standard economic variables alone. Nor can Japanese political performance and behavior be explained solely by political variables. The rules of the game, matters of policy, and the institutional environment are determined by the state—bureaucrats and politicians. Hence the political economy approach of these volumes. Yet even that is too narrow. A broader interdisciplinary, analytical approach is needed to take into account social and cultural variables, some of them changing significantly, others important for their very stability. In the short run it may be possible to isolate and analyze certain phenomena on the assumption that nothing else changes, but in the longer run one must take into account an intricate web of complex interactions between economic, political, social, and cultural forces and structures. However, social science has yet to develop generally accepted, comprehensive analytical frameworks that are operational. Each of the participants in this project found that even a political economy approach required substantial stretching beyond standard disciplinary boundaries.

What major changes marked the end of the postwar era? From a Japanese perspective, Japan in the 1970s had finally "caught up with the West." From a Western perspective, Japan had become a major affluent, industrial, high-technology power, the world's second largest market economy, and indeed the major challenger to U.S. industrial and technological supremacy. By 1970 Japan's domestic economic policies and performance had such an impact on the United States and Western Europe by way of trade that it could no longer be dismissed as a "small-country economy." Rather, U.S. and European government and business decision makers felt increasingly compelled to respond to Japanese competitive pressure; and Japan in turn could no longer take the world political-economic environment as a given. By the late 1970s, some Japanese large firms were at the technological frontiers in virtually every civilian goods industry and in the commercial application of basic scientific research, though not in basic science itself. By the mid-1980s, Japan had become the world's largest net exporter of capital in the now highly developed system of international financial markets.

Japan's economic prowess stands in sharp contrast to its modest military strength. Since World War II, Japan has persisted in a very low military posture of only limited self-defense capabilities. It has become an economic superpower, commensurate with the United States and Western Europe, while abjuring military power. Japan has depended for military security on its alliance with the United States, also by far its most important economic partner. This comprehensive alliance has been crucial for Japan; it has also become increasingly important for the United States.

The international political and economic environment has changed dramatically in the past fifteen years or so. Détente came to an end; the Soviet Union rose to nuclear parity with the United States. The hegemonic power—military and economic—of the United States declined but by no means disappeared. The Bretton Woods system of fixed exchange rates collapsed, to be replaced by a system of flexible exchange rates that has developed problems of its own. The two oil shocks of the 1970s contributed greatly to world inflation, a slowing of world growth, high interest rates, subsequent disinflation, an intractable Third World debt problem, and emergent protectionism in the United States and Western Europe. The international trading and monetary systems have come under immense strain. The sharp decline in world oil prices, interest rates, and the overvalued dollar in the mid-1980s continue the uncertain process of international adjustment and transition.

Japan has been as much affected by these international shocks and systemic changes as any other major nation. For these as well as internal reasons, Japan's formerly super-fast economic growth rate slowed sharply after 1973. Japan has nonetheless achieved more rapid economic growth than other industrial nations and has performed better in such areas as employment, price stability, productivity improvement, and structural adjustment. It has also fared better in terms of political and social stability. Even so, the sharp appreciation of the yen in the mid-1980s must have a substantial impact on domestic economic structure and performance, with implications for the rest of the world as well.

The question of where the present period of transition is leading pervades the papers in these volumes. Within Japan, we can anticipate an aging population; still further urbanization; and increased homogenization as mass media reduce regional and other variations, coupled, however, with the increased individuality of an affluent new middle class that forms Japan's great majority. Yet Japan's economy and institutions may well manifest greater decentralization, reflecting new opportunities as well as heterogeneity within a homogeneous society. Japan may well become the new, information-based society par excellence as a new technological era comes to dominate the turn of the new century. Undoubtedly economic, political, and social institutions will continue to evolve in response to changing needs and pressures. Basic values and behavioral patterns, however, change more slowly. Indeed, they are a major source of domestic stability; yet they are also a source of international misunderstanding, confusion, and even conflict. Nonetheless, values, and the behavior they shape, are not static. Will the transition be predominantly technological and economic? To what extent will the new era embody even more profound societal and cultural changes? Or will basic values and preferred behavior patterns provide the stability to make the transition easier to deal with?

The international system—economic, political, military—also appears to be in transition, with its future characteristics unclear. The U.S.-USSR confrontation continues to dominate the global military arena. The rise of Japan to major international economic prominence has generated pressures from the United States and Western Europe for Japan to play a far greater role in maintaining and strengthening the open international economic system, to prevent a systemic retreat into protectionism. The foreign desire for Japanese leadership has been matched so far by Japanese caution. Will a new era of reduced U.S.-USSR military tension emerge? Will Japan's economic role be stabilizing or destabilizing? Will protectionism become more significant, and if so, will it be sectoral rather than geographic? We do not pretend to answer these or a host of other questions comprehensively, but at least they are addressed.

The editors of each volume of *The Political Economy of Japan* expand upon the general themes raised here in their introductions to the volumes, setting the themes in their particular context. Volume 1, subtitled *The Domestic Transformation*, takes essentially a domestic approach, while recognizing the impact of the rest of the world on Japan and Japan's interaction with it. Volume 2, *The Changing International Context*, correspondingly takes an international approach, while examining the global effects on Japan's domestic political economy. Volume 3, *Cultural and Social Dynamics*, presents a quite different but equally essential perspective. Culture is the medium in which economic and political behavior rests; it embodies underlying norms, values, and tastes. Society and its institutions are essential features of any political economy. The linkages between Japan's political economy, society, and culture are clearly important. They are also extraordinarily difficult to analyze. In Volume 3, a wider range of social scientists analyze certain of these linkages. Whereas Volumes 1 and 2 aim to be definitive, Volume 3 is overtly exploratory. Its aim is to open new avenues of research for our understanding of Japan.

The basic themes and issues addressed in the volumes are broad and comprehensive. Every nation, like every individual, has its unique features. But far more important are the similarities, and the subtle degree and specific nature of the differences. In principle, these studies are explicitly comparative, interdisciplinary, and future-oriented. These are difficult goals to achieve, as anyone conversant with the current state of social science theory and methodology knows full well. In practice, most of the comparisons are between Japan and the major, market-oriented industrial democracies of the West, particularly the United States. In many respects they are the most appropriate comparison group. Financial and human resource constraints precluded an even more ambitious approach. The Japanese economy, polity, society, culture, and people are not nearly so monolithic, centralized, homogeneous, or vertically structured as they have on occasion been stereotypically portrayed in the West. Nor are they as unique as some Japanese would maintain. On the other hand, the United States stands at the opposite pole among the industrial nations in terms of heterogeneity and decentralization. A comparison between Japan and the United States, the world's largest market economies, is therefore of crucial importance in our search for insights into Japan's political economy.

The contributors to these volumes confronted a complex mixture of evolutionary change, discontinuous change, and enduring continuities in their analyses of Japan's current state and future possibilities. They bravely responded by delving beyond their normal, comfortable disciplinary limits. We believe that, thanks to their efforts, these volumes will contribute substantially to establishing both the substance and the approach of future social science research on Japan. Although these studies push forward the frontiers of our knowledge, we still have much to do.

In recognition that no one scholar could adequately address the array of topics and issues incorporated in these volumes, in 1982 the binational Japan Political Economy Research Committee was formed, with Yasusuke Murakami and Hugh Patrick as co-chairmen, in order to plan and carry out this comprehensive project. The committee, together with other scholars, held numerous planning workshops to prepare six substantive conferences between 1984 and 1987, two for each volume.

The committee members were: Takashi Inoguchi (Political Science, University of Tokyo), Kazuo Koike (Economics, University of Kyoto), Ryutaro Komiya (Economics, University of Tokyo), Shumpei Kumon (Social Systems Analysis, University of Tokyo), Yasusuke Murakami (Economics, University of Tokyo), Yukio Noguchi (Economics, Hitotsubashi University), Daniel I. Okimoto (Political Science, Stanford University), Hugh T. Patrick (Economics, Columbia University), Kenneth B. Pyle (History, University of Washington), Thomas P. Rohlen (Anthropology, Stanford University), Henry Rosovsky (Economics, Harvard University),

Seizaburo Sato (Political Science, University of Tokyo), Gary Saxonhouse (Economics, University of Michigan), Akio Watanabe (International Relations, University of Tokyo), Kozo Yamamura (Economics, University of Washington), and Yasukichi Yasuba (Economics, Osaka University). The committee benefited greatly from the participation of many other scholars in the planning, particularly Marius Jansen (History, Princeton University), Barbara Ruch (Japanese Literature and Culture, Columbia University), and Robert Smith (Anthropology, Cornell University).

The project and its scope were made possible by the visionary funding commitments made early in the planning stage by the National Institute for Research Advancement (NIRA) in Tokyo and the East-West Center in Honolulu. Their early enthusiasm and financial underwriting were crucial. Additional funding for various key components of the intellectual package was received from the Mellon Foundation, the Japan–United States Educational Commission, the United States–Japan Friendship Commission, and the Japan Foundation.

Our great debt, as co-chairmen of the committee, is to the scholars who have written, rewritten, and rewritten again the papers appearing in these volumes. This was no ordinary project and certainly no ordinary series of conferences. Each author made a deep intellectual commitment, reflected in immense amounts of time and energy devoted to planning and meeting as well as research and writing. We thank especially the editors of each of the three volumes for their dedication, leadership, and sheer hard work. By far the greatest financial source of support for this project, as with much social scientific research, was the cost of the scholars' time, borne by their universities; all too often we take for granted the universities' central role in making such research efforts possible.

The project had a rather loose, semiautonomous administrative structure, which worked—from beginning to final publication—because of the behind-the-scenes efforts of many persons, all of whom we deeply thank. We mention only three stalwarts by name: Mikio Kato, Executive Director of the International House in Tokyo, who administered the NIRA grant and the three conferences and many planning sessions held in Tokyo; Charles Morrison, Research Fellow at the East-West Center, who oversaw the East-West Center's role as conference host and funder; and Grant Barnes, Director of Stanford University Press, who personally shepherded these manuscripts through the publication process.

Yasusuke Murakami
Hugh T. Patrick

The Political Economy of Japan

Volume 1

Kozo Yamamura and Yasukichi Yasuba

Introduction

In the second half of the 1980s, few would dispute two observations about Japan. First, Japan is a stable democracy facing neither major political, economic, or social problems that could threaten the stability of its polity nor ideological and social schisms that are so pervasive as to hinder the smooth functioning of its democratic institutions. Second, by most of the important indicators of a nation's economic performance, Japan's performance ranges from demonstrably better to no worse than those of other large, advanced, industrialized economies. Indeed, there exists a broad consensus among the informed around the globe that postwar Japan's political and economic performance to date has been outstanding by most standards.

In sharp contrast to the consensus regarding its performance, however, views on how Japan has achieved its performance to date and what the future holds for Japan's polity, economy, and society vary widely. In broad terms, at one end is the view that much of Japan's performance results, in various direct and indirect ways, from conditions and characteristics unique to Japanese society. This view emphasizes one or more distinctive—or what many analysts holding such views believe to be unique—historical, political, or socioinstitutional characteristics or conditions. Those who offer this view, some with considerable subtlety and sophistication, tend to have an optimistic view of Japan's future. For them, these distinctive qualities will somehow enable Japan to cope with problems more effectively than other industrialized societies.

At the other end of the gamut is the view that Japan's postwar political and economic performance can be adequately explained by applying various theories used by political scientists and economists analyzing other polities and economies and that there is little need to emphasize distinctive conditions and characteristics. Those advancing this view—some with substantial analytic rigor and insight—tend to argue that political and economic developments (some of which can be reasonably anticipated on the basis of the analytic framework used) will determine Japan's future and that there is no reason to believe Japan's performance will be better or worse than those of other industrial nations solely because of Japan's distinctive social attributes.

Between these views lie many more that blend, juxtapose, or balance these two widely differing interpretations. The efforts of the proponents of these different views take varying forms as they seek to provide more satisfactory explanations. Some, for example, attempt to construct a new analytic framework to account more effectively for the political or economic behavior and institutional arrangements that played, in their judgment, important roles in postwar Japan's political and economic performance. Others may make imaginative revisions to, or introduce appropriate changes in, established theories in their efforts to analyze Japan's political and economic performance and to speculate about the future.

One crucial fact emerges from this spectrum of views: there exists today no single explanation for the performance of postwar Japan's political economy that a large majority of social scientists accepts as a satisfactory explanation. This fact also accounts for the diversity of views on Japan's future. By a "satisfactory explanation," we refer to an adequate analysis or explanation of the interaction and changes witnessed to date in both the politics and the economy of postwar Japan. We hasten to add that we are fully aware of the inadequacies and limitations of social scientists' analytical tools and that this fact explains the existence of diverse views regarding postwar Japan's political and economic performance, as well as its future.

The very existence of this diversity of views on the performance of postwar Japan's political economy—arguably one of the most significant developments in the world since the end of World War II—demands that social scientists continue to attempt to reduce this diversity. Their goal must be to forge an interpretation that is acceptable, at least in its essential parts, to a majority of social scientists and persuasive to many who are vitally interested in the reasons for Japan's postwar accomplishments and its future.

The importance of such a goal is obvious for two reasons. First, an increased understanding of Japan's political economy can help us better understand the present and future of all industrial economies. All industrialized economies today face many similar, or even identical, political and economic problems, and their futures will be even more closely linked. In the second half of this decade, apprehension and uncertainty concerning the future of industrial societies are being felt as acutely and collectively as at any time in the period since the early 1970s, which has seen oil crises, worldwide stagflation, seemingly abrupt changes in the political tides of several major industrial nations, and many other indications of political, economic, and social malaise.

All industrial nations are now asking: Can earlier economic resiliency be regained by somehow "revitalizing" their economies? Will they be able to avoid frequent and wrenching shifts in fundamental political ideology that would dictate a broad realignment of policy goals and the means to achieve these goals? How long will the existing international political and economic order be able to perform its essential functions as it continues to take bruising body blows? And, even more fundamentally, what will become of modern industrial civilization? Will it remain intact, or will it, or must it, be transformed into a new civilization based on new values, norms, and goals?

In attempting to answer these and other related questions, the significance and value of an increased understanding of the reasons for postwar Japan's accomplishments and an enhanced ability to anticipate Japan's future based on that understanding are evident. Like Japan's historical, socioinstitutional, and other characteristics, the performance of postwar Japan's political economy and the reasons for that performance differed in many ways from those of other industrial nations. Increased knowledge of the reasons for the achievements of postwar Japan's political economy can provide us with comparative knowledge crucial to a better understanding of the collective future of industrialized societies and the future of the world's political and economic order.

The second reason for reducing the diverse views social scientists hold on Japan is that the nation, having become a major world power in the economic and political arenas, now affects the political and economic realities not only of industrialized nations but also of all others in many direct and substantive ways. As the nation with the second largest GNP within the Western alliance, Japan today occupies a prominent position both in the world political order and in international trade and financial regimes. Japan's presence in international technology transfer and trade and in the world's political arena will in all likelihood increase even more. In analyzing the political and economic realities of the present and in hoping for a stable political and economic order in the future, we must understand Japan better.

An additional reason for social scientists to pursue this goal is that Japan offers a useful testing ground for competing social science theories and for new theories. Some of the questions that come to mind include Which theory among the several attempting to explain political change applies to Japan better than others? For those theories advanced by Western political scientists, how many changes and adjustments must be made in order to better explain political stability and political change in Japan? How satisfactorily can neo-classical economic theory explain the economic performance of postwar Japan? What aspects of which Japanese socioinstitutional characteristics must economists consider in order to explain Japan's economic performance? And, more important, what new, more broadly conceived politico-economic analytic framework could be evolved using, or taking account of, Japan's experience in the postwar years or even in the twelve decades since the Meiji Restoration of 1868?

Given the diversity of views on the reasons for postwar Japan's performance and the importance of understanding these reasons, the intent of this volume, as well as of other volumes in this series, is to provide (1) accurate and reliable descriptions of changes since 1945 in institutions, performance, behavior patterns, and other significant aspects of the Japanese polity and economy; (2) persuasive and balanced analyses of the reasons for the performance of the political economy of postwar Japan to date; and (3) credible and useful predictions and speculations about Japan's political economy in the years ahead. That is, an important goal of these volumes is to present descriptions, observations, and analyses that will help reduce the cacophony of explanations for the performance of postwar Japan's political economy and answer the major questions facing industrial nations today.

Aware of the ambitious goals of this volume and of the diversity of views and interpretations, the Japan Political Economy Research Committee (described in the Preface by the general editors) held several meetings—organizing committee meetings and conferences of all contributors and discussants—between 1982 and 1985. The aim of these meetings was to decide on the principal shared perspectives from which each contributor was to write his essay and to provide contributors with ample opportunities to comment on and criticize each essay in order to better define and broaden the scope of all contributions and to improve the technical analysis of all the essays.

This is not to say that each contributor is absolved of the ultimate responsibility for his analysis and conclusions. Rather, all the contributors, collectively and as individual scholars, made the utmost effort to make the most rigorous analysis possible; to critically examine and challenge established views and analyses; and to raise important issues for the future, even though definitive conclusions cannot yet be reached. As a result, some of the analyses and views presented are new and may even be surprising to many readers. They are likely to cause readers to reexamine widely accepted analyses and interpretations. Other contributions raise new questions that call for further studies, especially the contributions that are interdisciplinary or comparative.

The shared perspective from which all contributors were to write their respective essays had many elements (although not all were applicable because of their assigned topics). First, Japan, having completed its century-long process of "catch-up" industrialization sometime between the mid-1960s and 1970s, ceased to be a follower of the industrialized West. Some important analytic implications follow from this. One is that the end of catch-up industrialization cannot but have had profound and wide-ranging effects on the roles of the state, the behavior of all political actors from political parties and interest groups to individual voters, the character and strength of the party in power, and the nature and effectiveness of the policies adopted. And these effects, which have been apparent during the past two decades, are likely to manifest themselves even more visibly in the coming years.

Until the 1960s, the political realities of postwar Japan were shaped, in a very fundamental sense, by Japan's pursuit of catch-up industrialization. Summarized broadly, the most important of these realities were the thirty-year dominance of the conservative Liberal Democratic Party (LDP), which adopted policies that, above all else, were designed to promote rapid growth, and the broad political consensus regarding the desirability of achieving catch-up industrialization, to which the effectiveness of the policies owed much. The broadly shared desire to catch up with the West was the underlying political force majeure that the LDP fostered and harnessed to maintain power, providing the nation with a political stability unmatched by any other major industrial nation. The dynamic transformation of the devastated Japanese economy of 1945 into Asia's prosperous new giant was as much a cause as it was an effect of this political stability.

However, as Japan ceased to be a follower, the national consensus—the locomotive that pulled the Japanese polity along the track of political stability—eroded. To be sure, the LDP continues to remain in power and is likely to retain power into the near future as amply demonstrated by the results of the July 1986 elections (the party increased its strength from 250 to 304 seats in the lower house, which has a total of 512 seats). But, as the results of general elections since the mid-1960s have shown, the party's hold on power, despite the 1986 election results, is no longer as secure as it was in the 1950s and most of the 1960s. Policy goals are debated much more intensely now than in the past, the policymaking process has become significantly more politicized, and the bureaucracy no longer has the power it had in the rapid growth decades. Indeed, Japan is more likely to encounter many of the political problems and conditions experienced in the industrialized West.

These, of course, are only reflections on the fundamental changes occurring in Japan. The LDP, if it wishes to retain power, must increasingly and more effectively respond to the political demands of the largest possible number of voters. Japan now has a large number of affluent but ideologically uncommitted voters, and policymaking has become much more politicized, reflecting the maturing of Japanese democracy. In some ways, these changes are the Japanese versions of what has long been occurring in the West, but, in other ways, these developments differ significantly because of Japan's political and institutional legacies from the rapid growth era and even from the past hundred years of catch-up industrialization.

Here, we need not further describe the effects of the end of the catch-up era on Japanese political realities. All of the fundamental changes referred to above are fully described and analyzed in several papers in this volume. For the purpose at hand, we need only stress that what we are witnessing today and will see in the years ahead in Japanese politics cannot but profoundly differ from what we saw in the rapid growth decades: the locomotive that once determined the course of Japanese politics no longer exists, leaving Japan in the post–catch-up era to seek a new course.

The analytical implications of this historical perspective are even more important. The end of the catch-up period coincided roughly with the end of the postwar decades of rapid economic growth in all industrial nations. To be sure, there are many reasons for the visible decline in the performance of industrial economies that began in the early 1970s. No one, however, can deny that one of the most important is the gradual dissipation of the growth-promoting capabilities of the body of technologies that sustained the industrial growth of the past hundred years. Some may choose to perceive this simply as an end of the period in which economic performance was raised and maintained by such smokestack industries as iron and steel, chemicals, automobiles, and the like.

But it is possible to view this decline more historically and see it as the ending of the technological paradigm of the twentieth century. (By "paradigm," we mean a broadly identifiable body of knowledge that can be readily recognized, at least conceptually, as determining the essential characteristics of an economy.) The twentieth-century paradigm, we believe, consisted in, among other things, the knowledge of how to produce synthetic materials (cement, glass, rubber, and myriad chemical products), how to use new sources of energy (petroleum, gas, electricity, and nuclear power), and how to engage in mass production using large and powerful machinery.

No less important, we see, as others do, that the end of Japan's catch-up period and the end of a period of growth sustained by the technology of the past century coincided with the beginning of an era in which the industrialized economies can revitalize their performance by depending increasingly on a broader range of products from high-technology industries. That is, Japan completed its catch-up period just as the twenty-first century paradigm was beginning. The paradigm of blast furnaces, the Model T, supertankers, and petrochemicals is about to be replaced with that of fifth-generation computers, increasingly "intelligent" robots, "new materials," and novel "living" substances created through bioengineering.

These views imply that all industrialized nations, including Japan, are now in a difficult transitional phase of fundamental change in the technological base of industry. This change imposes serious problems of adjustments in productive capacities both domestically and internationally. As we are all aware, the process of adjustment gives rise to inexorable political and social problems that are extremely difficult to resolve.

This means that international conflicts, both economic and political, will increase in the transitional phase and that Japan, more than other industrial nations, will find itself involved in serious difficulties with its trading partners. Especially for the industrialized nations of the West that are undergoing the political and economic throes of the transition, the sudden emergence of Japan—yesterday's follower—as an effective competitor in the race to benefit from the new technological paradigm remains an unaccustomed and disturbing reality. But the reality is daily becoming more evident in the intensifying competition with the Japanese in their markets at home and abroad; in the political arena of Western nations, where more than a small number of voters are unemployed because of imports from Japan; and in the minds of many in the West who are being forced to ponder the possibility that their nations' industrial dominance is being challenged because of some fundamental weaknesses in their economy, polity, and even culture.

The foregoing suggests that the first understanding among the authors of this volume—to keep in mind that Japan, completing its catch-up industrialization, has just entered a new era—has a substantive implication for the analysis each author undertook. However, as stated in the general editors' preface, in this volume the authors focused on the significance and effects of the ending of catch-up industrialization on Japan's political economy as seen from "inside." Analysis of international political and economic issues raised by changes in the technological paradigm will be left to Volume 2, which is devoted to examining Japan in the international community.

This, however, is not to say that they ignored the changes in Japan's political economy that arise from increasing international political and economic tensions. Rather, they considered the many changes occuring and being made in response to the new international political and economic realities primarily in order to describe and analyze their effects on Japan's domestic political and economic performance. The changes referred to here include liberalization of trade and capital markets, changes made in the focus of industrial policy away from export promotion, and others occurring in response to the demands and concerns of Japan's trading partners.

The second understanding among the contributors to this and subsequent volumes is that they would describe and analyze their assigned topics from a broad politico-economic perspective. That is, in examining his assigned topic, each author considered the relevant political and economic aspects so that his analysis would not be limited to either politics or economics. Simply put, this understanding means that each contribution was to be an essay in political economy because such a broadly conceived approach is, as stressed earlier, required to reduce the diversity of views regarding the reasons for Japan's economic and political performance and its future.

Agreeing to contribute a paper that was an essay in political economy and writing such an essay to the satisfaction of all participants proved a challenging task for all the authors. The authors had little difficulty accepting the broad conceptualization that an essay in political economy is concerned with (1) the establishment and maintenance of the rules of the game (the basic politico-economic system) and the setting of its basic goals (individually, in groups, and by the basic system—the nation-state as a whole); (2) efficiency in resource allocation; and (3) distribution of output. (The considerations involving Japan vis-à-vis other nation-states are, for the purpose of this description, subsumed under the first heading.) Nor was it difficult for the authors to accept that there are three basic mechanisms by which a nation deals with each of these issues: the competitive (spot) market; the state (its legal system, bureaucracy, and interest group politics); and the "social" and "cultural" characteristics of each nation, which manifest themselves in formal and informal organizations, institutional arrangements (such as implicit long-term contracts), social relationships, societal values, and the like.

The challenge faced by some of the economists among the contributors was their inclination (which is, of course, substantially conditioned or limited by the analytical tools at their disposal) to take the rules of the game and goal setting as given—that is, to assume that they do not change or change only slowly (thus, in effect, "assuming away" the issues involved)—and to focus on questions concerning efficiency of resource allocation. Many economists also tend to deal with distributional issues only as outcomes of the working of the marketplace as affected by the state rather than with issues involving societal values or goals, thus leaving the latter considerations to moral philosophers and political scientists (or to Marxist economists and those neo-classical economists who discuss such issues not as economists but as philosophers and political scientists). Stated bluntly, but not inaccurately, most economists are inclined to focus on the market mechanism, taking the state (politics), society, and culture as unchanging and often regarding them as factors contributing to inefficiency in resource allocation and to the failure of markets to perform effectively.

Political scientists, on the other hand, usually show little interest in analyzing efficiency of resource allocation and focus on the creation, maintenance, and transformation of the "basic system" and on distributional issues. Their primary analytical goal is to test the validity of models formulated to explain political stability and changes in the political system and the distribution and use of power in political processes. Political scientists believe that, much as the invisible hand governs the market, the visible hand of politics affects the way a political economy functions. For them, politics sets forth the legal rights and responsibilities of all actors, establishes the basic rules of competition, aggregates interests, and adjudicates conflicts. All economic activity, including the allocation and distribution of resources, takes place within, and is shaped by, the political system.

Much more could be added, at varying levels of abstraction, about these differences in theoretical orientation. Here, let us add one further difference that is, analytically, closely related to those just noted and that contributes to making the task of writing essays in political economy on Japan especially demanding. There is an apparent difference in the definition, either implicit or explicit, of "rational behavior" or "rationality." This, in turn, reflects crucial and fundamental differences in the two professions' central concerns and the principal behavioral postulates used in their respective analytical approaches. Economists define these terms narrowly. Typically, rationality for them is demonstrated by the individual (or the family) or firms, each of which "knows" its goals and how to "weigh" the goals—that is, each has its own utility or profit-maximizing function. As envisioned by economists, the goal as a rule is materialistic—to maximize utility or profit; they measure the extent of goal attainment by the income, assets, profit, leisure, or the like that is gained. This, of course, is to be expected of economists, who, as already noted, emphasize allocative efficiency and the market mechanism. But because of this narrow focus, most economists fail to take other factors into account, such as the roles of group motivations and goals. Political scientists see this as a serious weakness, especially in economic studies of Japan (because, as described below, of the perceived importance of the group in the Japanese political economy).

In contrast, political scientists seem to define "rationality" much more broadly. They view group interests as more than mere aggregations of individual interests and give weight to nonrational forces (such as institutional rigidity and bureaucratic or organizational inertia). For them, groups of varying sizes that have specific interests of their own—political parties, labor unions, the bureaucracy, the middle class, or even the state—can and do make rational use of the political process to alter the distributive outcomes determined by the marketplace and, on occasion, even the very rules of the game. Thus, a crucial analytical problem for political scientists is how to accommodate and take account of the rational forces at work at the level of individuals, families, and firms.

That this difference is extremely crucial for authors attempting to write essays on the political economy of Japan is evident in several frequently studied and debated questions: What has determined the character of the relationship between government and business or between business and the bureaucracy? Do the relationships differ substantially from those existing elsewhere because of Japan's oft-noted group-orientedness? Alternatively, how much of the character of the relationships can be explained in terms of individual rationality? How much of interfirm relationships in Japan, to the extent they differ from those elsewhere, must be explained in terms of group rationality? That is, what determines the mixes of the different modes of interfirm relationships that the Japanese firms choose? Why do they use varying combinations of vertical integration, subcontracting, spot market transactions, or *keiretsu* (enterprise groups)? How much of the mix can be explained in terms of neo-classical economic analysis and how much, if any, must be explained in terms of interest groups that are formed, encouraged, or promoted in various ways by group rationality?

Further questions include How are the national goals of Japan set? How correct are the economists who, focusing on individual rationality, see the goals as the sum of individuals' and firms' rational desires? Or are the political scientists who emphasize the dynamics of interest group interactions nearer to answering this question more satisfactorily, even though they often fail to consider the effects of market forces on the character of groups and the outcome of intergroup dynamics?

As the papers in this volume demonstrate, these examples could be multiplied easily (and it goes without saying that many more examples can be added in relation to those topics dealt with in Volumes 2 and 3).

The third understanding among the contributors was that each would describe and discuss any socioinstitutional condition and characteristic that he deemed necessary to adequately examine his assigned topic. In this volume, we are not specifically focusing our attention on these conditions and characteristics. As described in the Preface by the general editors, this task is among the goals of Volume 3. Nonetheless, each author was free to, indeed encouraged to, discuss any relevant condition and characteristic. Readers will note that the authors have responded constructively, thereby strengthening their respective contributions.

Finally, as a logical extension of the first agreement among the contributors to write their respective essays from the historical perspective that Japan had completed its catch-up industrialization around 1970, the contributors agreed to make predictions about the future of the Japanese political economy. In short, the fourth understanding among the contributors was, in principle, to be forward looking and speculate about the Japanese political economy in the remaining years of this century.

In light of the implications of the first agreement discussed above and the many other political, economic, and social changes in Japan over the past two decades, the questions that a forward-looking contributor must attempt to answer are many. Although all questions are both political and economic, the more political include How will Japanese politics change as the LDP, no longer able to rely on the national consensus for rapid economic growth to maintain its hold over power, increasingly adopts more policies of a catchall party? How will the aging population and the cost it imposes on the national budget affect the politics of budget formation? How will the visible trend toward politicization of the policymaking process change the goals, character, and efficacy of policies? Will Japanese politics become more pluralistic, or will it continue to retain those characteristics specific to the Japanese polity? And what will take the place of the locomotive of the rapid growth era in shaping the character of Japanese politics in the years ahead?

The most salient among the economic questions are What problems will the Japanese economy face under the new technological paradigm and will it be more successful in adopting it than other nations? Will the structure and organization of industry change? Will Japan's high saving rate decline and, if so, with what domestic and international consequences? How will the politicization of the policymaking process affect macro- and micro- (including industrial) policies? How will the character and performance of firms and interfirm relationships change? What effects will Japan's new status as a major world economy and the ongoing liberalization of its economy have on economic policies and performance?

To describe the organization of this volume and also to aid readers who may not be particularly familiar with the topics dealt with in each chapter, we now present general observations about each section of this volume and a brief description of each of the papers included in the four sections.

Unlike subsequent parts, Part I, entitled "The Japanese Model," contains only one paper, "The Japanese Model of Political Economy" by Yasusuke Murakami. Given the broad and ambitious goal of this volume, we believe this contribution is important in acquainting readers with many salient analytical and empirical issues involved in the study of the Japanese political economy and in setting the intellectual stage, as it were, for the analyses that follow. The breadth as well as the depth of his analysis serves as a fitting setting to the subsequent parts.

In his carefully structured contribution, Murakami describes and analyzes (1) what he believes are the historical and sociocultural origins and the structural and behavioral characteristics of the Japanese political economy; (2) why and how these characteristics aided or determined the process of Japan's catch-up industrialization; and (3) how these characteristics are changing in the present post–catch-up period, altering the ways Japanese are responding to the newly emerging political, economic, and social realities.

To carry out this broadly conceived interdisciplinary analysis, Murakami begins with a discussion of what is meant by a politico-economic model. He presents (1) a rigorous definition and analysis of the historical origins of what he indentifies as an essential sociocultural characteristic of the Japanese model—namely, "group-orientedness"; (2) an analytical discussion of the factors that he believes contributed most to Japan's successful catch-up industrialization—that is, an analysis of why and how Japan, because of its sociocultural characteristics, was able to adopt policies and make use of a "cooperative" government-business relationship in ways that enabled firms to benefit both from the fruits of interfirm cooperation and market competition; (3) carefully structured examinations of the social and political changes affecting, and affected by, the successful catch-up industrialization; and (4) the many political and economic changes that will reshape the course of the Japanese political economy and society because of the coming of the technological paradigm of the twenty-first century and because of the rise of the "new middle mass"—a large group of ideologically uncommitted and increasingly affluent citizens whose presence is increasingly felt in other industrialized democracies as well.

Because Murakami's essay is tightly written and uses concepts and analytical tools from several disciplines, it is one that, to savor his analyses fully, must be read with care. Some readers may not be fully persuaded by his analyses and interpretations. But that is to be expected of such a broadly conceived and multidisciplinary undertaking. Whatever the final assessment that each reader makes of Murakami's analyses, his is the contribution with which we can most fittingly begin this volume.

Part II, "Macroeconomic Performance," presents four papers dealing with topics important for understanding the macroeconomic performance of Japan in the past few decades and in the near future. The first is "Economic Welfare" by Martin Bronfenbrenner and Yasukichi Yasuba. What has economic growth meant to Japan's citizens and how have the fruits of that growth been distributed among them? This is a critical question for examining the political economy of the resource-poor Japan that achieved rapid economic growth.

The authors ask Will the Japanese continue to be "workaholics living in rabbit hutches" and to bear the costs of rapid economic growth? Do they enjoy less economic welfare than their postwar economic performance would lead one to expect? Or, is it true, as some have asserted, that Japan has become a "welfare superpower" and that its citizens now have a higher level of economic welfare than do the peoples of the Western industrial nations? And, whatever the level of current economic welfare, what political and economic forces that are similar or different from those seen elsewhere are at work to change the level as well as the distribution of economic welfare? Bronfenbrenner and Yasuba attempt to answer these and other questions, making a thorough examination of comparative data and changes over time.

They find that the characterization of Japan as a "welfare superpower" is much closer to reality than that of Japan as a nation of "workaholics living in rabbit hutches," provided that one is careful to discount some of the exaggerated claims made by those subscribing to the former characterization. The authors demonstrate that most economic indicators show the level of economic welfare in Japan in the 1980s is no longer significantly behind, as it once was, those of the industrial countries of the West. Although the Japanese live in smaller houses and work more days in a year, their average income and wages are only slightly lower than those in the United States. Air and water pollution, once little controlled and a major social and political issue, was largely contained by 1980. The crime rate and other indicators of safety have improved significantly; they have long compared favorably with those of other industrial countries. Life expectancy has increased significantly, and today it is one of the highest in the world.

This is not to say, the authors stress, that Japan has become a welfare superpower and has little room for improvement. They see further needs for the Japanese to improve housing, strengthen the safety net for the poorest, make determined efforts to reduce discrimination against women and minority groups, further limit pollution, and decrease the number of hours worked per year.

This paper benefits from the authors' efforts to gather many types of comparative data and to pay due attention to the political forces at work in determining the level and character of economic welfare. It is a reliable and up-to-date study of what is, in the final analysis, most important in the daily lives of the Japanese as well as in evaluating the performance of the political economy of Japan.

The second paper in this section, Kazuo Sato's "Saving and Investment," examines Japan's high saving rate, a subject of economic and political importance. In his contribution, both an original technical analysis and a politico-economic study, Sato rejects the sociocultural explanation of the high saving rate because, in whatever way such an explanation is applied, it is, in Sato's judgment, unable to answer satisfactorily either of the following questions: Why did the personal saving rate decline appreciably less than the economic growth rate during the past decade or so, when the latter decelerated rapidly? And since Japan's personal saving rate was not notably high before 1955, what caused its sharp increase in the subsequent two decades? To Sato, the inadequacy of the sociocultural explanation is demonstrated by the fact that Japan's postwar saving rate was not exceptionally high; in many newly industrializing countries, the rate rose as it did in Japan during the rapid growth decades, and the rates in some developed countries, such as Portugal and Italy, have been comparable to that of Japan.

What explanation does Sato offer for the rise and fall of the household saving rate that occurred in Japan during the rapid growth decade and after 1973? He rejects what economists call the permanent income hypothesis because it explains neither the rise of the proportion of saving out of permanent income in the high growth period nor the failure of the saving ratio to decline quickly after 1973. He also rejects the so-called bonus hypothesis because, he believes, it mistakes form for substance. His answer is the target wealth hypothesis—individuals save as if they are attempting to acquire a targeted specific amount of wealth. (Technically expressed, the saving ratio in this hypothesis can be expressed as the sum of the change in the wealth–income ratio and the product of the wealth–income ratio and the growth rate.) Thus, in the high growth period, the saving ratio rose because both the growth rate and the wealth–income ratio were rising. After the mid-1970s, the saving ratio declined in response to the deceleration in the economic growth rate but the ratio did not decline rapidly because the wealth–income ratio continued to increase, albeit more slowly.

Sato believes that much of the incentive for wealth accumulation to date reflects the desire of families to own their own house, the prices of which have been rising continuously because of the steady increase in the price of land brought about by the concentration of population in urban areas. Sato speculates that in the future, land prices may stabilize because of the slowed growth of the population and an end of the trend toward concentration of population in limited urban areas. Thus, the saving ratio may continue to decline slowly as growth stabilizes at a lower rate and as demographic factors turn against saving.

Sato's essay is important for analyzing several currently debated issues. During Japan's rapid growth period, a large net saving by households constituted a crucial source of funds to meet the investment demands of rapidly growing firms. But after the mid-1970s, such demand declined sharply as profit rates of firms plummeted and growth prospects appeared less rosy. A result was the huge surplus of funds in the private sector, only a part of which was used, in the form of deficit financing, by the government. An inevitable consequence was the export surplus (flowing abroad as capital) and trade frictions with Japan's trading partners. The relatively modest dissaving by the government has nonetheless accumulated into a huge public debt, and trade frictions have grown more serious. Unless the rate of return and the growth rate are raised, Sato foresees that Japan will not be able to escape the dilemma of increasing public debt and intensifying trade friction. This paper, although the most technical in the volume, is important for understanding the changing patterns of, and motivations for, saving in the Japanese political economy and provides the essential foundation for those essays in Volume 2 treating Japan's trade and international financial issues.

The third paper in Part II is "Public Finance" by Yukio Noguchi. The author, whose intent is to deal equally with both the political and economic issues involved in Japan's public finance, begins by stressing that current issues have their origins in two major developments of the early 1970s: the exogenous shock of the first oil crisis in 1973 that marked the beginning of slower economic growth and the policy decision to increase social security benefits. For Noguchi, the twin results of these developments—the growth in the share of government in the economy (by 20 to 30 per cent in the past decade) and the huge budget deficit—did not result from slowed growth, as many maintain, but primarily from the sharp increases in social security payments. Tax revenues, previously a more or less constant proportion of GNP, began to increase steadily after the middle of the 1970s, but expenditures increased even more rapidly, mainly as the result of an increase in mandated social security expenditures (while government consumption and investment as a proportion of GNP remained remarkably stable). Thus, the fundamental cause of both the growth of the share of government and the increase in the deficit was the increase in social security expenditures.

For Noguchi, the real reason for this increase in the deficit is not difficult to see. In Japan, an important politico-economic rule is that decisions regarding public finance must be made much like those households make regarding consumption. Generous social security benefits were provided in 1973 when fiscal conditions appeared unusually favorable. Contributing to this decision were the growing national awareness of the need to improve the quality of life, the adoption by opposition parties controlling local governments of welfare policies in their communities, and a serious miscalculation of the costs of social security programs by the Ministry of Welfare. As the deficit soared because of the increased social security expenditures (primarily because of the aging of the population), the government tried to balance the budget by proposing the introduction of a general consumption tax. But the extreme unpopularity of this tax forced the government to turn to freezing expenditure levels to reduce the persistent huge budget deficits. This pattern continues to the present (1986).

Noguchi also analyzes the Japanese tax system, which is based principally on direct taxes. Since income tax is progressive, this may seem to favor egalitarianism. However, there are problems. First, whereas wages and salaries are almost fully included in taxable income, a large part of property, business, and farm income escapes taxation either legally or illegally. Second, despite the automatic tax increase that results from bracket creep, the gap between revenues and expenditures continues to remain wide principally because of the increased social security benefits mandated by a 1973 law. Noguchi argues that the government, sooner or later, will be forced either to cut expenditures or increase taxes, or both.

As is evident from the preceding, the character and health of Japanese public finance is crucially determined by the most recent changes in Japan's economic performance and by a delicate balancing of political forces—interest groups—each of which is acting to maintain or increase its share of what the central coffer has to offer. Prime Ministers Suzuki and Nakasone committed themselves to eliminating the budget deficit, which burgeoned to huge proportions in the latter half of the 1970s. The significance of Noguchi's analytic insights and politico-economic assessments are quite evident when his paper is read along with those by Murakami, Bronfenbrenner and Yasuba, and Sato and the papers by Kosai and by Muramatsu and Krauss in Part IV of this volume.

In the last paper in this section, "The Political Economy of the Financial Market," Koichi Hamada and Akiyoshi Horiuchi offer authoritative descriptions and analyses of the policies of the monetary authorities (the Ministry of Finance and the Bank of Japan) and the behavior of financial institutions, and they speculate about the likely future of Japan's financial market. They believe that the character and policies of the financial system of the rapid growth period were determined by the initial postwar conditions—the low level of accumulation of financial assets, small public debt, and the "closedness" of the economy.

In order to achieve rapid economic growth, in the decades up to 1973 business had to rely heavily on banks for funds. Since banks paid controlled low interest rates to depositors (who, of course, were "compensated" in various ways as the economy grew), the economy therefore grew at the expense of depositors. Rapid growth was also aided by the Bank of Japan (BOJ), which provided loans and which used them as an important lever to control financial markets. The ground that the authors cover may be familiar to some readers, but the authors' description and analysis are important because of their command of the behavior and motivations of financial institutions and the real effects of the policies adopted. One is, for example, more ready to be persuaded when Hamada and Horiuchi note that what businesses gained in borrowing from banks at the low controlled interest rates might have been smaller than often asserted because businesses had to deposit a substantial amount of the borrowed funds as compensating balances and that a large part of the rent—the gains resulting from the controlled interest rates—that accrued to the banks was used as a source of their financial power to form *keiretsu*.

The authors agree with most earlier students of the subject that in those decades the BOJ tried to control the financial market, but, because of the low level of the public debt, it had to rely on direct control of bank credit rather than on open-market operations. However, Hamada and Horiuchi argue, unlike many who have discussed the role of the BOJ, that it is not clear whether the often alleged goal of the BOJ of aiding the rapid growth of heavy and chemical industries was achieved. To the authors, the government also had to accommodate the financial needs of both stagnating and small and medium-size businesses; accordingly it did not possess sufficient resources to help the heavy and chemical industries to any significant extent.

Hamada and Horiuchi show that the financial system has entered an ongoing phase of domestic financial liberalization since the mid-1970s in response to changes in underlying conditions. As a result of both the growth of financial assets and the great increase in government bonds issued to finance deficit-financed spending programs, a more diversified financial structure has been and continues to be created. True to the way changes are made in Japan's financial institutions, the structural changes were first introduced in peripheral areas. The monetary authorities rarely led in introducing these changes; rather they usually played a rearguard, coordinating role, often with only limited success. Banks have become more eager to innovate; they have introduced many financial instruments, such as transferable certificates of deposit (CDs) and withdrawable time deposits, and the process has continued apace. The government was soon forced to issue medium-term bonds with interest rates increasingly determined by market forces, and these bonds became the basis for creating new, high-yielding financial instruments traded by stockbrokers. Liberalization has also occurred gradually in the field of international banking in response to the needs of the economy and to foreign pressure.

In the judgment of Hamada and Horiuchi, the efficacy of the BOJ's interventions in the past three decades to influence the allocation of funds is debatable, although the bank was largely successful in controlling inflation (except briefly in the mid-1970s). The authors believe that, in the coming years, the price mechanism will become of central importance in financial markets; large city banks, long-term credit banks, and government financial institutions will continue to lose their market share; market segmentation will continue to decline as financial institutions are allowed to engage in new activities; and changes in the instruments of monetary policy will occur. This is a knowledgeable and reliable overview of the financial markets in postwar Japan that demonstrates how markets evolved during the past decades by responding to changing economic and political realities. Some readers may take issue with the authors' overall assessment of the somewhat limited efficacy of the monetary authority in aiding firms in rapidly growing industries in the rapid growth period. However, they present strong analyses and evidence in support of their view; such revisionist views must be taken seriously.

Part III, "Firms and Employment," consists of four treatments of the important topics and questions most frequently discussed in examining the Japanese political economy at the level of the industrial firm. The first is Masahiko Aoki's "The Japanese Firm in Transition." As is well known, the ownership of large postwar Japanese firms listed on the stock exchange was characterized by widely dispersed ownership (shareholding) and interlocking controlling ownership of large firms by a number of other large, friendly firms that held shares in each other, thus creating enterprise groups (*keiretsu*). Aoki's task is to explain the reasons for, and the effects of, these ownership characteristics and to analyze why and how these characteristics are now changing.

Aoki first demonstrates that the development of these ownership patterns was a result of a series of historical events (dissolution of the *zaibatsu*, the serious and prolonged strikes of the late 1950s and early 1960s) and the risk-averse behavior of a technocratic management, especially its aversion to unfriendly takeovers. He argues that employees, after a series of disastrous strikes, became cooperative with management, which was also eager to develop peaceful labor relations. What emerged was a management that acted as a policymaking body, striking a balance between the interests of shareholders and employees; this new form of management succeeded in maintaining the balance by adopting the lifetime employment system. Aoki argues that this system, which in effect recognizes employees as an integral constituent body within the firm, made employees realize the importance of increasing their productivity by such means as actively adopting innovative methods on the shop floor. Managers, too, were motivated to maximize growth by making the most of these circumstances.

Aoki believes, however, that since the oil crisis of 1973, the difficult business conditions management has faced have forced it to make even more efficient uses of capital and labor. Management thus sought to reduce the number of workers at parent corporations by making increased use of subcontracting. The advantages of subcontracting, both vertical and horizontal, included the fact that such interfirm relationships enable parent firms and subcontractors to share risks and knowledge. He foresees that Japanese corporations will move closer to Western practices in the future because (1) innovation will come increasingly not from the shop floor but from laboratories, (2) interfirm labor mobility will increase, and (3) the balance of power will be tilted in favor of shareholders as more capital is raised in the form of equity instead of bank loans.

Aoki's analysis, broader in conceptualization than that of neo-classical analysis, attempts to explain how and why the behavior of Japanese firms has changed under the rapidly evolving economic realities of the past 15 years and is likely to change even further in the future. This is a contribution of crucial significance for understanding the economic performance of large Japanese firms and their subcontractors at present and in the coming years.

The next paper is Kazuo Koike's "Human Resource Development and Labor-Management Relations." For many readers familiar with the published research on Japanese employment and labor-management systems, Koike's paper will offer a new and perhaps surprising perspective. Explanations of "peculiarly Japanese" labor practices, such as worker interest in raising productivity or the cooperativeness of unions at the enterprise level, have often been based on Japanese sociocultural traditions. Koike rejects these explanations and attempts to explain the differences that exist between Japanese and Western practices by the differences in the ways skills are acquired and used.

To Koike, many of these so-called Japanese characteristics are simply myths. He offers evidence showing that older Japanese workers, even those who work for large-scale firms, are more vulnerable to layoff and hence early retirement because of the lack of seniority agreements; unions, too, were once as militant as in other countries but that had ended by the early 1960s; even the "dualism," or wage differentials by size of firms, that has long been seen as a hallmark of Japan's economy, he argues, is simply a statistical artifact; once workers are standardized by type, wage differentials by size of firm are no larger in Japan than in other industrial countries.

Many of the seeming peculiarities of Japanese employment practices and wage profiles can be explained, Koike argues, by the "white-collarization" of workers in the postwar years. That is, Japanese blue-collar workers in large enterprises acquire, unlike their counterparts in the West, a wide range of skills over their careers by experiencing many kinds of the jobs on the shop floor. Thus, the longer workers stay on the job, the higher their enterprise-specific productivity becomes, just as in the case of white-collar workers. Hence, the age profile of their wages becomes tilted as in the case of white-collar workers. Wage differentials by firm size show up in the statistics because in large Japanese firms most blue-collar workers are white-collarized, whereas only a small part of such workers in small firms are. Unlike in Japan, there are few white-collarized workers in large enterprises in Western industrial countries, and the unskilled and semiskilled tasks (performed extensively by subcontractors in Japan) are performed within large enterprises. This difference accounts for seemingly larger wage differentials in Japan.

Koike's view is that the presence of a large number of white-collarized employees is beneficial to management because employees (and unions) are more likely to be loyal to the firm and more motivated to raise productivity; it is also beneficial to workers because they can enjoy higher wages than otherwise. The termination of contracts is costly not only to workers but to society since accumulated enterprise-specific skill is wasted. As to the future, Koike speculates that white-collarization may spread to small-scale enterprises. The technical progress in an industry such as microelectronics may reduce the demand for traditional skilled and unskilled workers. But such a development may increase demand for blue-collar workers who can perform the jobs of technicians and engineers, thus possibly bringing about a net increase rather than a decline in the demand for blue-collar workers in the microelectronic and other high-tech industries.

In sum, according to Koike, Japanese workers and unions are not so different from their Western counterparts, but a peculiar method of skill formation developed among blue-collar workers in large enterprises creates many characteristics seemingly peculiar to Japanese workers and unions. Even though Koike's analyses and evidence may not persuade all readers, what he presents must be read with an open mind by all interested in Japanese employment practices and labor-management relations.

"Small-Scale Family Enterprises," coauthored by Hugh T. Patrick and Thomas P. Rohlen, covers a subject important for the study of the political economy of Japan but one that receives scant attention in the Western-language literature. Their contribution, dealing with small-scale family enterprises (SFEs), including those in agriculture, contains many descriptions and analyses that are new and highly informative.

As Patrick and Rohlen observe in their wide-ranging and well-supported essay, the continuous increase in the total number of SFEs attests to a continuing strong entrepreneurial drive in many Japanese. Yet, many SFEs are in declining industries, and their "mortality" rate is very high. One reason is they enjoy only limited assistance from the government. The major exception is farmers, who are protected by the government to the point of substantially affecting their resource allocation. In some industries, particularly in trade and services, SFEs have been rapidly increasing in number. In manufacturing, the bulk of SFEs are under subcontracting arrangements, giving, in some cases, monopsonistic power to parent companies. However, overall, subcontracting provides opportunities for SFEs and flexibility to parent companies. Comparatively speaking, SFEs are much more numerous in Japan on a per capita basis than in other industrialized countries. Important reasons include an abundant supply of entrepreneurs, significant economic advantages that can be realized by making use of well-established and often entrenched social networks, and the high cost of acquiring land and hence the benefit of extensive landownership. For some types of SFEs, availability of low-cost labor, too, is a significant cause of their persistence.

Unlike Koike, Patrick and Rohlen believe that wage differentials are larger than quality differences in labor, a major cause of which is discrimination against certain groups of workers, such as women, older (retired) workers, ethnic minorities, and those with inferior educational backgrounds. The authors hypothesize that Japan, given its historical and social patterns, will continue to have a comparatively large number of SFEs even though the wages they pay remain lower than what can be explained by differences in quality and productivity of workers. Patrick and Rohlen offer an insightful discussion of the significant roles SFEs play in Japan's social life and politics. In short, this chapter presents descriptions and analyses of an important segment of Japan's political economy that has to date failed to receive due attention in the English language.

Daniel I. Okimoto and Gary R. Saxonhouse contribute the final paper in Part III. Their study, entitled "Technology and the Future of the Economy," focuses on the issues and problems involved in Japan's future as a high-technology nation. Written by an economist and a political scientist, this highly informative chapter on a topic of vital interest succeeds in raising and answering many analytical questions important for anticipating the future of both the Japanese political economy and that of other industrialized nations.

The authors first examine several indicators of technological progress. In the number of patents granted, Japan's success is evident: the number of patents has increased not only absolutely but in comparison with the supply of scientists and engineers and in comparison with R&D expenditure. Okimoto and Saxonhouse, however, are inclined to think that the quality of Japanese patents might be lower, one indication being the very small number of major inventions made by Japanese. On the other hand, they note that the technological balance of trade, particularly that of new contracts, has recently shifted rapidly in Japan's favor. Here, too, however, the quality of technology being exported may not be high—many of Japan's exports have gone to developing countries.

The authors note that in a number of fields, such as iron and steel, agricultural chemicals, nuclear energy processing, semiconductors, office automation, robotics, biotechnology, and lasers, Japanese technology has reached the level of state-of-the-art technology. But, they also remind us that in other fields, particularly those where theoretical parameters for problem solving are highly complex and technological trajectories are not readily predictable, Japan's progress has been slower, and that in military-related fields Japan generally lags far behind the United States.

Going into analytically important issues that are also significant in policymaking, Okimoto and Saxonhouse find that the roles of small-scale enterprises have been quite different in Japan and the United States. In the United States, new venture capital has played a significant role in innovation; in Japan, although small-scale firms' share of total R&D expenditures is larger, this is mainly because small firms have a larger share of labor and sales than those in the United States. They observe that small Japanese firms' contribution to technological progress to date has been limited since important innovations tend to originate in large firms.

The authors then show, with persuasive evidence, that (1) the rapidity of technological progress in new fields in Japan results mainly from entries into new fields by firms in other fields; (2) differences between the United States and Japan result from the difference in the nature of labor and capital markets; (3) scientific information flows more freely in the United States than it does in Japan to the benefit of Japan; and (4) in Japan there have been significant vertical flows of scientific and technological information between large parent firms and small subcontractors or subsidiaries.

Also significant is their assessment that government R&D assistance has been far more important in the United States than in Japan, especially in defense and space technology. Such support in the United States has tended to concentrate in fields where spillover effects have been significant. In Japan, the government has had to rely on industrial policy and macro-policy to give direction to R&D. But, in general, R&D has been planned and carried out by the private sector, which emphasizes applied research with a reasonably high prospect of commercial feasibility. Related to this observation is that, although the rate of growth of the supply of scientists and engineers has been very high in Japan, the current number of qualified (Ph.D.) researchers is still small. Rather than graduate training in universities, Japanese firms have relied mainly on in-house training. This has been another reason why Japan emphasizes applied technology at the expense of basic science.

Okimoto and Saxonhouse conclude by speculating that Japanese firms, now at the forefront of technology in numerous industries, may have to emphasize basic R&D more if they are to contribute to the development of state-of-the-art innovation. The days when the Japanese could rely predominantly on imported state-of-the-art innovation have passed.

The final part of this volume, "Government and the Economy," presents four papers that examine political developments and the roles of government in the Japanese political economy. In its various manifestations, this subject is of wide and increasing interest. The first paper in this section is "The Future of Industrial Policy" by George C. Eads and Kozo Yamamura. They examine the role of Japan's industrial policy in the rapid postwar economic growth era and the future of industrial policy in Japan. Their subject is defined as a broad range of policies other than macroeconomic policy that influence investment and disinvestment decisions of firms, industries, or sectors, and they argue that, for industrial policy to be successful, three conditions must exist: (1) the nation must have a centralized, largely autonomous, elite bureaucracy capable of executing complex policies; (2) the bureaucracy must possess an appropriate and effective kit of policy tools; and (3) a political consensus on the basic goals of the policy must exist.

Applying these criteria to major industrial nations, the authors judge these three conditions were best met in Japan. Britain did not have a national consensus on policy goals, and the government had little direct control over its financial markets. In West Germany, where government intervention has become increasingly important, the bureaucracy did not possess policy tools comparable in effectiveness to those of Japan. France in the 1950s and 1960s came closer to meeting all these conditions, but it did not have the consensus on policy goals that Japan did.

In speculating on the future of industrial policy in Japan, Eads and Yamamura judge that its effectiveness will decline. The reasons they offer include (1) the institutional capabilities of the Japanese government have declined because of the growing influence of politicians in economic policymaking and of jurisdictional and policy conflicts now arising within and among several ministries; (2) fiscal stringency and international pressure to liberalize the economy have deprived Japan's bureaucrats of important policy tools; and (3) Japan has ceased to have a strong pro-growth policy consensus.

The authors suggest that Japan, in the coming decades, could follow one of two scenarios: aided by an industrial policy that will be less effective but still contribute to economic performance, the Japanese economy will continue to perform appreciably better than the OECD average; or Japan will perform relatively poorly, partly because of the negative effects of its industrial policy. The negative effects of industrial policy, the authors argue, result when it is pursued in the absence of the conditions necessary for the success of the policy. They speculate, however, that the underlying assumptions are not likely to hold fully for either scenario and that the actual outcome will be somewhere between the two. In other words, provided that Japan maintains a high rate of saving and transforms it into a high rate of domestic investment, Japanese labor remains relatively docile, and Japan promotes R&D, its economic performance is likely to be relatively good—at least as good as the better performers among the OECD nations—but industrial policy will not play a significant role.

Undoubtedly, parts of the analysis offered by Eads and Yamamura will be questioned. Nonetheless, theirs is a comparative politico-economic study of Japan's industrial policy that, when read with the other essays in this part, provides a broader and perhaps more balanced understanding of the reasons for, and the effects of, Japan's industrial policy than would a narrowly focused economic analysis in which policies are often regarded primarily as efficiency-reducing intrusions into effectively functioning markets.

In "Industrial Organization: The 1970s to the Present," the second paper in Part IV, Masu Uekusa reviews Japan's industrial organization during the past 15 years. For the author, the most salient change has been a clear and notable shift from heavy and chemical industries to knowledge-intensive and energy-conserving high-technology industries. Accordingly, he makes a special effort to examine the effects on the industrial structure of rapidly rising energy costs after the oil crises of the 1970s, the rapid technological changes, and the public demand for "clean" industries.

In evaluating the economic performance of Japan in the past 15 years, Uekusa credits Japan's ability to adjust its industrial structure more effectively than other advanced industrial nations. Facilitating these adjustments most has been the success of Japanese managers in lowering costs and improving product quality and the rapid expansion of private R&D expenditure, notably in high-tech industries. Government adjustment policy and the voluntary action of private enterprises, too, he believes, have aided Japan's efforts to cope with the problems created by declining industries and to encourage innovative activities. He stresses that the adjustment process has been eased by the increasing use made by large firms of subcontractors who are capable of providing the former with a high degree of flexibility. Significantly, the views expressed on subcontracting in Japan by Aoki, Koike, and Patrick and Rohlen are, in essence, consonant with those of Uekusa.

Uekusa provides an analysis demonstrating that Japan's industrial organization has become more competitive over time. There have been fewer cartels and mergers among large firms partly because of the 1977 revision of the Antimonopoly Law and partly because the Ministry of International Trade and Industry changed its policy and limited collusive activities among firms. Both trade liberalization and technological changes have made Japanese markets more competitive; new firms have quite readily entered high-tech and other industries. On the other hand, the gains from mass production and increasing output (learning curve effects) continue for semiconductors and other products, so that growing demand for them is likely to further encourage mass production, reinforcing the trend toward an oligopolistic market structure in these industries.

While these developments were occurring, Uekusa notes, Japan's industrial policy became passive and ineffective mainly because national priorities shifted from attaining maximum economic growth to raising the quality of life, because firms are no longer willing to be "guided," and because foreign pressure continues to force Japan to open its markets, depriving the bureaucracy of important policy instruments. He concludes that deregulation of industries will become a preoccupation of the Japanese government and that the trend toward a more liberal and competitive industrial organization will continue.

Uekusa's authoritative overview of the recent changes in Japan's industrial organization is especially valuable when read alongside the preceding study by Eads and Yamamura. These two contributions, examining many of the same recent developments and issues, provide one analysis made from a Japanese perspective and the other from an American, comparative perspective. The areas of agreement and disagreement— the differences in emphasis and in interpretation of the reasons for the same developments—themselves provide the reader rich insights and a better understanding of the roles of economic policy in Japan.

The third paper in this section is "The Conservative Policy Line and the Development of Patterned Pluralism," coauthored by political scientists Michio Muramatsu and Ellis S. Krauss. Their goal is to analyze the political causes of Japan's postwar economic growth. In the view of the authors, even those studies on Japanese economic growth that consider political factors all too often focus on only two variables: the elite bureaucracy striving for rapid growth and the national consensus supporting that goal. Muramatsu and Krauss argue that such studies present only a limited view of the contributions of politics to Japan's economic development because it is unwarranted to assume the existence of a consensus on developmental goals when the meaning of development in fact changed over time and because the influence of bureaucrats has declined over the past two decades. What must be stressed is the role of the dominant Liberal Democratic Party and its political strategy, the growing influence of interest groups, and the broadening of Japan's policymaking elite in building the context for economic growth and economic policy in general as it has evolved.

Most crucially, they argue that what they term the "conservative party line" (CPL) was developed early in the postwar period by Japan's conservatives in order to provide them with a new identity, to enlist the active cooperation of the bureaucracy, and to form a unified conservative party able to fill the political vacuum that existed after the decline of the opposition parties in the early 1950s. The basic tenets of the CPL are a close relationship with the United States, acceptance of the desirability and efficacy of government guidance of the economy, nonideological conservatism, and centrist policies designed to cushion domestic political confrontations. The CPL's aim, in short, has been to provide the political stability necessary for economic growth. The authors contend that economic success finally led to public acceptance of the CPL, thereby keeping the LDP in power for thirty years. That is, they maintain that "national consensus" was a result of the policy's success.

No less important, the authors argue that the LDP would not have remained the dominant party had the CPL not been flexible enough to respond to social and economic changes. With the emergence of the "new middle mass" in the 1960s, the LDP incorporated greater economic equality and social security into its program, and it has, in many other ways as well, broadened its base of supporters in order to become a catchall party.

Yet, the authors note, both the LDP's and the Japan Socialist Party's electoral strength have declined since the early 1970s, and new parties have emerged. The "one and a half party system" of the 1950s and 1960s has evolved into a power balance between a bare majority LDP and a multiparty opposition. Special interest groups with access to both politicians and bureaucrats have become more numerous and influential. Politicians of all parties are increasingly specialized and able to compete with the expertise of the bureaucracy. The ruling triad of the earlier rapid growth decades—the bureaucracy, the LDP, and big business—had to give way to a broader policymaking elite that has to accommodate the demands even of the opposition. Today various "subgovernments" to promote their common interest have emerged; these consist of segments of the bureaucracy, the LDP, and interest groups. Conflicts among and within different subgovernments have become a part of Japan's political life. Muramatsu and Krauss term this system "patterned pluralism" because there are many diverse actors whose alliances may shift, but the shifting coalitions occur within the framework of one-party dominance. And the bureaucracy still remains the pivot around which alliances and policymaking patterns are formed.

For the rest of the 1980s and perhaps beyond, the authors predict an increasing diversification of, and conflicts among, special interest groups that might even include foreign actors. The LDP, they speculate, will be forced to deal with more controversial political and economic issues; one result of such a development could be the abandonment of the party's centralist stance, one of the principles of the CPL. Such an anticipated development does not cause Muramatsu and Krauss to predict that the LDP will in the near future cease to be in power either singly or as a senior partner in a coalition. They suggest, however, that the CPL, and thus Japanese politics, will face serious challenges in the coming years.

This paper provides the reader with thoughtful descriptions and knowledgeable analysis of the nature and recent transformation of the party in power and its modus vivendi, which they call the CPL. This party also offers a dynamic account of Japanese politics, which has evolved from the ruling triad to patterned pluralism responding to the changing needs of the Japanese political economy and reflecting Japan's social and political legacies.

Yutaka Kosai's "The Politics of Economic Management," the final paper in Part IV, examines the process of economic policy formulation. Kosai's intent is to demonstrate that in Japan economic goals and the means to achieve them are determined politically, as in other democracies. He does not reject such models as the bureaucracy-led model and the ruling triad (bureaucracy, big business, and LDP) model that were earlier advanced to explain Japan's economic management. His view is that these models, once useful in explaining Japan's economic management in the immediate postwar years and in the 1950s, are no longer valid. For Kosai, to analyze the Japanese political reality since the early 1960s, the proper model is the patterned pluralism that Muramatsu and Krauss present in the preceding chapter.

Kosai argues that a more pluralist system in which politicians exert greater influence developed as a natural outcome of the maturing of the Japanese democracy. What made the ruling triad system obsolete was the rise of new interest groups whose demands the LDP must accommodate if it is to remain in power. And Kosai, agreeing with Murakami and Muramatsu and Krauss, notes that the emergence of the new middle mass is a crucial factor contributing to the politics of patterned pluralism because the middle mass is not tied to any specific political ideology or orientation.

As the central concern of his chapter, Kosai stresses that throughout the postwar period, Japanese political leaders have regarded economic policy as an important political issue and that politics has been an important factor in economic management both at the macro- and micro-levels. Kosai demonstrates the validity of this observation in his analysis of price stability, which has always been a major goal of macroeconomic policy pursued under the leadership of prime ministers attempting to respond to public opinion expressed in general elections.

Kosai further argues that, although the influence of the bureaucracy still remains strong on the micro-level, today politicians are exerting more power than before. This occurred, he believes, because politicians have acquired the experience and skills needed to exercise their power and because they have proved to be more flexible in solving intersectoral conflicts than the bureaucracy. He is convinced that, in the coming decades, the leadership in economic management will continue to shift away from bureaucrats and toward politicians. He adds, however, that the rapid social changes that could bring about a greater political instability and the changes that are expected to occur in the structure of the Japanese economy will require some institutional reforms to keep economic management effective.

Kosai's analysis is a carefully argued, politico-economic reexamination of the role of politics and politicians in the management of the Japanese economy. Like Muramatsu and Krauss, he does not deny that Japan's economic management had and continues to retain certain structural and behavioral features that differ from those of other industrial democracies. But he does argue persuasively that in Japan, too, the principal force determining economic policy has been politics and politicians. What has changed in recent years is that this has become more important as Japan's democracy has continued to mature.

For all who participated in this volume as editors and authors, the tasks involved were analogous, we felt, to those a group of painters encounters in attempting to paint a picture of a landscape on a huge canvas. In our case, we selected the Japanese political economy as the subject. Each of us agreed to sketch its contours using a pencil sharpened by the knives of differing disciplines; to draw in mountains, fields, and rivers, carefully mixing economics-red, politics-blue, and other colors; and to add structure, gardens, and people, taking pains to identify the details that make the scene Japanese. To complete the painting took nearly four years; many parts of the canvas were redrawn and repainted, benefiting from many hours of mutual criticism. How well we painted the landscape, capturing its subtle nuances and vibrant elan, is for the reader to decide.

We trust that this volume will stimulate the interest of readers to explore these and related topics further. For more detailed studies and for works offering differing views and interpretations, the reader is invited to examine the studies cited in each paper. Two companion volumes to this project will analyze the international dimensions of Japan's political economy and its social-cultural basis. In essence, all volumes are cut from the same cloth, but provide different perspectives and dimensions to many of the issues raised in this volume.

The editors of this volume wish to add that this volume is a product of a truly collective effort of the general editors, the contributors, and ourselves. In writing this introduction, we have also benefited substantially from the background essays (for discussion at our earlier planning conferences for this project) prepared by Yasasuke Murakami and by Hugh Patrick and Henry Rosovsky and by the comments of Daniel I. Okimoto and others. We also wish to express special thanks to Shumpei Kumon, Seizaburo Sato, and Ryutaro Komiya, who participated actively in the conferences and made comments that were most valuable in improving the various papers.

Finally, we, as volume editors, join the general editors in expressing our deep appreciation to those organizations and individuals mentioned in the Preface. We are also most grateful to Martha L. Lane and Karla E. Pearson, who played indispensable roles in editing this volume. To transform 13 manuscripts written on both sides of the Pacific into this volume, we needed all of their administrative abilities, editorial skills, and imperturbable sanity. The indexes were prepared by Sabine Seidler, *mit viel Eifer und Sorgfalt*.

Part I

The Japanese Model

Yasusuke Murakami

The Japanese Model of
Political Economy

A large number of models have recently emerged to explain Japan's postwar economic success. Although diverse in level of analysis, these models represent, on a theoretical level, different possible approaches. The purpose of this paper is to organize these models systematically and to summarize and evaluate each model in terms of its contribution to our understanding of the workings of contemporary Japan's political economy.

Broadly speaking, these models may be divided into two groups: those that emphasize economic factors and those that emphasize cultural factors. Economic models stress a set of factors in the "objective environment," such as the labor supply, diffusion of technology, or expansion of the world market. Cultural models, on the other hand, focus on factors in the "subjective environment," including various aspects of "traditional" Japanese culture such as group orientation or the inclination toward consensus. It seems clear that neither a purely economic model nor a purely cultural model is adequate for analysis of the postwar political economy (or, for that matter, any industrialization-oriented society, particularly a late developer). Postwar Japan's economic growth indisputably owes much to the favorable objective environment. At the same time, the imprint of Japanese culture on many characteristics of the politico-economic structure is clearly visible. Although much of the cultural determinism in the so-called *Nihonjinron* ("Japanese national character") literature is too one-sided or inaccurate, cultural influences are important in accounting for the differences between Japan's political economy and those of other industrial societies.

A suggested depiction of the relationship between political economy and the objective and subjective environments is shown in Fig. 1. The objective environment consists of the physical environment (nature-to-society relationships) and the international environment (society-to-society relationships). The physical environment includes not only such factors as climate, land, mineral resources, and other geographical conditions on and around the Japanese islands, but also such factors as the population or labor force at the beginning of the postwar reconstruction. An initial stock of available technologies is also an essential component of the physical environment. For the Japanese economy after the war, the technological environment meant the array of new technologies accumulated in other nations since the 1930s, particularly during the war. In the present analysis, the international environment is the Pax Americana, including the worldwide U.S. defense capability and the IMF-GATT economic system based on the principles of a fixed exchange rate and free trade. The stability of the Pax Americana until the oil crisis was a given condition favorable to Japan.

The subjective environment consists of the cultural environment and national goals. National goals are the broadest possible framework of national policies. Generally speaking, policies are endogenous variables determined within a society's political economy. Most specific postwar policies are explicable in terms of the internal dynamics of Japanese society. The basic policy orientation of postwar Japan was established in the first few years after the war, setting the locus of Japanese society in the following decades. This basic framework included the national consensus of catching up with advanced countries in economic policies. These policy stances constituted the national goals that conditioned the postwar Japanese political economy. There is no need to emphasize here the importance of the cultural environment. Its characteristic features are explained later in more detail.

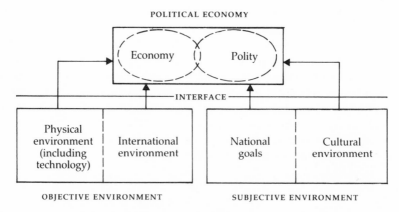

Fig. 1. The political economy and the environment.

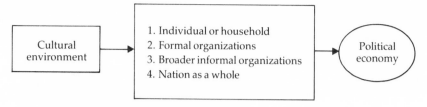

Fig. 2. Possible interfaces.

Within the framework of the system shown in Fig. 1, economic models focus on one set of factors in the objective environment (certain physical and technological factors) and cultural models focus on a set in the subjective environment (culture).

Much effort has gone into the elaboration of economic models, and cultural models have attracted much popular attention. Unfortunately, these efforts have proceeded separately from each other. This paper attempts to broaden the discussion to models that explicitly incorporate the effects of the cultural environment on the political economy with the effects of the technological and physical environments. In my view, such models can be classified into four types on the basis of where they locate the crucial *interface* or mediating sets of social actors between culture and the political economy (see Fig. 2). The next section presents a brief discussion of these interfaces.

Interfaces Between Culture and the Political Economy

Cultural Environment

The cultural environment is the latent basic pattern in society; that is, those principles governing the cognition, evaluation, and decision process of persons and the behavioral and organizational pattern embedded in a society as a whole or in a subgroup within it. The single most important characteristic of the Japanese cultural tradition is a particular type of organizational principle, which may be called the *ie* genotype (*ie* originally meant household) or, in some cases, the *mura* ("village") variant. As I argue later in this paper, many contemporary Japanese organizations resemble either the *ie*- or the *mura*-type organizational pattern. The two patterns may be defined as follows.[1]

1. The *ie* genotype is the tight version of the indigenous organizational principle and is defined as a group having the following characteristics:

    a. Collective goal: eternal continuation and expansion of the

group, which is often symbolized by stem succession to group
leadership.[2]

b. Membership qualification: "kintractship," that is, no member
should leave the group once he or she joins it.[3]

c. Hierarchy-homogeneity balance: all members are organized in a
hierarchy aiming at some functional goal, and various complementary measures further their homogeneity.[4]

d. Autonomy: the group encompasses all functions necessary to
its perpetuation.

2. The *mura* variant, the loose version of the indigenous organizational
principle, is defined as a group with the following characteristics:

a. Collective goal: very long term continuation and expansion of
the group.

b. Membership qualification: every member should stay with the
group as long as it continues.

c. Homogeneity-hierarchy balance: all members are considered to
be homogeneous and therefore treated equally, but they implicitly share a sense of ranking that reflects, by and large, functional capability.

d. Multifunctionality: the group achieves and reconciles diverse
interrelated functions.

These two organizational types share the principle that a group decision reached by long-term, multi-issue, often implicit agreements should
override a particular person's choice on a specific short-term issue. The
ie-type group originated in samurai organization in eastern Japan during
the eleventh century, reflecting the severe conditions besetting this agro-
military group in a frontier region. The *mura* in the sense outlined above
assumed its final form in the Tokugawa period (1603–1867) as semiautonomous social units constituting the society's substratum. Obviously,
the *mura* is a looser and more egalitarian organization than the *ie*.[5]

The Four Interfaces

The four key alternative interfaces are summarized below. (For the
sake of expository convenience, the explanation of the nation-focused
interface comes first.)

1. *Nation as a whole*. Western observers tend to argue that the interaction between culture and the political economy is consummated at the
national level by means of the Japanese government's conscious and consistent policy. According to this perception, the Japanese political economy mimics a single cohesive organization such as a family or a corporation. The popular "Japan, Inc." model, for example, represents the idea

that culture and the political economy are integrated at the national level rather than at a lower level. Another example is the notion of the family-state advocated by some ideologues in prewar Japan.

2. *Individual or household.* In any society, an average person's (or household's) economic or political behavior reflects an internalized cultural tradition. The average Japanese, for example, is often said to be hardworking, prone to saving, eager to acquire education, and skillful in imitation; presumably these traits arise from the cultural tradition. If culture influences economic performance mainly at this level, it should be possible to explain the Japanese economy as a whole by a standard market economy model in which cultural uniqueness is represented by unusually high values for certain structural parameters such as a high savings ratio, the high quality (high educational level) of labor, or a high speed of technological diffusion. As another example, the average Japanese is, according to many Western observers, docile, conformist, and obedient to authority. Based on this "trait psychology" presumption, a standard voting behavior model would predict, for example, the continued dominance of the governing party. In this way, the individual-focused interface assumption is likely to lead to the adoption of the classic individualistic models of society developed in the Western intellectual tradition.

3. *Formal organizations* (for example, firms, political parties). A firm is probably the most important economic entity that formally (with legal grounds) organizes a large number of people; a political party is a formal organization that plays the role of the key entity in the polity. The organization of these crucial entities probably reflects each society's cultural tradition, although the functional prerequisites for being a firm or a political party are likely to limit or transform to some extent the original cultural pattern. For example, if the Japanese firm is, as many people argue, a present-day embodiment of an organizational tradition unique to Japan, it will behave differently from the standard firm conceived in economic theory; for example, it might maximize its market share rather than its profit. A similar assumption might be made concerning Japanese political parties (see below). Under this firm- or party-focused interface assumption, the conventional individualistic model has to be at least partially revised. For example, the demand as well as supply of labor may not be adjusted in a standard market fashion. Similarly, the political party may not be a voluntary association based primarily on an agreed policy program.

4. *Informal organizations* (for example, administrative guidance, *keiretsu*, or *shitauke*). Another type of interface is those various agreements or policy arrangements that are broader in scale than a firm or a political party and are not legally institutionalized as formal organizations. In the economic sphere, examples of government-led informal organizations

are the policy setting (often called the "Japanese industrial policy") led by the Ministry of International Trade and Industry (MITI) or the Japanese financial system under the Ministry of Finance (MOF). Possible examples of private informal organizations are the *shitauke* ("subcontractor") system and the *keiretsuka* phenomenon (groupings such as the Mitsui group or the Mitsubishi group). In the political sphere, a similar example may be found in the relationship among parliament, the bureaucracy, and industry (see below). These semi-institutionalized practices appear to mirror the organizational tradition of the prewar era or a more distant past. If such informal organizations work as an additional restriction on the legal framework, the Japanese political economy will function differently from the classical model of market and parliament.

All of these four interfaces undoubtedly act to adapt the political economy to the cultural environment (and vice versa). Depending on which interface is viewed as crucial, however, various explanations of the postwar Japanese political economy arise. In the next two sections, I examine these alternative forms.

First, a few comments regarding the relationship between the polity and the economy in Japan are in order. It is necessary to weaken the basic presupposition of standard economic theory that an economy and a polity are separate entities. In British industrialization, separation of the economy from the polity was believed to be essential—the so-called laissez-faire principle. In the British case, political integration preceded industrialization and provided it with the required noneconomic setting. Once the setting was ready, any further political interference with the economy was thought detrimental to vigorous economic development. The same seems to be true of many former British colonies dominated by whites, such as the United States. In the case of late-developing countries, including such European examples as Germany, Italy, and in my opinion, France, however, political integration tended to lag behind industrialization. Political interference with the economy not only was unavoidable but also was often profitable in terms of implementing the lessons of the early developers' experience. Postwar Japan may be viewed as a variant of the late-developer case. The prewar Japanese economy had not caught up fully with those of Western industrial nations. The war isolated Japanese industry from much technological progress and in the end devastated it. For this reason, any analysis of the postwar Japanese politico-economic system should not preclude the possibility that an economy and a polity are linked more closely than standard economic theory assumes.

In order to make critical evaluation of the models explaining the relation between culture and political economy analytically manageable, however, it is most convenient to consider the economy and the polity separately for the time being and to examine the interface of each with culture. This is particularly appropriate for three of the models—excluding the nation-focused model—since they all view decision making in Japanese society as decentralized. I stress, however, that readers should not interpret this as an indication that the economy and the polity of postwar Japan are not closely linked.

Models Explaining the Economy

Nation-Focused Model

First, we can safely dismiss nation-focused models such as the "Japan, Inc." model. This once-popular notion asserts that the Japanese cultural tradition is most clearly manifested in the way Japanese society is controlled as a whole. According to this notion, Japanese society is monolithic and tightly regulated and thus resembles a single corporation run by a group of clever leaders, who mobilized the postwar Japanese populace for the sake of economic growth. Any closer examination, however, shows this to be a crude and simplistic stereotype.[6] All indications show that both the market mechanism and parliamentary democracy have been at work in postwar Japan, bringing about fierce competition and visible conflicts in many parts of society. The postwar Japanese economic experience has been replete with examples of competitive phenomena, such as the investment race, export competition, and competition among banks for depositors. Although continued rule by the conservative party has been a principal feature of the postwar political system, the conservative ascendancy faced serious challenges at least twice: in 1960, when the revision of the U.S.-Japan Mutual Security Treaty prompted riots in Tokyo, and around 1970, when the conservative party lost many major local elections. As I argue later, the seeming overall conformity of behavior in postwar Japan was a fortuitous outcome—under a set of favorable conditions unique to the postwar era—of interaction among various potentially conflicting interests. For this reason, the nation-focused model should be discarded.

Individual-Focused Model

This type of model by no means denies the influence of culture on the economy, but it regards each person (consumer, laborer, asset holder) as essentially the only link between the economy and the cultural environment. The interaction among individual economic actors can thus be explained largely by the classical market economy model, with cultural uniqueness presumably being expressed as the particular shape of each person's (or household's) demand or supply functions. Given these well-

defined functions, standard economic reasoning leads to familiar conclusions—for example, the classical propositions concerning comparative advantage or factor scarcity. In this market economy model, the factor endowments specific to Japan's objective environment explain the
apparent uniqueness of the Japanese economy. There are several variants
of this argument. Some people point to an abundant supply of hardworking, well-educated labor during the rapid growth period, at least in
the early phase. Others contend that the very high savings rate of Japanese households led to an ample supply of investable capital. Still others
emphasize that energy and basic materials were extremely cheap until
the first oil crisis.

There is no doubt that the abundance of these inputs proved beneficial
to the rapid growth of the Japanese economy. Had the labor force been
less abundant (that is, had there been less "disguised employment" in
agriculture) or less educated, economic growth would certainly have
been slower. Had households' savings been smaller, the growth rate
would have been lower. Higher world prices for petroleum or other mineral resources might have slowed industrial growth. As Denison-type
"growth accounting" shows, however, the imputed contribution of these
factor inputs accounts for less than half of Japan's economic growth.[7]
Thus, a difference in the abundance of inputs between Japan and other
countries accounts for an even smaller portion of Japan's economic growth.
(Recall that many other industrial countries could and did import capital
as well as immigrant labor.) Evidently, the issue of *absolute* scarcity (or
abundance) is not essential for explaining Japan's economic success.

The issue of *relative* scarcity of factor inputs is probably more important. To state it differently, a more important question is whether the vast
changes in Japanese industrial structure during the rapid growth period
can be explained in terms of relative factor scarcity. Indeed, there was an
ample supply or even an oversupply of labor in the 1950s and early
1960s. At that time, however, Japanese industrial structure was shifting
rapidly from the labor-intensive industries, such as textiles, that dominated the prewar era to capital-intensive (labor-saving) processing industries, such as steel, synthetic fibers, petrochemicals, and oil refining.
Three other new industries, automobiles, electric appliances, and shipbuilding, were also more capital-intensive than the prewar-type textile
industry. This structural shift remains, even if we take into account not
only the direct inputs to these industries but also the indirect inputs induced in all those industries that supplied intermediate products or materials to the industries in question.[8] If such factors as the quality of labor or capital vintage are considered, the picture might be somewhat
modified, but no empirical evidence has been given that revises this picture of relative factor scarcity.

Thus, in order to support the relative scarcity argument, we have to assume that capital was relatively more abundant than labor. This assumption, however, seems to contradict the facts. In the 1950s, when the shift toward the heavy and chemical industries occurred, the savings rate of Japanese households was still below 20 per cent (comparable to those in other industrial societies). Moreover, since the level of income in Japan was very low in the 1950s, even a savings rate above 20 per cent would have yielded a small amount of savings per worker (roughly one-tenth of the level in 1984). In short, there are no grounds on which to say that Japan in the 1950s and early 1960s was richer in capital (vis-à-vis labor) than other industrial nations.

The argument emphasizing the benefit of cheap energy and materials is not persuasive either. This argument could explain why the postwar industrial structure became more energy or material consuming and thus more centered on intermediate products than it would have been had higher energy or material costs prevailed. But it does not explain why the Japanese economy was relatively more inclined to energy- or material-consuming industries than other economies. Low energy costs were common throughout the world, and, it must be remembered, the Japanese economy incurred substantial social costs (including many serious labor disputes in the coal-mining industry) in switching from costly domestic energy sources to cheap imported ones. Without a conscious government policy, this kind of structural change would have been difficult.

The conclusions of Denison-type growth accounting make it necessary to explain the unexplained residual that constitutes more than half of Japanese economic growth. This residual is often attributed to technological progress, but it is, in fact, a collection of all those causes that cannot be explained by factor inputs. These causes probably are closely correlated with technological change or changes in industrial structure, and many scholars, such as Kazushi Ohkawa, Henry Rosovsky, Kazuo Sato, and others, have attempted to explain postwar Japanese economic growth in terms of technological progress.[9]

In the following, I attempt to clarify how this technological progress was brought to fruition at the macroeconomic level and how it was related to rapid shifts in industrial structure, governmental policy, and other relevant factors.

Organization-Focused Models

The argument above suggests that the individual-focused model, which is virtually the same as the classical market economy model, is inadequate to explain the essential characteristics (such as rapid growth) of the postwar Japanese economy. The two remaining approaches—the formal organization–focused model (firm-focused model) and the informal organization–focused model—explicitly involve considering economic organizations or systems larger than persons or households, such as firms, administrative organs, and markets.

Any organizational model of the economy can be broken down into three submodels: (1) a submodel explaining firm behavior; (2) a submodel explaining administrative intervention (which links the economy with the polity); and (3) a submodel explaining market structure. Both the formal organization–focused model and the informal organization–focused model must be specified at each level. In other words, each model is a collection of subhypotheses at these three levels. For the sake of convenience, each submodel is discussed below in terms of alternative hypotheses that constitute the formal and the informal organization models.

Firm behavior submodel. In my view, any model claiming to interpret the behavior of firms in the postwar Japanese economy must explain two important facts. First, Japanese firms in the leading postwar industries had, as many attitude surveys show,[10] a long-run managerial perspective as well as a strong motivation for growth (vis-à-vis profits) compared with those in other countries. Second, Japanese industries during the rapid growth period were frequently involved in unusually intense competition such as the investment race, the "downpouring of exports," or the competition among banks for attracting depositors; all of these were often termed "excessive competition."

The formal organization or firm-focused approach can be represented by the following now-celebrated notion about the Japanese firm.

1.a. *Japanese management hypothesis*
    The Japanese firm in the major postwar industries was a community-like organization that aimed at eternal expansion. In terms of economic performance, the Japanese firm sought to maximize its market share (subject to a certain minimum profit rate).

The hypothesis of market share maximization (which is close to sales growth maximization) can be derived from several more basic behavioral assumptions concerning the members of firms. Masahiko Aoki, for example, has formulated a rigorous model to explain why a firm may endeavor to achieve higher sales growth rather than endeavoring to maximize profits (share prices). His formulation is essentially a cooperative game model among members of the firm (employees, stockholders, and managers as arbitrators) reinforced by an assumption of promotional prospects for employees. (See his paper in this volume.) In order to guarantee the stability of this game-theoretic solution, his model presupposes a consensus about joint maximization that implies the existence of some group consciousness among firm members.[11] In this regard, Shumpei Kumon, Seizaburo Sato, and I have proposed that Japanese management is a present-day version of the *ie* principle; in other words, the indigenous organizational tradition in Japan provides contemporary Japanese firms with a basis of group consciousness and a certain type of organizational design. Space limitations unfortunately do not permit me to delve into the differences between Aoki's approach and ours. I note only that the maximization of market share or sales growth requires, under ordinary conditions, that some form of common group consciousness be shared by firm members.

Alternatively, the informal organization–focused approach to firm behavior may be represented by a hypothesis that emphasizes the favorable circumstances created by a set of informal policy arrangements (formulated later as the "weak guidance hypothesis").

1.b. *Pro-growth environment hypothesis*

The postwar Japanese firm faced favorable circumstances in the sense that the dynamic average cost schedule was declining. This cost-curve characteristic arose partly from the worldwide postwar surge of technological innovation, but more important it resulted from a set of risk-reducing environmental and institutional factors unique to postwar Japan.

These factors were related to technology, capital, labor, and demand. As latecomers, Japanese industries took advantage of the latest technologies, which had already been tested in more advanced economies. With respect to capital, the postwar Japanese financial system succeeded in shifting a substantial part of firms' risks to households. Labor was remarkably adaptable to rapidly changing technologies because of high interjob mobility and on-the-job training within each firm (see Koike's paper in this volume). Finally, the continued dominance of the conservative party guaranteed consistent pro-growth policies (announced as a series of "economic plans") that helped reduce uncertainty in demand.

This concept of dynamic cost schedule should be distinguished from the standard textbook notion of long-run cost function that describes a purely technological relationship between output and cost, given adjustable fixed equipment. It represents more realistically how managers estimate costs associated with various levels of output when they make decisions about long-run investments. The dynamic cost schedule may be limited to the levels of output that are immediately under consideration; a firm operating under decreasing average cost does not necessarily consider the increasing average costs that the firm will experience later. More important, the dynamic cost schedule should include "expectation variables"—the firm's forecast of such key variables as future capital costs, future wage costs, and future product prices (which reflect the firm's expectations about demand). The dynamic cost schedule is socio-economic—that is, it is dependent on how the economy as a whole deals with uncertainty. It probably differs from country to country.

In hindsight, decreasing cost was a global phenomenon in the postwar industrial world, which actively applied, refined, and systematized basic technologies born largely during the period 1925–50. Being latecomers, however, Japanese firms had the advantage of being able to detect and utilize, *ex ante*, this decreasing cost trend. Moreover, as I later discuss, the Japanese government encouraged key industries to take advantage of this latecomer status. Technological innovations could at least partly be expected, especially during the 1950s and 1960s, which were character-ized by technological application rather than creation. In this sense, technological progress is one of the expectation variables that can be in-corporated into the dynamic cost schedule. For latecomers such as Japa-nese firms, the risks surrounding this expectation variable were very low. In toto, the risk-reducing effects spelled out above resulted in the downward shift of long-run average cost (calculated as its expected value plus risk premium).

This decreasing cost phenomenon was most evident in industries with large-scale equipment such as steel, automobiles, oil refining, synthetic fibers, petrochemicals, and, to a lesser degree, electric appliances and other machinery industries. The cost decreases, however, resulted not merely from the large scale of fixed equipment but also from the late de-velopers' advantage in utilizing the consistent technological innovations characteristic of these industries in the postwar world. These two as-pects were inextricably interwoven. The standard economic argument—for example, the notion of "infant industries"—is too static to explain these volatile industries. In Japan, these leading postwar industries ac-counted for almost 40 per cent of the value added in manufacturing (ac-cording to the 1970 input-output table).[12] Moreover, all these industries generated a strong indirect demand, and they were generally sensitive to an increase in final demand.[13] These cost-decreasing industries were in-deed an engine of postwar Japanese economic growth.

The two hypotheses presented here—the Japanese management hy-pothesis and the pro-growth environment hypothesis—must be evalu-ated in terms of their relative ability to explain the existence of the long-run managerial perspective and excessive competition. In order to as-sess the hypotheses, we must consider two economic theorems regard-ing maximization and stability.[14] In these theorems, firms are price-takers and there is no new entry into the market (these assumptions are ex-amined later in the argument concerning the "competitive polyopoly hypothesis"). Each firm's supply behavior is represented by an aver-age cost (plus markup profit) curve if the firm is maximizing its market share (which is the same, under the price-taker assumption, as output maximization.)

Maximization theorem

Under decreasing average cost, market share maximization is, at a given price, behaviorally equivalent to profit maximization. The firm simply maximizes its output in both types of behavior.

Stability theorem

If firms operate under a decreasing average cost situation, market equilibrium is unstable in the sense of standard price theory (most typically, in the sense of Walrasian stability). Moreover, market share maximization does not necessarily cause market instability (as it would in the case of increasing average cost).

Either of the hypotheses proposed in this section can explain firms' orientation toward long-run growth. Excessive competition is the key test. Standard economic theory tends to disclaim the concept of excessive competition. The only definition the theory can permit is "cutthroat competition" among too many market participants under free entry. As discussed later, however, entry was restricted to a certain degree in the leading postwar industries. In the context of the postwar Japanese economy, the only theoretical way out is to define excessive competition as market instability, which implies that price reduction results in greater excess supply, which causes further price reduction, and so on—this is what the notion of excessive competition attempts to describe.

The pro-growth hypothesis may be more appropriate because it can account for both phenomena—growthmanship as well as excessive competition, whereas the Japanese management hypothesis is irrelevant in explaining excessive competition (see the stability theorem). But the first hypothesis does not contradict the second. In fact, together the two hypotheses may provide a more complete description of the postwar behavior of Japanese firms. The key point in the present context is that "Japanese management," or, in other words, market share maximization, did not cause excessive competition.

An important corollary of this argument is that the basic behavioral pattern of Japanese firms has probably been changing since the mid-1970s because, as many empirical studies indicate, the decreasing cost situation has been disappearing in such major industries as steel, automobiles, petrochemicals, and synthetic fibers. These industries have fully explored the scale effects, and technological progress has reached the level of saturation. The Japanese firm is now becoming more like those in other nations and no longer exhibits excessive competition, downpouring of exports, and other unusual behavior. This change will have, as argued later, crucial implications for industrial policy and antimonopoly policy.

Administrative behavior submodel. The following two hypotheses on government intervention are often found as prototypes in the literature and correspond to the nation-focused model and the informal organization–focused model in my terminology. The first hypothesis is less a formal organization–focused one than a nation-focused one. It is referred to here principally for the sake of comparison with the second hypothesis.

2.a. *Strong regulation hypothesis*
Postwar administrative intervention in the private sector of the economy was mandatory (that is, legally enforceable), discretionary, and specific to each industry—just like practices in a planned economy or those within each firm (as implied by the Japan, Inc. model).

2.b. *Weak guidance hypothesis*
Postwar administrative intervention was indicative (that is, not legally enforceable), based on fixed rules rather than discretion, and specific to each industry.

The misconception that any administrative intervention is necessarily of the "strong regulation" type is widely held. The experience of postwar Japan suggests, however, that there can be an intermediate mode of intervention between strong regulation and a laissez-faire system. The second hypothesis is an example of such an intermediate mode. The crucial concept in this hypothesis is that of "indicative intervention."

Any effective indicative intervention cannot be a mere indication of what the government has in mind. Rather, we could define it as "promotional intervention," that is, intervention dependent not so much on legal penalties (sticks) as on promotional measures (carrots), such as financing, tax concessions, subsidies, R&D grants, and government contracts. On the other hand, "mandatory intervention" means a prohibitive intervention by means of legal penalties rather than promotional measures. Obviously, promotional measures can exert no immediate prohibitive effects on firms. A government can restrain "undesirable" firm behavior only by causing a firm to fear that its behavior might produce long-run negative effects (suspension of promotional measures) or negative repercussions in other areas (for example, licensing troubles). In order for indicative or promotional intervention to be effective, some additional conditions must hold.

Theorem of long-term association: Mura *theorem 1*
Indicative intervention is effective only if all parties concerned, intervenor as well as intervenee, are involved in close interrelations based on implicit, long-term, and multi-issued agreements.

The basic fact that postwar interventions were rarely mandatory contradicts the strong regulation hypothesis. Except for the oil-refining industry, no regulatory statutes provided MITI or other ministries with legal grounds for penalizing violations by leading industries. In particular, although trade associations were essential for industry-specific administrative interventions no law made trade associations compulsory. In contrast to prewar Japan, postwar trade associations were, in a legal sense, voluntary associations. A corollary of this theorem is that securing the participation of all potential members in each trade association, and thereby maintaining the effectiveness of intervention, requires that intervention be impartial across all firms in that industry.

Theorem of fairness within an industry: Mura *theorem 2*
Indicative intervention can be viable only if it is sufficiently impartial or, more concretely, if it is based on rules that can be viewed as fixed for some reasonable length of time.

Many studies on specific Japanese industries testify that administrative intervention in major postwar Japanese industries was not only industry specific and largely legally unenforceable (that is, indicative), but also based on quasi-fixed rules (that is, it was impartial within each industry). A close informal relationship existed among all parties concerned, including the ministry of jurisdiction and all firms in the industry in question. This bundle of characteristics is aptly summarized in the concept of *gyōsei shidō* ("administrative guidance"), which may be viewed as the present-day variant of the *mura* principle because of the similarity in basic characteristics.

Indeed, industry-wide administrative guidance has a historical background. The trade associations were legally formed and assigned key roles in the wartime economy, retained some legal status in the impoverished rationing economy of the immediate postwar period, and then were legally terminated with the end of the import quota system. This background was undoubtedly one of the sources of *gyōsei shidō*, but the success of administrative guidance lay in its adaptation of the organizational heritage to the requisites of rapid catch-up growth and its more informal, flexible, and egalitarian structure compared to the *mura* prototype.

Industrial policy and the financial system. I have argued that the informal organization–focused model represented by the weak guidance hypothesis best explains the postwar system. Two important examples of the practice of administrative guidance were the Japanese financial system under the guidance of the Ministry of Finance (MOF) and the Bank of Japan (BOJ) and Japanese industrial policy under the Ministry of International Trade and Industry (MITI).

That regulation has played an important role in the postwar Japanese financial system has been a widely accepted idea in the academic community. Recently, however, a group of younger economists has challenged this conventional view, contending that the system might better be understood as being more akin to a competitive market. Specifically, the effective interest rate (the nominal interest rate adjusted to take account of the effect of compensatory deposit practices) was not artificially low compared with the market-clearing rate. In contrast to the old "regulation school," this new "market school" has provided insights and stimuli for further research. Even the strongest proponents of the market school would, however, hesitate to argue that the Japanese financial system as a whole was one big competitive market with perfectly arbitrated submarkets. Compensatory deposit practices were not available to individual depositors, who had to accept the artificially low nominal interest rates of savings deposits and bonds. Japanese households were, in this sense, unfairly treated vis-à-vis other lenders, mainly the banks. This implies that firms making investments transferred the risks on an enormous scale to households. This was mentioned in presenting the pro-growth environment hypothesis concerning firm behavior. The weak guidance hypothesis and the pro-growth environment hypothesis can thus be viewed as complementary.

Moreover, the artificially low interest rate resulted not from legal enforcement but rather from voluntary interest rate regulation (*jishu kinri kisei*) under the guidance of the MOF and BOJ. A bank lending at an interest rate higher than the BOJ advised would have faced serious inconveniences when it tried to borrow money at the BOJ's window or to get licenses to open new branches (growth money in postwar Japan used to be supplied mainly in the form of BOJ loans at favorable interest rates). In this way, the MOF and BOJ could effectively control the interest rate level as well as the direction of fund flows. On the other hand, the interventions were not really so strict, as indicated by the existence of compensatory deposit practices. The Japanese financial system was a typical example of indicative intervention.

But why did Japanese households tolerate such an unfair institutional arrangement? Their eagerness to save probably resulted from a combination of factors, including poor urban housing conditions and the inadequate welfare system (both improved vastly in the 1970s). Many economists argue that the savings rate may be insensitive to the interest rate—particularly if income levels are as low as they were for Japanese households in the 1950s and 1960s. The tax system in postwar Japan was designed to encourage saving. The unexpectedly high growth of income may have caused an increase in saving because of inertia in consumption and may have also compensated in part for a feeling of discontent with the unfairness that households had to bear. In my view, however, a crucial psychological factor—the national "catch-up growth" consensus—dwarfed other societal issues.

Another important example of *gyōsei shidō* is the now-famous Japanese industrial policy applied to the leading postwar industries. (With respect to relatively declining industries such as textiles and fertilizers, MITI managed to have protective statutes specific to each industry enacted.) In my interpretation, Japanese industrial policy consisted of four practices.

1. *Promotional measures and license controls.* The Firm Rationalization Promotion Act of 1952 authorized MITI to use policy instruments such as tariffs or tax exemptions, including favorable depreciation rules. MITI also played an important role in distributing the government's financial aid (through the Japan Development Bank and the Japan Export-Import Bank), subsidies, and government contracts. Besides these promotional measures, MITI controlled import authorization and other, more technical, licensing up until the early 1960s.

2. *Entry control.* MITI interfered with new entries in such leading industries as steel, oil refining, petrochemicals, synthetic fibers, and automobiles and, if less notably, in many other industries. In each of these industries except steel, the number of firms did increase during the rapid growth period, but MITI was influential enough to select and delay new entries. Up to the mid-1970s, it virtually prohibited entry by any foreign firm by invoking the Foreign Exchange Law.

3. *Investment guidance.* Each firm's investment in the leading industries was controlled, albeit loosely, by MITI's guidelines, which were based on quotas proportional to market shares or, in some cases (for example, petrochemicals), on equal quotas. MITI's investment guidance had the character of a fixed rule rather than of discretion, although the guidance was only loosely obeyed by firms.

4. *Recession cartels.* During each of the intermittent and short recessions, MITI-guided recession cartels were introduced in many industries. Evidence suggests that these recession cartels were, in the leading industries, short-lived because of strong pressures from excessive competition.

Entry control was essential to the stability of the long-term association between government and industry, on which the effectiveness of *gyōsei shidō* crucially depended. Freer entries would have made virtually impossible the implicit, long-term, multi-issued agreements among all parties concerned. In particular, entries by foreign firms would have destabilized the industry-wide interrelation because foreign firms would probably not have complied with the idea underlying administrative guidance—the fastest possible catch-up growth for the Japanese economy.

In my opinion, MITI's investment guidance and MITI-guided recession cartels were effective in avoiding or alleviating the adverse effects of excessive competition or market instability. During times of prosperity, the investment race could easily have gotten out of control if no coordination had been attempted. During times of (relative) recession, overcapacity would have caused cutthroat price competition, particularly in the export market, unless some kind of recession cartel had been introduced. If we accept the prevalence of decreasing costs in leading industries, there follows the important corollary that coordination was necessary to control the self-destructive forces of market instability. The four practices outlined above brought about a semi-institutional framework specific to each industry in terms of its content, timing, and strictness, thereby compartmentalizing the economy into industries. At the same time, however, a certain type of competition was set free and was fiercely at work within this framework. I have discussed this elsewhere under the rubric "compartmentalized competition."[15]

Irrespective of their tenets, most Japanese economists would admit that MITI bureaucrats did exercise, or at least attempted to exercise, these four practices. However, a totally different explanation is logically possible.[16] According to this explanation, the industrial policy gave rise to a vicious circle: MITI's effort to coordinate investment by the proportional quota rule intensified the competition for market share, which, in turn, intensified the investment race, which again further strengthened the need for investment coordination, and so forth. MITI intervention triggered a whole series of vicious circles and was the primary cause of excessive competition. To me, this interpretation is unacceptable as the main explanatory thesis because the vicious circle would have soon come to a halt had there not existed favorable underlying economic conditions, such as decreasing costs. Evidently, administrative intervention by investment quota does not always intensify competition irrespective of basic economic circumstances. Otherwise, such an intervention would be a panacea for any developing country aiming at faster growth at any cost. In my opinion, MITI intervention was not so much a cause of excessive competition as an attempted remedy for it.

Finally, *gyōsei shidō* can give rise to potentially serious problems in situations of increasing (instead of decreasing) average costs. First, there would no longer be any need for investment guidance or recession cartels because there would be no danger of excessive competition. In less growth-prone situations, the symbiotic association between business and government, if it continues to exist, is much more likely to become a defense to protect each industry's specific interest. If applied to once leading industries, Japanese industrial policy is likely to become a dead weight instead of continuing to be a core part of a vigorous growth mechanism. Second, *gyōsei shidō*, although impartial within each industry, was by no means impartial among industries or between firms and households. When economic growth was rapid and its benefits spilled over to virtually all sectors of the society, potential discontent with intersectoral unfairness did not surface. Under slower growth, however, each sector of the society will become less amenable to policies favoring other sectors. In fact, former leading industries such as steel, automobiles, synthetic fibers, and petrochemicals entered a phase beyond minimum optimal scale in the early 1970s, and technological progress in these industries has more or less subsided. Partly in response to this change (as well as to foreign pressures demanding more thorough going liberalization), institutions such as MITI, MOF, and BOJ seem to be abandoning *gyōsei shidō*, or at least its past style, at an unexpectedly high pace (see the last section of this paper).

I have so far contended that the weak guidance hypothesis is a far better explanation of Japanese administrative behavior than the strong regulation hypothesis. The success of the postwar Japanese economy resulted not so much from the fact that the government intervened as from the often overlooked fact that government intervention was minimal. Since strong regulation requires legal procedures, it is likely to stifle competitiveness, responsiveness, flexibility, and vigor in the economy. Japanese industrial policy—or, in other words, compartmentalized competition—is a successful example of how to combine two conflicting principles, competition and intervention, in order to achieve maximum economic growth.

Market structure submodel. The alternative hypotheses concerning the market structure of postwar Japan are largely corollaries of the previous hypotheses concerning both the firm and administrative behavior, and the following is, in effect, a summary of the foregoing arguments from a slightly different angle. The hypothesis reflecting the formal organization–focused model is the pervasive cartel hypothesis.

3.a. *Pervasive cartel hypothesis*
    The markets of major industrial products in postwar Japan were dominated by cartels or cartel-like practices.

The informal organization–focused model gives rise to two hypotheses.

3.b. *Pervasive quasi-conglomerate hypothesis*
    The markets of major industrial products were dominated by the so-called *keiretsuka* (groupings of large corporations) such as the Mitsui group or Mitsubishi group, which had some resemblance to the prewar *zaibatsu* conglomerates. Most large corporations were quasi conglomerates in the sense that each tightly controlled a number of small-scale subcontractors (*shitauke* or *kyōryoku kigyō*).

3.c. *Competitive polyopoly hypothesis*
    Each of the major industrial product markets consisted of a limited number of large corporations of comparable size. Any new entry

was subject to MITI's control, and each firm's investment was at least loosely under MITI's guidance. Within this framework of entry restriction and investment coordination, however, the product markets were highly competitive in terms of price, quality, and so on—except during the intermittent recessions when MITI-guided recession cartels were introduced.

These hypotheses are meant to describe those leading postwar industries in the manufacturing sector that were the engine of rapid economic growth in Japan. (Declining industries in the manufacturing sector, such as textiles and fertilizers, had a different market structure, as did industries in the nonmanufacturing sector.) These hypotheses are concerned primarily with the rapid growth period.

The pervasive cartel hypothesis seems too naive. It is true that the Antimonopoly Law in Japan is more lenient than U.S. antitrust laws. Since the 1953 revision, the Antimonopoly Law has permitted rationalization cartels as well as recession cartels. Some statutes (for example, the Medium- or Small-Scale Firm Association Law or the Export-Import Transaction Law) have exempted certain types of cartels from antimonopoly jurisdiction. Last but not least, the Fair Trade Commission in Japan was not powerful enough to curb MITI-guided cartel-like practices. In fact, there were several hundred to more than a thousand legal (recession or rationalization) cartels, depending on the year. Most of them, however, were cartels of small-scale firms in local markets or export cartels (which contributed mostly to restraining the downpouring of exports); legal cartels involving leading industries were few in number. This is not to say that cartel-like practices were not found in leading industries. As mentioned previously, in these industries, cartel-like practices under MITI guidance were often introduced during recessions, but were discontinued once prosperity returned. Considering the explosive expansion in demand as well as the marked rise in productivity, even the standard theory of industrial organization will predict dissolution rather than persistence of cartels formed during a recession. From the 1950s to the early 1970s, the prices of major industrial products generally declined. Moreover, no one can deny the existence of competition for market shares. These observations would be inconsistent with a hypothesis that simply assumes the pervasiveness of cartel practices in the usual understanding. As far as the leading postwar industries are concerned, competitive behaviors during prosperity alternated with cartel-like practices during recessions. Since most of the rapid growth period was an era of prosperity, the primary theme in the leading industries' market performance was vigorous competition rather than stagnant collusion.

The pervasive conglomerate hypothesis seems to explain only a part of the picture during the rapid growth period. A number of Japanese scholars, Marxists and non-Marxists alike, with bitter memories of prewar Japan, used to warn of the re-emergence of *zaibatsu*-type conglomerates in the form of bank-centered *keiretsuka*. There is, however, good evidence that each firm's dependence on a particular big city bank weakened from the 1950s through the 1970s.[17] It is also easy to point out many important examples of non-*keiretsu* firms: New Japan Steel, Toyota, Nissan, Honda, Matsushita Electric, Sony, and many others.[18] But *keiretsu* in which a network of close transactions and cooperation for risk sharing play some role do exist.[19] However, the *keiretsu* is an organization *across* industries (encompassing declining ones); the MITI-guided trade association is an organization *within* an industry. As Iwao Nakatani has shown,[20] the average *keiretsu* is not so much a system for faster growth as an organization aiming at minimal variability because the *keiretsu* as a whole pays to protect the declining industries under its umbrella. The *keiretsuka* phenomenon probably occurred more frequently in Japan than in most other industrial countries (because of the heritage from prewar times), but its contribution to invigorating the country's growth seems to have been limited in comparison with another type of interfirm relation—the MITI-guided trade association, which constitutes a crucial component of the weak guidance hypothesis.

The *shitauke* system is usually considered a management practice unique to big Japanese corporations. Many scholars used to argue that the parent firm had overwhelming bargaining power over its subcontractors and could therefore exploit them as a buffer. Masu Uekusa has formulated this exploitation theory clearly, but, as Uekusa himself correctly points out, this theory hinges on the assumption that the parent firm has monopoly over its product's market.[21] If product markets are competitive in the sense I have been arguing, the persistence of the *shitauke* system in leading industries should be interpreted not as a result of exploitation but as an outcome of rational choice by a parent firm and each subcontractor. Indeed, the *shitauke* system can benefit both sides as a device for risk sharing (the parent firm bearing the financial risk and the subcontractors bearing the unemployment risk) and as a scheme for retaining a certain degree of freedom on both sides. The system is, therefore, not particularly unusual because it is in effect a balance between complete vertical integration and complete independence of a subcontractor from a parent firm.

The postwar persistence of this balance is an intriguing theoretical problem. There seem to be several reasons for it. First, the system was an effective mechanism for transferring technology from a parent firm to subcontractors and, in some cases, even for establishing joint projects for technological development. During the rapid growth period, small-scale firms were not yet capable of importing and improving new technologies (this situation has radically changed since the mid-1970s). Therefore, this benefit was large enough to induce small-scale manufacturers to affiliate in the *shitauke* system. Second, the stability of this balance owed much to the belief of both parent firms and subcontractors in a long-run implicit relationship. In this sense, the *shitauke* system is an example of the informal organization–focused interface between the economy and the culture. But although the *shitauke* system was rational for parent firms as well as subcontractors in the rapid growth period, it was not a primary source of economic growth. The *shitauke* system is essentially a way of sharing, within an industry, the burdens of risk and, particularly, of technological adventure. The growth potential of the industry as a whole would not particularly be enhanced by changing the pattern of burden sharing within the industry. One piece of indirect evidence is that the *shitauke* system in postwar Japan was by no means limited to the fast-growing, leading industries but also extended to relatively declining industries such as textiles and printing.

The third alternative, the competitive polyopoly hypothesis, is, in effect, a summary of all foregoing arguments about the market structure in postwar Japan. No one would argue that a perfect competition model describes the core part of the postwar economy. The theory of perfect competition is, however, no more than an exercise in axiomatics. The key question is What are the conditions for maximizing competition in the real world—for example, where average costs are decreasing? Within postwar Japan's framework of entry restriction and investment control, however, product markets can be considered competitive, though not perfectly competitive. Although cartels did exist during the intermittent, short recessions, competition in terms of price and quality was intense during prosperity—probably more intense than that in the same industries in most other industrial nations.

Many empirical studies show that the degree of concentration in Japan was low, or at least not high, compared with that in other major industrial countries and has not exhibited any visible increase.[22] More specifically, the leading postwar industries may be said to have consisted of a relatively large number of firms (perhaps ten) of fairly equal size. This mode of competition may be located somewhere between atomistic competition and oligopoly. In order to contrast this situation with the widely used concept of oligopoly, I introduce another word, "polyopoly," a market composed of more than a few participants of similar size under some restrictions on long-run behavior such as entry or investment. In doing this, I have in mind an analogy with Robert Dahl's famous notion of polyarchy in political science. In fact, he posed a question analogous to mine: What are the conditions maximizing democracy in the real world?[23] Considering their total performance over the entire rapid growth period, the markets in the core part of the postwar economy were not in a state of collusive oligopoly but rather in one of competitive polyopoly. This competitive polyopoly was the substance of what I earlier called compartmentalized competition, and thus it is a reflection of the organizational tradition.

Summary

The nation and the individual are theoretically possible alternative interfaces between culture and the economy. There are, however, sufficient reasons to reject both of them. More complex interfaces of the formal and informal organizaton type yield more satisfactory arguments. The formal organization–focused model is synonymous with a firm-focused approach; informal organization can be either led by the bureaucracy as exemplified by *gyōsei shidō* or purely private as in the case of *keiretsuka* or *shitauke*. The relationships between these organizational interface assumptions and the various behavioral hypotheses at the submodel level are summarized in the Table 1.

In my opinion, informal organization provides the most useful explanation of the key feature of the postwar Japanese economy—strong growth accompanied by excessive competition. It is not that the Japanese-style firm (a typical formal organization) played no major role as an interface between the culture and the economy but that Japanese management per se cannot account for this key economic feature. I have also argued that another informal organization, *gyōsei shidō*, was more

TABLE 1

Organizational Interfaces and Behavioral Hypotheses

Focus of interface	Firm behavior	Administrative behavior	Market structure
Firm-focused model	Japanese management hypothesis (JMH) is essential	Administrative guidance hypothesis (AGH) is irrelevant	Quasi-conglomerate hypothesis (QCH) tends to be added
Informal administrative organization–focused model	JMH is irrelevant. AGH implies pro-growth environment for firms	AGH is essential	QCH is subject to AGH
Informal private organization–focused model	JMH tends to be added	AGH is subject to QCH	QCH is essential

instrumental to rapid, catch-up economic growth than either *keiretsuka* or *shitauke* (both private organizational forms).

Although these conclusions are open to debate, one broad picture seems obvious to me. Theoretically speaking, in order to achieve catch-up economic development, the best strategy is a proper combination of competition and regulation (that is, market mechanism and government planning) because the goal and the path to it are clearly defined by the experiences of more advanced economies, giving a definite guideline for government regulation or planning. In broader politico-economic terms, however, it is extremely difficult to maintain a proper combination of two conflicting principles or, more specifically, to preserve the vigor and flexibility of private initiative by keeping governmental regulation to a minimum. The Japanese catch-up attempt after World War II may be considered a rare example of success in maintaining this proper balance. In terms of regulation, the Japanese economic system during the rapid growth period was based on *weak* guidance, and, in terms of competition, it was a system of *compartmentalized* competition.

Two factors account for the maintenance of this duality. First, the technological paradigm of the twentieth century matured after World War II, setting an unmistakable target for late developers such as Japan (whereas recent explosive yet uncertain developments in microelectronics and genetic engineering will be difficult for a late developer to follow). Second, the cultural tradition of implicit, long-term, multi-issued agreements provided an organizational mold to combine competition and regulation. In this sense, the rapid postwar economic growth was a result of interaction between culture and the technological and economic structure. Furthermore, crucial to this success was the Pax Americana, which provided expanding markets for Japanese industries and tolerated the closed nature of Japanese domestic markets. All these environments, objective as well as subjective, constituted a fortuitous combination for the Japanese economy in the 1950s and 1960s. As of 1986, however, these environments were rapidly changing, and Japan was no longer a late developer.

Models Explaining the Polity

The postwar years may be divided into the three phases of political change.

Period 1 (the period of the Occupation and political realignment just after the war): 1945 to the early 1950s.

Period 2 (the period of the "one and a half party system"): the early 1950s to the late 1970s. One possible choice for the beginning of this period is 1952, when Japan regained independence. But a better choice is 1955, when the conservative parties merged, as did the socialist parties, establishing the so-called 1955 system or one and a half party system.

Period 3 (the period of conservative resurgence): from the late 1970s on. The beginning of this period was marked by a resurgence of the conservative party, which could be observed in 1977 in opinion survey data or in 1980 in the national election returns.

This section examines the Japanese political system mainly during Period 2, which roughly corresponds to the period of rapid economic growth.

The environment to which the Japanese political system was subject during Period 2 started from an initial condition of consensual national goals (formed during Period 1) of catch-up economic growth and non-activist foreign policies. Hence, its task was virtually limited to domestic economic issues. These involved solving the problem of establishing a framework to promote catch-up efforts and to take care of the social re-shuffling arising from economic changes. Essential to the task was, as emphasized before, adaptation of the cultural tradition (that is, the organizational heritage from the prewar years) to the requirements of the post–World War II political economy.

Any model claiming to interpret the postwar Japanese polity has to incorporate these interactions with the environment. Which type of interface between the polity and culture played the most crucial role in the postwar Japanese political system? In other words, should the model focus on the nation, formal organizations (parties), informal organizations, or the individual? A caveat should be mentioned here. As much as possible, the discussion follows the general outline of the four possible interfaces. The complexity of the issues involved, however, requires that the discussion follow a somewhat more fluid pattern when moving from one interface to the next. This is because, in the case of the polity, the overlap among interfaces is greater than in the case of the economy.

Any model should explain three crucial features of the postwar Japanese polity. First, it must explain the continued ascendancy of the conservative camp since 1948: in the post–World War II period, this record is rivaled only by the National Congress Party in India. Second, it must explain a decline after the mid-1960s in voter support for the Liberal Democratic Party (LDP) and the main opposition party, the Japan Socialist Party (JSP), and a remarkable increase in the number of independents (those who do not prefer any particular party in opinion surveys). Several minor opposition parties—the Democratic Socialist Party (DSP), the Kōmeitō (Clean Government Party; CGP), and the New Liberal Club

(NLC)—appeared during Period 2, but neither they nor the Japan Communist Party (JCP) could more than marginally challenge the two major parties. Then, almost unexpectedly, came the third feature, the conservative resurgence in the late 1970s. Any attempt to explain the Japanese political system should account for these trends.

From Nation-Focused Model to Individual-Focused Model

The analysis of the postwar Japanese polity has to tackle the same issue as the previous analysis of the Japanese economy: What was the key interface between the polity and culture? A typical early attempt to explain the Japanese political system was primarily based on the nation-focused approach.

4. *The "Japan as one big community" or "modernization" hypothesis*
Even after World War II, the Japanese had a traditional perception of group and social organization. Their characteristics of intragroup harmony, obedience to authority, and a sense of hierarchy ultimately culminated in the notion of a nation as one big cohesive community. The LDP was the only party that accepted and represented these traditional perceptions. Thus ensued the LDP ascendancy.
However, as the Japanese become more and more modernized and democratized, the dominance of the LDP will decline. This implies that the JSP or a JSP-centered coalition will rise to equal the LDP, creating a two-party system.

The notion of modernization in this argument is clearly equivalent to Westernization. Most proponents of this argument predicted the inevitable progress of modernization (= Westernization) in Japan—namely, the increasing applicability of the individual-focused model, including, above all, the classical notion of the two-party system. In this respect, this hypothesis was influenced either by an idealistic notion about the Anglo-American two-party system or by an ideology of class conflict. Modernization theorists thus believed, or wanted to believe, that Japanese society would converge with other "modern societies" so that, politically speaking, the classical two-party confrontation would emerge.[24] The hypothesis combines the nation-focused model and individual-focused model, or, more exactly, it involves an alternation from the former model to the latter.

A New Internal Dynamic: The Coming of the "New Middle Class"

For some time, the modernization hypothesis seemed to hold true. From the mid-1960s, however, this hypothesis began to lose credibility because of the marked decline of support for the JSP, including that of urban workers (though support for the LDP did decline as predicted). A new argument, greatly influenced by the line of argument from the "end of ideology" to those resulting from speculations about the future emerged in the popular writings in the second half of the 1960s.[25]

5. *The mass affluence hypothesis*

As mass affluence arrives or at least approaches, the slackening of ideology and the proliferation of diverse opinions and interests will become a central trend. The conservative party (LDP) and the ideological opposition parties (JSP and JCP) will decline, and the number of independents will significantly increase. New minor parties (such as DSP and CGP) representing the growing diversity in society will emerge. This argument suggests the emergence of the multiparty system rather than convergence toward a two-party system.

The background of this hypothesis was, of course, the phenomenal growth of the Japanese economy during the 1950s and 1960s. Mass affluence seemed to be approaching in the form of an explosive diffusion of consumer durables. However, this hypothesis soon faced a serious challenge. From the late 1960s to the early 1970s, mass affluence was unexpectedly accompanied by a flood of "pathological symptoms" (from the viewpoint of industrialism), such as large-scale student riots, massive protests against pollution, visible change in the lifestyle of young people, and persistent worldwide stagflation. These symptoms were visible not only in Japan but in virtually all advanced industrial societies. Mass affluence had given rise to criticism of, or pursuit of more than, the conventional modern values behind the postwar material prosperity. As a political manifestation of this countercurrent, the New Left movement emerged and was generally expected to revitalize the old left-wing parties such as the JSP and JCP. In fact, JCP support increased, compensating for the decrease in JSP support. Both parties were particularly successful in local elections, including the gubernatorial races in major cities such as Tokyo, Osaka, and Kyoto. However, this revival of the progressive parties was short-lived. Support for the JSP and JCP again started to decline from around 1973. One reason for this setback was that the new and old leftist groups were so far apart in their basic philosophical and historical perspectives: the New Left protested against industrialism as such; the old Left was opposed only to the particular form called capitalism. Another major reason was the effect of the oil crisis and ensuing depression, which I discuss later.

Mass affluence, unprecedented in history, thus has had two often mutually counteracting implications. On the one hand, it means a slackening of ideological confrontation based on the class struggle or, in political terms, a weakening of classical two-party politics between the conservative and the progressive parties. On the other hand, it implies a decline of conventional modern values (or, in other words, the values of industrialism), which may under certain conditions trigger a new type of political radicalism voicing a new set of values. In any case, mass affluence has introduced a profoundly new element into the politics of advanced industrial societies and into their sociological and cultural patterns. Basic value orientations appear to be moving away from the conventional modern virtues, such as hard work, frugality, efficiency, sanctity of marriage and family, and so on, that are "instrumental" in the sense that they are supposedly the means to some intrinsic end or final gratification. Instead, the trend seems to be toward something anti-instrumental or "consummatory" (in the sense that delayed gratification is no longer meaningful). Similar value trends have been pointed out in other affluent, industrial societies by a number of scholars, including J. H. Goldthorpe, Ronald Inglehart, Daniel Yankelovich, and many others.[26] These value changes are gradual, but some sociological symptoms, including an enormous change in marriage patterns especially in (formerly?) Protestant societies, are already observable. As another example, the class-based social structure is dissolving, and this process is, in my opinion, most visible in Japan.[27]

Essential to the dissolution of the class structure are certain economic conditions: virtually all people (except perhaps some ethnic minorities) in the advanced industrial societies now enjoy living standards well beyond the subsistence level, have access to a level of education and information that used to be the monopoly of the few, and are increasingly free from uncertainties in their life cycle thanks to welfare measures. Equally crucial are cultural factors such as lifestyles or values. In a capitalistic class structure, the middle class used to play an axial role—the virtues and lifestyle characteristic of industrial society were preserved and reproduced in the middle class. Under postwar mass affluence, however, the middle class has been losing this distinctiveness (vis-à-vis the working class) in living standards, lifestyle, education, and, above all, the value orientations that used to be summarized as "middle-class morality." The previous distinction between the middle class and the working class is blurring, and a new kind of "mass" is emerging, but the meaning of this term differs distinctively from what the same term meant, largely with negative connotations, in the mass society theories of the 1930s and 1940s. Since this new mass will occupy a vast central part of the society, it may be called the "new middle mass." It should probably not be viewed as a pathological phenomenon growing out of modern society but rather as a crucial component of the still amorphous post-industrial society.

The arrival of the new middle mass will gradually affect every aspect of advanced industrial societies: yet the political aspect will be more sensitive than most other aspects. Two-party politics, for example, will undergo basic changes, although no one can predict what political system will take its place. At least since the 1970s, Japanese politics has been experiencing this phase of political restructuring. The new middle mass phenomenon is not so much an environmental factor as defined above as an outcome of the internal dynamic of the postwar Japanese political economy. Any attempt to explain the postwar Japanese political system must account for the effect of this dynamic. The traditional analysis of conservative versus progressive confrontation should be replaced or at least supplemented by an analysis of the new middle mass politics. The decline of support for the two major parties and the concomitant increase in independents ultimately resulted from the emergence of the new middle mass.

The Formal Organization–Focused Model: The Political Party as Interface

The issue of the new middle mass became particularly important in Japanese politics after the late 1970s (Period 3). Before proceeding to that period, however, we still must explain the key features of the Japanese polity in Period 2 (the rapid growth period). Independents were increasing during this period. However, if the independents are put aside, LDP dominance still continued throughout this period, outweighing the support for all other parties combined. A comparison of the four types of interface assumptions illustrates this key feature of the political context underlying rapid economic growth.

Like the Japan, Inc. hypothesis in the economic sphere, the nation-focused approach of the Japan as one big community hypothesis is too simplistic a stereotype. It implies that Japanese society was politically well integrated because of its cultural uniformity. Be that as it may, the postwar Japanese political system was one of the more satisfactorily working parliamentary democracies. In respect to freedom of expression and association, postwar Japan compares favorably to any society and is better than most.[28] The "opposition-of-principle parties" (Otto Kirchheimer) such as the JSP and JCP always collected one-third of the vote.[29] The leading newspapers and journals were almost always critical of the conservative government. It was within this framework of pluralist democracy that the LDP managed to collect a sufficient number of votes to secure the majority of seats in the Diet. It was once argued that the LDP's strength was the result of bribes and gerrymandering. To deny these factors totally would be too extreme, but they cannot be the main reasons for LDP dominance, especially considering the high level of income and education reached by average Japanese voters in the latter half of the rapid growth period. There should be a better explanation for the success of the LDP. As recent major works on the Japanese political system suggest,[30] any such explanation should presuppose that pluralism worked in postwar Japan.

Yet there are elements of truth in the Japan as one big community hypothesis. In any society, cultural homogeneity contributes to political integration. Japanese society is a typical example of this. Having no significant ethnic or cultural minorities, preindustrial Japan was characterized by the dominance of one cultural pattern (the *ie*- or *mura*-type organizational principle) because of its historical and geographical isolation. By appealing to this cultural tradition, the LDP from its start in 1955 succeeded in collecting wide electoral support across all segments of Japanese society, including industrial workers. Important in this context was the conscious repudiation by the opposition parties, particularly the JSP and JCP, of all traditional elements as basic causes of prewar and wartime wrongs and miseries. The LDP was not simply a party of farmers and business interests but, as discussed more fully below, a tradition-based catchall party (in the sense of Otto Kirchheimer and Suzanne Berger[31]) like the French Gaullist coalition or the Italian Christian Democratic–centered coalition, whose traditional appeal lies in Catholicism or nationalism (in the case of France, "French glory" personified in General de Gaulle).

The pluralistic aspect of Japanese politics seems to be increasingly recognized, but the similarity to the French or Italian case has so far attracted little attention. The popular argument used to be that the LDP and the JSP were unique, emphasizing the difference between Japan and Western democracies. The basis of this argument was, in essence, that premodern culture heavily influenced Japanese party politics.[32] The political party—the formal organization in the political system—was viewed as a crucial interface between the polity and culture in this argument.

6. *Unique Japanese political party hypothesis* (party-focused model)

The two major parties in postwar Japan differed distinctively from the major parties in other industrial countries. On the one hand, the conservative party (the LDP) was not based on any organization of party members. It was, in fact, a coalition of factions (*habatsu*) that were fluid and voluntary associations of Diet members. Each Diet member or candidate had a personal support organization (*kōenkai*). The leader of each faction became, more or less through rotation, the party head (which virtually meant the prime minister). Thus, the LDP's organization was, in effect, a three-tiered hierarchy of personal (or *mura*-type) relations.

On the other hand, the JSP had its own party organization, but its size was small and its members were mostly trade union organizers. For the most part, it therefore represented union interests. For electoral support, however, the JSP depended heavily on the much broader, unorganized public who sympathized with the JSP's utopian ideas, such as the "socialist millennium" or the "eternally disarmed pacifist nation." The JSP's cadres with a union background were never eager to organize non-union members. Thus, the two major parties in postwar Japan were not organized parties based on explicitly agreed policy programs, or, in other words, they were not "modern mass parties" (Kirchheimer or Duverger).[33]

This hypothesis seemed to account for many important aspects of postwar politics. The LDP could indeed be viewed as a coalition of political groups, ranging from a nearly social-democratic faction to a traditional-nationalist faction. These factions shared a certain type of conservative orientation (which I later call "late-developer conservatism") rather than a systematic policy philosophy. By switching its party leadership from one faction head to another, the LDP's actual policy choices could be remarkably flexible and responsive to changes in circumstances (for example, the swing in the 1970s to support of a stringent antipollution policy, strengthened welfare measures, and reinforcement of antimonopoly law). Given the firm consensus on national goals, this policy tolerance provided an ideal setting for a harmonious relation between party and bureaucracy. Moreover, the rotation in party leadership worked as a surrogate for the alternative of rule by different parties.

The JSP's policy efforts occurred through negotiation with the LDP government and were largely limited to defensive reactions in support of union interests (for example, the JSP supported the interests of the government employees' union, which were often in conflict with those of consumers and taxpayers). Partly to compensate for this limitation, the JSP increasingly relied on a utopian appeal to the general public. In fact, the JSP's ideology tended to be less practical and more doctrinaire than that of the socialist or Communist parties in Western Europe. There was no *programme commun* or *compromesso storico* in Japan. A serious problem in this increasing dependence on utopian idealism was that the appeal of such ideals was fading because of vast changes in postwar conditions (for example, the socialist countries' poor economic achievement, limited individual liberty, and military intervention in neighboring small nations). The JSP has never presented any practical alternative policy program, but the LDP has adjusted its policy program to the needs of the increasingly affluent Japanese voters, that is, the new middle mass. The unique Japanese political party hypothesis appears to explain much of the LDP's strength vis-à-vis the JSP.

Are these features unique to Japan? The notion that any "modern" party should be a policy-oriented, organized party is closely related to the idealization of two-party politics in Anglo-American societies or to modernization theory up to the 1960s. In fact, late developers in the West, such as prewar Germany, France, or Italy, suggest a different perspective.

Theorem of late-developer conservatism

In late-developing countries, preindustrial social structures persist in rural areas as well as in traditional industries. Thus, a particular type of conservatism is necessary to promote catch-up industrial development and maintain some of the traditional heritage or give it leeway to adjust to economic changes. An essential feature of late-developer conservatism is its dependence on a strong bureaucracy, which, in contrast to the minimum government ideal of Anglo-American conservatism, intervenes in the economy.

Theorem of late-developer progressivism

In late-developing countries, progressivism seeks to eradicate traditional elements, accusing late-developer conservatism of preserving premodern elements and thereby distorting the course of modernization. Since the outcome of such idealistic eradication is highly uncertain, late-developer progressivism can include a wide range of variants ranging from classical liberalism to centralized socialism, depending on their future social scenarios. Since the progressives tend to be divided, it is difficult for them to unite against the conservatives. In such a late-developer polity, the ideological opposition-of-principle party always plays a significant role, and the parties in the center tend to be weak because of strong challenges from the more pragmatic conservative side and the more idealistic opposition-of-principle side.

These theorems describe features common to all reasonably successful late developers such as Weimar Germany, France, Italy, and Japan. The late-developer policy can exhibit diverse performances, depending on the relative strength of the conservative party, the parties in the center, and the opposition-of-principle parties. One possibility is a predominant conservative party system or a system with a dominant conservative coalition. The French Gaullist coalition, the Italian Christian Democratic–centered coalition, and the Japanese LDP became, in differing degrees, successful by appealing to traditional values: that is, they were tradition-based catchall parties.

Another possibility is that none of the three components of the late-developer polity may be dominant and an unstable multiparty system emerges. Parliamentarism may even collapse, as in Weimar Germany. The uncertain performance of a multiparty system, including the possibility of collapse, used to be viewed as a serious drawback of the late-developer polity. Under certain historical circumstances favorable to conservative predominance, however, the late-developer polity can provide more consistent policies, especially economic ones, than the two-party system with its alternation of governments. However, the tradition-based catchall parties now seem to be facing, as Suzanne Berger has pointed out, a crucial problem in that traditions such as Catholicism or certain forms of nationalism seem to be weakening under mass affluence.[34]

In summary, when compared with their French and Italian counterparts (instead of the Anglo-American parties), Japanese political parties do not appear particularly unique. The conservative parties in these countries shared some features, such as weak party structure, factionalism, an appeal to cultural traditions, and close cooperation with the bureaucracy. In all these countries, the opposition-of-principle parties, such as the French or Italian Communist parties and the JSP and JCP, played significant roles, often collecting more than 20 per cent of the total vote. They were all bound to union interests and were more or less ideologically rigid. Therefore, the formal structure of party organization cannot be a key factor in explaining why the performance of the Japanese political system, including the continued LDP dominance, has been quite different from that of the French or the Italian system.

Another factor is that electoral systems affect party organization. Electoral systems range from the small-electorate system of Britain, the primary system of the United States, the proportional representation system of West Germany, or the medium-sized electorate system with multiple-member districts of Japan. Party organization and discipline are arguably tight under the proportional representation system. Under the medium-sized electorate system or the primary system, each candidate has to form a close personal organization to compete against other candidates from the same party. Moreover, the medium-sized electorate system is likely to give rise to the formation of factions in the party's national center, reflecting the members' rivalry in each constituency (in the United States, personal organizations are not organized into national-level factions because one person represents one election district in Congress). In my view, many, though not all, characteristics of Japanese political parties are explainable in terms of Japan's late-developer status and its electoral system, and there is no particular need to refer to its cultural uniqueness.[35]

Broader Informal Organization–Focused Model (Bureaucratic Nexus Model)

Even compared with French or Italian politics, however, postwar Japanese politics exhibited a remarkable uniqueness: the LDP government holds the longest endurance record of any postwar political party in an advanced capitalist industrial society. Gaullist dominance began only in the late 1950s and ended in 1982 with the Giscardian attempt to woo the voters in the center,[36] and the Christian Democratic coalition in Italy was much more unstable than the LDP in Japan. As Berger has pointed out, the tradition-based catchall party generally loses its traditional support base amid value changes in an affluent society. What accounts for the remarkable persistence of LDP dominance?

One difference, albeit seemingly unfavorable to the LDP, is that traditionalism in postwar Japan was unorganized and much less explicit compared with the French or Italian case. It had neither an influential organization exhorting the traditional ideal like the Catholic church nor a charismatic symbol like General de Gaulle. In postwar Japan, no pronouncedly traditionalistic or nationalistic organization (let alone neofascist parties like those in Germany or Italy) has ever exerted influence on the general public: such an organization has never gained a seat in the Diet or in local legislatures. The emperor, the only conceivable example of a charismatic figure, has never played an active political role in postwar Japan. (In fact, one of the two most salient intergenerational trends in postwar opinion polls is a remarkable increase in indifference to the emperor, especially among the younger generation.[37]) The strict prohibition of patriotic organizations during the Occupation period was one reason for this. The main reason, however, was the average Japanese's deep-seated disillusionment with the prewar version of traditionalism with its heavy nationalistic overlay.

With this psychological background, traditionalism in postwar Japan has been divorced from the political context of nationalism and reduced to an emotional attachment to a certain pattern of everyday conduct and the organizational practices summarized as the *ie*- or *mura*-type principle. Tradition was manifested, if anywhere, not in politics but in organizational patterns such as Japanese management. This postwar traditionalism could thus never constitute a *positive* leverage in national politics. In a *negative* way, however, it played a certain political role in giving rise to a reaction against the progressive parties' rejection of everything uniquely Japanese. The LDP benefited from this widespread antipathy against the radical antitraditionalism of the progressive camp. And except for the Kishi cabinet (1957–60), the LDP consistently avoided any move toward an explicitly nationalistic policy program that would have reminded the average Japanese of the still lingering nasty memories about the pre-1945 period. (LDP policy documents after 1960 included little nationalistic rhetoric.[38]) In this context, the unorganized nature of postwar traditionalism worked in the LDP's favor. This implied that the LDP did not rely on organizations based on traditional ideology and, therefore, enjoyed more latitude in answering and manipulating various sectoral interests. Compared with its French or Italian counterpart, the LDP's policies were by and large less ideological, more flexible in choice of priorities, and more oriented to the manipulation of interests. The LDP is a tradition-based catchall party, but it had more of an interest orientation than similar parties in other countries. In short, the LDP's success may be attributed to its avoidance of an overcommitment to traditional ideology; this allowed it to retain policy consistency, particularly in respect to economic issues.

Generally speaking, any tradition-based catchall party faces the basic dilemma of how to deal with its two antipodal supporters, industrial interests and the traditional sector (agriculture, small-scale business for local markets, and so forth). Moreover, it cannot overlook a third category of supporters—those urban workers who are tradition oriented: this group is crucial for winning national elections. A catchall party that is too inclined toward industrial interests or openly behaves as such during parliamentary debates jeopardizes its image as a fair guardian of tradition. On the other hand, a party that is too protective of agriculture or the traditional sector destroys its overall consistency in economic policy and fails to achieve one of its two main goals, catch-up economic development. Balancing these dual tasks is evidently so difficult that a tradition-based catchall party often reaches the point of self-contradiction. These tasks imply a need for constant, subtle intervention and redistribution in order to bring about one compromise after another between the promotion of leading industries and the protection of traditional interests and ideals. The fulcrum for this maneuvering is "industrial policies" (including those for declining or traditional industries). Because of the enormity as well as the complexity of conflicting interests among industries, including agriculture and other traditional sectors, this task necessitates something more than open, rational parliamentary debates. This is a main reason for the tendency of late-developer conservatism to ally with a strong bureaucracy.

France, Italy, and Japan seem to have institutional or semi-institutional devices to cope with this task. In Italy and France, nationalized or semi-nationalized corporations play key roles in strategic industries, such as the Institute for Industrial Reconstruction or the National Hydrocarbon Organization in Italy or the nationalized banks and corporations (for example, Renault) in France. The ability to shape the character of industrial policy is, among other powers, in the hands of the management of these giant nationalized corporations, who consult closely with the conservative government. Although Japanese industrial policy has recently attracted broad attention, its counterparts in other countries are often more mandatory and more discretionary, such as in the French banking sector. On the other hand, in postwar Japan, there have been no nationalized firms in the leading industries.[39] As previously discussed in terms of the weak guidance hypothesis, the Japanese approach to industrial policy has had to take a different mode, which may be formulated from the viewpoint of the political system as follows:

7. Parapolitical nexus hypothesis

The political structure supporting the LDP included a wide-ranging informal nexus of close relations between government and industry based mainly on industry-wide trade associations. The LDP by and large delegated arbitration of interindustrial and interfirm conflicts to the central bureaucracy. The central bureaucracy performed this arbitrating function mainly by developing a long-term, multi-issued interrelationship between each industry and the ministry of jurisdiction, with minimal dependence on parliamentary legislation. This informal machinery contributed to the consistency and quickness of economic policymaking in postwar Japan.

The LDP and the bureaucracy formed an intertwined nexus. The conservative party, of course, indicated the main outline of policies and, in some crucial distributional issues such as the tax structure, welfare system, or price support for farm products (notably rice prices), intervened in the details of negotiations. However, economic policymaking and related interest negotiations were largely left to the central bureaucracy. More specifically, the central government was broken down into ministries, then bureaus, and finally into sections corresponding to industries. Each industry was thus linked with some particular unit of the central bureaucracy. Conflicts in all industries from manufacturing to agriculture were channeled into the hierarchical, industry-wide system of administrative guidance. The *gyōsei shidō* system was an informal but effective means of coordinating conflicts of interests in the rapidly changing Japanese economy.

This task of coordination meant that bureaucrats had to be responsible for drafting a consistent overall design for economic policies and to persuade the LDP politicians and the parties concerned to accept their plan by appealing to the catch-up growth consensus. During the rapid growth period, they largely fulfilled this responsibility through their ability to learn from the experiences of more advanced countries, their zeal in taking the initiative in policy formation, and their discipline, which by and large prevented serious corruption. Many facts seem to substantiate the bureaucracy's initiative in the policymaking process. For example, legislation was, in most cases, proposed to the Diet by the ministries of jurisdiction. Diet members seldom initiated important proposals, in sharp contrast to the practices of the U.S. Congress. Interest groups (including the Diet members supporting these groups) "lobbied" the bureaucrats in charge rather than Diet committees or their members, again in contrast to the U.S. practice. All in all, the LDP consciously assumed the role of protector of the bureaucracy against the opposition parties' interference, and the bureaucrats made full use of this substantial freedom of policy formulation and implementation under the LDP's umbrella.

However, the implementation process was not totally delegated to the bureaucracy. A notable idiosyncracy of the postwar political system was that every LDP Diet member was anxious to intervene into the final distribution (among regions) of government subsidies, public works, or other government services. For each LDP politician, the most readily effective way to increase voter support was to channel these benefits to his or her election district. The medium-size electorate system creates intense rivalry among fellow competitors in the same district, and each LDP politician is under constant pressure to take care of even minor local demands from voters. This pressure was obviously stronger in the case of the LDP than in the case of the smaller parties, which could have at most only one candidate in each district. The pressure also reflected a difference between Japan's electoral system and that of other countries.

Because of this local pressure from voters, roads, bridges, and community facilities were built in every rural area, and agriculture became a heavily subsidized industry. The same was true in cities and towns. Local small-scale firms and family-owned retail shops were similarly protected, and their owners formed the core of each Diet member's personal support organization. On the one hand, this local pressure can constitute a source of potential resistance against the reshuffling of national policies. As long as rapid growth continued and funds were abundant, such resistance could be appeased by further ample subsidization. On the other hand, this pressure was a source of responsiveness on the part of the LDP to the demands of a mass of people, including farmers, small-enterprise and small-shop owners, and the like, with the exception of the urban consumers in megalopolitan areas up until the mid-1970s. Given this constituency-level pressure, we may characterize the LDP as a "mass inclusionary" party.

The nature of the parapolitical nexus is intriguing because it contained two seemingly conflicting aspects. It appeared elitist because the actual mastermind of this nexus was the central bureaucracy, which pursued a consistent economic policy for the purpose of catch-up economic growth. But it was mass inclusionary because bureaucratic rationality was, through the LDP, subject to popular demands at the constituency level. These two aspects could often conflict. During the rapid growth period, however, they were largely harmonized by liberal redistribution of the gains from economic growth in the form of virtual subsidies financed by rapidly expanding government revenues. The LDP succeeded in collecting popular support for catch-up economic development by playing the role of intermediator and guardian throughout this process of interest coordination. In this way, the catchall efforts of the LDP were more interest oriented than those of its French or Italian counterparts. The whole system depended on the successful performance of the economy. One implication is clear: the LDP will face a serious challenge under slower growth if it continues to retain its so-far-effective pattern of parapolitical nexus.

As this suggests, the primary reason for the success of late-developer conservatism in postwar Japan compared with its French or Italian counterpart was the better performance of the economy under the LDP government. The remarkable performance of the Japanese economy was indeed the result of a fortuitous combination of environments, but the conservative government undoubtedly played a key role in combining these favorable factors. The informal nexus connecting the LDP, the bureaucracy, and industry was crucially instrumental to this process.

Summary

Many scholars, Japanese as well as non-Japanese, have characterized the Japanese political system as unique. Indeed, it was clearly different from the Anglo-American two-party system. When compared with the French or Italian system, however, the system of political parties in postwar Japan showed a key feature common to late-developer conservatism. What really differentiated the Japanese system from that in France or Italy was the nexus of party-government-industry relations specific to Japan. This parapolitical nexus was more informal and more mass inclusionary than similar practices in other countries, such as the more explicit and more mass-exclusionary *dirigisme* of the French bureaucracy. This systemic mode can also be differentiated from the typical corporatist state in that the interests were intermediated in a diffuse or rhizomic way—not only through interest groups but also at the constituency level.[40] The Japanese system is characterized by flexibility in policymaking as well as congruity with electoral politics. The feasibility of the same strategy in other countries is questionable because its stability in Japan relied on the implicit, long-term, and multi-issued agreements that reflected the *mura*-type organizational tradition in Japan. In this sense, the informal parapolitical nexus was a unique and crucial interface between the polity and culture in Japan.

In the final analysis, the LDP achieved what it had promised to bring about (as, for example, in the National Income-Doubling Plan in 1960), thereby vastly enhancing its credibility. Especially, the LDP and the bureaucracy obtained, thanks to rapid economic growth, sufficient funds to subsidize agriculture and other declining industries liberally so as to appease potential discontent in these sectors. The effectiveness of the parapolitical nexus was further increased by manipulation of these redistributional measures. Obviously, this informal machinery and its effectiveness were partly a cause and partly an effect of successful economic growth. The parapolitical nexus was an essential link in the "virtuous" circle called Japanese economic growth. Once a fortuitous set of favorable conditions started a virtuous circle, everything went smoothly. A circle may become vicious, however, and, once this happens, the parapolitical nexus may accelerate the whole process of economic slowdown. Slower growth, for example, implies fewer funds for distribution, which induces greater discontent in declining industries or less policy consistency, which further decelerates economic growth.

Indeed, the postwar Japanese polity may be viewed as a successful example of late-developer conservatism that managed to adapt an organizational tradition to the imperatives of twentieth-century industrial technology, which achieved full maturity after World War II. This uniquely Japanese system was characterized by a combination of a pluralistic system (market or parliament) and administrative intervention (bureaucracy). According to conventional wisdom, a combination of these two principles is simply inconceivable, but the postwar Japanese experience suggests that a viable combination can exist, at least under certain favorable conditions. From an economic viewpoint, I summarized this mode as compartmentalized competition. This view seems to be shared by several recent authors. For example, Ken'ichi Imai emphasizes the importance of "intermediate organization" (though he underrates, in my opinion, the role of relationships between government and industry).[41] From a political viewpoint, Michio Muramatsu and Ellis Krauss suggest the notion of "patterned pluralism," and Takashi Inoguchi offers the term "bureaucracy-led mass-inclusionary pluralism."[42] Seizaburo Sato and Tetsuhisa Matsuzaki use the term "canalized pluralism."[43] All these authors contend that the Japanese systemic mode proved viable under a combination of environments from the early 1950s to the late 1970s.

However, the question of how the Japanese political economy would behave when faced with two new impacts remains to be answered. The first is radical changes in the environment. The environment after the oil crisis differs basically from that in the past: the twentieth-century technology paradigm has ended; the Pax Americana has weakened; and, last but not least, the Japanese have accomplished catch-up development. The second impact is the emergence of the new middle mass as a result of the internal dynamic of the politico-economic system in postwar Japan.

The Period of Transition: The Post–Oil Crisis Recovery

The Economic Aspect

The first oil crisis in 1973–74 marked the end of the rapid growth period, but basic economic, political, and international changes loomed on the horizon before that date. In economics, the technological paradigm dominant during the last one hundred years (the twentieth-century paradigm) had started losing momentum throughout the industrial world, and the diffusion of this paradigm in Japan had reached completion in the early 1970s. In terms of my earlier argument, this implies that the decreasing average cost situation had largely disappeared in the previously leading industries. In politics, the emergence of the new middle mass seemed to be weakening the idea of ideological or class conflicts and undermining the classical notion of a two-party system. The drift toward post-industrial values became increasingly visible and the support for a tradition-based catchall party appeared to be declining or changing in pattern. In the area of international relations, the post-war world system, the Pax Americana, experienced major structural changes.[44] To Japan, this implied that reliance on U.S. hegemony should be abandoned and its external policy should be redefined in a more active direction. All these changes, economic, political, and international, added up to the conclusion that the phase of catch-up development was coming to an end. With these changes pending but not yet fully developed, the first oil crisis hit the Japanese economy.

Majority opinion about the future of the Japanese economy became pessimistic. Many people expected that the oil price hike would hurt the Japanese economy the most of all the major industrial societies because Japan's dependence on imported energy resources was the heaviest. However, this forecast was wrong: the Japanese economy adjusted to the oil crisis more successfully than other countries. The recovery of price stability was quicker, the unemployment rate stayed lower, and the growth rate was higher than that of other economies. In hindsight, this is not so mysterious. At the time of the oil crisis, Japanese industries and firms were at their prime in terms of the post–World War II technological and economic paradigm. Most of the advanced industrial societies had already exploited the potentials of technology as well as demand inherent in this paradigm. This was particularly true of the U.S. economy, which had experienced, as an industrial front-runner, the saturation of technology and demand ahead of other industrial societies. In contrast, Japanese industries were young, had the newest equipment as a result of high-powered investment in the preceding two decades, and were manned with scientists and workers who had accumulated a lot of experience in adjusting to the latest technology. The leading Japanese industries such as steel or automobiles were indeed entering maturity like those in other advanced economies but, relatively speaking, still maintained a high level of vigor. At this fortuitous moment, the first oil crisis hit. The oil embargo awakened a sense of crisis in the average Japanese, rebuilding something close to a national consensus: the agreed need to overcome "resource limitation." Firms in key industries mobilized their technological abilities to reduce costs, particularly the cost of energy. As a result of the oil crisis, Japanese industries were not crippled but reinvigorated.

Some people attribute the outstanding Japanese performance to factors specific to Japanese firms, industries, or government. For example, among the factors mentioned are (1) tight money supply policy and neutral fiscal policy; and (2) workers' compliance with real wage reduction. The early price explosion was curbed by the middle of 1975 because of the government's consistent macroeconomic policy of stopping inflation at any cost. The tight money supply policy was an essential part of such efforts, but most governments facing oil crisis stagflation adopted a policy of tight money (though the Japanese policy was more obstinate than that elsewhere). But the factor truly unique to Japan was that Japanese workers complied with a reduction in real wages. This was, in fact, a trade-off for guaranteed employment (that is, no unemployment or layoffs). Not only the workers but also the management in most big firms shared the idea that long-term stability in employment was more important than short-term profits or wages—one of the basic ideas of Japanese (*ie*-type) management. The role of enterprise unions, another feature of the Japanese management system, was also important: the average Japanese worker was, in this crisis situation, primarily concerned about the company he worked for.

Another notable fact was that the national labor organizations agreed to the government's informal request for a virtual incomes policy (this incomes policy negotiation has never been publicized, but there is evidence to substantiate its existence). Since the economy was in a depression, the employment guarantee meant a profit squeeze that industrial interests (the so-called *zaikai*) accepted in accordance with the government's request. The hidden incomes policy played a considerable role in curbing inflation. Compared with other industrial countries, the oil-crisis inflation in Japan was characterized by two facts: first, a drastic leap and then a quick fall in prices; and second, a small change in the unemployment rate. This contrasts with another successful case, West Germany, which experienced a small price change coupled with a big increase in unemployment.

These two factors were not the result of industry-wide administrative guidance. In fact, the experience in the oil crisis indicated that *gyōsei shidō* was ineffective when an unexpected event hit the economy. Under such catastrophic changes, informal, long-term, multi-issued agreements are no longer workable because past agreements are thrown out of context and future prospects are too uncertain to serve as a basis for new agreements. For example, wholesale prices in Japan skyrocketed just after the first oil crisis, but MITI was incapable of curbing this price explosion. The petroleum (refining and distributing) industry formed a price cartel, and this aggravated the situation. In spite of the close relationship between this industry and MITI (there was even a regulatory law specific to the industry), MITI failed to control it. This suggests that MITI's power over prices was weak, as I already suggested in discussing the competitive polyopoly hypothesis, and more broadly that administrative guidance based on long-term, multi-issued agreements can work only in a stably expanding economy.[45]

In hindsight, the oil crisis was not so fatal a shock to the Japanese economy as it first appeared. The oil crisis was, in essence, a sudden, one-time leap in the price of oil. Because of the tripled price, Japan's trade account recorded a sudden huge deficit, which naturally caused a sharp depreciation of the yen. This depreciation gave rise to a sharp increase in Japanese exports. This export increase, however, did not result in appreciation of the yen for more than two years (until the end of 1975). The current-account deficit was so huge that even an accelerated increase in exports took a long time to offset it. Moreover, capital imports, or the recycling of "oil money" into Japan, were limited by the widespread perception of Japanese "fragility" (Zbigniew Brzezinski) and by regulations on capital transactions.[46] Japanese exports thus kept expanding. As we can now see, the more heavily an economy depended on oil imports, the more expansion of exports would be allowed it because of the continued depreciation of that country's currency. (This continued depreciation implies a worsening of the terms of trade and thus the lowering of real income.) As we look back, the oil crisis was not necessarily unfavorable to a resource-fragile country such as Japan, which attempted an export-led recovery. This was particularly true when the pressure of rising resource costs was, as in the case of Japanese industries, absorbed by the intense technological efforts to reduce costs.

The process of recovery included several components not found elsewhere. Workers' compliance with real wage reductions, big business's acceptance of a profit squeeze, the surprising quickness of cost-reduction efforts, the LDP government's persistence in its deflationary policy, and a resurgence of the national consensus to overcome the economic crisis gave a unique coloring to the Japanese solution. Each of these components could be found in other countries, however. It was the average

Japanese's acute sense of crisis or deep-rooted anxiety about Japan's fragility on the one hand and the vigor of the young Japanese industries on the other that made the combination of these factors workable. In this sense, the timing of the oil crisis was fortunate for the Japanese economy: postwar Japanese society was not yet old enough to have forgotten the feelings of insecurity and inferiority of a few decades earlier, and its economy was sufficiently mature to have a competitive edge over other economies. But the important aspect of the recovery is that the core of the postwar Japanese politico-economic system—the industry-wide *gyōsei shidō* system—played no significant role in overcoming the oil crisis. The viability of this system for the future, however, was not really tested.

The Political Aspect: Sudden Conservative Resurgence

In politics, a visible watershed came about in the late 1970s. According to opinion poll data, popular support for the LDP showed a resurgence after 1977. (In retrospect, the first sign of this was in a 1975 opinion poll.) This turnaround did not materialize in the national elections of 1979, but in the 1980 national elections the LDP recorded a victory comparable to those of the 1960s. In 1983, however, the LDP again experienced a setback in the national elections. Therefore, what we have been observing since 1977 is probably not a simple conservative resurgence. Opinion poll results include declining JSP support as well as continued high support for the LDP, however, and the period since 1977 (Period 3) may still tentatively be termed a conservative resurgence. How can we interpret this turnaround?

I have already noted two undercurrents at work in the 1970s. First, the emergence of the new middle mass seemed to presage, as argued above, the decline of the classical two-party system. Conservatism appeared unlikely to gain support in the context of conservative versus progressive confrontation. Even a multiparty system was predicted. Second, "tradition," religious or nationalistic, seemed to be fading. None of these signs suggested a conservative resurgence. We clearly need a new hypothesis to explain the Japanese polity since the late 1970s.

Three hypotheses summarize the current attempts to explain this unexpected phenomenon.

8. *Revival of nationalism hypothesis*

The crisis conditions since the early 1970s—the oil crises, the growing trade conflicts, and the increasing Soviet military threats in the western Pacific, in sum the mounting anxiety about the alleged fragility of the Japanese political economy—stirred the Japanese out of the complacency resulting from the pre–oil crisis affluence. Along with their pride in their economic achievement, this crisis psychology led to an emergence of nationalism and to a reconfirmation of the traditional heritage disclaimed throughout the postwar period. The revival of nationalism reinforced the traditionalistic basis for the LDP as a catchall party.

From the analytical viewpoint, this hypothesis is a revival of the nation-focused model. Indeed, for the first time in postwar history, nationalistic arguments became visible in the so-called *rondan* (the world of professional critics and commentators), although they remained far from dominant. As shown by opinion poll data (see below), however, the *rondan* does not mirror the broader public's attitudes. The new type of writing, with its nationalistic veneer, may be viewed as an overreaction against the dominance up to that time of conventionally progressive ideology in major newspapers and magazines in postwar Japan.

9. *Catchall interests hypothesis*
   During the rapid growth period, the LDP was already mass inclusionary and responded to a wide spectrum of mass interests. In the 1970s, the LDP finally committed itself to an effort to catch all interest groups, particularly urban consumers, whom it had never seriously wooed. For example, the LDP brought the social welfare system up to a level equal to that of other affluent societies, established probably the strictest antipollution policies of any industrial country, and increased public spending for improving the urban environment.

From the 1960s to the 1970s, popular support for the LDP consistently declined, whereas the electoral performance of the JSP and JCP seemed to be improving in local elections. Amid these worsening circumstances and given the emergence of antipollution movements and New Left violence, the LDP had to switch its policy focus toward urban consumers. The antipollution measures, the upgrading of social welfare, the investment in large cities, and so forth all came into being in the early 1970s.

One problem with the catchall interests hypothesis is interpreting the time lag between the policy switch (which started around 1971) and the LDP's victory in the national elections (which came in 1980). It is plausible to assume that urban residents felt the effect of the new policy orientations only gradually in the late 1970s. This hypothesis implies that the LDP changed from a tradition-based catchall party to an "interest-oriented catchall party." Examples of interest-oriented catchall parties may be most major parties in a standard two-party polity such as Britain, West Germany, and the United States. The LDP in the 1970s came close to acquiring such an interest orientation.

The third hypothesis was first proposed by Inoguchi.[47]

10. *Adjusted expectation hypothesis*

The crisis conditions since the early 1970s—the oil crises, the persistent worldwide stagflation, and the all-too-visible damages caused by pollution, in sum the growing pessimism about the limits to growth of the industrial world as well as the fragility of the Japanese economy—shook the growth psychology of the Japanese and lowered their expectation level concerning economic achievement. Compared to this pessimistic expectation and, perhaps more important, to the performance of other economies, the LDP government's crisis management received wide recognition from the general public.

Although the revival of nationalism hypothesis and adjusted expectation hypothesis both assume a psychological reshuffling on the part of voters, they differ in many ways. The revival of nationalism hypothesis assumes a psychological upsurge or enhanced confidence, but the adjusted expectation hypothesis implies the adjustment of inflated expectations to reality. The latter hypothesis implies a passive acceptance of the extant conservative government; the former, active support or even instigation of the nationalistic component in the LDP policy.

Appraisal of the Three Political Hypotheses

The following appraisal of the three alternative hypotheses is based on national election returns and two large-scale, identical opinion surveys conducted by the NHK in 1973 and 1978. In terms of time coverage and reliability, these surveys seem most appropriate for the present analysis.[48]

The NHK surveys asked the question: "What political party do you usually support?" Those respondents who indicated they were independents were asked the further question: "If you had to support a party, isn't there one you could possibly choose?" Those who chose some party in response to this question can be called "weak supporters"; those who initially indicated party support can be called "strong supporters." The results are summarized in Table 2.

Support for the LDP or LDP and NLC did increase, but there was a significant growth of weak supporters. The revival of nationalism hypothesis assumed a reversal of the postwar trend in Japanese psychology, which should have resulted in an upsurge of nationalism and strengthened support for the conservative parties. Opinion survey data seem to contradict this hypothesis.

There was a resurgence of certain aspects of national pride among the average Japanese, however. NHK surveys also asked: (1) "Do you feel happy to have been born in Japan?"; (2) "Is Japan one of the first-class countries?"; (3) "Do you feel at home when looking at old temples or

TABLE 2
Party Support, 1973 and 1978
(per cent)

Party Support	1973	1978	Per cent difference, 1973-78
LDP			
Strong	34.3% (82.7%)	38.2% (80.8%)	3.9%
Weak	7.2 (17.3)	9.1 (19.2)	1.9
Total	41.5 (100.0)	47.3 (100.0)	5.8
NLC[a]			
Strong		1.4% (40.0%)	
Weak		2.1 (60.0)	
Total		3.5 (100.0)	
LDP and NLC			
Strong	34.3% (82.7%)	39.6% (78.0%)	5.3%
Weak	7.2 (17.3)	11.2 (22.0)	4.0
Total	41.5 (100.0)	50.8 (100.0)	9.3
Independents	31.6%	33.8%	2.2%
JSP			
Strong	19.8% (76.7%)	14.4% (74.2%)	−5.4%
Weak	6.0 (23.3)	5.0 (25.8)	−1.0
Total	25.8 (100.0)	19.4 (100.0)	6.4
JCP			
Strong	4.2% (64.5%)	2.1% (70.0%)	−2.1%
Weak	2.3 (35.4)	0.9 (30.0)	−1.4
Total	6.5 (100.0)	3.0 (100.0)	−3.5
JSP and JCP			
Strong	24.0% (74.3%)	16.5% (73.7%)	−7.5%
Weak	8.3 (25.7)	5.9 (26.3)	−2.4
Total	32.3 (100.0)	22.4 (100.0)	−9.9

NOTE: Numbers in parentheses are percentages of supporters within groups.
[a]The NLC was born in 1976 as an offshoot of the LDP; so there is no entry for it in 1973.

countryside houses?"; (4) "Do Japanese have good qualities compared to other peoples?"; (5) "Do you want to do something for Japan in your own way?"; (6) "Does Japan still have something to learn from other countries?"; and (7) "Do you feel respect for, favorable feeling to, indifference to, or antipathy toward the emperor?" For questions 1–6, positive responses were as follows (I forego comment on the appropriateness of the questions):

Year	1	2	3	4	5	6
1973	90.5%	41.0%	87.5%	60.3%	72.6%	70.0%
1978	92.6	46.9	88.4	64.8	69.0	70.2

Responses to question 7 were:

Year	Respect	Favorable	Indifference	Antipathy
1973	33.3%	20.3%	42.7%	2.2%
1978	30.2	21.9	44.1	2.4

As indicated by the responses to questions 1, 2, and 4, the evaluation by Japanese of their country's capability seems to have increased, probably because of the better performance of the Japanese economy. However, active feelings of nationalism weakened, as seen in the answers to question 5. Also notable is that positive feelings toward the emperor weakened (in fact, the younger the respondent, the greater the weight of indifference vis-à-vis respect; more than 70 percent of those under 25 indicated indifference toward the emperor). Although the national capability was valued higher in 1978, there seems to be no indication of an upsurge of nationalism or of support for tradition, as symbolized by the emperor. These changes were also observable among strong LDP supporters (though their rates of positive answers were generally higher than other respondents). For that matter, strong supporters of parties other than the JCP evinced the same trends. There seems to be little evidence to support the revival of nationalism hypothesis.

On the other hand, there seems to be good evidence to corroborate the catchall interests hypothesis. For example, affirmative answers to the question "How satisfied are you with your present life?" showed a significant increase (at the 95 per cent level of significance) from 1973 to 1978 despite the serious economic difficulties during this period, particularly in those groups ignored by the LDP up to that time: urban residents, people under 35, white-collar workers, and students. The increase in the ratio of positive answers was greater among wage- and salary-earners than among traditional LDP supporters such as farmers, the self-employed, and managers. In the same NHK survey, a change in the composition of LDP supporters paralleled this change in satisfaction. A significant change in *strong* LDP support came from residents of big cities, high school graduates, people aged 35–44, skilled workers, and housewives compared with residents of villages and the self-employed. A new trend was the significant increase in *weak* LDP support among residents of middle-sized cities, college graduates, people aged 25–39, and unskilled workers. According to the survey, there was a greater increase in satisfaction as well as in conservative support from 1973 to 1978 among urban, young, educated, and employed people than among other groups in society. The natural conclusion is that members of these categories found something that was satisfying to them, and, at the same time, this was positively correlated with the results of the LDP's shift in priorities toward urban consumers, as the catchall interests hypothesis asserts.

However, the catchall interests hypothesis is not the only hypothesis consistent with the opinion survey data. Positive answers to the question about satisfaction increased in all 74 nontrivial categories of people except those aged 50–54 (though the increases in certain categories were not statistically significant). Many sectors of Japanese society must have experienced economic difficulty in the years 1973–78, when acute inflation, the threat of unemployment, and other problems were strong. Therefore, the unusually uniform pattern of responses could not be attributed totally to improvements in social conditions, but was at least partly the result of changes in expectation levels or in comparative evaluations of what the Japanese economy can and did achieve, as the adjusted expectation hypothesis suggests. The two hypotheses—the catchall interests hypothesis and adjusted expectation hypothesis—can concur and, in fact, do complement each other.

To conclude this argument, I cite the results of factor analyses using the NHK survey data. According to Hiroshi Akuto, two important factors determined the political attitudes shown in opinion surveys.[49] The primary factor was whether a person was, as Akuto put it, "tradition oriented or anti–tradition oriented." Items contributing to this factor were responses to questions concerning respect for the emperor, place of employment (in the traditional or modern sector), religiosity, and nationalism, concern for order, and so forth. Akuto's "tradition" is thus close to the meaning of "tradition" in the revival of nationalism hypothesis. An amazing finding was that this factor differentiates strong LDP supporters from independents (which includes weak LDP supporters) rather than from progressives. On the axis of tradition versus antitradition, JSP and JCP supporters were located in the middle between strong LDP supporters on the traditional pole and independents on the antitraditional pole. That is, LDP voters consist of two heterogenous groups, traditional loyalists and new urban floating voters. An important corollary is that if the LDP becomes explicitly more tradition oriented by emphasizing respect for the emperor or nationalistic activism, the weak LDP supporters among the independents will defect. This finding is at variance with the revival of nationalism hypothesis but consistent with the catchall interests hypothesis.

Moreover, this corollary suggests that the findings of the factor analysis of opinion poll data are inadequate to explain actual voting behavior since the late 1970s. There must be some important, missing factor that can bring together the two poles of conservative voters. A possible explanation is that the tradition versus antitradition factor is much less influential in voting behavior than short-term conditions at the time of the election (such as choice of campaign topic, leadership image, the effects of election forecasts, or even weather conditions), which the NHK surveys, designed to study longer-term attitudes, do not take into account. Among these short-term conditions, probably the most important was the economic policy (for example, tax issues) proposed by the LDP in each election campaign. This suggests that conservative supporters as a whole are becoming increasingly fluid and interest oriented rather than tradition oriented.

Another factor analysis, by Kazuto Kojima, seems to support this conclusion.[50] He attempted to analyze contemporary Japanese attitudes in general, and studied not only political attitudes but various psychological inclinations. First, he cited two main factors as describing the attitude of contemporary Japanese: one, similar to Akuto's analysis, is whether a person is tradition oriented or anti–tradition oriented; the other is whether a person is *majime shikō* ("instrumental" in the sense defined earlier) or *asobi shikō* ("consummatory"). Second, he discovered that the tradition versus antitradition factor seemed to be declining in importance vis-à-vis the instrumental versus consummatory factor. In 1973, the tradition versus antitradition factor was dominant not only for the 50–54 age group but also for the 20–24 age group; in 1978 the instrumental versus consummatory factor became the primary factor for the young, although it still remained the secondary factor for older people. Younger Japanese seem to be less concerned with tradition in Kojima's sense (which is defined as a collection of items such as respect for the emperor, strong fatherhood, religiosity, objection to premarital sexual relations, and concern for order and justice). This finding substantiates the emergence of those value orientations characterizing the new middle mass discussed above. An interesting fact is that the instrumental versus consummatory factor cannot be found in Akuto's analysis of political attitudes, whereas it plays an increasingly important role in Kojima's analysis of Japanese attitudes in general. It follows that the value confrontation between instrumentalism and consummatorism is apolitical, although it supplied political energy to New Left radicalism a decade earlier. This may further imply that people's interest in politics in the conventional sense is weakening and that electoral politics is increasingly volatile.

Recent national election results seem to support this implication. The new middle mass is by and large protective of its material affluence and its immediate reaction is to preserve the status quo. Its members are less unwilling to support the LDP, which brought about affluence, than the opposition parties. Unless this anti-instrumental inclination becomes political, the new middle mass will continue to be a reservoir of weak LDP supporters. Such weak supporters are likely to choose whether to vote rather than which party to vote for. Election results will depend on the voter turnout rate. In the 1979 lower-house elections, pre-election opinion polls unanimously forecast a big increase in LDP representation. However, voter turnout was at a near all-time low of 67.9 per cent. The result was the LDP's "big defeat" (in comparison with pre-election forecasts), that is, a loss of one seat. Among the suggested causes were the effect of too favorable forecasts, cold rainy weather, and Prime Minister Ohira's allusion (later retracted) to the possibility of raising taxes. In the 1980 elections to both houses, the situation was reversed. During the campaign, the possibility of an LDP loss of majority control was widely discussed; the opposition parties even started negotiating about a possible coalition government. Fearful of radical political change, weak supporters turned out to vote for the LDP; the turnout rate of 74.5 per cent was one of the highest in recent decades. The short-term conditions were also favorable to the LDP: Prime Minister Ohira died during the campaign, resulting in a large sympathy vote, and the LDP exploited the technical advantage in this "double election" (both the lower-house and upper-house elections were conducted simultaneously). The outcome was a big LDP victory, comparable to those in the party's heyday. The same theory holds for the 1983 lower-house elections. Pre-election forecasts were generally favorable to the LDP, but voter turnout (67.9 per cent) was again low. The result was the LDP's loss of its lower-house majority and a coalition with the NLC. Short-term conditions were also unfavorable because Prime Minister Nakasone was thought to be under the influence of ex–Prime Minister Tanaka, who had been convicted in the Lockheed bribery case just before the election.

Indeed, the conservative ascendancy continues, but it is perhaps endangered. The new middle mass is enjoying affluence and does not want any radical change. At the same time, however, it is not committed to support the LDP, let alone the LDP's nationalistic-traditionalistic component. Rather, its members calculate what the LDP can do for them. The gradual value change toward anti-instrumentalism will enfeeble many elements of the LDP support. Resumption of tradition-based catchall efforts will be no solution, at least insofar as "tradition" is understood in the context of the past. More generally, late-developer conservatism can no longer be the prime mover of Japanese society. This implies that bureaucratic guidance will also lose its influence over society because its persuasiveness was based on the lessons of more developed societies and its effectiveness depended on the entry control of foreign firms. As a short-term result, the position of Diet members will be strengthened vis-à-vis that of the bureaucracy. This seems to be the case in recent years, as LDP politicians assume more and more of the decision-making role of bureaucrats.[51] In the long-term, the LDP faces a basic reshuffling of the whole postwar politico-economic system. The conservative ascendancy is now unstable in many ways—not only in terms of electoral support but also in the context of policy consistency. In this sense, the conservative resurgence since the late 1970s may be viewed as an interlude preceding an era of more volatile politics.

Future Prospects

In the mid-1980s, Japanese society is entering a new era after a century of modernization. The arrival of this era is partly a result of the development of Japanese society, but, more important, it is a result of major changes in the environment confronting Japanese society (see Fig. 3). Predicting the future is not the main task of this paper, but some issues related to its argument can be briefly discussed. The changes outlined above seem to be first-rate in magnitude; that is, of a type that occurs only once a century or even less often. By all indications, not only Japan but the whole world seems to be entering a new era.

The technological and physical environment. Since the mid-1970s, the technological gap between Japan and other industrial countries, above all the United States, has by and large disappeared. What is more, a radically new technological paradigm including microelectronics, biological engineering, and new materials is emerging in the advanced industrial nations. Some people are calling it "the third industrial revolution." This technological divide will differentiate the twenty-first-century paradigm from the twentieth-century paradigm symbolized by electricity, chemistry, automobiles, and consumer durables (the second industrial revolution as distinguished from the nineteenth-century paradigm symbolized by steam, iron, and railways). In this historical context, Japan is likely to be one of the technological front-runners and will no longer be able to take advantage of late-developer status. This change will probably cause

		Rapid growth period (to 1973)	Transition (1973-80?)	A new era? (from 1980?)
OBJECTIVE ENVIRONMENT	Physical/ natural	Ample labor force. Cheap resources	Oil crisis	Aging population. Resource limit?
	Physical/ technological	Maturation of 20th-century technology: phase of technological catch-up	Emergence of 21st-century technology: end of catch-up phase	
	International	Pax Americana Mark One: fixed exchange rate, free trade, U.S. military dominance. Closed Japanese markets	End of Pax Americana Mark One: flexible exchange rate, growing protectionism, increased Soviet strength. Liberalization of Japanese markets. Japan gains capital export capability	
SUBJECTIVE ENVIRONMENT	National goal	Catch-up economic growth. Passive diplomacy and defense policy	Resource saving	Technological leadership? More active diplomacy?
	Cultural factors	Explicit groupism. Instrumentalism. Hidden traditionalism	Implicit groupist psychology. Trend to consummatorism. Neo-traditionalism?	

Fig. 3. The evolution of Japan's political economy.

a basic reshuffling of the postwar Japanese political economy. First of all, the national consensus of catch-up growth has faded away, and no new alternative has appeared to take its place. Some might argue that enthusiasm for new technologies is high among Japanese, specialists as well as the public at large, and that this enthusiasm can constitute the basis for a national consensus regarding the next century. However, if consensus means agreement about the concrete design of the society such as the Japanese had during the rapid growth period, the Japanese, in facing the twenty-first century, will be able neither to have a consensus of this nature nor to develop a social system based on such a consensus.

More specifically, most of the parapolitical nexus of administrative guidance, such as Japanese industrial policy, or the Japanese financial system, will be impracticable because of the lack of preceding examples, the increasing entry of foreign firms, and the mushrooming of venture businesses. Moreover, target policies led by the bureaucracy may not only be unnecessary but even harmful because of the current uncertainty from a supply and demand perspective over which industry is to be targeted. A society based on new technologies will be vastly different from the one we know and beyond the imagination of any twentieth-century savant because of the enormous leaps in information technology. Perhaps all we can do is to prepare sufficient room for creative adventures, technological as well as social, without being afraid of the possible risks involved. This approach is liberal in a wide sense and is contrary in many ways to the Japanese approach in the catch-up phase. Unless the Japanese political economy can override the institutional inertia from the past, it is likely to be another example of a nouveau riche who fails to maintain the level he managed to reach. If it is to retain power, the LDP will have to create a "new conservatism" to replace the late-developer conservatism on which it has relied for so long. The bureaucracy will have to redefine its role in line with this new approach.

International environment. More than likely, the entire world system will have to undergo a basic restructuring. The cost of maintaining the world system has become too heavy for a single country to bear, even a country on the scale of the United States. The end of colonialism, the unthinkability of large-scale warfare, and the acceleration of technological diffusion that weakened the United States' economic dominance make the maintenance of a world order dependent on "hegemonic power" (Robert Gilpin) seem unlikely.[52] Along with the USSR's reinforced military strength, Japan's unexpected rise as an economic power (though similar impacts are likely to ensue from other quickly developing nations, for example, Korea and China) is a major factor disturbing the extant hegemonic order. A Pax Americana Mark Two is still conceivable, and most countries would welcome it under the present situation.

Even so, Mark Two will be structurally different from Mark One. A possible implication is that the major industrial powers including Japan will have to share joint responsibility for world leadership, if the world (or at least the Western world) is not to be divided. For Japan, this means a reversal of its foreign policies of the past four decades and indeed those of its whole history as a follower nation. New foreign policies should include, among others, liberalization of Japanese markets (goods, services, and capital), international coordination of macroeconomic policies, and international adjustment of worldwide capital flows (including aid to developing countries). Japan's more active participation in the Western security alliance system is also an unavoidable issue. Japan's postwar political system has consistently shunned each of these policies.

Cultural factors. The future of Japanese society is in the hands of the new middle mass. The LDP (or LDP-centered coalition) government will have to respond carefully to these people if the present bare conservative majority is to be maintained. Being pluralistic in many ways, Japanese society will no longer be controlled by any particular elitist group but will be subject to the choices of a vast, politically amorphous mass. We can hardly predict how these people, particularly the younger generation, will feel, judge, and behave. These young "new Japanese" are no longer motivated toward catch-up efforts. Nurtured in material affluence, they are freer from the conventional (instrumental) morality of hard work, efficiency, faith in marriage, strong masculinity, and more prone to a *homo ludens* mentality (consummatory values). Compared with the old Japanese, their loyalty to particular groups, especially firms, will be less intense.

The beliefs of these new Japanese are not, however, converging with classical Western values or individualism in the Western sense. Even younger Japanese will continue to embrace the idea of interpersonal harmony rather than that of the inviolability of the individual, as recent opinion surveys unequivocally show. Their group nature is indeed likely to be more amorphous and less institutional: for example, it will not necessarily take the form of typical Japanese management. The Japanese mode of decision making (long-term, multi-issued, often implicit agreements) is, however, unlikely to change very much. For example, Japanese society will still be more inclined than U.S. society to form intermediate, informal groupings within and across formal institutions, although increasingly closer contacts with the world outside Japan (for example, Japanese investment in other countries as well as foreign entries into Japanese markets) will gradually modify this inclination. As another example, Japan is less likely than many other societies to develop the strong personal leadership that is often essential to effective execution of active foreign policies.

A keynote for change can be found in the shift from instrumentalism to consummatorism. The *ie* tradition has so far been manifested as organizational know-how that incorporates the principle of achievement orientation (instrumental rationality) into a community-like organization. Japanese management is a present-day application of this organizational tradition. However, as instrumental virtues lose their grip over the minds of the new Japanese, Japanese management will develop in the direction of a workplace community rather than an organization devoted to instrumental rationality such as hard work or efficiency. The Japanese political economy during the rapid growth period, with all its formal and informal organizations, may be viewed as an efficient system targeted at catch-up economic development. This is not to say that postwar Japanese society was monolithic and tightly regulated. Compared with most other societies, however, it more efficiently achieved the goal of catch-up growth, although most of this growth can be attributed to a fortuitous combination of environments. The historical role of this instrumentally rational system now seems to be ending. As we have seen, this transformation mirrors the change in values among the new middle mass.

The Current Attempt at New Conservatism

Faced with these problems, the conservative government in Japan has been attempting in the 1980s to reform and redirect policies in response to the changes in the environment. The new policies include the curbing of government expenditures, administrative reform (*gyōsei kaikaku*), liberalization of Japanese markets, retightening of relations with the United States, educational reform (*kyōiku kaikaku*), and promotion of high technology. These efforts exhibit obvious parallels with the conservative governments' policies in the United States and Britain, that is, with the so-called neo-conservatism of the Reagan administration or Thatcher cabinet. Prime Minister Nakasone has been promoting new conservatism actively. As it gradually emerges, the new conservatism consists of market-oriented liberalism, more explicit confrontation with the socialist East, emphasis on new technological development, and a certain flavor of traditionalism. New conservatism is radical in that it attempts to overthrow the regulatory practices piled up during the permissive affluent era: the terms "deregulation" and "small government" thus symbolize the neo-conservative approach.

In the last phase of postwar prosperity, the two-party system in advanced (Anglo-American-type) societies often took the form of confrontation between two interest-oriented catchall parties. Progressive parties such as the Democratic Party in the United States or the German Social Democratic Party took most of the initiative in this stage of "interest-group liberalism" (Theodore J. Lowi).[53] The new conservatism in the 1980s may be viewed as an antithesis to this progressive initiative that dominated the period of postwar prosperity. In concluding this article, I appraise the potential of the new conservatism, given current politico-economic challenges, particularly those in Japan. This is not to totally deny the possibility of a "new progressivism," or an attempt at self-reform by the JSP or other progressive parties. I focus, however, on new conservatism because the chances for a government based on either old or new progressivism are slim in Japan (save for a catastrophe in international relations involving Japan).

As opinion surveys show, the Nakasone cabinet as of mid-1986 was receiving exceptionally strong support from the general public (the rate of support was nearly 50 per cent, an unprecedented figure). Does this mean that the Japanese accept the new conservatism? The majority of business interests seem to support Nakasone's policies because they favor the idea of small government (particularly, the reduction of welfare expenditures, dissolution of large public corporations, and the reduction of agricultural subsidies), at least so long as their industries or firms do not suffer too much economically. The bureaucracy is, of course, largely skeptical of the whole idea of small government, and its resistance to deregulation is by no means weak. However, bureaucrats seem increasingly aware that bureaucratic guidance is becoming outdated and internationally unacceptable; moreover, they cannot publicly oppose the idea of small government, given the current huge government deficit. The new middle mass is also complying passively because as taxpayers they prefer small government. Unlike in the United States, however, none of these groups believes in the neo-conservative philosophy, particularly its individualistic component. In my view, these groups form only a temporary coalition, and support for Nakasone is not as firm as that for Reagan, who can rely on the traditional "American ideal" of individual freedom. Nakasone or any other future conservative leader in Japan will not be free from the aftereffects of late-developer conservatism.

Nakasone or other future conservative leaders will have to persuade the Japanese public to bear a greater and more active international responsibility. The symbolic issue is the liberalization of Japanese markets (of goods, services, and capital). Liberalization clearly implies the reduction of bureaucratic power, the decline of heretofore protected industries, and, as a joint effect, the weakening of the parapolitical nexus of administrative guidance. Without introducing these deregulatory measures, the system of administrative guidance is likely to become a symbiosis between government and industry that serves only to protect specific interests and so will do much harm to the economy as a whole as well as destroy the perception of fairness throughout the society. In this sense, liberalization will become imperative as a response to foreign and domestic pressures. These efforts will weaken the LDP's traditional sources of support—farmers (over the issue of citrus and beef imports) and owners of small-scale firms (which will have to compete against imports from developing countries in Asia)—as well as the close link between the LDP and the bureaucracy.

Similarly serious is the issue of defense. For example, when a conservative government tries to move toward closer military ties with the United States, as the Nakasone cabinet has done, the reaction of the new middle mass is unpredictable because it is not yet prepared for Japan to take an active role in international affairs, particularly in the military sphere. The elder generation still remembers World War II. On the other hand, the younger generation is by and large indecisive and likely to defect from the LDP if conservative leaders try to appeal to prewar-style nationalism. If the Japanese public is determined to reject an increase in defense capability or closer military ties with the United States, it should instead accept another type of burden sharing among the world's economic leaders—greater aid to developing countries (including low-interest loans and emergency financing to debtor nations, based on explicit international agreements). At present, however, the new middle mass does not seem ready for this type of responsibility. In regard to defense issues, the conservative leadership will have to be extremely ingenious in handling the still confused, probably divided, and ill-prepared popular opinion.

Nakasone's fortune and the prospects of new conservatism in general hinge on the performance of the global economy, particularly that of the U.S. economy. If the U.S. economy continues to prosper as in 1983–86, all economies will benefit and many political tensions, domestic as well as international, will be eased: for example, the trade conflict between the United States and Japan is likely to be less serious than otherwise. However, prosperity per se is not enough. From 1983 to 1985, the United States prospered as a huge, consumption-prone economy with enormous deficits in government as well as trade: the dollar was overvalued in terms of purchasing power parity. Should the U.S. economy fall into deep recession, everything may go wrong and a vicious circle will occur—a rapidly weakening dollar, sudden capital outflows, greater government deficits, heightened interest rates, stifled investment. The world economy as a whole will face a system breakdown, and each economy will head for protectionism. Not being authentic believers in liberalism, all sectors of Japanese society, including business interests, the bureaucracy, and the voters at large, will lose their motivation for market liberalization and ask for an expansive fiscal or financial policy. The neoconservative program will disintegrate. In this sense, the new conservatism hinges on robust economic performance or, more specifically, on the expectation that a series of virtuous circles will come out of Reagan's tightrope walk over the huge trade and budget deficits. Under the present politico-economic situation, the neo-conservative recipe involves serious risk because of the potential instability in the world economy, particularly in the U.S. economy as its core. In order to remove this risk, the United States must revitalize its economy by rebuilding its industries' competitiveness and increasing its savings rate. If Japan or any other country liberalizes its economy, helps shoulder the burden of global defense and aid to developing nations, or coordinates the timing of its macroeconomic policies with other nations some of the difficulties will be solved. Without the revitalization of the U.S. economy, however, the potential instability may transpire, and Pax Americana Mark Two will never stabilize. In many ways, the neo-conservative attempts throughout the world hinge on whether the U.S. economy can be revitalized.

The new conservatism of Reagan, Thatcher, or Nakasone is meaningful in that it attempts to remove the psychological and institutional inertia from the historically unprecedented worldwide postwar prosperity. Particularly in the case of Japan, the deregulation of the parapolitical nexus is necessary and important, but domestic deregulation is not a panacea. New conservatism involves the serious problem of dealing with the potential instability in the world system. In order to build the society of the next century, we need something more than a new conservative philosophy. It is clear that some restructuring of the world economic order is in order. If each country is overly bound to nationalistic concerns, neo-conservative attempts will face serious inconsistencies in the worldwide context.

The tasks facing conservative governments, in Japan as elsewhere, are dual faceted and in a way conflicting. Domestically, government interventions in private activities and initiatives should be removed in order to create significant freedom for a wide range of attempts to meet the needs of the next century. Internationally, however, the coordination and reshuffling of burdens among the leading countries will be increasingly necessary. In Japan, the conservative leadership must gather stable support from the new middle mass for this dual-faceted political task. The new middle mass is largely conservative in the weak sense that it is unwilling to give up the material affluence it has come to possess since the rapid growth period. It is, however, not the "middle class" in the prewar sense of the word: its members do not view themselves as the mainstay of society or the bearer of its representative values. A resurgence of inequality in income distribution or visible divergence in lifestyle will disintegrate the new middle mass into divided, unsatisfied segments. It will then lose its conservative outlook. The new middle mass is indeed moderately traditional in the sense that it is searching for a Japanese cultural identity vis-à-vis the still overwhelming Western cultural impact. However, most of its members will be antipathetic to the return of prewar traditionalism. The new middle mass is not traditional in any simple sense of the word.

An increasing number of the new middle mass are apparently beginning to realize the necessity of assuming greater international responsibilities to protect Japan's present material affluence. However, they are still psychologically unprepared for the expansion of defense capability or aid to developing countries. Until the oil crisis, the LDP showed remarkable flexibility in coordinating the multiple targets of catch-up growth, passive foreign policy, and maintenance of tradition. Now, the LDP or LDP-centered coalition faces the dual tasks of deregulation and an active foreign policy. These new tasks are almost exactly opposite to those of late-developer conservatism. What is necessary in the new context is political leadership rather than bureaucratic initiative and voting strength based on a consensus about basic policy rather than on resource allocation and personal ties. The parapolitical nexus of *gyōsei shidō* will be of little use in the coming decades. The crucial question is Can Japanese society provide both flexible yet unfailing political leadership and voters with a broad perspective about international issues?

In the very long run, the new middle mass may be capable of creating a culture that differs from traditional Japanese culture as well as from Western culture but is still acceptable in the global context. In the more concrete, short-run context, however, the new middle mass is prone to complacency and unlikely to make any decisive departure from the past Japanese pattern. Politically, it will show only weak party loyalty and, therefore, unpredictable volatility in voting behavior. As a result, the government party, most likely the LDP or an LDP-centered coalition, will have to be hesitant in proposing sweeping changes in policy orientation. The challenges facing Japanese society in the coming decades will be enormous, involving the impact of radically new technologies and the transformation of the international politico-economic order. As in every other society, the success of Japanese society will be determined by how well the Japanese system copes with the political volatility of the new middle mass, particularly its younger component.

Part II

Macroeconomic Performance

Martin Bronfenbrenner and Yasukichi Yasuba

Economic Welfare

Japan has experienced a miraculous economic advance in the second half of this century. This paper addresses, without solving, the question To what extent has this advance been *enjoyed* as well as *experienced*? How has it affected the economic welfare of the average Japanese? Premier George Papandreou of Greece worried in the 1950s about "the figures prospering while the people suffered." Could Japan be another case in point?

On this important topic, there are two contrasting positions. One image, originating in a 1979 European Commission report, is of the Japanese as "workaholics in rabbit hutches." Yatsuhiro Nakagawa, however, called Japan a "welfare superpower" equal to any in the West, and Ezra Vogel wrote of Japan as number one (in social and economic organization and potential future welfare), whose performance offered "lessons for America."[1] This paper takes neither extreme position. We feel that "workaholics in rabbit hutches" is more wrong than "welfare superpower." At the same time, we recognize that Japan, especially urban Japan, has serious quality-of-life problems centering on housing, commuting time, and inadequate public facilities. Moreover, like other aspiring welfare states, Japan has not financed its welfare system adequately to prepare for the demographic revolution—the sharply increasing proportion of old-age pensioners in its population—in the next generation.

In the first section of this paper, we indicate what we mean by economic welfare. We then consider economic and to a lesser extent social indicators and indicate their limitations. We evaluate progress (or lack of progress) since 1955 and compare it with conditions elsewhere. (Historical trends are shown in order to facilitate understanding of the current situation.)

More specifically, we begin by considering real per capita GNP and some of its components (consumption and saving). We pass on to one of its alternatives, the concept of "net national welfare," to taxes as possible deductions, and to the underground economy as an important omission. This is followed by consideration of income distribution, such "costs of income" as hours worked, industrial accidents, other safety and health hazards, and environmental pollution. We then examine the problems of discrimination and alienation, which might also be thought of in part as costs of social and economic institutions. (For Japan's welfare-state institutions, see Noguchi's paper in this volume). Finally, we present some tentative conclusions.

What Is Economic Welfare?

Economists agree only imperfectly on the nature and constituents of economic welfare. We ourselves think in terms of six components, of which the first two are the most commonly emphasized.

1. *The current standard of living*, represented as a first approximation by real per capita GNP or GDP,[2] with the term "real" implying only statistical correction for price-level changes. In accepting this criterion, we reject the criticism that the average consumer "buys goods he does not want, at prices he cannot afford, on the basis of advertising he does not believe, to impress neighbors he dislikes." We also reject arguments that consumption is an addiction, a mindless search for a Nirvana of goodies consumers have neither time to enjoy nor space to store. (Neither do we believe that the average saver is pathologically afraid to spend or afflicted with Freudian "anal fixation.")

2. *The probable future standard of living*, as represented by real per capita GNP or GDP plus its growth rate.

3. The *distribution* of the society's income—and its wealth, a cumulation of past income—among classes of income receivers and wealth owners. Distribution can be made on many bases—age, race, sex, region, occupation, economic function. The most important here is by income size, the so-called personal distribution. People have widely different ideas on equitable distribution. These reflect varied views of the need and efficacy of economic incentives to work, save, and invest. They also reflect degrees of envy of "the rich" and of sympathy for "the poor." We personally would like to see distribution somewhat more equal than it is in either Japan or the United States and to see this equality increased more by better safety nets for the poor than by lower ceilings for the wealthy.[3]

4. *Security* of the standard of living from both the short-term shocks associated with business-cycle downturns and the longer-term ones associated with technological change, resource exhaustion, population ex-

plosions, and the like. (No economic system can protect Japan against the major earthquakes forecast for the near future or the world against nuclear holocaust.)

5. *Compatibility* of the standard of living with the *maintenance of physical and mental life and health*. The enemies under this category range from industrial accidents and environmental pollution to overwork and nervous breakdown. The issues include the possible costs of the standard of living. "There's no such thing as a free lunch," economists tell us; we apply this argument to the standard of living.

6. *Compatibility* of the standard of living with the *maintenance of civil liberties*. Here again the costs of prosperity issue arises, especially in systems of slavery or dictatorship.

Discussions of economic welfare as such concentrate on the first two items, the present and prospective standards of living, which between them capture the economic growth rate. Discussions of the welfare state, however, concentrate on the last four items, the prevention and cure of poverty and insecurity and the reduction of the costs of affluence. At least, these are the welfare state's ostensible purposes and the bases of its political support. Major beneficiaries of the welfare state's institutions may, of course, include members of the middle and upper economic classes, both as members of the welfare bureaucracy and as recipients of benefits. (Both U.S. and Japanese billionaires are entitled to social security benefits when they retire.)

Those who are born and live their life on welfare are members of an economic underclass. Their economic welfare is low, not high. Victorian England and the United States between 1900 and 1929 are examples of highly prosperous countries with underdeveloped welfare-state institutions. India and China, on the other hand, are poor countries attempting to construct widespread welfare-state institutions. A welfare superpower is not only economically prosperous but has well-developed welfare-state institutions.

Per Capita GNP and Associated Indicators

Wherever possible, we have chosen 1955 as the historical baseline for considering per capita GNP and associated indicators. In that year, Japan's per capita GNP regained its peak prewar value, attained in the 1934–36 period. A 1956 official *Economic White Paper* declared: "It is no longer 'postwar.' We now face a different situation, since growth through recovery is over. From now on growth will be supported by modernization."[4] Between 1955 and 1980, real per capita GNP grew by a factor of 5.2 (see Table 1). The annual growth rate was a phenomenal 9 per cent

TABLE 1
Per Capita GNP (in 1975 Prices) and Its Annual Rate of Growth, Japan, 1955-1980

Year	Per capita GNP (000 yen)	Growth rate (per cent)	Year	Per capita GNP (000 yen)	Growth rate (per cent)
1955	312	—	1970	1,123	9.8%
1960	455	7.8%	1975	1,319	3.3
1965	702	9.1	1980	1,621	4.2

SOURCES: Real GNP and growth rate, 1955-65, Kazushi Ohkawa, Nobukiyo Takamatsu, and Yuzo Yamamoto, *National Income, LTES 1* (Tokyo: Tōyō Keizai Shimpōsha, 1974), p. 214; 1965-80 and population, Japan, Economic Planning Agency, *Keizai yōran, 1983* (Economic survey) (Tokyo: Government Printing Bureau, 1983), pp. 15, 33.

during the 1960s, but fell to the 3-4 per cent range during the 1970s. There is no short-term prospect of a return to the 9 per cent rate, which amounts to a doubling every eight years.

It is to some extent tautologous to say that high GNP growth causes high GNP growth per capita, which is indeed the standard explanation. Although high GNP growth could have been diverted into a renewed population explosion similar to that in Japan from 1947 to 1949 or in Mexico in the 1970s, this did not happen in Japan after 1955. One can also argue, on basically Keynesian grounds, that high per capita GNP growth kept aggregate demand up and therefore led to high GNP growth.

A major methodological change in the international comparisons of real GNP (and GDP) has recently found general acceptance. Previously, the conventional method was to base international comparisons on market exchange rates. If the yen–dollar rate, for example, is ¥200 to $1 and per capita GDP is ¥2,000,000 in Japan as against $15,000 in the United States, the yen equivalent of the U.S. figure is ¥3,000,000 and Japanese real per capita GDP is 66.67 per cent of the U.S. figure. Despite the simplicity of such calculations, this system has serious disadvantages and is being discarded: (1) it does not reflect purchasing power vis-à-vis nontraded goods, particularly services, which influence exchange rates extremely indirectly or not at all; (2) it may be distorted by measures of trade protection and commodity taxation; (3) it may also be affected by capital movements and interest-rate differentials, which affect exchange rates much more than purchasing power; and, (4) disequilibrium exchange rates may be maintained for years by a number of devices known collectively as "exchange controls."

To counteract such deficiencies, a research team headed by Irving Kravis has developed a set of bilateral index numbers for direct purchasing-power comparisons between pairs of countries. Although sharing the imperfections of all index numbers, the results of the Kravis indexes are generally accepted as preferable to those of exchange-rate conversions. When the Kravis indexes are larger than the exchange-rate comparisons, the country's currency is undervalued against the U.S. dollar on a purchasing-power basis, as was the case for the Japanese yen in the 1960s (and vice versa, when the Kravis indexes are less than exchange-rate conversions).

Relying on the Kravis indexes, we find that all seven countries listed in Table 2 grew faster than the United States in terms of real per capita GDP between 1955 and 1980. Only South Korea, however, kept pace with Japan. Japan's per capita GDP rose from 21 to 74 per cent of the U.S. figure over this quarter-century. In the course of this spectacular rise, Japan passed Italy by 1970 and the United Kingdom by 1975. In 1980, Japan's Kravis figure was less than the estimate by exchange-rate conversion, reflecting the end in the 1970s of the systematic undervaluation of the yen vis-à-vis the dollar.

Both GNP and GDP are measured before taxes. Neither statistic includes the underground economy, which has arisen largely to evade taxes (and direct controls). Since both the tax burden and the underground economy have important welfare implications in many countries, we consider them together in a Japanese context.

One feature of the Japanese economy has been its relatively low level of taxes and levies for social security. Another has been the relatively

TABLE 2

Real Per Capita Gross Domestic Product (U.S. = 100), Selected Countries, 1955-1980

Country	1955	1960	1965	1970	1975	1980
Philippines	11.4	12.3	11.5	11.7	13.2	13.7
	(8.2)	(6.3)	(7.6)	(3.9)	(5.2)	(6.1)
South Korea	7.9	8.2	8.5	11.8	20.7	23.7
	(4.5)	(5.4)	(3.0)	(5.5)	(8.1)	(13.0)
Japan	21.2	29.8	38.6	58.5	68.4	74.1
	(11.1)	(16.5)	(26.1)	(40.6)	(62.0)	(87.1)
Italy	37.4	38.4	41.1	48.0	53.8	54.6
	(20.7)	(24.7)	(31.5)	(38.7)	(47.5)	(57.0)
United Kingdom	59.6	64.2	62.4	62.7	63.9	65.7
	(43.8)	(48.6)	(50.2)	(45.4)	(57.5)	(69.7)
West Germany	53.5	68.0	69.4	76.5	83.0	87.7
	(34.1)	(46.5)	(53.1)	(63.0)	(94.0)	(119.6)
France	50.1	59.2	62.6	71.9	81.9	83.6
	(47.1)	(47.0)	(51.9)	(57.2)	(89.1)	(103.3)

SOURCES: Irving B. Kravis et al., *World Product and Income* (Baltimore: Johns Hopkins University Press, 1982), pp. 327-29. For figures in parentheses, United Nations, *Yearbook of National Accounts Statistics, 1980*; and World Bank, *World Development Report, 1982*, pp. 110-11.

NOTE: Figures in parentheses are converted by exchange rates. Other conversions are by the Kravis method.

small size of its underground economy. The two features are probably not independent of each other. The ratio of total taxes and social security levies to national income was quite low until recently. Even in 1975, after substantial increases two years earlier, the figure was only 27.9 per cent, but it rose sharply thereafter, reaching 32.6 per cent in 1980. The figure remains considerably lower than that of the United States (38.4 per cent) or the United Kingdom (51.0 per cent), not to speak of West Germany and Sweden.[5] The Japanese ratio, however, is expected to rise rapidly in the near future, mainly because of the support provided to older members of a rapidly aging population. If no changes are made in support levels for social security beneficiaries, the level is expected to reach 40 per cent before the year 2000. So drastic a rise, which some insist is politically impossible despite north European examples, can hardly avoid triggering both class and generational conflicts. (For this range of issues, see Sawako Ariyoshi's 1984 novel *Kōkotsu no hito* [The twilight years] and Noguchi's paper in this volume.)

The recent growth of the second (or parallel, black, barter, or underground) economy seems to be a near-universal phenomenon, stemming largely from the desire to evade "unfair" taxes, at least in economies relatively free of direct controls.[6] It seems to have expanded as tax rates rose; whether it will decline if tax rates fall, we do not know. Its extent can be estimated only crudely. Participants avoid the statistician almost as assiduously as they dodge the tax collector.

Unrecorded underground transactions naturally result in an underestimation of GNP and other income measures; most countries make some attempt to include them. In Japan, for example, expense-account consumption, called "exhousehold consumption expenditure," amounted to ¥6.7 billion in 1975, or 4.5 per cent of GNP in that year.[7] A World Bank study estimates the proportion of underground income to reported income to be highest in India (9–48 per cent), followed by the United States (6–22 per cent), Italy (10–20 per cent), and Canada (5–20 per cent). Japan's underground economy, according to this estimate, was one of the world's smallest—less than 5 per cent of reported income.[8]

In several countries, statisticians have adjusted net national product (NNP) or net domestic product (NDP) figures—GNP or GDP less depreciation allowances on fixed capital—for a number of welfare considerations not included in national or domestic product estimates. For example, they deduct all taxes; adjust for environmental pollution, traffic accidents, and changes in leisure; spread the consumption of durable consumer goods over the estimated lifetimes of these goods; and add in the value of the unpaid, unrecorded labor of housewives. The result is called net national welfare (NNW) in Japan.[9] For Japan, Miyohei Shinohara and his associates estimated NNW at five-year intervals from 1955 through 1970, and Hisao Kanamori extended the series to 1975.[10] According to these estimates, between 1955 and 1970, NNW (total, not per capita) grew by 7.4 per cent per year, as against 8.8 per cent for GNP. This differential is not surprising. However, in the final quinquennium covered by the Kanamori study (1970–75), NNW grew faster than GNP by a wide margin, 9.3 per cent compared with 5.2. (Pollution reduction and the reduction in traffic accidents are given major credit for this reversal.) Kanamori has not extended his series, but judging from the movements of two indicators that we look at later—pollution and traffic accidents—we believe that the reversal continued at least until 1980.

Saving Patterns

Another feature of the Japanese economy in the twentieth century has been the size of its national saving ratio (saving by corporate and public bodies as well as by individuals and households). The saving ratio has declined slightly in recent years, but it was 31 per cent in 1980, much higher than in most Western countries (see Tables 3–5). Two other Asian countries, South Korea and the Philippines, have both shown steeply rising saving ratios, which may approximate the Japanese ratio in the future, as Singapore's appears to have done. Corporate saving in Japan, particularly in the form of depreciation reserves, is an increasingly important component of national saving, as it is in the United States.

It is clear that the Japanese saving ratio was pushed upward by high growth, especially in the 1950s and in the early 1960s when individuals may have regarded an increase in income as a temporary windfall. Another factor, stressed in Sato's paper in this volume, has been the desire to rebuild, renovate, and expand Japan's stock of industrial and residential assets that were destroyed or that deteriorated during World War II and the immediate postwar years.

Whether saving increases or decreases the growth rate is a complex

TABLE 3
Gross Domestic Saving as a Proportion of GDP, Selected Countries, 1960 and 1980

Country	1960	1980	Country	1960	1980
Philippines	16%	25%	United Kingdom	17%	19%
South Korea	1	23	West Germany	29	25
Japan	34	31	France	25	21
Italy	25	22	United States	19	17

SOURCE: World Bank, *World Development Report, 1982*, pp. 118-19.

TABLE 4
Personal Saving Ratios, Selected Countries, 1960-1980
(per cent of disposal personal income)

Country	1960	1970	1975	1980
Japan	17.3	20.0	24.9	19.2
United States	4.9	8.2	8.5	6.0
United Kingdom	4.7	5.6	10.0	12.3
West Germany	14.9	16.6	14.5	10.9
France	9.7	16.9	17.7	11.0
South Korea	−1.3	4.5	5.4	8.2

SOURCES: 1960-1975, Yutaka Kosai and Yoshitaro Ogino, *The Contemporary Japanese Economy* (London: Macmillan, 1984), p. 12; 1980 (except South Korea), Bank of Japan, *Nihon keizai o chūshin to suru kokusai hikaku tōkei, 1983* (Comparative international statistics on the Japanese economy) (Tokyo, 1983), p. 22; 1980, South Korea, United Nations, *Yearbook of National Accounts Statistics, 1981,* p. 1037.

TABLE 5
Sources of Japanese Savings, 1955-1980
(¥ trillion)

Source	1955	1960	1965	1970	1975	1980
Personal savings	0.9	1.9	3.8	9.6	24.5	33.8
Corporate retained earnings	0.2	1.0	1.0	4.8	−0.8	2.3
Depreciation reserves	0.8	1.7	4.2	9.9	19.3	31.5
Government savings	0.4	1.2	2.0	5.6	4.7	6.5
Current account surplus (−)	−0.1	0.0	−0.4	−0.8	−0.2	−2.5

SOURCES: 1955-70, Yutaka Kosai and Yoshitaro Ogino, *The Contemporary Japanese Economy* (London: Macmillan, 1984), p. 13; 1975-80, United Nations, *Yearbook of National Accounts Statistics, 1981,* vol. I, part 1, pp. 901, 904.
NOTE: In national accounting, gross private domestic investment is the sum of personal and corporate saving, the government surplus, and the current-account deficit.

issue. The Harrod-Domar growth formulas appear to imply that it increases the growth rate,[11] but since they are identities, the direction of causation cannot be determined. If the principal check to investment and capital formation is the absorption of the necessary resources by consumption, an increase in saving is a spur to growth. If the check to investment is inadequate demand for final products, the opposite is the case. Kazuo Sato, among other authorities, argues in this volume that Japan saves too much rather than too little.

Whatever its effect on the growth numbers, what does saving imply for economic welfare? Suppose that Countries A and B have identical GDP per capita and also identical measured growth rates. Country A has a negative saving ratio because its inhabitants are acquiring new durable goods on credit faster than they pay for the old ones. Country B outdoes Japan with a saving ratio of 50 per cent by limiting its consumption to basic human needs. Which country enjoys the higher level of economic welfare? We believe that economists can answer this question only by reference to their own compromises between the sybaritic life of Country A and the ascetic life of Country B. Both saving and consumption, as we have said, normally contribute to welfare. Saving, in particular, may represent a rational preference for future consumption, by oneself or one's family, over present consumption. It will provide streams of future income (or the pleasure derived from having accumulated assets, or "psychic income"), the present value of which may itself be an unrecorded consumption good.[12] Nevertheless, as suggested below for the years immediately following the 1973 oil shock, either a rise or a fall in the saving ratio may represent a panicky and irrational response to a crisis.

Perhaps the most remarkable feature of Japan's performance in saving is the exceptionally high saving ratios of worker families. Surveys of employee households show that the saving ratios of the four lowest income quintiles increased rapidly until 1975 (see Table 6). In that year, their combined average level was 26.2 per cent. Particularly noteworthy was the rise in the saving ratio of the first quintile (the lowest fifth of the employee-income distribution) from negative figures in 1955 and 1960 in cities with populations of 50,000 or more to the highest rate in Japan in 1975—28.2 per cent. The abnormally high saving ratios of the lower income classes in 1975—as compared with both 1970 and 1980—may reflect an irrational or panicky response to the energy crisis and the reces-

TABLE 6

Saving Rates of Employee Families, by Income Quintiles, Japan, 1955-1980
(per cent of disposable personal income)

Year	Average	Quintiles[a]				
		I	II	III	IV	V
1955[b]	9.3%	−24.3%	3.4%	9.4%	12.3%	17.9%
1960[b]	15.0	−14.4	7.9	12.6	17.2	24.1
1965	17.8	12.1	15.6	16.9	17.6	21.4
1970	21.2	14.2	17.8	20.5	22.3	24.2
1975	23.0	28.2	24.8	25.6	26.1	16.0
1980	22.1	13.2	18.9	22.2	23.9	26.0

SOURCES: 1955-60, National Livelihood Center, *Kokumin seikatsu tōkei nempō* (Statistical yearbook on national livelihood) (Tokyo: Shiseido), *1970*, p. 152; 1965-80, ibid., *1972*, p. 122, and *1982*, p. 96.
[a]Quintile I is made up of the lowest 20 per cent of income receivers among employees, Quintile V the highest 20 per cent.
[b]Cities with populations of 50,000 or more.

sion that followed. It may also represent a more rational intention to offset the erosion by inflation of the real values of that group's financial assets, such as deposits in the banks and the Postal Savings system.[13] By 1980, the normal pattern had resumed, with the saving ratios rising with income levels but with the overall value slightly below that in 1975. Still, the 13 per cent saving ratio in the lowest income quintile was remarkably high.

Consumption Patterns

The other side of saving is consumption. This has increased rapidly in absolute terms, despite the even faster rise in saving. Consumption expenditures for an average Japanese urban family household more than doubled in real terms, from ¥98,700 per month in 1955 to ¥230,600 in 1980, both in 1980 prices (see Fig. 1). Like real GNP per capita, this growth rate has fallen since 1970. As might be expected as a consequence of rising real income, the proportion of expenditures on food—the so-called Engel coefficient—fell from 46.9 per cent in 1955 to 29.0 per cent in 1980.[14] This compares with a ratio of above 90 for South Korea immediately after the Korean War and estimates of 20 per cent for the United States in recent years.

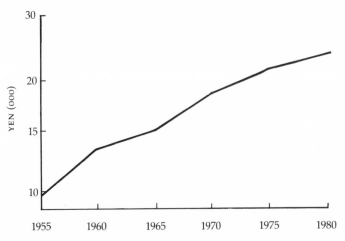

Fig. 1. Average monthly consumption of urban family households, Japan, in 1980 prices. Sources: Japan, Office of the Prime Minister, Bureau of Statistics, *Family Income and Expenditure Survey* (Tokyo: Nihon Tōkei Kyōkai), *1963*, p. 70, *1980*, p. 50. Consumer prices from Japan, Economic Planning Agency, *Keizai yōran, 1983* (Economic survey) (Tokyo, 1983), p. 21.

TABLE 7
Composition of Consumption, Japan, 1955-1980
(per cent)

Item	1955	1960	1965	1970	1975	1980
Food	46.9%	41.6%	38.1%	34.1%	32.0%	29.0%
Housing	3.2	4.0	4.4	4.9	4.9	4.6
Fuel, light, and water	5.6	5.6	5.0	4.4	4.5	5.7
Furniture and house-hold utensils	2.2	4.4	5.0	5.0	5.0	4.3
Clothing and footwear	11.7	12.0	10.1	9.5	9.2	7.9
Medical care	2.2	2.2	2.5	2.7	2.5	2.5
Transportation and communications	1.8	2.0	3.5	5.2	6.1	8.0
Education	3.5	3.4	3.9	2.7	2.8	3.6
Reading and recreation	5.4	6.1	7.1	9.0	8.4	8.5
Other	17.5	18.7	20.4	22.6	24.8	25.8

SOURCE: Japan, Office of the Prime Minister, Bureau of Statistics, *Annual Report on Family Income and Expenditure Survey* (Tokyo: Nihon Tōkei Kyōkai), *1963*, pp. 70ff, *1980*, pp. 50ff.

To the disgust of organized agriculture, which complains about society's unwillingness to pay its food bill, a decline in a country's Engel coefficient is a sign of increasing economic welfare. It means not only that the capacity of the human stomach is limited, but also that as income rises, tastes turn less to fancier foods than to a broad range of non-food conveniences and luxuries. In the Japanese case, the decline of the Engel coefficient has been relatively slow, reflecting the rise in the relative price of food (especially the government-supported price of rice) and the low price elasticity of the Japanese demand for food (see Table 7). Net caloric intake per capita per day increased slowly, from 2,104 calories in 1955 to 2,287 in 1971. Thereafter it tended to decrease, as the Japanese consumed a more balanced diet. Japanese daily net caloric intake per capita stood at 2,113 in 1979.[15]

The changing food-consumption pattern of Japan's urban families, summarized in the word "Westernization," probably represents a change in tastes more than a response to changes in relative prices or in income levels. For example, urban families have substituted wheat products, especially bread, for the traditional rice and meat for fish (see Table 8). Within the meat category, consumption of beef stagnated, whereas the consumption of pork and chicken increased. (This differs from the situation in the United States, where consumption of beef increased at the expense of pork.[16] A major reason for the difference is apparently a sharper rise in the relative price of beef in Japan.) Among alcoholic bev-

TABLE 8
Average Annual Consumption of Food, Urban Families, Japan, 1955-1980

Item	1955	1960	1965	1970	1975	1980
Rice (kg)	449.0	403.3	339.4	250.6	198.6	171.9
White bread (100 g)	—	202.4	173.8	195.9	246.4	260.4
Fish and shellfish						
(100 g)	845.6	752.7	616.5	554.3	548.2	504.8
Beef (100 g)	79.5	94.7	83.6	67.8	77.8	91.5
Pork (100 g)	31.5	44.4	88.0	140.0	182.2	208.7
Chicken (100 g)	—	19.8	46.9	86.5	111.2	145.1
Sake (100 ml)	—	149.2[b]	187.4	211.0	212.8	173.7
Beer (bottle)[a]	5.8	14.7	33.2	46.7	65.6	73.9

SOURCE: Japan, Office of the Prime Minister, Bureau of Statistics, *Annual Report on Family Income and Expenditure Survey* (Tokyo: Nihon Tōkei Kyōkai), *1955*, pp. 100ff; *1963*, pp. 158ff; *1980*, pp. 180ff.
[a] In terms of 633 ml bottles.   [b] 1962.

erages, the consumption of *sake* grew only slightly, and that of beer and whiskey increased enormously—further evidence of Westernization.[17]

Gross caloric intake in Japan at 2,916 calories per capita in 1978–80, though higher than that of the Philippines, was approximately the same as that in South Korea and considerably lower than the 3,300–3,650 figures for other industrialized countries. Japanese consumption of animal protein was also lower than that in other industrialized countries, with the exception of Italy (see Table 9). This does not imply, however, that many Japanese were suffering from either hunger or malnutrition. Because of the relatively high income of the poor and the absence of any large economic underclass, both circumstances to which we refer later, nearly all Japanese seem to have an adequate diet. A long life expectancy may be the best indicator of the adequacy of food consumption, and vice versa. (Possibly middle- and upper-class people in industrial countries are consuming excessive amounts of calories, animal protein, and alcohol—"digging their graves with their teeth," as the saying goes.)

Westernization in clothing began earlier and progressed even more drastically. By 1980, the traditional Japanese kimono had all but disappeared, even in the countryside. It is used nowadays only on such ceremonial occasions as weddings, funerals, and New Year's Day festivities, and then mainly by women. The daily wear of adults, particularly male office workers, is inconspicuously Western, with frequent flashes of haute couture among "office ladies." Youngsters wear jeans, T-shirts, and other informal Western clothes.

In addition to food and clothing, there are significant upward trends in real per capita expenditures for all other important consumption categories, including housing, transportation and communication, reading and recreation, and "miscellaneous," in which pocket money may be the most significant component. All of these increases obviously indicate increasing affluence.

For stock items like houses and consumer durables, however, there are better measures than the flow of expenditures. Housing, in particular, has been a target for unfavorable comment (witness the "rabbit-hutch" criticism). The change in actual housing conditions cumulate in a picture of small units and slow improvements (see Table 10).

1. Houses (including apartments, "mansions," and rented rooms)[18] have become steadily larger. The national average is now larger than 80 square meters per family dwelling unit.

2. The proportion of owner-occupied houses and other dwelling units declined annually during the housing shortage of the early postwar years. This trend appears to have been reversed in the 1970s, especially in the cities, where cooperative and condominium ownership has expanded.

3. Facilities for heating, cooling, and plumbing improved significantly. In particular, the proportion of dwellings with flush toilets grew rapidly. This did not require the parallel expansion of sewage systems since many houses with flush toilets depend on septic tanks. (Although the proportion of houses with flush toilets had risen to 45.9 per cent in 1978, the proportion of the population served by sewage systems was only 31 per cent three years later.[19])

4. Since the average size of newly constructed dwelling units (87.9 square meters in 1978) is larger than that of the typical existing unit, it is

TABLE 9
Per Capita Caloric Intake and Consumption of Protein,
Selected Countries, 1978-1980
(gross figures, including wastage and pet food)

Country	Calories	Protein (grams)	Percentage of animal protein
Philippines	2,315	51.7	35.8%
South Korea	2,946	80.4	19.9
Japan	2,916	93.4	53.6
Italy	3,650	104.0	47.6
United Kingdom	3,316	91.4	60.3
West Germany	3,537	90.4	63.3
France	3,390	105.3	64.2
United States	3,652	106.7	67.5

SOURCE: Japan, Office of the Prime Minister, Bureau of Statistics, *Kokusai tōkei yōran, 1983* (International statistical summary) (Tokyo: Government Printing Bureau, 1983), p. 67.

TABLE 10
Housing Conditions in Japan, 1963-1978

Dwellings	1963	1968	1973	1978
Total number (000)	20,372	24,198	28,730	32,189
Owner-occupied (per cent)	64.3%	60.3%	59.2%	60.4%
Rented (per cent)	35.7%	37.7%	40.8%	39.6%
With piped water (per cent)	67.9%	80.1%	86.9%	92.7%
With flush toilet (per cent)	9.2%	17.1%	31.4%	45.9%
Floor area (m²)	72.5	73.9	77.1	80.3

SOURCE: Japan, Office of the Prime Minister, Bureau of Statistics, *Japan Statistical Yearbook* (Tokyo: Nihon Tōkei Kyōkai, various issues).

anticipated that the average floor area of a Japanese dwelling unit will increase further. These newer units, however, are predominantly for middle- and upper-class occupancy. Unless there is a major change in housing policy, the cramped and overcrowded working-class dwellings in large cities will not disappear rapidly.

5. We cannot say categorically that Japanese housing conditions are improving. Urban land is increasingly scarce, especially in metropolitan Tokyo and Osaka, as witnessed by the sharp rise in land prices there. Much urban land is still used extensively, in ways befitting the lower land prices of earlier days. Considerable quantities of urban land are still held for speculative purposes, usually in such suboptimal forms as agriculture and single-family dwellings. In recent years, however, urban land has been used more intensively; high-rise buildings, both residential and commercial, are spreading from such centers in Tokyo as Ginza, Nihonbashi, and Shinjuku into areas that had previously been prairies of one- or at most two-story houses. The proportion of floor area of a house to the total area of its building lot increased from 38.4 per cent for houses built in the 1950s to only 42.7 per cent in 1982.[20] Housing developments in large cities and suburban areas feature not only "postage stamp"-size lots but dangerously narrow roads.

Japanese housing conditions in the 1970s were not greatly different from those in other industrialized countries, except that the proportion of dwelling units with flush toilets remains low despite improvements (see Table 11). (Japanese conditions are better than those in South Korea or the Philippines.) The size of the average Japanese room may be smaller than that in other industrialized countries; but again, judging from the dimensions of new construction, this difference should narrow in the future. Nevertheless, to repeat, the average is not the whole story, and "rabbit hutch" housing will not disappear soon in big cities, even for those whose computed real incomes would lead people to suppose that they lived in much better dwellings.

Another persistent sign of backwardness is the low acreage of Japanese public parks—only 1.9 square meters per person in Tokyo in 1980. Comparable figures are 8.4 square meters in Paris (1973), 19.4 square meters in New York (1967), and 26.1 square meters in West Berlin (1976).[21] Urban Japanese are forced to devise different lifestyles, including frequent short trips to crowded seashore and mountain areas, to cope with the urban problem of limited public space.

Table 12 documents the meaning of higher Japanese incomes in terms of the ownership of six leading consumer durables, all items of conve-

TABLE 11
Housing Conditions in Selected Countries, 1970s

Country	Year	Rooms per house	Persons per room	Owner-occupied (pct.)	Piped water (pct.)	Flush toilet (pct.)	Floor space[a] (m²)
Philippines	1970	2.4	2.3	83.3%	61.1%[b]	22.6%	—
South Korea	1975	3.1	2.0	63.6	35.2[c]	1.8[c]	—
Japan	1978	4.5	0.8	60.4	92.7[b]	45.9	93.6
Italy	1971	3.7	0.9	50.9	86.1	79.1	—
United Kingdom	1971	4.9	0.6	50.1	—	98.9	—
West Germany	1972	4.2	1.5	33.5	99.2	94.2	102.8
France	1975	3.6	0.9	47.1	97.3	72.5	—
United States	1977	5.1[c]	0.6[c]	64.8	99.3	96.0[c]	—

SOURCE: Japan, Office of the Prime Minister, Bureau of Statistics, *Kokusai tōkei yōran, 1983* (International statistical summary) (Tokyo: Government Printing Bureau, 1983), pp. 224-25.
[a]New houses, 1981.
[b]Includes houses with faucets only outside the house.
[c]1970.

TABLE 12
Household Durables per Hundred Households, Japan, 1957-1980

Item	Sept. 1957	Aug. 1960	Feb. 1965	Feb. 1970	Feb. 1975	Mar. 1980
Sewing machine	61.9	71.4	77.4	84.5	84.7	83.8
Electric washer	20.0	45.4	68.5	88.3	97.6	98.8
Electric refrigerator	2.8	15.7	51.4	84.6	96.7	99.1
Black and white television	7.8	54.5	90.0	90.2	48.7	22.8
Color television	—	—	—	26.3	90.3	98.2
Passenger car	—	1.2	—	22.1	41.2	57.2

SOURCES: National Livelihood Center, *Kokumin seikatsu tōkei nempō* (Statistical yearbook on national livelihood) (Tokyo: Shiseidō), *1967*, pp. 134ff; *1972*, pp. 106ff; *1982*, pp. 84ff.

nience or entertainment, by individual households. Indeed, the "three treasures" of the Japanese household a few years ago were the "three Cs," namely, the car (automobile), the cooler (air conditioner), and the color television, corresponding to "the sword, the jewel, and the mirror" of the Imperial household in Japanese prehistory.

At the same time, the only household durable for which expenditures (flows, as distinguished from stocks) show a sharp relative increase has been the automobile. Expenditures on private transportation increased from 1.0 to 4.1 per cent of disposable (aftertax) income between 1965 and 1980. (The number of automobiles purchased rose from 8 to 46 per 1,000 nonagricultural households in the same period.[22]) Spending on other individual household durables was not significant.

By 1965, ownership of black and white television sets had reached a saturation point of over 90 per cent; the field was quickly taken over by color television sets after 1970. By 1980, over 98 per cent of Japanese households owned at least one color television set. Both electric washing machines and refrigerators had reached saturation points of 99 per cent by 1980. Ownership of sewing machines was widespread at an early period (61.9 per cent in 1957) and reached a relatively low saturation point of 84.5 per cent by 1970. (This suggests a shift in Japanese demand toward ready-made clothing, plus increasing opportunities for paid labor by Japanese housewives outside the home.)

Passenger cars were the only consumer durable that had not reached saturation by 1980; the ownership ratio was then 57.2 per cent and was still rising quite rapidly. Japan's automobile ownership lags considerably behind European and U.S. levels (see Table 13). This comparison may be somewhat misleading, however, since the Japanese seem to use an unusually large number of commercial vehicles (vans and light trucks) for personal purposes as well. Also, Japan has good, if overcrowded, public transportation, although its road network for automobiles remains inadequate.

For smaller consumer durables, the Japanese ranking is lower than

TABLE 13
Ownership of Cars per 1,000 Persons, Selected Countries, 1979

Country	Passenger cars	All cars	Country	Passenger cars	All cars
South Korea	3	6	West Germany	367	395
Japan	196	313	France	344	410
Italy	309	335	United States	511	681
United Kingdom	309	—			

SOURCE: National Livelihood Center, *Kokumin seikatsu tōkei nempō, 1982* (Statistical yearbook on national livelihood) (Tokyo: Shiseidō, 1982), p. 205.

TABLE 14
Composition of National Income by Economic Activity, Japan
(1970-1980) and Selected Industrialized Countries (1980)
(per cent)

Country	Primary industry	Secondary industry	Tertiary industry
Japan			
1970	7.8%	38.1%	54.1%
1980	3.5	37.5	58.9
Italy	6.3	42.1	51.6
United Kingdom	1.8	39.3	58.8
West Germany	2.1	34.4	58.8
France	4.3	37.8	57.9
United States	2.7	31.5	65.7

SOURCES: Bank of Japan, *Nihon keizai o chūshin to suru kokusai hikaku tōkei, 1982* (Comparative international statistics on the Japanese economy) (Tokyo, 1982), pp. 47ff.

might be expected since single households in some countries may own two or more items of the same kind whereas Japanese are less likely to do so because Japanese homes are relatively small. Thus, for television sets, the number owned per 1,000 persons was 245 for Japan in 1979, as against 622 in the United States and 336 in West Germany.[23]

What increased most were services rather than goods, and most service expenditure was included in a "miscellaneous" category. Between 1955 and 1980, the share of "eating out" increased from 1.8 to 3.7 per cent of consumption expenditures, "reading and recreation" from 5.4 to 8.5 per cent, and the "other expenditures" catchall category (mainly services) from 17.5 to 25.8 per cent.

In national income statistics, too, the relative shares of both primary industry (agriculture, forestry, fisheries) and secondary industry (manufacturing, mining, construction) have declined since 1970, whereas the share of tertiary industry (services) has increased (see Table 14). This tendency toward what some sociologists call "post-industrial society" is observable in most industrialized countries, particularly in the United States, where the share of tertiary industry reached 65.7 per cent of national income in 1980. Japan was not far behind, with a figure of 58.9 per cent.

Income Distribution and Stability

Income Distribution

Much of Nakagawa's case for Japan as a welfare superpower is based on the relative equality in Japan's income distribution. This is indeed borne out by published statistics, which have been accused of under-representing lower-income and unmarried persons. Japanese equality arises from two sources, the first being the more important in comparison with Western countries and the more likely to endure in the future. First, Japan has, for practical purposes, no permanent economic underclass brought about by large-scale immigration of cheap labor, however much Japanese industry may be disadvantaged by rising wage rates. (There is a nationalistic element in its attitude, pinpointed recently by Japan's niggardliness in admitting refugees from Vietnam and Cambodia.) Moreover, although the Japanese constitution proclaims that "all the people shall have the right to maintain minimum standards of wholesome and cultural living," it is almost impossible to live on relief from the cradle to the grave. The smallest firms are in practice exempt from minimum-wage legislation and similar restrictions on employment practices. The "involuntary entrepreneurship" of low-level self-employment or family businesses replaces the relief system and reduces the size of the permanent underclass (see the paper by Patrick and Rohlen in this volume.)

The second source of Japanese equality may have been accentuated by

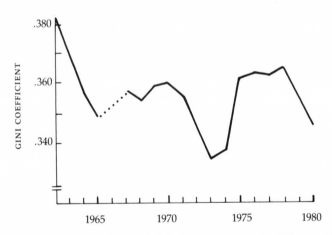

Fig. 2. Gini coefficient for all households, Japan, 1962–1980. Mizoguchi's estimate (1962–70) is spliced to Atoda's unpublished estimate (1970–80) at 1970. Sources: Japan, Ministry of Health and Welfare, *Kokumin seikatsu jittai chōsa hōkoku* (Survey of the state of the people's livelihood) (Tokyo: Kōsei Tōkei Kyōkai, various issues); for 1962–70, Toshiyuki Mizoguchi, "Wagakuni no zenshotai no shotoku bumpu suikei" (Estimates of income distribution of all households in Japan), *Keizai kenkyū*, Vol. 27, No. 3 (July 1976), p. 231; for 1970–80, Naosumi Atoda's unpublished estimate. We are grateful to Professor Atoda for permission to use his estimate.

high growth rates. Japan has had comparatively low lifetime-income gradients based on either education or skills, as compared with those for age and experience. This equalizes the distribution of Japanese labor income, especially in its upper range. (This income equalization, incidentally, does not imply equalization of overall social status.)

Distributional equality and inequality are commonly measured in terms of the Gini coefficient or ratio. This coefficient has the advantage of visible comprehensibility, which counteracts its several statistical bugs.[24] The Gini coefficient for all Japanese households declined gradually from 0.382 to 0.334 between 1962 and 1973 (see Fig. 2). It then stayed at approximately 0.360 until 1978, when it declined slightly; the 1980 figure was 0.346.

On the basis of international comparisons, Japan's income distribution is among the most equal in the capitalist world. An influential study by Felix Paukert found distribution most unequal in countries in the middle range of economic development and declining for the highest-income group (with per capita GDP above $2,000 in 1965).[25] The average Gini coefficient for the latter group was 0.365, considerably higher than the average Japanese figure. An OECD study by Malcolm Sawyer (see Table 15), confirms this result for Gini coefficients computed both before and after personal income taxes. The result is even more marked, according to Yasusuke Murakami, when distributions are adjusted by the "Atkinson correction" so as to place greater emphasis on the income shares of the lowest brackets.[26]

How has this come about? Yutaka Kosai and Yoshitaro Ogino have summarized the situation:

We think we can say that in Japan today income is fairly equally distributed. Japan's pre-tax income distribution [has] one of the highest degrees of equality among leading industrial nations, and for after-tax distribution of income Japan [is] also in the top group. Pre-tax distribution of income in particular is equal because [it] has been the result of labour market forces rather than a government redistribution policy. What is important here is that Japan's lower-income group is comparatively well off. In other words, redistribution has taken place from the bottom upwards, in contrast to countries where an increase in the degree of

TABLE 15
Gini Coefficients, Selected OECD Countries, Mid-1970s

Gini coefficient	Japan	Sweden	West Germany	United States	OECD average
Before taxes	0.335	0.346	0.396	0.404	0.366
After taxes	0.316	0.302	0.383	0.381	0.350

SOURCES: Malcolm Sawyer, *Income Distribution in OECD Countries* (Paris, 1976); and Yutaka Kosai and Yoshitaro Ogino, *The Contemporary Japanese Economy* (London: Macmillan, 1984), table 7.2.

equality has been achieved by reduction of the high-income group, leaving the numbers in poverty virtually unchanged.[27]

The welfare superpower thesis, however, stresses the leveling-off of higher incomes in Japan.[28] One claim is that lifetime incomes of middle school, high school, and college graduates are approaching equality for the country as a whole, although not within individual firms; these samples may not apply to the graduates of elite institutions, but only to those of ordinary universities. Another claim is that the salary of a *buchō*, a supervisor with some 500 white-collar subordinates, has fallen over a decade from 3.5 to 2.5 times that of a skilled worker (lathe operator) in the same company, whereas much higher ratios prevail in other countries.

It may be suspected that although personal income distribution is relatively equal, regional distribution is very unequal as between the cities, especially Tokyo, and the countryside. This was the case in the 1950s. In 1960, Kagoshima and Iwate, two of the poorest prefectures, had average prefectural incomes of 39 per cent and 44 per cent, respectively, of that of Tokyo. Public capital investment in the countryside and labor movements from the periphery toward metropolitan areas, however, corrected such disparities considerably. By 1975, the corresponding figures for these prefectures were 57 per cent and 62 per cent. Although low population densities in the periphery and congestion in the center create problems, Tokyo can no longer be criticized for exploiting the periphery.[29]

Turning from the distribution of incomes to a related problem, the structure of wage rates, we still find in twentieth-century Japan the so-called dual structure. Wages at larger establishments are higher than wages for similar work at smaller establishments; although labor quality is also higher in the large firms, we do not believe quality differences explain the wage gap completely. Male-female wage differentials were also very large. These differentials were reduced substantially through 1965. Since then, however, they have not been reduced further and may even have increased somewhat (see Table 16). Differentials by education and by age have moved in complex ways. Differentials by education have been small, seldom exceeding 20 per cent. For production workers, movement has been erratic; for salaried employees, differentials have tended to narrow in the past ten years. Differentials by age tended to narrow until 1970 or 1975, when the trend was slightly reversed (see Table 17).

Despite the persistence of these four systematic differentials—by firm size, sex, education, and age—the overall Japanese wage distribution was relatively equal and became more so during the period of high economic growth, which ended in the early 1970s. Since that time, with the loosening of the labor market, we can observe some tendency for labor

TABLE 16

Wage Differentials in Japan, by Size of Firm and by Sex, 1960-1980

Differential	1960	1965	1970	1975	1980
By size of firm[a]	46.3	63.2	61.8	60.2	58.0
By sex[b]					
Large establishment	37.4	52.4[c]	48.1	53.3	48.5[d]
Small establishment	48.3	53.1[e]	46.9	47.0	45.0[d]

SOURCES: Japan, Economic Planning Agency, Keizai yōran, 1983 (Economic survey) (Tokyo, 1983), p. 190; and Japan, Ministry of Labor, Rōdō tōkei yōran (Summary of labor statistics) (Tokyo: Government Printing Bureau, various issues).

[a] Average wages of regular workers employed in establishments with 5-29 workers as a percentage of average wages of establishments with more than 500 workers.

[b] Average wages of female workers as a proportion of those of male workers at (large) establishments with more than 500 workers and (small) establishments with 5-29 workers.

[c] At establishments with more than 1,000 workers.

[d] 1981.

[e] Establishments with 10-29 workers.

TABLE 17

Wage Differentials in Japanese Manufacturing Industries, by Education and by Age, 1960-1980

Differential[a]	1960	1965	1970	1975	1980
By education[b]					
Production workers					
Male, secondary	—	106.5	102.4	106.3	104.7
Female, secondary	—	112.1	104.8	102.2	100.5
Salaried employees					
Male, secondary	—	110.1	106.5	109.5	107.1
Male, tertiary	—	87.6	141.1	145.4	131.6
Female, secondary	—	107.4	112.2	107.5	112.5
By age[c]					
Production workers					
Male, primary	207.1	168.0	158.3	151.4	163.3
Male, secondary	204.2	179.4	163.4	154.4	174.0
Female, primary	100.2	94.6	93.8	95.1	102.6
Female, secondary	114.4	97.2	96.8	92.5	97.1
Salaried employees					
Male, primary	247.2	210.1	191.8	177.9	186.1
Male, secondary	275.2	245.7	212.4	197.9	220.1
Male, tertiary	348.1	294.2	270.8	246.2	273.4
Female, primary	147.4	129.0	93.8	120.6	120.5
Female, secondary	172.0	151.9	96.8	126.0	133.5

SOURCES: Differential by education, Japan, Ministry of Labor, Chingin kōzō kihon tōkei chōsa hōkoku (Survey of basic statistics on the wage structure) (Tokyo: Rōdō Hōrei Kyōkai), 1965, Vol. 1, pp. 190, 192, 194; 1970, Vol. 2, pp. 30, 32; 1975, Vol. 1, pp. 152, 154, 156, 158; 1980, Vol. 1, pp. 34, 36, 38, 40, 42. Differential by age, Japan, Ministry of Labor, Rōdō tōkei yōran (Summary of labor statistics) (Tokyo: Government Printing Bureau, various issues).

[a] Refers to money income only.

[b] With wages and salaries of primary school graduates as 100.0 among workers 40-49 years of age.

[c] Wages and salaries of workers 40-49 years of age with those of 20-24 as 100.0.

TABLE 18

Real Wage Index and Working Hours in Japanese Manufacturing Industries,
1955-1980

Category	1955	1960	1965	1970	1975	1980
Real wages index	30.4	36.5	45.7	69.5	92.2	100.0
Working hours per month	198.0	207.0	191.8	187.4	167.8	178.2

SOURCES: Real wages, Japan, Economic Planning Agency, *Keizai yōran* (Economic survey) (Tokyo, 1983), p. 22; National Livelihood Center, *Kokumin seikatsu tōkei nempō* (Statistical yearbook on national livelihood) (Tokyo: Shiseidō), *1967*, p. 32, *1977*, p. 26, *1982*, p. 28.

income distributions to become somewhat more unequal. This tendency is not yet clear-cut and may be reversed if business conditions improve substantially. Real wages have in general kept pace with per capita incomes. Real wages more than tripled between 1955 and 1980, at least in the manufacturing industry (see Table 18).

Many of the current complaints in Japan about maldistribution refer to net wealth rather than to income. Many people, even if they have middle-class incomes, consume at near-poverty levels since they are forced to save because of debts contracted to purchase real estate after 1970 or for the education of their children. In the 1984 *Kokumin seikatsu hakusho* (White paper on the people's livelihood), published by the Economic Planning Agency (EPA), more stress was placed on educational costs. Considering a demographically typical family with one male wage earner and two children, EPA figures indicated that the family dissaved during the breadwinner's late forties and early fifties because of the pressure of these costs as the children grew older. (It could avoid dissaving if the wife returned to paid work.)

Income Security

Unemployment in Japan has fluctuated in the 2–3 per cent level in good times and bad. A 1982 "recession" rate of 2.9 per cent compares favorably with rates like 7.1 in the United States, 7.4 in Great Britain, 3.8 in West Germany, and 7.6 in Italy.[30] But published unemployment percentages are among the least susceptible statistics for international comparisons. In the Japan–United States case, multipliers should be applied to Japanese percentages for comparability with those for the United States. To make matters worse, the multiplier is not a constant; we think it is higher in recessions than in periods of prosperity.

From an international viewpoint, the anomalies of the Japanese unemployment statistics come from the tendency of the Japanese to leave the labor force when they are unemployed. Young people, women, and many old people simply return to their families. They do not seek employment until it becomes readily available, and they do not register as unemployed. One reason for this behavior may be the derogatory connotation of the Japanese word for unemployed person (*shitsugyōsha*), but it is not possible to estimate the importance of such factors since the definition of unemployment is not much different between Japan and, say, the United States. Some indirect evidence of the unwillingness of Japanese to accept unemployment is the slang term for dismissal (*Kubikiri*, or "beheading") and strikes by workers against dismissals, even when these are disguised as early retirement and accompanied by augmented severance pay.

Another feature of the Japanese labor market that reduces published unemployment rates is the prevalence of subemployment and self-employment. The "unpaid family worker," often female, very young, or retired from a paying job, is an important element in Japanese labor statistics and not confined to agriculture. Nor should we forget that the smallest firms are for all practical purposes exempt from wage and work hour legislation and are free to pay poverty-level wages. (The Patrick-Rohlen paper in this volume explains this exemption on political grounds, as well as on the basis of administrative costs.)

Between 30 and 45 per cent of male workers are employed in firms whose tacit long-term employment policies are meaningful.[31] Lower down the economic scale, the self-employed and family workers are largely immune from unemployment (although not from drastic cuts in income). A number of overlapping intermediate categories—temporary workers, probationary workers, part-time workers, workers in weak companies (facing bankruptcy or shrinkage), married women, older workers—are subject to uncertainties even greater than those of similar workers in other countries.

Possible Costs of Income

Employment and working hours. Everything has a cost, not necessarily measurable in monetary terms, in other goods forgone or in undesirable effects associated with the good. Income and wealth are themselves no exceptions to this generalization, as witnessed by Japanese complaints, at the zenith of their nation's miraculous growth, about *seichō keizai no kunō* ("the anguish of a growth economy").

We shall not attempt a listing of all possible costs of income or of its growth. Instead, we select a sample of individual and social costs that critics have alleged to be important in the Japanese case. These include the loss of such goods as leisure, safety, and health and the growth of such undesirable effects as pollution, crowding, and wasted time (as in commuting between home and the work place).

Leisure. Workers in small-scale establishments do work longer hours than those in large-scale establishments. Working hours have, however, generally become considerably shorter. Between 1960 and 1980, average working hours per month in small establishments (5–29 workers) fell from 215 to 185 and in large establishments (500 or more workers) from 199 to 174. Working hours per month in the manufacturing industry tended to lengthen until 1960, when the trend was reversed substantially, from 207.0 hours in 1960 to 167.8 hours in 1975. Firms hesitated to reduce employment further, and working hours rose to 178.2 per month in 1980[32] (see Table 18). According to an NHK (Japan Broadcasting Company) survey of how people spend their time, daily working hours for a male in his thirties were 8.45 in 1965 and 8.20 in 1980 on weekdays, but hours on Saturday fell from 8.16 to 6.32 over the same period. This reflects the spread of the five-day week in Japanese industry. If the Japanese are workaholics, as frequently charged, it is difficult to explain the long *bakansu* and *rejā* booms that seem to have begun in the early 1960s and show no signs of abating. (*Bakansu* is a Japanization of the French *vacance* and *rejā* of the English leisure.)

On an annual basis, however, Japanese working hours remained comparatively long as recently as 1982; a Ministry of Labor survey estimated annual hours for that year to be 2,136 on average for all manufacturing industries. Roughly comparable figures for Western countries were over 10 per cent lower—1,888 in Britain; 1,851 in the United States; 1,707 in France; and 1,682 in West Germany.

How did the typical Japanese worker (age 30–39) spend his increased leisure? On weekdays, he watched television (2.45 hours per day in 1965 and 2.27 hours in 1980). Television had greater appeal for women age 30–39 (3.23 hours a day in 1965 and 3.37 hours in 1980). (The fall for men and the rise for women probably represent nothing more than sampling error.) Radio listening, lagging well behind television watching, increased in importance. For a male 30–39 years of age, it occupied on weekdays 29 minutes in 1965 and 51 minutes in 1980; for a female in the same age group, the figures were 28 and 55 minutes, respectively.

The pattern is different for Sundays. Television watching still constituted the most important activity, 3.26 (1965) and 3.56 hours (1980) for a male 30–39 years of age, and 3.40 hours (in both years) for a female of the same age. Radio-listening time was not much longer on Sunday than on other days; neither did the Sunday time allocation increase as the years passed. In any case, the Japanese spent much more time with TV and radio than the British.[33] Time spent in socializing, household work (for males, called *nichiyō daiku*, or "Sunday carpentry"), and the catchall category of "leisure time activities" increased significantly on Sundays.[34]

Another use of so-called leisure is commuting time, which is indeed used by many Japanese for sleeping, reading, or listening to music on portable radios or cassette players. Like New York and London, Tokyo and Osaka have sprawled and become suburbanized at explosive rates. The recent reductions in urban population density and increases in over-all area per dwelling unit reflect this suburbanization. The improvement may well extend to health in some degree, although this is uncertain. The reverse side of these gains is increased travel time to and from work. In Tokyo and Osaka, commutes of 90 minutes, two hours, or more each way are not uncommon and are often complicated by two or more trans-fers in crowded, labyrinthine train stations and other traffic nodes. Tokyo and Osaka differ from Chicago and Los Angeles—more than from older New York and London—in that more commuting is done by public transportation (chiefly surface and subway electric lines) and less by pri-vate automobile. The Japanese system involves more crowding than the U.S. one, but less nervous strain and accidental death. Who knows which is the more destructive of total time and energy?

Japan's older generation has a special employment problem. Most medium-size and large firms have compulsory retirement systems. The traditional age of retirement has been 55, reflecting the demographic fact that male life expectancy at birth was less than 50 years. In the post-war years, however, it has increased to over 70; part of this change results from lowered infant mortality rates, but the remainder is reflected in the life expectancies of adult males. The retirement system has been slow to adjust to this demographic change. Movement toward retirement at 60 started only recently. Although 43 per cent of firms surveyed in 1982 set the retirement age at 60, 35 per cent still set it at 55.[35]

Partly by choice and partly by economic necessity, Japanese workers have remained in the labor force until old age despite the compulsory retirement systems. The participation rate for ages 60–64 has been 81–85 per cent (male) and approximately 40 per cent (female). The ratio for ages 65 and over declined from 56.5 per cent in 1955 to 46.0 per cent in 1980 for males and from 20.7 per cent to 16.1 per cent for females (see Table 19).

These ratios may be affected by changes in demographic variables and social insurance provisions for the aged, but at present the typical Japa-nese laborer works until an extremely old age, say, 70 or older. Old-age labor-force participation ratios have been considerably higher in Japan than in other industrialized countries (see Table 20). (They have been somewhat lower in the agrarian Philippines.)

Safety and Health. Safety and health have sometimes been jeopardized by economic growth. It is not at all clear in Japan whether threats to safety and health are costs of income or of growth. Industrial injuries, including deaths, are most closely related to the economy. Despite the

TABLE 19
Labor Force Participation Rates of Workers over 55, Japan, 1955-1980
(per cent)

Age	1955	1960	1965	1970	1975	1980
Male						
55-59	91.1%	90.5%	93.8%	94.2%	94.7%	94.0%
60-64	82.5	82.5	85.2	85.8	85.4	81.5
65-	56.5	54.4	55.1	54.4	49.7	46.0
Female						
55-59	45.8	46.8	56.1	53.7	50.9	50.7
60-64	38.5	39.2	39.5	43.3	39.2	38.8
65-	20.7	21.0	17.6	19.6	15.8	16.1

SOURCE: Japan, Office of the Prime Minister, Bureau of Statistics, *Jinkō no shūgyō kōzō to sangyō kōzō* (Employment structure of population and industrial structure) (Tokyo, 1983), p. 43.

TABLE 20
Labor Force Participation Rates of Workers over 55, Selected Countries, ca. 1980

Country	Males aged			Females aged		
	55-59	60-64	65+	55-59	60-64	65+
Philippines[a]	89.6%[b]		62.1%	46.1%[b]		27.8%
South Korea	96.8[c]		39.0	56.5[c]		11.8
Japan[d]	94.0%	81.5%	45.5	50.7%	38.8%	16.1
Italy[d]	83.1[e]	39.6	12.6	27.7[e]	11.0	3.5
West Germany	81.9	44.4	7.0	39.0	13.3	2.8
France	78.7	42.2	5.3	45.1	23.3	2.6
United States	80.5	57.8	17.7	49.0	32.3	7.5

SOURCE: ILO, *Yearbook of Labour Statistics, 1982*, pp. 13-15.
[a] 1978.   [b] 55-64.   [c] 45-64.   [d] 1980.   [e] 50-59.

quickening pace of economic activity, the rate of industrial injuries has decreased sharply over time from 24.5 per million man-days in 1955 to 11.3 in 1970 to 3.2 in 1981. The corresponding figures for industrial deaths were 0.20, 0.06, and 0.03.[36] These results compare favorably with both the United States among industrial countries and with South Korea among developing nations.

Japan's low crime rates and high arrest rates have long attracted attention. Homicides and robberies per 100,000 population have decreased since 1955, reaching in 1980 levels less than half of those recorded for 1955 (see Table 21). Rapes increased in number in the first decade; since 1965, they, too, have declined. Arrest rates have declined somewhat since 1965, but in 1980 remained at the relatively high level of 70–80 per cent for major violent crimes.

Crime rates for each crime category are much lower in Japan than in other industrial countries, particularly the United States (see Table 22). Japanese policies toward private handgun ownership and drug trafficking are among the world's most severe. Arrest rates, in addition, were considerably higher in Japan; we believe that high probability of arrest deters the commission of such crimes. Urban Japan has, however, been plagued for years by protection, extortion, and other rackets (which often go unrecorded), carried on by organized criminal gangs (*bōryoku-*

TABLE 21
Crime and Arrest Rates, Japan, 1955-1980

Category	Homicide	Robbery	Forcible rape
Crimes (per 100,000 population)			
1955	3.434	6.584	4.532
1960	2.834	5.564	6.789
1965	2.322	3.954	6.765
1970	1.915	2.593	4.976
1975	1.874	2.055	3.309
1980	1.691	1.866	2.230
Arrests (per 100 offenses)			
1965	97.6	84.4	95.2
1970	97.0	81.0	92.0
1975	96.5	79.7	91.5
1980	82.7	75.5	89.5

SOURCES: Japan, Office of the Prime Minister, Bureau of Statistics, *Japan Statistical Yearbook* (Tokyo: Nihon Tōkei Kyōkai, various issues).

TABLE 22
Crime and Arrest Rates, Various Countries, 1981

Country	Homicide	Robbery	Forcible rape
Crimes (per 100,000 population)			
Japan	1.5	2.0	2.2
England and Wales	2.4	36.3	7.2
West Germany	4.8	44.9	11.2
France[a]	4.2	65.8	3.5
United States	9.8	250.6	35.6
Arrests (per 100 offenses)			
Japan	97.4	81.5	89.3
England and Wales	82.6	24.7	89.6
West Germany	95.3	52.3	71.6
France[a]	79.4	26.4	76.6
United States	71.6	23.9	48.1

SOURCES: Economic Research Center, *Japan, 1983: An International Comparison* (Tokyo, 1983), p. 80.
[a] 1980.

dan). These hoodlums are now said to operate nationwide. Resistance to their activities, plus warfare between the various gangs, may raise some recorded crime rates in the mid-1980s.

Traffic accident statistics also suggest Japan's relative safety in recent years. Deaths in traffic accidents increased for a time, but declined through the 1970s. Since 1980, as motorcycles have increased in number, deaths have again shown a slight upward trend. (A 1983 estimate was 9,500, of which a third were drivers of bicycles or motorcycles.)[37] Particularly when expressed in numbers per 10,000 motor vehicles, without regard to the number of miles or kilometers driven per car-year, the decline in the death rate is substantial—from 43.6 to 2.2 (see Table 23). Japan's accident level was also low by international standards (see Table 24). Several causes have been conjectured for this favorable record, but we know of no tests of their relative importance. First, Japanese laws for the licensing of drivers and the periodic inspection of vehicles are among the world's strictest. Second, penalties for drunken driving are severe, and the drunk driver is a rarity in Japan. Third, annual mileage per car is lower in Japan, a small country, than in a large country like the United

TABLE 23
Deaths from Traffic Accidents, Japan, 1955-1980

Year	Deaths	Per 100,000 persons	Per 10,000 motor vehicles
1955	6,379	7.1	43.6
1960	12,055	12.9	34.9
1965	12,484	12.7	15.8
1970	16,765	16.1	9.0
1975	10,792	9.6	3.7
1980	8,760	7.5	2.2

SOURCE: Japan, Office of the Prime Minister, Bureau of Statistics, *Japan Statistical Yearbook, 1982* (Tokyo: Nihon Tōkei Kyōkai, 1982) p. 716.

TABLE 24
Deaths from Traffic Accidents, Selected Countries, 1970s

Country	Deaths per 100,000 persons	Country	Deaths per 100,000 persons
Philippines (1974)	3.2	West Germany (1978)	23.1
Japan (1978)	10.5	France (1977)	21.9
Italy (1972)	25.9	United States (1976)	21.9
United Kingdom (1977)	11.9		

SOURCE: Same as Table 23, p. 748.

TABLE 25
Population per Physician and per Hospital Bed, Selected Countries, 1970s

Country	Per bed	Per physician	Country	Per bed	Per physician
Philippines (1973)	639	2,793	West Germany		
South Korea (1976)	1,406	905	(1977)	85	490
Japan (1977)	94	845	France (1976)	97	613
Italy (1976)	97	—	United States		
England and			(1977)	159	569
Wales (1977)	—	632			

SOURCE: United Nations, *Statistical Yearbook, 1979/80*, pp. 846ff.

States—or for that matter than in Europe, where international driving is easy. In particular, relatively few cars are used for daily commuting.

The problem of safety in Japan is complicated by considerations related only indirectly (through population density and urbanism) to the Japanese economic and social system. The Japanese archipelago is geologically among the youngest land areas in the world. It is therefore subject to earthquakes, landslides, and volcanic eruptions to a greater degree than Western Europe or North America (with the exception of the Pacific Coast). The Kanto area, comprising both Tokyo and Yokohama, for example, has not suffered a major earthquake since 1923 and is allegedly overdue for another. Lying to the east of the continental Asian landmass, Japan is also more subject to typhoons or hurricanes than Europe or North America (with the exception of the Caribbean–Gulf of Mexico region).

Traditional Japanese buildings were not fire resistant. As Edo (now Tokyo) grew to become perhaps the world's largest city in the eighteenth century, its conflagrations were called the "flowers of Edo." Although both Japanese construction and fire-fighting technologies have made great strides since 1945, the congested areas of Japan's large cities still remain potential firetraps.

As for health, nobody would expect a trade-off relationship with growth. As income levels rose, the number of doctors per 1,000 population increased, and more hospitals were built. Japan's position on these matters does not differ greatly from those of other industrialized countries (see Table 25). There is criticism about the quality of medical care and the system of medical insurance (see below), but the improvement in the standard of medical care is beyond doubt.

Two standard indicators of the health of a population are the infant mortality rate and the population's life expectancy at age five. (Usually life expectancy at birth is compared, but since this is affected by infant mortality, we chose an independent indicator—life expectancy at age five.) In both of these indicators (Fig. 3 and Tables 26–27), Japan's records improved greatly in the postwar years, and the nation now ranks at the top among the major industrial countries considered in this chapter.

Japanese firms were permitted to pollute the environment quite freely until the early 1960s. Osaka, for example, was called "Smokeopolis" by its citizens, who thought the term meant "great industrial center." Only in the 1960s, after the concentration of population and industry into cities caused disastrous environmental hazards, and after the "Minamata disease" and other scandals,[38] were vehement protests raised against air and water pollution. Foreign observers stated that "by the late sixties, Japan had become one of the most polluted countries in the world."[39]

Social attitudes changed quickly after Minamata, causing changes in pollution abatement policy. The policy itself became more drastic than elsewhere, under the so-called PPP or polluter pays principle. As illustrated in Table 28, sulfur dioxide air pollution and organic water pollution abated quickly after 1970 in large cities. Japan still has serious problems of air pollution by various nitrogen compounds, and there are a growing number of complaints about noise pollution. It can, however, be said that pollution as a major social problem was largely contained by

Fig. 3. Infant mortality in Japan, 1955–1980. Sources: Japan, Office of the Prime Minister, Bureau of Statistics, *Japan Statistical Yearbook* (Tokyo: Nihon Tōkei Kyōkai, various issues).

TABLE 26
Infant Mortality, Selected Countries, 1981

Country	Deaths per 1,000 live births	Country	Deaths per 1,000 live births
Philippines[a]	58.9	United Kingdom	12.1
South Korea[a]	36.7	West Germany	12.6
Japan	7.5	France	10.0
Italy	14.3	United States[b]	12.5

SOURCE: United Nations, *Demographic Yearbook, 1981,* pp. 293ff.
[a] 1979.   [b] 1980.

TABLE 27
Life Expectancy at Age 5, Selected Countries, ca. 1979

Country	Male	Female	Country	Male	Female
South Korea (1978-79)	60.3	68.2	West Germany		
Japan (1981)	69.6	74.8	(1979-81)	66.1	72.7
Italy (1974-77)	66.5	72.5	France (1978-80)	66.1	74.1
United Kingdom			United States		
(1978-80)	66.6	72.6	(1979)	66.3	73.9

SOURCE: United Nations, *Demographic Yearbook, 1982,* pp. 438ff.

TABLE 28
Pollution in Japan, 1965-1980
(parts per million)

Year	Sulfur dioxide pollution[a]	Organic water pollution[b]
1965	0.057	—
1970	0.043	23.11
1975	0.021	13.52
1980	0.016	9.20

SOURCES: Japan, Economic Planning Agency, *Keizai yōran* (Economic survey) (Tokyo, various issues); and Yano Touneta Kinenkai, *Nihon kokusei zue, 1983* (Summary of Japanese social conditions) (Tokyo: Kokuseisha, 1983), p. 526.
[a] 15 monitoring stations.   [b] 11 urban rivers.

1980. It is hoped that at most places the levels of pollution will fall further as new industrial plants and new automobile models replace older ones.

Education. Education is treated in conventional economic statistics exclusively as a service or benefit, a form of consumption, or human capital formation. This treatment makes good sense, but can nevertheless be one-sided when the education or schooling is poorly adapted to students' needs and when it is seen as both financially and psychologically costly while remaining semicompulsory. These circumstances are common in contemporary Japan.

Free public education in Japan is limited to nine years of primary and middle school. Public high schools and universities charge tuition, although their fees are lower than those of private institutions. Japan's system of public education is criticized for being single-track (academic) and slanted toward competitive examinations for the next higher level. These defects are blamed for the so-called examination hell, which is itself blamed for neuroses, psychoses, and even suicide among youth. The many untalented students—the so-called *ochikobore* (dropouts in all but name)—resent the system, and their revenge on unsympathetic teachers and intellectually inclined classmates takes such forms as vandalism and violence. These problems are by no means peculiar to Japan, but should be kept in mind when the Japanese system's emphasis on "educational fundamentals" is praised (by Ezra Vogel and others) as a model for countries with less demanding systems.

The race for high examination scores has led to the proliferation of private preparatory or cram schools. In addition to nervous strain and deprivation of leisure for the children themselves, these institutions impose financial strains on lower-income parents. Wealthier and more educationally ambitious parents in most public school districts try to send their children to elite private schools, whose graduates receive the top examination scores, or which are affiliated directly with private universities and offer at least their better graduates relief from the examination hell. At the other end of the educational scale, there are prefectures with too few public high schools for all applicants, so that the academically untalented and their parents must choose between expensive, but low-rated, private schools and dropping out of the educational system with only a middle-school diploma.

Discrimination and alienation. All the countries and regions we consider here, including Japan, have minorities, and with them, minority problems. The income, wealth, and quality of life—including the physical safety—of these minorities are usually inferior to those of the majority population. Japan's lack of an economic underclass means that Japan's minority problems are quantitatively less important than those of the United States and Western Europe;[40] it also means that we expect Japan's restrictive immigration policy to keep them so.

The prehistoric inhabitants of the Japanese islands may well have been as anthropologically heterogeneous as those of China or the British Isles. Japanese folk history and mythology can be interpreted as dealing with centuries or millennia of racial conflict between Ainu aborigines and waves of later invaders from East and Southeast Asia. In historical times, however, displacement and intermarriage isolated the Ainu in Hokkaido "reservations" and homogenized the invaders into a single Japanese race.

Modern Japan has numerous minorities, including *hisabetsu buraku-min*, Koreans, Chinese (including Formosans), *konketsuji*, and, of course, the Ainu. The *hisabetsu burakumin*, the most numerous, are ethnic Japanese descended from families segregated by feudal authorities for engaging in activities deemed "unclean."[41] The *konketsuji* ("mixed-blood children") of the Occupation and post-Occupation years have been absorbed into Japanese society with less difficulty than had been anticipated.

We shall not compare the minority policies of Western and Japanese governments. Our point is that since minorities account for little more than 3 or 4 per cent of the Japanese population, minority resentments are quantitatively less serious there. There have indeed been antiminority riots in Japan, notably against Koreans in Tokyo and Yokohama at the time of the great earthquake of September 1923. Minority groups, especially the *hisabetsu burakumin*, are discriminated against in employment and marriage. Affirmative action in their favor is being taken particularly in the Kansai area, where these people are concentrated, but a backlash has also followed.

Japan's largest group of discrimination victims is its working women, particularly those educated beyond the junior-college or finishing-school level and hoping for long-term and eventually high-level careers either alongside or instead of marriage and motherhood. "Office ladies," or "OLs," and female factory workers are both expected to quit work after marriage or after they become pregnant. They have limited opportunity to return to work, especially to white-collar jobs, when their children are older. As temporary employees before marriage, they seldom receive significant on-the-job training. Furthermore, their (or their families') educational choices often handicap them in competition with men. (They tend to choose 14 years of education, not 16; attend inferior universities with easy entrance examinations instead of the prestigious ones; and stress gentility over practicality in selecting an academic concentration.)

Success stories of women in Japanese economic life are increasing year by year and go beyond mere tokenism. But women are still concentrated in the independent professions less constrained by set working hours, in education and the arts, and in small-industry entrepreneurship in such fields as fashion design, cosmetics, interior decoration, and retailing (particularly boutiques). (In many of these cases, women have combined their own entrepreneurial skills with capital supplied by their families.)

Even less often than in Europe or America has the woman executive without family connections risen from the ranks to a high position in a large-business hierarchy.

Poverty is often associated with discrimination. In the United States, it is increasingly concentrated among single women and female-headed households. It "bears a female face" as well as a nonwhite and Spanish-speaking face. The rising labor-force participation rates of married women in the United States have crowded a number of low-skilled and semiskilled "female occupations" (typist, clerk, secretary), and the 40 per cent sexual wage differential represents more than the higher percentage of part-timers in the female labor force. In Japan, the proportion of married women working outside the home is comparable with that in the West and creates similar problems.

Sexual controversy has nevertheless remained muted in Japan. A woman's movement featuring pink helmets for its militants achieved more publicity than results in the halcyon days of demonstration politics, but quickly subsided in the later 1970s and shows no immediate signs of revival. An antidiscrimination bill enacted by the Diet in 1985 lacks enforcement provisions and relies on negotiation. Meanwhile, one sign of female dissatisfaction is the divorce rate, which has been rising for a generation. Its current level of 1.22 divorced persons per 1,000 is considerably lower than in other industrial countries. (This low rate may have improved the quality of life for the Japanese male by keeping his wife in her place and muting domestic discord. Its effect on the quality of life for Japanese women is more problematic.) For the present at least, Japan remains a man's country.

Apart from its minorities and women, Japan is accused of neglecting both its physically and mentally handicapped, who might be thought of as a semi-underclass. Public hospitals are overcrowded, private facilities unaffordable for the poor, and families overwhelmed by the burdens handicapped members impose on them. (We can again cite Ariyoshi's *Twilight Years*, which focuses on the problem of senility.) As a result of general neglect, urban districts like Tokyo's Ginza and Shinjuku attract *furōsha* (street people) to their back alleys, garbage cans, subway stations, and underground arcades. Their numbers are unknown—the 1980 census count of 700 in all Tokyo was ridiculously low. Neither do we know how many are actually mentally deficient or otherwise handicapped, how many enjoy what may be called a lazy life, and how many are aggressively alienated from Japanese society. The Shinjuku ward office, following complaints by merchants and residents, has conducted patrols against the ward's *furōsha*. The patrols offer invitations to the ward's public hotels, but find few takers even in cold weather. Also, the patrols urge merchants not to feed *furōsha* and throw water or wet sawdust on places where they sit or sleep outdoors in winter. (One is reminded of campaigns against insects, rodents, or stray cats and dogs.)

Following Karl Marx, radical critiques of capitalist societies have stressed the concept of "alienation" of working people from their work, their families, their society, even from themselves, as a feature of life in capitalist countries. Alienation manifests itself in many forms—from laziness and enervation through alcoholism and drug addiction to crime, violence, and suicide. Some forms of alienation—school violence and youth suicide—are relatively common in Japan. Other forms—drug addiction and child abuse—seem less common than in, for example, the United States.

The suicide rate may be taken as a sign of alienation, although this interpretation could be contested. Suicides among teenagers and the elderly receive much publicity in Japan, but the overall suicide rate is not high. Japan nevertheless had one of the higher rates (17.6 per 100,000 in 1980) along with West Germany (20.9), compared with the United States (12.5) and Britain (8.8).[42]

Alienation, whether or not we accept the Marxist doctrine of its causation and importance, does not lend itself easily to the quantitative investigation and analysis on which we rely. It is dangerous to judge its extent and severity by answers to ordinary journalistic questionnaires about happiness and satisfaction. Whether people, assumed honest, report themselves as "happy and contented" or "unhappy and discontented" depends on their expectations as well as their alienation. In the same United States (mid-nineteenth century) that repelled foreign visitors by its arrogance, provincialism, conceit, and braggadocio, Thoreau claimed that the common folk led lives of "quiet desperation." Could these visitors—Charles Dickens, for example—and Thoreau both have been right?

What we cannot measure we find hard to compare. Is alienation more or less of a problem in Japan than in the West? What proportions of suicidal youths, fanatics in the National Students Federation (*Zengakuren*), and members of juvenile gangs (*bōsōzoku*) are equivalent to x per cent of hippies, y per cent of junkies, and z per cent of gangsters?

As we have seen, the material living standard of the Japanese improved sharply from 1955 to 1980. Many less material social indicators have also shown improvement. These indicators suggest that Japan has caught up with the welfare levels of the other industrialized countries. An international poll conducted by the London *Economist* (Table 29) in 1983 compared 23 countries, combining various welfare indicators of its staff's devising. The final result put Japan third, tied with Australia overall as a country in which (other than their own) those polled desired to live—after France and West Germany, but ahead of Britain and the United

TABLE 29
Indicators of Welfare, 23 Countries, 1982
(score)

Country	Political	Cultural	Social	Health	Economic	Climate	Total[a]
France	204	140	167	173	171	179	1,034
West Germany	196	147	157	162	195	179	1,028
Australia	192	156	160	175	175	154	1,002
Japan	188	132	168	184	186	160	1,002
Italy	190	129	169	173	154	188	989
Switzerland	182	153	113	179	168	186	980
Sweden	181	150	153	179	164	142	978
United States	181	160	147	149	181	150	974
Britain	187	160	156	161	160	152	965
Canada	180	147	147	175	175	110	950
Spain	177	134	153	183	143	154	944
Israel	176	113	154	180	141	162	911
Mexico	176	114	149	110	146	173	882
Bahamas	175	142	142	147	135	134	880
Hungary	172	132	145	139	147	165	879
Russia	168	135	166	152	143	127	856
China	161	81	139	150	131	184	828
Sri Lanka	151	94	130	143	134	126	802
Singapore	148	108	127	159	166	101	792
Brazil	143	93	146	114	139	159	782
Kenya	133	83	135	105	112	159	762
India	131	73	109	94	108	164	729
Saudi Arabia	131	77	115	112	158	113	721

SOURCE: *Economist* (London), Dec. 24, 1983, p. 59.
[a]Indicators are weighted in computing total and do not necessarily add to total shown.

States. Japan's score was particularly high in health indicators (first), social indicators (second), and economic indicators (also second). In culture, politics, and climate, Japan did not rate so highly. (The rankings are not without some apparent anomalies, France ranking first in political indicators, for example, and Italy in social indicators.)

Whereas the *Economist* polled *kokusaijin* ("international people") throughout the world, the Japanese prime minister's office frequently samples public opinion in Japan itself.[43] The attitudes of the Japanese toward their lives, as expressed in opinion polls, has shown no marked change despite material improvements. (Expectations may have risen in step with real incomes.) The percentages of those more or less satisfied decreased little if at all during the high growth period, although remaining in the majority. In the low growth period after 1973, the percentage of those satisfied seems to have increased slightly, possibly responding to the expansion of welfare-state institutions. The latest (1984) poll shows a slight decline (see Fig. 4). On the other hand, a *marukin, marubi* lifestyle became a status symbol among young people at the same time.

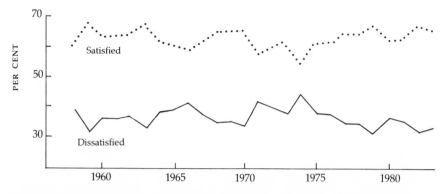

Fig. 4. Per cent of survey respondents expressing satisfaction and dissatisfaction with their lives, Japan, 1958–1983. Sources: 1958–73, Japan, Office of the Prime Minister, "Kokumin seikatsu ni kansuru yoron chōsa" (unpublished report); 1974-83, *Gekkan yoron chōsa*, Oct. 1983, p. 8.

(*Marukin* means keeping one's accumulation of wealth through saving and investment as secret as one can; *marubi* is a kind of shabby gentility one step removed from poverty.) The results imply a turn to leisure and saving and away from conspicuous consumption—hardly a sign of active dissatisfaction, although hardly conducive to high measured growth.

In judging their own relative positions, a large and increasing majority of Japanese—approximately 90 per cent—report themselves as belonging to the middle class, rather than to either the upper or the lower classes. (Alternatives such as "capitalist class" and "working class" were not presented.) Some changes over time become apparent when the middle class is further subdivided (see Fig. 5). The proportion of respondents who feel themselves "middle-middle class" has risen over time, whereas the "upper-middle" proportion has remained constant and the "lower-middle"—possibly a code word for "working class"—has fallen.[44] These results suggest decreasing polarization along class lines, in conformity with the conservative attitude in the Japanese electorate. Such results tell us little about the breadth and depth of alienation in Japan. They indicate only that, whatever its breadth and depth, it is not becoming broader and deeper.

Welfare-State Institutions

Social security systems, like tax systems, have become detailed and complex. It is natural to think of one's own country as having a reasonably simple system, considering its history, and sometimes to be critical of a foreign system for being unnecessarily complicated. In fact, many

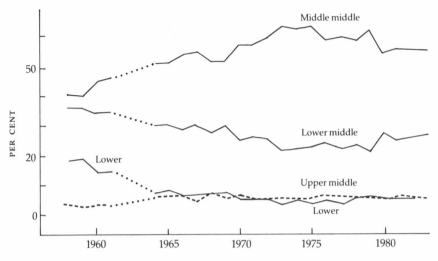

Fig. 5. People's self-classification in terms of living standard, Japan, 1958–1983. "Upper class" (not shown) comprised about 1 per cent. Sources: 1958–73, Japan, Office of the Prime Minister, "Kokumin seikatsu ni kansuru yoron chōsa" (unpublished report); 1974–83, *Gekkan yoron chōsa*, Oct. 1983, p. 7.

complications everywhere have grown out of special provisions for favored minorities (civil servants, for example) at one end of the scale and for the indigent at the other end. It is difficult to fit a single system to the special problems of the employed wage earner, the self-employed farmer, storekeeper, or professional, and the unemployed pauper. Even the definition of "social security" may be called into question (in Japan, government contributions to regular civil service pension funds are sometimes so classified). Since this essay is not an extended study of the Japanese social security systems, we concentrate our attention on the plans applying to wage earners in private employment. In general, the plans applying to civil servants are usually more generous, whereas the plans applying to the self-employed and unemployed are usually less so. (More detail may be found in Noguchi's treatment of public finance in this volume.)

As in most systems, care for the elderly is the centerpiece of the Japanese welfare state. There are many reasons for this. Even in the best of times, some people do not accumulate sufficient assets during their working years to provide for their later support. Some find themselves rejected by children or other relatives on whom they had relied, or these relatives find themselves with insufficient income or housing space for their care. Another group of elderly outlives the provisions its members had made for their own support, for reasons such as inflation, longer lives, and the rising relative cost of medical care. And finally, the elderly—more than other beneficiaries of the welfare state—vote and can be organized into pressure groups or lobbies.

In Japan, the public pension system began in 1941 for employees and in 1961 for the general public. These systems accounted for a small percentage of GNP until 1973 (see Fig. 6). There were three reasons for their relative cheapness: (1) there were comparatively few old people in the Japanese population; (2) full pensioners, who had paid premiums for 20 years or more, were even fewer; [45] and (3) benefit levels were low, even for full pensioners.

Legislation in 1973 increased the size of pensions. Furthermore, that portion of the pension independent of wages was indexed to consumer prices, and the wage-related portion was indexed to current wage rates. Pensioners did not need to fear inflation and could anticipate real increases in pensions as real wages rose. The background of this major policy change was more than humanitarian.

First, 15 years of high growth had increased Japan's capacity to finance

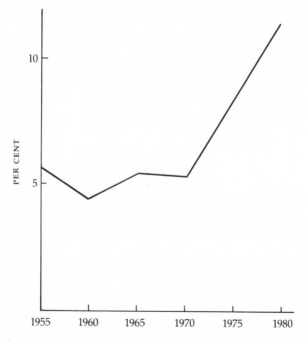

Fig. 6. Social security expenditure as a proportion of GNP. Sources: Japan, Office of the Prime Minister, Bureau of Statistics, *Japan Statistical Yearbook* (Tokyo: Nihon Tōkei Kyōkai, various issues).

social security programs, including pensions. Second, this growth was expected to continue, further reducing concern with the cost of the reforms. (Had the OPEC oil shock come early in the year—instead of in October—the legislation might have been less costly.) Third, few if any Japanese realized the implications of the demographic revolution already under way. The conjunction of rising life expectancies and continued low birthrates meant a future of decreasing numbers of working-age people per old-age pensioner and therefore increasing financial pressure on the pension system. Fourth, the government party (Liberal Democratic Party; LDP) was concerned with the erosion of its voting strength, especially in urban areas. Finally, the LDP prime minister, Kakuei Tanaka, not only headed a "populist" faction within his party, but was not himself of elite background. (His concern for increasing welfare is reflected in the influential reformist volume *Building a New Japan*, which was released over his signature.[46])

By the end of 1973, pensioners in the *Kōsei Nenkin* (the system for wage earners, administered by the Ministry of Welfare) received an average monthly payment of ¥38,200, or 40.8 per cent of the average wage of the previous year. This exceeded the West German and British percentages for the same year (36.7 and 34.5, respectively). Individual pensioners who had paid premiums for 25 years could obtain ¥66,600 per month, 71.1 per cent of the basic wage (exclusive of bonuses) if both husband and wife were of pensionable ages.[47] (By 1981, the average pensioner received ¥108,000 per month, 44.2 per cent of the average monthly wage.[48]) Workers paid relatively small portions of their wages as premiums, 3.8 per cent in 1973, rising to 5.3 per cent in 1980, with equal contributions by employers. (Government workers, covered by another plan, received more.)

An academic study that treated both employer and employee contributions as deductions from what wages would have been in the absence of deductions for social insurance and that applied a 6.5 annual discount rate to future payments estimated the intergenerational transfer (from younger to older worker families) as ¥16.8 million in 1980, or 87 per cent of the present value of pensions receivable under the program. It estimated the internal rate of return on contributions at 20 per cent per annum, as compared with an inflation rate of 4 to 6 per cent.[49] This unusually high real return can be defended on the basis of the older generation's contribution to the human and public capital of the nation. It can also be defended on the ground that the present elderly had taken care of their parents privately during their own working years. Whether these theories are right or wrong, it will not be easy to finance future pension payments.

As the proportion of the elderly in Japan's total population increases—

and the proportion of full-fledged pensioners among the elderly also rises—the ratio of pension payments to estimated national income will rise until, in the year 2010, premiums amounting to 31 per cent of the average annual wage (or 16.9 percent of national income) would be required to keep the system solvent.[50] If worker and employer contributions are kept constant, the great bulk of payments must come from the general budget.

As a political matter, this solution will not be accepted easily, however correct the above estimates may be. In an amendment passed in 1985, the eligibility age was raised to 65, the norm in most industrial countries. Furthermore, the benefit level was scaled down somewhat. This is not sufficient, however, and Japan may adopt some "more easily collected" sales tax or value-added tax to defray the increasing costs. Japan may also adopt austerity measures. That is to say, real pension benefits may be cut further; worker and employer contribution rates may be increased; and eligibility may be tightened, as, for example, by means tests. It is not easy to forecast such alternatives in a representative democracy. The Japanese can hardly derive much comfort from the fact that Japan is not alone and that similar problems have come to affect so many other welfare-state pension systems.

Japanese unemployment insurance dates from 1947. The present system ("employment insurance") protects the unemployed from starvation while financing their search for better jobs than they may first be offered. It dates from 1976. The program is tilted in favor of older workers, for whom a job search is more difficult under the Japanese systems of long-term employment, age-related wages, and promotion from within. The unemployment benefit is 60 per cent of the worker's last wage, with a maximum of ¥200,000 per month. For a worker under 30, it is payable for 90 days, but workers over 55 may collect benefits for 300 days. In addition, workers in a number of special categories—the physically handicapped, ex–coal miners, and those over 45—receive lump-sum payments worth up to 30 days' wages if re-employed as full-time regular workers. Kosai and Ogino state categorically that "the transfer of income to those unable to work (the physically handicapped, the aged, fatherless families) [is] insufficient."[51] (We have already considered the case of the aged.)

Japan has nothing corresponding to the large Aid to Families with Dependent Children program in the United States. The neediest families in Japanese society are protected by the public assistance program of the Ministry of Welfare, sometimes supplemented by grants from local communities. The percentage of people protected under the Ministry of Welfare system fell from 2.0 per cent in 1955 to 1.2 per cent in 1980.[52] For a standard (four-person) household, the nominal amount of assistance has increased sharply, from ¥8,200 per month in 1955 to ¥114,500 in 1980.[53] These payments are means-tested; one hears complaints about social workers' intrusions into clients' privacy, and there are limitations on clients' ownership of automobiles and amount of bank deposits. A minimum living standard is available to almost everyone, even though the resulting "safety net" does not meet the standards of Kosai and Ogino.

As with old-age pensions, Japan has several medical care programs. There is a public health-insurance program (*Kumiai Kenkō Hoken*) for employees, which formerly fully covered the medical expenses of the insured and paid 70 per cent of the additional expenses resulting from hospitalization. Like the corresponding *Kōsei Nenkin* pension system, it is funded by payroll deductions paid by workers and employers. For the general public, there is another system, *Kokumin Kenkō Hoken*. Its benefits are somewhat greater; until 1983 it included a special old-age medical care program that provided free care to all persons over 70 (in some places, 65). An additional system for the aged was established in 1983.

The payment system was changed in 1984 to slow or counteract the rising cost of health care. Previously, the insured paid ¥800 for a first visit to each physician or dentist consulted, with subsequent visits free. The 1984 legislation eliminated the initial fee, but in principle added a 10 per cent charge for all medical treatments (including medicines). There are reductions to these changes in the cases of poor patients or particularly expensive treatments. This change was expected to reduce malingering by patients, and early reports suggest that it has reduced the number of visits to doctors. We do not yet know whether it has also meant any failure to treat dangerous illnesses in their early stages, with higher costs in the long run.

Complaints against the Japanese health care system abound, including the usual ones of malingering by patients and profiteering by doctors and hospitals. Some hospitals are obsolete and inadequately staffed. Some doctors are overworked; some refuse to undertake difficult, risky, or costly treatments without (illegal) side-payments. Such complaints, of course, are not peculiar to Japan; they are common to every system of expanded medical care for the masses of the population. One problem, the refusal of some hospitals to treat patients at night, appears to be more widespread in Japan than in other industrial countries. Yet, as we saw before, Japan's records on infant mortality and life expectancy at age five are among the best in the world.

In the long run, the overly sanguine pension system for the elderly is the principal cause for concern about the Japanese social security system, largely because insufficient account has been taken of the shift in the country's age distribution. Rising demand for improved provisions for the physically and mentally handicapped is anticipated and will also be difficult to finance. On the other hand, the problems of the general public health insurance scheme, the *Kenkō Hoken*, which had for years been one of the "three Ks" of the public deficit, along with *kome* (rice) and *kokutetsu* (the National Railways), were alleviated at least temporarily by new legislation in 1983 and 1984. Indeed, the system was in the black for the fiscal year ending March 31, 1984, but only because health insurance for the elderly had been shifted to another account.

Tentative Conclusions

Of the rival positions mentioned early in this study, the "workaholics in rabbit hutches" thesis may be ignored, despite the several grains of truth in it. The "welfare superpower" and "Japan as number one" theses are smug and complacent exaggerations, but we can use them as baselines. What needs to be done for Japan to indeed become a welfare superpower—not necessarily number one but still a superpower?

1. First and foremost, we believe, the set of issues involved in industrialization and urbanization should be met head on—as they should have been two decades ago. The most important of these involve the quantity and quality of housing and therefore the high price of urban land. Only slightly less important are the issues of commuting time and discomfort and the shortage of urban public facilities.

We would like to see urban land used much more efficiently, as under a system of urban land taxation based on its potential rental value at its estimated best use. The tax rate could be lower than the present 1.7 per cent of assessed value in urban areas, but the assessed value should be much closer to market value so as to facilitate efficiency.

The present plan of creating small developed centers of the university town and "technopolis" variety seems reasonable. (Tsukuba, in Ibaraki Prefecture, is an outstanding example.) Former Prime Minister Tanaka's 1972 *Building a New Japan* was correct in this respect, although unfortunately ahead of its time and too closely connected to pork-barrel politics.

2. Japan's welfare-state institutions are in trouble. In particular, the potential problems of old-age pensions for a graying society need somehow to be solved. They may wreck the economy just as "bread and circuses" debilitated ancient Rome. All welfare states, not merely Japan, face similar problems. We hope that they can be solved within the political constraints of implied contracts within representative democratic governments. If they cannot be, there is trouble ahead, in Japan as well as in the West.

3. At the same time, Japan's welfare safety net for the poorest of the poor remains weak and needs improvement. Some, notably Nobel economics laureate Milton Friedman, believe this problem, along with the

problem of an aging society, can be solved by restructuring the welfare system to cover only the payment of money income—rather than subsidizing housing or health care—and to apply only to the poor. This reform could, we think, hardly avoid major sacrifices by middle-aged or middle-class beneficiaries of existing welfare-state institutions.

4. The economic position of Japanese women, particularly educated and ambitious women, should be improved. This improvement, we believe, will come about in Japan much as it has in the West, and Western examples will accelerate it. How many years or generations may be required, we do not dare forecast.

5. Efforts to improve the lot of racial and other minorities should be continued. However unimportant minority members may be as a proportion of the Japanese population, they should be treated as equals.

6. We have said that environmental pollution has been largely contained in Japan. This is true for sulfur dioxide pollution and also for organic water pollution. Public sewage systems, however, should be extended and improved, and further action should be taken against types of presently uncontained pollution, such as noise and nitrogen oxides.

7. In a welfare superpower, the standard workweek should contain fewer hours and fewer days than the Japanese now work. The 40-hour week should be extended to most of the society, and more people should have realistic options for more vacations and earlier retirement. Present Japanese work practices are not models for other countries.

Japan in the mid-1980s is stable and almost serene, purse-proud, and inclined toward smugness internally and condescension toward external criticism. (Condescension is, however, combined with concern about what envious foreigners unable to understand Japan's special position may do to the economy.) Can such a society, ignoring some of its troubles and blaming the rest on foreigners' misunderstanding, summon the political will to address its problems in the remainder of the present century? We fear that it cannot, barring further miracles. A major split between mainstream factions and their opponents within the LDP or a compromise between the reformist and revolutionary opposition parties may change this situation—but perhaps for the worse rather than for the better. But we do not see either of these political breakthroughs occurring in the near future—even though we could explain them easily enough when and if they surprise us by happening.

Kazuo Sato

Saving and Investment

The macroeconomic balance between saving and investment is crucial in maintaining an economy's equilibrium at any given time and in promoting its growth over time. The saving and investment rates are influenced by different factors and do not necessarily behave in a complementary manner. How these two variables are brought into accordance with one another sets the basic tone for an economy's macroeconomic performance. Those who adhere to the notion of a classical macroeconomic system may argue that equality between saving and investment is achieved at the level of full employment through the effective working of the price mechanism. This does not seem to have been the case in real life—or in Japan after World War II.[1]

Over the four decades since the end of World War II, the Japanese economy has experienced four major macroeconomic phases: recovery in the late 1940s from the economic setbacks caused by the war, a return to normalcy in the 1950s, rapid growth through the 1960s and early 1970s, and decelerated growth following the first oil shock in 1973. Saving and investment rates changed in response to these fundamental macroeconomic phases. The economic miracle of the 1960s owes much to the steady rise in the saving ratio as the demand for investment steadily increased. Much of the trouble experienced since the mid-1970s has been caused by the slow decline in private saving compared with a sharp fall in investment relative to GDP.

The role of saving in Japan has changed, and popular views of saving have altered drastically. Until a few years ago, foreign commentators unconditionally praised the Japanese virtue of saving, as well as the success of Japan's supply-side policies in general. Now, they often cite excess saving as the root cause of Japan's international economic conflicts.

In this paper, I present a general account of Japan's postwar performance with respect to saving and investment, describe the general

TABLE 1
Investment and Saving in Japan, 1885-1983
(per cent of GNP [GDP])

Years	(1) Gross domestic investment	(2) Foreign saving	(3) Gross national saving	(4) Consumption of fixed capital	(5) Net national saving	(6) Household saving	(7) Corporate saving	(8) Government saving
Series A (per cent of GNP)								
1885-1889	12.6%	0.0%	12.6%	10.0%	2.6%	-0.8%		3.4%
1890-1894	13.7	-0.1	13.6	9.0	4.6	3.5		1.1
1895-1899	17.9	-1.1	16.8	9.0	7.8	9.6		-1.8
1900-1904	12.4	-1.0	11.4	8.6	2.8	4.0		-1.2
1905-1909	14.7	-2.6	12.1	8.8	3.3	3.7%	0.4%	-0.8
1910-1914	16.3	-1.7	14.6	8.6	6.0	0.2	0.4	5.4
1915-1919	17.6	7.0	24.6	9.5	15.1	9.6	1.2	4.3
1920-1924	17.3	-2.2	15.1	11.0	4.1	0.5	-0.1	3.7
1925-1929	15.9	-1.0	14.9	9.7	5.2	0.5	0.2	4.5
1930-1934	13.8	0.1	13.9	9.6	4.3	4.9	0.1	-0.7
1935-1939	17.3	-0.3	17.0	9.7	7.3	9.6	2.1	-4.4
Series B (per cent of GNP)								
1930-1934	13.0%	0.6%	13.6%	6.6%	7.0%	8.1%	0.1%	-1.2%
1935-1939	18.3	0.9	19.2	7.2	12.0	14.6	2.2	-4.8
1940-1944	18.0	-0.7	17.3	7.1	10.2	22.3	3.8	-15.9
1946-1949	13.2	0.6	13.8	4.6	9.2	0.4	0.1	8.7
1950-1954	24.6	1.5	26.1	6.8	19.3	8.7	3.6	7.0
1955-1959	29.3	0.1	29.4	9.6	19.8	10.7	3.6	5.5
1960-1964	38.4	-0.7	37.7	11.3	24.4	12.1	4.8	7.5
1965-1969	35.7	0.8	36.5	12.9	23.6	12.4	4.9	6.3
1970-1974	38.7	0.9	39.6	13.4	26.2	15.3	3.7	7.3
Series C (per cent of GDP)								
1965-1969	33.8%	0.8%	34.6%	13.6%	21.0%	10.6%	5.0%	5.4%
1970-1974	37.5	0.9	38.4	13.7	24.7	13.5	4.7	6.5
1975-1979	31.5	0.6	32.1	13.0	19.1	15.6	1.2	2.3
1980-1983	30.5	0.7	31.2	14.0	17.2	13.6	0.9	2.7

SOURCES: Series A, Kazushi Ohkawa, Nobukiyo Takamatsu, and Yuzo Yamamoto, Kokumin shotoku (National income) (Tokyo: Tōyō Keizai Shimpōsha, 1974), tables 1, 6. Series B, ibid., Tables 1A, 6A; for 1970-74, Japan, Economic Planning Agency, Annual Report on National Income Statistics, 1978 (Tokyo: Government Printing Office, 1978). Series C, idem, Annual Report on National Accounts, 1984 and 1985; OECD, National Accounts, 1970-82 (Paris, 1984).
NOTE: (1) + (2) = (3) = (4) + (5). (5) = (6) + (7) + (8).

macroeconomic climate in Japan, and provide a basis for predictions for the coming decades. In the first section, I present a broad historical overview of saving and investment in Japan. In the second section, I discuss several salient features of Japan's capital and wealth accumulation. Then I examine household saving and investment behavior in the third section and business saving and investment behavior in the fourth. After reviewing the overall balance of saving and investment in Japan by looking at the government and the external sectors, I end by making some predictions of future trends.

Historical Overview

Although the principal focus of this paper is the postwar period, Japan's long-term record over the past hundred years is of interest. Table 1 outlines gross domestic investment and components of gross national saving as a per cent of GNP or GDP in quinquennial averages. The saving ratio was relatively modest before World War II except in such extraordinary periods as 1915–19, when the World War I superboom brought about huge export surpluses, and 1935–39 and 1940–44, when private saving was mobilized to finance the war (see Fig. 1). When such unique situations are discounted, net national saving was about 5 per cent of

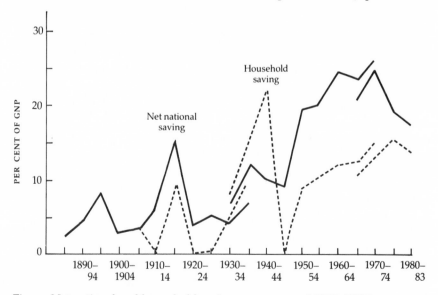

Fig. 1. Net national and household saving, as per cent of GNP (GDP), 1885–1983. See Table 1 for sources.

GNP, which corresponds to the low growth rate of 3.0 per cent per annum between 1885–89 and 1935–39. The capital–output ratio implied by these figures is 2.0.[2]

In contrast to the modest prewar record, the saving ratio in the postwar period was remarkable. After a precipitous fall in private saving in the immediate postwar years, the saving ratio steadily recovered through the early 1970s. In the rapid growth period of the 1960s and the early 1970s, net national saving was nearly 25 per cent of GDP. Correspondingly, the growth rate was also high—a little over 10 per cent per year. The capital–output ratio rose to a level slightly greater than 2. The saving ratio began to decline in the late 1970s in response to slower economic growth, but this decrease can be attributed primarily to a decline in government saving. Private saving also declined but at a slower rate.

This brief overview illustrates the interaction among saving, investment, and economic growth. If the saving ratio had not increased rapidly after World War II, Japan's remarkable postwar economic growth could not have been achieved. The increases in the saving ratio may be explained by the rapid increases in income experienced by most Japanese households. Such a point must be carefully examined. Another condition often cited as an explanatory factor is that Japan's high saving ratio reflects the frugality of Japanese households under the strict discipline of the *ie* ("family") system.[3] Saving claimed a much smaller fraction of household income in the heyday of the *ie* system, however. The saving ratio is apparently a variable conditioned principally by macroeconomic forces rather than by cultural factors.

When the war ended on August 15, 1945, Japan's economy was in shambles. Productive capacity was devastated, agricultural production plummeted, and with real income about half its prewar level, households faced starvation. Many urban families, including overseas repatriates, were forced to return to villages for temporary shelter. The population in rural areas rose to above 50 per cent of the total population, reversing the steady downward trend since the early Meiji period. Private saving was virtually nonexistent. The shortage in the supply of goods ignited rampant inflation, which took the entire Occupation period to bring under control. Meanwhile, the Occupation authorities implemented a number of economic "democratization" measures: land reform, dissolution of the *zaibatsu*, and unionization.

The peace treaty restored sovereignty to Japan in 1952, and inflation was finally quenched. The prewar peak level of production was regained early in this period, and the economy began to function normally. Industry began to expand, and the population started to return to the cities from rural areas. By the end of the decade, the proportion of agricultural labor fell to 30 per cent of the total labor force. Saving and investment continued to rise as a per cent of GDP. The major constraint on growth at this time, as well as in the early 1960s, was the balance of payments.

The miraculous economic growth of Japan took place in the brief span of 14 years from 1960 to 1973. GDP grew at an average annual rate of 10 per cent, quadrupling total GDP. Behind this spectacular growth were massive imports of technology, especially in manufacturing, that raised Japan's international competitiveness enormously. By the mid-1960s, the balance-of-payments constraint on growth was removed. Growth acceleration required that a large fraction of GDP be devoted to capital formation. Japan's so-called miracle lies in the mobilization of saving in greater amounts to match the demand for investment, which kept the economy from overheating. Industry expanded at a tremendous rate, absorbing most of the population from rural areas. The agricultural labor force had declined to about 10 per cent of the total labor force by the end of the period.

Like other advanced economies, Japan entered a new era of decelerated growth after the first oil crisis of 1973–74. Japan managed a swift recovery, however, and has maintained a reasonably good growth rate (at least compared with other countries), kept inflation under control, and experienced relatively low rates of unemployment. But the Japanese economy faced a new set of problems. As economic growth declined, the demand for new capital fell drastically. Saving, however, did not fall at a comparable rate, and an excess of saving over investment began to appear in the private sector. At the same time, government revenues and expenditures became structurally imbalanced as slower economic growth resulted in the stagnation of government revenues and government expenditures continued to rise. This shortfall of revenues was financed by deficits. Although this development helped absorb excess private saving without incurring unemployment, it resulted in a mounting accumulation of public debt.

Over the postwar decades, the balance of saving and investment has undergone several transitions reflecting the changes in Japan's macroeconomic climate. The Japanese government has remained steadfastly pro-saving—an attitude with a historical basis, but notable in the postwar decades. It kept the tax burden relatively low, especially on property income and capital gains.

Japan's Accumulation in International Perspective

Saving and investment accumulate into wealth and capital, respectively. In this section, I compare Japan's flow and stock of wealth and capital accumulation with that of other countries.

Overall Saving Ratio

Neither too little nor too much saving is beneficial in sustaining economic growth. A certain balance among saving, investment, and growth must be attained. High potential growth can be realized only if the economy succeeds in mobilizing an adequate supply of savings or in reducing the amount of investment required.

Japan was able to expand saving in the rapid growth period. In this regard, Japan's performance is not unique. Confronted with equally high potential growth, a few newly industrializing countries have allocated a large proportion of national output to capital formation. Even a few developed countries have higher saving ratios.[4]

Capital–Output Ratio

When the supply of funds (saving) is less than the demand for funds (investment), a balance may be attained by reducing the latter. For this to take place without lowering the growth rate, the capital–output ratio must be lowered. Since saving was in short supply in Japan throughout the rapid growth period, did Japan, in fact, reduce its capital–output ratio? Although capital estimates are subject to statistical pitfalls, statistics now available for a number of OECD countries allow the comparison of broad orders of magnitude.

A comparison of the ratio of net fixed capital stock to total GDP in 1970 and 1980 in current prices for several countries reveals that, of the six countries for which complete data are available, Japan had the lowest aggregate capital–output ratio (see Table 2). The ratio was especially low in 1970, suggesting that the capital supply was still limited at the end of the rapid growth period.

As for the stock of producer durables, the capital–output ratio in Japan was not markedly different from that of other countries, especially by the end of the 1970s after substantial increases in the ratio over the decade. Thus, Japan is more or less similar to other major industrial countries in the employment of productive capital.[5]

The contrast is much sharper in the case of housing stock. The housing stock–output ratio was definitely low in Japan in 1970. Even after a substantial expansion in housing in the 1970s, the ratio was still low by international standards in 1980. This finding is by no means surprising; it is generally acknowledged both inside and outside Japan that Japan's housing conditions lag far behind its general standard of living, thus justifying the European Community's sarcastic description of Japanese dwellings as "rabbit hutches" a few years back.[6] In short, Japan econo-

TABLE 2

Capital–Output Ratios, Selected Countries, 1970 and 1980
(net fixed capital stock/GDP)

| Country | Dwellings | Nondwellings | | | Total |
		Private	Public	All	
Japan					
1970	0.28	0.76	0.30	1.06	1.34
1980	0.56	1.10	0.58	1.67	2.23
United States					
1970	0.76	0.82	0.52	1.34	2.10
1980	0.96	0.98	0.58	1.58	2.53
Canada					
1970	—	1.42	0.36	1.77	—
1980	—	1.59	0.39	1.97	—
France					
1970	—	0.88	0.19	1.07	—
1980	—	1.02	0.23	1.25	—
Germany					
1970	1.14	1.22	0.20	1.41	2.55
1980	1.37	1.28	0.24	1.52	2.90
United Kingdom					
1970	0.72	1.38	0.31	1.69	2.41
1980	1.02	1.72	0.50	2.22	3.24
Norway					
1970	0.84	2.20	0.66	2.86	3.70
1980	0.83	1.98	0.69	2.67	3.49
Sweden					
1970	1.06	1.16	0.37	1.53	2.59
1980	1.12	1.37	0.47	1.84	2.96

SOURCES: Capital stocks from OECD, *Flows and Stocks of Fixed Capital, 1955-1980* (Paris, 1983); GDP from OECD, *National Accounts, 1964-1981* (Paris, 1983). For Japan, Economic Planning Agency, *Annual Report on National Accounts, 1983* (Tokyo: Government Printing Office, 1983). For the United States, *Survey of Current Business*, Mar. 1980, Feb. 1981, and Oct. 1982.

NOTE: All figures in current prices except data for Sweden, which are based on 1975 prices.

mized on housing in order to deploy its limited supply of capital in more productive areas.[7]

Household Wealth

Although wealth and capital are two sides of the same coin, they must be considered independently except at the level of the national economy. In the household sector, wealth includes land, which is not considered capital because it is not reproducible. Aside from land, household wealth consists primarily of financial assets (less liabilities). Physical assets included in household wealth are dwellings owned by households as residences and business capital stock employed by unincorporated businesses, which are considered a part of the household sector. In Japan, the composition of household wealth differs considerably from other countries.

First, because land is unaugmentable in quantity, its market value tends to rise in a growing economy as the demand for land increases. This fact makes land an important component of private wealth. In Japan, inhabitable land constitutes only a small fraction of total area.[8] Furthermore, metropolitan areas are overcongested. Consequently, urban land, both residential and commercial, is extremely expensive in Japan.[9] Although Japan's total land area is only a twenty-fifth that of the United States, the former would cost more than the latter. For this reason, land occupies an overwhelming position in Japan's household wealth portfolio.

Another well-known feature of personal portfolios of wealth in Japan is the small position of corporate equities. Household financial assets are largely of fixed-claim types that are vulnerable to inflation. Individuals hold their financial savings primarily in bank deposits, postal savings, and the like. On the one hand, this financial structure has given special

TABLE 3

Household Wealth, as Multiples of Household Disposable Income, Japan and the United States, 1980

Household wealth	Japan	United States
Land	2.90	0.33
Reproducible assets	0.98	1.22
Financial assets	1.99	3.06
Fixed-claim	1.59	1.22
Equities	0.41	1.83
Corporate	0.16	0.56
Others	0.25[a]	1.27[b]
Total assets	5.87	4.61
Liabilities	0.76	0.81
Net worth	5.11	3.80

SOURCES: For Japan, Economic Planning Agency, *Annual Report on National Accounts, 1983* (Tokyo: Government Printing Office, 1983). For United States, R. Ruggles and N. Ruggles, "Integrated Economic Accounts for the United States, 1947-80," *Survey of Current Business*, May 1982, pp. 1-53.

[a]Life insurance.

[b]Noncorporate nonfarm equity, farm business equity, estates, and trusts.

power to financial intermediaries in their role as providers of credit.[10] On the other hand, the special tax treatment of interest income is significant.

Expressed as a per cent of disposable income, household debt is currently about the same in Japan and the United States.[11] Financial assets, however, make up a smaller proportion of the household wealth portfolio in Japan (see Table 3). Therefore, net financial assets are significantly lower in Japan than in the United States.

Household Income, Saving, and Capital Formation

Analyses of household saving often emphasize the functional distribution of income among different types of households—workers, rentiers, proprietors, retired workers, and the like—since they tend to exhibit different propensities to save. The advanced economies differ from one another in this regard; the income of proprietors is relatively high in the continental European countries and very low in North America, with Japan somewhere in between. Since a substantial portion of proprietors' income may be imputed to their labor services, labor income within household income is comparable among these countries, ranging from 70 to 80 per cent of total household income. Any remaining differences in the income share of labor can be attributed primarily to the differences in the importance of transfer income among these countries, especially in social security payments. By the end of the 1970s, social security payments were as developed in Japan as in Canada, the United States, and the United Kingdom, although much less so than in continental Europe.[12]

With respect to household saving and capital formation, macroeconomic theories often neglect the absorption of a large part of household saving into household capital formation. The ten OECD countries for which household gross saving and capital formation statistics are available can be divided into two groups. In the high-saving group (Italy, Japan, and Portugal), household gross saving is about 20 per cent of GDP, with household gross capital formation and net lending each accounting for about half of this figure. In the low-saving group (Canada, the United States, Austria, Finland, France, Sweden, and the United Kingdom), gross saving is about 10 per cent of GDP, most of which goes to gross capital formation, with net lending making up only a small fraction of total saving. In Japan, the household sector has been an important source of funds for the rest of the economy.

Government Consumption, Saving, and Investment

The government sector takes an increasingly larger share of national income all over the world. The fiscal scale of the Japanese government, however, has remained relatively small with respect to public consumption. The share of total GDP going to the final consumption expenditure of the general government is lower in Japan than among other advanced countries—it was about 10 per cent in the early 1980s as against 20 per cent in Canada, West Germany, and the United Kingdom, with the United States, France, and Italy falling in between. Japan's low level of government consumption can be attributed partly to its nearly nonexistent defense expenditure (barely 1 per cent of GDP as against 6 per cent in the United States). Japan's low government share may be somewhat overexaggerated in national accounting statistics, especially because of the understatement of national health expenditures.[13] With proper adjustments, the share of government consumption expenditures may realistically be raised by 4 percentage points, reducing the gap between Japan and other countries.

Another factor that may make the Japanese government's economic activities larger than they may seem at first glance is the sizable public expenditure on capital formation—6 per cent of GDP in the early 1980s as compared with 3 per cent in France, West Germany, Italy, and Canada and 2 per cent in the United States and the United Kingdom. Until the mid-1970s, government capital formation was more than fully financed by government saving under the balanced-budget principle, making the government an important source of net national saving in the postwar period. All factors considered, the government claims nearly as much of GDP in Japan as elsewhere.

The Cost of Funds

The cost of funds influences both saving and investment. Has the cost of funds been lower in Japan than elsewhere? In 1982–84, nominal rates of interest were relatively low in Japan (see Table 4).[14] Real rates of interest have not been particularly low, however, since the rate of inflation has also been low in Japan.[15]

For businesses, the corporate income tax rate is another important cost element. This tax rate continued to rise through the 1970s and is now among the highest internationally.[16] In addition, considering the relatively high depreciation cost, the user cost of capital has not been low in Japan.

Demographic Conditions

The structure of the population is an important determinant of personal saving behavior. Although the Japanese population is still younger than American and European populations (see Table 5), it is expected to age rapidly over the next quarter century. It is projected that the propor-

TABLE 4
Rates of Interest and Inflation, Selected Countries, 1982-1984
(per cent)

Country	Nominal interest rate		Inflation rate		Real interest rate			
	Short-term	Long-term	WPI	CPI	Short-term		Long-term	
					WPI	CPI	WPI	CPI
Japan	6.8%	7.4%	−0.2%	2.2%	7.0%	4.6%	7.6%	5.2%
United States	10.5	12.2	1.9	4.6	8.6	5.9	10.3	7.6
Canada	11.3	12.9	4.5	7.0	6.8	4.3	8.4	5.9
France	13.1	13.8	11.8	9.6	1.3	3.5	2.0	4.2
Germany	6.9	8.2	3.4	3.7	3.2	3.2	4.8	4.5
Italy	18.8[a]	18.0	11.3	14.0	7.5	4.8	6.7	4.0
United Kingdom	10.5	11.5	6.4	6.1	4.1	4.4	5.1	5.4

SOURCE: IMF, *International Financial Statistics*, Aug. 1985, series numbers 60b, 61, 63, 64.
[a] 1984, first two quarters only.

TABLE 5
Population and Labor Force, Selected Countries, 1974-1982

Country	Life expectancy (years)	Old-age dependency ratio (per cent)[a]	Labor force participation ratio, 1982 (per cent)[b]		
			Male	Female	Male, 65+
Japan	73.8 (1981)	9.3 (1981)	89.2	55.9	38.3
United States	69.9 (1979)	11.4 (1981)	88.1	63.1	17.8
Canada	70.2 (1975-77)	9.5 (1981)	86.2	59.7	13.8
France	70.1 (1978-80)	13.5 (1982)	79.8	56.0	5.9
Germany	69.9 (1979-81)	15.3 (1981)	80.6	49.6	6.0
Italy	69.7 (1974-77)	13.5 (1980)	81.3	40.0	11.7
United Kingdom	70.4 (1978-80)	15.3 (1981)	89.2	58.1	7.8

SOURCES: Life expectancy and dependency ratio, Tōyō Keizai Shimpōsha, *Keizai tōkei nenkan, 1985* (Yearbook of economic statistics) (Tokyo, 1985). Labor force participation ratio, OECD, *Labour Force Statistics, 1970-1981* (Paris, 1983).
[a] 65 and older population/total population.
[b] Figures for Germany, Italy, and United Kingdom are for 1981.

tion of the population age 65 and over will rise from the current level of 10 per cent to 13.6 per cent in 1995 to 17.1 per cent in 2005.[17] Also important is that many older workers, especially males, continue to work after retirement age, even though the proportion of aged persons engaged in paid labor has been falling,[18] reflecting slackening demand for older workers. Now that Japan's life expectancy is one of the highest in the world (80 for females and 74 for males, as of 1984), satisfying older workers' willingness to work will be a difficult question. Their desire to remain in the labor force may even be stronger in the future since the aging of the population is sure to result in lower social security benefits because the burden on the working population of providing social security payments must be kept to a reasonably tolerable level.[19]

A related problem is the increased female participation in the labor force. The female labor force participation rate rose from 45.7 per cent in 1975 to 49.0 per cent in 1983, in response to the increasing need to supplement household income, which ceased to improve in the late 1970s as the income tax and social security burden continued to rise.

Household Saving and Investment

A major hurdle in aggregate studies of household saving is the diversity of demographic, economic, and social characteristics among households. First, households must be divided into distinct groups of different economic status—such as farmers, nonfarm proprietors, workers, rentiers, and so on. Even within the relatively homogeneous group of worker households, distinctions must be made among young unattached worker households, households with a working male head, households with both husband and wife employed, households with no male head, and households of retired workers. Family size is an important variable, as is house ownership, because the household budgets of homeowners and renters differ considerably. Ideally, households should be cross-classified for a complete analysis, but such detailed data for individual households is not readily accessible to researchers.[20] Although the available studies in this field are less than satisfactory, the rest of this paper relies heavily on their results and observations.

In Table 6 and Fig. 2, I examine the changes in household saving ratios. I applied statistics from two series taken directly from their original sources—one from the family budget survey of worker households (Family Income and Expenditure Survey; FIES) and the other from that of farm households (Farm Household Economy Survey; FHES). The others are from the official National Income and Product Accounts (NIPA) prepared by the Economic Planning Agency, both the new and old series.[21] Since income and saving are defined differently in these sources, the saving ratios are not strictly comparable in terms of levels. Their movements over time, however, are broadly similar, enabling us to draw broad generalizations from the data.[22]

Following the period of reconstruction (1945–51), when rampant inflation made household savings worthless and income levels were severely depressed, the 1950s saw a rapid increase in the saving ratio. By

TABLE 6

Ratio of Household Saving to Disposable Income, Japan, 1951-1984
(per cent)

Year	(1) Worker	(2) Farmer	(3) NIPA old[a]	(4) NIPA, new[a,b]			
				Saving	Consumption of fixed capital	Gross savings	Gross capital formation
1951	2.0%	11.3%	12.8%[c]				
1952	4.4	8.1	10.3				
1953	5.8	6.2	7.8				
1954	7.4	3.4	9.6				
1955	9.2%	10.0%	13.4%				
1956	11.8	3.6	13.7				
1957	12.5	6.2	15.6				
1958	12.6	7.3	15.0				
1959	13.9	8.7	16.7				
1960	14.9%	12.2%	17.4%				
1961	16.5	10.8	19.2				
1962	16.2	13.6	18.6				
1963	16.2	13.6	18.0				
1964	17.1	14.4	16.4				
1965	17.2%	15.6%	17.7%	15.8%	4.6%	20.4%	11.7%
1966	17.6	17.1	17.4	15.1	4.7	19.8	11.8
1967	18.4	18.9	19.0	15.5	4.9	20.4	13.1
1968	18.6	16.6	19.7	16.7	5.0	21.7	14.3
1969	19.2	15.8	19.2	17.4	5.1	22.5	14.7
1970	20.3%	15.5%	20.4%	18.2%	5.1%	23.3%	14.6%
1971	20.1	14.7	20.7	18.2	5.3	23.5	14.3
1972	21.6	18.8	21.7	18.6	5.4	24.0	15.5
1973	22.5	22.0	25.1	21.2	5.2	26.4	16.3
1974	24.3	24.6	25.7	23.9	5.1	29.0	15.1
1975	23.0%	25.8%	25.1%	22.5%	5.4%	27.9%	14.4%
1976	22.6	24.1	24.3	22.7	5.7	28.4	15.0
1977	22.8	28.5		21.3	6.0	27.3	14.2
1978	23.0	22.6		21.0	6.2	27.2	14.2
1979	22.4	20.6		19.2	6.5	25.7	14.6
1980	22.1%	18.1%		19.6%	6.7%	26.3%	13.6%
1981	20.8	18.7		20.0	6.8	26.8	12.5
1982	20.7	19.3		18.0	7.0	25.0	11.9
1983	20.9	19.4		17.2	7.0	24.3	11.1
1984	21.3						

SOURCES: (1) Japan, Prime Minister's Office, Family Income and Expenditure Survey. (2) Japan, Ministry of Agriculture, Forestry, and Fisheries, Farm Household Economy Survey. (3) Japan, Economic Planning Agency, *Annual Report on National Income Statistics, 1978* (Tokyo: Government Printing Office, 1978). (4) Idem, *Annual Report on National Accounts, 1985* (Tokyo: Government Printing Office, 1985), and earlier issues.

NOTE: Saving and disposable income variously defined in sources.

[a] All households including individual proprietors and nonprofit institutions.

[b] 1965-69, excluding nonprofit institutions.

[c] Based on fiscal-year data.

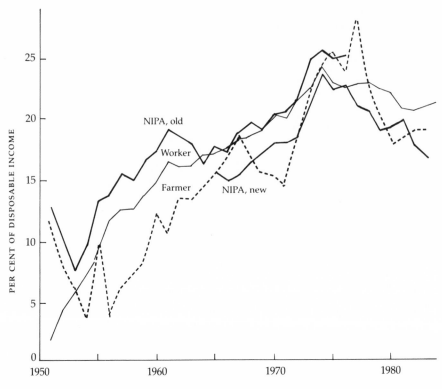

Fig. 2. Household saving ratios, 1951–1984.

1952, inflation had been brought under control, the economy started to function more normally, and people began to think once again about family savings. In an attempt to recover lost ground in asset accumulation, the saving ratio rose year after year throughout the 1950s. By the end of the decade, the saving ratio had attained and then exceeded the prewar level.[23] This observation led to the popular belief that the saving ratio would soon stop rising.[24]

This prediction seems to have been realized in the early 1960s, but the saving ratio began to rise with renewed vigor in the mid-1960s. A possible explanation of this resurgence is that consumers, facing a rapid increase in income during the rapid growth period, failed to make swift adjustment in their consumption level, which lagged behind income, causing a rise in the saving ratio.[25] Other possibilities include demographic and institutional factors, such as the underdeveloped social security system (forcing individuals to increase saving for retirement since anticipation of a higher consumption level in the future necessitates increased current saving) and the underdeveloped consumer credit system (forcing individuals to save in order to purchase houses and consumer durables). For whatever reasons, the saving ratio continued to rise throughout the rest of the rapid growth period, peaking in 1974, the year of double-digit inflation (a 24 per cent increase in the CPI).[26]

The saving ratio began to decline from its peak in 1974 as income growth slowed. In fact, since the burdens imposed by income tax and social security payments increased at the same time, the growth of disposable income was minuscule.[27] If the permanent income hypothesis held for the rapid growth period, the saving ratio should have fallen swiftly. The decline, however, has been relatively small. Although the NIPA saving ratio has continued to decline, the FIES and FHES saving ratios were stable in the last two years studied. In addition, although both social security benefits and the consumer finance system have recently been developing at a respectable rate, they apparently have not been strong enough to further accelerate the decline in the saving ratio.

Composition of Saving by Source

If we could determine the composition of saving by source, that is, by type of income, it would better facilitate our understanding of the mechanics involved in saving. Because of the poor quality of available basic data, I have been forced to indulge in highly conjectural guesswork. What is important is not the actual figures, but rather the broad orders of magnitude of the results. For this exercise, I classified household income into three types: labor income, capital income, and transfer income. For Japan, this classification is appropriate because of its income tax system, which taxes incomes separately by source (see Table 7).[28]

TABLE 7

Composition of Japan's Household Saving, 1979-1981 (conjectural exercise)

Income type		Before-tax income, ρ_i	Average tax rate, t_i	Aftertax income, $(1 - t_i)\rho_i$	Average saving rate, s_i	Saving, $s_i(1 - t_i)\rho_i$	Percent of total saving
1. Labor		.571[a]	.080[b]	.525[b]	.140[b]	.074[b]	41%
2. Capital		.237[a]	.140	.203	.374	.076	42
3. Transfer and							
other	a	.031[a]	.000[c]	.031[c]	1.000[c]	.031[c]	17
	b	.161[a]	.000[c]	.161[c]	.000[c]	.000[c]	0
TOTAL		1.000[a]	.080[a]	.920[a]	.197[a]	.181[a]	100%

[a] Observed value.
[b] Conjectural value, based on some evidence.
[c] Conjectural value, assumed.

Labor income. Labor income is the total of wages and salaries less employee contributions to social security (which are nontaxable). Income taxes, both national and local, are withdrawn at the source from paychecks. Property income, such as interest and dividends, is either wholly exempt from tax (under the small-saver tax-exemption program)[29] or separately taxed at the source at a flat rate, justifying the segregation of labor and property income.

Capital income. This classification covers proprietors' income and property income. Proprietors are classed as quasi corporations in the income tax code, and their incomes (after the exclusion of wages and salaries to themselves and family labor) are taxed as corporate income. For this reason, proprietors' income can be lumped together with property income. Property income consists of interest, dividends, and rent receipts. Under the small-saver tax-exemption system, a large part of interest and dividend incomes is not subject to taxation (legally or illegally),[30] with the residual being taxed at the source at a flat rate.[31] Imputed rent on owner-occupied dwellings (net of capital consumption) is excluded here from capital income.

Transfer income. Transfer payments such as social security benefits, social assistance grants, employer contributions to private pension funds, and imputed rent are included in this classification, and interest on consumer debt is deducted. Although social security benefits are a major source of disposable income for the retired and are taxable in Japan, it is likely that these benefits usually lie below the taxable limit, and savings from this type of income are probably small. It may be assumed that no tax and no saving are made out of social assistant grants to the poor and indigent. Imputed rent is free of tax and consumed fully. These entries are lumped together as the second component (3b) of "transfer and other income" in Table 7. Employer contributions to private pension funds, which, by definition, are not taxed or consumed,[32] are entered independently under 3a.

The composition of household income after these manipulations is shown in Table 7. In order to determine the aftertax income by source, the individual tax rates must be known, in addition to the average tax rate for the sector. I assumed above that the tax on income type 3 (t_3) is zero as a first approximation. If either t_1 or t_2 is known, the other can be determined residually. Since income tax on wages and salaries is withdrawn at the source, t_1 can be determined from tax statistics. As reported elsewhere,[33] it has been found that t_1 closely approximates t. Based on this fact, I have set t_1 equal to t, or 8 per cent; therefore, t_2 equals 14 per cent. The t_2 rate is low but by no means implausible since a large part of interest and dividend income is nontaxable.

The same steps must be repeated with respect to saving. The sectoral average of s is known. I assumed that s_{3a} is equal to 1 and s_{3b} is equal to 0. Then, if either s_1 or s_2 is known, the other can be determined residually. The NIPA definition of s_1 is estimated at 14 per cent in the FIES, leaving an assumed value of 37 per cent for s_2. In interpreting the size of s_2, note that the retired households may spend their accumulated savings. Their dissaving is netted out of saving from capital income.

The last column of Table 7 shows the composition of saving by type of income. The proportion of employer contributions to private pension funds is sizable; of the remainder, labor income and capital income claim about equal shares of saving. Thus, saving by worker households is an important component of total personal saving. In contrast to ordinary worker households in the United States, those in Japan save a considerable amount, accounting in part for the high personal saving ratio in Japan.[34]

Income Tax and Saving

When the proposed implementation of the green card system was hotly debated a few years ago,[35] the main controversy centered on whether the discontinuation of the small-saver tax-exemption program would reduce saving. It was feared that the expected increase in tax revenue might sap economic vitality. In general, it is believed that a heavier tax on household income discourages saving.[36] Is this supposition correct?

An increase in taxes on labor income (t_1) naturally reduces disposable income. If the stream of lifetime disposable income retains its initial time profile, consumption is reduced by an equal proportion. Therefore, the ratio of saving to disposable income remains virtually unchanged, and saving from labor income (s_1) is not likely to be greatly affected.

A rise in taxes on capital income (t_2) also reduces disposable income. If the savings of small savers are mostly for retirement and saving out of property income is earmarked for that purpose, they may find it necessary to raise their saving ratio out of capital income. However, for large savers interested in saving for saving's sake—namely, to accrue wealth as a status symbol—the heavier tax bite deteriorates their relative wealth position. In the face of such an unwelcome development, they may decide to increase savings. As s_2 increases, saving out of before-tax income may remain unchanged.[37] Therefore, the expected adverse effects of an increased tax on saving may be minimal.

Social Security and Saving

It was once widely believed that Japanese households tended to save for old age because of Japan's underdeveloped social security system.

Now that the social system has attained a respectable position in the national economy, has total saving declined?

It is argued that since the social security system provides spendable income to households after retirement, social security contributions made during working years substitute for private saving. The national accounting convention excludes social security contributions (by employers and employees) from household income and saving figures. Therefore, all things being equal, an increase in households' social security saving should be accompanied by a reduction in personal saving.

There are at least two reservations to this intuitive argument. First, although an increase in social security contributions may reduce working households' personal saving, an increase in social security benefits helps retired worker households to reduce dissaving. It is therefore not entirely clear whether total saving is thereby reduced or raised. Second, the availability of social security benefits may induce workers to retire early. Workers may then be encouraged to increase their saving during their working years to make up for a shorter working life. These two opposing effects may or may not lower the personal saving ratio.[38]

It seems, especially in Japan, that empirical evidence is not yet conclusive on the effect of social security on saving.[39] I tentatively conclude that the development of social security has had a relatively minor effect, if any, on the personal saving ratio. Other factors must have exerted an overridingly strong influence on saving.

Popular Saving Hypotheses

How can the movement of Japan's personal saving ratio over time, as seen in Fig. 2, be explained? This question has proved to be a challenging topic that has attracted many explanations by economists. Here, I discuss two of the principal hypotheses found in the empirical literature—the permanent income hypothesis and the bonus hypothesis. For other views, readers are referred to the competent surveys available elsewhere.[40]

The permanent income hypothesis. This hypothesis has been applied extensively in econometric literature. Its simplest version states that consumption is a certain proportion (k) of permanent income (Y^p) Thus, saving (S), which is a residual from current income (Y), is given by $S = Y - kY^p$. The saving ratio then is $s = 1 - kY^p/Y$. If expectations are adaptive, Y^p falls short of Y when Y has been growing at a high rate,[41] leading to a rise in s. In other words, households are slow to adjust their consumption level when income is rising rapidly. This argument may account for the rise in the saving ratio experienced through the rapid growth period. However, as the rise continued, there must have been a corresponding fall in k—the propensity to consume out of permanent income. Reasons for this fall are not properly explained.[42] Conversely, when income growth slows, the saving ratio should fall relatively swiftly. The fall in *s*, however, has been comparatively slow since the mid-1970s. It seems that the permanent income hypothesis is too simplistic to explain the changes in household saving behavior in Japan.[43]

The bonus hypothesis. Another popular explanation for Japan's high personal saving ratio is the well-known bonus hypothesis. This hypothesis, often favored by the general public, maintains that Japan's worker households save mainly from their semiannual bonuses. Studies comparing the proportion of bonuses in total annual earnings have found a strong covariation between this proportion and the household saving ratio.[44] Many economists favor this hypothesis.[45]

Bonuses are paid twice a year, in summer and winter, and on average amount to a couple months' salary. These payments make family budgeting easier, given the pronounced seasonality in household spending for summer and winter festivities, as well as the custom of exchanging gifts among relatives, friends, close business associates, and clients. Although bonuses were originally a reward for meritorious service, the actual practice today is to base bonuses on monthly pay. For civil servants, this proportion is stipulated by law. In private companies, however, it varies from year to year. The proportion is determined by collective bargaining and is positively related to each company's performance.

According to the bonus hypothesis, these fluctuations or uncertainties endow bonuses with the characteristics of transitory income with respect to the permanent income hypothesis. Wage earners consider regular wages and salaries to be permanent or normal income and use them primarily for regular consumption, thereby aligning regular monthly expenditures with regular monthly paychecks. Workers consider bonuses to be supernumerary income and allocate this income substantially to saving. Whatever they save, therefore, is saved out of their semiannual bonuses.[46]

In response to positive business performance during the rapid growth period, the size of bonus payments increased at a faster rate than did regular wages. Thus, the proportion of bonuses to total annual earnings rose steadily until 1974. For the opposite reason, it has been falling since then, and the saving ratio of worker households has followed suit. The bonus hypothesis, therefore, seemingly explains the saving behavior of Japanese workers.

Bonus payments may make it psychologically and practically easier for workers to save by eliminating the necessity for self-discipline in budgeting.[47] But it would be an error to insist that bonuses are therefore the primary source of saving. If the bonus system were eliminated, workers would be forced to be much stricter in their monthly budgeting but would continue to save as much as before, as long as their need to save remained as powerful. The bonus hypothesis appears to mistake form for substance.[48]

Why then have the personal saving ratio and the bonus-earnings ratio covaried so closely? Yutaka Kosai and Yoshitaro Ogino offer an intriguing explanation.[49] Knowing that it is easier to save out of bonuses, workers opt to save more out of bonus payments than out of regular wages as a portion of given income. This explanation, however, misses an important point—the bonus–earnings ratio itself has changed in response to changes in economic conditions, especially the tightness of the labor market. Faced with a shortage of labor, firms offered greater bonuses to attract more workers. In such a situation, the firm's productive capacities tend to be fully utilized, providing the wherewithal to pay bonuses. The bonus–earnings ratio peaked in 1974, when the labor market was at its tightest. The saving decisions of worker households must have been influenced by the same set of influences that determined the bonus–earnings ratio. In other words, the covariation between the saving ratio and the bonus–earnings ratio does not necessarily imply that one determines the other, but that the two ratios may have been simultaneously influenced by common factors.[50]

The Target Wealth Hypothesis

Neither the permanent income hypothesis nor the bonus hypothesis satisfactorily explains household saving behavior. I propose that the target wealth hypothesis—individuals save in order to attain a certain target of wealth relative to income—better explains the character of household saving in Japan. The steady rise in the target wealth–income ratio in Japan profoundly influenced the saving ratio, and changes in this ratio will determine future trends. This approach allows both financial saving and capital formation to be dealt with in a single framework of analysis, and the effect of capital gains on saving can also be easily taken into account. Furthermore, not only economic and demographic factors but also sociological and even cultural factors can be examined insofar as they affect the target wealth–income ratio.

The formal model. Each person sets a different wealth target (W^*) relative to current income (Y), depending on the stage in the life cycle and current economic status. These individual wealth targets can be aggregated relative to aggregate income, and the population as a whole saves as if to attain the target wealth. Let w^* be this aggregate target wealth–income ratio; that is $W^* = w^*Y$.[51] Note that w^*, as the average target wealth over all persons, may change in response to general trends in the desired target wealth–income ratio, as well as in response to compositional changes in the demographic, economic, and social characteristics of households.[52]

Disregarding capital gains for the moment, we have the identity $S_t \equiv \Delta W_t$, where W_t is the stock of wealth at the end of period t.[53] If the wealth target is instantaneously achieved, we have

$$S_t \equiv \Delta W_t = \Delta W^*_t = w^*_{t-1} \Delta Y_t + Y_t \Delta w^*_t$$

Dividing this relation by Y_t, we have

$$s_t = w^*_{t-1} (\Delta Y_t / Y_t) + \Delta w^*_t$$

where $s_t = S_t / Y_t$. In this simple case, the saving ratio depends on two factors: income growth and changes in target wealth. Thus, when the saving ratio rises while income growth is stable, the rise must be attributed to a steady increase in w^*. When income growth is deflected downward, the saving ratio may not fall as quickly since w^* continues to rise. This seems to describe events in Japan through the rapid growth period and the slow growth period. If wealth adjustment is relatively quick, the actual wealth–income ratio (w) closely follows the target wealth–income ratio (w^*).[54] Fig. 3 and Table 8 illustrate the changes in w over time.

Types of wealth. As wealth is not homogeneous, it is necessary to ex-

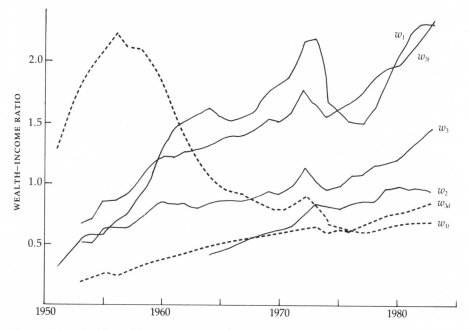

Fig. 3. Household wealth–income variables, 1981–1983. See Table 8 for explanation of variables.

TABLE 8

Japanese Household Net Worth, Yearend 1953-1983

	Fractions of household disposable income								
Year	(1) w_1	(2) w_2	(3) w_3	(4) w_{3f}	(5) w_{3d}	(6) $w_2 + w_3$	(7) w	(8) w_2	(9) P_2/P
1953	2.52		0.51	0.68	0.18				0.953
1954	2.75		0.50	0.71	0.21				0.962
1955	2.88		0.63	0.86	0.24				0.923
1956	3.13		0.64	0.87	0.24				0.952
1957	3.08		0.64	0.91	0.27				0.994
1958	3.24		0.71	1.02	0.31				0.981
1959	3.28		0.80	1.14	0.34				1.021
1960	3.38		0.85	1.22	0.37				1.035
1961	3.26		0.84	1.22	0.39				1.128
1962	3.11		0.83	1.26	0.43				1.113
1963	2.96		0.81	1.27	0.46				1.071
1964	2.88	0.41	0.84	1.32	0.48	1.25	4.13	0.38	1.064
1965	2.72	0.44	0.86	1.36	0.50	1.30	4.02	0.43	1.018
1966	2.64	0.48	0.86	1.39	0.53	1.34	4.00	0.47	1.021
1967	2.66	0.53	0.87	1.41	0.55	1.39	4.05	0.50	1.046
1968	2.67	0.56	0.89	1.46	0.57	1.45	4.12	0.54	1.030
1969	2.76	0.59	0.94	1.54	0.60	1.53	4.29	0.58	1.024
1970	2.80	0.62	0.93	1.51	0.59	1.55	4.35	0.62	1.007
1971	2.88	0.65	0.99	1.60	0.62	1.63	4.51	0.67	0.967
1972	3.30	0.76	1.15	1.79	0.64	1.90	5.20	0.69	1.101
1973	3.27	0.84	1.02	1.66	0.64	1.86	5.13	0.69	1.208
1974	2.62	0.81	0.95	1.54	0.59	1.76	4.39	0.75	1.068
1975	2.46	0.80	0.98	1.61	0.63	1.78	4.24	0.80	1.000
1976	2.32	0.84	1.07	1.67	0.61	1.91	4.23	0.85	0.997
1977	2.29	0.85	1.08	1.75	0.67	1.93	4.22	0.89	0.955
1978	2.41	0.87	1.15	1.85	0.70	2.02	4.44	0.92	0.947
1979	2.69	0.97	1.18	1.94	0.75	2.16	4.85	0.95	1.026
1980	2.89	0.98	1.21	1.97	0.76	2.19	5.08	0.98	1.002
1981	3.11	0.97	1.30	2.09	0.79	2.27	5.38	1.00	0.974
1982	3.20	0.97	1.39	2.21	0.82	2.36	5.56	1.01	0.963
1983	3.17	0.95	1.46	2.33	0.87	2.41	5.58	1.01	0.945

SOURCES: Japan, Economic Planning Agency, *Annual Report on National Income Statistics, 1978* and *Annual Report on National Accounts, 1985*; Mitsuo Saitō and Takashi Ōga, "Kakei no shisan juyō hōteishiki no keisoku" (Estimation of household asset demand equations), *Keizai bunseki*, No. 68 (Oct. 1977), pp. 1-34. 1969-1983, based on Economic Planning Agency (1985); 1953-1968, (1) see table 7, (2) extrapolated by the household sector's gross capital formation, (4) and (5) extrapolated by *Flows of Funds* data reported in Saitō and Ōga (1977).

NOTATION: (1) land, consisting of w_{1f} (farmland) and w_{1u} (urban residential land). (2) tangible reproducible assets. (3) net financial assets (4-5). (4) gross financial assets (equities at market value). (5) debt. (6) (2) + (3). (7) total wealth (1 + 6). (8) (2)/(9). (9) P_2 (implicit asset deflator)/P (implicit consumption expenditure deflator).

amine its major components separately. In this analysis, I distinguish three components, namely; land (w_1), which consists of farmland (w_{1f}) and urban residential land (w_{1u}); tangible reproducible assets (w_2), which consist of dwellings and business assets of noncorporate businesses; and net financial assets (w_3), the difference between gross financial assets (w_{3f}) and debt (w_{3d}). These components of wealth are divided by household disposable income to yield the respective wealth–income ratios.

In analyzing changes in w, it is necessary to consider capital gains (KG). The identity $S_t + KG_t \equiv \Delta W_t$ gives the following relation:

$$\Delta w_t = s_t + x_t - w_{t-1} (\Delta Y_t / Y_t),$$

where $x_t = KG_t / Y_t$. (All variables are in nominal terms.) Thus, capital gains raise the actual wealth–income ratio without any saving. The degree of appreciation that can be accredited to capital gains varies by type of asset. For land, the new supply is negligible; observed changes in w_1 can be attributed almost entirely to capital gains. For reproducible physical assets, capital gains result from general inflation. Changes in w_2 therefore are attributed only marginally to capital gains and primarily to increases in supply. For financial assets and debt, capital gains have been nominal because these financial instruments are almost wholly of fixed-claim types and are susceptible to erosion in value during inflation.

Land. Changes in w_1 exhibit somewhat complicated patterns.[55] It was at a peak in 1960 and, after a fall, peaked once again in 1972–73. A subsequent decline and comeback followed. These changes arose as a composite of two components: farmland and urban land (see Table 9).

With respect to farmland, w_{1f} peaked in the mid-1950s and has declined steadily ever since, except in 1972–73. A simple explanation for this phenomenon is that the total area of farmland has declined only slightly over time. The price of farmland recovered rapidly in the early 1950s, because of the land reform initiated by the Occupation forces, from its very depressed level after World War II. Thus, the value of farmland increased far more rapidly than household income. However, the increases slowed to the pace of the general price index. Since real household income was expanding, w_{1f} steadily declined. The small hump in 1972–73 was the outcome of the land speculation boom caused by the Plan for the Remodeling of the Japanese Archipelago of Prime Minister Kakuei Tanaka.

In contrast, the ratio of urban (residential) land to household income, w_{1u}, exhibited a strong upward trend until 1973. An explanation for this phenomenon is that the population, forced back to rural areas after World War II, began to return to the cities, in particular, to the three metropolitan areas of Tokyo-Yokohama, Kyoto-Osaka-Kobe, and Nagoya. The three areas together account for only 10 per cent of the total area but

TABLE 9

Land–Income Ratios, Japanese Households, Yearend 1951-1983

Year	(1) Private urban land/ household Total (m²)	Residential (m²)	(2) Land-income ratio Residential	Farmland[a]	Subtotal	Total	(3) Households + nonprofit institutions
1951	304		0.31	1.28	1.59		
1952	300		0.42	1.55	1.97		
1953	299		0.53	1.81	2.34		
1954	299		0.56	1.99	2.55		
1955	298		0.57	2.10	2.67		
1956	293		0.68	2.22	2.90		
1957	291		0.75	2.11	2.86		
1958	287		0.89	2.11	3.00		
1959	284		1.03	2.00	3.04		
1960	286		1.32	1.81	3.13		
1961	283		1.47	1.55	3.02		
1962	281		1.53	1.35	2.88		
1963	288		1.58	1.16	2.74		
1964	289		1.63	1.04	2.67		
1965	291		1.56	0.96	2.52		
1966	290		1.52	0.93	2.45		
1967	291		1.55	0.93	2.47		
1968	293		1.62	0.86	2.48		
1969	299		1.75	0.80	2.56	2.72	2.76
1970	304		1.82	0.79	2.61	2.76	2.80
1971	306		1.89	0.80	2.69	2.83	2.88
1972	314		2.17	0.91	3.08	3.25	3.30
1973	322		2.19	0.86	3.05	3.22	3.27
1974	325	213	1.68	0.67	2.36	2.51	2.62
1975	332	216	1.61	0.65	2.26	2.42	2.46
1976	333	217	1.52	0.61	2.13	2.28	2.32
1977	334	216	1.51	0.59	2.10	2.25	2.29
1978	335	216	1.62	0.61	2.22	2.38	2.41
1979	333	216	1.85	0.64	2.49	2.65	2.69
1980	332	215	2.03	0.66	2.69	2.84	2.89
1981	331	214	2.23	0.68	2.91	3.06	3.10
1982	329	212	2.31	0.69	3.00	3.15	3.18
1983			2.31	0.67	2.98	3.12	3.17

SOURCES: (1) Japan, Office of the Prime Minister, Bureau of Statistics, *Japan Statistical Yearbook*, various issues. (2-3) 1969-83, computed from Japan, Economic Planning Agency, *Annual Report on National Accounts, 1985*, and earlier issues; 1951-68, land values estimated by the product of land area and land price index, spliced to the 1969 benchmark values, original data from *Japan Statistical Yearbook*.

NOTES: In (2-3), land is the market value, income is household disposable income where households include nonprofit institutions. Except for (3), land refers to that owned by households excluding nonprofit institutions. In (2), farmland includes pastures, etc., total includes forests.

nearly half of the population (36 per cent in 1955 and 47 per cent in 1984). As people migrated into the narrow Pacific Coastal Belt Area, farmland was converted into residential sites. The continuous demand for new residential land forced urban land prices up at an astronomical rate, especially during the rapid growth period. The land speculation boom raised urban land prices sky-high in 1972–73. The bubble broke in 1974, and urban land prices declined for the first time—in the midst of double-digit inflation. A lull followed for the next few years since the housing demand was low. A recovery in w_{1u} began in 1977.

This brief explanation of the movements of w_{1f} and w_{1u} clearly indicates that the fundamental determinant of changes in them is industrialization and urbanization. They are, however, essentially determined by demand; w_1 is only indirectly the result of accumulation. Rather, the process of accumulation is conditioned by w_1 (see below).[56]

Physical assets. The physical assets of the household sector consist of dwellings (50 per cent), buildings and structures used by unincorporated businesses (30 per cent), and other business assets including inventories (20 per cent). As a first approximation, let us identify w_2 with housing. The relative price of real assets remained secularly stable (see Table 9). Therefore, the persistent increase in w_2 in the past two decades is mostly the result of real increases. The average size of dwellings has increased only moderately.[57] Therefore, the real increase in w_2 resulted primarily from more expensive buildings of the same size—namely, from more costly qualitative improvements.[58] Needless to say, such improvements were made possible by rising income.

Yet, as I noted above, Japan has a long way to go before housing conditions reach the level of North America and Europe. Since the over-congestion of metropolitan areas will continue, it is unlikely that the average size of dwelling units will expand dramatically. The Japanese must continue to live in "rabbit hutches."[59] They can and will spend more on furnishings and the like,[60] but definitely not on additional space.

Financial assets. Both total assets and liabilities have increased, the former more than the latter—resulting in an increase in the difference denoted by w_3. For worker households, the Family Saving Survey reveals that most debt arises from housing loans. Furthermore, w_{3d} has been roughly of the same order of magnitude as w_2. Changes in w_3 represent the household sector's net lending to the rest of the economy.

As for gross financial assets in general, the ratio of assets required for transactions (currency and demand deposits) to household income has been stable. Ownership of corporate equities (at market value) has, however, declined steadily over time. The observed increase in w_{3f} is attributable to holdings of time deposits, long-term securities, and life insurance equity.

Having examined each w independently, let us consider them together. Since w_1 is primarily demand determined, it should be excluded
from total w in considering the wealth target. However, w_2 and w_3 are
supply determined. Although w_2 stopped increasing in 1979, w_3 continued to rise even in the depressed conditions of recent years. I argue
that w_3 has been rising (as a target) partly because of the continued increase in w_1 and partly because of the demographic transition occurring
in Japan.[61] The rise in households' equity in social security has apparently had no detectable effect on private saving. As long as w^* continued
to rise, s fell only slowly even when income growth slowed. This accounts for the relatively sluggish downward adjustment in s since 1974.

Housing demand, wealth target, and saving behavior. Subject to life-cycle
phases,[62] the two major incentives for worker households to save are
housing and retirement.[63]

The first need arises in workers' early to mid-careers. Japanese families
strongly desire to live in their own house even though housing is expensive. The proportion of owner-occupied dwelling to all dwellings has
steadily been slightly above 60 per cent, a level comparable to that in the
United States where homeownership was until recently easier. In Japan,
a house and its site are as a rule one package. This, of course, makes the
unit price of a dwelling extremely high relative to income.[64] By the same
token, homeownership is not only a good hedge against inflation but
also a good investment as long as land values are expected to continue
rising. In any event, ordinary citizens tend to buy houses (if they ever
buy) in their thirties and forties. For that purpose, they must have sufficiently large financial savings beforehand because of the relatively high
down payments required.[65] And, once a house is bought on mortgage,
repayment of the principal constitutes an important reason for household saving.[66]

Most new houses are built on residential sites converted from farmland. A substantial part of the proceeds accrues to the sellers of land
(primarily farmers in the metropolitan suburbs). Because of the continued increases in land prices, they have become wealthy. Thus, financial assets are transferred from the relatively poor to the relatively rich.
The latter enjoy more income and wealth. Through this process, w_{3f}
tends to move along with w_{1u} and w_2 (see Fig. 3). From these observations, one can conclude that land prices (relative to the CPI) are a good
explanatory variable of the personal saving ratio.[67]

Why then has w^* (excluding land) continued to rise? Initially in the
1950s, as households attempted to recover what they had lost in the postwar confusion, w^* was set high (by the standard prevailing at that time).
While w was catching up to that level, s continued to rise. Once the target was achieved in the early 1960s, s stabilized for a while. However, the

rapid growth period began, and population migration intensified. Not only the very young but also middle-aged farmers began to move to the cities in this decade. This mass exodus of the population from rural areas is reflected in the resurgence of w_{1u} following the mid-1960s. Real income growth gave rise to a strong demand for improved housing, and residential land prices soared. This led to another round of saving. Household capital formation accounts for about half of household gross saving—the two tend to move together. Interestingly enough, the collapse of the land speculation boom in 1974 is reflected in a similar fall in w_3. However, the demand for wealth soon recovered, and w^* returned to its upward path.[68]

Saving for retirement. Provision for old age is an important component of w_3. This component involves a timing problem. A plausible life-cycle sequence is that a working family first saves for acquisition of housing—possibly while the spouses are in their thirties or so. In the meantime, children grow up, and paying for their college education eats up much of the household income when the parents are in the late forties and early fifties. Finally by their late fifties, the couple is free of major financial obligations. Sizable separation allowances received at the time of mandatory retirement (now more often at 60 years of age than 55) add to the family nest egg. The worker often moves on to a second career. Social security and pension benefits help the couple into retirement living. By the time the life cycle is complete, the household has barely broken even apart from housing ownership.[69] Now that people live longer, they have to increase their means of support. They must be supported either by themselves, by their children, or by their fellow citizens.

To achieve self-support, old people must have ample employment opportunities. The mandatory retirement age has been rising from the traditional 55 to 60 in nearly half of the firms enforcing mandatory retirement. Still, following mandatory retirement, second careers are needed for reasonable self-help. As noted earlier, old workers still work in substantial numbers in paying jobs. There will be more old people looking for jobs. Will there be enough job openings for them?

There have been substantial modifications in the seniority (*nenkō*) wage system in recent years, as firms began to extend the length of "life-time" employment. Obviously, senior workers are more expensive than new employees, even though their wages are often frozen or even debased when they are past the former mandatory age. Firms have coped with this development in a number of ways. One is to lower the tilt of the age-wage profile, relative to the entry pay, so that older people are no longer paid as much as before. The other is to reduce severance pay.[70] These changes imply that workers have to modify the life-cycle sequence and reconsider their long-term consumption-saving plan.

The family system in Japan is in a state of transition. Even though three-generation families remain a dominant mode of family life in Japan, unlike in America and Europe,[71] the trend toward the nuclear family has been proceeding slowly but steadily.[72] Even when parents live with their grown children, budgeting is often separate, and they sometimes have separate living quarters under the same roof.[73] Mass-media columnists advise the elderly against depending on their children's spontaneous support.

As the dependency ratio is expected to rise, the working population must support an increasingly larger number of retired workers. The social security burden on workers will rise to an intolerable level if the present benefit level is maintained. A debasement in the benefit structure is inevitable if the social security system is to remain solvent.

Predicting the saving ratio. Under the target wealth hypothesis, the saving ratio is subject to long-term influences—the growth rate of nominal income and changes in the target wealth–income ratio. In 1979–83, household disposable income increased at an average rate of 6 per cent per annum (2 per cent in real terms and 4 per cent in the consumption deflator). Barring any unforeseen events (such as another oil shock), this average growth rate may be expected to continue in the foreseeable future. The wealth–income ratio (excluding land) was 2.4 in 1983. If this ratio remains unchanged, the saving ratio would be 14 per cent because of the long-term growth of income. An observed saving ratio above this level must result from a concurrent rise in the target wealth–income ratio pursued by households in general.

In order to predict the behavior of w^* in the future, the individual components of w must be considered. As for the land value (w_1), the population influx into metropolitan areas has virtually ended,[74] and the natural increase in the population has slowed.[75] In view of these developments, the demand for new residential sites will not be as strong as previously, and urban land prices will rise only slowly. Under these circumstances, increases in w_{1u} will slow even more. In fact, urban residential land prices reached such a high level that new housing demand was depressed, and w_2 has been stationary since 1979.

Changes in net financial assets (w_3) will be crucial, therefore, in influencing changes in the target wealth–income ratio. Over the past ten years, w_3 has been on an upward trend, surpassing the European level but still below that of the United States (see Table 3).[76] Can w_3 be expected to continue to rise? Some factors, particularly those related to the demographic transition Japanese society is experiencing, are important in this regard. It is anticipated that life-cycle needs will change as people begin to live longer. However, life-cycle factors are double-edged, having both positive and negative effects on household saving.

As the population ages, workers must save more to prepare for a longer expected retirement life. They cannot expect as much family support as before in view of the continued erosion of the traditional family system; and since social security benefits are expected to be less generous, they cannot depend as heavily on public support. How much a worker saves depends on how long he expects to continue working. Employment in a second career after the age of 60 depends on future job opportunities for the elderly—which cannot be predicted with any certainty. Corresponding to this positive effect of increased worker saving, the negative saving of retired workers will increase. The net effect may be an eventual downward pressure on the household saving ratio—a view currently gaining popularity in Japan. Another important issue is the tax reform expected to be undertaken in an attempt to balance the national budget.[77]

Business Saving and Investment

In the national accounts, unincorporated businesses are included in the household sector. The business sector, therefore, consists of corporations (both private and public), which can be further divided into financial and nonfinancial enterprises. Since certain arbitrary and artificial adjustments are made to the income-outlay accounts of financial corporations, it is difficult to perform ordinary economic analyses on their books. Therefore, the following analysis is restricted to the nonfinancial business sector.[78] The bulk of this analysis concentrates on the period from 1970 on because the extensive revision of NIPA data made the old and new series not readily comparable.

The Capital–Output Ratio, Capital's Share, and the Aggregate Production Function

The first estimate of the capital- output ratio in Table 10, for the nonfinancial business sector from 1970 to 1983, is the ratio of net fixed capital stock to GDP at factor cost, both in 1975 prices. The second, for the secondary sector extending further back in time, is the ratio of gross fixed capital stock to GDP in purchasers' value, both in 1975 prices. The two estimates exhibit quite comparable movements over the overlapping years (see Fig. 4),[79] thus allowing us to study the movements of the capital–output ratio since the mid-1950s. The ratio fell through the late 1950s, stabilized through the 1960s (though with a small rise in the first half and a small fall in the second half), rose sharply from 1970 to 1975, and then stabilized at a higher level.

Capital's share is the ratio of gross returns on capital (defined as the sum of the consumption of fixed capital and operating surplus) to GDP

TABLE 10
The Capital–Output Ratio (K/Y) and Capital's Share (P/Y), Japan, 1955-1983

	Nonfinancial corporations		Secondary sector		
Year	K/Y	P/Y	K/Y	P/Y	
1955			1.80	0.412	
1956			1.62	0.423	
1957			1.51	0.459	
1958			1.64	0.436	
1959			1.52	0.438	
1960			1.42	0.479	
1961			1.39	0.489	
1962			1.48	0.467	
1963			1.51	0.468	
1964			1.49	0.466	0.518
1965			1.58	0.443	0.498
1966			1.54	0.447	0.502
1967			1.46	0.462	0.515
1968			1.44	0.478	0.529
1969			1.44	0.481	0.534
1970	1.19	0.487	1.42	0.481	0.533
1971	1.34	0.456	1.51	0.455	0.496
1972	1.33	0.447	1.56	0.443	0.484
1973	1.41	0.425	1.54	0.414	0.474
1974	1.52	0.377	1.71	0.374	0.438
1975	1.57	0.347	1.82		0.401
1976	1.56	0.349	1.77		0.409
1977	1.58	0.354	1.79		0.408
1978	1.54	0.357	1.76		0.427
1979	1.53	0.349	1.72		0.426
1980	1.48	0.357	1.68		0.429
1981	1.48	0.346	1.70		0.429
1982	1.49	0.345	1.72		0.420
1983	1.52	0.343	1.72		0.409

SOURCES AND NOTES: *Nonfinancial corporations,* K = net fixed capital stock (end of year), from Japan, Economic Planning Agency, *Annual Report on National Accounts, 1985,* and earlier issues; Y = GDP at factor cost in 1975 prices, from K. Sato, "Shifts from high-growth to low-growth steady states . . .", mimeo., 1985; K/Y in 1975 prices; P = consumption of fixed capital + operating surplus; P/Y in current prices.

Secondary sector, (mining, manufacturing, construction, electricity/gas/water, transportation and communications), K = gross fixed capital stock (end of year), (installation basis), from Economic Planning Agency, *Gross Fixed Capital Stocks;* Y = GDP, taken from Economic Planning Agency, *Annual Report on National Accounts,* and OECD, *National Accounts, 1983,* and earlier issues; K/Y in 1975 prices; P = consumption of fixed capital + operation surplus, Y = P + employee compensation; P/Y in current prices. The earlier series for 1955-74 is from T. P. Hill, *Profits and Rates of Return* (Paris: OECD, 1979).

at factor cost. Capital's share has covaried inversely with the capital–output ratio over the past three decades, suggesting the existence of an aggregate production function.[80]

How can observed changes in the capital–output ratio and capital's share, especially in the first half of the 1970s, be explained? The two ratios together imply that the marginal product of capital (MPK) was considerably different in the years prior to 1970 from that after 1975. The MPK was higher before 1970 because firms attempted to economize on capital, which was in short supply.

In Japan, households' financial savings have been placed principally in bank deposits, postal savings, and life insurance policies. Financial institutions that served as depositories of personal savings made loans to borrowers—principally business firms. The government adopted a low-interest-rate policy immediately after World War II and placed ceilings on loan rates.[81] Thus, when an unusually strong demand for investment funds emerged in the 1960s, the demand for funds exceeded the supply of funds at the given maximum loan rate, and financial institutions engaged in credit rationing.[82] Since fewer funds were available than de-

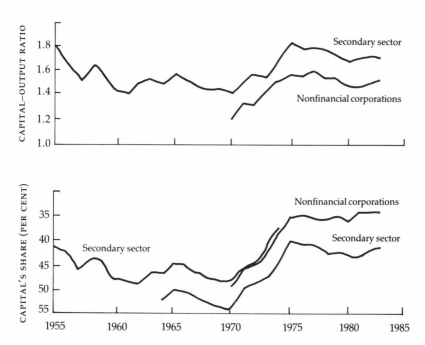

Fig. 4. The capital–output ratio and capital's share, 1955–1983.

sired, firms tried to keep their capital–output ratio low. The other side of this story is that the rate of return on capital was higher than the cost of capital.

The economy's growth rate began to decline in 1970. Hence, the demand for investment started to fall. The supply of saving, however, continued to rise. In the funds market, excess demand disappeared. With more funds available, firms could now raise their capital–output ratio. At the same time, industry faced an acute labor shortage, especially for new workers, since the agricultural labor force that had been the major source of new labor was nearly depleted.[83] The labor market became very tight, especially for new school graduates.[84] The labor shortage induced firms to substitute capital for labor, thereby tending to raise the capital–output ratio. This rise had already begun in 1970 and was completed by 1975, suggesting that contrary to popular belief, the oil shock did not cause this increase in capital intensity.[85]

Business Investment

While the capital–output ratio was rising through the early 1970s, the capital formation proportion was maintained at a higher level than would have otherwise been the case. To see this point, consider the following identity:

$$I/Y = \Delta(K/Y) + (K/Y)(\Delta Y/Y + \delta)$$

where I is gross fixed capital formation, K is net fixed capital stock, and δ the depreciation ratio. The identity shows that the amount of total output devoted to capital formation depends on (1) a change in the capital–output ratio, (2) the growth rate, and (3) the depreciation ratio, given the capital–output ratio. During the early 1970s, the positive change in K/Y averaged 8 percentage points per year. When fixed investment is maintained at a high level, the growth rate is sustained through the multiplier effect, even though the potential growth rate has been lowered. A high growth rate, in turn, generates investment demand through the accelerator effect.

The capital–output ratio cannot continue rising indefinitely. The marginal product of capital begins to decline. When it declines to a sufficiently low level consistent with the prevailing cost of funds, the capital–output ratio reaches a plateau, as occurred in 1975. Both the multiplier and accelerator effects cease to function. The growth rate is now constrained to the potential growth rate. I/Y now stabilizes at a lower level, although the higher capital–output ratio helps to make I/Y a little higher than might otherwise occur. A comparison of quinquennial average values of I/Y for the nonfinancial corporate sector and the entire

TABLE 11
*The Investment/GDP Ratio and the Growth Rate, Japan,
1960-1983*

Period	Investment/GDP ratio[a]		Growth rate[b]
	(1)	(2)	
1960-64	—	0.194	0.124
1965-69	—	0.180	0.116
1970-74	0.335	0.189	0.081
1975-79	0.255	0.150	0.052
1980-83	0.251	0.153	0.051

SOURCES: Japan, Economic Planning Agency, *Annual Report on National Income Statistics, 1978,* for 1960-64; idem, *Annual Report on National Accounts, 1985,* for later years.

[a](1) Gross capital formation/GDP at factor cost, in current prices both relating to the nonfinancial corporate sector. (2) Business gross fixed capital formation/GDP in purchase value, in current prices, all economy.

[b]Growth rate of GDP in 1975 prices, industry excluding agriculture.

economy shows that business investment continued to claim a constant share from the 1960s to 1974, despite a fall in the growth rate (see Table 11). Since 1975, both the growth rate and the capital formation proportion have declined to lower levels.

Business Profits and Saving

The rise in the capital–output ratio has brought drastic changes in corporate income statements. First, capital's share decreased. Capital's share of GDP at factor cost declined from 43.8 to 35.0 per cent between 1970–74 and 1975–83 (see Table 12). At the same time, consumption of fixed capital fell by 3 percentage points, even though the capital–output ratio rose, because of a substantial fall in the depreciation ratio (from 12.2 per cent to 8.5 per cent).[86] Direct taxes maintained a stable fraction, although taxable corporate income (as a per cent of GDP) fell because of the continued rise in the corporate tax rate. Since Japanese firms borrow heavily, they make sizable interest and rental payments. Since interest rates remained stable throughout the period under study (except during the oil shock years), the net property income paid by firms claimed a stable proportion of corporate GDP. Subtracting these items and an additional entry for miscellaneous items from capital's share gives net profits. Net profits declined from 8.9 per cent to 3.0 per cent. This decline understates the actual fall in profitability since net profits fell rapidly through the early 1970s. Capital's share fell from 46.8 per cent in 1960–69 to 43.3 per cent in 1970–74 in the secondary sector (see Table 10). Thus, the fall in the share of net profits must have been from a little over 12 per cent in the 1960s to 3 per cent in 1975–83.[87]

Net profits (NP) are divided between dividends and corporate saving (CS). Dividends not only were a relatively small fraction of GDP because of the relative unimportance of equity financing but also changed relatively little over the years. This means that corporate saving took the full brunt of the fall in net profits (see Table 13). Movements in corporate saving may be explained by net profits and net worth (NW). After adjusting for time lags, the following relation is derived:[88]

$$CS/GDP = .813 \; NP/GDP - .034 \; NW/GDP + .068$$

This equation shows that a decrease in corporate profits leads to a reduction in corporate saving, almost yen for yen, and that an increase in net

TABLE 12

Capital's Share, Nonfinancial Corporate Sector, Japan,
1970-1983
(per cent of GDP)

Capital's share	1970-74	1975-83
Consumption of fixed capital	16.5%	13.6%
Operating surplus		
Direct taxes	6.4%	6.1%
Property income, paid − received		
− dividends paid	11.5	12.1
Miscellaneous	.4	.2
Net profits	8.9	3.0
Total	27.3%	21.4%
Gross operating surplus	43.8%	35.0%

SOURCES: Japan, Economic Planning Agency, *Annual Report on National Accounts, 1985* and earlier issues. For GDP, see K. Sato, "Shift from high-growth to low-growth steady states . . .", mimeo. 1985.

TABLE 13

Net Profits, Dividends, Saving, Net Investment, and Net Worth, Nonfinancial
Corporate Sector, Japan, 1970-1983
(per cent of GDP at factor cost)

Period	Net profits	Dividends	Saving	Net investment	Net worth
1970-74	8.9%	3.7%	5.3%	25.8%	226%
1975-79	3.0	2.7	0.5	12.9	218
1980-83	2.9	2.2	0.8	12.8	238

SOURCES: Same as Table 12.

worth gives rise to a fall in saving because of an increase in dividend payments. Corporate saving claimed as much as 12 per cent of corporate GDP in 1970 but fell to less than 1 per cent on average over the past decade. Since the depression of profits has persisted, the low level of corporate saving has become chronic.[89]

Rates of Return

It is useful to compute realized rates of return in order to show how depressed business profits have been. For this exercise, the structure of corporate finance becomes important. Total assets are equal to the sum of a firm's liabilities and its net worth. A firm does not employ all of its assets in its operation, but lends some on the outside, corresponding to the nonmonetary financial assets that the firm holds. The firm's balance sheet is thus represented by total assets less nonmonetary financial assets (1A) = net worth (2A) + liabilities (3A) − nonmonetary financial assets (4A). Correspondingly, its income statement would be operating surplus after tax (1B) = net profits (2B) + interest and rentals paid (3B) − property income received (4B).

Let us define four rates as follows: r_1 = 1B/1A = aftertax rate of return on total assets less nonmonetary financial assets; r_2 = 2B/2A = aftertax rate of return on net worth; i_d = 3B/3A = implicit rate of interest on liabilities; and i_a = 4B/4A = implicit rate of interest on nonmonetary financial assets. The rate of return most closely related to the marginal product of capital in our production function analysis is r_1 except that monetary assets, inventories, and land are included. It is not r_1, but r_2, which is the rate of return on net worth after adjusting for payments and receipts of interest, that is compared with the net cost of funds. The following identity illustrates this point.

$$r_1 (\text{NW} + D - A) = r_2 \, \text{NW} + i_d D - i_a A$$

where NW is net worth, D is liabilities, and A nonmonetary financial assets. This adjustment is of particular importance in the case of Japanese firms because property income paid and received is a sizable wedge between r_1 and r_2.

Both i_d and i_a remained stable in the period under study (see Table 14); i_d has been around 6 per cent, slightly lower than the average bank loan rate.[90] In contrast, i_a has been about half of i_d, presumably reflecting the fact that interest rates charged on interfirm trade credits (about two-thirds of nonmonetary financial assets) have been kept below the market rates as a disguised subsidy to subcontractors.

Recall that the capital–output ratio rose and capital's share fell from the 1960s to the late 1970s. In that process, the marginal product of capital

TABLE 14
Rates of Return and Implicit Interest Rates, Nonfinancial Corporate Sector, Japan,
1970-1983

Period	r_1	r_2	i_d	i_a	D/NW	A/NW
1970-74	6.0%	4.1%	5.9%	3.5%	134%	81%
1975-79	4.5	1.4	6.0	3.3	138	80
1980-83	4.1	1.2	6.0	3.3	122	73

SOURCES: Japan, Economic Planning Agency, *Annual Report on National Accounts, 1985,* and earlier issues.

NOTATION: r_1, aftertax rate of return on total assets less nonmonetary financial assets. r_2, aftertax rate of return on net worth. i_d, implicit rate of interest on liabilities. i_a, implicit rate of interest on nonmonetary financial assets. NW, net worth. A, nonmonetary financial assets.

declined by nearly half (see Table 10). This fall is reflected in the fall of r_1, which also fell by half (r_1 was 8.6 per cent in 1970). Since i_d and i_a were stable during this period, the fall in r_1 was more than fully transmitted to a fall in r_2. The following identity illustrates this point more clearly.

$$r_2 = r_1 + (r_1 - i_d)D/NW - (r_1 - i_a)A/NW$$

which is derived from the preceding identity. Both $(r_1 - i_d)$ and $(r_1 - i_a)$ fell, but as D/NW was in excess of A/NW, the fall in r_2 was greater than the fall in r_1. In 1970, r_1 and r_2 were nearly equal at 8.6 and 8.0 per cent, respectively; r_2 probably exceeded r_1 in the 1960s. The severity of the profit squeeze became obvious when r_2 fell from above 10 per cent in the 1960s to a little over 1 per cent in recent years.

The Corporate Financial Structure

The analysis above is based on the NIPA, which make full adjustment to capital-asset valuation. Corporate balance sheets differ substantially from those reported by corporations and the reconstructed one given in the NIPA, principally because of the significant undervaluation of physical assets, especially land, which are recorded at original acquisition cost in corporations' financial records. The undervaluation is magnified far more in net worth than in total assets. This means that the realized rates of return recorded in the annual financial reports of corporations are overstated.[91]

A direct corollary is that debt is overstated in book values. The debt–asset ratio is as high as 85 per cent in Japan, compared with about 55 per cent in the United States. When assets are properly revalued, the ratio falls to around 45 per cent in both countries (see Table 15). Thus, in terms of stock, the composition of total assets is not much different today between Japanese and U.S. corporations.[92]

This does not mean that Japanese firms have ceased to depend as heavily on debt financing. An analysis of new flows of business funds by source reveals that internal sources became slightly more important in the early 1980s (see Table 16). But when depreciation charges are netted out, external sources have actually gained in importance because of the diminished role of retained profits. Financial institutions account for 90 per cent of external financing sources—a proportion that has not varied since the late 1960s.

It has often been noted that Japanese corporations have earned much less than U.S. corporations in recent years.[93] Such comparisons are in book values. When proper valuation adjustments are fully applied, the U.S.-Japan profit disparity is likely to be far greater. In fact, Japanese rates of return (r_2) may have been negative. How can such low rates of return be compatible with a viable business environment? How can capital formation be maintained even at the present level?

The reason gross capital formation has remained at a stable fraction of GDP since the mid-1970s under such adverse conditions may be sought in the sizable capital gains accruing to the firms' real assets—namely, inventory, fixed capital, and land. From 1975 to 1983, their price deflators increased at the annual average rates of 3.0, 3.3, and 11.5 per cent, respectively. When weighted (0.1:0.5:0.4), the average price increase was 6.6 per cent per annum. Since the ratio of real assets to net worth stands

TABLE 15
Financial Structure of Corporations, Japan and the United States, 1980
(per cent of total assets)

	Japan		United States	
Category	Current value[a]	Book value[b]	Current value[c]	Book value[b]
Assets				
Inventory	8%	17%	7%	14%
Net fixed capital	30	21	30	51
Land	25	6	12	8
Monetary	4	14	1	2
Nonmonetary financial	33	42	50	25
Total	100%	100%	100%	100%
Liabilities	45%	85%	44%	37%
Net worth	55%	15%	56%	63%

SOURCES: *Japan* (current value), Economic Planning Agency, *Annual Report on National Accounts, 1983;* (book value), Ministry of Finance, *Hojin kigyō tōkei nempō* (Corporate enterprise statistics annual), 1980. *United States* (current value), R. Ruggles and N. Ruggles, "Integrated Economic Accounts for the United States, 1947-80," *Survey of Current Business,* May 1982, pp. 1-53; (book value), Department of Commerce, *Statistical Abstract of the United States, 1984,* Nos. 903 and 904, p. 538.
    [a]Nonfinancial corporations (private and public).
    [b]Nonfinancial corporations (private).
    [c]All enterprises.

TABLE 16
*Net Supply of Industrial Funds to Private Japanese Nonfinancial Corporations,
by Source, 1965-1983*
(per cent)

Sources	1965-69	1970-74	1975-79	1980-83
Internal				
Depreciation	34.7%[a]	33.45%	46.8%	50.3%
Retained Profits	14.8[a]	9.7	5.6	4.1
Total	49.5%[a]	40.0%	51.9%	54.3%
External	50.4%[a]	57.0%	48.1%	45.7%
TOTAL	100.0%[a]	100.0%	100.0%	100.0%
External sources as per cent of total external				
Equity	6.0%	6.0%	7.0%	8.0%
Bonds	3.5	3.1	5.1	2.9
Financial institutions	90.5	91.0	87.8	89.1
Private	(81.2)	(82.9)	(74.5)	(78.3)
Public	(9.4)	(8.0)	(13.4)	(10.9)
TOTAL	100.0%	100.0%	100.0%	100.0%

SOURCES: Bank of Japan, *Economic Statistics Annual, 1984* (Mar. 1985) and earlier issues.
[a]1965.

at 1.1, capital gains amount to 7.2 per cent of net worth. This high rate of capital gain results primarily from land.

In the neo-classical theory of investment,[94] the marginal product of capital is equated to the user cost of funds. The user cost of funds consists of depreciation charges of fixed assets, corporate profit taxes, financial cost of borrowed funds, and adequate returns on invested funds. What may be considered an adequate rate of return on net worth is the real interest rate (nominal interest rate minus capital gains accruing to net worth). Thus, the user cost of funds depends, among other things, on the depreciation ratio, the corporate income tax rate, the loan interest rate, and the rate of real asset appreciation. Since interest cost (as well as depreciation cost) is nontaxable, the less sensitive the unit user cost is to the tax rate, the more heavily firms depend on borrowed funds.[95] In the case of Japanese firms, the corporate tax rate edged upward, but the interest rate remained stable. Firms still depend heavily on borrowed funds. The depreciation ratio as recorded in national accounts fell because of the neglect of valuation adjustments of capital assets; in reality, there was no such fall in capital consumption (see note 86). Components of the user cost attributable to these elements have therefore been more or less stable since the 1970s through the early 1980s. The only volatile element was capital gains. The rate of inflation (in the implicit GNP deflator) was 5.1 per cent in 1965–69, 8.4 per cent in 1970–74, 4.7 per cent in 1975–79, and 1.1 per cent in 1980–84. It follows that the user cost was sizable in the 1960s but fell sharply toward zero in the early 1970s and then rose to a high level in the early 1980s. The sharp increase in the capital–output ratio in the early 1970s must have owed much to this temporary fall in the user cost.

The Saving-Investment Balance in the Business Sector

In summary, the capital–output ratio rose and capital's share fell in the nonfinancial corporate sector during the early 1970s. As profits were squeezed, corporate saving fell sharply. The decline in the growth rate resulted in an even sharper fall in the capital formation proportion, despite the rise in the capital–output ratio. Hence, the sector's need for external funds diminished sharply in the late 1970s.

These findings also hold for the business sector when financial institutions are considered. Since financial institutions receive more income than they pay out, they are a source of funds.[96] Thus, in the business sector, the excess of investment over saving is further reduced, although the sector remains a net borrower. Over the past two decades, the business sector's net borrowing fell from 9 per cent of GDP in the early 1970s to 5 per cent after 1975 (see Table 17).

TABLE 17
Saving and Investment by Business Sector, Japan, 1965-1983
(per cent of GDP)

Sector	1965-69	1970-74	1975-79	1980-83
Nonfinancial				
Saving		3.0%	0.2%	0.4%
Consumption of fixed capital		9.7	8.0	8.2
Gross saving		12.7	8.2	8.6
Gross capital formation		21.5	15.4	15.4
Net lending		−10.2	−5.8	−5.9
Financial				
Saving		1.7%	1.0%	0.6%
Consumption of fixed capital		0.2	0.2	0.2
Gross saving		1.9	1.2	0.8
Gross capital formation		0.4	0.3	0.3
Net lending		1.3	0.9	0.8
Business				
Saving	5.0%	4.7%	1.2%	1.0%
Consumption of fixed capital	10.0	9.9	8.2	8.4
Gross saving	15.0	14.6	9.4	9.4
Gross capital formation	21.9	21.9	15.7	15.7
Net lending		−8.9	−4.9	−5.1

SOURCES: Japan, Economic Planning Agency, *Annual Report on National Accounts, 1985*; OECD, *National Accounts, 1983*.

In view of the stability of the proportions reported in Table 17, the business sector seems to have been in a steady state at a low level of economic growth since the mid-1970s. Both corporate saving and investment are related to the sector's aggregate production function. Hence, unless there is a drastic change in the latter, one cannot anticipate much further change in these proportions. Changes in the production function relate to the rate and bias of technical change. The center of gravity in the Japanese economy has been moving steadily toward the tertiary sector and away from the secondary sector. This so-called service revolution has two implications.[97] First, the rate of productivity growth will slow further because, traditionally, productivity growth has been much more limited in the tertiary sector than in the primary and secondary sectors. Second, the bias of technical change may also be affected by this shift in the industrial structure because the capital–output ratio varies considerably from industry to industry. A statistical examination reveals that the tertiary sector is much less capital-intensive.[98] Hence, all things being equal, the aggregate capital–output ratio may fall as the tertiary industries become a larger contributor to GDP. Developments that may offset this tendency are office automation, quality upgrading in service facilities, and the like. However, these may not be enough to maintain the aggregate capital–output ratio at its present level.

The Macroeconomic Balance

In order to complete this discussion of saving and investment in the Japanese economy, the saving and investment behavior of the government and the external sector must be discussed. For the economy as a whole, saving and investment are equal. This is not so at the various sector levels. For the domestic sectors, the identity for each sector is

Saving (S) + consumption of fixed capital (CFC)
= Gross capital formation (GCF) + net lending (NL) + adjusting items[99]

For the external sector, the corresponding identity is

Receipts on current account (X) − payments on current account (M)
= Net lending (NL) + adjusting items[100]

The investment-saving identity for the economy as a whole can be restated as an identity of net lendings in the domestic economy as a whole and the external sector (see Table 18). The same is true of adjusting items.

Before the mid-1970s, the household sector was a net lender and the business sector a net borrower of funds. The demand for and the supply of funds were near the equilibrium between these two sectors of the private economy. This may have been a primary factor in Japan's rapid

TABLE 18

Saving, Investment, and Net Lending by Sector, Japan, 1965-1983

(per cent of GDP, in current prices)

Sector	1965-69	1970-74	1975-79	1980-83	1980	1981	1982	1983
Household								
Saving	10.6%	13.5%	15.6%	13.6%	14.2%	14.3%	12.9%	12.8%
Consumption of fixed capital	3.1	3.4	4.3	5.0	4.9	4.9	5.0	5.1
Gross saving	13.7	16.9	19.9	18.6	19.1	19.2	17.9	17.9
Gross capital formation	8.6	10.1	10.6	8.9	9.8	9.0	8.7	8.0
Net lending		9.0	9.7	9.5	7.8	10.3	10.1	9.7
Business								
Saving	4.9%	4.7%	1.2%	1.0%	1.7	0.7	0.9	0.5
Consumption of fixed capital	10.0	9.8	8.2	8.4	8.0	8.2	8.5	8.9
Gross saving	14.9	14.5	9.4	9.4	9.7	8.9	9.4	9.4
Gross capital formation	21.9	21.9	15.7	15.7	16.0	15.9	15.9	15.0
Net lending		-8.9	-4.9	-5.1	-5.1	-5.4	-5.7	-4.1
Government								
Saving	5.5%	6.5%	2.3%	2.7%	2.6%	3.0%	2.8%	2.4
Consumption of fixed capital	0.5	0.4	0.5	0.7	0.6	0.6	0.7	0.7
Gross saving	6.0	6.9	2.8	3.4	3.2	3.6	3.5	3.1
Gross capital formation	4.4	5.2	5.7	6.0	6.2	6.2	5.9	5.6
Net lending		0.8	-4.2	-3.9	-3.8	-4.5	-3.7	-3.7
Domestic								
Saving	21.0%	24.7%	19.0%	17.2%	18.5%	18.0%	16.6%	15.7%
Consumption of fixed capital	13.6	13.7	13.0	14.0	13.5	13.7	14.2	14.7
Gross saving	34.6	38.4	32.0	31.2	32.0	31.7	30.8	30.4
Gross capital formation	34.9	37.2	32.0	30.8	32.0	31.1	30.5	28.6
Net lending	0.8	0.9	0.6	0.5	-1.1	0.5	0.7	1.8
External								
Receipts on current account	11.2%	12.0%	13.4%	16.1%	15.2%	16.6%	16.8%	15.8%
Payments on current account	10.1	11.1	12.8	15.6	16.2	16.1	16.1	14.0
Net lending	0.8	0.9	0.6	0.5	-1.1	0.5	0.7	1.8

SOURCES: Japan, Economic Planning Agency, *Annual Report on National Accounts, 1985;* OECD, *National Accounts, 1983.*

growth. Indeed, saving was growing faster *ex ante* than investment, as indicated by the gradual easing of credit rationing. I have argued that this longitudinal behavior of household saving is an outcome of industrialization and urbanization. The process of economic growth itself generated private saving in an amount sufficient to support the capital formation required to maintain that growth, as it did through the 1960s up to 1973 in Japan. Capital shortage, therefore, did not constrain growth.

Operating under the balanced-budget principle and benefiting from rapidly growing tax revenues, the general government maintained a small budget surplus. Since the private economy balanced saving and investment, the government budget surplus matched a surplus in the current account of the balance of payments. By the mid-1970s, this was no longer the case. As economic growth slowed, business investment fell sharply, and even though business saving fell, the business sector's net borrowing diminished greatly. In the household sector, the saving ratio started to decrease, primarily in the capital formation area. Hence, the household sector remained as much of a net lender as before, and saving came to exceed investment in the private economy.

Japan was at a critical turning point—from a neo-classical economy in which saving overwhelmed investment to a Keynesian economy in which investment conditions saving. In the latter, *ex ante* excess saving is eliminated by the reduction of aggregate supply and the emergence of large-scale involuntary unemployment. To avert unemployment, either the government must engage in deficit spending or capital must flow to overseas investments, thereby enabling the private economy to maintain its excess saving. In the late 1970s, the former solution seems to have been followed; in the early 1980s, the latter situation seems to have developed.[101]

The Government Sector

Although one effect of government deficits was to sop up excess saving in the private sector, this development was more a coincidence than an outcome of a deliberate stabilization policy. The emergence of government deficits was inevitable because of structural problems encountered under slowed growth.

First, there has been a strong upward pressure on the government's purchase of goods and services in both consumption and investment. Second, the economic activities of the government are often very labor intensive, and a large part of its expenditure goes to its wage bill. Even though the Japanese government maintained a relatively small public administration, its work force increased at a somewhat faster rate than the total labor force. At the same time, the wage scale of civil service jobs, especially those of local governments (accounting for 70 per cent of total government employment), continued to improve at a faster rate than the wage scale of the private sector (before the recent pay freezes in the national civil service). This relative expansion of the government's labor cost partially accounts for the increase in government expenditures.

Third, transfers have been increasing even more markedly (see Table 19). Over the period under study, transfer payments rose by nearly six percentage points. In this regard, there are two notable features: the balance of the social security system has turned adverse, and interest costs have been rising at a rapid rate because of the sharp expansion of outstanding public debt since the late 1970s.

Revenues did not keep pace with disbursements. Disbursements increased by nearly 11 points, but revenues increased by only 6 points. Nearly half of the revenues collected were from direct taxes on households. This increase was achieved by maintaining the personal income tax schedule at its 1974 level for subsequent years. Previously, personal income tax cuts were enacted annually as rapid income growth increased tax revenues. As inflation and real growth pushed nominal income upward, individuals moved into higher income tax brackets, and more low-income workers began to pay taxes. At the same time, social security contributions increased by 4 per cent. Household disposable income virtually stopped growing in real terms.

Large deficits were financed by new bond issues, and the outstanding balance of national debt grew to alarming proportions—46 per cent of GDP in March 1983, a level exceeding the level of the U.S. national debt

TABLE 19
The General Government Account, 1965-1983
(per cent of GDP)

Category	1965-69	1970-74	1975-79	1980-83
Disbursements				
Expenditure[a]	11.7%[b]	13.7%	15.9%	16.5%
Transfer paid, net[c]	2.0	2.6	5.4	8.3
Total	13.7%[b]	16.3%	21.3%	24.8%
Revenue, total[d]	15.2%	17.2%	17.7%	21.3%
Deficits		−0.9	3.9	3.9

SOURCES: Japan, Economic Planning Agency, *Annual Report on National Accounts, 1984* and *1985*.
[a]Final consumption expenditure + gross capital formation − consumption of fixed capital + purchases of land, net.
[b]Excluding purchases of land.
[c]Social security benefits − social security contributions + social assistance grants + subsidies + property income payable.
[d]Indirect taxes + direct taxes + property income, receivable.

in 1984.[102] With bonds yielding above 7 per cent (in 1984), debt servicing alone claimed nearly 3 per cent of GDP. If the present level of government deficits continues, the debt–income ratio is likely to rise further.[103] Thus, government deficits have helped the Japanese economy escape the Scylla of extensive unemployment, but the government faces the Charybdis of bankruptcy. Fiscal reform has been and will remain an important issue on the public agenda.

The External Sector

An economy faced with excess domestic saving can dispose of its surplus capital by exporting it. By becoming a major capital exporter, Japan can solve its internal imbalance and benefit the capital-short world economy.[104]

Japan's net overseas lending has been only slightly above 1 per cent of GDP over the past two decades, after accounting for year-to-year fluctuations (see Table 18). This means that, by and large, Japan's excess saving in the private economy has been absorbed by its fiscal deficit. In the early 1980s, however, the current account of the balance of payments began to show an increasing surplus. This surplus was as high as 3.0 per cent of GDP in 1984 and 3.8 per cent in 1985 (see Table 20).

Interpreting this recent development as an indication of a new long-term trend, government economists in Japan argued in the summer of 1984 that decelerated growth in Japan has led to a decline in rates of return on domestic investments and weakened incentives to invest at home.[105] Owners of capital, which is in excess supply, look for better investment opportunities abroad, resulting in capital exports. Deficits in the capital account are matched by surpluses in the current account because of the trend in Japan toward a chronic trade surplus. This tendency can be attributed to the high income elasticity of about 2 for exports with respect to foreign income and a low income elasticity of about 0.66 for imports with respect to domestic income.[106]

There are at least two major questions regarding this argument. Is the recent rise in the trade balance of a short-run nature? And is the balance-of-payments position determined principally by internal forces or external forces?

Japan's trade balance, which dominates the current-account balance, has fluctuated widely over the past two decades. During the two oil shocks (1973–74 and 1979–80), Japan's trade balance turned adverse as its import bill rose sharply. Exports then caught up as the terms of trade became more favorable for manufactured goods. Thus, Japan's trade balance has proved to be more sensitive to imports than to exports in its year-to-year fluctuations. External shocks play an important role in influencing Japan's current-account position.

TABLE 20

Japan's External Balance, 1965-1984

(per cent of GDP)

Year	Exports				Imports				Net lending	Capital account[a]		
	Goods (fob)	Services	Factor receipts	Total	Goods (cif)	Services	Factor payments	Total		DOR	KO	KI
1965	9.2%	1.3%	0.3%	10.9%	8.0%	1.2%	0.6%	9.8%	1.0%	0.12%	0.49%	-0.42%
1966	9.2	1.4	0.4	11.0	7.9	1.1	0.6	9.7	1.2	-0.03	0.67	-0.55
1967	8.4	1.3	0.4	10.1	8.4	1.1	0.6	10.1	-0.2	-0.06	0.71	0.76
1968	8.8	1.3	0.3	10.5	7.9	1.1	0.6	9.7	0.7	-0.61	0.75	0.64
1969	9.2	1.4	0.4	11.0	7.8	1.2	0.7	9.7	1.2	-0.35	0.88	0.00
1970	9.4	1.4	0.5	11.3	8.2	1.3	0.7	10.3	1.0	0.44	0.94	0.41
1971	10.3	1.3	0.5	12.3	7.6	1.4	0.7	9.8	2.5	4.74	0.91	3.16
1972	9.2	1.3	0.6	11.3	6.9	1.4	0.6	9.0	2.2	1.03	1.59	0.45
1973	8.8	1.2	0.7	10.8	8.5	1.5	0.7	10.8	-0.0	-1.47	2.05	0.61
1974	12.1	1.5	0.9	14.5	12.5	1.8	1.1	15.5	-0.9	0.26	0.89	2.14
1975	11.2	1.6	0.9	13.7	10.8	1.9	1.0	13.8	-0.1	-0.15	0.68	0.67
1976	11.9	1.7	0.8	14.4	10.8	2.0	0.9	13.7	0.6	0.68	0.81	0.84
1977	11.6	1.6	0.7	13.9	9.7	1.9	0.7	12.3	1.5	0.86	0.75	0.07
1978	9.9	1.3	0.7	11.9	7.8	1.6	0.6	10.2	1.7	1.08	1.52	0.88
1979	10.3	1.4	1.0	12.8	10.7	1.9	0.9	13.7	-0.9	-1.28	1.62	1.24
1980	12.3	1.6	1.2	15.2	12.8	2.1	1.2	16.2	-1.1	0.44	1.03	2.56
1981	13.4	1.7	1.5	16.6	12.1	2.2	1.7	16.1	0.5	0.27	2.01	1.83
1982	13.1	1.8	1.9	16.8	11.9	2.2	2.0	16.1	0.7	-0.49	2.56	1.40
1983	12.7	1.6	1.5	15.8	10.1	2.5	1.5	14.0	1.8	0.11	2.79	1.11
1984	13.6			17.1	10.1			14.1	3.0			

sources: Japan, Economic Planning Agency, *Annual Report on National Accounts, 1985* and earlier issues; 1984, preliminary estimates.

[a] DOR, change in official reserves; KO, capital outflow; KI, capital inflow.

External shocks ought to result in a substantial shift in the exchange rate under the flexible exchange rate regime if the current account is to be balanced swiftly. This did not occur in Japan because the capital account helps overcome deficits in the current account. When a deficit appears in the current account, it tends to be temporarily absorbed by a reduction in the monetary authorities' official reserves or an increase in the country's foreign liabilities. The opposite occurs when a surplus emerges in the current account.

Capital flows, however, are not merely accommodating to the current account. Capital flows, especially capital outflows, are sensitive to international interest differentials, especially with respect to the United States. When U.S. interest rates were high in international terms in the early 1980s, capital flowed to the United States, causing an increase in the price of dollars. The cheaper yen then stimulated Japanese exports, especially to the United States. Again, this development arose from an external shock.

Hence, external shocks—whether through the current account or the capital account—greatly influence Japan's balance-of-payments position and largely account for the recent increases in Japan's current-account surplus. In addition, Japan's trade balance is largely dependent on the world's terms of trade.

Contrary to what Japanese government economists maintain, there would be no tendency toward a surplus in the trade balance if the terms of trade remained at a level that equalized exports and imports in Japan. First, according to almost all available econometric estimates, the income elasticity of imports is closer to 1.0 than to the 0.66 espoused by government economists. Second, since Japan's export prices tend to fall relative to the domestic price level because of the more rapid productivity growth in the export sector, the export growth rate will be less in nominal terms than in real terms. Moreover, if Japan's domestic growth rate should fall toward the world's growth rate, its export growth would decline since the rate of export expansion depends on the growth of domestic supply capacity.

Altogether, Japan's balance-of-payments position has been and will be more strongly influenced by external forces than by internal forces. Suppose, for example, that internal forces are strong enough to push excess domestic saving into capital outflows.[107] The resulting deficit in the capital account must be matched by a surplus of equal magnitude in the current account. Japan is currently the leading industrial exporter and tends to concentrate its exports to a few major destinations (the United States, Southeast Asia, and the Middle East) and in a few major commodities (automobiles, steel, electronics, and, increasingly, high-tech products). It will become more and more difficult for Japan to expand its international market share as protectionist sentiments rise in the United States, Europe, and elsewhere. Under such circumstances, Japan's excess saving will remain locked within the country.

This does not mean, however, that internal forces have been wholly without effect. On the contrary, such forces have expressed themselves in the form of export drives—another cause of recurrent trade friction. Whenever Japan's domestic demand weakens, Japanese exporters attempt to sell their goods overseas. External demand is forced to increase, thereby helping the country to moderate the intensity of recession. This development has led to foreign criticism of Japan's short-term macroeconomic policy, for example, in the spring of 1985. This phenomenon, however, is of a short-term nature. The export drive also works in reverse.

Concluding Remarks

What will the macroeconomic balance look like in the near future?

The growth rate is unlikely to rise above the 4 per cent level. Economic activities will continue to gravitate toward the tertiary sector, where productivity growth has been relatively slow. Unless there is a sudden improvement in efficiency in this sector, its future growth rate will not exceed the historical trend.

Given expectations of low growth and high capital costs, business investment will at best remain at the level of the past several years. If there is no marked change in technology, the capital–output ratio will decline overall as the tertiary sector continues to gain in importance within the national economy.

The future trend in household saving is more difficult to predict. An important factor is expected changes in the target wealth–income ratio in the future. As population migration into the metropolitan areas is completed and population growth slows, the land–GDP ratio in current value may finally stabilize. The housing and financial asset–income ratios may become stationary. Since social security benefits are expected to decline and employment opportunities for the elderly to remain poor, the incentive to save will remain strong for working households. At the same time, dissaving by retired workers will increase as their proportion in the total population rises. It seems plausible that the household saving ratio will gradually fall. It is not clear, however, how far this overall reduction in saving will lead to a fall in households' net lending or how soon it will be realized.

As long as excess private saving continues, it will be difficult for the government to balance the budget unless it is willing to jeopardize (reasonably) full employment. If the government must continue deficit spending, public debt will increase at a considerable rate. If the public becomes reluctant to absorb this ever-increasing public debt, the interest rate will rise. The government will have to pay more for debt servicing and therefore will be forced to enlarge its deficits further—a vicious circle.

Increased government revenues may reduce future deficits. Such a solution would entail an overhaul of the present tax system since piecemeal changes would not be sufficient. Should the government rely more on indirect taxes, despite lukewarm public response? Should it increase the personal income tax rates or raise corporate income taxes, already very high? Or should the government discontinue the small-saver tax-exemption program? Concrete measures are still in the formative stage despite a great deal of public debate.

It is difficult to reduce government expenditures in the face of rising economic and social needs, despite the efforts at administrative reform. One example is the social security system, which is threatened by structural imbalance unless some fundamental changes are adopted.

A portion of private saving may be exported as capital outflows. By engaging in capital export full scale, Japan can mitigate its chronic domestic macroeconomic imbalance. This solution is difficult, however, since capital exports must be matched by a surplus in the current account. A large surplus in the trade balance has emerged since the early 1980s because of the decline in the prices of oil and other primary goods, which lowered Japan's import bill relative to domestic output, and because of the high interest rates prevailing in the United States, which attracted overseas capital to finance its huge fiscal deficits. The high price of the dollar has encouraged Japanese exports to the United States. Japan has become the number one industrial exporter, overtaking West Germany and the United States in 1984. As evidenced in the emergence of intense economic conflicts between Japan and the rest of the world, there will be stronger resistance to further expansion of Japanese exports. Since Japan's comparative advantage has been moving into technology-intensive goods, especially in the high-tech field, Japanese exporters must make significant inroads into foreign markets. Such an intensive effort has already given rise to trade frictions.

Furthermore, foreign pressure for increased imports of manufactured goods into Japan, which have been low by international comparison, is growing. If imports into Japan are to be increased, there must be a corresponding increase in exports from Japan (or increased imports of fabricated products matched by a decline in imports of crude materials). Both are difficult to achieve on a short-term basis.

It is evident that maintenance of the macroeconomic balance at full employment will remain a serious challenge for Japanese policymakers in the foreseeable future. There has been no dearth of proposals on how to meet this challenge.[108] Methods to stimulate "vitality in the private sector" have been actively debated. It is argued that administrative measures taken in this direction will stimulate private economic incentives. Some indirect measures already initiated are deregulation of the cumbersome government controls in many economic spheres and privatization of public enterprises dominated by inefficient government monopolies in order to introduce competitive forces. Other, more direct measures may include increasing the scope of public investment. It is believed that such measures would stimulate domestic demand and thereby reduce Japan's dependence on export expansion to support economic growth. However, this would entail further expansion of fiscal deficits. Good intentions notwithstanding, it is doubtful that these measures can be effective in stimulating economic growth if potential growth remains as subdued as in the past decade.

In this paper, I have examined the behavior of saving and investment in Japan. During the rapid growth period, the private sector met the rising demand for investment with its own saving. In the decelerated growth period, private investment fell more than private saving. The resulting surplus of saving was absorbed first by government deficits and later also by current-account surpluses. With economic growth expected to remain at a modest level and the population aging rapidly, the macroeconomic imbalance in the private sector may persist for some time.

Will the government succeed in balancing the budget through tax reform without jeopardizing the macroeconomic equilibrium? Can Japan continue to be a capital exporter, despite strong protectionist sentiments abroad? These are some of the important questions facing the Japanese economy. It will not be easy to devise satisfactory solutions. This is the crossroads at which the Japanese economy now finds itself.

Yukio Noguchi

Public Finance

My purposes in this paper are twofold: to summarize the facts about Japanese public finance during recent decades and to identify major structural changes in this period, analyze their causes, and consider their implications for the future. I focus primarily on the post-1970 period, both because the 1960s have been covered by other works[1] and because the changes during the 1970s have important implications for the current and future management of Japanese public finance.

The basic story of Japanese public finance—in the recent past, the present, and the foreseeable future—springs from two major events between 1973 and 1975. One was the exogenous shock of the first oil crisis, inflation, and sustained slower growth of the economy. The other was the policy decision to increase social security benefits (health insurance and public pensions) substantially. These events had fundamental impacts on the structure of the public finance system, as reflected in the government's increased share in the economy and the huge budget deficit. The tax and expenditure structures have also changed significantly.

In the popular view, the oil shock of 1973 was the main cause of structural change during this period. According to this view, the public sector deficit is simply a result of economic changes caused by the oil shock. The view presented in this paper is different, however; I emphasize the structural changes in the social security system as the essential cause of the present deficit. I show in the first section that changes in the expenditure structure occurred before the first oil shock and that the oil shock simply made this change visible in the form of deficits by causing a recession that made tax revenues drop sharply. I argue that the deficit would have grown even if there had been no oil crisis.

An important politico-economic problem is to clarify the behavioral rules of the government in budget making. The basic view developed in this paper is that it resembles household consumption decisions in that

perceived fiscal affluence leads to adoption of new programs and perceived fiscal crisis leads to austerity. Following this line of thought, I
argue that the most important factor for the changes in the social security system in the 1970s was the favorable fiscal situation. Although
these two views are not contradictory, the view presented here contrasts
with that emphasizing political factors in the budget-making process.

I compare this view with the Buchanan-Wagner hypothesis, which
claims that, in a democratic society, increased borrowing tends to lead to
an expansion of expenditures because deficit financing creates the illusion that fiscal benefits can be obtained without assuming burdens. I
argue that this hypothesis cannot be verified in Japan and show that
increased dependence on deficit financing has compelled fiscal authorities to adopt a tight budget policy, contrary to the Buchanan-Wagner
hypothesis.

The sharing of fiscal burdens is another important topic of the political
economy of public finance. Usually, distribution of burdens across different income groups (vertical equity) is emphasized. In this paper, I examine different issues. One is the distribution of burdens across different occupational groups (horizontal equity), which is usually called the
9-6-4 problem in Japan. I argue that the automatic increase in income
taxes (bracket creep) has aggravated this problem.

Another issue is the distribution across generations, to which traditional arguments have not paid sufficient attention. The shifting of fiscal
burdens to future generations takes place in an implicit way through
public pension programs. In fact, it can be argued that the greatest problem in Japanese public finance is the intergenerational or intertemporal
distribution of fiscal burdens. The crucial point in this discussion is
whether households adjust to changes in fiscal burdens by changing
their savings pattern.

Although the budget deficit is already huge, the full effect of the
changes made in the social security system in the 1970s has not yet been
realized. In fact, even in recent years, the relative size of the government
in the economy has been small in Japan compared with European countries. In the coming decades, however, the share of transfer payments in
national income will more than double because of the aging of the population and the maturing of the public pension system. Moreover, there is
a possibility that saving ratios will fall. These observations imply that the
true fiscal crisis is a problem for the future.

The Growth of Government

One of the most significant changes in industrialized countries after
World War II was the growth of government activities in the economy.[2]
Table 1 shows the ratio of general government expenditures to GDP for

TABLE 1

General Government Expenditures and Social Security Transfers, Japan and Other
Countries, Selected Years, 1955-1980

(per cent of GNP)

Country	General government expenditures			Social security transfers		
	1955-57	1974-76	1980	1955-57	1974-76	1980
Japan	—	26.6%	32.9%	3.7%	7.0%	10.9%
France	33.5%	41.6	45.7	13.2	19.9	22.9
West Germany	30.2	44.0	45.0	12.0	15.4	15.3
Italy	28.1	43.1	44.3	9.7	19.4	15.8
Sweden	—	51.7	—	7.4	17.1	—
United Kingdom	32.3	44.5	44.3	6.1	11.3	11.7
United States	25.9	35.1	32.7ᵃ	4.1	10.9	11.1
OECD average	28.5	41.4	—	7.5	13.9	—

SOURCES: Japan, Economic Planning Agency, *Yearbook of National Account Statistics* (Tokyo: Government Printing Bureau, annual); OECD, *Public Expenditure Trends: OECD Studies in Resource Allocation* (Paris, 1978); and idem, *National Accounts of OECD Countries* (Paris, 1980).
    ᵃ 1979.

selected OECD countries.[3] The average figure for the OECD countries was 28.5 per cent between 1955 and 1957, but rose to 41.4 per cent between 1974 and 1976. As shown in Table 2, the ratio of tax and social security contributions to national income has also risen dramatically.[4] In some countries, such as Sweden, this ratio has been nearly 70 per cent in recent years; that is, about two-thirds of national income is collected by the government and used or distributed according to public decisions.

A similar phenomenon has also occurred in Japan. The indexes in Table 3 demonstrate that the relative size of the government in the economy has increased substantially during the past ten years. The ratio of general government expenditures to GNP, which was below 20 per cent until 1970, steadily increased during the 1970s and is now approaching 35 per cent. The ratio of tax and social security contributions to GNP increased from about 18 per cent during the 1960s to above 27 per cent. The general account expenditures of the national budget have increased from about 10 per cent of GNP to 18 per cent.

Several facts deserve attention. First, unlike in European countries in which the growth of government occurred in the 1950s and 1960s, public sector growth in Japan has occurred since the 1970s.[5] Second, the relative size of government in Japan, as measured by the above indexes, is still smaller than that in European countries.[6] The growth of government in European countries was caused mainly by an increase in transfer payments; the ratio of transfer payments to GDP grew faster than that of total expenditures (see Table 1).[7] The same phenomenon has occurred in

TABLE 2

Tax and Social Security Contributions, Japan and Other Countries, Selected Years, 1955-1980
(per cent)

Country	Taxes and social security contributions (ratio to GNP)			Social security contributions (ratio to GNP)			Ratio to national income (1980)		
	1955-57	1974-76	1980	1955-57	1974-76	1980	Total	Taxes	Social security contributions
Japan	18.0%	22.1%	26.0%	2.2%	5.0%	7.6%	32.2%	22.8%	9.4%
France	30.9	37.2	44.7	9.7	15.2	20.2	58.6	32.1	26.5
West Germany	31.4	38.3	40.0	7.4	13.4	15.5	51.8	31.7	20.1
Italy	24.9	31.8	—	7.4	13.7	—	—	26.3	—
Sweden	26.2	47.0	—	2.2	9.9	—	64.1	44.5	19.6
United Kingdom	28.6	36.0	37.7	3.1	6.6	7.3	51.0	41.1	9.9
United States	24.8	27.5	30.3	3.1	6.7	7.8	37.7	28.0	9.7
OECD average	24.6	33.9	—	3.4	7.6	—	—	—	—

SOURCES: Same as for Table 1.

Japan (see Fig. 1). Although government consumption and government investment do not exhibit clear trends in terms of their ratios to GNP, that of transfer payments has increased remarkably during the past ten years.[8]

As in other areas of social and economic change, Japan was a latecomer in expanding its social security system: in European countries, major changes in the system had been completed by the 1960s. In Japan, substantial changes were made in the early 1970s. Before this period, social security in Japan was far inferior to that of Western countries, and various piecemeal programs, such as subsidies to low-productivity sectors, functioned as substitutes. This was the main reason why the relative size of the government in the economy remained small until the 1960s.

Why, then, is the size of government still small in Japan? Needless to say, this does not imply governmental efficiency in Japan. Nor does it

TABLE 3

Growth of Government Expenditures and Revenues in Japan, FY 1965-1983
(per cent of GNP)

	Expenditures		Taxes and social security contributions			
FY	General government	General account	Taxes (1)	Social security contributions (2)	(1) + (2)	National taxes
1965	19.03%	10.90%	14.39%	4.01%	18.40%	9.24%
1966	19.33	10.93	13.77	4.08	17.85	8.78
1967	18.75	10.72	14.18	4.14	18.31	9.13
1968	18.50	10.64	14.45	4.09	18.54	9.27
1969	18.35	10.39	14.72	4.13	18.85	9.56
1970	19.47	10.59	15.35	4.41	19.75	9.99
1971	21.09	11.38	15.33	4.71	20.04	9.85
1972	22.07	11.89	15.98	4.73	20.71	10.43
1973	22.03	12.25	17.61	4.87	22.48	11.74
1974	25.07	12.39	17.38	5.68	23.06	11.16
1975	26.91	14.02	14.93	6.09	21.02	9.66
1976	27.69	14.27	15.49	6.43	21.91	9.48
1977	29.12	15.10	15.60	6.88	22.48	9.47
1978	30.83	16.59	17.15	7.07	24.22	10.88
1979	31.78	17.38	17.56	7.23	24.79	10.97
1980	32.95	17.70	18.39	7.55	25.95	11.45
1981	34.10	18.43	18.83	8.08	26.91	11.69
1982	34.44	18.63	18.88	8.28	27.16	11.71
1983	34.23	17.88	19.05	8.47	27.52	11.76

SOURCES: Japan, Economic Planning Agency, *Yearbook of National Account Statistics* (Tokyo: Government Printing Bureau, annual); and Japan, Ministry of Finance, *Fiscal and Monetary Statistics* (Tokyo: Government Printing Bureau, monthly).

NOTE: Figures are those of the settlement basis, except for the general account expenditures, which are initial budget figures (same for other tables and figures unless otherwise noted).

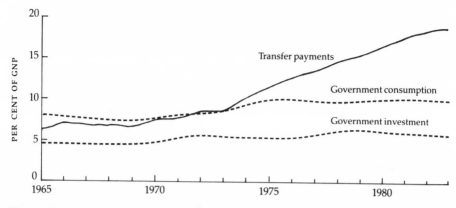

Fig. 1. General government expenditures, FY 1965–1983. See Table 3 for sources.

imply an insufficiency of public services. This is particularly true for social security programs. In fact, improvements in the 1970s made the Japanese social security system comparable, and in some respects even superior, to those of European countries. The essential reason for the relatively low level of social security expenditures is that the relative number of elderly people is still small and that the public pension system has not yet matured (that is, the number of people satisfying the eligibility requirements is small). The smallness of government in Japan is essentially the result of time lags between the introduction of the new programs and the actual increase in outlays.

Because it is a lagged phenomenon, the situation will change if the underlying conditions change. This will in fact occur in the coming decades. The pension programs will automatically mature as time passes. Moreover, the aging of the population is expected to take place rapidly in the future. These factors would increase social security expenditures considerably even if no improvements were made in the system. In this sense, the potential size of the Japanese government is already as big as that of many European countries, and what we are observing now is only the beginning of the growth of government in Japan.

In addition to total expenditures, including transfer payments, the growth of government purchases of goods and services is important because it represents the portion of the national product used directly by the government. As shown in Fig. 1, the ratio of government consumption to GNP has been quite stable, except for a one-time increase in FY 1973 and 1974 caused by a steep increase in government employees' wage rates, especially those of elementary and secondary public school teachers.[9] The ratio of government investment to GNP, on the other hand, shows cyclical variations, rising in 1965–67, 1970–72, and 1976–79. However, no significant upward trend can be observed. Consumption by the central government has remained almost unchanged in terms of its ratio to GNP. This reflects the constant ratio of defense expenditure to GNP and the almost unchanged number of central government employees. On the other hand, consumption by local governments increased remarkably in FY 1974, reflecting the increase in personnel expenditures.

The Growth of the Deficit

The current state of public finance in many countries is symbolized by huge budget deficits.[10] Japan is no exception. In fact, in terms of the ratio to GNP or to the budget size, Japan's figure is among the highest.[11]

For many years after 1949, the general account of the national budget was based on a balanced-budget policy and not on long-term borrowing, even though the Fiscal Act of 1947 allowed the issuance of bonds.[12] In FY 1965, the balanced-budget policy was abandoned, and long-term bonds were issued as a means to supplement tax revenues. Until FY 1974, however, borrowing was only a marginal source of revenue: the average bond dependency ratio (the ratio of bond revenue to total revenue) was about 10 per cent during this period (see Fig. 2).

A significant change occurred in the supplementary budget of FY 1975. Tax revenues, especially corporation tax revenues,[13] dropped sharply because of the recession caused by the oil shock. As a result, it became necessary to increase the bond dependency ratio from the initial budget level of 9.4 per cent to 25.3 per cent. As shown in Fig. 2, the bond dependency ratio has never fallen below 25 per cent since.

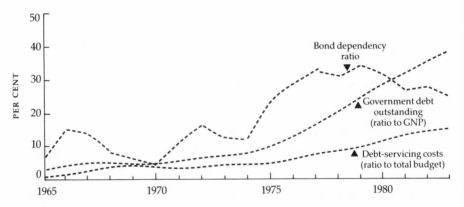

Fig. 2. Growth of the deficit, FY 1965–1983. See Table 3 for sources.

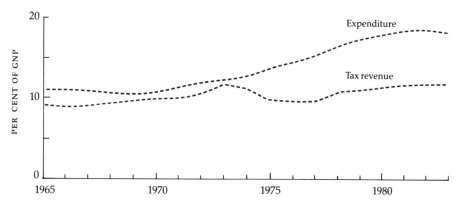

Fig. 3. Tax revenues and expenditures of the general account, FY 1965–1983. See Table 3 for sources.

Because the Fiscal Act limits bond issues to the amount of public works expenditures and because deficits have continued to exceed this ceiling since FY 1975, a special law is passed every year in order to legalize the issuance of bonds exceeding the ceiling. These bonds are usually called "deficit-financing bonds" (*akaji kokusai*), even though they finance only a part (about half in recent years) of the total deficit.[14]

Although the direct cause of the deficit increase in FY 1975 was a fall in tax revenues, from a somewhat longer perspective, the true cause of the deficit can be found on the expenditure side rather than on the revenue side. As shown in Table 3 and Fig. 3, the ratio of tax revenues to GNP, which certainly fell during fiscal years 1975–77, soon returned to the pre–oil shock level and is now significantly higher than it was in the 1960s. (The mechanism behind this—the automatic increase in income taxes—is discussed in the next section.) But expenditures have increased steadily, even in terms of their relative magnitude to economic activity during this period. This tendency had begun in the early 1970s. Until FY 1974, however, the deficit did not grow because tax revenues were also expanding. In other words, the rise in tax revenues in FY 1973 and 1974 had the effect of concealing the potential gap.

Some people regard the expansionary fiscal policies undertaken in FY 1977 and 1978 as the main cause of the present deficit. However, as is apparent in Fig. 2, this view is incorrect. Although the bond dependency ratio rose in FY 1977, the change was quite marginal compared with the magnitude of the dependency ratio itself. Therefore, the increase in the deficit was not the result of a deliberate decision to begin a Keynesian expansionary policy.

The increase in expenditures was structural. As mentioned above, the major changes were the continuous increase in social security expenditures and the one-time increase in salary-related expenditures (in the general account of the national budget, the latter were included in education-related expenditures and in "other items"). In terms of the general account expenditures of the national budget, debt-servicing costs also increased significantly.

If neither the oil shocks nor the economic slowdown had occurred, would there still be a large government deficit, given the change in the social security system? Answers to this question are inherently speculative. It is, however, useful to explore this issue in order to clarify the nature of the deficit.

Had there been no slowdown in economic growth, tax revenues would not have fallen, and the deficit would not have expanded as sharply as it did in FY 1975. This would have reduced debt-servicing costs in subsequent years and hence have prevented the vicious circle of expenditure expansion.

Even in that case, however, the increases in social security expenditures would have changed the budget balance significantly. The ratio of general account expenditures for social security programs to GNP has risen by about two percentage points during the past decade. The extent to which the budget balance is affected by this change depends on the tax policy. If the tax burden as measured by the ratio to GNP were held constant, as was the case in the 1960s, the deficit would have increased. The increase in the deficit would be greater than the increase in social security because an increase in debt-servicing costs has accelerating effects on the deficit. The magnitude of this effect would be around 1 per cent of GNP after ten years of deficit expansion. The deficit, then, would have become somewhere around 3 per cent of GNP, which is not much different from the actual figure in recent years—4.2 per cent in FY 1984.

Needless to say, the deficit would become smaller if tax burdens were raised. Even in that case, however, the deficit would increase because of the accelerating effects of debt-servicing costs if there were time lags between expenditure expansion and tax increases.

James Buchanan and Richard Wagner have argued that in a democratic society budget deficits tend to grow because people feel little or no fiscal burden if expenditures are financed by borrowing rather than by taxes.[15] They further argue that, because of this fiscal illusion, increased bond dependency leads to fiscal irresponsibility and hence to increases in expenditures. The second statement can be interpreted as a hypothesis that attempts to explain public sector growth in a modern society.

Does this argument hold in Japan? The bond dependency ratio does correlate positively with the ratio of the general account expenditure to GNP. Thus, one may be tempted to accept this hypothesis. A careful examination, however, reveals a considerably different picture.

First, amortization and interest payments on national bonds should be excluded from expenditures because it is obvious that they will increase if bond issuance increases. It is also appropriate to exclude grants-in-aid to local governments (*chihō kōfuzei*) because they are not a discretionary item. When these modifications are made, the increase in Japanese government expenditures is not so apparent, especially before 1974 (see Fig. 4). This means that the positive correlation mentioned above is, to a large extent, superficial.

True, the data after 1975 are positively correlated, but this does not necessarily imply causality. The series would be positively correlated if the direction of causality were precisely the opposite from what Buchanan and Wagner insist—that is, if an increase in spending caused a passive increase in the deficit. In fact, the data after fiscal year 1979

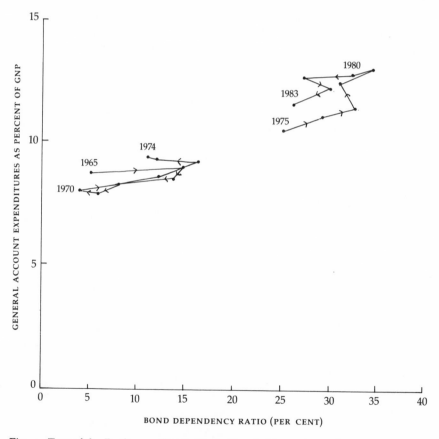

Fig. 4. Test of the Buchanan-Wagner hypothesis. Expenditure figures are those of the initial budget. See Table 3 for sources.

show a movement toward the origin, which is difficult to explain by the Buchanan-Wagner hypothesis. It is more natural to interpret this movement as representing a mechanism whereby an increase in the deficit forces fiscal authorities to adopt a tight budget policy, which in turn causes the bond dependency ratio to fall. Indeed, the reduction of bond issues has been regarded as one of the most important policy objectives in recent years. (The details of this process are reviewed below.)

So far I have used the word "deficit" as a synonym for "bond revenue," but depending on the definition of "deficit," there might be a difference between the two.[16] This is especially important for public pensions, which I discuss in the last section.

Changes in the Tax Structure

As mentioned in the previous section, the ratio of tax revenues to national income, which fell in FY 1975 because of the recession caused by the first oil shock, quickly recovered its previous level and is now higher than the pre–oil shock level (see Tables 3–4). The ratio of total tax reve-

TABLE 4
Changes in Japan's Tax Structure, FY 1965-1983
(per cent of national income)

FY	National and local taxes		National taxes			
	Direct taxes	Indirect taxes	Income taxes	Income tax on salaried income	Corporation taxes	Indirect taxes
1965	7.41%	7.33%	2.89%	—	2.76%	3.58%
1966	7.00	7.06	2.75	—	2.61	3.42
1967	7.35	7.16	2.79	—	2.83	3.51
1968	7.60	7.21	2.95	—	2.91	3.42
1969	7.92	7.15	3.09	1.52%	3.10	3.37
1970	8.51	7.17	3.23	1.61	3.42	3.34
1971	8.49	7.01	3.49	1.68	3.09	3.27
1972	8.99	7.04	3.86	1.90	3.10	3.47
1973	10.58	7.19	4.57	2.25	3.87	3.29
1974	11.03	6.86	3.88	1.90	4.21	3.08
1975	8.95	6.49	3.61	1.80	2.72	3.33
1976	9.14	6.79	3.65	1.98	2.81	3.02
1977	9.25	6.89	3.48	1.86	2.95	3.03
1978	10.48	7.19	3.75	1.98	3.83	3.31
1979	10.52	7.52	4.18	2.28	3.33	3.47
1980	11.35	7.53	4.49	2.48	3.71	3.26
1981	11.67	7.62	4.72	2.66	3.48	3.50
1982	11.66	7.62	4.79	—	3.40	3.53
1983	11.60	7.57	4.90	—	3.53	3.32

SOURCES: Same as for Table 3.

nues (the sum of national and local tax revenues) to GNP, which was 14.4 per cent in FY 1965, rose to 19.2 per cent in FY 1983 (in terms of the ratio to national income, from 18.5 per cent to 23.9 per cent). If social security contributions are included,[17] the increase in government receipts is even more dramatic: their ratio to GNP rose from 18.4 per cent in FY 1965 to 27.5 per cent in FY 1983 (in terms of the ratio to national income, from 23.2 per cent to 34.3 per cent). These observations support the contention that the fundamental reason for the recent increase in the deficit is increased expenditures rather than diminished revenues. Moreover, tax burdens were quite stable during the 1960s. In other words, the increase discussed above is a relatively recent phenomenon.

Not only the magnitude but also the composition of taxes has changed significantly. Although the ratio of indirect taxes to GNP in recent years has been about the same as that in the 1960s, that of direct taxes has increased considerably during the past decade.[18] As a result, the share of direct taxes, which was about one-half in the 1960s, has risen to about 60 per cent in recent years. The same trend can be observed more clearly in national taxes.[19] In FY 1955, the share of direct taxes in national taxes was 51.4 per cent. In FY 1983, it had risen to 70.7 per cent.

Among the national taxes, income taxes have increased the most sharply. In FY 1965, the ratio of income taxes to national income was 2.9 per cent, whereas in FY 1983, it had risen to 4.9 per cent. Social security contributions, which can be regarded as a kind of direct tax, have also increased dramatically. Their ratio to GNP increased from 4.0 per cent to 8.5 per cent over the same period (in terms of the ratio to national income, from 5.1 per cent to 10.6 per cent).

Increases in income taxes and social security contributions can also be identified in data from the Family Budget Survey (*Kakei chōsa*). In 1981, salaried workers' before-tax household income rose by 5.2 per cent, but their income taxes rose by 12.9 per cent, leaving real disposable income to grow by only 3.9 per cent. A similar trend has been under way since 1977. As a result, the ratio of income taxes to income rose from 2.6 per cent in 1970 to 4.0 per cent in 1981.

In the case of social security contributions, the increase in the burden is the result of explicit revisions in the system. For example, the rate of contribution to the Employees' Pension Fund (*Kōsei Nenkin*) was raised (in several stages) from 3.5 per cent in FY 1960 to 10.6 per cent in 1985 (including the employers' share).[20] In the case of income tax, however, the increase in the burden in recent years is not the result of explicit revisions in the income tax law. Rather, it was a result of bracket creep, which occurs when a progressive tax structure is not indexed to offset inflation or economic growth.[21]

Until the early 1970s, the income tax law was amended almost every year in order to prevent this mechanism from operating: a tax reduction of about 2 to 5 per cent of tax revenues was undertaken in most years until FY 1974.[22] Since the first oil shock, however, the amount of tax increases has become greater than that of tax reductions. This was particularly true in FY 1981, when the corporation tax rate was raised two percentage points. Adjustments to the income tax law were not undertaken for seven full years, starting in FY 1977. Only in FY 1984 was a substantial revision made.

Automatic increases in income taxes have the effect not only of raising the overall income tax burden but also of distributing the burden unevenly among different categories of income. Wage earners cannot avoid being caught by this mechanism since nearly all of their income is subject to taxation. In contrast, people who receive business and other nonwage incomes can avoid this mechanism by declaring increased expenses.[23]

As a result, revenue from self-assessed incomes went almost unchanged in terms of its ratio to national income (0.97 per cent in FY 1965, 1.26 per cent in FY 1983),[24] but revenue from withheld income taxes rose from 2.67 per cent in FY 1965 to 4.7 per cent in FY 1983. This implies that the increase in income taxes is mainly attributable to an increase in withheld income taxes, about 70 per cent of which are taxes on salaried income.

Thus, the share of taxes from salaried income in total income tax revenues rose from 49.9 per cent in 1975 to 56.3 per cent in 1981. In contrast, the share of taxes from business income fell from 3.7 per cent to 2.7 per cent during the same period.

The increase in income taxes on salaried income is achieved not only through bracket creep but also through increases in the number of taxpayers as the number of workers whose income exceeds the minimum taxable level increases. The number of salaried workers paying income taxes increased from 21 million in FY 1972 to 33 million in FY 1981. Because the burden of social security contributions is borne mainly by wage earners, the combined effect of increases in income taxes on salaried income and increases in social security contributions has increased the burden on labor income significantly.

I have focused on equity across occupational groups (horizontal equity). If the focus is on equity across income group (vertical equity), direct taxes (especially income taxes) are generally more progressive than indirect taxes (although social security contributions are generally regressive because of the fixed contribution rate and the maximum assessed income). It appears, however, that in Japan the increased equity across income classes that results from a higher share of direct taxes is considerably offset by the decreased equity across occupational groups.

The basic principle of the Japanese income tax is comprehensive taxation—that is, all categories of income are added together and are subject to the same rate schedule. It is frequently pointed out, however, that the burden of the income tax is unevenly distributed among different categories of income. This is commonly called the 9-6-4 (or 10-5-3-1) problem, meaning that the portion of income subject to taxation is 90 per cent of actual earned income for salaried income, 60 per cent for business income, and only 40 per cent for agricultural income (or 100 per cent for salaried workers, 50 per cent for the self-employed, 30 per cent for farmers, and 10 per cent for politicians).

The ratio is uneven because of differences allowed by income tax law and differences in actual assessment. The most important difference in the tax law is that deduction of actual expenses is allowed in the cases of business and agricultural income, but only a fixed proportion determined by law can be deducted from salaried income. Moreover, a de facto double deduction is allowed for business income because salaries for family workers can be deducted as expenses from business income and a fixed proportion is further deducted from that salary income.

As for the actual assessment, almost 100 per cent of salaried income is captured by the tax authorities because the collection system withholds at the source. However, since business or agricultural income is taxed according to the taxpayers' self-assessment, it is difficult for the tax authorities to capture the entire income. The probability of being audited has fallen considerably in the past decade, and it is now only about 2–3 per cent because the number of taxpayers has grown significantly whereas that of tax officials has remained almost unchanged.

It is difficult to analyze the 9-6-4 problem quantitatively, however, because most of the necessary data are unavailable. Hiromitsu Ishi conducted such an analysis by comparing the tax statistics and the national account statistics.[25] His basic assumption was that the latter reflect true income. By applying various adjustments to the data and making several additional assumptions, he concluded that the portion of income subject to taxation is almost 100 per cent for salaried income, 60 to 70 per cent for business income, and 20 to 30 per cent for agricultural income. This result validates the popular belief on this issue. Thus, the automatic increases in income taxes aggravate the uneven distribution of tax burdens.

This inequality across different occupational groups probably reflects interest group politics: certain occupational groups such as farmers, small businessmen, and doctors have succeeded in receiving preferential treatment because members of the same group have similar interests and because they have political channels to realize their demands. But salaried workers are left out because they share few common interests among themselves and because they are politically unorganized.

The inequality is to a large extent, however, a reflection of the difference in the properties of income. It is possible to tax salaried income without much administrative cost through the withholding method. For such incomes as business income, the self-assessment method is inevitable. As the number of taxpayers increases, it becomes more and more difficult for tax authorities to tax the latter kind of income completely. To this extent, inequality across occupational groups is a result of taxing techniques rather than of a political process.

Another important problem is special tax measures. As pointed out by George Break, this problem is important when discussing the role of government in an economy because if fiscal benefits are provided in the form of preferential tax treatments rather than explicit expenditures, measurements such as those employed in the first section of this paper do not correctly represent the true size of the government in an economy.[26]

According to materials prepared by the Ministry of Finance, the loss in revenue because of special tax measures in terms of its ratio to total tax revenues was 8.2 per cent in FY 1965 but has been reduced steadily to about 3 per cent in recent years. The absolute amount of revenue loss was ¥1.3 trillion in FY 1984,[27] of which ¥0.9 trillion was from income taxes and the rest from corporation taxes. Most of the reduction in income taxes results from the special treatment of interest earned on small savings accounts.

These figures are considerably lower than the estimate of "tax expenditures" in the U.S. federal budget, which amount to as much as about one-third of total federal receipts.[28] Despite the formal resemblance, the definition of "special tax measures" in Japan is significantly different from that of "tax expenditure" in the United States. The Japanese definition uses the actual income tax law as its basis and includes only those provisions allowed in separate laws as "special tax measures." Thus, for example, the provision to exclude interest earned on postal savings from the tax base is not regarded as a special measure because it is included in the income tax law. On the other hand, the U.S. definition adopts the ideal income tax as the basis and then classifies a wide range of provisions as tax expenditures. For example, special treatment of retirement savings and of capital gains, not included in the Japanese definition of special measures in spite of their existence, are included in the U.S. definition and account for about one-third of total tax expenditure. If a different definition were adopted in Japan, the results would be substantially different from the official estimates.

As for corporation taxes, the most important point is whether to regard provisions for tax-free reserves as special measures. In the Japanese corporation tax system, accumulation of certain kinds of reserves can be deducted from the tax base. For example, a firm can accumulate a tax-free fund up to 40 per cent of the amount necessary for paying lump-sum retirement benefits for employees. Thus, if the necessary amount increases because of an increase in the number of employees or in the payment level, the difference from the previous year can be deducted from income.

The Ministry of Finance's definition of special tax measures does not include such treatments on the grounds that they are admitted in the corporation tax law. However, it is possible to regard them as special measures because they reduce the tax base. If such measures are included, then the loss of revenue can be estimated at around 15 per cent of the total corporation tax revenue for the 1970s.[29]

Although increasing in recent years, the tax burden in Japan is still low compared with that of European countries. However, a significant increase in the tax burden will become unavoidable in the future in order to finance increases in social security expenditures.

Changes in the Expenditure Structure

In terms of their ratios to GNP, only two major expenditure items in the general account budget—social security expenditures and debt-servicing costs—show significant upward trends (see Table 5).[30] The ratio of the former rose from 1.5 per cent to 3.2 per cent, and that of the latter from 0.1 per cent to 2.9 per cent, between FY 1965 and FY 1983. The ratio of total expenditures in the general account budget to GNP has risen during the same period from 10.9 per cent to 17.9 per cent, and these two items account for about two-thirds of the total increase.

The increase in debt-servicing costs (amortization and interest payments on national bonds) is indeed remarkable.[31] In FY 1985, they became the largest expenditure item, surpassing even social security expenditures. They are, however, a result of past increases in other expenditures. In order to see the real factors of expenditure expansion, they should be excluded from the analysis. When this is done, the ratio of the general account budget to GNP rose by 4.2 percentage points from 1965 to 1985; of this, the increase in social security accounted for 40 per cent. It is apparent that the most fundamental change during this period was the increase in social security expenditures. In view of their importance, the details of social security expenditures are discussed separately in the next section. Here, I review the other expenditure items in the general account.

The amount of grants-in-aid to local governments is set at 32 per cent of the total of income tax, corporation tax, and liquor tax revenues. Thus, its ratio to GNP rises when the ratio of revenues from these taxes to GNP rises. The recent increase in grants-in-aid is a result of increases in income tax revenues.

TABLE 5
Major Items in the General Account Budget, FY 1965-1983
(per cent of GNP)

FY	Total budget	Social security	Public works	Education	Debt-servicing costs	Government employees' pensions
1965	10.90%	1.54%	2.18%	1.42%	0.07%	0.50%
1966	10.93	1.58	2.21	1.38	0.12	0.48
1967	10.72	1.56	2.16	1.35	0.25	0.47
1968	10.64	1.49	1.95	1.28	0.37	0.46
1969	10.39	1.46	1.85	1.24	0.43	0.41
1970	10.59	1.52	1.88	1.23	0.39	0.40
1971	11.38	1.62	2.01	1.30	0.39	0.41
1972	11.89	1.71	2.23	1.35	0.47	0.39
1973	12.25	1.81	2.43	1.35	0.60	0.40
1974	12.39	2.09	2.06	1.40	0.62	0.42
1975	14.02	2.59	1.92	1.71	0.68	0.50
1976	14.27	2.82	2.07	1.74	0.98	0.58
1977	15.10	3.01	2.27	1.78	1.24	0.62
1978	16.59	3.28	2.64	1.86	1.56	0.64
1979	17.38	3.43	2.95	1.94	1.84	0.68
1980	17.70	3.41	2.77	1.88	2.21	0.68
1981	18.43	3.48	2.62	1.87	2.62	0.71
1982	18.63	3.41	2.50	1.82	2.94	0.71
1983	17.88	3.24	2.36	1.71	2.91	0.67

FY	Grants-in-aid to local governments	Defense	Official development assistance	Subsidies to small and medium firms	Agriculture related	Others
1965	2.13%	0.90%	0.08%	0.06%	0.31%	1.70%
1966	1.90	0.86	0.13	0.07	0.31	1.89
1967	1.94	0.82	0.12	0.08	0.27	1.70
1968	2.00	0.77	0.10	0.07	0.44	1.70
1969	2.06	0.74	0.11	0.07	0.46	1.55
1970	2.21	0.76	0.11	0.07	0.51	1.52
1971	2.48	0.81	0.11	0.07	0.56	1.62
1972	2.28	0.83	0.11	0.07	0.54	1.93
1973	2.38	0.80	0.11	0.07	0.46	1.82
1974	2.81	0.79	0.13	0.07	0.52	1.47
1975	2.90	0.87	0.13	0.08	0.60	2.04
1976	2.24	0.89	0.12	0.09	0.53	2.21
1977	2.45	0.90	0.11	0.09	0.44	2.19
1978	2.61	0.92	0.13	0.10	0.41	2.44
1979	2.38	0.94	0.15	0.11	0.40	2.57
1980	2.72	0.93	0.16	0.10	0.40	2.45
1981	3.18	0.95	0.17	0.10	0.39	2.34
1982	3.46	0.97	0.18	0.09	0.37	2.19
1983	2.60	0.98	0.18	0.09	0.32	2.82

SOURCES: Same as for Table 3.
NOTE: Expenditure figures are those of the initial budget.

Expenditures for education also increased relative to GNP during this period because of the improvement of teachers' salaries and the introduction of subsidies for private schools. As I pointed out above, the former was the major reason for the increase in local governments' consumption.[32]

Although the ratios of these two items to GNP have increased, the magnitude of the increase is small relative to the increase in social security expenditures and debt-servicing costs. For other items, no significant upward trend can be observed during this period. This stability is remarkable in light of the tremendous structural changes in the private sector after the oil shocks.[33]

In particular, there is no long-run upward trend in public works expenditures. Although they fluctuate from period to period, their ratio to GNP does not tend to deviate from an average level of about 2.5 per cent. This provides evidence against the hypothesis that there is an expansionary bias in Keynesian macroeconomic demand management that leads to a long-run tendency for the relative size of public works expenditure to increase.[34] In Japan, years of expansionary policy are followed by years of contractionary policy, leaving almost no trend in the relative size of public works expenditures. The past several years can be interpreted as belonging to a contractionary phase.

The ratio of agriculture-related expenditures to GNP increased during the late 1960s and early 1970s, but has been falling significantly in recent years. This results primarily from the reduction in the discrepancy between the producer and consumer prices of rice. Other major items have also shown declining trends in their ratios to GNP during the past several years because of the tight budget policy adopted since FY 1980.

Only a few items have been allowed to increase during this period: defense expenditures, energy-related expenditures (not shown in Table 5), and official development assistance (ODA) expenditures. Defense expenditures are increasing mainly because of pressure from the United States and other countries on Japan to assume its share of defense efforts. The level of defense expenditures as measured by their ratio to GNP decreased significantly in the 1950s and 1960s, however. The recent increases can be regarded as a return to the previous level.

Another important element of Japanese public finance is local public finance.[35] Its importance has been increasing in recent years, especially in those areas closely related to daily life. It is difficult, however, to discuss local public finance because of the large number of local bodies (over 3,000) and because their characteristics vary considerably. For example, the budget of the Tokyo metropolitan government was ¥3.4 trillion in FY 1983, whereas some municipalities had budgets under ¥10 million.

The relationship between the national government and local governments is complex. There are many subsidies, in addition to the general-purpose grants-in-aid, from the former to the latter. As a result of these subsidies and grants, the expenditures of local governments are about twice that of the central government (excluding transfers to local governments), even though local tax revenues are only about half of national tax revenues.

One of the largest items in local public finance is personnel expenditures, which account for about 30 per cent of total expenditures. (Personnel expenditures are about 6 per cent of the national government's total expenditures.) There are two aspects to this problem: the number of personnel and the level of salaries. The number of local government employees, which was 2.3 million in FY 1967, has increased rapidly in the past decade and is now about 3.2 million.[36] In contrast, the number of national government employees remained almost unchanged at about 1.2 million.

The average salary level of local government employees is about 6 per cent higher than that of national government employees. In FY 1982, the salary level in 33 municipalities was more than 20 per cent higher than that of the national government. These higher wage levels suggest that local governments are less responsive to the welfare of the electorate. This is somewhat surprising because theoretically the electorate has more interest in, and knowledge about, local politics, and local governments would thus be forced to be more responsive to the welfare of the electorate than would the national government.

Although some grass-roots movements have sought limitations on retirement payments to local government employees, there has been no movement comparable to California's Proposition 13. The basic reason is that, because of national subsidies and grants, a reduction in local expenditures does not necessarily lead to a reduction in the local tax burden.

Theoretically, one remedy would be to grant fiscal autonomy to local governments. Many people, while admitting this possibility, feel that there is a danger in doing so because the actual political process does not necessarily function as theory predicts and fiscal resources may be used to increase government employees' salaries rather than the welfare of residents.

Changes in the Social Security System

As noted above, the most fundamental change during the past decade was the growth of social security expenditures caused by major changes in the system during the 1970s. Since these changes are so crucial for the present and future state of public finance in Japan, it is worthwhile considering their background.[37]

Figure 5 shows the general account outlays for the three major social security programs in terms of their ratios to GNP. Although the ratio of public assistance expenditures stayed at almost the same level, that of health insurance and public pensions increased dramatically during the past decade, reflecting the remarkable changes in the social security system during the early 1970s.

For example, such new programs as free medical care for the aged and subsidies for expensive medical treatments were introduced. In addition, the part of health insurance for the self-employed covered by the government was raised from 50 per cent to 70 per cent.

Public pension programs were also improved significantly. Before this period, public pensions were insufficient. Even in terms of "model benefits"—those a representative recipient satisfying eligibility requirements could expect—the old-age benefits were only about 20 per cent of the average salary. In 1973, the ratio jumped to 43 per cent, and an indexation provision for inflation was introduced. Still other social security programs, such as the children's allowance, were introduced during this period. In fact, FY 1973 is called "the first year of the welfare era" because so many new programs were introduced.

There were several reasons why the social security system was improved so dramatically during this period. One was the growing consciousness of the quality of life. After years of rapid economic growth, Japan had reached a stage at which it could allocate resources to areas not directly related to productivity increases.

Another reason was changes in local politics. In the late 1960s, non-

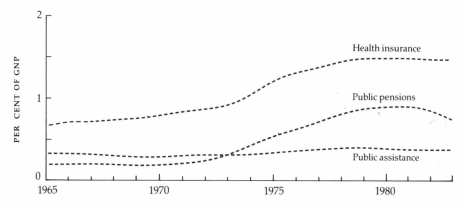

Fig. 5. Social security expenditure (general account), FY 1965–1983. Expenditure figures are those of the initial budget. See Table 3 for sources.

conservatives (in most cases, Socialist-Communist coalitions) gained control of many local governments. The most symbolic event was the Minobe administration in the Tokyo metropolitan government in 1967. These nonconservatives actively introduced welfare programs, under the political slogan "Improvements in Welfare." These changes were infectious: once one local government introduced a new program, its neighboring governments were forced to adopt similar programs. Once welfare programs had spread to a certain number of local governments, pressures arose for the national government to adopt them as national policies financed by national revenues. An example of a program adopted in this way was free medical care for the aged.

Moreover, fiscal conditions were exceptionally favorable during this period, as shown by the remarkable "natural increases" in tax revenues.[38] Natural increases are resources fiscal authorities can use without much constraint. Usually, they are used to reduce bond issues, as was the case in FY 1969–71 and 1980–83.

However, natural increases in the 1970s occurred under different circumstances. The bond dependency ratio was not extraordinarily high compared with its previous levels, and the magnitude of natural increases was greater than the previous levels (see Fig. 6). Thus, although a portion was used to reduce bond issues, a greater portion was used to improve social security programs.

The introduction of new social security programs by local govern-

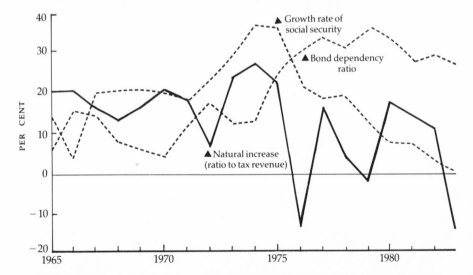

Fig. 6. Natural increase and social security, FY 1965–1983. The figures for natural increases and expenditures are those estimated in the initial budget. See Table 3 for sources.

ments was made possible by similar conditions in local tax revenues. The essential factor causing the great changes was fiscal affluence. In fact, it is possible to construct a model of the public sector on the hypothesis that the basic behavioral rule of the public sector is similar to household consumption decisions in the sense that expenditures expand when perceived "permanent income" increases. This model explains fairly well the actual trends of various expenditures, including social security expenditures.[39] If such an explanation is correct, political factors are not as important as is usually emphasized because a similar phenomenon will occur regardless of political situations if fiscal conditions are similar.

When the major changes were made in the early 1970s, many people, including budget examiners, believed that the new programs would not cause serious financial difficulties in the future. It is an irony of history that the oil shock hit the economy immediately after the first year of the welfare era.

As noted above, the fiscal crisis precipitated by the dramatic changes in social security would not have been so serious had the oil shock not occurred and had growth continued at high levels. To that extent, the fiscal crisis can be blamed on bad luck or bad timing rather than on bad management or bad judgment. Nonetheless, the folly of financing a long-term commitment such as social security (especially public pensions) using a volatile source of funds such as natural increases in tax revenues can be criticized with the benefit of hindsight.

In the case of public pensions, an important but somewhat unbelievable factor contributed to the expansion of the system. A theoretical mistake led to a serious underestimation of the required contribution rate. Since the calculations involved are difficult for nonspecialists, this mistake has not attracted popular attention.

The required contribution rate is calculated by setting the sum of the present value of future contributions, the present value of future subsidies from the general account, and the value of the existing fund equal to the present value of future payments. Needless to say, assumptions concerning the future economic growth rate and discount rate affect the results of such calculations greatly. The Ministry of Welfare assumed the former to be zero, and the latter to be 5.5 per cent. This assumption is unacceptable from an economic point of view: a static economy implies a low discount rate. A discount rate close to the historical rate should be accompanied by a realistic growth rate. The Ministry of Welfare's assumption was wrong because the discount rate was too high relative to the growth rate.

Surprisingly, the Ministry of Welfare was not aware of these problems. In a document explaining its calculations, the ministry stated that it had adopted the zero-growth assumption because "this assumption has the advantage of excluding uncertainty." It also said that "a fairly low discount rate of 5.5 per cent" was used.[40]

The high discount rate introduces a bias toward undervaluing future events. In a steady-state economy, this does not imply an underestimation of required contributions since future contributions are undervalued as well.[41] The Japanese economy is, however, not a steady-state economy. On the contrary, adverse events such as the aging of the population and the maturing of the pension system will arise in the future. The Ministry of Welfare's assumption undervalues these events and hence underestimates the required contribution rate greatly.

Because of this underestimation, people believed that public pension programs would not impose many burdens and therefore welcomed the expansion of the system. Had the contribution rate been calculated correctly, it is doubtful that the major changes would have been made.

To what extent was the required contribution rate undervalued? As mentioned above, assumptions concerning the economic growth rate and discount rate are crucial for such calculations. Here, I assume that the two rates are equal. Consider a representative male worker who begins his work career at age 25, retires at age 60, and dies at age 75, and whose wage equals the average wage.

If the present benefit-contribution structure remains unchanged, the present value of his lifetime contributions is about ¥10 million, including the employer's share. On the other hand, the present value of his lifetime benefits turns out to be as much as about ¥40 million, including survivor's benefits to his wife.[42] If the demographic structure stabilizes, which is an approximation of the Japanese situation in the next century, equality between revenues and outlays must hold for a representative individual. Since 20 per cent of the benefits are covered by subsidies from the general account, the lifetime contributions of an individual must cover 80 per cent of his lifetime benefits on a present-value basis. My calculation implies that the rate should be more than three times as high as the actual rate.

If the same calculation is done for the benefit formula in 1973, the required rate turns out to be about 25 per cent. The "theoretical rate" calculated by the Ministry of Welfare at that time was only 10.5 per cent (the actual rate was 7.6 per cent). Therefore, undervaluation was in fact serious.

The financial structure of public pensions has other important implications. One is the intergenerational distribution of burdens. According to the official explanation, public pensions in Japan are based on the "modified-funded method," which means that the contribution rates are set at levels slightly lower than the levels required for a full-funded method. This suggests that there is little intergenerational transfer in the present system. Many people believe that most of the benefits are in fact financed by the accumulated contributions of the beneficiaries.

This is far from the actual structure, however. Most benefits are financed by current contributors and taxpayers, and huge intergenerational transfers are created through public pension programs. In FY 1982, total payments from the Employees' Pension Fund amounted to ¥4.5 trillion. If three-fourths were transfer payments, the amount of transfer payments was ¥3.4 trillion, or about 1.6 per cent of national income. This is more than three times as large as the general account outlays for the public assistance program.

Other implications of the present structure of the public pension system are financial crisis and the necessity of increasing burdens in the future. The present system has thus far not been in deficit, despite the huge imbalance between contributions and benefits, simply because the number of beneficiaries is far smaller than the number of contributors. This situation will change dramatically as the population ages and pension programs mature. Thus, the system cannot be managed without raising the contribution rate significantly above the present level (and possibly reducing benefits). This will increase not only social security contributions but also tax burdens significantly.

Fiscal Reconstruction

Since the increase in the budget deficit in FY 1975, reducing the deficit has been the most important objective of the budget preparation process. In fact, many regard this as one of the most important objectives of overall economic policy. In this section, I review recent efforts to reduce the deficit, usually called "fiscal reconstruction."

The first strategy of the Ministry of Finance was to reduce the budget deficit by introducing a new tax. In October 1977, the Tax Council (Zeisei Chōsakai) released a report recommending the introduction of a general consumption tax (*ippan shōhi zei*), similar to the value-added tax in European countries. In September 1978, the details of the tax were publicized in another report from the Tax Council. The Ōhira administration, which took office in December 1978, declared that it would introduce the new tax in FY 1980. This became the most important issue in the general election of October 1979, which resulted in a setback for the Liberal Democratic Party (LDP). Since then, discussion of a general consumption tax seems to have become a political taboo.

Why is it so difficult to introduce a general consumption tax, especially since the burden of income taxes, corporation taxes, and social security contributions has increased? It is usually argued that increasing indirect taxes is relatively easier than increasing direct taxes because taxpayers perceive the burden imposed by the former incompletely. There are several reasons why this argument does not apply directly to the present case.

First, the true reason for the resistance to a general consumption tax is not necessarily the general taxpayers' concern about the increased burden but apprehension among small firms that it will make all transactions transparent to the tax authorities, who may in turn use the information to assess taxes on them (corporation tax or individual income tax on business incomes). In this sense, the resistance is against increases in direct taxes. Second, although explicit action is needed on the part of the tax authorities to introduce a new tax, increases in income tax revenues can be achieved by doing nothing, through the automatic increase mechanism. Inaction is far easier than action in the politico-administrative system.

Public documents have emphasized the need for a radical re-examination of the expenditure structure ever since the deficit increase in FY 1975. Until FY 1979, however, actual policy did not move in this direction for two reasons: the Ministry of Finance intended to reduce deficits by introducing a new tax, and the demand for expansionary fiscal policy (the so-called locomotive theory) was strong for several years after the first oil shock.

Since the introduction of a new tax turned out to be politically infeasible, however, it became necessary to change the strategy toward expenditure cuts. Other factors contributed to the realization of this change. One was the increase in bond issues. The bond dependency ratio exceeded the symbolic level of 30 per cent as a result of the expansionary policies of FY 1977–78 and rose further to a record level of nearly 40 per cent in the initial FY 1979 budget. The need to reduce the deficit became urgent. Another factor was that public opinion concerning the role of the government changed gradually but significantly after the second oil shock. Those favoring a smaller government gained influence, especially among businessmen, because of their fear that future tax increases will fall on them, while benefits will go to such areas as agriculture and small business. These factors gradually reoriented basic policy toward the suppression of expenditures.

The first step was the establishment of a deficit reduction objective. The Suzuki administration, which took office in July 1980, declared that the issuance of deficit-financing bonds would be terminated by FY 1984. Since FY 1980, the amount of bond issue reduction has been the first decision in the budget preparation process.[43]

The next step was lowering the ceiling for increases in budget requests by each government ministry or agency. Between FY 1961 and FY 1974, the ceiling had been set at 20 per cent over the previous year's budget. Although lowered in FY 1975, it was still greater than the actual rate of increase in the budget. In FY 1980, the ceiling was reduced to 10 per cent. In FY 1982, it was further reduced to zero, and in FY 1984 a "minus ceiling" was imposed on various items.[44]

The third step was the establishment of the Ad Hoc Council on Administrative Reform (Rinji Gyōsei Chōsakai) in March 1981, the most recent administrative reform commission. The council's task was to review all government activities and to recommend ways of rationalizing government.[45] The council released its first set of recommendations in June 1981, including the zero-growth ceiling mentioned above. It made several sets of proposals before it was dissolved in March 1983.

Its most important achievement was the basic policy orientation of "fiscal reconstruction without tax increases"; the reduction of bond issues was to be achieved through expenditure cuts, not tax increases. Other proposals included the revision of the social security system and the privatization of public corporations such as the Japan National Railways and the Nihon Telephone and Telegraph Corporation.

As a result of these policies, the rate of increase in expenditures has fallen significantly since FY 1982.[46] The rate of increase in general expenditures (the total budget minus debt-servicing costs and grants-in-aid to local governments) fell to 1.8 per cent in FY 1982, to zero in FY 1983, and then to −0.1 per cent in FY 1984.

Bond issues have also declined steadily since FY 1980.[47] Since the objective of the Suzuki administration turned out to be infeasible because of stagnant tax revenues in FY 1981–82, the Nakasone administration adopted the objective of terminating the issuance of deficit-financing bonds by FY 1990. This is one of the basic policy objectives of the current economic plan, "Outlook and Guidelines for the Economy and Society," formulated in August 1983.

The tight budget was, however, merely superficial for many items. For example, subsidies to public pension programs were reduced in FY 1982—but only for three years on the condition that the reduction be repaid later with interest. Some expenditures were financed by borrowing from special accounts, and the debt-servicing costs in the general account budget were "reduced" by cutting transfers to the debt-servicing special account. A considerable part of the declines visible in Table 5 resulted from such stratagems.

Of course, budget austerity was substantial for some items. Public works expenditures are one example. Government employees' salaries and subsidies to private schools were cut considerably, at least in terms of their growth rates. In FY 1984, a substantial revision in the health insurance program for employees in the private and public sectors reduced the insurance coverage ratio for household heads from 100 per cent to 90 per cent; a further reduction to 80 per cent is scheduled.

These developments reveal the basic workings of the fiscal system: substantial reform is undertaken when fiscal conditions as represented by the bond dependency ratio become serious. This is contrary to the Buchanan-Wagner hypothesis, as I argued above.

Public Finance and the Macroeconomy

A convenient way to analyze changes in macroeconomic structure is the sectoral saving-investment gaps in the national account statistics. Until the mid-1970s, the excess saving of the household sector was absorbed mostly by the excess investment of the corporate sector, and the private sector's excess saving was on average negative.[48] During this period, the excess saving of the general government was positive, and the general government was a net supplier of funds.

The structure has changed significantly since the first oil shock. The excess saving of the private sector has become positive, the ratio to GNP being around 2 to 5 per cent (see Fig. 7). During this period, household investment remained almost unchanged, and the sum of household and corporate savings decreased in terms of their ratio to GNP. The major factor behind the increase in private sector excess saving was a fall in corporate investment. Its ratio to GNP has fallen from over 20 per cent during

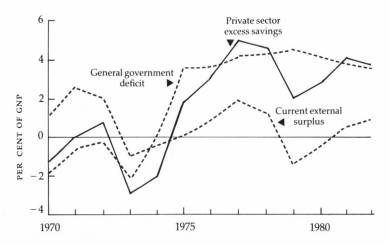

Fig. 7. Private sector excess savings and external balance, FY 1970–1982.
Source: Japan, Economic Planning Agency, *Yearbook of National Account Statistics* (Tokyo: Government Printing Bureau, annual).

the early 1970s to about 15 per cent in recent years. This decrease is closely related to the fall in corporate profits. These changes had already occurred before the first oil shock.

According to a basic macroeconomic identity, the excess saving of the private sector must be equal to the sum of the government deficit and current external surplus. Although the excess saving of the private sector has increased, most of this has been offset by increased government deficit (see Fig. 7). Even in 1972–73, when Japan's external surplus reached a record level, the public sector absorbed over half of the private sector's excess saving.

Expansion of the government deficit had a strong impact on demand and supply conditions for funds. Until the mid-1970s, the basic function of the financial system was to channel the excess saving of the household sector to the corporate sector, which was the only net demander of funds in the economy. A fundamental change after the first oil shock was that the general government became an important source of demand for funds. In such years as 1977 and 1978, the government absorbed almost half the excess saving of the household sector. (In recent years, the share of the government has been about one-third.)

Some people regard the expansion of the government deficit as a result of an intentional demand management policy to cope with the increase in the private sector's excess saving. I noted above that this is not the case (see Fig. 1 for confirmation). The ratio of government investment to GNP was remarkably stable during this period, in contrast to corporate investment. Although government investment increased considerably as a result of an expansionary fiscal policy in FY 1972–73, it did not bring about a change in the saving-investment structure of the economy. Government saving decreased significantly during this period in terms of its ratio to GNP. As discussed in the preceding sections, this was caused by an increase in transfer payments.

It is interesting that while the government deficit has increased in terms of its ratio to GNP, household saving has also increased.[49] The sum of government deficit (saving-investment gap) and household saving has been remarkably stable in terms of its ratio to GNP except in FY 1974.[50] It may be possible to interpret this as evidence of the mechanism suggested by Robert Barro; that is, people regard expansion of the government deficit as implying a future tax increase, and they increase saving rather than consumption.[51] If this interpretation is correct, intergenerational transfer caused by the public sector is offset by increased household saving, as far as the explicit government debt is concerned.

However, corporate saving decreased significantly during this period. The sum of household saving and corporate saving has also been fairly stable. We can infer the presence of a mechanism first noted by Martin

Feldstein, and later advanced in a somewhat different form by Paul David and John Scadding.[52] The increase in household saving may have been an adjustment to the drop in corporate saving, rather than to the increase in the government deficit. Actually, the ratio of total saving in the economy to GNP has decreased.

It is still possible to argue that household saving has adjusted to both the drop in corporate saving and the increase in government deficit, but only insufficiently. This is probable considering that changes in corporate saving and government deficit do not necessarily cause one-to-one changes in household's perceived permanent income.

Although the effect of changes in fiscal variables on short-run economic performance is an important problem, I do not undertake a rigorous analysis here and make only some preliminary observations.

Although the growth rate of real government investment has fluctuated greatly from year to year, the growth rate of GNP has been relatively stable, especially since 1975 (see Fig. 8).[53] The view that the expansionary fiscal policy of 1977–78 was the basic factor behind the Japanese economy's recovery from the recession caused by the first oil shock cannot be supported by the information in Fig. 8: the growth rate had already reached the 5 per cent level before the expansionary policy was undertaken in FY 1977, and the policy had no significant effect on the real

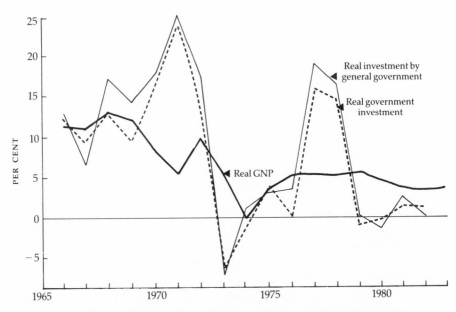

Fig. 8. Growth rates of real GNP and real government investment, FY 1965–1982. See Fig. 7 for source.

growth rate of the economy in subsequent years. One may then wonder where the increased demand generated by the expansionary fiscal policy disappeared. One possibility has been suggested above: increased household saving absorbed the increased demand. As mentioned above, this adjustment may have been incomplete.

Another possibility is that the increased government expenditure crowded out net exports. In an open economy where international movement of capital is free, this is quite possible: interest rates rise because of increased bond issues, causing capital inflow and appreciation of the currency and reducing net exports. In fact, the yen began to appreciate dramatically shortly after the expansionary fiscal policy of 1977, and the external surplus (national account basis) fell in 1978. (Needless to say, the external surplus is affected by various factors other than those mentioned here, and a more rigorous analysis is necessary.)

Future Problems and Prospects

The relative size of the government in the economy is still small in Japan compared with European countries. The main reason is that the share of social security expenditures in national income remains small in Japan, despite the remarkable changes of the early 1970s. Social security expenditures will, however, increase further in the future because of the aging of the population and the maturing of public pension programs. This will increase overall government expenditures because the share of social security expenditures in the total budget is significant. There is some possibility that the gap between revenues and expenditures will grow. This will become a serious problem because it is likely that saving ratios will fall. In this sense, a true fiscal crisis is a problem to be faced in the future.

Various attempts have been made to estimate future social security expenditures; the most comprehensive was made by the Economic Council in 1982 (see Table 6).[54] The ratio of social security transfers to national income will increase from the present level of 13.7 per cent to 25.3 per cent in the year 2000 and to 31.2 per cent in 2010. Most of the increase will result from the growth of public pension payments: their share in national income will rise from 4.8 to 17.1 per cent of national income between now and 2010. This accounts for about 70 per cent of the total increase in social security expenditures.

Social security burdens will increase significantly. Contributions, now 10.1 per cent of national income, will rise to 15.6 per cent in the year 2000 and to 21.4 per cent in 2010. (The difference between benefits and contributions corresponds to subsidies from the general account.)

According to a separate estimate by the Ministry of Welfare the contri-

TABLE 6

*Projected Growth of Social Security Benefits and Social Security Contributions
in Japan, FY 1981-2010*

(per cent of national income)

Category	1981	1990	1995	2000	2005	2010
Social security benefit	13.7%	18.4%	21.3%	25.3%	29.8%	31.2%
Public pension	4.8	8.7	11.1	13.8	17.1	17.1
Health insurance	5.0	5.9	6.3	7.2	8.2	9.3
Social security contribution	10.1%	11.2%	11.6%	15.6%	19.0%	21.4%
Public pension	5.4	6.0	6.2	9.7	12.6	14.5
Health insurance	3.8	4.2	4.4	4.9	5.4	5.9

SOURCE: Japan, Economic Planning Agency, *2000 nen no Nihon* (Japan in the year 2000) (Tokyo: Government Printing Office, 1982).

bution rate (the ratio of contributions to earnings excluding bonuses) to the Employees' Pension Fund will rise to 38.8 per cent in 2030 if the present benefit formulas remain unchanged.[55] Since this apparently exceeds a tolerable limit, some reforms must be made to reduce the burden to a reasonable level.

In FY 1986, a "fundamental" reform was made in public pension programs. The plan introduced a "basic pension" covering everyone regardless of their employment status and a complicated reduction in the effective rate of government subsidies. However, the plan incorporated few revisions in the basic benefit-contribution structure. Virtually the only substantial change was a moderate increase in the contribution rate (in the case of the Employees' Pension Fund, from 10.6 per cent to 12.8 per cent). Basic revisions such as raising the eligibility age or lowering the replacement ratio were left to the future.

The growth of social security expenditures will have a significant impact on the overall budget. In the following, I assume that (1) the elasticity of tax revenues with respect to national income is 1.1; and (2) the growth rates of expenditures other than for social security and of current revenues other than tax and social security contributions will be the same as that of national income. The assumption concerning expenditures probably causes an underestimation bias since it neglects the fact that debt-servicing costs will increase faster than national income. Thus, the result should be interpreted as a lower limit.

There are several important points about the results, which are summarized in Table 7. First, the relative size of the government in economy will increase dramatically in the coming decades, reaching about the same level as that in European countries today, both on the expenditure and the revenue sides. Second, the share of social security in public finance will grow. On the expenditure side, the share of social security benefits in total expenditures will increase from the present level of 32.1 per cent to 51.7 per cent by the year 2010. On the revenue side, the relative weight of social security contributions, which is now 26.6 per cent of total revenues, will grow to 39.3 per cent by 2010. Among the social security programs, the growth of public pension programs is the most important factor (see Table 6). Third, the gap between revenues and expenditures will grow in the future. This gap must be closed by tax increases, expenditure cuts, and/or bond issues.

Budget deficits have not caused serious economic problems so far in Japan, mainly because of the large savings of the household sector. In fact, the huge external surplus of the Japanese economy results from the ability of the excess saving of the private sector to absorb the general government deficit.

This condition is likely to change. One factor is the aging of population. Since people save while young in order to dissave after retirement, an increase in the number of elderly people will reduce total savings. In addition, there is a possibility that public pension programs may reduce household savings further because an important reason for saving loses its meaning if retirement life is made secure by public pensions.[56] Unless public pension programs are managed according to the full-funded method—the method of financing pensions by accumulated funds—no increase in government savings will offset the reduction in household savings, and total savings will be reduced.

TABLE 7
Projected Growth of Expenditures and Revenues of the General Government,
FY 1981-2010
(per cent of national income)

Category	1981	1995	2000	2005	2010
Expenditures					
Social security					
benefits	13.7%	21.3%	25.3%	29.8%	31.2%
Other	29.1	29.1	29.1	29.1	29.1
TOTAL	42.7%	50.4%	54.3%	58.9%	60.3%
Revenues					
Taxes	24.2%	26.8%	27.6%	28.6%	29.4%
Social security					
contributions	10.1	11.6	15.6	19.0	21.4
SUBTOTAL	(34.3)	(38.4)	(43.1)	(47.5)	(50.9)
Other current					
revenues	3.7	3.7	3.7	3.7	3.7
TOTAL	38.0%	42.1%	46.9%	51.3%	54.5%
Gap (revenues −					
expenditures)	−4.7%	−8.3%	−7.5%	−7.7%	−5.7%

Thus, fiscal deficits will become a serious macroeconomic problem. The necessity of reducing the deficit will become urgent, not only for political and administrative reasons to increase the degree of freedom in budget making, but also for macroeconomic reasons. The problem is how to accomplish this. Apparently, there are only two ways to reduce a structural deficit: cutting expenditures or increasing tax revenues.

In theory, there is room for expenditure cuts. For instance, many agricultural expenditures are difficult to justify on efficiency grounds. Also, many public works expenditures, especially those in rural areas, could be reduced. It is, however, difficult to implement such measures, given the present system of budget making. As mentioned above, there have been many superficial elements in the recent fiscal austerity. Of course, there is a possibility of achieving stronger austerities if tight budget policies are continued. However, it may well be that national government expenditures can be reduced only by transferring burdens to local governments.

Another measure to reduce deficits is tax increases. Politically, the easiest way to increase the tax burden is to rely on the automatic increase mechanism of the income tax, and it is likely that the tax burden will be increased through this mechanism. However, this will aggravate the distortions in the tax structure mentioned earlier. Thus, the introduction of a new tax, such as the general consumption tax, will become necessary. It is uncertain, however, whether this will be done in the near future because of the political difficulties.

Finally, it is necessary to consider the timing of reforms. Here again, the basic issue is the funding of public pension programs. Many people believe that the problems of public pensions are not urgent and that gradual reform would be best. This belief is incorrect. If reforms are carried out gradually, future generations will suffer from both increased contributions and reduced benefits (if the reduction in benefits is undertaken earlier, the need to increase contributions will be alleviated). The relationship between lifetime contributions and lifetime benefits needs to change significantly. It is possible that, under a plausible reform plan, the lifetime benefits of someone who is now young will be less than lifetime contributions, on a present-value basis.[57] This implies that the internal rate of return on public pensions will become lower than the interest rate—that is, that people can receive higher pension benefits from private programs than from public programs, with the same amount of contributions.

However, it is unlikely that this will occur because people will demand benefits that correspond to their contributions. Politically, this scenario seems likely because, in the twenty-first century, more than one-third of all voters will be pension beneficiaries. But this will trigger a vicious circle because this demand can be met only by transferring even more of the burden to subsequent generations. In order to prevent this, reforms must be undertaken at the earliest possible date.

Appendix A: An Outline of the Japanese Budget System

The Japanese public finance system can be divided into the national system and the local system.[58] Since the budget system of each local government is similar to that of the national government, the latter is described here.

The national budget consists of the general account budget, special account budgets, and budgets of government-affiliated agencies. The revenues of almost all national taxes, as well as those of long-term bonds, become revenues of the general account. Most general account outlays are transfers and subsidies to various special accounts and to local governments (in fact, few outlays are directly disbursed from the general account except for the salaries of government employees). Although the general account is only a part of the entire public finance system in terms of its size, it can exert considerable influence over the entire system, including local governments, through these transfers and subsidies. In this sense, the figures of the general account can be regarded as representing the whole picture of Japanese public finance, at least as far as policy changes are concerned.

Special accounts are established when it is necessary to distinguish the related flow of funds from that of other government activities. Government enterprises such as the Government Printing Bureau and social insurance such as public pensions are managed by special accounts. The number of special accounts has risen to nearly 40 in recent years. Many special accounts have their own sources of revenues. For example, social security contributions become revenues of social insurance special accounts. However, some special accounts are financed entirely by transfers from the general account.

Government-affiliated agencies have separate legal status from the state. They include the Japan National Railways, the Japan Development Bank, and the Japan Housing Loan Corporation. Their budgets constitute a part of the national budget and must be approved by the Diet.

In addition to the above, there are many public corporations such as the Japan Highway Corporation and the Japan Housing and Urban Development Corporation. Significant portions of their activities are financed by the Fiscal Investment and Loan Program, a government-operated financial system. There are government regulations on their activities and personnel decisions. Their budgets are not subject to Diet approval.

Many features of the Japanese budgetary system are different from those of other countries. The following points are noteworthy, especially in comparison with the U.S. system.

1. Long-term bond revenues are included in the general account revenues. Thus, at the budget stage, the total amount of expenditures must be equal to that of revenues (in the settlement, there could be a difference between the two). In spite of this, the amount of bond revenues is usually called the "deficit."

2. Social security contributions do not become revenues of the general account, as mentioned above. On the expenditure side, only subsidies for social security programs appear in the general account. Thus, in order to find the total revenues and outlays of social security programs, one must include those of the related special accounts.

3. As a consequence of this treatment, the nature of the deficit in Japan is different from that in the United States, where entire revenues and outlays of social security programs are included in the federal budget. Since public pension programs in Japan yield surpluses at present, the magnitude of the deficit would be considerably smaller if a definition similar to the one used in the United States were adopted.

Appendix B: An Outline of the Social Security System

The Japanese social security system consists of three major components: public assistance, social insurance, and other welfare programs. The social insurance system, which consists of health insurance, public pensions, and unemployment compensation, is the most important of the three, especially from a fiscal viewpoint.

The social insurance system in Japan is complex because people of different employment statuses belong to different programs. The basic distinction made in the system is among employees of private firms, government employees, and the self-employed. In the case of public pensions, employees of private firms belong to the Employees' Pension Fund (*Kōsei Nenkin*), the self-employed to the People's Pension Fund (*Kokumin Nenkin*), and government employees to the Cooperative Pension Fund (*Kyōsai Nenkin*).

Administrative arrangements vary as well. Health insurance for the self-employed is operated by local governments, that for employees of large private firms is operated by cooperatives in each firm, and all other programs are operated by special accounts of the national government. For most programs, subsidies are provided from the general account budget; that is, the programs are financed both by social security contributions and taxes. In the case of the Employees' Pension Fund, the subsidy is 20 per cent of benefits.[59]

Appendix C: The SNA Data and the General Account Data

Trends in public expenditures can be analyzed using several statistical sources. In the text, both the system of national account (SNA) data and the general account data are used extensively.

In the SNA, the government sector is classified into five categories:

1. Central general government—the general account and non-enterprise special accounts of the national budget;

2. Central social security fund—social insurance special accounts;

3. Local general government—general accounts and non-enterprise special accounts of local governments;

4. Central public corporations—government enterprise special accounts, government-affiliated agencies, and other government-related corporations;

5. Local public corporations—public enterprise special accounts and agencies affiliated with local governments.

In most published tables, public corporations are included in the corporation sector, and only the general government data are shown separately. The central government and local governments are not distinguished in most tables of the general government.

It would be convenient if either the SNA data or the general account data could be used throughout the discussion. But this is not always possible because both series have advantages and shortcomings. The merits of the SNA data include the following:

1. Because the SNA data are based on internationally common standards, they are convenient for international comparisons;

2. It is also appropriate to use the SNA data in macroeconomic discussions becaues duplications between various accounts and between various levels of government are eliminated and because consumption, investments, and transfers are distinguished;

3. In order to see total outlays for social security programs, it is better to look at the general government accounts rather than the general account of the national government for the reasons mentioned in Appendix A.

However, the SNA data are not appropriate for some policy discussions for four reasons:

1. Although a breakdown of public expenditure figures by policy area is made in the SNA data ("Outlay of General Government Expenditures

by Purposes"), the grouping is too aggregated for most policy discussions. For example, expenditures for agriculture cannot be distinguished from those for other industries. Nor is a breakdown of public works expenditures into such categories as roads, sewers, and flood control available. In many instances, one is forced to use more detailed data such as the general account data.

2. The problems of the national government and those of local governments are in many cases considerably different, but it is not always possible to distinguish these two levels of government in the SNA data.

3. In discussing the government deficit, we are usually interested in the deficit in the general account budget of the national government because this is related to the issuance of long-term national bonds. Even if central government data are available, the saving-investment gap in SNA differs considerably from the amount of national bonds issued because of the surpluses in the social insurance special accounts.

4. Although some data are available from 1965, most of the SNA data are available only from 1970. There are discontinuities between the SNA data and the national income data that cover the earlier periods.

For these reasons, both series of data are used in the text. The SNA data are used for international comparisons and for macroeconomic discussions. The general account data are used for discussions of most policy matters. With regard to expenditures, the "General Account Budget by Major Items," prepared by the Ministry of Finance, is used. Although the general account of the national budget covers only a part of the entire system, its analysis reveals the essence of public finance in Japan because it has substantial influence on various aspects of the entire fiscal system. Moreover, data for a fairly long period (since the 1950s) are available (although the grouping of items changes slightly from year to year, historical figures rearranged according to the most recent standard are calculated and published).

It is important not to confuse the general government and the general account of the national budget. As mentioned above, the former includes not only the latter but also local governments and non-enterprise special accounts such as social insurance special accounts. Also, the "general expenditure" category in the general account of the national budget (defined in the section entitled "Financial Reconstruction") should not be confused with general government expenditures.

Koichi Hamada and Akiyoshi Horiuchi

The Political Economy of the
Financial Market

The Japanese economy experienced remarkably rapid growth from the mid-1950s to the early 1970s. Since the mid-1970s, economic growth has clearly slowed. Reflecting the changes in the real economy during the past three decades, Japanese financial markets have undergone substantial changes.

In this paper, we focus on developmental processes in postwar Japanese financial markets and examine three questions. First, did the Japanese financial system, in fact, promote economic development, and, if so, how and to what extent? Not only is the macroeconomic question of whether the Japanese financial system and the management of it promoted greater savings and capital accumulation worthy of our attention, the microeconomic question of whether it helped foster a desirable industrial structure by selectively channeling funds to the more important sectors of the economy also deserves some attention. In particular, we investigate the roles of the monetary authorities and their influence on the financial system and examine the conventional but highly problematic view that Japanese policymakers deliberately and successfully controlled financial markets in order to promote economic growth.

Second, who gained from the regulation of financial markets? Financial intermediation involves savers as fund suppliers, users of funds ranging from large ex-*zaibatsu* enterprises to small and medium-size firms to borrowers from the notorious consumer loan companies, and various intermediaries. This question concerns the distribution of the benefits and the costs to the parties involved in the financial intermediation process.

Third, what has been the driving force behind financial development? Financial innovation and reform are based on agreement, negotiation, and mediation between conflicting interests represented by various sectors of society. If the gains from reform appear unlikely to outweigh the costs, the status quo will prevail, reflecting a political equilibrium among all the parties involved. If such exogenous shocks as technological innovations in the financial industry and the steady accumulation of government debts occur, as in the late 1970s, the cost-benefit structure for the participants will change (the disintermediation of the banking sector is a good example). A movement toward change will arise because the status quo has become intolerable for some participants and political pressures for reform have mounted.

In this sense, a near crisis in the financial structure is often considered a requirement for the institutional development of financial markets and practices. Although the government usually intervenes to protect the status quo, the government itself rests on a balance among various political forces. If a substantial change occurs in the cost-benefit structure because of the adoption of reforms, greater political pressure to change the structure and workings of financial markets will result.

In Tables 1–2, we summarize the changes that have occurred in the Japanese financial system since World War II. A comparison of the assets and liabilities held by the nonfinancial sectors shows that incorporated businesses were by far the largest borrowers in financial markets, and individuals, by contrast, borrowed much less.[1] Private financial institutions collected savings from individuals mainly in the form of safe and highly divisible deposit accounts carrying low rates of interest. These institutions, in turn, supplied funds to incorporated businesses primarily through loans.[2] The obvious question is, Was there a correlation between Japan's "miraculous" economic growth and the dominance of private financial intermediaries? Some scholars argue that the government successfully controlled the financial intermediation process undertaken by private financial intermediaries, primarily the big city banks.[3] In this paper, we present an alternative view.

As Tables 1–2 show, a substantial shift in the structure of the flow of funds occurred in the mid-1970s. This change resulted from the government's (including local governments') entrance into financial markets as a large-scale borrower. The influence of this shift on the Japanese financial system is an important topic of this paper.

Governmental financial institutions also played a significant role as lenders of funds (see Table 3) although their relative importance declined from the late 1950s to the early 1970s. Precisely what role they played, especially during the high growth period, is an important issue.

As Table 3 further shows, the share of the city banks (toshi ginkō), the leading figures among private financial institutions, declined during the high growth period, and that of financial institutions catering to small and medium-size businesses (chūshō kigyō kin'yū kikan) remained steady. The former were important as the main suppliers of funds to businesses in the modern sectors, particularly the heavy and chemical industries.

TABLE 1
External Finances of Nonfinancial Sectors, 1954-1983
(annual average, billion ¥)

Period		Government				Corporations						Individuals			
		Bonds	Loans	Other	Total	Stocks	Bonds	Loans	Trade Credits	Other	Total	Loans	Trade Credits	Other	Total
1954-58	Billion ¥	112	104	1	217	224	43	857	302	60	1,486	208	150	0	358
	Per cent	(51.6)	(47.9)	(0.5)	(100.0)	(15.1)	(2.9)	(57.7)	(20.3)	(4.1)	(100.0)	(58.1)	(41.9)	(0.0)	(100.0)
1959-63	Billion ¥	215	214	18	447	617	196	2,529	1,815	240	5,397	603	471	0	1,074
	Per cent	(48.1)	(47.9)	(4.0)	(100.0)	(11.4)	(3.6)	(46.9)	(33.6)	(4.5)	(100.0)	(56.2)	(43.8)	(0.0)	(100.0)
1964-68	Billion ¥	1,417	492	10	1,919	443	211	4,429	2,191	371	7,645	1,454	665	60	2,179
	Per cent	(73.8)	(25.6)	(0.5)	(100.0)	(5.8)	(2.8)	(57.9)	(28.7)	(4.8)	(100.0)	(66.7)	(30.5)	(2.8)	(100.0)
1969-73	Billion ¥	2,604	1,564	20	4,188	992	483	12,326	8,078	449	22,328	4,676	1,758	27	6,461
	Per cent	(62.2)	(37.3)	(0.5)	(100.0)	(4.4)	(2.2)	(55.2)	(36.2)	(2.0)	(100.0)	(72.4)	(27.2)	(0.4)	(100.0)
1974-78	Billion ¥	12,276	5,183	71	17,530	1,031	965	12,930	5,433	295	20,654	7,969	1,682	0	9,651
	Per cent	(70.0)	(29.6)	(0.4)	(100.0)	(5.0)	(4.7)	(62.6)	(26.3)	(1.4)	(100.0)	(82.6)	(17.4)	(0.0)	(100.0)
1979-83	Billion ¥	17,425	7,415	−140	24,700	1,667	1,307	16,530	7,616	43	27,163	10,190	1,872	9	12,070
	Per cent	(70.5)	(30.0)	(−0.6)	(100.0)	(6.1)	(4.8)	(60.9)	(28.0)	(0.2)	(100.0)	(84.4)	(15.5)	(0.1)	(100.0)

SOURCES: Bank of Japan, *Flow of Funds Accounts in Japan*: *1954-1964* (Nov. 1983), *1965-1974* (Dec. 1977), *1970-1977* (Sept. 1978), *1975-1981* (Sept. 1982); and *Chōsa geppō*, June 1983 and June 1984.

TABLE 2
Increments of Main Financial Assets of Nonfinancial Sectors, 1954-1983
(annual average, billion ¥)

Periods	Government				Corporations					Individuals				
	Deposits	Securities	Other	Total	Deposits	Securities	Trade credit	Other	Total	Deposit	Trust and insurance	Securities	Other	Total
1954-58														
Billion ¥	66	10	71	147	302	74	452	-21	807	612	167	151	91	1,021
Per cent	(44.9)	(6.8)	(48.3)	(100.0)	(37.4)	(9.2)	(56.0)	(-2.6)	(100.0)	(59.9)	(18.4)	(14.8)	(8.9)	(100.0)
1959-63														
Billion ¥	178	10	167	355	1,149	228	2,286	-52	3,612	1,380	461	588	269	2,694
Per cent	(50.1)	(2.8)	(47.0)	(100.0)	(31.8)	(6.3)	(63.3)	(-1.4)	(100.0)	(51.2)	(17.1)	(21.8)	(9.8)	(100.0)
1964-68														
Billion ¥	519	5	233	757	1,742	293	2,856	413	5,304	3,299	1,080	490	762	5,630
Per cent	(68.5)	(0.7)	(30.8)	(100.0)	(32.8)	(5.5)	(53.8)	(7.8)	(100.0)	(58.6)	(19.2)	(8.7)	(13.5)	(100.0)
1969-73														
Billion ¥	1,490	59	859	2,408	5,222	699	9,835	665	16,420	9,236	1,977	1,428	1,657	14,298
Per cent	(61.9)	(2.5)	(35.7)	(100.0)	(31.8)	(4.3)	(59.9)	(4.0)	(100.0)	(64.6)	(13.8)	(10.0)	(11.6)	(100.0)
1974-78														
Billion ¥	3,151	279	2,048	5,479	5,553	783	7,115	984	14,436	17,584	5,628	3,570	1,203	27,984
Per cent	(57.5)	(5.1)	(37.4)	(100.0)	(38.5)	(5.4)	(49.3)	(6.8)	(100.0)	(62.8)	(20.1)	(12.8)	(4.3)	(100.0)
1979-83														
Billion ¥	4,892	371	1,457	6,719	5,936	2,143	9,497	908	18,483	21,847	9,772	5,122	530	37,271
Per cent	(72.8)	(5.5)	(21.7)	(100.0)	(32.1)	(11.6)	(51.4)	(4.9)	(100.0)	(58.6)	(26.2)	(13.7)	(1.4)	(100.0)

SOURCES: Same as for Table 1.

TABLE 3
Relative Shares of Various Financial Institutions, 1953-1983

End of year	Total assets (billion ¥)	Relative shares (per cent)						
		Private institutions				Public institutions[b]		
		City banks[a]	Fin. inst. for small firms	Other	Total	Gvt. fin. inst.	Other	Total
1953	5,163	51.1%	11.8%	16.7%	79.6%	9.7%	10.7%	20.4%
1954	5,947	46.3	12.2	19.7	78.2	10.2	11.6	21.8
1955	6,858	46.6	13.0	18.4	78.0	10.0	12.0	22.0
1956	8,534	50.1	13.0	16.0	79.1	9.1	11.8	20.9
1957	10,594	48.1	13.0	19.0	80.1	8.5	11.4	19.9
1958	12,564	45.2	13.3	22.0	80.5	8.6	10.9	19.5
1959	15,103	43.1	13.6	24.7	81.4	8.2	10.4	18.6
1960	18,626	42.6	13.9	25.8	82.3	7.8	9.9	17.7
1961	23,219	42.6	14.6	26.2	83.4	7.2	9.4	16.6
1962	27,797	40.8	16.0	26.9	83.7	7.2	9.1	16.3
1963	34,110	42.3	16.6	25.3	84.2	6.8	9.0	15.8
1964	39,923	42.2	17.0	25.2	84.4	7.0	8.6	15.6
1965	46,838	40.3	17.1	27.0	84.4	7.1	8.5	15.6
1966	54,754	37.6	17.2	29.3	84.1	7.2	8.7	15.9
1967	64,094	35.2	17.7	30.8	83.7	7.3	9.0	16.3
1968	74,494	35.4	17.1	30.5	83.0	7.5	9.4	17.0
1969	88,563	35.8	17.4	29.6	82.8	7.5	9.6	17.2
1970	104,228	35.4	17.7	29.7	82.8	7.2	10.0	17.2
1971	127,168	34.3	17.3	31.2	82.8	7.0	10.2	17.2
1972	158,989	34.3	17.5	31.2	83.0	6.5	10.5	17.0
1973	190,853	34.0	18.0	30.5	82.5	6.6	10.9	17.5
1974	219,872	33.2	18.4	30.0	81.6	7.0	11.4	18.4
1975	255,891	31.6	18.3	30.7	80.6	7.2	12.2	19.4
1976	296,660	30.4	18.1	31.2	79.7	7.4	12.9	20.3
1977	337,832	28.2	17.8	32.5	78.5	7.6	13.9	21.5
1978	384,392	27.0	17.7	32.8	77.5	7.7	14.8	22.5
1979	428,188	26.0	17.6	32.8	76.4	8.2	15.4	23.6
1980	475,707	25.8	17.3	32.1	75.2	8.6	16.2	24.8
1981	527,343	24.9	17.2	32.6	74.7	8.9	16.4	25.3
1982	583,558	24.3	16.9	33.0	74.2	9.0	16.8	25.8
1983	648,437	24.0	16.4	33.7	74.1	8.9	17.0	25.9

SOURCES: BOJ, *Flow of Funds Accounts in Japan*, various issues; and *Economic Statistics Annual*, various issues.

[a] The city banks' total assets are estimated from the Bank of Japan's *Economic Statistics Annual*.

[b] Public financial institutions comprise governmental financial institutions, Trust Fund Bureau, and postal savings, postal life insurance, and postal annuity.

In the first section, we examine conditions in Japan immediately following World War II. Those conditions largely determined the fundamental features of Japan's financial mechanism in the period of high economic growth.

In the second section, we explain the monetary authorities' intervention in financial markets during the high growth period. Although the intervention was quite comprehensive, the purposes of the authorities were diverse because of various political pressures. Contrary to conventional wisdom, the authorities failed in many cases to intervene on behalf of industrial pioneers. In our judgment, the government was important, not as a designer of well-conceived plans for allocating funds, but as a coordinator of various interests in the financial markets.

We then investigate the structural changes in Japanese financial markets since the mid-1970s. We suggest several basic causes of the changes and explain the responses of the monetary authorities to the changes. We argue that the recent liberalization of financial markets was an inevitable response by the monetary authorities to the fact of structural change.

In the last section, we suggest some prognoses for the future of the Japanese financial system, even though such an attempt is admittedly fraught with uncertainties, given the ever-changing financial environment.[4]

Financial Mechanisms in the High Growth Period

Several features of financial mechanisms immediately after World War II through the period of high economic growth, or from the 1950s through the early 1970s, are important. First, the Japanese financial structure was relatively stable. The extraordinarily rapid economic growth was achieved under this stability, implying that the structure was consistent with rapid economic growth. How did this structure develop? And what was the role played by Japanese policymakers in exerting intentional control? Our basic contention is that the financial structure of this period was largely determined by several conditions faced by the Japanese economy following World War II. The characteristics of the Japanese financial system were, we believe, the inevitable market responses to these conditions.

In our view, two conditions determined the Japanese financial structure: the low level of financial assets held in the nonfinancial sectors and the small size of the public debt.

The Low Stock of Financial Assets

The level of financial assets held by households and firms at the end of World War II was quite low. As of 1953, by a simple comparison using the conversion rate of $1 equals ¥360, total financial assets held by Japanese nonfinancial sectors were a thirty-fourth of the corresponding figure for the United States. By 1979, this ratio had risen to one-half, using the exchange rate ($1 = ¥225) applicable at that time (see Table 4). Also, the distribution of income and wealth, due to economic democratization after the war, became relatively equal. In effect, only a very few households held large blocks of financial assets.

TABLE 4

Financial Assets Held by the Private Nonfinancial Sectors,
Japan and the United States, 1951-1982

End of year	Japan[a]		United States[c]	
	¥100 billion	per GNP (%)[b]	$100 billion	per GNP (%)[d]
1951			6.2	1.88 (1.47)
1952			6.6	1.90 (1.58)
1953	71.6	0.95 (0.46)	6.8	1.85 (1.46)
1954	82.8	1.06 (0.54)	7.8	2.12 (1.71)
1955	95.6	1.08 (0.56)	8.8	2.19 (1.77)
1956	118.7	1.19 (0.61)	9.3	2.20 (1.79)
1957	140.9	1.25 (0.65)	9.2	2.08 (1.67)
1958	167.0	1.42 (0.73)	10.7	2.38 (1.95)
1959	210.3	1.55 (0.72)	11.5	2.37 (1.94)
1960	255.5	1.58 (0.78)	11.8	2.34 (1.92)
1961	327.6	1.65 (0.77)	13.4	2.56 (2.13)
1962	396.0	1.83 (0.86)	13.3	2.35 (1.94)
1963	492.0	1.92 (0.85)	14.8	2.47 (2.05)
1964	579.1	1.96 (0.89)	16.0	2.51 (2.09)
1965	672.4	2.00 (0.92)	17.6	2.55 (2.13)
1966	783.5	1.99 (0.90)	17.7	2.34 (1.93)
1967	936.4	2.03 (0.92)	20.1	2.52 (2.11)
1968	1,078.2	1.97 (0.90)	22.7	2.60 (2.19)
1969	1,284.7	1.98 (0.91)	22.5	2.39 (1.97)
1970	1,489.2	1.98 (0.91)	23.4	2.35 (1.94)
1971	1,738.9	2.10 (0.98)	26.0	2.41 (2.00)
1972	2,100.0	2.18 (1.03)	28.9	2.43 (2.01)
1973	2,597.1	2.23 (1.02)	28.7	2.17 (1.73)
1974	2,930.0	2.12 (1.02)	27.7	1.93 (1.53)
1975	3,383.3	2.23 (1.10)	31.6	2.04 (1.65)
1976	3,865.0	2.27 (1.15)	36.1	2.10 (1.71)
1977	4,259.4	2.25 (1.20)	38.5	2.00 (1.63)
1978	4,806.1	2.32 (1.26)	42.5	1.96 (1.58)
1979	5,379.4	2.42 (1.33)	47.7	1.97 (1.58)
1980	5,974.7	2.48 (1.36)	56.2	2.13 (1.72)
1981	6,600.9	2.60 (1.45)	59.9	2.04 (1.65)
1982	7,100.4	2.69 (1.54)	65.6	2.14 (1.76)

SOURCES: BOJ, *Flow of Funds Accounts in Japan*; Japan Economic Planning Agency, *Annual Report on National Income Statistics*, and *Annual Report of National Accounts*; Federal Reserve System, Board of Governors, *Flow of Funds Accounts: Assets and Liabilities Outstanding*; Council of Economic Advisers, *Economic Report of the President*, Feb. 1983.

[a]Corporations + personal.

[b]The parentheses show the ratio of the personal sector's financial assets to GNP.

[c]Nonfinancial business + household.

[d]The parentheses show the ratio of household financial assets to GNP.

Economies of scale are recognized in financial transactions. Transaction costs in financial markets tend to increase more slowly in proportion to increases in trading volume. The Japanese nonfinancial sectors with their small amounts of financial assets faced substantial transaction costs, which prevented them from diversifying their assets and greatly biased their portfolios toward both safe and divisible assets such as bank and postal savings deposits.[5] Thus, the low level of accumulated financial assets and the associated transaction costs allowed the banking sector to become a predominant influence in postwar financial markets.

The Small Size of the Public Debt

A salient feature of Japanese financial markets that distinguishes them from those in the United States or the United Kingdom was that the stock of outstanding public bonds was quite low during the period of high economic growth, especially during the 1960s. The accumulated public debt held by the private sectors totaled only a small percentage of GNP. In contrast, the corresponding ratio for the United States was well over 50 per cent of GNP in the early 1950s, though it gradually declined through the end of the 1970s (see Table 5).

The scarcity of public bonds was crucial to the financial mechanism of this early period; secondary markets for bonds were not developed and suitable substitutes for bank deposits were not introduced.[6] This constrained liquidity adjustment by the Bank of Japan (BOJ). Without well-developed secondary markets for public bonds, the BOJ had to rely either on operations in the interbank money market (the call money market, where the market mechanism was relatively developed) or on the adjustment of its loans to private banks, particularly the city banks, as a means of monetary control. In light of the above, the financial markets of the high growth period were broadly characterized by a scarcity of public bonds.[7]

Some Features of Financial Mechanisms

Immature capital markets. Since the low stock of assets held in the nonfinancial sectors made transaction costs in financial markets quite substantial, the nonfinancial sectors, especially households, tended to concentrate their savings in a few safe and liquid assets such as bank and postal savings deposits. The essential role of the financial system was to transform, in an efficient manner, these short-term liabilities into the long-term credits that the business sector eagerly desired. Admittedly, Japanese financial institutions were active in maturity transformation of financial assets. If, however, the commercial banks had been the only financial institutions to provide nonfinancial businesses with long-term funds, the degree of maturity transformation would have been so drastic as to threaten their viability.

The long-term credit banks (*chōki shin'yō ginkō*) were established in 1952 to overcome this limitation. These banks supply long-term funds by issuing bank debentures whose maturities are relatively long compared

TABLE 5
Government Debt, Japan and the United States, 1951-1982

End of year	Japan		United States	
	¥100 billion	per GNP (%)[a]	$ billion	per GNP (%)
1951			218.2	66.0
1952			223.6	64.3
1953	6.2	8.8 (6.3)	230.6	62.9
1954	7.6	9.7 (5.7)	233.0	63.5
1955	8.6	10.0 (4.9)	233.2	58.3
1956	9.0	9.2 (4.2)	227.8	54.0
1957	7.3	6.6 (3.6)	226.9	51.1
1958	9.2	8.0 (3.5)	235.8	52.4
1959	11.1	8.6 (3.6)	244.8	50.2
1960	11.3	7.3 (2.9)	243.1	48.0
1961	8.5	4.5 (2.3)	250.8	47.8
1962	9.2	4.3 (2.0)	259.1	45.9
1963	10.5	4.3 (1.8)	264.7	44.4
1964	12.8	4.4 (1.5)	271.4	42.6
1965	14.5	4.2 (0.9)	275.3	39.8
1966	23.3	5.9 (2.9)	284.5	37.6
1967	32.9	7.1 (3.9)	297.7	37.2
1968	42.3	7.7 (4.4)	315.1	36.1
1969	50.3	7.8 (4.4)	321.2	34.0
1970	55.3	7.4 (4.2)	343.0	34.6
1971	63.3	7.7 (4.7)	373.8	34.7
1972	95.1	9.8 (6.2)	397.4	33.5
1973	103.4	8.9 (6.5)	425.7	32.1
1974	127.4	9.2 (6.8)	457.6	31.9
1975	185.7	12.3 (9.2)	552.5	35.7
1976	264.4	15.6 (12.8)	636.7	37.1
1977	371.4	19.7 (16.1)	716.7	37.4
1978	545.3	26.4 (20.4)	807.1	37.3
1979	660.3	29.8 (24.2)	893.2	36.9
1980	812.9	33.8 (28.0)	1,016.1	38.6
1981	972.5	38.3 (32.0)	1,149.1	39.1
1982	1,086.6	41.2 (35.4)	1,375.0	45.0

SOURCES: Same as for Table 4.
[a]The parentheses show the ratio of the medium- and long-term government bonds outstanding to GNP.

with those of bank deposits. Commercial banks, especially city banks, bought most of these debentures. Since bank debentures were much more liquid than nonfinancial business liabilities (long-term loans to corporate firms), they helped commercial banks avoid an extreme degree of maturity transformation.

Government funds were important in the immature capital markets. These are collected mainly by means of postal savings deposits, postal life insurance, and postal annuities, and they are supplied to various industries mostly in the form of long-term credit. The proportion of government funds to the total amount of long-term equipment funds supplied to private businesses was high, particularly in the first half of the high growth period. It can safely be said that the government funds functioned to complement the immature capital markets. (We shall discuss the complementary role of government funds in the next section.)

The connection between banks and firms. Even if businesses in the nonfinancial sectors had been permitted to raise funds freely in the capital markets, by selling securities directly to the nonfinancial sectors, the extent to which they could have satisfied their financial demands would have been limited. Moreover, Japanese firms were, in general, conducting their businesses under extreme uncertainty. Their securities not only were devoid of homogeneity but also were risky for investors in the nonfinancial sector. Firms had to rely on financial institutions, particularly commercial banks, in order to collect the necessary funds for business activities. Under these conditions, they found it desirable to create and maintain intimate relationships with a few banks.

Long-term relationships with firms, especially those whose performance was good, were equally beneficial to the banks. Such relationships were useful in reducing transaction costs such as the examining and monitoring costs. During periods of tight monetary control, many banks decrease their lending but continue to supply necessary funds to main customers.[8]

Indeed, the *zaibatsu* conglomerates originated some customer relationships between banks and firms. New firms were, however, able to create such relationships without assistance from the *zaibatsu*. Such connections between banks and firms, or *keiretsu* (business liaisons between banks and groups of nonfinancial firms), are not peculiar to Japan.[9] Because of the long prewar history of *zaibatsu* groups and the primitive postwar financial structure, however, such groups were more conspicuous in Japan.

The system of corporate finance based on bank loans was partially supplemented by a relatively important network of trade credit (see Tables 1–2). Some of the major nonfinancial corporations, especially large trading companies, supplied financial services through trade credits. Trade credits were a particularly important substitute for bank loans as a method of supplying funds to many small businesses.

Keiretsu did not, however, maintain exclusive relations with one bank. Individual firms did borrow substantially from banks other than their main bank.[10] Certainly, the possibility exists that the patterns of fund allocation for groups of firms differed from those that might have resulted from atomistic competition in financial markets. It is not certain, however, that the patterns of fund allocation were in themselves growth stimulating.[11] At any rate, the connections between banks and firms in the nonfinancial sector should be regarded as the spontaneous responses of markets to the specific financial conditions immediately after World War II.

The marginal role of the equity stock market. Japanese capital markets in the period under discussion, particularly the equity stock market, were relatively important until the mid-1960s. By the early 1960s, the funds raised by Japanese firms in the nonfinancial sector by issuing equity stocks accounted for around 13 per cent of the total of their externally financed funds. This figure was slightly larger than the corresponding figure for the United States (see Table 6). The volume of equity stocks held by the individual sector was significant, accounting for about 20 per cent of that sector's total financial assets during the period (see Table 7).

Equity finance, therefore, played a marginal role in the Japanese financial mechanism. In particular, during periods of tight monetary policy, firms tended to increase their reliance on equity financing, thereby sharply depressing stock prices.[12] This had a destabilizing effect on the stock market. Tight monetary policy implied not only a decline in asset demand, but also an increase in asset supply in the stock market. In other words, a substantial part of the burden created by tight monetary control fell on the stock market. The extremely tight monetary policy of

TABLE 6

*Nonfinancial Corporations' Net Increase in Liability and Its Components,
Japan and the United States, 1953-1982*

| Period | Net increase per annum | Components (per cent) | | | | | | | |
		Net new equity issue	Corporate bonds	Loans by private fin. insts.	Loans by public fin. insts.	Trade debt	Foreign debt	Other
			JAPAN (¥100 billion)					
1954-57	14.0	15.1%	2.7%	50.5%	6.2%	21.0%	4.5%	
1958-62	41.5	13.4	4.2	42.1	3.9	32.7	3.6	
1963-67	72.9	6.2	2.8	51.4	5.9	30.5	2.9	
1968-72	169.5	5.0	2.1	56.8	4.7	28.4	3.1	
1973-77	238.3	4.4	3.3	51.6	6.8	32.8	1.1	
1978-82	257.7	6.3	3.0	49.3	7.9	31.2	2.3	
			UNITED STATES (billion $)					
1953-57	13.0	13.0%	30.2%	13.8%	−0.2%	25.7%	1.3%	16.2%
1958-62	16.2	9.7	26.2	12.2	0.5	25.3	0.8	25.3
1963-67	29.7	3.0	25.7	23.0	0.7	30.4	0.3	16.9
1968-72	59.4	10.6	25.7	14.8	0.3	27.0	0.8	20.8
1973-77	90.0	7.7	24.6	16.3	0.5	24.0	2.6	24.3

SOURCES: BOJ, *Flow of Funds Accounts in Japan*; Federal Reserve System, Board of Governors, *Flow of Funds Accounts, 1948-1978*, Dec. 1979.

TABLE 7

Components of the Personal Sector's Financial Assets, Japan, 1954-1983

End of year	Total (¥100 billion)	Cash and demand deposits	Time deposits	Postal savings deposits	Trust and insurance	Securities Total	Government bonds	Stocks	Securities investment trust
1954	43.6	28.6%	30.0%	9.7%	9.0%	19.8%	1.7%	15.7%	1.6%
1955	52.6	26.8	31.1	9.7	10.6	19.4	1.3	16.2	1.0
1956	65.2	25.3	30.8	9.6	10.9	21.5	0.8	18.6	0.9
1957	76.4	22.7	32.7	9.6	11.6	19.9	0.6	16.5	1.6
1958	91.8	20.5	33.3	8.9	12.5	22.0	0.7	17.8	2.0
1959	116.3	18.9	32.0	8.3	12.7	25.3	0.5	20.5	2.5
1960	143.4	18.4	31.1	7.8	12.9	28.2	0.3	21.9	3.8
1961	169.8	18.8%	31.0%	7.5%	13.6%	29.1%	0.2%	20.5%	6.3%
1962	207.1	17.8	29.4	7.2	13.7	29.0	0.1	20.9	5.6
1963	235.5	18.5	30.9	7.5	14.6	26.7	0.2	18.8	5.2
1964	276.4	18.4	31.4	7.8	15.1	24.2	0.3	16.6	4.5
1965	333.8	17.3	31.2	7.8	15.1	24.3	n.a.	17.6	3.2
1966	385.9	17.6	32.3	8.2	16.1	23.5	n.a.	16.6	2.4
1967	450.4	17.7	33.0	8.7	16.6	20.6	n.a.	13.7	1.9
1968	539.7	17.2	32.3	9.0	16.6	22.1	n.a.	15.4	1.5
1969	666.1	17.0	31.1	9.1	16.2	24.1	n.a.	17.5	1.5
1970	724.9	18.0	33.7	10.2	18.0	19.0	0.5	11.7	1.7
1971	862.9	17.9%	32.9%	10.7%	18.2%	19.7%	0.5%	11.7%	1.7%
1972	1,119.4	17.8	31.5	10.5	16.9	23.0	0.5	15.4	1.5
1973	1,279.5	19.2	33.8	11.6	17.4	17.9	0.5	10.2	1.6
1974	1,486.9	18.4	34.5	12.4	17.8	16.7	0.6	8.8	1.8
1975	1,787.7	16.6	34.5	13.1	17.8	17.9	0.5	9.9	1.7
1976	2,092.9	16.0	34.0	14.0	18.1	17.6	0.8	9.0	1.6
1977	2,397.7	15.1	33.9	15.2	18.3	16.9	1.5	7.8	1.8
1978	2,781.7	14.8	33.0	15.7	18.2	17.6	2.1	8.2	1.8
1979	3,123.9	14.1	33.5	16.3	18.6	16.8	2.3	7.6	1.7
1980	3,468.5	12.5	33.9	17.4	19.0	16.4	2.5	7.3	1.5
1981	3,880.9	12.0%	33.9%	17.5%	19.6%	16.4%	2.8%	7.1%	1.6%
1982	4,292.3	11.6	33.2	17.8	20.5	16.6	3.0	6.8	1.8
1983	4,797.1	10.5	32.2	17.7	20.9	18.3	3.0	7.9	2.5

SOURCES: BOJ, *Flow of Funds Accounts in Japan*, various issues.

the early 1960s caused a mini-crisis in the stock market, a crisis that the monetary authorities had to resolve by issuing special BOJ loans to a few securities companies in 1965.

This disorder greatly impaired the functioning of the equity stock market. Firms in the nonfinancial sector reacted by sharply reducing their reliance on equity finance in the latter half of the 1960s (see Table 6). The nonfinancial sectors became extremely conscious of the risks involved in stockholdings. Many investors withdrew entirely from the stock market (see Table 7). This served to further strengthen the predominant role of banks in the financial markets during the latter half of the 1960s and the early 1970s.

Mechanisms of liquidity adjustment. Primarily because of the conditions outlined above, Japanese money markets were underdeveloped. The interbank call money market was the only market in which price mechanisms were effective.[13] No open money markets in which the nonfinancial sectors could directly participate existed.

This feature of Japanese money markets strongly influenced the BOJ's specific procedures for monetary control. Since open bond markets, especially for public bonds, did not exist, the BOJ could not engage in the open market operations observed in the United States or the United Kingdom. Except for adjustments through the call money market, banks adjusted their liquidity by borrowing from the BOJ, and the BOJ's loans to private banks were important instruments of monetary control.

Japan's rapid economic growth was associated with steep increases in the demand for capital. To match this demand, the BOJ had to expand its loans to private banks generously, a situation termed "over-loan." In light of the financial structure during the period under consideration, it is not an exaggeration to state that the over-loan phenomenon was inevitable.[14]

Importance of Intervention by Public Authorities

How did public authorities intervene in financial markets during the high growth period? Were the interventions effective in promoting economic growth? Generally speaking, in most industrialized economies, the financial industries are more heavily regulated than other industries. The primary reason for this is to protect the monetary system against financial chaos. This is also true of the Japanese financial system.

Functional Specialization

For the purpose of controlling financial allocation, the Japanese financial system is divided by law into several functionally specialized sectors, for instance, the division between short-term and long-term financing and the division between financing for big businesses and financing for small and medium-size businesses. Since the specialization has not been very rigorous, its effects on fund allocation seem to have been ambiguous.[15] Instead, the monetary authorities have used specialization to support existing financial intermediaries in each specialized sector. This specialization has been to some extent effective in preventing financial institutions in one sector from entering other sectors, thereby restraining intra- and intersectoral competition.

During the period of high economic growth, the members of each sector established vested interests. The monetary authorities have not been able to ignore those interests. The relatively stable financial structure during the period under consideration helped the authorities to balance the interests of various groups within the financial sectors.

Regulation of Interest Rates

The regulation of interest rates has been very comprehensive during the past three decades in Japan. Interest rates for bank deposits and short-term bank loan rates are regulated by the Temporary Interest Rate Adjustment Law, enacted in 1947. Based on this law, private banks fix the short-term prime rate at a constant margin above the official discount rate. Long-term loan rates and bond-issue interest rates are, although not directly regulated by law, determined by an implicit cartel arrangement among large financial intermediaries. The authorities can directly influence the determination of those interest rates. Thus, at least on the surface, most interest rates in Japan have been rigidly regulated, and price mechanisms do not appear to have been effective in financial markets. Not all of these regulations, however, have been effective.

The Temporary Fund Adjustment Law of 1937, which provided for legal control over bond financing, was abolished in 1948. Nonetheless, the public authorities continued to guide bond financing. Their control lever was the Bond Issue Committee (Kisaikai), which consisted of representatives of the largest banks and major securities companies. At the low interest rates set for newly issued bonds, the committee arranged bond financing for major nonfinancial businesses and public corporations. In short, the committee effectively rationed credit in the bond market. In general, even big businesses could not obtain sufficient funds at such low rates of interest, but the committee gave favorable treatment to bonds issued by electric power companies and banks.

The amount of funds allocated through the bond market was relatively small, and the bond issue arrangement seemed to hinder the development of bond markets. The arrangement worked against a financing method for business firms as a substitute for bank loans. This implies that the mechanism favored the banks. At any rate, since the bond market played only a minor role in this period, the effects of credit rationing in the market on general economic growth were, to say the least, not very important.[16]

The regulation on deposit rates seems to have kept rates on deposits lower than the levels that would have prevailed in the absence of any regulation. The call money rate, freely determined in the interbank money market, was almost always higher than the regulated deposit rates, and the banks could compete to some extent for deposits by nonprice means. The Ministry of Finance (MOF), however, restricted nonprice competition through administrative guidance.[17] This guidance was not unfavorable to the banks because no suitable substitutes for bank deposits were available to the majority of savers. Under the regulation of deposit rates, branch offices were crucial to bank management. The MOF officials responsible for branch administration determined the number and geographic distribution of branch offices of each bank and were, therefore, both powerful and important.

Did the regulations keeping deposit rates at relatively low levels contribute to Japan's economic growth? Since they reduced the rates of return on major financial assets, it is implausible that these regulations increased the amount of savings. The regulation served as an effective means of taxing holders of bank deposits, particularly small savers, because they could not obtain access to suitable financial instruments other than bank and postal savings deposits. Therefore, the regulation almost certainly transferred income from savers to the banks. (We discuss whether this transferred income eventually reached the recipients of bank loans, especially business firms, in the next section.)

The tax incentives for savings may have ameliorated this situation to some extent and encouraged savings. Savers extensively utilized the *maru-yu* system, which, by exempting interest earned on small deposits, raised aftertax rates of return. Because the privilege was often abused beyond its formal ceiling, the system gave added incentives to savers to keep money holdings in the form of bank and postal savings deposits.

Can the *maru-yu* system be regarded as a forerunner of the supply-side policy encouraging capital accumulation? Academic studies investigating this possibility are virtually nonexistent.[18] If it had been effective, however, the regulation fixing deposit rates at relatively low levels would have weakened the stimulatory effect of the *maru-yu* system because, as we have argued, the regulation worked to reduce the rates of return on bank deposits. In this sense, the *maru-yu* system and the regulation of deposit rates were fundamentally inconsistent with each other as supply-side policies.

Most economists claim that the practice of requiring a "compensating balance" (*kōsoku yokin*) reduced the effectiveness of the regulation of bank loan rates,[19] and it is evident that banks used compensating balances to a great extent during the high growth period. In 1964, for example, the ratio of compensating balances to loans was 11.1 per cent for city banks, 21.6 per cent for local banks, 40.6 per cent for savings banks, and 41.9 per cent for credit associations (compared with 1.5 per cent, 1.9 per cent, 3.0 per cent, and 8.9 per cent, respectively, in 1980).[20] This raised the effective interest rates on bank loans to a level much higher than the regulated nominal rates. If the compensating balance requirement adequately adjusted the effective loan rates, the banks could retain much of the income transferred from savers by the regulation of deposit rates.

The profit rate was significantly higher in banking than in industries in the nonfinancial sector during the 1950s and 1960s. Average annual after-tax profits for all banks ranged above 12 per cent in these decades, and banks consistently outperformed industry. This suggests that adjustment through the compensating balance process was to some extent effective.

The Japanese loan market cannot be regarded, however, as one of perfect atomistic competition. As we discussed in the previous section, the relationship between banks and firms implies a more complicated mechanism of fund allocation than that of perfectly competitive loan markets.[21] Under the mechanism, the surplus profits that the regulation of deposit rates conferred on the banks might have been transferred in part to some borrowers, thereby promoting their investment expenditure. In consideration of those bank-firm relationships, what effects did the regulation of interest rates have? Did the regulation influence the allocation pattern of funds? If so, in what ways? These are difficult questions to answer.

Many foreign economists as well as many Japanese argue that public authorities in Japan were able to control fund allocation in order to promote economic growth through intervention in the credit-rationing process supposedly created by the regulation of interest rates. Our main argument in this paper is that the specific procedures utilized by the authorities and the effectiveness of these procedures remain to be adequately explained.

Policymakers' Control of Financial Allocation

Besides the close relationship between private financial intermediaries, particularly big banks, and business corporations, there were several alternative channels for the flow of funds that were relatively less important than the banking sector. The government played a substantial role as a financial intermediary during the late 1940s and early 1950s. As shown in Table 8, however, its importance declined during the high growth period. During this period, the share of funds provided by government financial institutions in the total amount of funds raised externally by the business sector was, at its greatest, 8 per cent.

This financial structure, in which savings were channeled to firms primarily through the banking sector, allowed public authorities to influence the flow of funds by controlling banks' lending behavior. The Japanese government has continued to intervene in the banking sector. The mode of control, however, has changed over time.

Before the early 1950s, the monetary authorities announced explicit intervention objectives and intervened directly in the particular channels through which savings were transferred. Most controls in force at that time had their roots in controls imposed during the 1930s and World

TABLE 8

External Sources of Industrial Funds, 1947-1981

(annual average, per cent)

Period	Stocks & shares	Corporate bonds	Private financial institutions' loans	Government funds[a]	Foreign loans[b]
1947-52	11.5%	3.2%	71.7%	13.6%	n.a.
1953-57	16.3	3.6	70.9	9.3	n.a.
1958-62	16.6	5.6	70.1	7.8	1.9%
1963-67	8.4	3.6	79.8	8.1	0.8
1968-72	6.5	2.7	82.8	8.0	1.2
1973-77	5.9	4.3	78.5	11.1	n.a.
1978-81	8.3	4.6	73.0	14.2	n.a.

SOURCES: BOJ, *Economic Statistics of Japan*, and *Economic Statistics Annual*, various issues.

[a]Sum of the amount supplied by governmental financial institutions and the Special Accounts for Financial Purposes.

[b]The proportion of foreign loans based on the Law Concerning Foreign Investment in the total of industrial funds raised in the domestic markets and through foreign loans.

War II. For example, private financial institutions were obliged to supply loans to those industries designated by the government as being of national importance. These designations were contained in the Rules of Financial Institutions' Fund Supplies, legally based on the Emergency Ordinance on Financial Measures of 1946, and in the Order of Priority in Industrial Loans. According to the order, the essential industries were mining, metalworking, chemicals, electric power generation, oil supply, and transportation. Private financial institutions could make loans to industries designated as "unimportant" or "not urgent" only with permission of the MOF.[22]

For its part, the BOJ could monitor the funds it lent to banks, especially to city banks. From the late 1940s to the early 1950s, the loan mediation system of the BOJ was of some importance. The objective of the system was to favor financial allocation to essential industries through the use of cooperative financing arranged by the Loan Mediation Bureau of the BOJ. In addition to this semipublic financing arrangement, the BOJ's system of investigation of corporate bonds eligibility, effective from 1949 to 1955, was a rather powerful control lever for financial allocation through the bond markets. BOJ loans were available to those holding predesignated corporate bonds and debentures as collateral. This meant, of course, a discriminatory promotion of selected corporate bonds and bank debentures.

Most direct controls over private financial institutions disappeared in the first half of the 1950s.[23] The investigation system was abolished at the end of 1955. The Rules for Financial Institutions' Fund Supplies had already become ineffective by the early 1950s, after several alterations, though they continued to be formally in effect until 1963. The BOJ gradu-

TABLE 9
Comparison of Investment Plans Approved by the
Industrial Finance Committee and Their Results,
1961-1963
(per cent)

Industry	FY 1961	FY 1962	FY 1963
Electric power	−3.9%	−8.5%	−6.6%
Coal mining	−13.5	−7.2	−15.3
Iron and steel	−7.3	−5.8	−0.4
Petroleum refining	−9.5	−16.5	−6.4
Petrochemicals	−10.1	−14.9	−16.8
Ammonium sulfate	−5.4	−13.4	−4.3
Synthetic textiles	−1.5	3.3	11.7
Automobiles	−3.9	−4.4	−0.1
Electric machine	5.7	7.9	−18.0
Electronics	−9.8	−12.9	−2.5
Paper and pulp	−21.1	−14.1	−8.3
Cement	−11.9	−11.9	5.7
Other industries	−3.0	17.1	−7.1
TOTAL	−5.7%	−1.1%	−5.6%

SOURCE: Data presented by MITI to the Industrial Finance
Committee.
    NOTE: (Actual investment − planned investment) ÷ planned in-
vestment. The industries covered by this table are those under the
jurisdiction of MITI.

ally withdrew from loan mediation around 1950 and then stopped completely in February 1954.

The main instruments used by the monetary authorities to intervene
in financial markets during the high growth period were neither direct
controls based on legislative regulations nor the imposition of direct administrative guidance on private financial institutions. The monetary authorities, in particular the MOF and the BOJ, attempted to control the
supply of funds by indirectly supporting cooperation among private financial institutions. These indirect controls were pursued through many
institutional arrangements, such as the Bond Issue Committee mentioned above, the Financial Institutions' Fund Council (Kin'yū Kikan
Shikin Shingikai), and the Industrial Finance Committee (Sangyō Shikin
Bukai) of the Ministry of International Trade and Industry (MITI). These
public or semipublic organizations consist of representatives of major
banks and major users of funds (business corporations). Through these
organizations, the attitudes of policymakers toward desirable financial
conditions and fund allocation were clarified. At the same time, the authorities supported the formation and maintenance of cooperative behavior, including quasi cartels among financial institutions.

For example, the Industrial Finance Committee supervised investment and associated finance plans of major industries under the jurisdiction of MITI. The investment plans approved by this committee reflected the basic intentions of MITI. However, during the high growth period, such plans did not seem to have been executed rigorously. As shown in Table 9, actual investment undertaken by individual industries differed widely from the planned levels. These deviations were great enough to cast some doubt on the effectiveness of the Industrial Finance Committee. Nevertheless, this committee may have been useful as a means of transferring government policy information to the private sector and coordinating the behavior of private firms.

The Bank of Japan's Monetary Policy

As illustrated above, the BOJ was heavily involved in the public control of financial allocations for several years following World War II. This involvement not only increased the effectiveness of public control, but also seems to have made the BOJ itself politically powerful. Naoto Ichimada, the BOJ's governor from 1946 to 1954, was often called a pope. However, when Eikichi Araki became governor in late 1954, the BOJ began to retreat from its commitment to direct public control. Thereafter, it played only a minor role in controlling the allocation mechanisms of the financial system.

It is not clear why the BOJ stopped intervening directly in specific financial allocations by influencing loans to particular firms. One explanation may be the runaway inflation of the immediate postwar period when direct intervention often culminated in an excessive supply of money (see Table 10). Perhaps the BOJ considered it better to concentrate on ag-

TABLE 10

Average Rates of Increase in Money Supply, Real GNP, and Price Levels, 1947-1982
(annual rate, per cent)

Period	Money supply[a]		Real GNP	Wholesale price index	Consumer price index
	M1	M2			
1947-52	46.9%	50.2%	11.2%	80.6%	37.9%
1953-57	10.0	17.3	7.4	1.1	3.1
1958-62	18.3	20.1	10.1	−1.0	3.6
1963-67	17.1	17.8	10.2	1.4	5.4
1968-72	21.0	19.8	9.7	1.3	5.8
1973-77	12.0	13.5	3.8	11.4	13.1
1978-82	6.0	9.7	4.2	5.1	4.6

SOURCES: BOJ, *Economic Statistics of Japan*, and *Economic Statistics Annual*; Japan, Economic Planning Agency, *Annual Report on National Income Statistics*, and *Annual Report of National Accounts*, various issues.

[a]Estimates by the BOJ cited in R. W. Goldsmith, *The Financial Development of Japan, 1969-1977* (New Haven: Yale University Press, 1983), p. 136.

gregate monetary control in order to stabilize inflation. In fact, the policy stance of the BOJ during the high growth period was not very conducive to growth.

During the period of high economic growth, especially prior to 1970, the BOJ's primary objective was to attain equilibrium in the balance of payments under the fixed exchange rate regime.[24] The strong investment demand of business was a powerful driving force behind economic growth. At the same time, it often brought a deficit in the balance of payments, depleting the already scarce stock of foreign reserves. The BOJ, in order to ensure that the domestic economy did not overexpand, often adopted a tight monetary policy. The call money rate that was freely determined in the interbank money market was almost always significantly higher than both the regulated deposit rates and the official discount rate, a joint product of the strong demand for funds and the restrictive stance of the BOJ.[25]

The Diverse Purposes of Public Intervention

Among the many objectives of public intervention in the financial markets, that of promoting economic growth was especially important. The government officially announced time and again that it aimed to promote the heavy and chemical industries within the Japanese manufacturing sector. Not all interventions were, however, intended to encourage industries on the technological frontier. It was also necessary to pay due attention to depressed or stagnating industries, small and medium-size businesses, and so on. The objective of achieving effective monetary control was also important. In order to pursue these objectives, the monetary authorities had to rely in part on policy measures that did not conform to the objective of high economic growth.

Financial policy had many objectives, each of which reflected the interests of various sectors or bureaucratic organizations (see examples below). The monetary authorities attempted to protect those interests simultaneously by reconciling the interests of many groups. It was not too difficult for the authorities to balance diverse interests because the cost-benefit structure related to the financial markets was relatively stable during the high growth period.

We mentioned above the important role of government financial institutions in the immature capital markets of postwar Japan. Most of the government's funds—provided by both government financial institutions and the special account for financial purposes (*yūshi tokubetsu kaikei*)—were supplied to industries at interest rates significantly lower than the long-term interest rates determined through negotiation between financial institutions and policymakers. It is obvious that policymakers utilized government funds to subsidize private businesses and others. Therefore, we can infer the purposes of government financial policy from the pattern of government fund allocation.

Government funds were most important in coal mining, agriculture, and merchant shipping (see Table 11). These industries were, during the high growth period, stagnant or declining. Government funds were, of course, provided to leading industries as well, but because of political pressures on the allocation of funds, the government allocated funds to all kinds of industries, including significantly declining or stagnant ones.

This kind of diversification was inevitable. In general, the organizations or committees that planned the allocation of funds did not appear to have played a decisive role. For declining industries such as coal mining, agriculture, and merchant shipping, however, the influence of relevant committees was direct and strong. For instance, the Council for the Coal Mining Industry (Sekitan Kōgyō Shingikai) and the Council for the Modernization of the Merchant Marine and Shipbuilding (Kaiun Zōsen Kindaika Shingikai) were successful in providing funds for their respective industries. It can safely be argued that government funds complemented the immature capital markets in supporting some industries that could not have obtained a sufficient amount of funds had capital markets been well developed.

During the high growth period, branch offices were an extremely important element in banking business. The number and the location of

TABLE 11

Proportions of Government Funds to Total Supply of Industrial Equipment Funds, 1954-1967

Industry	Per cent[a]
Coal mining	49.8 (0.2)
Iron and steel	4.1 (7.0)
Machinery	10.4 (4.7)
Chemicals	7.4 (6.4)
Textiles	14.8 (1.2)
Agriculture, forestry, and fishery	50.0 (0.5)
Water transportation[b]	41.8 (5.1)
Land transportation[b,c]	15.5 (1.7)
Electric power	26.8 (4.4)
TOTAL (incl. other industries)	18.8 (3.1)

SOURCES: BOJ, *Economic Statistics of Japan*, and *Economic Statistics Annual*, various issues.
[a]The parentheses show the proportion of the amount of foreign loans based on the Law Concerning Foreign Investment in the sum of the industrial equipment funds each industry acquired in domestic markets and through foreign loans, 1957-67.
[b]Since the amount of funds acquired by issuing stocks and shares in 1964 is not available for water and land transportation, estimates for these industries exclude the year 1964.
[c]1965-67.

branches crucially affected the fund-raising capabilities of financial institutions. Their importance was reinforced by the ceiling on deposit rates, as well as by the MOF's restrictive guidance on nonprice competition. Financial institutions could not, however, freely choose the number and location of their branch offices. The MOF had to approve the establishment of a new branch and its location. This powerful control is called branch administration.

From the standpoint of promoting economic growth, the MOF could have given preferential treatment to large city banks that had better access to the leading industries; however, this was not the case. The MOF tried to give preferential treatment to small and medium-size firms, as the higher growth rate of branches approved by the MOF for small and medium-size financial institutions suggests. This preferential treatment enabled those banks to keep a stable position in the financial markets (see Tables 3 and 12). This is evidence for the belief that Japanese policymakers had to consider the political pressures exerted by the small and medium-size firms since they were an important part of the Liberal Democratic Party's constituency.

The BOJ often adopted a policy of quantitative control as a means of macroeconomic policy. When it wanted to pursue a tight monetary pol-

TABLE 12

Changes in the Number of Branch Offices, Deposits, and Loans, 1951-1980

(annual average, per cent)

Bank	1951-55	1956-60	1961-65	1966-70	1971-75	1976-80
City						
Branch	−0.1[a]	−0.4	3.1	1.1[b]	0.9	1.2
Deposit	18.8[c]	18.5	17.7	14.3	17.2	10.4
Loan	6.2[c]	20.5	18.3	14.9	17.2	8.4
Local						
Branch	4.4	−0.1	1.9	1.2[b]	2.7	2.6
Deposit	14.5[c]	20.0	19.5	15.4	18.3	12.1
Loan	11.7[c]	20.0	19.3	16.4	18.0	10.4
Thrift[d]						
Branch	8.4[c]	4.0	5.6	3.1[b]	3.3	3.3
Deposit	19.4[c]	24.3	26.2	17.8	20.3	11.8
Loan	16.6[c]	24.5	24.9	19.1	18.9	11.2

SOURCES: BOJ, *Economic Statistics of Japan*, and *Economic Statistics Annual*, various issues.

[a]In 1955, Nihon Kangyō and Hokkaidō Takushoku were reclassified as city banks. This reclassification increased the number of city bank branch offices by 230. The effect of this reclassification is adjusted for in this table.

[b]In 1968, Nihon-sōgo, the largest of the mutual loan and savings banks at that time, was converted to a city bank. Saitama was converted from a local to a city bank in 1969. The effects of these conversions are adjusted for in this table.

[c]1954-55.

[d]The thrifts comprise the mutual loan and savings banks, the credit associations, and the credit cooperatives.

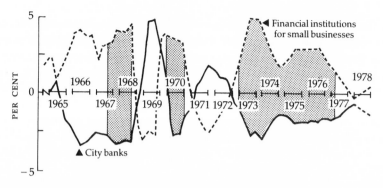

Fig. 1. Changes in the shares of city banks and financial institutions for small businesses in the loan market, 1964 (fourth quarter) to 1978 (first quarter), a year-ago comparison. Shading indicates periods in which the BOJ adopted window guidance. Sources: BOJ, *Economic Statistics Annual*, various isues.

icy, the BOJ put ceilings on new lending by some private banks, in addition to using more conventional means of controlling the monetary base. This measure is called window guidance (*madoguchi shidō*). The rationale for this guidance was that by controlling the major channels of funds through the banks, the BOJ could safely manage the flow of funds as a whole.

The BOJ has consistently applied window guidance to city banks and long-term credit banks, although it began to apply such guidance to a wider range of institutions around 1970. This policy measure had a clearly discriminatory impact on the pattern of fund allocation through financial intermediaries: in periods of tight monetary policy and window guidance, the relative share of the flow of funds through both city banks and long-term credit banks declined and that of funds through small and medium-size financial institutions increased (see Fig. 1). This indicates that at least some of the effect of window guidance was offset by compensating increases in the amount of funds supplied by small and medium-size financial institutions exempted from the direct regulation of window guidance.[26]

This fact is not necessarily congruent with the view that monetary policy was designed chiefly to achieve high growth because the financial institutions that were tightly controlled by window guidance were in a position to provide most of the funds to the industrial sectors expected to promote economic growth. This may show that the BOJ put more emphasis on stabilizing aggregate demand than on promoting the modern sectors of the economy.

Structural Changes Since the Mid-1970s

Just as the real economy has shifted into a new phase of low economic growth, the Japanese financial system has experienced drastic changes since the mid-1970s. The relatively stable financial structure of the high growth period began to deteriorate, and many of the cooperative relationships that existed before the early 1970s began to wane. The structural changes in the financial markets have primarily resulted from the gradual erosion of the immediate postwar conditions.

The Diversified Demand for Financial Services

The steady growth of the Japanese economy since the early 1950s has rapidly increased the total level of financial assets held by the private sector. According to the flow of funds accounts, the level of financial assets held by both corporate firms and individuals increased sevenfold between 1953 and 1963 and fivefold between 1963 and 1973; the corresponding figures for the United States are 2.2 and 1.9 times, respectively (see Table 4). This rapid accumulation of financial assets has, by substantially reducing transaction costs, led to a diversified demand for financial instruments. This corresponds to the fact that financial assets other than bank deposits have gradually become more important in the portfolios of the private sector.

If financial institutions could introduce money market instruments that were highly substitutable for traditional bank deposits, those instruments would threaten the viability of the banks, which have enjoyed the lion's share of postwar financial markets. Such new financial instruments would create incentives for the banks to respond, altering the financial mechanism in Japan. For instance, the development of the *gensaki* market made it possible for many businesses to shift part of their funds from banks to open money markets.[27] Eventually, the banks were forced to introduce the negotiable certificate of deposit (NCD) in 1979 to prevent their business customers from diverting funds to the *gensaki* market.

The remarkable increase in postal savings deposits can also be regarded as a manifestation of diversified financial demand associated with assets accumulation. Not only do postal savings deposits pay slightly more favorable interest rates than comparable bank deposits, they also provide the wealthy with a means of decreasing their tax burden. Although private banks are under the jurisdiction of the MOF, which is responsible for taxation, postal savings deposits are under the jurisdiction of the Ministry of Posts and Telecommunications. The latter is widely believed to be relatively free from supervision by the Tax Administration Agency. In 1982, to counteract postal savings deposits, the banks introduced a new kind of time deposit in which the depositor designates the maturity of the time deposit (*kijitsu shitei teiki yōkin*). Such deposits respond to the needs of customers seeking high-yield deposits and the freedom to designate a maturity date.

The *gensaki* market and postal savings deposits illustrate one feature of financial evolution in Japan. Financial change has tended to start, not at the center, but on the peripheries of the financial system. Securities companies developed the *gensaki* market to finance their inventories of securities because they had lost access to the interbank money markets after the mini-crisis in the securities markets in the mid-1960s.[28] Postal savings deposits played a relatively minor role during the high growth period. Competitive pressures from abroad, which we discuss below, can also be regarded as peripheral changes in the Japanese financial system.

Financial institutions, such as big city banks and long-term credit banks, tend to respond only when menaced by peripheral developments. Only then do the public authorities begin to coordinate or intervene in the establishments' responses. In other words, if changes on the peripheries had been suppressed, the Japanese financial structure might not have been substantially altered.

Escalating Government Debts

Until the mid-1970s, corporations were overwhelmingly engaged in deficit financing. They borrowed a vast amount of funds in the financial markets to close the huge gap between their investment expenditures and savings (see Tables 1 and 13). The government, including local authorities and public corporations, gradually became an important net borrower after the mid-1960s, but far less so than corporations. With the sharp decline in Japanese economic growth, however, the government overtook corporations as the most important net borrower. Large amounts of national bonds have been floated since FY 1975, with the outstanding stock of national bonds jumping from less than 7 per cent of GNP in 1974 to about 35 per cent in 1982. This ratio of outstanding national bonds to GNP is comparable to that of the United States (see Table 5). Since the BOJ has monetized only a small amount of the national bonds, the bulk of them, in particular long-term national bonds, have been absorbed into the portfolios of the private sector.

A syndicate of national bond underwriters—banks and other financial institutions—has underwritten most national bonds. This method of issuing national bonds allowed the government to force high bond prices on underwriters. Furthermore, before 1977, the MOF prohibited the underwriters from selling national bonds on a secondary market, probably because the MOF believed that the development of such a market would

TABLE 13

Financial Surplus or Deficit of Nonfinancial Sectors, 1954-1982

(per GNP, per cent)

Year	(1) Central govt.	(2) Local authority[a]	Total government (1) + (2)	Corporations	Personal	Foreign
1954	−0.0%	−2.2%	−2.2%	−4.7%	5.9%	0.2%
1955	−0.6	−1.6	−2.2	−5.0	7.6	−0.9
1956	1.2	−1.3	−0.1	−8.0	7.0	0.1
1957	1.9	−1.2	0.7	−10.9	7.1	2.0
1958	0.8	−1.2	−0.4	−5.4	6.3	−1.4
1959	0.2	−1.0	−0.9	−8.7	9.5	−1.0
1960	1.5	−1.0	0.5	−10.1	8.9	−0.3
1961	2.4%	−1.6%	0.8%	−12.2%	8.8%	1.8%
1962	1.5	−2.6	−1.1	−8.7	9.0	0.1
1963	1.1	−2.5	−1.4	−8.4	7.7	1.1
1964	0.3	−2.6	−2.3	−8.3	9.3	0.6
1965	0.3	−3.0	−2.7	−3.9	7.5	−1.0
1966	−0.6	−3.0	−3.7	−3.6	8.4	−1.1
1967	−0.6	−2.3	−2.9	−6.2	8.9	0.1
1968	0.1	−2.7	−2.5	−5.5	8.5	−0.7
1969	0.6	−2.1	−1.5	−5.4	8.0	−1.2
1970	1.3	−2.1	−0.9	−6.7	7.7	−0.9
1971	0.9%	−2.7%	−1.9%	−6.1%	9.2%	−2.4%
1972	0.6	−3.2	−2.6	−7.6	11.1	−2.1
1973	1.0	−3.8	−2.8	−7.4	8.6	0.0
1974	0.7	−4.3	−3.6	−8.3	10.0	1.0
1975	−2.7	−4.5	−7.2	−4.0	10.3	0.1
1976	−3.2	−4.1	−7.3	−3.9	11.2	−0.6
1977	−3.9	−3.2	−7.1	−2.5	10.9	−1.5
1978	−5.3	−3.7	−9.0	−1.0	10.9	−1.7
1979	−4.4	−3.4	−7.9	−3.0	9.1	0.9
1980	−3.2	−3.5	−6.7	−3.5	8.1	1.1
1981	−3.8%	−3.6%	−7.4%	−3.1%	11.1%	−0.5%
1982	−4.0	−3.1	−7.1	−3.9	11.0	−0.7

SOURCES: BOJ, *The Flow of Funds Accounts in Japan*; Japan, Economic Planning Agency, *Annual Report of National Accounts*, and *Annual Report on National Income Statistics*, various issues.

[a] Includes public corporations.

make it difficult to enforce the artificially high issue prices of national bonds on the syndicate.

This prohibition did not follow the natural dictates of market forces. The development of a secondary market was indispensable to the smooth absorption of a large volume of national bonds by the financial markets. In 1977, the MOF had to permit banks and financial institutions to sell national bonds they had underwritten, although under some constraints. Members of the syndicate were obliged by administrative guidance from the MOF to hold national bonds for a prescribed period of time. This time period, however, has gradually been shortened.

As the MOF feared, the development of a secondary market for national bonds made it more difficult to issue long-term bonds through the system of syndicated underwriting. Because of disagreements between the MOF and the syndicate on issue prices and other conditions, the MOF has often had no choice but to postpone issuing long-term bonds. In order to avoid such difficulties, the MOF began to offer medium-term bonds at public auctions in 1978. The medium-term bonds are attractive instruments for the nonfinancial private sector and for investment trust funds (*chūkoku* funds). The issuance of medium-term bonds can, therefore, be regarded as a supply-side response to the public's diversified demand for financial assets.

On the whole, the increase in national bonds has stimulated an extraordinary expansion of bond trading in the secondary markets during the past decade. Before 1977, less than 5 per cent of the total volume of national bonds was sold on the Tokyo market; in 1982, 62.3 per cent. This expansion of secondary bond markets clearly results from the rapid increase in national bonds and indicates a noteworthy change in adjustment mechanisms in the Japanese financial system.

Changing Patterns of Corporate Finance

Corporate firms have sharply reduced the intensity of their net borrowing in financial markets since the mid-1970s. At the same time, by extending their activities abroad, they have obtained access to foreign financial markets. These changes greatly influenced the mechanisms of financial markets, especially those of bank loans and bond markets. In short, the relationships between banks and firms have become weaker, and the influence of the big banks on those connections have been greatly reduced.

Reliance by big businesses on bank loans dropped from an annual average of 30.2 per cent of total investment funds in 1973–77 to 17.5 per cent in 1978–82. As the reliance on bank loans declined, the traditional prime rate system became obsolete. The prime rate system was originally intended to reduce the loan rates for prime borrowers such as big businesses by mechanically fixing both long-term and short-term prime rates slightly above the official discount rate.[29] Prime rates have, however, become unfavorable for the prime borrowers, who have developed alternative methods of financing.

Competition among banks for prime borrowers has become so fierce that many have reduced their loan rates to levels below the prime rates. Along with this development, small businesses have become increasingly important customers for banks. In 1974, 36.9 per cent of all bank loans were to small businesses; the comparable figure in 1982 was 48.8 per cent. Large city banks have been competing much harder than before with both regional banks and other financial institutions for the loan business of small and medium-size firms.

The increased borrowing in foreign capital markets by Japanese corporations is a result of their rapid expansion overseas. This implies that corporations have effective alternatives to borrowing in domestic markets, and domestic financial markets are inevitably receiving impacts from abroad. This is especially true of corporate bond markets.

As explained above, the Bond Issue Committee has arranged and controlled corporate bond issues. As members of this committee, banks have been influential both as trustees who undertake surveillance over collateral and as large buyers of new corporate bonds. It is not surprising, therefore, that the committee's stance has not been liberal regarding the promotion of corporate bond issues that might threaten the predominance of bank loans in the financial markets.[30] Japanese corporations have, however, gradually increased the relative share of funds acquired by overseas issues in their total bond financing over the past decade (from 20.8 per cent of all bonds issued in 1977 to 47.6 per cent in 1982). This has created competitive pressure in domestic markets, thereby contributing to the deregulation of these markets. During 1981 and 1982, Japanese firms increased their issuance of convertible bonds in Switzerland so rapidly that their bond issues in the domestic market declined. In 1983, this decline induced some liberalization in the conditions applying to bond issues in the domestic market.[31]

Technological Developments in Electronic Communication Systems

Recent technical developments in electronic communications have reduced various financial transactions costs. This development allows combined packages of complementary financial services to be produced more cheaply. For example, some financial institutions could confer payment services on money market instruments, if granted permission to do so. At present, such packages remain only a possibility in Japan. This possibility, accompanied by the diversification of financial demand, will, however, exert serious pressure on the existing Japanese financial system.

The extent to which these technological possibilities are actually exploited and their accessibility will be essential elements in the development of the financial system. In this respect, the Japanese monetary authorities and above all the MOF have played an important role. The authorities have effectively controlled both the degree of utilization of recent technological possibilities and their accessibility in order to preserve the existing financial structure characterized by functional specialization.

The authorities view technological developments as forces that may be detrimental to the functional specialization of the present financial system. It is expected that it will become increasingly difficult for the MOF to control them. The deliberate and overly cautious introduction of these technological possibilities seems to have widened the gap between their potential application and their actual utilization.

Inflation and the Financial Markets

Inflation in the past decade has been responsible for drastic institutional changes in U.S. financial markets.[32] However, the impact of inflation has been only moderate in Japan. This is mainly the result of the BOJ's successful suppression, except during 1973–74, of inflationary pressures by controlling the supply of money and partly the result of the greater flexibility of ceilings on deposit rates in Japan than in the United States. The difference between competitively determined money market rates and the regulated deposit rates remained within the range of one or two percentage points on average. The incentive for financial markets to circumvent the regulation on deposit rates was, therefore, relatively weak. In contrast to those in the United States, the recent structural changes in the Japanese financial markets are not the result of inflationary pressures but of other factors.[33]

Responses of the Public Authorities

The simple structure of the financial system in the period of high economic growth and the balance among the interests of various participants in the financial markets have been seriously shaken by developments since the early 1970s. The Japanese monetary authorities seem to recognize the growing difficulty of preserving the functionally specialized system inherited from the high growth period. Maintaining the status quo is no longer consistent with the interests of financial market institutions and prevents the authorities from pursuing new policy objectives, particularly precise control over the money supply by the BOJ and efficient debt management by the MOF.

Most of the so-called liberalization policies adopted by the MOF and the BOJ since the mid-1970s reflect their recognition that their ability to preserve the existing system is weakening. Some obstacles still remain to the smooth transformation of the financial system. One is the monetary authorities' continued consideration of the vested interests of financial institutions. Another is the dispute among public authorities concerning financial reforms.

Liberalization of the National Bond Market and Monetary Control

The MOF was forced to liberalize the national bond market to enable financial markets to absorb the vast amount of national bonds. The BOJ's virtual refusal to monetize national bonds, as evidenced by its adoption of a stable money supply target in July 1978, has contributed to the development of a secondary bond market. Since then, the BOJ has announced its forecast (de facto target) for the quarterly growth rate in the money supply. By adopting this target, the BOJ has taken a precautionary measure against MOF pressure to monetize the national debt.

The BOJ has succeeded in closely controlling the money supply. The actual growth rate of the money supply has virtually agreed with the target values forecast by the BOJ, usually differing by less than a percentage point. This success has clearly resulted in disinflation since the mid-1970s. In the process of controlling the supply of money, the BOJ has continued to engage in window guidance, closely monitoring bank lending behavior. This guidance seems anachronistic. With the sharp decline in the importance of bank loans in the financial system and the development of alternatives to traditional bank loans in corporate financing, the effectiveness of window guidance as an instrument of monetary control seems to have declined substantially. The continuation of window guidance has served to maintain the relative shares of individual banks in the loan market, an attempt by the BOJ to preserve the status quo.

Liberalization of the MOF's Banking Administration

In June 1981, the amended Banking Act was promulgated, and the MOF has gradually liberalized its banking administration to conform with this new law. Regulation of bank branching has been relaxed to some extent, and the range of permissible activities widened. Banks were allowed to sell newly issued national bonds to their customers in April 1983 and then to act as dealers in the national bond market in June 1984.

As explained above, the MOF permitted banks to introduce new instruments such as negotiable certificates of deposit and time deposits of specified duration. The MOF, however, tried to minimize the impact of these new instruments on the financial system. It delayed their introduction to give financial institutions time to adjust and persuaded innovators to make the new instruments less revolutionary. Negotiable certificates of deposit had only limited negotiability, for example, and were offered only in very large denominations (¥500 million), reflecting the MOF's administrative guidance.

The medium-term government bond (*chūki kokusai*) investment trust funds initiated in 1980 were another example of controlled financial innovation. These funds, similar to U.S. money market mutual funds, were expected to put extreme competitive pressure on the banks. By order of the MOF, however, initial sales of the funds were not permitted to exceed ¥10 billion. This was the MOF's response to the banks' fears that free sales of these funds would seriously undermine the existing order in the financial markets.

In April 1984, a small financial institution (shin'yō kinko) in Kyoto began to offer a cash management account in collaboration with a securities company, which was a substantial success for the financial institution. The MOF, however, exerted some control over this financial innovation, and some time lapsed before the association was permitted to introduce this new instrument.

Postal savings deposits have become increasingly important in the portfolios of the private sector since the late 1960s (see Table 7). The monetary authorities, specifically the MOF and the BOJ, are not totally pleased with this development. This increase in postal savings deposits, under the jurisdiction of the Ministry of Posts and Telecommunications, means that financial markets are expanding outside the monetary authorities' jurisdiction.

The Ministry of Posts and Telecommunications can legally set, through the Council of Postal Enterprise, the interest rates on postal savings deposits. Even after the deregulation of interest rates, the ministry is expected to utilize this power to set postal savings deposit rates at levels significantly higher than those on bank deposits, giving rise to serious financial disintermediation from private banks. The monetary authorities fear that this disintermediation will make the Japanese financial system much more unstable under liberalized interest rates. Therefore, they argue for integration of determinations of interest rates if the deregulation of interest rates, especially those for small deposits, is to be introduced. This integration would obviously mean limiting the financial power of the Ministry of Posts and Telecommunications.

Some of the arguments against the Ministry of Posts and Telecommunications may be justifiable, but at the same time, the existence of postal savings deposits seems to be an excuse for postponing financial reforms. In any case, as of mid-1986, an agreement was still to be reached between the monetary authorities and the ministry concerning the integration of rates.

Internationalism

During the high growth period, the Japanese monetary authorities closely regulated capital inflows and outflows in order to maintain sufficient levels of foreign reserves under the fixed exchange rate regime. Since the late 1960s, however, these regulations have been gradually relaxed as the Japanese balance of payments improved, although the authorities have sometimes tightened capital controls in an attempt to restrict undue fluctuations in the yen exchange rate under the flexible exchange rate system adopted in 1973.

At the same time, internationalization has proceeded gradually in the domestic financial markets. The monetary authorities have not taken a positive stance on the internationalization of financial markets, perhaps because of concern over the possible destabilizing effect of internationalization on the domestic financial structure. Thus, they have retained many regulations that they feel are necessary to preserve the system of functional specialization in domestic financial markets. For example, the MOF's Banking, Securities, and International Finance bureaus agreed to impose regulations on the underwriting activities of Japanese banks in foreign markets. These regulations correspond to those in domestic markets separating securities activities from banking activities. This agreement, called the Three-Bureau Agreement (*sankyoku gōi*), was first made in 1974 and is still in effect. Moreover, except for long-term credit banks, Japanese banks are prohibited from using in Japan funds acquired by issuing long-term liabilities in foreign markets. The purpose of this regulation is to support the position of long-term credit banks in domestic financial markets.

These regulations tend to postpone the adaptation of the Japanese financial institutions to the internationalization of the markets. With the comprehensive amendment of the Foreign Exchange Law in December 1980, these regulations have been somewhat relaxed. Moreover, as a result of negotiations between the United States and Japan, the Japanese government liberalized some restrictions on transactions in the Euroyen markets. These liberalizations are expected to accelerate the internationalization of Japanese financial markets and to promote structural change in the financial system.[34]

The BOJ and Liberalization of Money Markets

Essentially, the BOJ's monetary control has been based on its control over the relatively closed interbank money markets—the call money market and the discount market—through six discount houses (money market dealers). The discount houses have acted as bridgeheads from which the BOJ can directly supervise the behavior of financial institutions in the interbank money markets.

The development of the *gensaki* market in the early 1970s could be regarded as a development in financial markets not amenable to direct BOJ control because financial institutions can exchange funds through these markets without the intermediation of the discount houses. The BOJ had endeavored to connect the open money markets directly with the interbank money markets that it has efficiently controlled for many years, an endeavor reflected in a series of recent measures liberalizing the money markets.[35]

In one measure in 1980, the BOJ allowed some securities companies to borrow in the call money market. Since the securities companies have been the main borrowers in the *gensaki* market, this move was expected to make arbitrages between the interbank and the open money markets more efficient and, thereby, to enhance the BOJ's ability to control money market interest rates. Since 1978, the BOJ has also to a certain extent liberalized the restrictions on the workings of the interbank money markets. Such liberalization may have strengthened the relationship between the interbank and the open money markets.

The BOJ is eager to develop the treasury bill market. The BOJ and the governmental financial organization (the Trust Fund Bureau) have underwritten almost all treasury bills because their issue prices have always been higher than their free market prices. Private agents have not been overly attracted to these bills, which could have been viable instruments in the open money markets. If the public held a sufficient number of treasury bills, the BOJ could directly influence the open money markets by buying or selling them through open market operations, as is done in the United States and England.

In 1981, the BOJ began to sell some of its treasury bills to private financial institutions at interest rates comparable to the interbank money market rates, hoping to promote the development of a treasury bill market. The MOF reportedly opposes the development of a treasury bill market because it wants to adjust its short-run financial needs free of market constraints. At present, a substantial disagreement seems to exist between the MOF and the BOJ concerning the necessity of a well-developed treasury bill market for efficient monetary control under the rapidly changing structure of the financial markets.

On the other hand, the BOJ has restricted quite rigorously *direct* transactions by financial institutions in the money markets—that is, transactions without intermediation by the discount houses. For example, the BOJ has refused to liberalize interest rates on interbank deposits because these deposits could become the main channel for direct exchange of funds among institutions. The regulation of interbank deposit rates has substantially prevented the expansion of such transactions.

It is quite natural for bankers to seek to economize on brokerage fees and avoid the inconvenience of BOJ interference associated with traditional interbank transactions. The relaxation of regulation of yen conversion (*yen tenkan kisei*) in June 1984 raised the possibility of direct interbank transactions in the form of foreign currency deposits with unregulated interest rates.[36] A bank could supply its surplus funds to another bank in the form of foreign currency deposits with a forward cover instead of deposits in yen. With free yen conversion, a bank with foreign currency deposits can use the funds in swap operations as if they were denominated in yen. Thus, this relaxation has had the effect of neutralizing the regulation of interbank deposit rates.

It was reported in the press that the BOJ had asked the city banks to refrain from engaging in direct transactions through foreign currency deposits. Thus, the BOJ is still restricting the natural arbitrage through foreign currency deposits even after yen conversion liberalization. The BOJ's bias against direct transactions between private banks results from its belief that monetary control is only effective through intervention by discount houses, which the BOJ regards as its subsidiaries.

Conclusions

On the surface, every social system appears to be designed explicitly to promote public welfare. The evolution of the social system is, however, always connected to the interests of particular agents and the groups they represent. A social system can be maintained even when a relatively small number of these groups benefit from the existing system at the expense of the other constituents of the community, if the burden is not too large. At the same time, even though it is possible to improve economic welfare, reform cannot be introduced smoothly when it seriously damages those groups receiving the most benefit from the system. Although those groups with vested interests easily draw attention to the burdens imposed by reform, the smaller benefits accruing to a greater number of constituents tend to go unnoticed. Therefore, there is inertia in the system to maintain the status quo.

External disturbances to a society that change the cost-benefit structure of the system must render the status quo intolerable to supporters of the present system before a society will adopt social reform. In general, unless certain exogenous shocks occur and the socioeconomic situation becomes critical, significant reform will not proceed. It is only when the cost-benefit structure shifts drastically, seriously undermining the interests of a certain group, that changing the rules of the game can obtain sufficient support. Political leadership and entrepreneurial effort in drawing a suitable design can work as catalysts to realize structural reform.[37]

These observations are generally true of financial reform. Financial reform can be explained as the result of serious disturbances created by environmental changes in the cost-benefit structure that supports the existing financial system. If a new development in technology or in assets accumulation damages some interest groups—as exemplified by disintermediation from the banking sector in the United States and a similar development in Japan—afflicted groups may exert political pressure strong enough to change the current rules of the game. The relative stability of the financial system in the period of high economic growth can be regarded as a result of an equilibrium among the various interests in the financial markets at that time.

We have emphasized several exogenous shocks as subverting the political impasse that dominated the Japanese financial system during the high growth period: (1) changes in the financial markets brought about by economic growth, in particular the rapid accumulation of financial assets by nonfinancial sectors; (2) the surprisingly rapid increase in public bonds because of drastic changes in the flow of funds since the mid-1970s; (3) the progress in electronic telecommunications technology, which, at least potentially, facilitates the joint production of financial services; and (4) the internationalization of financial markets, which has exerted increasing pressure to open and deregulate the Japanese financial system and made it impossible to sustain cartel-like behavior in the banking sector supported by the monetary authorities.

Moreover, we have stressed the important role of the monetary authorities in the financial system. Admittedly, the Japanese authorities have played an active role in the development of the financial markets in the postwar period. They have, however, been important and active not so much as designers of specific plans for economic development but as coordinators among various agents in the financial markets, particularly among financial intermediaries. The influence of the authorities on financial allocation was far more indirect and ambiguous than some observers suggest.

Perspectives

We now have some insight into the future development of the Japanese financial system, but a precise prediction is beyond our scope. We attempt only to provide a probable scenario of the future of the financial system.

1. The price mechanism will become much more important in financial markets. The accumulation of financial assets accompanied by rapid economic growth has provided an essential basis on which full-scale capital markets can function. The internationalization of Japanese business finance will promote interest rate arbitrage between domestic and foreign capital markets, stimulating the efficient working of price mechanisms in the domestic financial markets. Under these circumstances, it will be difficult for the authorities to continue regulating domestic interest rates; indeed, deregulation has already begun.

The most important problem for the Japanese authorities will be to preserve stability in a much more competitive atmosphere. Strengthening the power of the deposit insurance system will most likely be an efficient means to cope with this problem.

2. We expect the structural changes in financial markets to further lessen the predominant role of private banks as suppliers of funds to major industries. Since the latter half of the 1970s, the ties between banks and firms have gradually loosened. Big businesses have reduced their dependence on bank loans. In the near future, therefore, small and medium-size businesses, as well as households, will be more important as borrowers in bank loan markets.

Of course, loans to consumers are always accompanied by problems of asymmetric information; it is difficult for lenders to identify poor credit risks among the thousands of potential borrowers. Many of the recent problems associated with consumer finance companies are related to this difficulty. Some organizational changes will have to be introduced to enable the consumer loan market to expand smoothly. The expansion of consumer loans may depress the saving rates of Japanese households, thereby reducing the gap between savings and investment.

3. Japan's financial evolution will render some institutions obsolete, particularly those institutions that complemented immature capital markets during the high growth period. The long-term credit banks, for instance, are losing their significance as suppliers of long-term funds. They may have to utilize their accumulated expertise in the field of investment banking in order to survive.

The role of governmental institutions as suppliers of long-term credit is also declining. Recently, a governmental institution, the Housing Loan Corporation, has gained importance in the residential loan market since private financial institutions have delayed responding to increases in demand in this market. At the same time, however, the share of government funds in the supply of equipment funds to private businesses has increased since the mid-1970s. This suggests that governmental financial institutions are competing with private financial institutions in the business loan market. Political demands from private bankers to reduce the role of governmental financial institutions will undoubtedly grow stronger, although existing government institutions and the Postal Savings system will continue to resist. On balance, however, we expect that the government will reduce the extent of its lending activities in the future.

4. The BOJ will have to recast its monetary policy instruments. Indeed, we have already observed some indication of change. During the high growth period, the BOJ relied heavily on quantitative control methods. The penetration of price mechanisms into the financial markets,

however, will make those methods less effective. The BOJ's more recent promotion of money market liberalization reflects its recognition that change in its policy procedures is imminent.

Will the BOJ be able to maintain its precise monetary control over financial markets? It is possible that heightened capital mobility will introduce various disturbances from abroad, thus hampering domestic control. There may be a trade-off between economic welfare gains from deregulation and the costs of the reduced effectiveness of monetary policies. Whether such a trade-off will occur and whether there will be any plausible method of shifting the trade-off relationship to a more favorable position are issues to be investigated in the future.

5. As we have already emphasized, the Japanese government was most important as a coordinator of the various interests represented in the financial markets. We do not believe that the government will cease to be a powerful coordinator in the near future. Although coordination may have contributed to stabilizing the financial structure during the high growth period, it is less clear what role such involvement would play in a rapidly changing environment. Because of government intervention, Japanese financial markets may be able to operate efficiently in the face of drastic changes. It is more likely, however, that governmental arbitration among the various existing interests will hinder adaptation to the new circumstances.

The Japanese government will surely be unable to preserve the various vested interests, given the growing importance of price mechanisms and increasing influence from abroad. The government will be forced to promote both deregulation and internationalization of domestic financial markets lest Japanese financial institutions and businesses be barred from foreign capital markets, which will become increasingly important as their spheres of activities broaden.

This scenario implies that the Japanese financial system will not be able to build a wall around itself. Most of the features that have characterized it for the past three decades seem destined to disappear gradually. Of course, it is not certain that our scenario will prove correct. The inertia in the financial system may be much stronger than we expect.

We conclude this paper with some subjective and speculative judgments concerning politico-economic aspects of Japanese financial markets. First, the Japanese financial system has been supported at the expense of consumers and individual savers. They are so numerous and their interests so diverse that it would be difficult for them to form a single pressure group. The interests of individuals, especially small savers, as suppliers of funds have been damaged by the ceiling on deposit rates. This regulation does not allow them to enjoy the fruit of their savings fully.

Many of the problems associated with consumer finance companies indicate that individuals or households have not been treated fairly as financial borrowers. The authorities often discourage extending credit to households through the ceiling on consumer loan rates and by administrative guidance. This stance seems to have prevented banks from fully entering the consumer loan market. A portion of the vacuum has been filled with the rapid development of consumer finance companies, which could charge borrowers interest rates above 50 per cent per annum. If the financial system were restructured to give individuals freer access to consumer finance, Japanese society might become more consumer oriented. This could also help reduce the current surplus in the balance of payments, thereby easing international tensions.

Foreign pressure to deregulate could play an important role in realizing the interests of consumers in the financial system. As mentioned above, consumer interests are difficult to present in the political process. Exporters may sometimes unknowingly represent consumer interests by supporting import liberalization. But such cases are limited. By pushing for further deregulation or liberalization, foreigners work for the benefit of domestic consumers.[38]

For good or ill, the coordination of the authorities, or *nemawashi* (laying the groundwork), has been an indispensable part of the financial process in Japan. Since *nemawashi* tends to take time, the process of coordination will seem to foreigners to be stubborn adherence to the traditional rules. Because of this long process of coordination, however, most participants will be prepared to conform smoothly to the new rules.

It is quite unlikely that the basic structure of the financial process will change abruptly in the near future. Admittedly, the Japanese financial structure will be forced to react to several of the environmental changes we have considered. The changes may seem radical to those in Japan, but the process may appear much too sluggish to foreigners. This divergence of views will persist at least for a while.

Part III

Firms and Employment

Masahiko Aoki

The Japanese Firm in Transition

Lifetime employment, a seniority system, and enterprise unionism are the three pillars of Japanese industrial relations." "Japanese firms grow rapidly because they are able to raise investment funds from banks on easy terms." "Large companies exploit smaller firms as a business-cycle buffer." These are some of the generalizations about the Japanese firm and its management bruited by popular writings. Although some aspects of these statements may be true, many recent works seek to modify these oversimplified notions and to demystify "Japanese management."

Informed readers know that (1) long-run employment, if not "lifetime employment," is prevalent not only in Japanese corporations but also in large, well-managed corporations elsewhere; (2) seniority is not necessarily the sovereign principle governing layoff decisions in Japanese corporations, and in times of business hardship expensive senior employees are often the most vulnerable; (3) on average, companies having close connections with large city banks do not perform as well in terms of profitability as companies that do not, even before interest payments;[1] and (4) subcontractors maintain stable, long-term relations with prime manufacturers and are somewhat like in-house supply divisions.[2]

Thus, the differences between the Japanese firm and its Western counterpart seem to be much more subtle than popular writing suggests. But subtleties aside, is there some characteristic unique to the Japanese firm and its management? More specifically, having demystified Japanese management, can we settle comfortably into a belief that the neo-classical postulate of profit maximization is the guiding principle of the Japanese firm?

Academic and bureaucratic circles have never taken the concept of "Japanese management" seriously. The neo-classical postulate of value maximization (the maximization of a firm's value on behalf of the shareholders as a long-run analogue of profit maximization) has been accepted without much reflection in most econometric studies aimed at explaining and predicting the behavior of Japanese firms. For example, the econometric model developed under the supervision of the Econometric Committee of the Economic Council (comprising 14 noted academic econometricians) for use in ecomonic planning by the Economic Planning Agency is explicitly based on the value-maximization postulate.[3] But the model performed so poorly that, in order to improve its statistical fitness, researchers resorted to adding ad hoc variables to the derived equations for estimating and predicting firms' investment, employment, and other behavior.

At issue is not simply the statistical fitness of this or other models, but rather the aptness of the fundamental conception of the modern corporate firm that lies behind most econometric model building. I would suggest that in general the modern corporate firm is not a simple entity maximizing a single objective such as its share price. In a series of recent works, I have developed a conceptual and analytical framework for analyzing and interpreting the structure and behavior of the modern firm on the premise that the firm is a complex organization within which the partly harmonious and partly conflicting interests of diverse constituents, including employees (and even suppliers), are brought into equilibrium.[4] In this essay, I attempt to apply this framework to the recent historical development of the Japanese firm.

In the first section of this paper, I summarize some basic structural and behavioral characteristics of the Japanese firm. This characterization relies on my previous work, to which readers interested in further analytical and empirical support for the characterization may refer.

In the second section, I pinpoint a few important historical events that seem to have contributed to the institutionalization of the Japanese firm as characterized in the first section. I then discuss the roles of individual shareholders and corporate shareholders. Specifically, I argue that labor market imperfections (the establishment of the internal labor market) and the relative illiquidity of corporate shareholdings (because of the formation of corporate groups) are twin prerequisites for, as well as twin consequences of, the kind of management that has developed in Japan. The imperfect labor and capital markets reinforce and complement each other. This is followed by a discussion of the adaptation of the Japanese firm to the increased environmental uncertainties that followed the first oil shock, focusing on the tendency of the Japanese firm to hive off quasi-independent subsidiaries and to utilize long-run subcontracting relations with smaller firms. This tendency toward quasi disintegration hints at the Japanese firm's ability to commercialize high technology in spite of imperfections in the capital market (specifically the lack of a venture capital market). I conclude by speculating on the future of the Japanese firm and conjecture that the dual imperfection of the labor and capital markets is beginning to recede and that this will somewhat modify the workings of the Japanese firm while preserving its fundamental characteristics.

The Japanese Firm

In neo-classical economics, the "firm" is identified with the entrepreneur, who performs the dual functions of control and risk taking. In the modern context, "entrepreneur" is usually taken to mean the shareholders, who exercise ultimate control over corporate affairs by selecting managers and take the uncertain residual income of the firm after the payment of contractual rewards to other factors of production. Employees are *not* considered members of the firm, and their rights are supposed to spring only from individual or collective contracts. I propose that this characterization does not elucidate the workings of the Japanese firm, which rather must be understood in the following terms:

Characterization A
The body of employees is, together with the body of shareholders, explicitly or implicitly recognized as a constituent of the firm, and its interests are considered in the formation of managerial policy.

The consideration of the employees' interests is not unique to the Japanese firm. The actual institutional frameworks that make it possible are diverse. Employees' interests may be voiced through a collective bargaining apparatus, while management serves as an agent of the shareholders, as in unionized Anglo-American firms (the *collective bargaining model*). Employees' directors, side by side with shareholders' directors, may supervise management through a supervisory organ, as in West German and Scandinavian firms (the *participatory management model*), or employees with an employees' stock ownership plan may express their preferences through such corporate organs as shareholders' meetings (the *employee part-ownership model*). But the way in which employees' preferences are accommodated in managerial policymaking in the typical Japanese firm differs from all of these and may be considered an instance of what I call the *corporative managerialism model*, characterized as follows:[5]

Characterization B
Management acts as a mediator in the policymaking process, striking a balance between the interests of shareholders and those of employees. The enterprise union functions as a substructure of the firm and represents employees in the decision-making process.

These characteristics may exist latently in firms elsewhere, but they are conspicuous features of the representative Japanese firm. (The reason the typical Japanese firm is structured in this way is largely historical. See the next section.) This characterization of the Japanese firm is perhaps akin to the sociological structure Ronald Dore labeled "hierarchical corporatism," in which management is supposed to act as "the benevolent guardians of the interest of the company as a whole (including the interests of the workers as well as the shareholders)."[6] But in my view, management is a "mediator" that weighs and equilibrates both the implicit and explicit bargaining powers of the firm's constituents. Employees make their interests known to management through the enterprise union, but informal and implicit pressures exercised by subordinates on management may also play an important role. Shareholders may communicate their interest to the management through the stock market, shareholders' meetings, informal personal contacts (in the case of large shareholders), and so on.

The differences between the characterization given here and Dore's are not simply semantic. My own contribution, if any, lies in the construction of analytical notions of the bargaining powers of the constituent bodies and their intrafirm equilibrium within the framework of cooperative game theory.[7] I was thus able to show that some of the firm's behavior, as it is described or prescribed by neo-classical economists, may not be internally efficient from the viewpoint of existing shareholders and incumbent employees. Specifically, in the context of the Japanese firm, or of any large firm administering an internal labor market, the efficient behavior of management cannot be explained in terms of the neo-classical synthetic postulate, which holds that management unilaterally chooses its employment and investment policy in order to maximize share price *posterior* to individual or collective wage bargaining.[8] Rather, it must be explained in terms of the efficient mediation postulate, according to which management, possibly in cooperation with the enterprise union, coordinates wage determination and managerial policymaking simultaneously in order to achieve an efficient outcome. Specifically, efficient management chooses to employ more employees and strives for higher sales growth than share-price maximization posterior to the wage determination would dictate.

This claim assumes that the technology employed by the firm is such that employees' skills are formed and transmitted on the job and in a team context, as emphasized in the illuminating works of Kazuo Koike.[9] In order to motivate employers and employees to share the costs of investment in such team-oriented human capital, seniority-related benefits to employees in the form of seniority wages, retirement compensation (*taishokukin*), and the like have been developed as devices through which both partners can reap returns from their respective investments over time. Without such contrivances, employees might quit in the middle of their careers, causing the value of the human capital accumulated within the firm to be lost. These devices bind employees to the firms in which they are trained, and once they are instituted, the employers are guaranteed returns to shared investment in specific training. On the other hand, the employees are able to substitute expected utilities derivable from job security and better prospects of career advancement within the firm for the immediate satisfaction derivable from current wages. This trade-off between current wage levels and managerial policies favorable to the welfare of employees is the basis for the efficient mediation postulate.

Under this circumstance, if the employees make wage concessions, management, in its employment and investment decisions, may in turn consider the benefits accruable to employees in the form of job security and improved chances for career advancement in addition to possible capital gains accruable to shareholders. Without such mutually beneficial (or more technically, Pareto-improving) trade-offs, overly high current wages, too low growth, and insufficient levels of employment will be the inevitable outcome of maintaining a certain level of employee satisfaction at the expense of share price (or vice versa).[10]

Some caveats about this characterization of Japanese management and its behavioral implication are in order. First, this argument by no means implies that Japanese management is a passive agent that merely reconciles the partly conflicting, partly harmonious claims of employees and shareholders. In order to mediate efficiently, management must account for the extra benefits from the growth of the firm accruable to employees in the form of better prospects for promotion. Moreover, in an uncertain world, the possibilities for the firm's growth do not become known through exogenously given data; they are something that must be explored at considerable expenditure of resources and entrepreneurial energy. If management can organize the activities of the firm in such a way as to realize higher growth at lower cost, it will improve employees' opportunities for promotion within the firm and increase capital gains for shareholders. This will in turn enhance the legitimacy and the reputation of the manager. Efficient managers in Japanese firms are even more aggressive and growth exploring than the neo-classical paradigm would suggest. In this connection, it may be pointed out that the growth-seeking behavior of Japanese management is not assumed *a priori* in our theory, but rather is derived as an equilibrating outcome of the utility-seeking behavior of the constituents of the firm.

Second, a casual reading of the efficient mediation postulate may lead one to wonder how the firm can maintain its competitiveness when it does not maximize share price (profit). But the postulate maintains only that efficient management will not maximize share price with wages taken as given. It is consistent with this claim that management should maximize the share price for a certain level of employee welfare by coordinating both wage level and managerial policy instruments simultaneously. The firm may be able to maintain and enhance its competitiveness in the market be restraining current wage levels while preserving and accumulating firm-specific human capital. Gains from such efficient mediation can be shared between shareholders and employees over time to enhance their long-run utilities.

The Formation of Japanese Management, 1945–1965

Before Japanese management as characterized in the preceding section could become viable, at least three prerequisites had to be met. First, management had to be freed from the institutional setup of classical capitalist control and from the ideology that supports it—namely, that management should passively serve the interests of owners. Second, a framework of collective bargaining had to be established to facilitate explicit and implicit trading between current wage levels and managerial policy choices affecting the welfare of employees, and both management and employees had to adopt ideological stances to support this framework. Third, management had to be protected, to a certain extent, from the inefficient stock market discipline of incessant share-price maximization as described in the neo-classical synthetic postulate. In other words, it had to be protected from excessive threats of unfriendly takeovers. Such prerequisites were met over the course of the postwar period (before World War II in the case of the first point[11]), and Japanese management as I have characterized it had firmly established itself by the middle 1960s. In this process, several notable events encouraged the development of Japanese management.

Removal of Classical Capitalist Control

The first, and probably the most important, impetus for the formation of Japanese management was given by the postwar reforms directed by the Occupation, especially the dissolution of the *zaibatsu* and the purge of the prewar and wartime leaders of the business community. In the period between August 1946 and August 1947, 83 companies were designated as holding companies, and in 1947 the ten families controlling these and other companies were designated as *zaibatsu* families. Most of the shares held by the holding companies and the *zaibatsu* families were transferred to the Holding Companies Liquidation Commission. The total value of the shares transferred in this operation combined with those transferred to the government to pay taxes amounted to ¥18.4 billion, which was about two-fifths of the total value of stock outstanding at that time. In the absence of an open stock exchange, the Security Liquidation Coordination Council sold these shares.

Two of the council's policies are worthy of note. First, company employees and then local residents were given the first opportunity to purchase the liquidated shares at prices set by the council. Second, no person was allowed to acquire more than 1 per cent of any company. As a result of these policies, 29.3 per cent of the employees in the affected companies purchased 38.5 per cent of the total shares sold. At the end of fiscal year 1949 (March 1950), individual holdings reached nearly 70 per cent of the total outstanding stock. Thus, family control, which had governed many strategic companies through holding companies, was effectively removed.

Parallel to the *zaibatsu* dissolution, in November 1946 the General Headquarters of the Occupation purged the wartime officers of 200 important companies. In addition, a January 1948 law banned all members of the ten *zaibatsu* families and high-ranking directors of 240 *zaibatsu*-related companies from assuming directorships of related companies for ten years. As a result of these two measures, more than 3,600 business leaders were expelled from the business community.

The dispersal of shareownership through the dissolution of *zaibatsu* holding companies and the replacement of previous managers by relatively young managers, who were not as loyal to the *zaibatsu* families as the older leaders, were a "managerial revolution from above." The new breed of technocratic managers, together with the aggressive founder-managers who became prominent during the turmoil following the war by exhibiting extraordinary entrepreneurial abilities, would lead Japan's economic recovery and high growth.[12] I examine certain attitudinal differences between the two types of managers in greater detail below. Briefly, the successful founder-managers were generally more technologically innovative and growth oriented than the career managers in the ex-*zaibatsu* companies, who tended to be more prudent about entering new lines of business. Notwithstanding these differences, however, founder-managers never developed into controlling families of the old *zaibatsu* type. The Antimonopoly Law of 1947 outlawed holding companies outright, and no revision of this provision was ever attempted. Not only were successful founders prevented from extending direct capital controls, they even voluntarily decreased their relative shares in the stock of their own companies by developing employee stock ownership plans, making new equity issues available to the public, and so on. They showed more overt pride in being public minded, albeit socially influential, managers of ever-growing organizations than in being men of great wealth.

With this qualification, it may be postulated for the purpose of analysis that the representative Japanese manager is not the classical manager who single-mindedly endeavors to maximize profit, taking wages and other employment conditions as a given in the outside marketplace. Rather, he coordinates managerial policy decisions with wage and other employment decisions in such a way as to strike a balance between the interests of shareholders and employees. Of course, this does not mean that every firm gives employees' and shareholders' interests equal weight. In firms where founder-managers preside and most employees are younger than those in ex-*zaibatsu* firms, the weight is likely to be less in favor of employees. In my view, this difference in relative weighting is, however, a quantitative rather than a qualitative matter.

Enterprise Unions

Even after unilateral control by a few dominant shareholders ended, two steps were necessary for employees to be recognized as legitimate members of the firm and for efficient bargaining on current wages and managerial policy choices to be conducted. The confrontational attitudes of both managers and unionists had to be altered, and a framework for collective bargaining at the enterprise level had to be developed. Efficient coordination of wage determination and managerial policymaking is unlikely if wages are set at the supra-enterprise level or in a noncooperative atmosphere.

In Europe, important bargaining still takes place at the supra-enterprise level, partly for such ideological reasons as emphasis on worker solidarity (as in Sweden), a traditional suspicion of syndicalism on the part of unionists (as in West Germany), and ideological cleavages leading to weaker grass-roots union organization (as in France). But one of the major causes for the persistence of supra-enterprise-level bargaining is historical inertia, as typified by the case of England. In England, a supra-enterprise bargaining apparatus was firmly established as early as the 1870s, when the internal labor market was still underdeveloped and workers were still mobile between firms in particular localities. As the internal labor market developed, supra-enterprise collective agreements were supplemented by sporadic and unorganized wage bargaining at the workshop level (1950 and 1960s). But after it was observed that this unofficial bargaining had generated an inflationary "wage drift," a shift toward more formalized enterprise-level bargaining came to be recognized as an urgent necessity, and in the 1970s this shift in fact began to occur. The shift, however, has not been smooth precisely because of institutional inertia: the bargaining apparatus remains adapted to bargaining at the supra-enterprise level.[13]

In contrast, in U.S. manufacturing industries, where a large-scale union movement started in the 1930s after an internal labor market had already developed, bargaining at the enterprise/plant level between a single employer and the local affiliate of a trade union became the dominant pattern. Japan benefited even more from this "late-development effect." Only after the end of World War II did a large-scale labor movement resume. Because of the vacuum created by the war, there was no institutional inertia to hamper the formation of enterprise-based unions congruent to firm-specific employment structures.

An interesting point is that, because of its own interest in union control of enterprises, even the Japan Communist Party, which exercised a dominant influence in the militant union movement immediately after the war, did not object to enterprise-based unionization. When, however, management's "red purge" swept ruthlessly through union ranks with the strong backing of the General Headquarters of the Occupation Army, revolutionary zeal subsided. Either more moderate unionists assumed the leadership of enterprise-based organizations, or competing enterprise-based organizations led by such unionists superseded more militant organizations through intrafirm union rivalries.

Two noteworthy events marked the transition to the new era of co-operative enterprise unionism: the defeat of a three-month strike led by leftist leaders in the steel industry in 1959 and the end of a strike-lockout at the Mitsui Mining Company's Miike Mine in 1960, which had lasted more than 300 days. In an election following the steel strike, the militants lost to leaders of a more moderate slate, and the new leaders created a bargaining framework in which single-offer bargaining (*ippatsu kaitō*) in the steel industry every spring set a pattern for wage settlements elsewhere. This framework has proved favorable to efficient bargaining by motivating both partners to clarify the objective circumstances that will influence the outcome—the company's ability to pay, the union's willingness to compromise, and so on. Clear understanding of these circumstances helps the partners find an appropriate bargaining solution. As was made clear in the discussion regarding the efficiency implications of the neo-classical synthetic postulate and the efficient mediation postulate, annual wage revision through the spring offensive is more conducive to efficient bargaining than a situation in which wages are fixed for a longer period and management unilaterally revises such policy instruments as those affecting employment and growth for the purpose of immediate capital gains.

The Miike dispute was the last in a series of serious management-union confrontations arising out of management's attempts to reduce the work force. Since it was contemporaneous with the political turmoil surrounding the renewal of the U.S.-Japan Mutual Security Treaty, however, the dispute had a far-reaching impact. During this dispute the Ikeda cabinet was formed, with Politics of Generosity and Conciliation as its slogan, and the first act of the cabinet was to intervene in the Miike dispute in an effort to bring about a conciliatory settlement. Two years after the settlement, a disastrous explosion in the mine took the lives of 458 miners. It was generally believed that the scars of poor morale and negligence of safety provisions left by the confrontation were indirect causes of the disaster. By the time the incident occurred, most Japanese managers had accepted the philosophy of cooperative and conciliatory labor relations.

Insulation from Takeover

Another historical development contributing to the formation of Japanese management was the development of mutual shareholding between companies and financial institutions, notably city banks. Although Japanese banks had been allowed to hold stock in nonfinancial corporations during the prewar period, city banks did not become targets of the *zaibatsu* dissolution. The Antimonopoly Law of 1947 imposed a 5 per cent ceiling on city bank holdings in the stock of any single company, but subsequent legislation raised this ceiling to 10 per cent in 1953. Bank holdings in listed companies stood at 9.9 per cent at the end of fiscal year 1949 but increased to more than 20 per cent by the end of 1956. Intercorporate shareholding also increased, from 5.6 per cent in 1949 to 15.7 per cent in 1956. Except for single-layer holdings of technologically related subsidiaries, the Antimonopoly Law of 1947 virtually prohibited intercorporate shareholding. But in 1949 this stringent restriction was repealed, although the provision making holding companies illegal remained intact. Through the operations of the Holding Companies Liquidation Commission, securities companies purchased a substantial number of shares and eventually resold them to city banks and other corporations. Further, shareholders had no statutory preemptive rights, and a substantial portion of the new equity issues of business corporations were mutually subscribed among companies related to each other either through old *zaibatsu* connections or through city banks.

A historical event that accelerated mutual shareholding was the stock market crash of 1964–65, which nearly drove one of the largest security companies, Yamaichi Shōken, bankrupt. In this period, Shōken Hoyū Kumiai (Securities Holding Union) and Nihon Kyōdō Shōken (Japan Cooperative Securities) were created with the backing of the government. Financed by the Bank of Japan, these organizations purchased securities from the market and security companies, as well as from ailing investment trusts, and then froze them in order to stabilize market prices. After this objective had been achieved, the shares were to be liquidated in the market.

But during this period, Japan was liberalizing foreign investment, and managers who feared possible unfriendly takeovers by foreign investors tried to counteract this threat.[14] Since with minor exceptions a company is barred from acquiring its own stock (Commercial Code, Article 220), related companies utilized mutual shareholding as a substitute and, in mutually agreed, concerted "stockholder stabilization operations," purchased most of the stocks offered.

By the end of 1968, shareholding by financial institutions had climbed to 30.3 per cent of the total outstanding stock of all listed corporations, and shareholdings by other business corporations had risen to 21.4 per cent. I discuss other aspects of intercorporate shareholding later; here it is important to note that this development has effectively insulated the management of the typical large Japanese company from outside take-overs. This has three important implications. First, although management is immune from the disciplinary actions of the stock market, excessive pursuit of its own interests at the expense of shareholders is limited by other monitoring mechanisms, particularly mutual monitoring by the managers themselves.[15] Second, conflicts of interest may arise between individual shareholders and corporate shareholders because individual investors are more likely than corporate shareholders to be concerned with stock prices. I discuss these issues in later sections.

Third, insulation from takeover may have the unintended effect of mitigating the pressure on managers to maximize share price. Such maximization may result in internal, short-run inefficiency for the period of a wage contract. As pointed out already, once an internal labor market develops and employees can benefit from better opportunities for promotion and job security within the firm, it is better for them to reach some explicit or implicit accord with management in regard to the choice of a combination of wage and managerial policy variables. For instance, they may agree to trade wage increases for job security or better opportunities for promotion made possible by the growth of the firm. In order, however, to maintain efficiency from the viewpoint of the incumbent employees and existing shareholders, once such an accord is reached, the agreed-on managerial choices should not be changed unilaterally. Management may be tempted, however, to make such a change if it is under strong pressure to maximize the short-run share price because, once wages are fixed, there is normally room to enhance the share price of a company by manipulating managerial variables. If management does so, the union, knowing this, will press for higher wages to compensate for management's subsequent inclination to choose an inefficient combination of managerial variables (say, lower employment and lower growth, implying fewer promotional opportunities). This suggests that management and the union can bargain efficiently and will be willing to abide by a cooperative agreement only if there is sufficient mutual trust for each party to believe that the other will abide by it. It further suggests the necessity that neither party be susceptible to pressures that might make it default on an effective cooperative agreement. Stock market pressure for unilateral, short-run share-price maximization would constitute such a pressure. Only if it is removed will the union's trust in managerial conduct and management's unwillingness to act unilaterally and exclusively as the agent of the shareholders become well established.

But the lack of stock market discipline may pose a problem—it may generate collusion between management and the union (employees) at the expense of the shareholders. From the standpoint of efficiency, management's insulation from stock market discipline is thus double-edged.

The Relative Importance of Individual Shareholding

As indicated in the last section, in the 1950s, the proportion of individual holdings of stock of listed corporations declined gradually, and the proportion of intercorporate holdings, especially the holdings of banks, rose significantly. As shown in Fig. 1, this tendency continued into the 1970s. What implications can we derive from this observation? One important question regarding this phenomenon is whether there is a unanimity of interest between individual shareholders and corporate shareholders. Although above I treated shareholders as a homogeneous group, unanimity of interest among them cannot be taken as a dictum. Individual investors and corporate shareholders are subject to different tax obligations and have access to different financial markets. This can be a source of disagreement over what policies a corporation in which they both own stock should adopt. If there is no unanimity, management faces a more complicated task of interest mediation. I investigated this problem in another paper by building a simple general financial equilibrium model incorporating stylized features of the Japanese tax and financial systems.[16]

The basic actors in my model are a representative individual investor, a representative nonfinancial corporation (the firm), and a representative bank. The level of investment by the firm is exogenously given but the firm faces a choice between internal financing and debt financing. The savings of individual investors are also exogenously given, but they too, face a choice—investing their savings in the stock of the firm or depositing them at the bank. The bank can lend investment funds to the firm as well as invest in its stock. The deposit rate is regulated, but

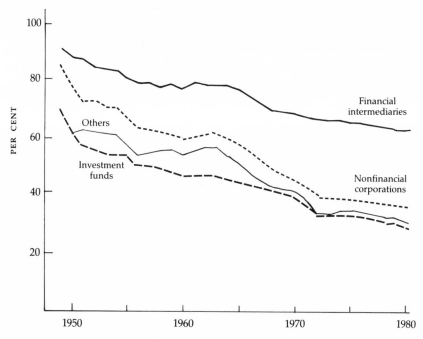

Fig. 1. Distribution of shareholdings of all listed corporations, 1949–1981.

the bank's effective lending rate is determined by bargaining between the bank and the firm over the amount of the compensatory balance the firm deposits with the bank. The stock price is determined endogenously on the market. There is uncertainty in regard to returns on the firm's investments. The individual investor and the bank are risk averse. They both exercise certain controlling powers over the financial decisions of the firm between internal and debt financing, depending on their relative influence in the corporate governance structure, in the absence of unanimity of opinion about the decision. Is there such unanimity? If not, how has the balance of power changed over the past two decades or so?

Analysis of the model indicates a lack of unanimity. The representative individual investor wants the corporation to maximize the share price, but the bank as shareholder wants the corporation to finance its investment by borrowing from it beyond the level that value maximization would warrant. In other words, if the relative power of bank as shareholder is stronger than that of individual shareholders in the corporate governance structure, then from the viewpoint of individual shareholders the firm is likely to borrow too much. My statistical analysis indicates that Japanese firms did overborrow, particularly in the 1960s, even though there is evidence that the power of banks as shareholders declined substantially in the 1970s. This decline suggests that despite the decreasing number of individual shareholders in relative terms, a situation favorable to individual shareholders has recently been created. I return to this later.

Another question regarding the relative decline of individual holdings concerns the distributional consequences. Are individuals deprived of opportunities for sharing fully in the wealth generated by the corporate sector because they hold a comparatively small proportion of stock? If there is no tax and if the capital market is complete and perfectly competitive, the existence or nonexistence of intercorporate shareholding should be immaterial to the opportunities open to individual investors. The benefit Company A derives from holding shares in Company B would eventually accrue to the individual shareholders of Company A, and within their budget constraints, investors could mix the stock of Company A and Company B as they pleased. This must be obvious to neo-classically trained economists. However, the decreasing proportion of individual shareholding coupled with the smaller and smaller proportion of profits paid out as dividends in Japan has led many people to feel that individual shareholders are "exploited" [17] and that the corporate sector gains at the expense of individual shareholders. But, after all, what is the "corporate sector" anyway? Can it not be decomposed ultimately into individual shareholders as the neo-classicists presume?

In the next section, I give an explanation more acceptable to neo-classicists and demonstrate that what a company gains through intercorporate shareholding may not completely accrue to individual shareholders. The argument has some bearing on the characteristics of Japanese management. Here, I point out a fallacy, often associated with the popular view of shareholder exploitation; namely, that returns to individual shareholding have been declining because of the declining propensity of companies to pay out dividends.

As is evident from Table 1, the ratio of average dividends to the average share price for all listed nonfinancial corporations has declined steadily from more than 5 per cent in the early 1960s to 1.5 per cent in the early 1980s. According to an estimate by the National Tax Agency, the proportion of before-tax profits paid out as dividends by the entire corporate sector has been around 10 per cent in the past several years (10.4 per cent in 1982). The corresponding figure in the United States is estimated at about 40 per cent. However, returns to shareholding are composed of dividend receipts *and* capital gains. Since dividend income is taxed separately at 20 to 35 per cent and capital gains are not taxed in Japan, from the viewpoint of individual shareholders it is rational for companies to reduce dividend payments and retain profits internally, provided that the share price reflects the value of retained profit. In fact, as Table 1 shows, the annual rate of capital gains has been substantial for the past 20 years (averaging 13.1 per cent); during the same period, the one-year deposit rate remained at only 6.0 per cent on average.

Why then do typical individual investors hold a substantial portion of their wealth in the form of safe assets such as bank deposits and postal savings? According to the Family Saving Survey of the Statistical Bureau, shareholdings (including holdings of investment fund certificates) constituted only 6.8 per cent of the total assets of households in 1983, whereas deposits and similar assets constituted 63 per cent. The bureau estimated that only 16.9 per cent of all households own shares. The total number of individual shareholders has, however, been increasing recently. From 4 million in 1949, it increased to 18 million by 1973. After that there were ups and downs, but a record high of 19.6 million was reached in 1981.

TABLE 1

The Annual Rate of Return to Shareholding, Nonfinancial Corporate Shares Traded on the Tokyo Exchange, 1st Section, 1963-1983

(per cent)

Year	(1) d/V	(2) $\Delta V/V$	(3) $1 - t$	(4) $(1) \times (3)$	(5) $(2) + (4)$	(6) $\Delta P/P$	(7) $(5) - (6)$
1963	5.6%	13.6%	90%	5.0%	18.6%	6.1%	12.5%
1964	5.2	−9.0	90	4.7	−4.3	4.7	−9.0
1965	5.8	−0.1	95	5.6	5.4	6.4	−1.0
1966	5.6	22.7	95	5.3	28.0	4.2	23.8
1967	4.9	1.2	85	4.2	5.4	5.8	−0.4
1968	5.2	11.0	85	4.4	15.4	3.8	11.6
1969	4.9	32.5	80	4.0	36.4	6.3	30.1
1970	4.1	8.2	80	3.3	11.5	7.9	3.6
1971	4.4	15.4	80	3.5	19.0	4.6	14.4
1972	3.6	68.6	80	2.9	71.5	5.3	66.2
1973	2.4	28.0	80	1.9	29.9	19.2	10.2
1974	2.1	−13.5	75	1.6	−11.9	21.9	−33.8
1975	2.4	3.7	75	1.8	5.5	7.8	−2.3
1976	2.4	13.9	75	1.8	15.7	10.4	5.3
1977	2.2	9.6	70	1.5	11.1	4.8	6.3
1978	2.2	12.9	65	1.4	14.3	3.6	10.7
1979	1.8	9.0	65	1.2	10.2	5.7	4.5
1980	1.7	6.7	65	1.1	7.8	7.1	0.7
1981	1.5	19.3	65	1.0	20.3	4.3	16.0
1982	1.5	0.6	65	1.0	1.6	1.8	−0.3
1983	1.5	21.5	65	1.0	22.5	1.8	20.7
Average	3.4%	13.1%		2.8%	15.9%		9.1%
Standard error		16.5			16.6		17.6

NOTE: d/V = dividend-price ratio (Japan Securities Research Institute estimate); $\Delta V/V$ = capital gain rate (Japan Securities Research Institute estimate); t = maximal separate tax rate on dividend incomes; $\Delta P/P$ = the rate of increase in consumer price index (Japan, Office of the Prime Minister, Bureau of Statistics).

Shareholding has become an increasingly important portfolio component for some persons.

One probable reason shareholding has not become a more important means of storing individual assets is the high risk costs and high transaction costs associated with it. As Table 1 shows, the standard error in the annual rate of capital gains was 16.5, and that of total aftertax returns was 16.6 (17.6 in real terms) over the period 1962 to 1982. Moreover, the broker's fees charged by securities companies for trading shares are regulated and highly regressive. The rate for transactions not exceeding ¥1 million in value per stock is 1.25 per cent of the value of the transaction, whereas the rate for transactions of more than ¥100 million is 0.55 per cent. The hypothesis that risk costs are higher for small investors than for large ones (that is, small investors are more risk averse) may imply, together with the regressiveness of broker's fees, that the relative insignificance of shareholdings in individual assets in Japan is partly attributable to the lower degree of financial accumulation by the typical Japanese household relative to U.S. households.[18]

Why have investment funds (Japanese-style mutual funds) for overcoming the risk and transaction costs associated with small shareholding not developed in Japan? One of the main reasons may be found in the security crash of 1964–65. Before that, investment funds were clearly on the upswing. At the end of 1963, 11.9 per cent of all households owned investment fund certificates (and 20.3 per cent held shares). The proportion of shareholding in investment funds increased from 3.9 per cent in 1956 to 9.5 per cent in 1963. After the relatively minor stock crash in 1961, security companies borrowed heavily from the call market, the Japan Security Finance Corporation, city banks, and the like. They used securities deposited by customers as collateral and incurred high financial costs. In order to maintain the prices of securities that were apt to tumble, the major security companies utilized their controlling power over portfolio selections of investment funds.

This only made the 1964–65 crash worse. Most investment funds suffered heavy capital losses and cancellation of contracts by individual investors. As a result, the proportion of households holding investment fund certificates dropped to 4.8 per cent in 1967. This crash had two enduring effects. First, resentful small investors came to distrust security companies. Second, the Securities Department of the Ministry of Finance (MOF) introduced tighter regulations in order to control the conflict-of-interest problem. Entry into the securities business began to be tightly controlled by licensing, and the number of securities companies decreased sharply, from 484 in September 1965 to 277 in April 1968. Under the administrative guidance of the MOF, investment fund portfolios came to include substantial amounts of national bonds (government-guaranteed long-term bonds issued by long-term credit banks and the like), and they became a not particularly attractive form of asset holdings from the point of view of individual investors.

In summary, the relatively small number of shares held by individual investors in Japanese firms may be explained by the relatively low level of individual financial accumulation as well as by the (yet-to-be established) standard of business ethics in the investment community. In spite of the apparently weak role they play in the corporate governance structure, however, individual shareholders should be regarded not as "exploited" but as viable members of the Japanese firm. Increasing financial accumulation by households and increasing competition among security brokers and investment trusts accelerated by the ongoing financial deregulation are likely to make shareholding a more important component of individual portfolios.

The Role of Intercorporate Shareholding

As noted above, there are roughly two types of managers: bureaucratic managers found predominantly in established firms of *zaibatsu* origin (or firms with *zaibatsu* connections) and the entrepreneurial founder-managers of newer firms. Although a line cannot be drawn neatly between the two types, firms managed by the former are usually interconnected through mutual shareholding, whereas in many cases firms managed by the latter remain independent.[19] My concern here is with a theoretical inquiry into a certain aspect of corporate groupings.

There may be many motives behind intercorporate shareholding, but the one emphasized here is their role as an insulator against unfriendly takeovers. The management of each member-firm in a corporate group is subject to reciprocal monitoring instead of the market discipline of share-price maximization. As seen in the recent Mitsukoshi incident, when misconduct becomes apparent, not even an extremely powerful chief executive officer can resist a sanction led by outside directors who are themselves managers of other firms in the same group.[20] It often happens that the management of a financially ailing business corporation is taken over by a major bank that belongs to the same group and at the same time is the principal lender. Since any board member may be replaced at any time by an ordinary resolution at a shareholders' meeting, reciprocal monitoring within a corporate group, which collectively holds 15 to 30 per cent of the total stock of each member-firm, provides a powerful means of discipline.

On what criteria do member-firms exercise collective discipline over peer members? Do they impose a value-maximizing (profit-maximizing) discipline? According to a pioneering econometric study by Richard

Caves and Masu Uekusa, the hypothesis that member-firms of corporate groups on average enjoy higher profit rates than independent firms is not supported statistically.[21] A recent econometric study by Iwao Nakatani reaffirms this conclusion.[22]

Lately an alternative theory has been advanced that purports to explain the function of corporate groups as reducing transaction costs through intragroup exchanges of information, repetition of transactions between members, and the like.[23] But if the transaction-cost savings accrue exclusively as premium profits to member-firms, this hypothesis is reduced to the profit-maximizing postulate and thus is not empirically supportable. It is hard to explain why profitable independent firms exist alongside corporate groups if cost savings are the only motive for the group's formation. Thus, a need arises to introduce some corporate characteristic as an explanatory variable. One attractive hypothesis would be that member-firms of corporate groups are more risk averse than independent firms and that grouping functions as a mutual insurance scheme.[24] However, what is meant by the "risk averseness" of a firm? Why can't the capital market function as an optimal risk-shifting mechanism? Can mutual shareholding by firms create new opportunities for risk diffusion? Do the special characteristics of Japanese management have any bearing on this possibility?

First, a purely theoretical observation. If the capital market is complete and perfectly competitive, and if there are no transaction costs and no tax, the efficient allocation of risk bearing can be achieved through the market. Neither intercorporate shareholding nor any other mechanism can expand the opportunity already available to all wealthholders through the capital market. But suppose that individual holders cannot sell some wealth associated with a firm freely through the capital market. Under this "no-sales" constraint, the role of intercorporate shareholding changes. The individual wealthholders associated with that firm are constrained in their capacity to trade shares in order to realize subjectively optimal risk diversification. But if the firm itself can trade that wealth for the stocks of other companies and if the owners of the weath in the firm have similar attitudes toward risk, then this action can be substituted, albeit incompletely, for unrealizable individual diversification of risk.[25] Furthermore, corporate grouping linked by intercorporate shareholding may function as a mutual insurance scheme, albeit suboptimally, when individual holders cannot sell the wealth associated with member-firms.

In the above, the no-sales constraint was an imaginary hypothesis, but, in my view, the typical employee and manager of the Japanese firm are engaged in de facto capital participation in the employing firm, and this wealth is not perfectly salable. Under the seniority wage system, employees bear a portion of the cost of investments in firm-specific, collective human capital when they are junior employees and reap returns on the investments when they become senior employees. Further, around 70 per cent of retirement benefits of employees at all publicly listed corporations are paid as lump sums at the time of retirement. Reserves for these compensations are accumulated within the firm and investable at management's discretion. Reserves for retirement compensation amount to a little more than 15 per cent of the value of paid-in capital in all publicly listed nonfinancial corporations. Employees who voluntarily quit the firm in mid-career receive a substantially lower sum than if they had stayed on until mandatory retirement.

The important point here is not only that the potential wealth of employees associated with the employing firm is unportable, but also that it is undiversifiable. In Western firms as well, an employee who quits a firm in mid-career may be penalized by a reduction in the pension benefits provided by the firm. But as long as a person continues to work for the firm, that person's and the firm's pension contributions would normally be funded and diversified in the capital market by a professional pension manager. The so-called prudent man rule is imposed on pension managers in their portfolio selections, and the employee is freed from firm-specific risks. In contrast, a substantial amount of the wealth owned by the employees of a Japanese firm is at stake in the employing firm. In this situation, mutual shareholding by member-firms within corporate groups would mitigate firm-specific risks. In fact, major corporate groups centering around city banks are composed of many firms, not necessarily related through close business relations. These firms are engaged in diverse lines of business and thus belong to diverse risk classes.

Of course, mutual shareholding is an incomplete substitute for risk diversification by individual investors in an efficient capital market, but it does provide an important safety net for members of participating firms. First of all, stock owned by member-firms serves as an important reserve and can be cashed, mostly by other member-firms and banks, in the case of substantial losses. For instance, when the Sumitomo Bank incurred an estimated loss of ¥113 billion in the first half of 1977 because of the virtual bankruptcy of Ataka Trading Company (a then important member of the Sumitomo Group), it apparently sold stocks with an estimated value of ¥26.2 billion in order to report a profit.[26] There are many other conceivable methods by which member-firms might come to the rescue of an ailing company, such as employing redundant employees or offering extraordinary business opportunities. For instance, when Tōyō Kōgyō, the maker of Mazda automobiles, was on the brink of bankruptcy in 1979–80, the entire Sumitomo group switched its auto purchases to Mazda. Tōyō Kōgyō sources estimate that the 600-member group purchased 3,000 vehicles per year (or 18,000 vehicles over the six years 1975 to 1981).[27]

For such mutual insurance schemes to work, a long-term relationship among the member-firms is necessary. Mutual shareholdings provide an effective bond for such relations. Furthermore, interlocking directorates and regular meetings of the presidents' club (*shachō-kai*) of the corporate group provide mutual monitoring mechanisms to help prevent wrongdoings of top managers insulated from takeover threats.

Iwao Nakatani's recent findings that variations in the profits and the earnings of employees at member-firms of corporate groups are on average significantly lower than those at independent firms may be partly explained by the greater internalization of the labor market in member-firms (that is, the average tenure of employees is longer at those firms) and their greater accumulation of nonsalable, nondiversifiable wealth.[28] Also, it is often observed that as they mature, even relatively new firms of non-*zaibatsu* origin seek more stable relationships with particular banks, suppliers, and so on. The theory and empirical testing of the risk-sharing function of corporate groupings are yet to be developed, but they seem to be worthwhile subjects for further exploration.

Quasi Disintegration: The Post–Oil Shock Period

If risk diversification were the only concern, the member-firms of corporate groups might as well have merged into integrated, highly diversified firms. However, mergers are rather rare in Japan. In fact, although the 1960s witnessed several noteworthy mergers, the last major merger came in 1970 with the creation of the largest steel-manufacturing corporation, the New Japan Steel Manufacturing Company. Since the first oil shock, emphasis has noticeably shifted from economies of scale to the merits realizable from the so-called streamlined management (*genryō keiei*). Specifically, larger firms started to rely more and more on subcontracting and to hive off various activities in the form of subsidiaries in order to trim the number of their employees as much as possible. What is the motivation for this tendency toward the "quasi disintegration" of large Japanese firms? How should the industrial organization emerging out of this tendency be characterized?

Let us first look at subcontracting relations. Unfortunately, no data are available regarding the extent to which large firms act as prime contractor or prime manufacturer (*motouke*) in the subcontracting relationships. But the Small and Medium Enterprise Agency (SMEA) surveys the ratio of the number of subcontractors to the total number of small and medium-size firms with 300 or fewer employees every five years on a detailed industrial basis.[29] According to this survey, the proportion of sub-contractors in the manufacturing sector has increased as follows:

1966	53.1%	1976	60.7%
1971	58.1%	1981	65.5%

Figures for the electric machinery and electronics industries are even more impressive. In 1981, 85.3 per cent of small and medium-size firms entered into subcontracting relations with (presumably larger) firms.

As regards the ever-increasing subcontracting relations, at least three points deserve mention.[30] First, small and medium-size subcontractors tend to increase the number of larger firms with which they enter into subcontracting relationships. According to the SMEA survey, the average number of firms with which small and medium-size subcontractors have subcontracting relations is four. This number increases as the size of the subcontractor increases. For instance, the average number of sub-contractees per medium-sized subcontractor (200–300 employees) is 11. The typical relationship between larger and smaller subcontractors is not that of exclusive monopsony, but involves a considerable degree of over-lapping. According to a recent survey on subcontracting, the results of which were partially published in the SMEA's White Paper in 1983, the proportion of small and medium-size subcontractors that want to in-crease the number of their prime manufacturers exceeds 50 per cent, and this tendency is expected to grow. Multiple relationships give subcontrac-tors more bargaining power in their dealings with prime manufacturers.

Second, subcontracting relationships are not necessarily used exclu-sively to lower labor costs. In many cases, small and medium-size firms that have had long-term relations with larger prime manufacturers have accumulated their own technological and managerial expertise as well as the ability to develop new part products. Such situations involve a cer-tain degree of "knowledge sharing" between prime manufacturers and subcontractors, with the general direction of research and development being determined by the former.[31]

Third, the exclusive absorption of shocks by subcontractors in terms of fluctuating earnings and employment does not seem to be as wide-spread as it used to be: various types of risk sharing between prime manufacturers and subcontractors seem to have become more prevalent. According to the SMEA survey, the buffer function is regarded as the pri-mary factor behind the spread of subcontracting by fewer than 10 per cent of the subcontractors and prime manufacturers surveyed. Instead, about one-third of the prime manufacturers thought that subcontracting reduced the cost of production, and about three-quarters of the sub-contractors regarded "reliable long-term relations" as the primary factor. This indicates that, contrary to the stereotyped dual-structure hypothesis, larger prime manufacturers with diversified finished products and financial viability act as partial insurers of business opportunities, earnings, and employment for smaller subcontractors in exchange for insurance premiums in the form of semimonopolistic gains.

In view of these three points, the typical subcontracting relationship is neither appropriately described as a rigid hierarchy, nor as a "tree structure" in which a larger prime contractor (the trunk) exercises unidirectional and exclusive control over small subcontractors (the branches). In present-day subcontracting relations, we see more overlapping: subcontractors have multiple relations with many prime manufacturers and vice versa. There is also increasingly more sharing of knowledge and risks between the two. Elsewhere, I termed such a structure a "quasi tree."[32] Robert Cole and Taizo Yakushiji called it a "semihorizontal relation."[33]

As for the development of subsidiarization, among manufacturing corporations listed on the Tokyo Exchange, the ratio of investments in subsidiaries to paid-in capital has steadily increased (see Table 2). A simple regression analysis reveals that the larger the size of the firm in terms of sales (or assets), the higher the degree of subsidiarization. For instance,

TABLE 2

The Ratio of Investment in Subsidiaries to Total Paid-in Capital in Selected Industries, Tokyo Exchange, 1st Section, 1965-1984
(per cent as of end of March)

Year	All industries	Manufacturing industries	Autos and auto parts	Electric machinery and electronics
1984	37.2%	44.0%	85.5%	72.6%
1983	36.0	42.7	79.9	76.6
1982	33.2	39.1	59.2	72.0
1981	30.9	34.8	45.1	62.4
1980	29.1	32.3	40.3	56.9
1979	27.7	30.3	38.3	53.0
1978	26.5	28.1	35.3	46.8
1977	25.3	27.1	41.4	41.0
1976	24.3	25.8	43.2	36.8
1975	24.2	25.4	32.3	37.7
1974	22.2	23.0	32.3	32.2
1972	19.6	20.0	28.7	26.2
1971	17.3	17.6	26.9	21.4
1970	16.3	16.4	28.1	20.0
1969	15.1	15.0	25.3	19.4
1968	13.9	13.8	21.8	17.6
1967	12.6	12.9	20.5	16.7
1966	11.8	12.3	17.4	14.8
1965	10.7	10.9	12.5	13.8

SOURCE: Computed from Nikkei Electronic Economic Data System corporate data.

a 10 per cent increase in firm size in the electric machinery and electronics industry is estimated to accelerate the ratio by 1.5 per cent. With
the size of firms controlled, the exogenous rate of increase in the ratio in
the same industry was 0.89 per cent per annum from 1967 to 1972, but
jumped to 1.45 per cent after the first oil shock (1973 to 1982). Such acceleration has the effect of keeping the number of employees at the parent
corporation low. By controlling the effects of economies of scale in the
use of labor and exogenous labor-saving technology, the 43.2 per cent
increase in the subsidiarization ratio in the electric machinery and electronics industry between 1973 and 1982 is estimated to have reduced the
number of employees per sales by as much as 5.7 per cent.[34] Thus, as
they grow in terms of sales and assets, typical large firms have limited
their employment growth by hiving off more subsidiaries.

The increasing use of semi-independent subcontractors and subsidiarization, though different from the point of view of corporate structure,
may be summed up as "quasi disintegration" in that a highly integrated
form of business organization is in effect avoided and the parent firms or
prime contractors retain a considerable degree of control over their subsidiaries or subcontractors. This quasi disintegration is certainly different from the spinning-off of venture business firms from established
large firms recently observed in Western countries since the initiative for
the move is in the hands of the larger firms. There are, however, some
similarities: Japanese subsidiaries and subcontractors could utilize the
relative merits of small scale, such as the more direct exposure to high-
powered market incentives, the creation of an atmosphere favorable
to individual autonomy, the reduced cost of informational exchanges
achieved by reducing hierarchical layers, and the flexible and ad hoc adjustments of labor conditions.

One of the motives behind the quasi disintegration of large firms is the
desire to keep employees as homogeneous as possible in terms of career
prospects, labor conditions, and so forth, thereby making human resource management easier. In most large Japanese firms, enterprise-
based unions represent blue-collar workers as well as white-collar workers. If the union were to represent an overly heterogeneous group of
employees, the problem of aggregating and reconciling the diverse preferences of members would become too formidable for union leaders. In
some cases, even maintaining the conventional rule of "one enterprise,
one union" might become problematic. This would also make it difficult
for management to assimilate employees' preferences in corporate decision making efficiently and effectively through the channel of collective
bargaining. Decentralizing human resource management by creating
subsidiaries and using subcontracting extensively seems to abate the
difficulties of preference aggregation inevitable in large integrated firms.

This argument might appear similar to the old-fashioned dual-structure theory, which holds that large firms utilize subcontracting in order to maintain the practice of lifetime employment throughout business cycles and to place the brunt of employment adjustments on the shoulders of smaller firms. But the homogeneity that concerns me here is a broader notion involving job content, prospects for promotion, and so on. There is a fairly clear demarcation between the jobs of subcontractors and those of subcontractees as a result of quasi disintegration, and it would be difficult for larger firms to introduce or do away with a certain job depending on the state of business cycles. Moreover, if larger and smaller firms share knowledge, it becomes difficult for larger firms to maintain smooth operations throughout business cycles without the cooperation of smaller firms. Therefore, adjustments in employment may occur at both smaller and larger firms. In fact, although the speed of adjustment is likely to be much slower in the latter, in the mid-1970s, a notable degree of employment adjustment occurred at many large firms.[35]

The Future

As for the future of Japanese management, the fundamental pattern of employees, as an element of the firm, exerting an important impact on managerial policymaking will not be altered significantly. On the contrary, this tendency is observed worldwide, albeit in such diverse guises as codetermination, collective bargaining, and employee stock ownership plans. In this respect, Japan has succeeded in finding its own way to incorporate the interests of employees into the decision-making process in a relatively efficient way.

Actual human resource management, however, is expected to undergo a substantial change. From the 1950s to the 1970s when the processing industry and machinery industry were the leading sectors, piecemeal improvements in labor efficiency on the shop floor, as well as improvements in design of total processes by engineers, contributed substantially to aggregate cost reduction. In this regard, the organization of the internal labor market, supported by expectations of lifetime employment, handsome retirement compensation, seniority wages, and so on, has been efficient in stimulating employee initiative, as well as in generating, preserving, and transmitting employees' abilities to contribute to efficiency. If in the future Japan succeeds in the mass application of high technology in order to be competitive in the world market, this picture will not be altered significantly. Yet, in the age of high technology, innovation in laboratories will, and must, gain in importance relative to piecemeal improvements on the shop floor. It may happen that certain types of skills fostered over time and on the job will suddenly become obsolete, at least for employers. On the other hand, given the Japanese work ethic, a prolongation of working years will become inevitable if the aging of the population proceeds as expected. Considering these supply and demand factors, one may conjecture that, instead of expecting to spend a lifetime at a single firm, people may become more accustomed to changing jobs and employers at various stages of their lives.

This possibility may have some interesting financial implications for the firm. As workers' mobility increases, their presently nonsalable, nondiversifiable wealth, fixed in the employing firm in the form of future claims for retirement compensation, seniority premiums, and the like, may become more liquid. For instance, instead of reserves being accumulated within the firm to pay retirement compensation, pension funds managed by insurance companies and trust banks outside the firm will gain importance as a form of retirement benefit provided by the firm. Furthermore, with the development of high technology–oriented industries for which general education becomes the most effective method of training employees the seniority wage differential will lose some of its merits. This implies that opportunities for the individual accumulation of wealth will improve for the younger generation. Also, there are growing indications that the importance of fixed assets such as land and houses is declining vis-à-vis financial assets because the stocks of housing improved substantially in the 1970s and the capital gains from landholding have been somewhat less than expected. As younger employees and others accumulate financial wealth, the relative risk costs of engaging in the capital market may decline for them. The relatively wealthier older generation is already more active in the stock market. Also, the liberalization of security regulations will bid down transaction costs.

All of these developments will make shareholding a more important component of individual portfolios and reinstate more competitive investment funds. Moreover, as the financial market becomes more integrated into the competitive international market, threats by banks to withdraw cooperation will become less effective, and the balance of power within the corporate structure may tilt further in favor of individual shareholders and other institutional shareholders such as investment trusts and insurance companies. This may imply greater pressure on the management for share-price maximization. If the corporate sector as a whole is able to grow at a steady speed, as in the 1960s, the mediating role played by management will be relatively easy. But as growth opportunities become scarcer and individual and institutional shareholders become more active members of the firm, management's function of exploring potential growth opportunities on behalf of every constituent of the firm, as well as assigning appropriate weight to the diverse interests of different constituents, will become more complicated and demanding. The performance of these increasingly difficult entre-preneurial and mediating roles will require decisive leadership.

As the no-sales, nondiversifiable constraint on the wealth of employees weakens and as risk-taking entrepreneurship becomes more highly val-ued, the raison d'être of corporate groupings as a mutual insurance scheme may also weaken somewhat. The quasi disintegration of large firms will continue, however, because it provides an efficient and effec-tive means of quality-cost control. Even in multidivisional integrated firms, a monitoring device that simulates market discipline can be insti-tuted. It is obvious, however, that discipline for cost reduction and quality control is much more self-enforcing in smaller, quasi-independent firms than at in-house divisions because a smaller firm's failure to meet a cer-tain standard in these respects may affect its viability directly. If, how-ever, smaller firms accumulate their own managerial and technological resources through the quasi-disintegration process and if the capital market becomes more accessible to them, the quasi-tree structure may gradually be transformed into a more horizontal network system.

Needless to say, all of this remains highly speculative. But to the de-gree that these predictions are realized, the difference between Japanese and Western firms (particularly U.S. ones) will lessen, provided that cor-responding adaptations by Western firms occur as well. As the 1984 col-lective agreements between the United Auto Workers and U.S. auto manufacturers exemplify, the possibility of efficient trade-offs between the current wage level and job security has begun to be overtly recog-nized by management and union alike, even in the United States. There is a growing indication that U.S. auto manufacturers have started to reor-ganize their relations with suppliers (particularly with subcontractors) in a more systematic way. In this era of increasing internationalization, there seems to be a growing convergence of certain aspects of the firm. It is, however, too early to predict whether this will lead to the emergence of a new corporate paradigm.

Kazuo Koike

Human Resource Development and Labor-Management Relations

There is a consensus that human resource development and labor-management relations have contributed crucially to the performance of the Japanese economy. Yet the operation of the industrial relations system and how it has contributed to Japan's economic success raise questions. Why are Japanese workers keen to promote productivity? Why are they eager to conduct quality-circle activities? And why are Japanese labor unions so cooperative with management? The most popular answers stress the uniqueness of both the institutional setting, including permanent employment and seniority wages, and behavioral patterns, such as the so-called group-oriented nature. However, a short look at practices is enough to raise doubts whether these unique factors can exist in a highly competitive industrial society such as Japan. An alternative explanation, minimally dependent on assertions of social and cultural uniqueness, is needed.

The main purpose of this paper is to present such an alternative explanation by highlighting a long-neglected and vitally important technical aspect: workers' skills on the shop floor. Within a general framework and with minimal recourse to unique institutional and cultural variables, I try to account for the behavior of Japanese workers as well as labor-management relations that might at first glance appear characteristic only of Japan. My central proposition is that a portion of Japanese blue-collar workers have intellectual work skills similar to those of "white-collar" technicians and engineers. These blue-collar workers effectively employ these skills to deal with the frequent nonroutine or unusual operations on the shop floor. These white-collarized skills form a crucial foundation for economic growth and contribute greatly to productivity. Contrary to the common perception, however, these intellectual skills raise serious problems in case of redundancy. Further, these skills form the base for cooperative unionism as well as the "new middle mass" in contemporary Japanese democracy.

In the first section of this paper, I examine this most important variable, the content of intellectual skills on the shop floor. In the next section, I study how these skills are acquired. Next, I analyze the working of intellectual skills, especially their contribution to economic growth and the problems that arise when output declines. This analysis makes it clear, in contrast to the popular view, that Japanese industrial society has a smaller capacity for adjustment to economic contraction than other industrial societies. Based on this analysis, I try in the fourth section to explain Japanese labor-management relations, which appear different from normal textbook models. All discussion to this point is confined to practices in large firms, which overall employ about one-third of Japanese workers. Whether "white-collarization" of blue-collar workers is prevalent in small and medium-size firms, and if not, what labor practices are employed, and the relationship between large and small firms are the subject of the fifth section. In the final section, I project the future of the white-collarization of skills, speculate whether these skills can develop in the face of new technology, such as microelectronics, and discuss an important political implication—workers with intellectual skills are the foundation of the new middle mass of Japanese democracy.

Let us begin by examining the current popular view of industrial relations, which clarifies the reasons an alternative explanation is needed that focuses on workers' skills on the shop floor.

The most popular view of Japanese industrial relations highlights two unique aspects of its systems: Japan's particular institutional setting (permanent employment, seniority wages, and enterprise unionism) and the Japanese way of thinking and behaving (group orientation). In this view, these institutions guarantee both employment and wages for workers, and with their security assured, employees work diligently.[1] But why do people work industriously when their wages are guaranteed regardless of their performance? Here enters the second part of the popular argument—attitudes toward work. Proponents of this argument maintain that Japanese characteristically behave in a group-oriented way. If their group protects them from risk, they are loyal to their group. Since the most important grouping for contemporary Japanese workers is their firm, once the firm guarantees employment, it is natural for workers to be loyal and hardworking. And because the most important group for workers is the enterprise, enterprise unionism results, and cooperative industrial relations encourage the workers' high morale.

It follows from the culturalists' view of Japanese industrial relations that Japanese workers will continue to work hard in the future because their culture makes them industrious and culture changes only slowly.

However, this argument does not explain certain features of Japanese industrial relations. It fails to recognize the variety of experience with industrial relations, both historically and across firms. Not a few of its assumptions are unsupported by reliable statistical data. If cultural variables were as powerful as the culturalists presume, then the features to be explained should be shared by most, if not all, of the work force and should continue over a fairly lengthy period, just as culture is pervasive and continuous.

Although quality-control (QC) circles are said to symbolize the high morale of Japanese workers, workers' attitudes toward QC circles vary, as Table 1 indicates. The larger the firm, the more QC circles prevail. This difference is emphasized when combined with the results of Table 2, which shows management's assessment of the success of QC circles. In 1977, nearly two-thirds of the largest firms (more than 5,000 employees) had active QC circles, but only one-sixth of the smallest firms (under 300 employees) had active QC circles. If we had data on firms with fewer than 100 employees, the gap would definitely be greater; only a few QC circles would be working well in small companies. This coincides with information obtained in my own case studies; most small firms I visited

TABLE 1

Percentage of Workers in Establishments with QC-Circle Activities, by Size of Firm and Existence of Trade Unions, 1977

Number of employees in firm	Total	With trade unions	Without trade unions
5,000 and over	77.2%	77.4%	67.3%
1,000-4,999	58.5	59.1	53.6
300-999	42.9	43.9	39.1
100-299	33.3	34.6	31.7

SOURCE: Japan, Ministry of Labor, *Survey on Communication Between Management and Labor for 1977* (Tokyo, 1979).

TABLE 2

Assessment of QC Circles by Management, by Size of Firm, 1977
(per cent)

Number of employees in firm	Successful	Not successful	In between	Unknown
5,000 and over	83.4%	7.6%	8.6%	0.4%
1,000-4,999	67.2	15.9	16.4	0.5
300-999	52.7	28.2	18.9	0.2
100-299	45.3	37.6	15.6	1.5

SOURCE: Same as Table 1.

had inaugurated but not maintained QC circles. In sum, workers' attitudes in contemporary Japan vary greatly. We have to explain not only the high percentage of active QC circles in large firms but also the comparative rarity in small firms.

Table 3 shows the size of strikes between 1955 and 1980 in terms of working days lost through industrial disputes in selected industrialized countries. Strikes are undeniably one of the most crucial aspects of industrial relations. It is clear that the number of working days lost in Japan during the latter half of the 1950s was far greater than that in the late 1970s. Also, it is clear that the figures for the second half of the 1950s and the first half of the 1960s differ little from, or are even greater than, those for the United Kingdom and France, but in the second half of the 1970s, only West Germany had a lower figure.

This finding strongly contradicts the assumption of the popular view that Japanese industrial relations are exceptionally cooperative and peaceful. It is clear from the table that Japan's strike record did not become peaceful until the first half of the 1970s. If Japanese industrial relations can be called cooperative, then German and Swedish industrial relations would have to be called super-peaceful. It is true that lost time in Japan has decreased since the mid-1970s, but this trend is of recent origin. It is only in comparison with the United States and Italy that postwar Japanese industrial relations can be termed peaceful.

(A word of caution is necessary here. The definition of strikes differs from country to country. The main variation lies, however, in the smallest strikes. Some countries exclude those involving fewer than ten men and lasting less than ten days; others exclude strikes shorter than one day. These differences cause serious problems when we analyze the number of strikes. If we take working days lost, however, such differences are unlikely to affect the general trend.)

TABLE 3
Number of Working Days Lost Through Industrial Disputes per 1,000 Employees, Selected Countries, 1955-1980

Country	1955-59	1960-64	1965-69	1970-74	1975-80
Japan	254	177	107	151	69
United States	615	301	513	539	389
United Kingdom	220	146	175	624	521
France	180	197	163	201	195
Italy	433	932	1,204	1,404	1,434
West Germany	47	23	7	55	41
Sweden	19	6	38	69	222

SOURCES: International Labor Office, *Yearbook of Labor Statistics* (Geneva, various issues).

The assertion that seniority wages are unique to Japan is also unsupported by the most reliable statistical evidence. Since the mid-1970s, high-quality statistics on wages by age have been available for the European Community (EC) countries.[2] Japan has had similar detailed yearly data since 1954. Seniority wages for male white-collar workers in EC countries are apparent in the EC statistics. A comparison with Japanese statistics reveals that EC age-wage profiles differ little from those of male blue-collar workers in large firms and male white-collar workers in all sizes of firms in Japan, both of which have been thought as typically having seniority wages.[3] Consequently, we cannot say that seniority wages are peculiar to Japan. Rather, the Japanese feature, if any, is that some blue-collar workers have an age-wage profile similar to that of white-collar workers.

A similar argument is applicable to permanent employment. Again, the EC statistics supply reliable data on the distribution of workers by length of service. And an EC-Japan comparison reveals that the immobility of male blue-collar workers in large Japanese firms—long the symbol of permanent employment—is equal to, or even less than, that of male white-collar workers for all sizes of firms in EC countries. Once more, white-collarization of a section of the Japanese blue-collar work force is visible.[4]

It is therefore of prime importance to analyze the content and basis of this seeming white-collarization of male blue-collar workers in large Japanese firms. Two of the crucial variables affecting wages are undoubtedly the nature of skills and career development.

Unusual Components of Work

No definitive approach to the problem of analyzing the content of skill has yet been presented. This does not imply a lack of achievements in the study of skill; a variety of methods have been employed in its analysis. Among them, however, economic methods seem to have achieved the least. They concentrate on costs and returns of investment in human capital and rarely investigate the content of skills. The discipline with the longest tradition in the study of skill is undoubtedly psychology. However, it tends to be an exact science, confining itself to the simplest jobs or work in an accurately controlled laboratory in order to produce exact academic results. Most jobs on the shop floor in large firms in contemporary Japan, however, are complex. Industrial engineering, which employs the method of job analysis, is successful in observing the physical activities of work. For modern industrial work, however, the core of the skill lies not in physical activities, but in mental processes, to which this method of job analysis is not so well suited. The only way to approach the mental content of skill is to ask many questions of veteran workers.[5] This method is adopted here.

There are several types of technology in industry. Here, three major types are analyzed: mass production machinery or assembly workshops, non–mass production machinery or assembly workshops, and production workshops in the processing industry. At first glance, mass production workshops would seem to require little skill because of the repetitive nature of the work. This is deceptive, however. A close look at the work and intensive interviews with veteran workers reveal much of the work content. The discussion below essentially applies to large firms with 1,000 or more employees.

We can categorize the major components of work on the shop floor in large firms as (1) usual operations and (2) unusual operations to deal with troubles or changes. With mass production machinery or in the processing industry, usual operations are supposedly repetitive and monotonous, and people are apt to conclude that little skill is necessary. But in any mass production workshop, changes occur more frequently than is generally conceived; variation occurs in the ratio of inferior products to total output, the types of defects in goods, and the extent of defects, along with variation in products, product mix, and the method of production. The labor mix varies in two ways. One is daily changes because of absences, which cause changes in deployment within the workshop. The other is changes in the weight of experienced workers within the workshop, which makes variation in deployment easier and more efficient.

Dealing with such changes comes under the rubric of unusual changes. Operators in Japanese workshops are required to locate the smallest problems or defects in goods or parts as soon as possible, to determine the causes, and to eliminate them. Ideally, they anticipate any problems from the smallest indication, so that no actual damage results.

This component of shop floor work is more important in mass production, where speed is critical; the longer it takes to deal with and eliminate troubles, the longer the production line stops and hence the greater the cost. Quick responses are of prime importance; ideally problems are solved while the production line remains in motion.

Some might argue that a careful study of unusual troubles would reveal patterns and that standard ways to deal with them could be described in a manual, so that not much time, or skill, would be required. According to veteran workers, however, problems are so varied that standardization in the form of a manual is impractical. And even if it were possible to compile a manual analyzing problems in terms of many standard patterns, the number of patterns would be too large to enable quick response.

More important, standardization may lessen efficiency. An example is illustrative. In a biochemical plant where the volume of oxygen is crucial to a process, minute adjustments in the flow of oxygen are vital. Practical standardization cannot formalize these minute adjustments, but rather at best simply sets upper and lower limits; only when the figures exceed these limits would the volume of oxygen be adjusted. Highly skilled workers, however, can make minute adjustments between these two limits.

Another characteristic is that in the firms observed, the operator who conducts the usual component of work also performs these responses to unusual situations. Another group of workers such as technicians or even engineers could conceivably make such responses because they require a high level of skill. In such a separated system, one operator would perform the usual work while different workers responded to changes or unusual circumstances. The Japanese system, however, is integrated: the same operator is in charge of both components of work. This does not imply that Japanese operators deal with all problems. There are naturally many problems that they cannot solve.

There is another aspect to unusual work. The causes of problems may lie in the machinery or in production facilities. Overall maintenance is clearly out of the job sphere of operators, but maintenance on a minor scale is in their hands. To give an example, in one biochemical plant, ten workers, divided into five teams, are in charge of one section. Each two-man team conducts usual work (component 1) and the nonmaintenance part of unusual work (component 2) in shifts. Three shifts of eight hours are covered by four teams, one of which is resting. The fifth team works in the daytime only, mostly on maintenance, searching for pinholes in pipes and mending as many as possible. The workers contact maintenance men for larger repairs. Another example is the pasting machine workshop of a battery producer. This process involves pasting plates for battery boxes. Since most of the process is automated, the weight of component 2 would seem to be small. Here, however, the work of the operator includes disjointing, cleaning, and reassembling parts of the pasting machines in order to keep them in good condition. Overall disjointing and repairs are done by maintenance men.

What skills are necessary to perform these two components? Although it might be thought that no skills are needed to conduct component 1, exact operation at high speed is demanded; for mass production work, the speed with which work is carried out is important. Component 2 involves a series of skill requirements. First, an accumulation of experience with unusual patterns is needed. Because the patterns are unusual, there is no way to know them other than from experience. This does not imply that no other skill is necessary. The causes of problems are either in the structure of products or in the machinery that makes them. In order to reason about the causes and to fix the problems, operators need knowledge of the structure, functions, and mechanisms of the machinery and products. Operators share this second requirement with engineers or technicians, whose formal role is to know the mechanism of machines and products and improve them for higher efficiency. Japanese operators can, in this sense, be said to share this crucial element of skill with these white-collar workers. In other words, Japanese blue-collar workers in large firms are partly white-collarized in terms of skill, as well as in terms of wages and length of service.

How Skills Are Acquired

The nearly 400 training schools in Japan sponsored by local or central government give one year of full-time training to high school graduates and two years to junior high school graduates. The number of trainees amounts to about 30,000 per year. At least for large firms, however, these training schools have played a small role in developing workers' skills. Large firms appear to recruit few training school graduates, although no truly reliable statistics are available. The apprenticeship system went into decline around World War I. School education, particularly for the period after World War II, has been heavily inclined to general education. Although there are many vocational high schools, they are unable to recruit bright pupils, and accordingly, the main sources for blue-collar recruits in large firms is the pool of high school graduates of general education courses.

This does not imply that most recruits for blue-collar jobs are new graduates from high school. It is an established myth that Japanese workers enter a firm directly after completing school and rarely move to other firms. Reliable statistics show that for firms with 1,000–4,999 employees, only one-third of male blue-collar recruits are new graduates and that the remainder have some work experience in other firms.[6] It does not follow, however, that the majority enter firms as skilled workers. Rather, most recruits lack specific skill qualifications. In other words, the number of employees quitting in their first years with a firm is extremely high. Turnover figures in large firms for male workers in their early twenties have been around 20–25 per cent. Again, much of the common perception of Japanese industrial relations is far removed from fact.

Most job training occurs after workers join a firm. Generally there are two types of training: off-the-job training and on-the-job training. Off-the-job training is easier to observe because of its formal structure. In a typical case—one of the largest plants of a giant heavy electrical machinery firm—the off-the-job training begins with two, completely different entry courses. One is a one-year, full-time course; the other can be as short as one week. The one-year courses are for those recruited directly after they finish senior high school; the shorter courses are for those who have had some experience in other firms.

The former type of course dates to around World War I, when large firms typically began to establish their own training schools, recruiting extremely promising young students just completing compulsory education (elementary school at that time). Since social mobility was not high in those days, many promising youths could not proceed to higher education because it was too costly. Consequently, large firms were successful in recruiting promising youths of high aptitude. Companies provided three or four years of full-time technical training as well as further general education somewhat paralleling the secondary education received by the 10–20 per cent remaining in the regular school system. The young recruits were expected to and did become core workers and later foremen on the shop floor. As such, they were a major source of trade union leaders in the 1950s and 1960s. During the 1960s, companies gave up this practice because they were unable to recruit promising youths because of the diffusion of secondary education.

Thus, instead of the three-year course for promising trainees, companies typically maintain only one-year, full-time courses for senior high school graduates. The plant described here has a training center for 40 boys gathered from several plants belonging to this company in the area. Training is divided into three courses: machining, machine assembly, and electrical machine assembly. The 975 hours for practice and 710 hours for theory in one year are equivalent to government training schools and are certified under the Vocational Training Act. This type of formal training for one full year is probably exceptional, although formal systems seem to prevail in not a few large firms. In practice, however, a large part of the one-year course tends to be allocated to shop floor practice rather than formal off-the-job training. This means firms do not, in fact, depend much on formal classroom training.

The other course is too short to be important in skill acquisition. A one-week, formal course cannot teach trainees any technical skills for work on the shop floor. A short lecture on the products of the plant constitutes the main content of the course. This short course has, contrary to popular perception, drawn most of the new recruits because many enter the company not directly after completing school but after working briefly in other companies.

These are not the only off-the-job training courses in this plant. About every five years, blue-collar workers attend short courses designed especially for them. The courses are connected to the ranking system, which is of a type common in large firms. In this company, blue-collar workers, including group leaders as well as foremen, are divided into five ranks: master and first, second, third, and fourth class. Promotion through these ranks depends partly on achievement in these training courses.

The duration of these courses is short. The course for the fourth class is 32 hours long, for the third class 44 hours, and for the first 16 hours, amounting to a total of less than a hundred hours. Even when other voluntary courses in preparation for skill tests (see below) are added, the total barely exceeds 120 hours. This is extremely short in comparison with the whole occupational career, which extends to about thirty years. Given this short duration, can these courses be effective for acquiring the special skills described above? (There are lengthy courses of 600 hours, consisting of one or two days per week over one or two years. However, these are only for supervisors and hence for a small minority, which in turn permits their length.)

Moreover, the topics in these courses do not always seem relevant to work on the shop floor. The course for the fourth class, who have had only a little work experience, includes a lecture on sales as well as other, more expected topics: materials, safety, work efficiency, and problems on the shop floor. Still, there is little in the course aimed at teaching skills directly necessary for conducting daily work. The same applies to the course for the third class. The 44 hours consist of 4 hours of lectures on plant management policy by the plant manager; 20 hours of lectures on quality control, cost control, and betterment of work methods; and another 20 hours of theory in each participant's field, such as basic machining theory. Except for the last, these topics seem suitable not for blue-collar workers but for white-collar. The 16 hours for the first class are devoted to a series of lectures on current demand, which products' sales are expanding, the production situation, and the development plan for machinery as well as a group discussion on the roles of the first-class men. In all the courses, it is difficult to find a training course designed to teach the skills described above. The question arises why the main topics in these courses are so general and so concerned with management problems far beyond the workers' sphere. To put it another way, why do blue-collar workers learn much of what is of concern for white-collar workers?

A part of each course is concerned with theories of work in the workers' own field. As mentioned above, 20 hours for the third class, in preparation for upgrading to the second-class workers, are devoted to learning theory, such as that of machining. Here, the national skill test must be noted as a functional equivalent. (The national skill test is regulated under the Vocational Training Act and consists of a demonstration of skills and a written test on theory.) The screening procedure for the second class comprises two parts: achievement in work performance to date and a written test on each worker's field, such as assembly of electrical machines. The test follows the pattern of the national skill test, and therefore those with a second-class certification in the national skill test are exempted from taking the written test.

The national skill test covers 119 occupations, only a small part of all occupations on the shop floor. In other words, the national skill test can test only general skill, not the many specific skills needed on the shop floor in large, mass production companies. For example, the staff of a large mass production company estimates that only 20 per cent of workers have skills covered by the national skill test. Even in this electrical machinery plant, which is not a mass production plant, not all workers are covered by the skill test, and this is the reason the firm's test is independent of the national one. In those cases where the character of work fits the national skill test, the plant encourages its workers to take it by presenting a series of lectures on theory and by making plant facilities freely available to workers preparing for the practical test.

This type of off-the-job training, for recruits or incumbents, is effective not only for acquiring general skills easily transferred to other firms, but also for acquiring specific skills. Each job consists mainly of general skills; in a rough estimation, 10–20 per cent for specificity in job content would be the maximum. Hence, the training in general skills is useful. Also, there is constant variation on the shop floor. Minor changes in products, product mix, and production methods are followed by changes in job content. The skills required are not confined to what is needed to conduct specific work, but include those for coping with these variations.

Another type of variation might be more crucial; as explained later, a worker tends to hold not one position but, over time, a series of positions closely connected with each other. Training in the theory of one occupation during an off-the-job training course could be a good basis for adjusting to these variations. Yet, a course on theory is too general to teach workers the structure and functions of each machine they operate daily. Nor can the accumulation of experience in dealing with problems be taught in a course. We can conclude that short off-the-job training courses are supplementary to acquiring intellectual skills.

The final feature of these short courses is that they are made available to employees of firms supplying parts to the firm offering the course.

A comparison of Toyota and Ford demonstrates the greater dependence on parts suppliers by large Japanese firms. Although Toyota produces slightly more cars, it hires far fewer employees: only one-seventh of those employed by Ford. Needless to say, productivity differentials cannot explain such a large gap. The main reason for this difference is the degree of dependence on parts suppliers; large Japanese firms tend to produce a smaller proportion of intermediate products. This feature can explain why large Japanese firms open training courses to the workers of parts suppliers. If the workers of parts suppliers could not acquire the skills necessary to make the needed products, or if the quality of the parts deteriorated, the quality of the final product could not be guaranteed. It is common practice for a large firm to circulate among its parts suppliers a list of available training courses. In return, the parts suppliers pay a minimal fee for the courses they participate in; usually these fees barely cover the direct cost. The most popular courses among parts suppliers are said to be on QC-circle activity and computer programming.

My description so far has been based largely on a few case studies. Without more widely based evidence, these results cannot be considered reliable. Although not in-depth, two statistical surveys are available on vocational training, one of large scale in terms of the number of observations and the other somewhat smaller. Here, the smaller one is utilized since it is more relevant to the points in this article.

Table 4 indicates the diffusion of vocational training courses in firms by size of firm and for recruits and incumbents. Some 98 per cent of larger firms (over 1,000 employees) offer these courses. Although the figures drop with the size of the firm, more than half of the smallest firms (30–99 employees) have courses. The figures are highest for new graduates, next highest for incumbents, and lowest for those recruits who have been out of school for some time. For the largest firms, even the lowest

TABLE 4
Percentage of Establishments Conducting Vocational Training, 1979

Number of employees in firm	Total	Training for recruits		Training for incumbents
		New school graduates	Other	
1,000 and over	98.2%	95.0%	71.0%	92.3%
500-999	93.0	92.2	62.1	85.6
100-499	87.0	88.4	48.0	68.8
30-99	57.6	66.4	27.9	42.9
All firms	82.0	86.8	50.1	69.7

SOURCE: Japan, Ministry of Labor, Bureau of Vocational Training, *Jigyōshonai kyōiku kunren* (A survey on in-plant vocational training) (Tokyo, 1981).

TABLE 5
Percentage Distribution of Training Courses by Number of Hours, 1977

Type of training; size of firm	Hours of training					
	Less than 10	10-49	50-99	100-199	200-499	More than 500
Training						
For Recruits	9.5%	49.5%	20.2%	9.3%	7.3%	4.2%
New School Graduates	6.7	47.9	22.5	10.0	8.1	4.8
Other	23.9	58.2	8.5	5.7	2.8	0.9
For Incumbents	20.8	63.0	8.2	4.5	2.2	1.3
Number of employees						
1,000 and over	10.3%	58.2%	14.0%	8.2%	6.0%	3.3%
500-999	16.2	58.9	14.2	5.7	3.0	2.0
100-499	21.9	59.5	10.0	4.3	3.0	1.3
30-99	30.4	54.6	7.1	4.0	1.8	2.1

SOURCE: Same as Table 1.

figure, for new workers who are not recent graduates, is 71 per cent. Thus, the firm described above was not exceptional in having vocational training courses within its plants.

Another feature of vocational training courses in the case cited above is their short duration: 16 to 44 hours. Table 5 supports this feature; the mode of distribution is clearly located in the interval 10–49 hours, which is almost equal to the figures presented above. Along with such short courses, there were two long-term courses in my example: one for those just out of school and the other for supervisors. In the column for the longest courses (over 500 hours), the highest percentage is for recent graduates, 4.8 per cent; other recruits rarely take such courses; for incumbents the figure is still very small, 1.3 per cent. Unfortunately, no specific figures are available by type of worker and size of firm, although I would guess that the long courses for foremen in the case discussed above are not exceptional. When we aggregate the figures for courses of more than 100 hours for the largest firms, they amount to over 18 per cent.

Table 6 shows the location of training. Differences by size of firm are remarkable. In the largest firms, around two-thirds of the courses are given in the plant. This indicates that the case described above was not exceptional for a large firm. In the smallest firms, those given outside the firm are greater: training seminars and courses held in consultant companies are about 30 per cent, and the figure for courses given within the company drops to 19 per cent. Training courses "in other firms" occupy significant percentages and the smaller the size of firm, the larger the

TABLE 6

Percentage Distribution of Courses by Place of Training, 1977

Type of training; size of firm	Within firm	Training courses in other firms	Public voca- tional training schools	Private voca- tional schools	Univer- sities	Seminars and courses in training consultant companies	Other
Training							
For recruits	60.5%	8.2%	1.2%	0.1%	0.4%	5.3%	24.2%
For incumbents	46.0	13.0	3.4	0.9	1.2	18.0	16.8
Number of employees							
1,000 and over	68.1%	8.3%	2.2%	0.6%	0.9%	5.4%	14.5%
500-999	49.6	11.5	2.0	0.5	0.7	12.3	23.4
100-499	39.1	13.7	3.0	0.8	0.9	22.8	19.7
30-99	19.4	16.5	5.2	0.8	1.4	29.8	26.9
All firms	51.2%	11.3%	2.6%	0.6%	0.9%	13.9%	19.5%

SOURCE: Same as Table 1.

figure. In part this reflects the participation of parts suppliers' workers in the parent company's courses and workers' participation in courses arranged by and in the plants of machine manufacturers. It is not uncommon for manufacturers, in order to promote sales, to prepare training courses to teach workers to operate new machines.

An additional comment on this table is necessary. "Public vocational schools" in Table 6 differ from those described above. The latter offer one- or two-year full-time training courses for youth. This table focuses on another type of course, as short as 10 or 20 hours for incumbents, called module training.

The other finding in the cases described above was firms' encouragement to employees to complete off-the-job training courses to take the national skill test. As indicated in Table 7, the percentage of establishments responding positively to the question "Does your establishment encourage those workers who finish the training course given in your firm to take the national skill test?" distinctly shows that the smaller the firm, the more likely it is to encourage workers to do so. This would imply that the skills required in small firms tend to be of the general type tested in the national test. However, 9 per cent of large establishments also encourage workers to do so. In short, many of the features observed in my example are generally supported by statistics.

Next, the series of questions raised in connection with my example must be tackled: why off-the-job training courses cover topics seemingly irrelevant to daily work, such as sales, quality control, and the business situation of the company; how workers acquire skills necessary to deal with unusual work; how they obtain skill and knowledge of the structure and functions of products and machinery; and how they accumulate experience in unusual problems.

The primary means of skill formation in contemporary Japanese firms is undoubtedly on-the-job training (OJT) on the shop floor. It is extremely difficult to describe OJT with quantitative data. First, it is informal and inseparable from work itself—neither classroom nor full-time instructor exists. Second, we have to observe a series of jobs rather than a single job. The cost of using OJT rather than off-the-job training is inefficiency or inferior products because of inexperience in the job. These costs can be minimized by letting a worker start at the lowest grade of job and by moving him to a slightly more difficult and closely related job so that the cost of inexperience is minimized. Thus, a series of jobs closely related in job content tend to make a career. A possible way to approach workers' skill is to identify the extent of the career because it reflects the extent and depth of skill. One difficulty lies, however, in the scarcity of records or documentation on the careers of workers. And if there is any competition for promotion among workers, then room for discretion makes career patterns vague. Third, a career is apt to be enterprise specific. Firms with many veteran workers are likely to broaden the careers, or work experience, of those veterans in order to better utilize that experience. Without documentation and given their enterprise-specific character, it is not feasible to collect statistical data on workers' careers.

The only feasible way is to observe practice on the shop floor carefully. Because this requires an in-depth investigation demanding much time and energy, it can cover only a small number of cases, too small in terms of sample size to have statistical reliability. Yet the insights into practice are of prime importance. I conducted such an investigation in a comparative study of the United States and Japan during the first half of the 1970s.[7] Since no recent research is available, let me summarize the results

TABLE 7
Percentage of Establishments Encouraging Workers to Take National Skill Test, 1977

Number of employees in firm	Firms encouraging testing	Number of employees in firm	Firms encouraging testing
1,000 and over	9.4%	30-99	33.1%
500-999	11.6	All firms	16.4%
100-499	20.0		

SOURCE: Same as Table 1.

of this study, which analyzed shop floor practices in heavy industries in the United States and Japan.

First, in both countries the main part of skill formation is OJT in one plant after entry into a firm. Except for a few occupations, such as maintenance and craft jobs, most workers enter the plant without any significant experience in their own occupation. They start their career from the bottom of the job ladder in a plant and are promoted to higher grades of jobs as their service becomes longer. In both countries, the majority of workers in large firms are hired unskilled and acquire the skills needed through experience.

Second, the major difference between U.S. and Japanese firms is the extent of workers' careers. In the case of OJT, experience defines skill, so that by observing the extent of the career we can identify the skill. The extent of a worker's career can be measured horizontally and vertically. The horizontal span indicates how widely the worker moves from one position to another within one workshop under the leadership of a subforeman, whether he moves widely beyond the subforeman's unit, and whether he moves to other workshops closely related in terms of technology or in the way skill is acquired.

In the United States, a worker's career tends to be within a single workshop or even a part of a workshop. Because strict seniority controls promotion and deployment of workers far more strongly than is described in collective agreements and than is generally thought, it takes a long time for a worker to be promoted to the highest grade of job in the job ladder, and no time is left for him to move to another line of progression. Transfer to another workshop is strictly prohibited by seniority; a vacancy in a job ladder is filled solely from within the ladder, and no room remains for accepting transfers from other workshops.

In contrast, mobility on the shop floor in Japan is far less rigid, and seniority functions feebly, contrary to popular belief. Rather, an egalitarian method of deployment prevails. A kind of rotation system covers most of the positions in the workshop. This frequent mobility can extend even beyond a workshop to similar workshops in the neighborhood. For example, workers in an integrated steel plant in the United States cover nearly a dozen jobs in their career, but their Japanese counterparts will experience about three dozen positions.

This mobility is completely different from transfers to dissimilar workshops that occur in a recession to lessen the number of workers laid off by moving them from declining workshops to growing ones. Transfers to dissimilar workshops are not effective in elevating skills because workers cannot utilize skills acquired elsewhere. In the case of mobility between similar workshops, however, workers utilize acquired skills because the former workshop and the new one are closely related in terms of technology and hence in terms of skill acquisition. Any small differences between the two workshops would be an attractive opportunity to add a new skill.

Some simple questions might be raised. It is common for a worker to be reluctant to move to other positions or workshops. Are Japanese workers in large firms less reluctant to move? And if so, why? Observation affords a simple answer. Workers may ordinarily be reluctant to move, but when management policy encourages moves by promoting to subforeman or foreman those who have experienced the most positions in one workshop or similar workshops, workers are willing to accept this wide range of mobility.

This wide horizontal extent of a career presents the best opportunity to acquire needed skills as described above: knowledge of the structure and functions of both machinery and products and accumulation of experience on unusual problems. Wide mobility allows a worker to cover not just one workshop but those ahead and behind it in the flow of production, giving him a better opportunity to know the flow of production and to learn the mechanism of production. Even within a workshop, a worker experiencing most positions will deal with most product parts.

Although firms give workers plenty of opportunities, no formal course exists to ascertain and theorize the experience. A finding from a biochemical plant is suggestive. Workers newly transferred from a neighboring workshop are, along with their main job of conducting normal operations, assigned the task of describing the chart of the piping facilities in the workshop; another assignment is to write a manual of job operation in the workshop as informal off-the-job training. These new tasks are so demanding that only those with long experience in a similar workshop can do them. Clearly, it is an extremely valuable opportunity for workers to acquire skills for dealing with unusual work. Yet, these are informal courses given on the shop floor and are never recorded in the office of production management or in the training department. Consequently, we cannot guess the prevalence of this informal type of course.

In summary, the typical method in Japan for acquiring the skills to deal with unusual problems is a wide range of OJT covering a cluster of similar workshops. Through this OJT, workers can obtain knowledge of the structure and function of production facilities and products. A series of short off-the-job training courses, inserted into a worker's career every five years or so, affords at least in part a knowledge of the theory of production, which supplies a foundation for dealing with problems. A career developed in workshops also supplies ample opportunity to accumulate experience in coping with problems. Thus, employees can obtain

most skills needed to tackle troubles, even though companies are unlikely to have established courses on the operation of particular machines or on products.

The Workings of White-Collarized Skill

Two aspects of the workings of white-collarized skill are important
here: its contribution to increasing output and the problems that arise
when output declines. Included in the former are reasons for high worker
morale, and in the latter, the problems of redundancy.

The contribution of skill to increases in output can mostly be found in
two forms: skillful operation of and adaptation to new machines and
more efficient methods of work and production. Activities in the latter
category have been given many names, including QC circles or zero-
defect (ZD) activities; here the term "QC circle" is used.

A lot has been said about loyalty or attitudes toward work as forming
the foundation of QC circles. Little has been noted of the technical bases
that make QC circles feasible. Most suggestions and plans arising from
QC circles are highly technical. Without a certain background in technology, continuous QC circle activities cannot be maintained, even though
a few marvelous suggestions might come out. Workers with white-
collarized skill have knowledge of the mechanisms of production and of
principles or theories in their own field, though not as much as engineers. With this background, workers can devise better methods of work
and production.

The same argument can be applied to handling new machines. Even
though a machine may be new, the principles employed in its mechanism rarely are completely new; principles hold true through changes.
Those workers with knowledge of the principles can operate new machines with less difficulty.

It is true, however, that technical skill alone is not sufficient to promote QC circles. An important feature of QC circle activities is the implementation of a plan by the workers themselves on the shop floor. For
implementation, workers must have the power to change their deployment and work methods in their workshop. If they do not have this
power, they must get approval from their supervisors every time they
think of, and wish to implement, a new plan, which would definitely
make them reluctant to do so.

Observation of shop floor practice reveals that worker groups on the
shop floor have some discretion, particularly in two aspects. One is deployment within the workshop. As stated elsewhere,[8] the deployment or
mobility of workers within a workshop varies. Even in one plant in the
same year, some workshops adopt a regular rotation system covering all

positions in the workshop, others have irregular or partial rotation, still others have no rotation at all. This suggests that deployment within the workshop depends partly on shop floor custom, rather than on regulation by management or by unions.

The often-made remark that there are no manuals in Japanese industry might also be suggestive. This famous remark itself is not exactly true. When new machinery is introduced, there is always a manual that describes how to operate a particular machine or conduct a job. As time passes, however, workers are apt to devise better ways to do the job and surpass the manual. This is why it is usually said there are no manuals in Japanese firms. Again, this shows that in practice workers on the shop floor have the power to change the way jobs are conducted, which is one of the foundations of QC circles.

Even when workers have the ability and power essential to the success of QC circles, they do not form QC circles unless they feel a necessity to do so. The most crucial source of such a feeling is a career widely developed in a firm or, in other words, skill formation. With this type of skill formation sysem, workers' skill development largely coincides with the prosperity of the firm. When the firm grows quickly, workers can be promoted quickly, and the opportunity to attain higher skill levels comes earlier. Conversely, if the firm grows slowly, workers' skill development tends to be delayed. And when the firm suffers from reverses or decline, workers may be laid off. To a worker with a specific skill, layoff or redundancy represents great damage; it is not only an interruption in skill development, but it is a sacrifice because he is often compelled to find a job in another company that cannot utilize the skills he has acquired. In order to protect his own skill development, the worker must be interested in the economic situation of the firm. Even without any loyalty to the firm, he has to pay attention to the firm's productivity to prevent it from being bested by rivals.

This simple explanation for workers' attitudes is also effective in explaining seemingly cooperative trade unionism. It is natural for union officials to conform to the desires of union members because otherwise they will not be re-elected to their posts.

This tendency has been encouraged by the drastic changes in the society caused by defeat in World War II. The defeat destroyed the establishments that owned most of the giant prewar firms. Consequently, it is now hard to find large firms owned by one or a group of families, except for new entrants. Even in Matsushita and Toyota, two relatively new firms, the founders' families own less than 3 per cent of stock holdings. This is a well-known phenomenon in management capitalism. In contemporary Japan, it is true of almost all large firms. In such firms, employees feel they are working not for the profit of the owners but for their own employment. If the workers feel that the profit they have created is used not for promoting their employment but for the personal consumption of the owners, why would they work willingly?

This attitude is common, irrespective of country, to workers who experience career development within a single firm. Since this type of career worker can be equated to most male white-collar workers in the EC, similar reasoning should be applicable to them. In other words, workers tend to work well when they have a promising career, even one of limited prospect, and the Japanese blue-collar workers in large firms share this type of career with white-collar workers, and they work as diligently as, if not more diligently than, male white-collar workers in the EC.

Although white-collarized skill has worked well in periods of growth, what problems arise with a decrease in output? Decreases in output lead in general to layoff or redundancy, and layoff, as mentioned above, is of great consequence to workers with specific skills.

Two myths have prevailed in explaining adjustments to decreases in output: extreme labor hoarding and the so-called dual structure of labor markets. Certainly, the strongest myth of Japanese industrial relations is permanent employment. Firms suffering a large contraction in output are said to hold to the principle of permanent employment and retain the surplus labor within their own firm. In return, workers must pay the cost; that is, they must accept transfers to other workshops within the establishment or within the firm, transfers from declining workshops to less declining ones being the usual method of preventing layoffs. Such mobility is clearly unfavorable for workers from the viewpoint of maintaining skills, although some say that Japanese workers lack a developed sense of attachment to an occupation, either because of a delay in establishing the concept of occupation or because of their way of thinking. This type of argument typifies the culturalist view, which is seldom accompanied by logical reasoning. Transfers to dissimilar workshops often occur in time of output decrease, and these are utilized because the wide range of skills developed enlarges the adjustment ability of workers. But these are short-term measures. They do not work well if the contraction lasts longer than a year or so. This is clearly shown in an analysis of the adjustment process of firms over the long term.[9] One of the sources used in that analysis is a statistical survey of firms' behavior in the face of decreases in output for the period 1975 to 1978.[10] Only a few of even the largest firms employed internal transfers or other policies of labor hoarding in the long term, but many adopted them for short-term adjustment.

The second myth is the theory of the dual structure of labor markets. To maintain permanent employment in the face of long-term decreases in output, all redundancy is borne by the lower segment of labor markets. It is suggested that in the Japanese situation, the many ancillary firms surrounding a giant firm act as a shock absorber in the case of contraction. Research has not yet furnished enough evidence to assess this dual theory with sufficient hard data. We can, however, safely maintain that this practice occurs not only in Japan; indeed, the extent of shock absorbing by low-grade workers would seem to be smaller in Japan than in the United States.

For example, compared with Ford, more of Toyota's parts are produced by parts suppliers, some of which are ancillaries, and some of which are independents. We also know that layoff practices in the United States follow strict criteria of reverse seniority. And according to my own case studies in the United States,[11] for blue-collar workers promotion depends mostly on seniority, to a far greater extent than indicated by the language of collective agreements.

These two facts mean that large U.S. firms allocate layoffs to the lower grades of workers. The latest entrants are engaged in jobs equivalent to those of Japanese workers in parts supplier firms. Those core workers with jobs similar to those of Japanese workers in Toyota itself are never laid off, unless the firm is at the door of bankruptcy. If large Japanese firms completely stopped their orders to parts suppliers in case of contraction, then they could be said to shift layoffs to the lower grade of workers as much as their U.S. counterparts. However, according to a brilliant piece of research on the relationship between large firms and parts suppliers,[12] this is not the case. To the contrary, once a new model is launched, or even before launching, the relationship between the firm and its parts suppliers is stable. When demand decreases, the damages are shared by both. The large firm does not produce parts manufactured by parts suppliers in order to maintain its own employment even when there is large decrease in output. Although this research has not been extended to smaller firms, it is sufficient to say that the degree to which the burden of layoffs is borne by the lower grades of workers is less in Japanese firms than in similar U.S. firms.

With a similar shift to the lower segment of the work force in large Japanese firms, redundancy is unavoidable even in the largest firms. This is shown in Table 8, based on a valuable and unique survey by the Ministry of Labor on adjustment to decreases in output from January 1975 to June 1978. The survey covered a somewhat lengthy period and can thus reveal what is hidden in short-run data, and it classified adjustment by the degree of decrease in output.

From Table 8, it is clear that the diffusion of redundancy in large firms is not much less than, or is even equal to, that in small firms in the case of the largest contraction in output. At first glance, it seems strange that those firms whose output has increased have conducted redundancy programs, but during the three and a half years covered by the survey it

TABLE 8

Percentage of Establishments Conducting Redundancy, by Size of Firm and Grade of Change in Output in Manufacturing Industry, January 1975 to June 1978

Number of employees in firm	Grade of change in output, June 1978[a]				
	Aggregate	150+	120-149	100-119	0-99
1,000 and above	20.3%	17.6%	22.5%	14.6%	35.3%
300-999	30.7	35.6	28.1	35.1	20.4
100-299	29.5	27.6	27.6	27.4	37.8
30-99	26.1	26.1	26.0	24.1	28.9
5-29	16.7	15.5	18.3	14.6	19.4
All firms	19.4%	19.5%	20.7%	17.0%	21.6%

SOURCE: Japan, Ministry of Labor, *Koyō hendō sōgō chōsa* (A survey on employment adjustment) (Tokyo, 1979).

[a]January 1975 level = 100.

was possible for firms that suffered decrease in output in the short term to increase output for the whole period. Nevertheless, in the case of firms that experienced a contraction in the period of observation, as many as 35.3 per cent of the largest firms conducted redundancy programs; a similar, or even a lesser, proportion of smaller firms did likewise. Another piece of research on adjustment to changes under contemporary Japanese industrial relations reveals that when a deficit in the balance sheet of a firm lasts for two years, nearly 30 to 40 per cent of large firms tend to conduct layoffs.[13] Redundancy is not rare in large Japanese firms.

In the practice of redundancy in large Japanese firms, a feature of crucial importance is apparent: redundancy tends to be concentrated among workers to whom redundancy is most costly, in contrast to the United States. Consequently, social tension is apt to be higher even at low redundancy levels. In other words, the capacity for adjustment to output contraction might be less than in the United States. This feature has long been overlooked because of the myth of permanent employment.

The social cost of redundancy depends not only on the number of workers laid off but also on who is laid off. Redundancy by and large implies a period of unemployment, during which workers cannot utilize their skills. Hence, the cost of layoff is related to the level of skill; the higher the skill, the greater the cost. Since unemployment benefits do not last indefinitely, workers have to find another job. Here is another possibility for loss; if workers taking another job cannot fully utilize their acquired skills, there is a loss due to specificity of skill. Because we are discussing workers in large firms where high and specific skills prevail, these costs are important.

In the United States, layoffs tend to be concentrated among workers to whom redundancy is least costly, particularly when there are trade unions. As mentioned above, layoff practice in the United States is heavily dependent on seniority. Since promotion is dependent on seniority, laid-off workers are from the lowest rank of jobs, which demand little skill. Therefore, workers of least cost are made redundant.

The Japanese practice of redundancy is quite unlike the U.S. practice. It abides by no seniority rule. In fact, there have been no hard and fast rules as to who should be laid off. Historically, there have been roughly two stages in the practice of redundancy, before the mid-1950s and after the mid-1970s. In the first stage, there were many strikes against layoffs in large firms. Once depression came, even large firms not infrequently had to conduct redundancy in order to protect the firm and the employment of the majority of workers. First, the firm proposed to its trade unions that it advertise for volunteers who would accept premium redundancy payment. Trade unions ordinarily opposed these offers, perhaps in part because of the Marxian ideology that governed trade union leaders in those years. However, to survive, the firms could not cancel the redundancy plans. Therefore, they nominated workers to be laid off. The trade unions were bitterly opposed, and lengthy strikes ensued. Some strikes lasted for more than six months. Naturally, the unions could not hold out, and those workers nominated by the firms had to leave. The criteria for nomination were commonly "inferior achievement in work" and "older than 45 years of age." In large firms, workers over 45 have long served their firm and accordingly are highly skilled. Thus workers to whom costs were highest were most vulnerable to being laid off.

In the mid-1970s, firms avoided nomination of redundant workers, and no severe strikes developed. Some leaders in both management and unions still remembered the bitterness and tragedy of the first stage, which imposed enormous costs to both sides. The firms advertised for volunteers who would accept redundancy in return for premium payments. Contrary to firms' expectations, young workers frequently volunteered, although many volunteers were workers over 45 years of age, to whom higher premium rates were offered. In both periods, workers to whom costs were highest seemed vulnerable to redundancy.[14]

The above description is based on case studies, but not enough for statistical reliability. No statistical material directly concerned with this point is available; indirect figures showing the age distribution of laid-off workers in 1977 and 1979 are shown in Fig. 1. A comparison with the age distribution of workers in general reveals that redundancy is concentrated in older groups. Among those workers laid off, the figures indicate a higher concentration of redundancy within the group older than 45, which clearly supports the conclusions of our case studies.

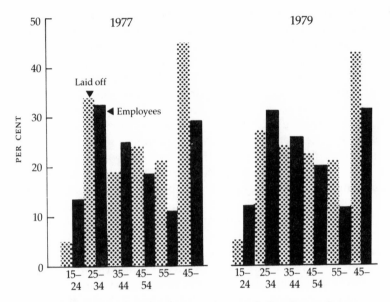

Fig. 1. Age distribution of laid-off male workers and of male employees, 1977
and 1979. Source: Japan, Office of the Prime Minister, Bureau of Statistics,
Rōdōryoku tokubetsu chōsa (Labor force survey: A special report).

The reason for such a high concentration of redundancy in workers
over age 45 is complicated. As stated above, most workers in large firms
tend to invest highly in their human capital. Based on the simplest human capital model, it is reasonable to assume that the aggregate sum of
wages paid over a long period equals the aggregate sum of marginal productivity for that period, provided that both figures are discounted. The
equality of the aggregate sums over the long term necessarily produces
the gap between productivity and wages; productivity is higher than
wages in the earlier period and lower in the later period. This gap in the
later period causes the concentration of redundacy among workers over
age 45, though at the costs of destroying long-term equality and, accordingly, of discouraging worker morale.

To sum up, one of the crucial defects of Japanese industrial relations in
large firms lies in their redundancy practices; workers to whom the costs
are highest are the most vulnerable to redundancy. Consequently, only a
small increase in unemployment is sufficient to raise social tension to an
intolerably high level. In contrast, the United States tends to concentrate
layoffs among the least costly workers, and social tension may not be as
high even though the volume of unemployment may be larger. Any industrial society is obliged to bear a certain amount of unemployment

when adjusting to changes in industrial structure or technology. Contemporary Japanese society has a limited ability to adapt to changes because of the practice of shifting the burden to workers who suffer large losses from redundancy. If redundancy in large Japanese firms were to occur beyond a certain level, industrial relations would likely become as militant as those in the 1950s, when long strikes were not rare.

Enterprise Unionism

Analysis of workers' skills sheds light on labor-management relations, which have been subject to much misunderstanding. The greatest misunderstanding arises with respect to enterprise unionism. Observers note that the basic unit of a labor union is enterprise-wide and consequently maintain that unions are feeble, not conducting strikes and being too cooperative to be effective in regulating wages and working conditions. Behind this view is the idea that in order to be workable, labor unions must organize the whole field in which workers are competing with each other. Many interpret this thesis to mean that it is necessary for labor unions to cover an occupation or an industry and have coverage wider than a single company. Those choosing this interpretation naturally expect enterprise unions to be powerless and submissive to management and argue that one of the most crucial contributors to Japanese economic performance is the feeble voice of workers, or, in other words, the exploitation of workers.

As we will see, however, insight into the character of workers' skills on the shop floor affords a completely different explanation for cooperative, enterprise-based unionism. This viewpoint sees it as a natural outcome of reasonable union behavior dedicated to securing the largest net gains for workers. A word of caution is necessary. Many popular conceptions are contradicted by statistical facts. Japanese labor unions conducted, as shown in Table 3, as many strikes as those of France and the United Kingdom in the 1950s and 1960s, and many more by far than those of Germany and Sweden for most periods. No one can claim that Japan is uncommonly free of industrial disputes.

The "feebleness" of Japanese unions might be attributed to a lesser extent of union organization. The percentage of employees with union membership, however, has been higher in Japan than in the United States for all of the postwar period. At present, a declining trend is common to both countries, although the decline began in the United States in the mid-1950s but not until about 1970 in Japan. In 1984, the number of union members in Japan was 12.5 million, or 29.1 per cent of all employees.[15] The major cause of the decline is structural change in industry; shifts to tertiary industry result in a greater number of smaller establishments that are not easily organized. (There is not space here to touch on historical aspects of unionism in Japan, but Japanese labor unions do have a fairly long history, reaching back to around the 1890s, shortly after Japan's industrial revolution. As in most other industrial countries, labor unions appeared just after their industrial revolution.)

Central to misunderstandings about Japanese industrial relations is the misconception that all Japanese unions are enterprise unions. This is doubly erroneous. First, Japanese unions are multilayered organizations, consisting of both work-place and industry affiliations. It is true that most labor unions organize themselves at the work place, that is, at the plant and at the company level. This is, however, only a part of the whole labor union structure; most work-place unions do not stand alone but affiliate with industrial-level union federations.[16] The distribution of industrial unions by the number of members in the United States and Japan is similar in both nations (see Fig. 2): two peaks occur, one around 100,000 and the other at more than 500,000, suggesting much comparability in terms of the scale of industrial unions.

Second, there are craft unions in contemporary Japan. Although they were the dominant form of organization before World War I, they are now very much in the minority. Yet, the largest craft union is in the building trades, with a membership of 290,000, equivalent to its U.S. counterpart in terms of percentage of the population. Indeed, in both countries, craft unions exist mostly in the building trades.

These similarities between union organization in the West and Japan

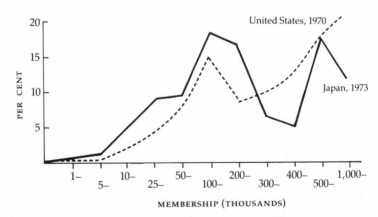

Fig. 2. Percentage distribution of union membership by size of industrial unions, United States (1971) and Japan (1973). Sources: For Japan, Ministry of Labor, *Rōdō kumiai kihon chōsa, 1973* (Basic survey of labor unions) (Tokyo, 1974); for United States, Department of Labor, Bureau of Labor Statistics, *Directory of National Unions and Employees Associations* (Washington, D.C., 1971).

may, however, be the only ones. Japanese industrial unions may exist only in name, not doing anything effective in regulating wages and working conditions, whereas their Western counterparts are active. Before forming any conclusions, we need to examine carefully the functions and activities of Japanese labor unions.

Most issues that crucially interest rank and file members of labor unions are negotiated at the enterprise and/or plant level. To workers on the shop floor, issues relevant to skill formation are of prime importance because these ultimately affect wages and working conditions. Promotion, transfer, and redundancy are the main issues concerning skill formation. Promotion is movement from lower-grade jobs to upper-grade jobs in a career, which is virtually synonymous with skill formation because it results from on-the-job training. Transfer is deviation from a path of skill formation because it represents movement from one career line to another that requires different skills; transferred workers lose the opportunity to utilize many of their acquired skills and must learn a new set of skills. Redundancy is a breakdown of skill formation for those workers with white-collarized skills; redundant workers have to find new jobs in other companies, and it is not easy to find ones in which acquired skills can be fully utilized. All these issues arise from events specific to a plant or an enterprise, and industrial unions cannot effectively handle them. Work-place unions must play the main role.

Each wage rate for each job or for each worker is negotiated in the work place. When workers' careers are developed within a single company, the composition of a career tends, to some extent, to be enterprise specific. As a result, no uniform wage rate can be set across companies, and hence, work-place unions must deal with them.

This does not imply that industrial unions have no role. Their role is to negotiate general changes in wages, scheduled working hours, and other industry-wide conditions. Although skills include elements specific to an enterprise, the major part of each skill remains general in character. Because of this, there is a foundation for wage levels in competing companies to be equalized, and competition in product markets is a compelling force. General changes in wages and working conditions, therefore, are handled at industry level.

This does not necessarily mean that an industrial union negotiates with the employers' federation of the industry. In some industries, such as textiles and private railways, industrial unions themselves do sit around the table with the relevant employers' federation. But in other industries, negotiation of general wage changes is conducted at the enterprise level. A closer examination of the process, however, discloses de facto industry-level bargaining. For example, the five giant firms in the iron and steel industry, which has set the pattern in Japanese wage rounds for three decades, negotiate and sign contracts individually. However, the content of the Japanese companies' offers and of the agreement on the amount of wage changes are exactly the same across the five major firms. More curiously the offers of the five are revealed simultaneously. Clearly there has been a long series of informal talks at the industry level before the ritual takes place.

Those familiar with bargaining procedures in U.S. industrial relations may be astonished by the striking similarities between the United States and the above description of the division of labor in union activities. It is the local unions in the United States, that is, work-place unions, that negotiate promotion, transfer, and redundancy, but the industrial unions that bargain for general changes in wages.

Despite these similarities, it may still be asked whether there are differences between Japan and the United States in the functions performed by unions. Those arguing that industrial unions are merely nominal bodies cite the distribution of full-time union officials as well as union funds, both of which seem to be heavily concentrated at the enterprise level in contemporary Japan. Although it is extremely difficult to find statistics on the distribution of union officials and union funds at various levels, it can safely be said that Japanese labor unions allocate the greater portion of these two important resources to the enterprise level. Japanese industrial unions do have full-time officials and union funds, but enterprise unions have more officials and money.

However, it would be dangerous to assert that Japanese enterprise unions have more full-time officials and money than their Western counterparts. The remarks above refer only to those whose wages are paid from union funds. There are many full- or part-time officials whose wages are paid not by labor unions but by companies in the West. In the United States, a large portion of work-place union officials are at least partly paid by the company. To mention just two examples, shop stewards in automobile plants, who are paid completely by the company, are allowed to engage in union activities after only one hour's work on the shop floor, and the ratio of shop stewards to union members is about 1 to 250, an extraordinarily large figure for any industrialized country. Another common practice is that work-place union officers, such as committeemen, have obtained vested rights to engage in union activities for a half-day on company pay; unions can pay for another half-day to let the officers act as full-time officials.

In the United Kingdom, the leaders of work-place union organizations, such as conveners or senior shop stewards of workshop organizations, although they are formally supposed to work on the shop floor, often devote all their time to union activities. Formal German labor unions have no full-time officials at the enterprise or plant level, but German workers' organizations do not lack full-time officials at these levels. Rather, the members of workers' councils are full-time worker-officials and are paid by the company. These workers' councils are legally not labor unions and are prohibited from affiliating with industrial unions as well as from conducting industrial disputes, but they have the right to, and do, negotiate redundancies, transfers, and promotions as well as wage rates. They are de facto labor unions at the work place in terms of their function. When we take into account all these de facto labor unions in the work place, it is not certain that Japanese labor unions allocate more resources and power to the enterprise level than do their counterparts in the West. If there is any feature peculiar to Japan, it is that full-time union officials at the work-place level are paid wholly by labor unions, and consequently, the distribution of union money is necessarily relatively concentrated at the work-place level in comparison to the West.

Even if labor union resources are allocated reasonably, this does not guarantee effective functioning of the union. One of the most popular arguments with respect to Japanese labor unions is that they are weak in exercising their voice in regulating wages and working conditions. In other words, the Japanese economy has grown mostly at the sacrifice of the workers' voice. One way to measure the size of the workers' voice quantitatively is to compare the extent of industrial disputes in terms of working days lost, as done in Table 3. Of course, the problem remains that though strikes are not rare, they might not be effective. All we can do here is to describe the process through which Japanese labor unions negotiate and regulate issues crucial to union members. Here, transfer is selected as an example; it occurs more frequently and widely than redundancy, which is undoubtedly the most crucial issue for union members. Transfer is also important because it deviates a worker's career from skill development.[17]

Transfers in contemporary Japanese industry fall into two categories: within a plant and between plants within a company. Although no statistical figures are available, intraplant transfers are far more common than interplant ones. Intraplant transfers represent mobility between different workshops not closely related in technology or in terms of skills. Mobility between closely related workshops promotes the skill development process described above. For example, a move to the next workshop, which makes the same parts of a different size or model, where workers can utilize skills acquired in the former workshop, can enable them to learn new skills. In contrast, transfers between unrelated workshops do not afford such opportunities because the skills required in the new workshop are so different from the former ones. The workers transferred have to learn new skills almost from scratch. Since this represents great damage to the workers transferred, naturally the labor unions at the work place try to regulate closely the conditions of transfers.

If transfers are so costly, why do labor unions not reject them completely? The answer is simple: there is clearly another cost—redundancy. Transfers are needed when there is fear of redundancy. In a large plant with a variety of departments making different products, it is not unlikely that one department will decline and another prosper temporarily or permanently. If the labor union rejected transfers, the declining department would have to lay off workers, and the other department would recruit from outside the firm. Transfers can reduce redundancy, and this is why both labor unions and their members accept transfers.

There are two types of both intra- and interplant transfers: temporary and permanent. Temporary transfers guarantee that the workers transferred will return to their former workshops within a certain period, say three months; permanent ones offer no such guarantee. Since the cost of transfers to workers is larger in permanent transfers than in temporary ones, union regulation is naturally most intense and detailed in cases of permanent transfer. From which workshop to which, who is to be transferred, guarantees of former wages for each worker, and training programs are the major issues negotiated in detail by the labor unions. By way of illustration, let me examine guarantees of wages because these are easily visible. In order to explain this type of guarantee, we have to begin with a brief look at wages in large Japanese firms.

Contrary to the popular perception that Japanese wages lack incentive components because they are based not on jobs or on performance but on length of service, wages for blue-collar workers in large corporations provide as much incentive as, for example, wages for banking employees in the United Kingdom.[18] In fact, wage payment systems are very similar in both groups; yearly wage increments with additional merit payments are common to both. Since the merit rating depends on the assessment of workers' performance by their supervisors, the size of the merit rating becomes crucial in regulating wages in case of transfers. When a worker moves to a new workshop, his merit rating in the new workshop naturally becomes lower than that in the former shop because he has not yet acquired the skills necessary for the new shop. Labor unions at the work place, therefore, seek not only to guarantee the wage rate of the former shop, but also to secure the same merit rating in the new shop as in the former one for a certain period, say three years.

The working out of the crucial problem of who is to be transferred also runs contrary to the popular belief that the Japanese workshop is governed by seniority: no seniority rule operates in these cases. Consequently, who is to be transferred is a delicate issue, and the criteria applied to the issue are not always clear. One established practice is that the labor union at the work place accepts permanent transfers only with the approval of the worker involved. Usually, a full-time official of the labor union meets with the worker and discerns the wishes of the candidate for transfer. Most permanent transfers require the signature of the president of the labor union at the work place.

Temporary transfers are more common than permanent ones and are utilized when adjustment to changes in output is necessary. Labor unions at the work place set the maximum period through negotiation with the company, say three months, in addition to other conditions. Because temporary transfers invite less damage than permanent ones, the burden of transfers tends to be equally distributed.

Interplant transfers are a different story. Here, there are also two types. When a new plant opens, mobility is between the same kind of workshops. Workers apply for transfers if they feel the benefits outweigh the costs. The benefits would include a better opportunity for promotion to supervisory positions; the costs would arise from changes in place of residence. This type of voluntary interplant transfer is more common in processing industries such as chemicals and steel, in which the work units are smaller than in other industries. Because of this smaller scale, the probability of promotion to supervisory positions naturally becomes larger, and workers tend to be more expectant of becoming supervisors than in other industries. In other words, when there is little opportunity for workers to be promoted to supervisory positions in one plant, because of, say, the age composition of the work group, transfer to a new plant can be promising. Since this type of transfer is beneficial, no serious problem is presented.

The other type of interplant transfer occurs when there is a permanent decrease in output in one plant. The main reason for this type of transfer is simply avoidance of redundancy. Job compatibility is seldom assured. As a result, the cost to the worker resembles that involved in intraplant transfers to a different kind of workshop. Because the cost is generally large, regulation by labor unions is most intensive.

One feature in the working of Japanese labor unions is their voice in management. Formally, there is no legal framework for worker participation in management, unlike the German system, for example. No workers' representatives are allowed to sit in the boardroom. In spite of this, workers are extremely vocal about management, and joint consultation between labor unions and the company at the enterprise and/or plant level is remarkably widespread.

Table 9 shows the percentage of workers who answered yes to the question whether they wanted to have a voice in management. The source is a government survey that is extremely valuable because of its large sample size (120,000 workers) and because the individual workers were surveyed directly. The results are clear; an overwhelming number of workers, particularly males, express a desire to have a voice in making managerial policy.

Table 10 shows the diffusion of joint consultation machinery in the work place. The larger the firm, the higher the percentage of establishments with such machinery; it exceeds 90 per cent in large firms. Even in firms with 100–299 employees, the figure is 70 per cent. Such machinery exists in firms without labor unions, though to a lesser extent. A variety of functions are performed by joint consultation. First, it is utilized in preparing for collective bargaining on wages and working conditions for those firms with labor unions and substitutes for collective bargaining in companies lacking labor unions. Second, and more important here, it works as an important channel through which labor union officials and management discuss managerial policies. This feature has become more noticeable since the first oil shock, when employment was severely threatened. This is indicative of the reason why Japanese labor unions, as well as workers, are so eager to have a voice in management. Workers with specific white-collarized skills are naturally interested in management because their employment security depends heavily on the company's prospects: when the company grows quickly, promotion becomes speedy; when the company declines, not only do they face delays in promotion, but also, in extreme cases, they are threatened by redundancy. They lose the prospect of being promoted in the company in which they have worked, and, more important, they experience difficulty in finding jobs in other companies in which they can utilize their acquired skills fully. Workers seeking to protect their interests are interested in having a voice in management.

Examination of Japanese labor union activities has revealed both similarity and dissimilarity to labor-management relations in the West. Although at first there appears to be a great difference between the two, the

TABLE 9

Percentage of "Yes" Answers to the Question "Do You Think It Necessary for Rank and File Workers to Have a Voice in Management?" 1977

Age	Men	Women	Age	Men	Women
19 and younger	87.6%	78.9%	40-44	90.5%	78.0%
20-24	90.8	85.0	45-54	87.5	78.0
25-29	89.9	82.4	55 and older	81.3	61.7
30-34	90.1	79.1	All ages	90.0%	81.7%
35-39	92.9	79.5			

SOURCE: Japan, Ministry of Labor, *Survey on Communication Between Labor and Management for 1972* (Tokyo, 1978).

TABLE 10
Percentage of Establishments with Joint Consultation Machinery, 1977

Number of employees in firm	Firms with labor unions	Firms without labor unions	Number of employees in firm	Firms with labor unions	Firms without labor unions
5,000 and more	94.1	67.2	100-299	69.8%	38.0%
1,000-4,999	90.6	46.3	All firms	82.9%	40.3%
300-999	82.3	42.4			

SOURCE: Same as Table 9.

emphasis on work-place activities is not specific to Japan, but is common in Western nations if we take into account de facto labor unions as well as formal labor unions. Yet there is some difference: Japanese labor unions and their members are very interested in having a voice in management, and, in the aggregate, Japanese unions emphasize the work place relatively more than do their Western counterparts.

What is the basis of the similarity and dissimilarity in labor-management relations? A theory of workers' skill type or career type is outlined here in answer to this question.[19] Career type is classified according to the nature of a worker's skills and skill development. In the long history of economics, only one dichotomy has been employed for classifying skills: skilled and unskilled. This dichotomy neglects the possibility of change in skill over time; it is more natural and reasonable to consider that workers elevate their skill levels through experience. Adding this possibility of changes in skill to the traditional dichotomy, we obtain four career types.

1. *Craftsman.* The grade of skill is high, and there is no change in skill over time. Most skilled trades in the building industry in the United States or Japan are examples.

2. *Laborer.* The grade of skill is low, and there is no change in skills over time. These are unskilled workers.

3. *White-collarized.* Skills increase as experience increases over a long period, mostly within one enterprise, which forms a career with late and high ceilings in terms of the extent of remuneration obtained, made through a lengthy promotion-from-within process. One example is white-collar workers in the West, such as banking employees. Because "intellectual" skills tend to require development over a long period of time, they are generally of this type.

4. *Semiskilled.* Skills increase to a lesser extent and for a shorter period than for the white-collarized type, often taking the form of a shorter period of promotion from within.

These four career types produce different kinds of labor-management relations. The craftsman accompanies craft unions; laborers tend to be left unorganized; and the semiskilled and those promoted internally form industrial unions that include work-place unions, as explained below.

All four types exist both in Japan and the West, and this yields similarity in labor-management relations. The basis for common work-place unionism is that types 3 and 4 represent the majority of workers in large firms both in Japan and the West. Both types take the form of promotion from within, which is most crucial in skill development. Once this phenomenon is present in an enterprise or a work place, naturally work-place labor unions are required to deal with it.

Dissimilarity between Japan and Western nations results from the difference in the weight of these four types. Japan, seems to have fewer craftsmen than the West, although clearly there are craft unions in contemporary Japan. This is one example of differences in labor-management relations. Even among workers in large firms, Japan has more workers of type 3 than the West; although type 3 is confined to white-collar workers, such as banking employees, in the West, in Japan this category includes not only white-collar but also blue-collar workers of large firms. In other words, promotion from within leads to wider and deeper careers for Japanese blue-collar workers than it does for their Western counterparts. These workers realize that there is a strong connection between their skill development and the business situation of the company. Hence, Japanese labor unions are obliged to emphasize work-place activities as well as a voice in management.

The description above is confined to workers in large firms in Japan, who constitute only a minority of the work force. Apart from the self-employed, who are examined in the paper by Patrick and Rohlen in this volume, those who work in large firms—that is, those with white-collarized skills—account for less than one-third of all employees. The majority of employees are workers in small firms and female workers, each numbering slightly more than one-third of all employees, respectively. Are workers with white-collarized intellectual skills confined only to large firms or are they also found in the other two groups of workers?

Questionnaire surveys and in-depth interviews reveal that workers in small and medium-size firms are composed of three groups with different types of skills:[20] (1) "core workers" with intellectual skills, (2) semiskilled workers (the majority), and (3) the unskilled. Core workers have intellectual skills equivalent to those of male workers in large firms. Their careers are as wide as, or even wider than, those of male workers in large firms. Employees of small firms can work in several main workshops that require different kinds of skills during their careers. For example, it is rare to find machinists in large firms who have also experienced assembly work in their career, but such workers are common in small firms.

In addition to the width of career, depth of career can differ between large and small firms. Because there is less of a bureaucracy in small firms, blue-collar workers with intellectual skills are more likely to be promoted to positions in middle management, which rarely occurs in large firms. However, when we compare the number of subordinates and supervisors' functions, middle management in small firms does not differ much from lower management in large firms. But we can say that there are workers in small firms with intellectual skills whose careers are at least equivalent to those of workers in large firms in terms of both depth and width. I have summarized the relevant evidence elsewhere.[21] Here, I repeat only some of the discussion on wage profiles. The wages of workers with intellectual skills in small firms coincide with those of workers in large firms both in terms of wage levels and age-wage profiles, with wage profiles having a positive slope until workers reach their late forties or early fifties.

The most important discrepancy between large firms and small ones is the percentage of workers with intellectual skills; they are the minority, say 5–10 per cent, of all employees in small firms, but they account for nearly all production workers in large firms. The majority of workers in small firms are undoubtedly members of the next group, the semiskilled. This does not mean that the firm places its recruits into different categories. Rather, these two groups are not separated for the first couple of years; after that, management sorts out who is to be in the first group and develops their careers accordingly by rotation among workshops.

The majority, the semiskilled workers, acquire skills through on-the-job training, but of shorter length than that of the core workers. Hence, their wage profiles differ from those of the core workers; after nearly ten years of experience, unlike the core workers, little difference in wages is observed.

Unskilled workers constitute another minority, though their weight varies with industry. Reflecting their skills, wage profiles are almost flat irrespective of experience. Female workers are found in all three of these groups; a few belong to the first group, and many to the second and third.

One of the important consequences of the fact that workers with intellectual skills form only a small minority in small firms is workers' reluctance to participate in QC circles. Evidence of the small extent of the diffusion of QC circles in small firms was presented in Tables 1 and 2. However, this does not imply that no attempts have been made to initiate

QC circles. According to my field work, many small firms have launched them, only to have them founder because of workers' lack of interest. Clearly, without workers with intellectual skills, it is difficult to maintain QC circles for extended periods.

The greatest divergence between large firms and small ones is that workers in large firms are of a single type—namely, white-collarized workers with intellectual skills—and that small firms employ a variety of workers. This does not imply that large firms do not need workers in groups 2 or 3. On the contrary, large firms have work for the semiskilled and for the unskilled. Here is revealed one of the most crucial characteristics of contemporary Japanese industry—large firms submit work for group 2 and group 3 workers to small firms.

This reflects the most vital difference in contemporary industrial organization between Japan and the West; large Japanese firms have a greater dependence on parts suppliers. The number of workers in giant corporations in the United States and Japan is enough to confirm this.

The high degree of dependence on small firms in Japan has long been criticized as representing a dual structure in which large firms exploit small ones. An alternative view, however, suggests that the Japanese system is more decentralized, leaving more room for discretion by small firms.[22] Which view is appropriate depends on wage differentials by size of firm, for which Japan has been notorious. Consideration of the differences in work force composition between large firms and small firms is, however, crucial in this regard.

With variation in the degree of dependence on parts suppliers, even the same wage differentials by occupation across countries can produce greater variation in wages by size of firms in the country with the higher dependence on parts suppliers. For example, suppose that the U.S. and Japanese auto industries employ equal numbers of three worker groups, X, Y and Z, and presume that wage differentials among these three groups are equal in the two countries, say 2 for X, 1.5 for Y, and 1 for Z. Now, assume that a large corporation in the Japanese auto industry, say Toyota, employs only those workers belonging to group X, and its parts suppliers employ only workers of groups Y and Z. The large U.S. firm, Ford, for example, employs half of each worker group, the other halves being employed by parts suppliers. Wage differentials by size of firm do not appear in the United States because worker groups are equally distributed between large and small firms. Conversely, in Japan wage differentials by size of firm are of the order 2:1.25, or 100:63, solely because of unequal distribution of the three worker groups between large and small firms. To summarize, the large U.S. firm has a larger wage differential within the company than its Japanese counterpart, and Japanese firms have greater wage differentials by size of firm than their U.S. counterparts, although there is no real discrepancy in wage differentials between the two countries.

This model cannot be tested directly since no exact statistics are available on the degree of dependence on parts suppliers or on the composition of worker groups by company or size of company. Indirect evidence, however, can be brought to bear on the problem. Statistics on the number of employees for each large corporation in the two countries with similar output both in terms of amount and quality suggest great differences in the degree of dependence on parts suppliers between the two countries. Wage structure surveys in the two countries tell us that wage differentials by occupation and by grade of education are far larger in the United States than in Japan.[23] This also suggests that intracompany wage differentials in large U.S. firms would be larger than in their Japanese counterparts. This indirect evidence is at least sufficient to indicate the dangers of assuming a dual structure simply because of wage differentials by size of firm, without knowledge of the structure of industrial organization.

Since 1954 Japan has produced detailed annual statistics on the wage structure; these provide wage differentials by size of firm, length of service, age, grade of education, sex, occupation, and industry. For a long time, equivalent statistics were lacking for the West. Fortunately, the EC statistics on wage structure for 1972 mentioned above provide higher-quality data than ever before. Although the classifications are less detailed than those of the Japanese survey, wage differentials by size of establishment, sex, white-collar or blue-collar status, and industry, but not by length of service or age, are available. Data for both surveys were collected directly from establishments, have large sample sizes, and cover firms with ten or more employees. It is rare to find data with such comparability as well as reliability when conducting international comparisons.

The data shown in Fig. 3 are confined to manufacturing industries. The largest worker group is male blue-collar workers, for whom Japanese wage differentials by size of firm fall in the middle of the range plotted for EC countries. For male white-collar workers, the Japanese wage differential by firm size appears to be one of the largest, although it is equal to, or even less than, that of Italy. The size of the gap is only 15 per cent, which is even smaller than the average differential for blue-collar workers of the EC. With respect to female blue-collar workers, Japan exhibits slightly lower than middle-rank differentials, and for female white-collar workers, Japan belongs to the group of countries with the smallest differentials. To sum up, Japan's wage differentials by size of firm are not unusual and are comparable to those of EC countries when we examine the data by worker skill classifications.

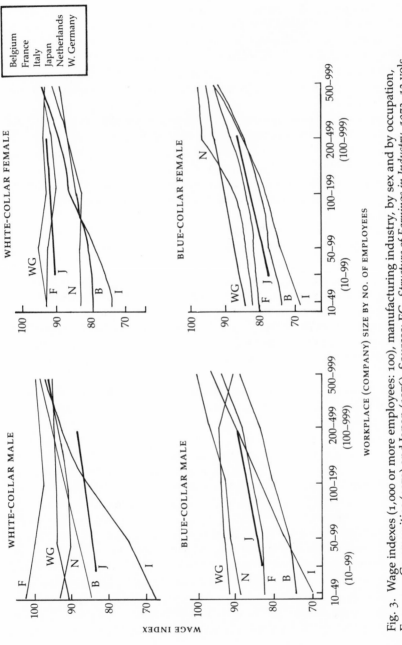

WHITE-COLLAR MALE

WHITE-COLLAR FEMALE

BLUE-COLLAR MALE

BLUE-COLLAR FEMALE

Belgium
France
Italy
Japan
Netherlands
W. Germany

WORKPLACE (COMPANY) SIZE BY NO. OF EMPLOYEES

WAGE INDEX

Fig. 3. Wage indexes (1,000 or more employees: 100), manufacturing industry, by sex and by occupation, European Communities (1972) and Japan (1976). Sources: EC, *Structure of Earnings in Industry, 1972*, 13 vols. (Brussels, 1975–76). Japan, Ministry of Labor, *Chingin kōzō kihon tōkei chōsa* (Basic survey of wage structure) (Tokyo, 1976).

Concluding Remarks

By focusing on the nature of skill, we can easily explain many features of Japanese industrial relations. The most famous are undoubtedly seniority wages and permanent employment. Seniority wages simply reflect the nature of skill; skill is developed in a career over a long period within a firm, and accordingly the age-wage profile is positively sloped. This profile is not peculiar to Japan in two senses: it is confined to only a minority of Japanese workers, and it is common to male white-collar workers in the West. This similarity is also explained by the nature of skill; the skills of Japanese blue-collar workers in large firms are partly of an intellectual character—determining the causes of problems and adjusting to minor changes on the shop floor—and this intellectual character of skill is shared with white-collar workers in general. Therefore, seniority wages are not a uniquely Japanese feature; the Japanese feature, if any, is the extension of white-collar wages to a section of blue-collar workers.

With this type of skill, it is natural that both management and workers benefit from long-term employment, which has long been thought of as Japan's unique "permanent employment." For workers, it is beneficial to stay with one firm because skills can be developed; for management, finding and training substitutes takes time and is costly. And again, this long-term employment is not unique to Japan in two senses: it is confined to large firms, and it is also common for male white-collar workers in Europe. A Japanese feature is the extension of the white-collar characteristics to a section of blue-collar workers. In short, the white-collarization of a section of blue-collar workers is a Japanese feature.

Returning to a point raised at the beginning of this paper, skill development over a long career with one firm can account for high worker morale. It not only is the foundation of high morale but also is necessary to it. The essence of the contribution of high morale is not in long work hours or in a heavy work load, but in devising better work methods and production, which in turn demand technological knowledge by workers for maintenance; without proper technological background, no effective program can last long. This kind of wide-ranging skill contains such knowledge and promotes the ability of workers to determine the causes of problems on the shop floor and thus to contribute to productivity.

Even if workers can devise better ways to work, they do not practice them unless they sense a necessity, which is also a matter of skill. As stated above, this type of skill can be better developed through promotion within a single firm. In order to elevate their own skills quickly, workers take an interest in the growth of their firm. If the company declines, promotion will be delayed and skill development slowed. In an extreme case, a firm has to lay off workers, and this represents great damage to workers with specific skills. To promote their skills, therefore, workers must maintain high morale lest their company lose out to rival companies and endanger their careers.

Again, high morale is not unique to Japanese workers, but shared with white-collar workers with promising prospects in the West. A common impression of Japanese workers' attitudes is that promising white-collar workers are hardly more industrious than their Western counterparts. Generally speaking, it is clear that without a promise of a career to some degree, no worker will make substantial efforts. The Japanese feature, if any, is that blue-collar workers prospects are raised, and, accordingly, morale is high.

Trade unions adopt a policy of cooperativeness with respect to production because they are democratic and reflect the members' desires. The apparent difference between Japanese and Western unions results mostly from a simple fact. Formal trade unions in European countries still consist, by long tradition, mostly of blue-collar workers (although the situation is changing and unions now include more white-collar workers). This was common, too, of Japanese unions in the prewar days. Defeat in the war brought new organization and the inclusion of both blue- and white-collar workers in the same work-place union. Formal trade unions in Europe usually do not include white-collar and white-collarized workers in the same organizations as blue-collar workers, and consequently, formal unions are not so cooperative as in Japan. If we compare Japanese unions with Western white-collar workers' organizations, more similarities emerge. In other words, a comparison of Japanese unions with workers' councils in Europe might be meaningful because the latter include white-collar workers.

One of the problems of Japanese industrial relations is finding ways of adjusting to contractions in output. Contrary to the popular belief that Japanese systems are flexible in adapting to changes, redundancy happens in Japan just as it does in the West. A big difference lies in the fact that Japanese firms lay off workers who suffer the greatest costs when unemployed. Workers with the longest service, aged 45 and over, are most vulnerable to redundancy. Consequently, social tension is high even with a small volume of redundancy; more redundancy would make industrial relations as militant as they were in the late 1940s and the 1950s. The upper limit of redundancy or unemployment that can be endured in an industrial society is lower in Japan than in the West. This makes the capacity for adjustment to change smaller because changes, in industrial structure, for example, require a certain amount of unemployment.

The white-collarization of blue-collar workers has great implications for contemporary politics in Japan. Along with white-collar workers, blue-collar workers with intellectual skills are the economic foundation of the new middle mass described by Murakami in his paper in this volume. Members of the new middle mass think of themselves as belonging to the middle class. Wage differentials by grade of education and by occupation are, as mentioned above, smaller in Japan than in other industrialized countries because blue-collar workers in large firms have some skills similar to those of white-collar workers.

If workers with intellectual skills are only a small minority, why can they be considered a "mass" in politics? Two reasons deserve mention. First, although they are the minority, they are dominant in organized labor. In general, blue-collar workers in large firms are the easiest to organize into labor unions in industrialized countries. In addition, since their country's defeat in World War II, Japanese white-collar workers have been organized into labor unions with blue-collar workers. Needless to say, organized labor has a bigger voice in politics than the unorganized majority.

Second, even small firms have core workers with intellectual skills. Although they are a small minority, they occupy central positions in production on the shop floor. Consequently, they naturally influence and lead other workers on the shop floor.

As I have stressed many times, only a minority of Japanese blue-collar workers, mainly in large firms, are white-collarized. A rough estimation suggests that at most they constitute one-third of all workers. Whether this minority will grow is a question of crucial significance. The hypothesis adopted here is that, with appropriate policies, the number of workers with this skill type could grow slightly, mostly in small firms and among female workers. Small firms have difficulty in developing this type of skill among employees because workers in small firms are often mobile, making them unsuited for skill formation of this type, and because small firms are not stable enough to have the long horizon necessary to develop this type of skill. In practice, however, they have succeeded in letting their key workers acquire this type of skill. Only 5 or 10 per cent of all employees in small firms have careers similar in terms of breadth to those in the large firms. Even though it is unfeasible to extend this skill development to all workers, it is reasonably feasible to consider that this core group may grow from 5 or 10 per cent to 15 per cent, with a proper policy. A simple reason is that the weight of long-serving workers has constantly been increasing even in small firms and among female workers. The most detailed Japanese statistics on wage structure provide figures on length of service of workers by age, sex, occupation, industry, and size of firm. For almost all age groups irrespective of sex, industry, and size of firm, the average length of service has been rising consistently for the past two decades.[24] At the same time, however, careful examination of the most reliable data makes it clear that Japanese workers were more mobile to start with than is generally conceived. Japan had an equivalent or smaller weight of long-service workers than the United States in the first half of the 1960s.[25] Now, Japan has more long-service workers than the United States. Economic assessment of this trend is not easy, but it is evident that this is a most favorable foundation for development of intellectual skills even in small firms and among female workers.

What might be the impact of microelectronics and technological change in general on this type of skill? No one can give definite answers, but based on the findings and analysis above, let me venture a suggestion. According to my field surveys, the demand for knowledge of the mechanisms of production and machinery seems to grow, and demand both for manual skilled labor and for routine work to decrease. Microelectronics can do the minute work that once required high manual dexterity, and hence, the classic type of skilled worker might diminish. These machines cannot, however, work by themselves without orders, or programs. To make programs, knowledge of computer software is not sufficient. Even a worker with excellent knowledge of programming cannot make effective programs without knowing the work itself. Imagine a case of writing a program for cutting a part by machining. There are several factors involved—the order of cutting, the speed of cutting, movement of both the work and the cutter, and the angle of cutting. Depending on the character of materials and on the forms of cutting, the most efficient way to proceed can be selected. This selection can never be made by studying computer programming, but only on the basis of experience in machining and learning the theory of machining. These elements are the essence of the skill of Japanese blue-collar workers in large firms. In other words, the demand for engineers and technicians will grow, and in Japan a section of blue-collar workers can fit this demand.

Generally, an integrated career of routine jobs and intellectual work would be effective in dealing with new technology and would also encourage workers to learn the necessary skills because an integrated career implies a promising career, at least one slightly more so than that of ordinary blue-collar workers. And this is exactly the way in which blue-collar workers have been white-collarized in Japan.

It is evident that in industrialized countries, white-collar jobs have consistently expanded both among male and female workers. White-collarization is, in that sense, a long-term trend dating from the end of the nineteenth century. The Japanese extension of white-collarization to some blue-collar workers may be a part of this long, worldwide trend.

Hugh T. Patrick and Thomas P. Rohlen

Small-Scale Family Enterprises

$\mathbf{A}$ll too frequently big business has dominated popular perceptions of the Japanese economy. Large firms are deemed to have powered Japan's growth through their successes in generating output, raising productivity, absorbing and creating innovations through large-scale R&D, and creating and developing the "Japanese management system" of industrial relations, internal decision making, and close intragroup affiliations. Big business plays a highly visible, broad political and social role, financing political leaders and their factions, influencing national economic and other policy, serving as a role model, and preaching its business ideology. It is a system of male managerial elites dealing on equal footing in carefully developed formal and informal networks with counterpart elites—central government bureaucrats, elite politicians, and others holding power at the top of the pyramid of Japan's hierarchical society. Some characterize big business as the brain and the central nervous system of Japan's economy.

If that is the case, then small enterprise is the economic, political, and social heart and backbone of Japan. In particular, small-scale family enterprises have long been and continue to be a large and dynamic element in the political economy of Japan—in entrepreneurship, job creation, output, and political clout. Small business makes up the bottom two-thirds (or more) of Japan's social and economic pyramid. It is a curious mixture of seething activity, often turbulent change, and calm, quiet, even stoic inertia. Small business is the main provider of employment for the Japanese and thereby the source of consumer demand; it engages in almost half of business investment as well. Small business, as comprehensively defined here, is extremely heterogeneous and not unified politically or in other ways; nonetheless, subgroups are effective in exercising political power to achieve well-defined, typically economic, goals.

Small business is at once the source and repository of great social stability, the locus of a considerable range of tolerated behavior (what Westerners might even term "individualism"), and the carrier and implementer of social and cultural change. Many small businessmen are conformists, but few are company men of the sort that prevails in large enterprises.

A big-small classification of enterprise size is obviously too simple, as is any delimitation in the consideration of small-scale enterprise to a few sectors. In principle, we consider here the role of small-scale units of ownership and production—enterprise in the broadest sense—in all sectors of the economy, farming, manufacturing, construction, retail sales, and personal services. Enterprises range over a continuum of sizes; obviously, in numbers most are very small, and only a few (2,040 or 0.2 per cent of total incorporated enterprises) employ more than 1,000 workers.[1] Where to divide the continuum into segments depends on the purpose. Here, we are concerned primarily with enterprises of fewer than 100 workers, especially units of fewer than 30 workers and minuscule units of fewer than 5 workers.

Small-scale enterprise is quantitatively as well as qualitatively important in Japan's economy. In a three-size classification, small enterprises in 1982 provided jobs for 36.5 million Japanese men and women, 68.7 per cent of private sector employment; medium-size firms (100–999 workers) accounted for 16.2 per cent; and big business 15.0 per cent.[2] Small enterprises, with more than two-thirds of the labor force, produce close to half of the GNP originating in the private sector.[3]

Japan is a country teeming with small-scale family enterprises, more so than any other advanced industrial country. Many are entrepreneurially vigorous; many others are content, or doomed, to drift along. Small-scale family enterprises (SFEs), typically located in or near the family home, represent a complex economic, social, and psychological phenomenon.[4] Our focus is primarily on its economic features, particularly in terms of the owner-operator and his or her immediate family. (The intrafamilial dynamics of the owner-operator and family workers are complex, fascinating, and beyond the scope of this study.) Even among SFEs, size makes for qualitative differences. A 100-worker firm is probably more similar to a 300-worker firm than to a 30-worker firm. Moreover, minuscule enterprises of fewer than 5 workers are qualitatively distinctive: the workers consist almost entirely of owner-operators and family members; fewer than 15 per cent are wage-earning employees.

Our main interest here is in the ownership and operation of SFEs with fewer than 30 workers. There are some 9.5 million owner-operators of such SFEs throughout Japan, almost one-fifth (18.0 per cent) of the labor force. Of these, 2.4 million are farmers, 6 million run unincorporated nonfarm businesses, and almost 1.1 million head small incorporated enterprises. In addition, there are about 6.5 million unpaid and paid family members. Almost one-third (31.2 per cent) of Japan's labor force works as owners and family members of SFEs.[5] When their hired employees are included, these SFEs employ more than half the labor force (see Table 3, next section).

These macroeconomic facts, though illuminating, conceal the tremendous diversity and heterogeneity of small-scale family enterprises—in goals and behavior, success and failure, innovativeness and conservatism, flexibilities and rigidities, and sectoral differences and similarities. Two polar-opposite kinds of SFE stories can be told.

One story is premised on the positive pull of opportunity, ambition, ability, and the preference to be one's own boss. In it a reasonably favorable environment provides identifiable opportunities; individuals possess entrepreneurial drive, ambition, and freedom of choice; and they obtain and use resources productively and efficiently. The ultimate result is economic and personal success. It is a story of optimism and hope.

The negative story is one of lack of opportunities; limited choices under adverse circumstances, inefficiency, and defensiveness; survival by taking advantage of imperfect land or labor markets; and low wages and incomes. Families may own assets, especially land, whose implicit rental value they can obtain most effectively through some inefficient type of production. Persons may be discriminated against—especially women, older persons, Burakumin, and Koreans. Or they may be people of marginal ability, skills, personality, or motivation. It is a story of resignation, even despair. At its extremes, this is a story of exploitation, of workers and petit bourgeois families striving desperately to subsist however they can while high incomes accrue to the owners, managers, and workers of large enterprises.[6]

In real life the two stories are mixed. Moreover, the stories do not indicate much beyond material well-being; there are after all many anxious, unhappy, "successful" people and many others who are content no matter how plain or simple their lives. The negative story of engaging in marginal activities may prevail temporarily for a family who, because of dire circumstances, is waiting for something better or who is amassing a little capital to start anew. It is difficult to assert *a priori* which story is likely to prevail and under what circumstances because of the heterogeneity of individuals and families, their circumstances, and the specifics of such opportunities as may exist. In general, the negative situation characterizes industries or sectors declining because of inefficiency and an inability to compete, such as part-time agriculture and minuscule retail shops. Owners and their families are in general probably better off than their wage-earning employees. A core of quite skilled, regular (male) workers are paid substantially higher wages than middle-aged females and part-time workers (the last two categories overlap substantially).

The subject of SFEs raises a host of issues involving the economy as a whole. Why is the SFE sector so large? What does its large size mean for the political economy as a whole? More speculatively, what are its likely prospects and its effects on Japan's future? Is the large share that small-scale enterprise holds in Japan's economy mainly a lagged phenomenon, requiring a generational process of adjustment to an earlier phase of Japan's economic development? Or does it reflect an effective way to organize production in Japan's current, and future, affluent economy? Do SFEs survive mainly because of "exploitative" wage rates that are the consequence of labor market dualism, or do lower wages reflect the heterogeneity of labor in relatively competitive labor markets? Can the multitude of small-scale entrepreneurs best be described as successful utilizers of existing assets, as ambitious people seeking independence, or as people who lack better alternatives? Is government protection a major factor in the persistence of so many SFEs?

As already stated, our central focus is on the ownership and operation of small family enterprises: how they come into being, exist, transform themselves, and in some cases disappear. By "small" we usually mean enterprises with fewer than 30 workers, including the myriad of very small unincorporated enterprises. Although the operation of labor markets, firm-size differentials in wages and other forms of remuneration, and the well-being of workers in SFEs are important elements in our story, they are not central. Hence, this is more an essay on the political economy of small-scale industrial organization than on that of labor.

In contrast to those who propound the "exploitation" and "lagged" interpretations, we view small-scale family-owned and -operated enterprises mostly in a positive light. Although some sectors are clearly marginal or failing remnants of an earlier era, some are dynamic and growing; many provide sound, stable incomes. SFEs are a dynamic source of flexibility for the Japanese economy. In many instances they prove efficient and responsive to market demands. The individuals and families that make up SFEs combine their human attributes—entrepreneurship, labor, skills and knowledge, ambition, willingness to take risks, networks of social relationships—with ownership of land and other physical and financial assets. This, indeed, is their essence and their economic and social rationale. The successful persistence of small business also results in substantial part from the distribution of landownership and land's high value, the heterogeneity of labor (and to some extent segmentation of labor markets), and supportive government policies, especially in tax treatment. Perhaps most of all, it reflects the depth of entrepreneurial ambition and talent in Japan.

Several cautionary notes are in order. First, the smaller the scale, the more fluid and less reliable the data. In particular, most successful SFEs underreport their true economic profits through tax avoidance and, in many cases, tax evasion. Accordingly value added, family income, implicit wage rates, and return on investment are understated. Second, the heterogeneity among SFEs is so great that generalizations are certain to require significant exceptions. We focus on agriculture, manufacturing, and retailing, the three largest sectors. (For small high-tech venture firms, see Okimoto and Saxonhouse, this volume.) The construction industry is not considered, even though small local firms play a particularly active role in the political economy of public construction contracts and the financing of politicians.[7] Third, the data problems associated with scale within SFEs are serious. Government statistics typically lump small and medium enterprises together; the Census of Manufactures no longer collects data on the smallest firms (one to four workers); frequently manufacturing data refer only to firms with 30 or more employees; and financial data are mainly for incorporated enterprises.

In the next section, we provide a descriptive overview, first in macroperspective and then specifically for agriculture, manufacturing, and retailing. In the following section, we examine economic, social, and political reasons for the persistently high proportion of small family enterprises in the Japanese economy. In the final section, we discuss the future role of small business in Japan.

A Descriptive Overview

Surprisingly little cross-country comparative research exists on small-scale enterprise. The quality of data apparently is directly related to the degree of importance attached to small firms. Although the level of rhetorical support is substantial everywhere, Japan and the United States have the best data and the most extensive programs of financial and other support; Western European countries seemingly have less interest.[8]

Japan's small-scale enterprise sector is large in comparison with its counterparts in other advanced industrial societies. Self-employed workers and unpaid family workers constitute a far larger proportion of the labor force in Japan (29 per cent) than in France (17 per cent), Germany (14 per cent), the United States (9 per cent), or the United Kingdom (8 per cent).[9] The differences lie not so much in agriculture as in manufacturing and retailing. In Japanese manufacturing, 46.5 per cent of workers have jobs in establishments with fewer than 50 workers, slightly more than in

Italy (44.4 per cent) and much more than in the United States (15.2 per cent) and the United Kingdom (15.9 per cent). The other Western European countries fall between 16 and 40 per cent but are closer on average to Italy and Japan.[10] The same pattern is even more pronounced for establishments with fewer than 10 workers. Furthermore, in comparison to the United States, West Germany, and the United Kingdom, value added per worker is considerably lower in small firms than in large firms in Japan.[11] Subcontracting is more prevalent in Japan than elsewhere. Similarly, although lower in productivity, Japan has many more retail stores relative to population than the United States or Western Europe.

Interestingly, the share of businesses with 100 or fewer employees was remarkably constant at 40 per cent in the United States between 1963 and 1977, but rose modestly in Japan from 51 per cent in 1962 (and 1971) to 56 per cent in 1979. The Japanese government provides far more financing to small business than the U.S. government; it had about $66 billion in outstanding loans in 1982 versus $3.8 billion for the U.S. Small Business Administration, and loan guarantees of $21.8 billion versus $1.6 billion.[12] However, the interest subsidy was substantially farther below market rates in the United States than Japan.

As Kiyonari stresses, the two decades of high growth ending in the early 1970s completely transformed small business.[13] For many firms, profits increased, technology improved, investment deepened; SFEs grew rapidly, and so, too, did their number. Buyer-supplier relationships, especially in subcontracting, deepened and became more stable.

Between 1971 and 1982, the share of small-scale enterprises (fewer than 100 workers) in total employment remained essentially constant since increases in retail and wholesale trade and other services offset the decline in agriculture. Table 1 provides detailed information on SFEs with fewer than 30 workers for 1971 and 1982. The absolute number of workers increased, although the ratio decreased slightly, but there were significant changes in composition. An overall decrease in self-employed individual proprietors and family workers took place solely in agriculture; the numbers increased in all other sectors. This occurred even though for tax and other reasons many SFEs incorporated themselves. Indeed, the total number of SFEs has risen significantly. Between 1960 and 1981, incorporated enterprises increased from 414,000 to 1,187,000; not surprisingly, almost all were small, but firms with fewer than ten employees accounted for over three-quarters of the increase.[14] Unincorporated enterprises also increased, from 3,467,000 in 1969 to 4,178,000 in 1981.[15] These are net figures; birth, growth, and death (or transformation) are treated later.

There are three kinds of participants in small-scale enterprise: self-employed owner-operators; family workers; and wage-earning em-

TABLE 1
Private Sector Employment by Form of Organization, Status, and Industry for
1-29 Workers, 1971 and 1982

Private sector employees[a]	1971			1982		
	Number (000)	Pct. of total workers	Pct. of industry workers[b]	Number (000)	Pct. of total workers	Pct. of industry workers
Self-employed						
Agriculture and forestry	3,790	8.1%	100%	2,420	4.6%	99.1%
Construction	716	1.5	100	873	1.7	99.7
Manufacturing	1,396	3.0	100	1,608	3.1	99.9
Wholesale and retail	2,162	4.6	100	2,393	4.5	99.7
Finance, insurance, and real estate	142	0.3	100	178	0.3	100.0
Transportation and communication	103	0.2	100	150	0.3	98.7
Services	1,393	3.0	100	1,725	3.3	99.8
Other	193	0.4	100	164	0.3	100.0
TOTAL	9,899	21.3%	100%	9,513	18.1%	99.8%
Family workers						
Agriculture and forestry	4,202	9.0%	100%	2,529	4.8%	99.9%
Construction	158	0.3	100	300	0.6	99.7
Manufacturing	654	1.4	100	633	1.2	99.4
Wholesale and retail	1,479	3.2	100	1,662	3.2	99.8
Finance, insurance, and real estate	25	—	—	47	0.1	100.0
Transportation and communication	22	—	—	32	0.1	97.0
Services	404	0.9	100	533	1.0	99.6
Other	132	0.4	100	164	0.3	100.0
TOTAL	7,076	15.2%	100%	5,856	11.1%	99.8%
Employees						
Agriculture and forestry	108[c]	0.2[c]	NA	178	0.3%	75.1%
Construction	1,717	3.7	55.1%	2,546	4.8	59.4
Manufacturing	2,910	6.3	24.8	3,394	6.4	28.3
Wholesale and retail	2,974	6.4	49.0	4,387	8.3	50.0
Finance, insurance, and real estate	189[c]	0.4[c]	NA	310	0.6	15.8
Transportation and communication	314[c]	0.7[c]	NA	516	1.0	17.5
Services	1,806	3.9	NA	2,915	5.5	44.5
Other	85[c]	0.2[c]	NA	118	0.2	24.2
TOTAL	10,103	21.7%	32.2%	14,365	27.3%	38.6%
GRAND TOTAL	27,078	58.2%	58.2%	29,734	56.5%	56.5%

SOURCES: Japan, Office of the Prime Minister, Bureau of Statistics, 1971 and 1982 Employment Status Survey.

[a] Includes part-time workers.

[b] Self-employed and family workers are assumed to be affiliated with firms having fewer than 29 workers.

[c] Estimated by applying a pro rata allocation from 1982 employment figures for the same industry.

ployees. Of the total labor force (57.8 million in 1982), some 15 per cent, almost all women, define themselves as working part-time (less than 200 days per year) with their main activities elsewhere, almost always in housework. More than four-fifths of part-timers work in very small enterprises. Further basic data on labor force allocation appear in Tables 2 and 3. We have already noted that over half of Japan's total labor force works in enterprises of fewer than 30 workers. The largest share (28.2 per cent) is in wholesale and retail trade, followed closely by agriculture (27.6 per cent), and then by services (16.0 per cent) and manufacturing.

Yet the most startling, and perhaps most distinctive, feature of Japan's SFEs is the immense share of minuscule enterprises with one to four workers (including the proprietor). Some 30.6 per cent of the total labor force works in minuscule units; since three-fifths of part-timers work in these enterprises, minuscule units account for a smaller share (12.3 million workers, 15.6 per cent) of full-time workers. Indeed, almost all the self-employed (93.7 per cent) and unpaid family workers (89.3 per cent) are in minuscule enterprises. Only one-fifth of the workers in minuscule

TABLE 2
Workers by Type of Organization and Scale of Enterprise, 1982
(thousands of persons)

| Category | Number of workers | | | | | |
	1-4	5-29	30-99	100-999	1,000+	Total
Private sector						
Unincorporated[a]						
Self-employed	8,931[b]	582	20	—	—	9,356[b]
Family workers	5,243	613	11	—	—	5,869
Employees	2,026	2,555	250	—	—	4,827
SUBTOTAL	16,201	3,754	271	—	—	20,232
Incorporated						
Directors and ordinary employees	1,216	6,728	4,860	6,803	6,478	26,100
Temporary and day workers	89	868	649	629	318	2,556
SUBTOTAL	1,305	7,597	5,509	7,432	6,796	28,656
Other organizations	208	674	700	1,061	1,108	3,754
TOTAL	17,719	12,027	6,457	8,520	7,906	52,691
Government services[c]	—	—	—	—	—	5,197
GRAND TOTAL	—	—	—	—	—	57,888

SOURCE: Japan, Office of the Prime Minister, Bureau of Statistics, *1982 Employment Status Survey—Whole Japan*, Table 4.
NOTE: Items do not sum to totals because a few workers are not reported by enterprise size.
[a]Unincorporated firms with 30 or more employees assumed to be in 30-99 category.
[b]Includes 1,072 pieceworkers at home (841 in manufacturing and 231 in services).
[c]Government service is not disaggregated by number of employees.

TABLE 3
*Private Sector Labor Force by Status, Industry, and
Scale of Enterprise, Small Firms, 1982*
(thousands of persons)

Industry	1-4	5-9	10-29	Subtotal, 1-29
Agriculture and forestry	4,930	146	54	5,130
Fisheries and aquaculture	270	48	87	380
Mining	7	11	24	43
Construction	1,576	978	1,166	3,720
Manufacturing	2,521	1,157	2,069	5,638
Wholesale and retail	4,990	1,729	1,725	8,444
Finance, insurance, and real estate	355	84	97	536
Transportation and communication	220	112	367	699
Electricity, gas, water, steam	0	0	2	2
Services	2,839	990	1,293	5,122
TOTAL	17,719	5,264	6,763	29,746

Industry	Subtotal, 1-99	Total	1-29 ÷ total	1-99 ÷ total
Agriculture and forestry	5,163	5,264	97.5%	98.1%
Fisheries and aquaculture	417	457	83.2	91.2
Mining	63	118	36.4	53.4
Construction	4,497	5,470	68.0	82.2
Manufacturing	7,880	14,255	39.6	55.2
Wholesale and retail	9,828	12,886	65.5	76.3
Finance, insurance, and real estate	665	2,207	24.3	30.1
Transportation and communication	1,185	3,576	19.5	33.1
Electricity, gas, water, steam	11	347	0.6	3.2
Services	6,448	11,193	45.8	57.6
TOTAL	36,203	52,691	56.4%	68.7%

SOURCE: Same as Table 2.
NOTE: Items do not sum to totals because a few workers are not reported by enterprise size.

enterprise are wage-earning employees. Such minuscule production units include almost all Japanese in agriculture (93.7 per cent) and 38.7 per cent of those in wholesale and retail trade. Some three-fifths of small businesses and four-fifths of retail stores are "home businesses" in which owner and family constitute more than half the labor force. Moreover, about one-fifth of small enterprisers engage in a secondary line of business; in rural areas a quarter of those are in farming or fishing, in urban areas "apartment rental is popular."[16]

Other important features of the small-scale family-enterprise sector are their sex and age compositions. Females are particularly concentrated in small enterprises. Four-fifths of the family workers are women. Almost one-third (3.0 million) of those classified as self-employed are women, and one-third of those do piecework at home at extremely low wages.[17] Even so, some 2 million women run their own enterprises. Almost a quarter of them are in agriculture, but many more are in services, especially those catering primarily to other women—Avon ladies, life insurance, and so on.[18] As Hill has shown, for married women the choice is not "to work or not to work," but threefold: to work as a wage-earning employee, to work in a family enterprise as an unpaid family member or as its proprietor, or to engage in housework.[19]

Other workers are also drawn to, or end up in, small-scale operations. One-third of workers age 55–64 are in minuscule (one to four workers) enterprises, as are almost half of those still working after 65. Minuscule enterprises have disproportionately more older workers and fewer younger workers; yet otherwise the age distribution by firm size does not vary greatly except for large firms, where young workers are disproportionately numerous. A far higher proportion of old people work in Japan than in other industrial nations.

Small-scale enterprises are dominant in terms of employment and of great importance in terms of output in agriculture, forestry, fisheries, construction, retail and wholesale trade, and personal services. They comprise a significant share of manufacturing[20] and a dominant share in many manufacturing industries. Wholesale and retail trade has the largest share (27.2 per cent) of SFE employment, followed by manufacturing (19.2 per cent), personal services (17.8 per cent), and agriculture (14.2 per cent).

Excluding agriculture, SFEs on average are substantively less productive than medium and large firms, which, with 30 per cent of the labor force, produce about half the GNP. The evidence is overwhelming that value added per worker and income per worker increases monotonically with enterprise size and that a substantial gap persists between the extremes of firm size. On the other hand, especially with tax evasion, the rate of return on capital may well be higher in smaller enterprises. In manufacturing in 1981, value added per worker in establishments of over 1,000 employees was 2.39 times that of a worker in establishments of 4–99 workers, though the wage gap was substantially narrower.

Nonetheless, over the past two decades, the growth in value added per worker in small enterprise has been at least as rapid as in large firms (the minuscule one-to-four-worker firms always constitute a special problem, not only of data but of comprehending the underlying reality). The initially wide gap in value added between large and small firms narrowed until the mid-1970s, but has widened subsequently. The similarly large gap in capital per worker also narrowed until 1975 and has continued to narrow since, albeit modestly. Wage differentials by firm size narrowed sharply from the late 1950s to the mid-1960s and leveled off until 1972–73, but they have since widened modestly. (See Bronfenbrenner and Yasuba, this volume.)

In sum, small business is not a lagging sector; on the whole, it is prosperous and healthy and growing as rapidly as the rest of the economy. But it is not correct to regard small business as the engine of GNP growth; it has not been the major source of R&D and innovation.[21] Nonetheless, SFEs do contribute significantly to growth—as the recipients of technological diffusion, as sources of on-the-job innovations, as active investors in new (and used) equipment, as major suppliers of consumer goods and services, and as flexible users and absorbers of most of the labor force.

Agriculture

Farming is a special and extreme case of small-scale family enterprise. Although in many respects it is very different from small-scale family enterprises in manufacturing and the tertiary sector, there are numerous reasons for some considerations of agriculture, especially for comparative purposes, since European and other countries also have policies to maintain family farms, however inefficient.

The two key factors making possible the continuation of so many family farms have been the farmer's ownership of his land and the government's policies of restraining import competition and of providing huge direct subsidies while allowing domestic agricultural prices to rise substantially.[22] In these respects agriculture stands in clear contrast to most other SFEs. The benefit to farmers has been high—rising incomes and growth in the value of their main asset: land. The benefit to the Liberal Democratic Party (LDP) has been a strong base of political support. Society in general has benefited from a more equal income distribution and a greater degree of food self-sufficiency. But the economic costs have been enormous, equivalent to more than half the value added in the agricultural sector. These have been borne by consumers and taxpayers. The costs include not only high prices for agricultural products but inefficient and excessive allocation of capital, land, and perhaps even labor. More efficient policy packages could achieve the same goals at substantially lower costs, but organized agriculture resists them since farmers know the benefits of the present system and fear that changes might undermine that commitment.

The basic economic problem is that major improvements in technology and financing and the rapidly increasing opportunity cost of labor have sharply enlarged the minimal size of family farms required for inter-nationally competitive production far beyond anything even contem-plated today in Japan. Achievement of optimal size (of competitiveness) is further impeded by Japan's mountainous terrain. By the criteria of world prices for agricultural products, much submarginal land is cur-rently in production. Land consolidation is impeded because land is overpriced. Since the renting of land confers de facto ownership rights, owners are unwilling to lease it. And since idle land is taxed at higher rates, farmers feel something should be grown. Farmers and others have rationally held land for speculative purposes, in the anticipation that land will increase in value more rapidly than other assets—reflecting, in part at least, a higher opportunity cost of land in some areas for fac-tories, office buildings, and housing, as well as lenient tax policies.

Yet in a social and political sense, agrarian policy has been remarkably successful. Rapid and sustained growth has made it inevitable that agri-culture became an uncompetitive, declining industry; labor and savings had to be absorbed elsewhere, and the costs of structural adjustment had to be borne. On the whole, the government has managed this process brilliantly. Income has been redistributed and equalized. The so-cial infrastructure has vastly improved, especially roads and transporta-tion to nearby towns and cities where jobs were being created by rapid growth. No economy has ever gone through so rapid a decline in the agrarian labor force as Japan has since 1955. Essentially all (97 per cent) of the new generation take nonfarm jobs; their parents now commute to nearby nonfarm jobs while continuing to live at home, reducing the de-mand for urban housing and infrastructure.

The problem is that government policy has gone too far. It raised agri-cultural prices and incomes too much and gave too many tax exemp-tions. It has retarded structural adjustment through crop diversification and land consolidation. Yet, rhetoric to the contrary, government policy toward agriculture has fundamentally changed from the late 1970s. The decision not to raise the government purchase price for rice (it has risen on average far less than the CPI since 1976) and to hold the line on sub-sidy payments while cutting back on acreage under cultivation has set the policy terms by which the attractiveness of farming will gradually but steadily decrease. The future of small family enterprise in agricul-ture is that of a economically inefficient, politically powerful sector about to embark on major generational change.

A crucial question is whether a similar pattern is or will be found in the case of those elements of small manufacturing and retailing that are declining. Given the numbers of people involved, this is indeed a signifi-cant political issue.

Manufacturing

We have already provided data demonstrating the important share of small family enterprises in manufacturing output and employment (see Tables 1 and 3). There are, of course, substantial differences by industry, depending on specific technology and capital-scale requirements. Not surprisingly, small enterprises predominate in labor-intensive industries. The popular view that most small-scale manufacturing involves specialized production or assembly of specific components or parts for much larger producers of final products for domestic or foreign markets is substantially true. Slightly more than three-fifths of SFE manufacturers are subcontractors. That means that almost two-fifths of the SFEs produce final products for domestic consumption or investment or for export markets. The share of direct exports in production by small and medium enterprises is only about 6.5 per cent;[23] however, firms producing exports specialize greatly in their specific export products.[24]

Several types of manufactures and organizations are often distinguished. Traditional goods (such as kimonos, lacquerware, paper fans) catering to predominantly Japanese tastes are one. The success of traditional goods industries depends on income, the price elasticities of domestic demand, and changes in tastes; exports are negligible, and the possibility of import competition limited. Products (including food products) that serve local or regional markets are another type. Small-scale producers for local markets face increasing competition, both from larger Japanese producers and from imports. A third type consists of labor-intensive modern products generated for the national market by geographically clustered SFEs. Handbags, pencils, toys, flatware, and printing are examples. Certain types of machinery are produced by small, or at most medium-size, enterprises.

A closer examination of several cases is instructive.[25] About 2,000 companies are listed as briefcase manufacturers, of which 80 per cent are located in Tokyo, primarily in two wards of the city. The average firm has seven workers. Some prepare and dye the leather; others make parts such as metal fittings. Central to the arrangements are coordinating contractors (*ton'ya*) who take orders, purchase materials, delegate the manufacturing, and manage the storage and shipping of the finished products. The actual construction of the briefcases goes to a "maker" firm that typically utilizes from 10 to 20 separate subcontractors for the majority of work involved. Most of these, in turn, circulate piecework to women to do at home (*naishoku*). All elements of the system are owner-operated businesses, with subcontractors being almost entirely minuscule family units comprising husbands and wives, occasionally with a relative or employee added. Nearly all produce at home. Hours are generally long (10–12 hours on busy days), but vary a good deal with the level of business. Gross sales figures also vary widely, but the average monthly income in 1976 was about ¥300,000 ($1,200) for subcontractors, which amounts at most to ¥1,000 ($4.00) per hour in a husband-wife operation, hardly better than the average wage level in the industry.

Briefcases could be manufactured in larger factories as a unitary operation. A larger piece of land would be required and a large, consolidated initial investment would be needed for equipment. A means of gathering and keeping labor with requisite specific skills, namely, an attractive employment system, would be necessary. All this would presumably require a high confidence in the size of initial demand.

Yet, since the variety of styles is great, briefcases are not manufactured by highly mechanized processes. The savings in production costs of consolidated, longer runs would amount to very little, whereas an operation under one roof would entail higher costs due to increased inflexibilities of labor utilization, greater pressure on wages, and greater investment costs. Moreover, in light of the preferential tax treatment of small SFEs, corporate profits taxes would undoubtedly be higher. The dispersion versus consolidation of processing steps raises the further issue of coordination and reliability. Can independent units keep in synchronization as styles, costs, and so forth shift? Can they remain part of a single system without unified ownership and management? The answer appears to be yes for many of these cluster industries.[26] New forms of labor-saving mechanization might make larger-scale units efficient; yet given the present arrangement, mechanization of individual steps in the process is accomplished by existing small firms (assuming loans and technical advice are available). A system of larger-company (bureaucratic) management would not benefit from the competition among suppliers that keeps costs down while delivering quality in each step of production.[27]

Once established, such "cluster" industries often go far in modernizing on the basis of integrated small-scale operations. In some instances, such as the flatware industry in Niigata Prefecture, the entire system has successfully shifted from one kind of metal product to another with the common threads being production technologies and the production network of participating families. An industry of this kind, once set down in history (tied to the land and socially organized), has strong incentives to adapt and unite to protect itself.

Their niches are often quite marginal, however, and are threatened by cheaper foreign imports and new manufacturing processes. Korea, Hong Kong, Taiwan, and Singapore, for example, are capable of making quality briefcases at wage rates roughly one-quarter of those in the Tokyo industry. Both kinds of threats create downward pressure on wages and costs in an already competitive industry, and the niches left to exploit are ones involving responsiveness to narrower, high-end market segments. Large-scale and foreign competition also creates pressure for government protection, intensified by the local density of cluster industries. Some medium-size cities, for example, depend almost entirely on a particular industry.

Although some small-scale industries are in decline, others are growing. From 1968 to 1978, the number of metal-fabricating machine shops with four or fewer workers increased in Tokyo by 62 per cent, and larger shops (those with ten or more workers) declined by nearly 25 per cent. The industry's ten-year growth resulted almost entirely from the creation of nearly 5,000 new SFEs in Toyko. How did this occur, and why was growth primarily in the smallest-scale segment of the industry?

Most small machine shops develop in small incremental steps. Experienced individual operators typically first shift to subcontracting for their former employers, often borrowing space and machinery from him to accomplish this. The next stage is to move into separate rented space (often in another machine shop). Used machinery can be bought on relatively accommodating terms, but an independent space rental involves "key money" (typically equivalent to ten months' rent). As business expands, an employee and a second machine may be taken on. If expansion continues, the point will be reached when the entrepreneur, in turn, agrees to set up one of his employees as a subcontractor.

Why would he want to do this? It is difficult to keep skilled workers satisfied in this industry after they have six to eight years of experience. Limited wage increases and growing skill create a strong desire for independence. There are also severe space limitations to consider since the average factory size is but 25–40 square meters. To make a virtue of necessity, owners help the spin-out process in hopes of gaining benefits from the continuing relationship. That is, "offspring" companies form part of the "parent's" network through which new orders and valuable information are exchanged; frequently the parent entrepreneur serves as a broker for new orders, guaranteeing the product's reliability and delivery date and receiving a fee for his services.

The notable point is that productive efficiency is not apparently affected by the overall scale of the operation. Whether there is one machine or many does not matter. What matters is the operator's skill and whether more expensive, more efficient machines will drive out such a small-scale approach. If loans are available and demand is steady, there is little that precludes such minute subcontractors from acquiring the new machines. However, a higher initial investment will necessarily mean higher barriers to entry. It follows that stable production technologies bring down the barriers to small-scale entry in forms of manufacturing that involve separate small processes. Equally important are the ways social ties and an initially minuscule starting point keep the barriers to entry low for insiders.

The basic question concerning SFE subcontractors for large assembly firms is their extensiveness. The question strikes at the heart of industrial organization, at issues of organization versus market, of factor market imperfections, and of technological innovation and dissemination. (These issues are also addressed in the papers in this volume by Aoki and Uekusa.)

About 60 per cent of Japan's small manufacturers exist primarily on parts production (or subassembly) for larger design, assembly, and marketing companies. As such, they are quasi-independent members of large, complex systems typically involving many subcontracting companies of varying sizes gathered around a central large company. Although subcontracting is found in every economy and is common to a broad range of products, in Japan subcontracting is notable for (1) its extensive role in a large number of industries, (2) its highly evolved character, and (3) its capacity to adapt to rapid technological change. All of this implies comparative efficiency.[28]

Subcontracting relationships run from the simple (a one-time agreement to supply a component part at a fixed price between two firms that have no other relations) to the complex (an ongoing, cooperative relationship centering on the creation of products of a particular type at prices and terms that are periodically renegotiated, in which the two firms' personnel regularly interact over many functional areas including cost control, design engineering, finance, manufacturing engineering, and R&D in a manner approaching cooperative efforts internal to a single firm). Japanese subcontracting is impressive in its inclination to and its capacity for highly complex, "evolved" relationships, ones that presumably generate higher levels of efficiency, over longer time periods, by taking advantage of many complementarities between the contracting and subcontracting firm (or, more often, many subcontracting firms). Particularly in the more complex relationships, labor costs differentials are but one reason for the use of subcontracting.

The basic complementarities involved are (1) manufacturing specialization versus design and marketing specialization; (2) specialization within production technology; (3) investment specialization in production equipment; (4) R&D specialization; (5) different labor costs; (6) differentials in overhead costs; (7) different capacities for flexibility and change (staffing, systems, low-volume product runs); and (8) different financing advantages (including access to financial markets, extended and at times flexible payment terms, and shifts in inventory burdens). Small subcontracting manufacturers survive by exchanging one or more of these complementary advantages with a total subcontracting system. The more developed the arrangement, the greater the potential for more kinds of complementarities.

There are, at the same time, many arm's-length aspects and contractual protections involved in subcontracting relationships (see Uekusa, this volume). Information sharing is far from perfect, and risk management necessitates some price and quality guarantees over extended periods when large investments are involved.

How well large companies manage their subcontracting network has become a major aspect of competition.[29] The proportion of external manufacturing costs has risen well above 50 per cent for many important products (for example, electronics, autos). Close cooperation is necessary in the design stage, and managerial leadership is needed to effect systemwide changes and cost improvements.

The best management strategy when the capacity of production is great and the product is constantly changing appears to differ considerably from country to country. In Japan the tendency has been to create a deepening bond with suppliers, allowing for closer cooperation and supervision. Assemblers have avoided high fixed costs, but they have also grown dependent on external supply systems. The Japanese basically chose to seek efficiencies of a long-term relational kind rather than to maximize market efficiencies in which many arm's-length suppliers compete in what are essentially spot markets. This has meant that the capacity to maximize coordination between firms is a major management skill. The entrepreneurial activity of small suppliers is encouraged within a narrowly defined context, one determined and guided by the larger firms. Coordinated interdependence results in the creation of value that makes both parties more independent in other markets.

The Japanese government measures the subcontracting system in a number of ways that highlight its notable qualities. It asks about the number and weight of important customers in total sales. The weight of a parent firm or firms in the world of each subcontractor indicates the character of the relationship.

Two-thirds of the smallest manufacturing enterprises—those with one to three employees—engage in subcontracting, and for them the significance of a single "parent" firm is overwhelming.[30] Eighty per cent of their production goes to one customer. We can best imagine operations as if they were based in a family, with the entire operation oriented to manufacturing since a single parent takes virtually all the output. Overhead and labor costs are low (and also difficult to determine accurately because of the family basis of operations). In many cases, the parent firm supplies raw materials, designs, and even machinery and technical advice. The existence of tiny subcontractors of this kind, in other words, is a highly dependent one; yet the enterprise has some degree of autonomy in the areas of technical learning and cost management and thus some control over its profitability. In many instances, however, even these areas are supervised by the parent firm. Yet, since healthy subcontractors are a goal of parent firms, a well-run subcontractor can gain more autonomy and more business over time through good performance.[31] Moreover, since minuscule subcontractors use relatively general-purpose equipment, the barriers to going to a different parent firm are low. This sets a competitive level to profits below which a parent may find it difficult to push its supplier for any sustained period of time.

Most subcontracting enterprises begin with some form of patronage in the form of an initial sales base (and other technical and financial assistance). This social asset determines the real level of initial risk. It is not a permanent form of security, but it induces risk taking on the part of people with little means and modest skills. Insight into future development is a matter more of affinity with larger players than a product of independent calculation. Start-ups apparently occur by a number of mechanisms: a manufacturing employee may be encouraged to set up as a supplier; a trading firm or other go-between may promise initial business; or a parent firm may seek out an individual in order to establish a needed supplier. Large firms devote much time to developing new subcontracting links. In all such instances, relational qualities are prior and initially dominant, and the dependence of the subcontractor is high.

Business growth brings with it greater autonomy and a shifting balance among the factors of production. Among manufacturing subcontractors with 4–9 employees, only 40 per cent report selling to only one parent firm; a mere 20 per cent of those with 50–99 employees have only one main customer. On the other hand, the number of reported parents increases. Most larger subcontractors (those with 50–100 employees) have succeeded in establishing themselves as integral elements of the manufacturing systems of four to eight larger parent firms. We must assume they achieved this position by their competence in a technology, their overall efficiency, and their ability to integrate well with the needs of more than one parent firm. Along the way they have developed increased proprietary technology and capacities to protect or increase profitability. One form of this capacity is innovative cost reductions within longer-term supply contracts.

A process of growth and transformation can be seen in this pattern. Tiny subcontractors that master a technology and manage costs can grow as a result of the specialized competence they achieve. In time this can also mean that they gain advantages based on their investment in specialized production equipment. In turn, these make the subcontractor more attractive to other parent companies. Growth also hinges on the successful management of increasingly complex labor, financial, and other inputs. Accountability (for product and profits) has, in effect, been shifted to the lowest levels of the production process. Every step is its own profit center and subject to the market. If performance becomes unsatisfactory, there is no guarantee of continuing in business. Changes in technology or market demand can make a subcontractor obsolete. What is notable are the numerous instances in which a parent firm helps a subcontractor of basic worth to achieve greater efficiency or convert to supplying a different product. By growing and diversifying, subcontractors begin to manage more of the risk and attendant possibilities for gain themselves.

Small subcontractors, like other smaller firms, do not offer long-term security of employment and are much less inclined to offer special benefits. Flexibility in staffing (including a greater reliance on family and part-timers) and great caution in making any investments other than those for production equipment also characterize these firms. Attempting to gain autonomy quickly by engaging in new areas or by emphasizing independent sales is quite uncommon. The emphasis is on the development of production technology. On the parent side, the pattern is to cultivate a stable of strong subcontractors as a means of borrowing their strengths without incurring the fixed costs that doing the same work internally would entail.

Large firms have unions that defend not only permanent employment, but a seniority-based wage system and many benefits for both blue- and white-collar employees. Large firms thus have rather inflexible labor costs and other fixed overhead costs. In many instances it takes them a long time to develop in-house expertise, given their reluctance to hire mature skills on the open market. Such employment inflexibilities favor a major role for subcontracting. As the age profile of large firms matures (a common phenomenon, given both slower growth and the aging of the population as a whole), assembly firms adapt by increasing subcontracting (as well as by automating and rearranging seniority pay). Since 1973, total manufacturing employment in Japan has dropped by about 10 per cent, and the proportion of manufacturing stemming from the small and medium sector has increased. Most of this rationalization thus appears to result from large-scale enterprises' cutting staff and resorting to subcontracting.

Retailing

The single largest category of SFEs in Japan is retailing. Small stores constitute 29 per cent of all businesses with four or fewer workers; when agricultural households are excluded, the proportion of stores in the total rises to about 35 per cent. Indeed, most retail stores are very small, with few workers and low sales per worker.[32] Compared with other advanced industrial societies, Japan has far and away the highest number of retail outlets per capita, with nearly twice as many relative to population as the United States, West Germany, France, or England, and low productivity in distribution. Like agriculture, Japanese distribution appears to be seriously inefficient. Retailing is filled with underemployed workers who in other societies might well be unemployed. Finally, being so numerous, shopkeepers are a significant political force. About as many families today own shops as own farms. If there is a populist focus in the next decade's electorate, it will be retailers.

The distribution networks are complicated by extensive wholesaler chains. In some industries manufacturers maintain exclusive dealerships that handle only their products. For example, of the some 7,000 retail outlets selling consumer electronic goods, about 5,000 are integrated into the exclusive distribution system ("distribution" *keiretsu*) of particular manufacturers.[33] They try to offset the lower prices of high-volume outlets such as department stores and discount houses by locational advantage and by intensively providing repair and other services.

The majority of shops are quite small.[34] Eighty-five per cent of all stores have fewer than six workers. Sixty per cent have only one or two workers, implying that no one outside the family is involved. The place of very small stores in total retailing is slowly decreasing, but it remains central to any discussion of Japanese small business.

What patterns characterize family shops? Three-quarters of one- and two-person operations are located in the family residence. Even among shops with between 10 and 20 workers, 30 per cent of the owners live on the premises. In most instances husbands and wives work together. Most shops originate when the husband and/or wife are in their thirties or forties, the early thirties being the most common age. The usual intent is for the shop to be a long-term proposition. But a sizable minority (about one-quarter) are oriented initially to income production in the retirement years. In one large survey, 26 per cent of shopkeepers gave security in old age as a reason for opening a store and 10 per cent mentioned the impending retirement of the husband. If we add to this the unmarried and widowed women running shops (2 to 3 per cent of the total), we can see the role of small retailing in personal planning for old age. Fully one-quarter of all owner-operators are over 60 years old.

Although only one-quarter of the listed owner-operators are female, surveys show that most wives put in long hours in the shop. Four out of five women operators are married, but their husbands tend to have other jobs. Women tend to run stores oriented to female customers. Entrepreneurship among middle-aged women is not uncommon. As a means of supplementing family income, it is preferred to low-status part-time work for a large company. Given a solid base of social contacts as a customer base, female entrepreneurs are often in excellent positions to build up small businesses while their husbands continue as wage earners. In the event of considerable success, husbands may shift to managing part of the wife's business.[35] On the other hand, wives of shopkeepers typically adjust the degree of their assistance to childrearing and housekeeping demands. The combination of spousal labor input shifts over the life cycle, with business and family needs being periodically readjusted. The notable point is the great flexibility of the system as long as the SFE is part of the residential arrangement. Also, some 20 per cent of married women working in family enterprises become wage-earning employees elsewhere as their children grow up.[36]

Obviously the role of the store in total household income varies greatly. Surveys indicate that about half of the unincorporated stores (typically one to four workers) provide at least 50 per cent of the household income and one-tenth of the smallest shops provide under 10 per cent of the total. One competitive advantage is that small stores can and do keep long hours; the hours of large stores are legally restricted. Even so, only 20 per cent of small stores report utilizing part-time hired labor.

The reported average gross sales for all unincorporated retail and wholesale operations in 1982 was about ¥21.5 million ($86,000). We assume that wholesale operations inflate this average, but underreporting probably also deflates it. From this sales base, an annual average net profit of ¥3,462,000 ($13,848) was reported in 1982. The profit/sales ratio of 15 per cent is before the "wages" of family workers are calculated. If we assume that on average one and a half family workers are engaged in the business and allocate the profits as labor income for the year, the return would come to about ¥700 or $2.80 per hour (assuming ten hours a day, 330 days a year). This return is somewhat above wages paid female part-timers by large firms and further above those paid by the smaller firms in which women are more likely to find employment. An implicit hourly wage of ¥550 would leave only $2,950 as return to capital and entrepreneurial profits. However, sales and net income are typically underestimated substantially, and our assumptions may overstate the actual hours of work. No clear judgment can be made. Estimates of the efficiency or inefficiency of distribution in Japan obviously rest on the value of the labor input in family-based retailing. Is the high-quality service but low value added the retail industry's analogue to a technically efficient but economically inefficient system of agriculture (with far higher subsidization of output and incomes in the latter)?

A calculation of the actual return to owner-operators is complicated by other factors: (1) the household residence (or part of it) is carried as a business expense, (2) shop goods may be an unaccounted form of income, (3) sales and profits may be underreported for tax purposes (the average total tax payment for all unincorporated wholesale and retail establishments was only ¥182,000 [$728] annually, and most of this was probably paid by the larger unincorporated businesses in the sample), (4) the purpose of some stores may be more to protect claims on land and to maintain advantageous property tax arrangements than to generate current income, and (5) an important objective may be to continue the present occupation and way of life, as long as income remains at a comfortable level.

Surveys find that roughly half of all shops were founded by their present manager-owners; the rest were inherited. Eighty-five per cent of the successors are family or relatives; the remainder are former employees. The buying or selling of retail businesses is not common, and one in five owners say they do not intend the shop to continue past their tenure, giving as reasons the low status of the work and declining sales and income. Indeed, there probably is little of value to sell other than the land itself. Another 30 per cent would like to see their stores remain in operation, but as yet have no successor. An interesting pattern is that children are not raised to succeed to the shop, but are encouraged to set their sights on higher education and employment in larger firms. Yet, as the parents reach their late fifties and early sixties, succession becomes a serious issue, and some children do return.

Why the High Proportion of Small Businesses?

The preceding description has suggested various explanations for Japan's relatively high proportion of small businesses, a subject to which we now turn. Two caveats are in order. First, any hypothesis here is in principle comparative and properly should be considered through careful investigation of leading Western economies; however, comparative data and studies are slim at best, and our comparisons are unfortunately more implicit than explicit. Second, satisfactory explanations will differ by economic sector and by particular industry. Many useful generalizations have inevitable exceptions.

We propose a broad, syncretic model (or framework) through which to understand small-scale family enterprise behavior and performance. It is a model of demand and supply, but includes more than the standard factor and output markets. The small enterpriser has his own mixture of skills, labor, ownership of land and capital, network of social connections, and entrepreneurial drive and ambition. He utilizes family resources and hires resources (labor, capital, land) in factor markets. A market niche is essential for selling his product. Friends and relatives are the traditional and most important form and source of venture capital, social as well as financial. We probably cannot overestimate the importance of social networks and personal contacts—the conveying of information and the conferring of patronage—in making markets function effectively for SFEs. That many markets—for sales and for inputs— are mediated by personal and social relationships implies that long-term contacts (implicit or explicit) are the main way of doing business for Japanese SFEs. All this takes place in a changing external environment shaped by general economic conditions, government policies, and Japan's cultural heritage.

We assume small-scale enterprises and their workers behave rationally in the classic economic sense: they have a sense of their own self-interest and try to maximize it. However, self-interest is neither entirely individualistic nor entirely materialistic (that is, maximization of income and wealth over some life cycle); it is largely defined in the context of the family's well-being. Survey data suggest that Japanese start an enterprise for a wide range of reasons—not just to obtain a job or to generate income and wealth; but to be one's own boss; to utilize and develop one's perceived talents, knowledge, and skills; to utilize existing assets (experience, land, connections); to capitalize on existing networks as well as to build and enhance a network of relationships valued in its own right;[37] and so forth. They also choose to stay in economically marginal businesses for reasons that reflect the importance of other satisfactions; frequently mentioned are the social ties in an industry and a neighborhood.

The substantial and persisting differences between smaller and larger production units in output, real capital, and wages per worker present an ongoing analytical puzzle for understanding the structure and performance of the Japanese economy. Terms such as "dual economy," "dual structure," and "differential structure" have become value-laden phrases that incorporate a number of stereotypes and myths. They imply the exploitation by large firms of cheap labor located in smaller firms through factor market imperfections; and they imply that the persistence of smaller firms is primarily a lagged consequence of technical, educational, and financial imbalances in a rapidly changing economy and society. The inequalities, in other words, are neither voluntary nor efficient. The symbiotic rise of subcontracting in manufacturing in the postwar period has been explained mainly in terms of these market imperfections and scale differentials. In the postwar era of rapid growth, "unskilled labor surplus" dualism gave way to big business capitalism that shares oligopolistic rents derived from superior technology and relatively cheap capital with unionized regular (male) employees. The small-scale sector was seen as the passive but flexible absorber of redundant or less qualified labor, which, in order to exist, offset limited access to and expensive cost of capital (even adjusted for default risk) and lesser command over technology by the payment of even cheaper wages (relative to labor quality).

In our view, "economic dualism" has become an outmoded phrase because the underlying economic conditions that determined the terms of the dual-structure analysis have changed substantially over the past two decades. We see on the one hand an erosion of traditional dualistic features, but on the other hand the growth in importance of new imperfections. We also find great economic interdependence among small, medium, and large enterprises and increasingly complex interactions in the sphere of public economic policy. Interdependence goes far beyond subcontracting relationships or sales networks; it permeates the economy in the standard input-output sense of interindustry relations. Further, as well as producing its own products, each category of enterprise generates labor and profit income used to purchase the products of others.

To succeed, the small-scale entrepreneur must have certain special assets to produce specific goods or services and a market in which to sell them. In some output markets, he has to compete both with SFEs of his own size and with much larger firms, which are likely to have superior technology, superior access to labor skills and cheap capital, or other inputs that make them cost competitive. Larger Japanese firms, on the other hand, often choose to work with, rather than compete directly with, smaller firms in a wide range of activities. This is part of the phenomenon of competition across groups in which competing larger firms organize sets of medium and smaller firms in manufacturing and, to a lesser extent, in retailing. We find that most smaller enterprisers work in a complex but generally supportive economic, sociocultural, and political environment in which most competition is between enterprises of similar scale. While we attempt to generalize, we must always recall that we are dealing with a huge number of specific micro-contexts, with persons of differing and on occasion idiosyncratic characteristics, and that random events (luck or stochastic processes, depending on one's way of perceiving destiny) often are important determinants of outcomes. The unusually large number of Japanese SFEs is a product of numerous factors that appear *in degree* to distinguish the Japanese situation.

Entrepreneurship: Historical, Social, and Cultural Perspectives

The long-standing proportion and centrality of small businesses to the economy is itself a basic, if tautological, consideration. There is no better nursery for small business than being raised in a small-business environment.[38] Small-scale farming, family entrepreneurship, and business networking are not recent developments, and yet in many nations they have not adapted well to modern requirements; Japan's adaptation of these social forms to the requirements of a modern economy is notable. Furthermore, despite the draining off of a large percentage of the working population into large organizations with higher status, the pool of entrepreneurs has apparently not diminished. In the midst of this century's rapid and profound sectoral shifts, the small-scale element has remained, as the children of farmers, artisans, and shopkeepers have populated manufacturing and new service industries.

How Japan produces its petite bourgeoisie is worth noting. The crucial points include the near absence of sociocultural barriers and the large supply of people who have small business experience before they are 30. Japan has few minorities, and they find niches in specialized small businesses. Ethnicity is not a barrier to them in small business, only in large.

The average Japanese is also highly educated by cross-national standards.[39] Insufficient education can be a significant barrier to the generation of small businesses, especially in an advanced economy where such characteristics as illiteracy, poor work habits, or an inability to grasp technological or business complexities preclude successful entrepreneurship. The high average level of education in Japan assures the society a large pool of well-trained potential entrepreneurs and helps explain the relatively small percentage of incompetent ("unemployable") workers in the labor pool. This benefits small business. Since educational performance is an important means to the realization of career aspirations, the educational system, especially at the high school level, serves to sort out career options and to shape expectations. Concurrently, family characteristics (occupation, educational level, income level) and personalities play a strong role in defining options.

Welfare and employment policies that increase insecurity about old age also play a role by (1) encouraging self-help, (2) inducing workers to work even for low wages, and (3) causing people to view entrepreneurship as a means to greater security in retirement. Big businesses do not hire mid-career job changers, and their early retirement programs throw out many people who wish to continue to work. The still limited level of government as well as private retirement benefits have, thus far at least, offered relatively little income security even for the retired employees of large firms. (See, however, Bronfenbrenner and Yasuba, this volume.) The extension of life expectancy and the reduction of three-generation families because of urbanization are parallel trends that add to the overall level of insecurity, an insecurity that motivates participation in the small business sector since there is nowhere else to go.

Social Networks

Social connections (relatives, friends, former schoolmates, former employers, industry colleagues, and neighbors) are an important means of minimizing information costs and of reducing the uncertainties of unreliability, incompetence, or fraud. In Japan, social relationships are regularly mentioned as key ingredients of start-up businesses. They provide the initial demand for a product or service and help secure other assets. Patronage of this sort can provide capital or access to it, access to markets, and access to others with needed connections. Even as the small enterpriser seeks independence, he or she is often very dependent on the personal goodwill and support of others. Enterprisers assiduously cultivate personal networks as an economic asset. What distinguishes Japan is the regularity with which social networking and small business interact for such large segments of the population. Just as jobs often are not allocated solely by impersonal processes, so business opportunities, small-scale investments, and other assistance are channeled along social networks. Where small enterprise is an accepted framework for new developments, it is commonplace for social networks to provide assets and opportunities that increase their vitality. These social assets alone are not sufficient to generate business success. Without good service and a competitive price, personal relations and connections alone cannot enable many small businesses to survive, but they enhance the opportunity to compete in particular niches.

Market niches are the sine qua non for most small businesses, and specialization is the adaptive response. As discussed above, many traditional manufactures are conducted by clusters of tiny symbiotic units, each occupying a functional role in processes that elsewhere might fall under the roof of a single firm. In retailing and wholesaling, small operators typically occupy either locational niches or differentiate themselves by products in ways that make them competitive other than by price alone. For many services, locational advantages are important; so, too, are customized, personalized service and, indeed, a high level of customer service. The demand for certain types of "customized" products is also worth noting (components for ambulances, for example). Small producers can achieve efficiencies of scale by long production runs of a single item, such as eyes for fishing rods or hands and dial faces for wristwatches. In consumer markets, local brand differentiation has always been important, especially in food products. The point here is that as prosperity encourages increased social complexity, it creates opportunities that can be met by small-scale entrepreneurs if they are available and barriers to entry are not prohibitive. On the other hand, new products have transformed some industries to the acute disadvantage of SFE producers; Coca-Cola, for example, replaced hundreds of small local bottlers.

Finally, there is no question that as an economic unit and a nexus for human social relations, the cooperative, working household (*ie*) is a deep-seated part of Japanese culture. Not only is it a product of Japan's Confucian heritage and hundreds of years of ideological emphasis as the key metaphor for Japanese morality, but modern popular media have regularly idealized the small, family-run business as the place where work and human affection can find a proper balance. Japanese culture and history provide fundamental patterns of thought, value, and action that encourage small business. Such issues are difficult, at best, to deal with on a comparative basis, and we suggest only that without such a base of positive factors, the number and vitality of SFEs in Japan would be less. Together, these cultural and historical factors add a dimensional richness to the significant economic factors supportive of a vigorous small-scale family enterprise sector.

These considerations suggest the hypothesis that Japan will continue to generate a comparatively large proportion of small businesses simply by virtue of its history and sociocultural patterns and that only where larger-scale production is more efficient and competitively superior and government protection insufficient will the share of small-scale activities decline. Japanese do not enter small business with an expectation of failure, nor are they only in business to make a better return than their skills would earn in the employ of larger firms. They engage in small businesses and patronize small businesses by choice, and this preference has a foundation in historical patterns as well as in economic opportunity.

Support, albeit untestable, for this hypothesis comes from the fact that, despite enormous economic transformation, small-business activity has not substantially decreased in the postwar era. As agriculture has declined, small-scale activities and employment in manufacturing and services have grown proportionally. The immense productivity gains in manufacturing have been responsible for overall growth and now quite high levels of income and thus have supported the employment shift between the primary and other sectors. The role of small-scale manufacturing has not diminished in the course of productivity growth within the manufacturing sector. In no other advanced industrial nation has this occurred, and this leads to questions (alternative hypotheses) of a more particular kind regarding factor market efficiencies (especially in manufacturing) and, of course, government protection.

Factor Markets

The basic structure and evolving characteristics of markets for labor, capital (finance), and land provide both opportunities and obstacles for small-scale family enterprises. Labor markets and wage differentials by firm size have been studied voluminously since they are core themes in the dual-structure analysis. The higher cost and lesser availability of finance for small firms relative to large firms has received less attention, and the nature and implications of the markets for land and rights to its use have scarcely been analyzed at all.

We cannot analyze any of these markets in detail here; fortunately, labor markets and financial markets are treated in the papers by Koike and by Hamada and Horiuchi. Nonetheless, we do have a point of view about the special effect of each of these factor markets on SFEs in Japan today. They can be stated, rather baldly, in three hypotheses.

1. Certain wage differentials do provide a special opportunity for SFEs, but not in the labor markets usually analyzed; rather, special pools of abundant, productive, low-wage labor are available—notably middle-aged married females, workers over 55 separated (retired) from larger firms; workers desiring part-time employment, and workers in remote or inconvenient locales.

2. Any higher costs of capital (borrowed funds) to SFEs now reflect essentially only differences in default risk, collateral, and transactions costs; the historic high interest rate differential in excess of competitive costs has now disappeared.

3. SFEs' access to land through ownership or long-term lease at below-market rental rates provides a special opportunity, given the widespread distribution of landownership and tenant rights, both urban and rural.

Labor. Much attention has been devoted to explaining the substantial differentials in wages, bonuses, and fringe benefits for male employees by firm size—the Japanese dual labor market.[40] Earlier explanations centered on labor market imperfections, notably the industrial relations system in large firms of entry-level hiring, so-called permanent employment, and seniority-based promotion and wage increases (*nenkō*). Paternalistic or other noneconomic reasons were given for the creation and development of these institutions, and "culture" was invoked without specifying variables or causal mechanisms.

Others have sought more direct economic explanations of the phenomenon. Several neo-classically based theoretical arguments have been advanced, although so far empirical testing has been limited. There is evidence that part of the increasing wage differential with seniority is payment for investment (by large firms and their workers) in the development of firm-specific skills needed for particular technologies.[41] A second argument, supported by the extensive use of entrance examinations and interviews for the hiring of both blue-collar and white-collar entrants, is that large firms select the more able and better motivated within each educational cohort; accordingly, unequal pay reflects unequal quality even after adjustment is made for education, age, occupation, industry, and gender. A more recent theoretical contribution is that large firms have greater monitoring costs to keep workers motivated and prevent them from shirking on the job—and one way to monitor is to pay higher wages and to get rid of those caught shirking.[42] Further, a considerable amount of research shows that turnover is greater than the stereotype implies, with considerable differences by age, education, and status.

A quite different strand of analysis emphasizes that almost all Japanese empirical research is limited to comparisons of full-time male employees in large and small firms, but the significant wage differentials are the consequences of discrimination, especially against women, older persons, and ethnic minorities. Discrimination occurs at three sequentially more subtle levels: entry-level wages for the same or comparable work; occupational segmentation and exclusion; and institutionally generated differential access to opportunities to develop on-the-job skills.

With rapid growth, changing industrial structure, higher productivity and wage levels, and increasing levels of education, labor market conditions have evolved considerably on both the demand and supply sides. The steepness of seniority-age wage profiles has flattened somewhat. Over time the wage gap by firm size for average workers comparable in age, education, gender, and experience has narrowed for all age groups, and the difference as of 1983 was only about 10 per cent (except for older workers).[43] Therefore, the much larger gap in actual average wage is due to heterogeneity of labor within a common base and to a substantial degree of labor noncomparability between large and small firms. Small firms disproportionately hire less educated, female, or older workers as well as those who did less well at school. Starting wages are now higher in small firms than in large ones in all sectors, but wage increments and lifetime earnings are substantially lower.

Kazuo Koike argues in this volume that Japan's labor markets are not dualistic, at least no more so than those of Western Europe.[44] He asserts that the Japanese pattern of wage differentials for male employees of comparable age, education, and experience by firm size follows the Western European pattern except for blue-collar male workers and that the blue-collar differential is due to the even greater on-the-job training that male workers receive in large Japanese firms. He also argues that male workers are paid more than female workers in all firm sizes because of greater skills developed through on-the-job training. For Koike, Japan's labor markets are neo-classical: wage differentials reflect skill and hence productivity differentials.

A different approach asserts that oligopolistic large firms pay higher wages than required in order to maintain labor peace and good relations with the enterprise union. Large firms earn quasi rents through technological prowess and, in some industries, through the exercise of market power; employees capture part of those rents through union power.

In a bargaining process (see the paper by Aoki), management allocates profits to employees, major (financial) institutional stockholders and financiers, and individual stockholders. Permanent, regular (predominantly male) employees receive seniority-related high wages and bonuses, extensive fringe benefits, and large lump-sum retirement benefits and work shorter hours for which, in turn, they work reasonably hard, develop skills assiduously, propose improvements, and maintain labor peace.

By screening out certain groups and by retiring workers early (before they want or can afford to stop working), large firms create large pools of certain kinds of labor available at lower wage rates. Deeply embedded institutional rigidities in hiring, firing, and retiring result in de facto occupational, promotion, and career segregation, which is reinforced—particularly in the case of females—by social values and the socialization process.

Two major pools of underutilized labor are thereby created: middle-aged, married females who re-enter the labor force after years away for bearing and rearing children and males over age 55 who have been forced to retire from large firms but wish to continue working. A third category overlaps these two groups—namely, those seeking part-time employment and scheduling flexibility. Many part-timers are middle-aged women or older workers, but this group includes college students and younger women with small children. Smaller pools of labor are also tapped, including persons residing in less developed (lower-wage) rural regions and minority ethnic groups. It is the very heterogeneity of labor supply, combined with institutional rigidities in education, socialization, and large firms' employment systems, that provides SFEs access to relatively low wage labor.

However, the essential issue is not low wage rates per se, but that for several reasons productivity differentials appear to be narrower than wage differentials for these differentiated pools of underutilized labor. On the supply side, holding quality constant, the preferences, age, gender, geographic location, and other characteristics of workers do not match fully the large employers' demand for labor. The screening and retention process of large firms is not perfect: certain types of labor are screened out, or cast out, regardless of ability, and, of course, others are mistakenly hired. There is a wide range of tasks where ascriptive variables such as education, age, or even intelligence probably have only modest correlation with productivity. To be on the safe side, large firms may simply overpay for certain attributes since they find it difficult to measure individual productivity. (In contrast, SFEs are likely to have a much better sense of individual capabilities and productivity.) For many labor-intensive jobs such as assembly operations, skills are learned relatively easily and quickly.

The large employers' rationale for retiring older workers at a relatively early age, given health and projected life spans, is that the seniority wage structure makes them expensive relative to their current productivity. Yet older workers do not lose all their skills, nor do those skills become fully obsolete, when they retire from large firms and move into small ones. Moreover, labor laws (including fringe benefit requirements) are not seriously applied to SFEs. Although wage rates of other workers on average are much lower than those in the 50–55 age group, this may be a problem of composition; few old persons work in large firms. Lower wages no doubt reflect lower productivity, but tasks assigned to older workers may not take full advantage of their skills. This is a topic that will be of increasing importance as the aging of the population leads to more and more working old persons.

More attention has focused recently on the large wage differentials between males and females, especially in the 30–55 age group. Middle-aged, married females re-entering the labor force are paid about the same as young, single females. The female-male wage differential (54.1 per cent in 1981) is far greater than in other industrial countries; the ratio (1980) is 66 per cent in the United States and 70–90 per cent in Western Europe.[45] Koike's explanation that this results from differences in skill based on experience is not fully satisfying, in part because women are never provided the opportunity to develop appropriate skills. Moreover, Yashiro found that 54 per cent of the female-male wage differentials was due to human capital (46.8 per cent to work experience, 7.2 per cent to educational level), leaving an unexplained residual of 46 per cent.[46] Kawashima has addressed these issues directly. She analyzes blue-collar and white-collar wages in concentrated industries in terms of worker characteristics (such as education and work experience) and labor market structure (sex discrimination). She finds that for blue-collar female workers sex discrimination explains 78 per cent of the wage differential in competitive sectors and 65 per cent in concentrated sectors, and for white-collar female workers 28 per cent in competitive sectors and 86 per cent in concentrated sectors.[47]

Although more women work full time than part time in all age categories, women constitute 93 per cent of all part-time workers, more than half (55 per cent) of them in the 35–54 age group. Labor costs of part-time workers to employers, overwhelmingly SFEs, are much lower than for full-time workers. For example, in 1980 a woman working six hours per day received an hourly wage rate 24 per cent below that of a comparable full-time worker.[48] Moreover, part-time employees receive little, if anything, in bonuses and fringe benefits and require less in employer social security contributions. Women constitute a vast reservoir of low-cost labor. Although more than half of married women work, more than 8 million women (and 2 million men) not employed desire to work (mainly part time), although most are not actively seeking a job and do not show up in unemployment statistics.[49] Most housewives are motivated by straightforward economic goals: to supplement household income, to support the household, and to add to savings. Personal development and career goals are not strong motivations.[50]

In our view, labor market discrimination, broadly defined, against women and older persons has replaced labor market dualism as the main source of low-cost productive labor. Small firms, especially in manufacturing and services, have responded flexibly to these labor market opportunities. Their ability to locate and utilize cheap yet productive labor continues to be one of their most important advantages over large employers. Nonetheless, two points must be emphasized. First, these labor market interactions must be viewed in the dynamic context of changes in both supply and demand; basic market forces push toward a narrowing of wage differentials commensurate with skill and productivity differentials. It is no accident that large firms in fairly labor-intensive activities are beginning to hire substantial numbers of middle-aged, female, part-time workers. Second, it is not by cheap labor alone that Japanese SFEs survive and even prosper. They must offer quality products and responsiveness to markets and customers as well as be price competitive. They require a core of skilled workers, beginning with the owner-operator, who assume the technical and business responsibilities of the operation. Wages and opportunities for skilled core workers are of a different order. If low labor costs were the dominant explanation for most small businesses, then large-scale producers would rely much more on offshore subcontracting based on truly cheap labor, and imports of labor-intensive goods would be substantially greater.

Capital. The second major factor market for the small enterpriser is the capital market. Until recently small enterprises had to pay higher interest rates than large ones and had less access to finance.[51] This situation is not unique to Japan, of course. Two facts stand out: most loans to small enterprises have been backed by collateral, typically land, and until recently interest rate differentials were substantially greater than transactions costs and risk premiums would warrant. The degree of the differential depended on the degree of institutional development and the tightness of funds; the system of segmented financial markets allocated credit preferentially to larger firms in a quite competitive top-tier market, but small enterprises tended to face oligopolistic lenders.[52]

However, over the past decade, conditions have changed more in finance than in virtually any other market in Japan, as the papers by Sato and by Hamada and Horiuchi make clear. As a result, financial institutions awash with relatively low cost funds and facing inadequate customer demand now actively seek small as well as large borrowers. In addition, the loan programs of government financial institutions have been vigorously redirected to small business; as of December 1983, loans outstanding to small business from these two sources alone amounted to about $20.7 billion and $19.4 billion, respectively. More important, total loans to small business amounted to $676 billion; and the share of small business in the total loans of the financial system increased sharply from 43.0 per cent in 1963 to 58.9 per cent in 1983.

These changes have dramatically improved the access to and cost conditions for borrowed funds for almost all small enterprises, particularly those with some land or other real collateral. This leads to our basic proposition: there is now no substantial discrimination in financial markets against small enterprises once adjustment is made for transaction costs and risk.

That does not mean that all small enterprisers have ready access to borrowed funds or that the great importance of trading companies as a major source of external funds (often in the form of goods to be processed) has substantially diminished. In Japan as elsewhere, the capital for small-scale start-ups comes overwhelmingly from family savings and borrowing from relatives, friends, and patrons.[53] Early growth is financed by retained profits and further personal infusions. Only after a SFE has developed at least a brief track record is it likely to be able to borrow significantly from a financial institution. Accordingly, the unreported but very real assets of landownership, personal networks, and individual qualities and skills of the small-scale enterpriser count heavily in establishing and maintaining a business.

Land. The widespread distribution of both urban and rural land has endowed many families with a physically small but valuable, increasingly high priced asset. Land is by far the most important asset of those families that happen—by history, circumstance, or wise investment—to own land. The redistribution of farmland to tenants in the postwar land reform and the ongoing legal difficulties in recombining farmland into larger units are the most important reasons for the persistence of such a large number of family farmers. Landowning urban households use most of their land for their residential purposes. At the same time, the land and house become an asset to exploit for business purposes, a major and seriously underreported form of investment input into very small businesses. Thus, in 1978 some 2.4 million homes were used as stores and other commercial establishments. A high proportion (78.8 per cent) of the self-employed owned homes, and presumably most use these as a base of operations. Many small industrial and commercial enterprises probably obtain their viability through the high implicit rent (in opportunity cost terms) accruing on land rather than through substantial productivity of labor or capital inputs. These "rents" show up as SFE income attributed in part to their labor inputs; part is probably bid away through the competitively determined sales prices of SFE goods or services to their customers.

However, ownership of land is by no means the full story. Tenants have very strong rights: in urban areas land for business use often is under long-term (20–30 year) contract; under the Civil Code, tenants have vested rights and cannot be forced out; rent increases have to be mutually acceptable. As a consequence, rental payments by long-situated tenants are low. Land reform and tenant rights have virtually eliminated land rental in agriculture and have seriously inhibited land consolidation for farming purposes. In urban areas much land, in ever smaller plots, is under lease. Frequently the ownership of a building is separate from that of the land on which it stands, which the owner leases out. Thus, tenant user rights have become very valuable—between 40 and 70 per cent of the total land value in urban areas (the Tokyo ratio is apparently on the order of 70 per cent)—and the capital (market) value and rental income of landownership, where rented out, are correspondingly lower.[54] Thus, SFEs that have tenant rights (the more long-standing the better) also hold a valuable asset.

In a pure world of neo-classical equilibrium, these rents and quasi rents would be capitalized, the land sold and put to its most efficient use. Why does this occur only very slowly? In part it is a matter of lifestyles and generational changes in tastes; operating a small business out of one's home may be more efficient than simply using it as a residence. Part has to do with the complementarity of family landownership and family labor. Women can work at home, on their own schedules (in some occupations) and with greater flexibility than would be possible working elsewhere as wage-earners. Or specific labor skills complementary to landownership may be developed, as, for example, with small wholesalers. But why not retire, sell land or tenant rights to its use at a high price, use part to buy an apartment, and live comfortably on the income from the remainder? There are good reasons: capital gains taxes on land sales (let one's inheritors take care of the happy problem of land wealth); low returns to depositors in Japan's financial markets; and the various tax advantages of maintaining or strengthening potential claims on land. Indeed, Japanese seem to respond quite rationally in ways to protect their claim on landownership or tenancy. Family residences and other land used for business purposes receive favorable tax treatment, especially at times of transfer at death of the owner; it may well be wealth maximizing to have *obaasan* ("granny") running a tiny store that generates virtually no value added or income.

We hypothesize that land—its highly dispersed ownership, tenant rights to its use, its high price, its role as the main source of wealth for most landowning families, its security as an asset—is an important reason why there are so many small-scale enterprises and especially why they will tend to persist longer than income and value-added measures of economic efficiency would imply. To some undetermined degree, high implicit land rent compensates for inefficiency in labor and capital use and makes it possible for the SFE to stay alive or even do reasonably well. Indeed, it is empirically very difficult to know when and to what degree entrepreneurial drive counts for more than ownership of land.

At the same time, although ownership of land or tenant rights make it easier for a small business to become established and to remain in business, apparently a lack of such assets is not a serious barrier to new entry. New SFEs seem to be able to find space at affordable rents. We find this surprising, given the reported high values of land. Land markets are clearly imperfect; they are constrained by legal and customary restrictions on rights, subject to considerable fragmentation, affected by tax regulations, and probably involve special deals and arrangements. Land values, markets, and use are one of the puzzles of Japan's political economy.

We do not mean to imply by this discussion of factor markets that small-scale enterprise involves an optimal or even efficient allocation of economic resources. A major issue is the optimum scale of production, organization, or marketing. Indivisibilities of physical capital, technology, and managerial abilities in many products mean that economies of scale overwhelm the advantages of small-scale production. Although lower labor productivity and wage may arise substantially from labor heterogeneity, that certainly is not the whole explanation. As we have stressed, many small entrepreneurs have taken advantage of their own areas of competitive advantage *and* have responded creatively to (and thereby ameliorated) specific inefficiencies in the Japanese system as a whole—imperfect land markets, differential government legislation and its implementation, labor market discrimination and local conditions, institutional and bureaucratic rigidities of large firms and their system of industrial relations, and so on.

Many other SFEs have responded defensively to situations of inexorably declining economic competitiveness. Examples include most of agriculture, much labor-intensive manufacturing of standardized products subject to strong import competition, and many varieties of small retailers faced with competition from large stores. For some it is a matter of living off the continuing but declining rents of their ownership of land, machinery, and specific skills. Others adjust. Mom and pop stores join franchise convenience chains, and small producers shift to new products or change businesses entirely (using the same location and labor). But others, especially when there is generational change, simply go out of business and convert their assets in land and building to rental income.

The Political Economy of Government Policy

The large number of small businesses make them potentially of great significance to the electoral process.[55] Unlike white-collar voters, but like farmers,[56] small entrepreneurs (and their families and employees) are sensitive to particular economic issues and quite capable of voting single-issue concerns. Business self-interest is a paramount factor. On the other hand, and quite unlike agriculture, the diversity of interests in the small business sector is enormous. There are over 50,000 industrial associations representing small businesses in diverse industries and localities. The political potential of small businesses is realized on a national scale only when unity is forged around general issues. The government naturally seeks to avoid activating such issues.

Small-scale entrepreneurs are inherently pragmatic, and their interests are often local. As businessmen they may be rather conservative on most issues, but they are quite capable of supporting local opposition party candidates who respond to their particular needs. They also are responsive to the criticism that the LDP favors big business, a regular opposition party theme; however, it is best to view the small business vote as inherently independent.

Interests combine and can become politically influential (1) when inclusive issues such as taxes, labor policies, or environmental protection are raised in a manner that adversely affect the small business sector as a whole, (2) when sectors of small business decline and seek protection, and (3) when localities seek particular economic benefits.

The government avoids raising general issues by assuming a hands-off administrative posture.[57] Tax laws and environmental and labor standards, in particular, are stringently applied to large firms, whereas smaller enterprises are rarely subject to scrutiny. In the case of health and sanitary inspections, a consortium of small business associations launched a massive and successful lobbying effort to preserve quasi autonomy when administrative incursions increased. In cities, furthermore, zoning laws that would inhibit small business activity are seldom proposed. Further, the government can rarely enforce its depression cartel limitations on the production of smaller firms. Comparatively speaking, the government follows this approach to small business for reasons both of politics and of administrative efficiency. In this respect, Japan seems like Italy and appears to be in direct contrast to the United States, where small business finds onerous the imposition of a plethora of hiring, safety, environmental, and other regulations. The relatively large size of the small business sector means that a comparatively larger part of the Japanese economy escapes significant government involvement, the reverse of recent international ideas about Japanese industrial policy and its influence in directing the economy.

The greatest, though most invisible, form of government support for small-scale family enterprises relative to large corporations is through the lenient tax treatment of their personal and corporate incomes. The law provides substantial benefits for smallness, most notably the deduction as expenses of wages paid to family members in both incorporated and unincorporated enterprises without requiring tax withholding so long as annual wage income is below the personal exemption level. Moreover, reporting requirements are lax. Most important perhaps (it is impossible to know), the opportunities for and exercise of tax evasion by SFEs are substantial. We presume that most SFEs with income above minimum statutory levels underreport net income and evade taxes.[58]

We infer an implicit political decision (within the LDP, not the Ministry of Finance) to tolerate widespread tax evasion by SFEs, with only modest efforts of rectification through audits and punishment of tax evaders. There is an implicit political exchange: support us and we won't tax you. This arrangement was probably not conceived of in such terms initially, but simply emerged as small business grew, prospered, and became an increasing source of financial support for local politicians and their leaders. Few politicians are willing to alter the present tacit agreement. The passage (and then unprecedented revocation) of legislation to tax interest income and the evasion of these taxes through illegal multiplication of interest-free deposit accounts (the "green card" system of personal identification) is an excellent example of the political pressures exercised by small businesses, among others.[59]

Inevitably data on tax evasion are fragmentary and not readily available. The *Nihon Keizai Shimbun* ran an informative series of articles between May 1983 and May 1984,[60] from which the following information is derived. Although 88.4 per cent of wage earners paid income tax (through withholding), only 39.5 per cent of the heads of nonfarm unincorporated enterprises and only 14.6 per cent of farm household heads did. Of the 1.75 million corporations, 1.1 million showed a loss or otherwise paid no corporate income tax. Indeed, many of the self-employed are not legally required to keep books, and they do not file tax returns. The chances of a serious audit are small: one in 25 for farmers and other self-employed persons, one in ten for a corporation (less for very small corporations). More than a third of the enterprises in the following categories audited in 1981 and 1982 had seriously understated tax returns:

bars (53 per cent), *pachinko* parlors, *sushi-ya*, moneylenders, fish stores, realtors, construction, coffeehouses, gravel landfills, foreign food restaurants, souvenir sellers, and love hotels. The average amount evaded ranged between $12,000 and $65,000. The extensive use of cash in settlement of transactions makes evasion difficult to trace. Tax audits indicated that the most common practice (50 per cent) is to hide sales revenues; 12 per cent of the audited firms reported wages paid to nonexistent employees; 11 per cent padded expenses, and 10 per cent padded purchases. There is a business of selling forged receipts to increase stated expenses (some receipts are inadequate to pass even cursory inspection by tax auditors).

This does not mean that all SFEs evade taxes. The tax evaders cited are mainly service establishments, where it is difficult to measure either output or material inputs or their relationship is not close. Where material input-output relationships are relatively fixed—flour and sugar and bread and pastries for a baker, for example—auditing is easier, and evasion is correspondingly more difficult. Some SFEs find themselves directly involved with local regulatory agencies. For example, all car sales are registered, and most repairs are done to meet annual inspection requirements and so are reported to the local authorities.

To what extent does preferential or lenient tax treatment for SFEs confer such advantages that new SFEs are deliberately started, or deliberately remain small enough, to avoid tax exposure? How important a reason is this, relative to the benefits of specialization and entrepreneurial independence, for the existence of clusters of the minuscule SFEs that subdivide the production of one product rather than integrating into one operation? How important is it in subcontracting arrangements? We do not know and doubt that anyone does. Tax treatment probably is not a dominant reason for starting or maintaining an SFE, but it does make their activities more profitable and hence enters into the cost-benefit calculus of any entrepreneur.

The early 1970s witnessed a significant intensification of LDP interest in small business precipitated by the success of the People's Association of Commerce and Industry (Minshū Shōkōkai, or Minshō), an organization affiliated (informally) with the Japan Communist Party.[61] Minshō proved to be an effective force in recruiting small business people to the opposition cause in Japan's larger cities, where in key instances mayoral and gubernatorial positions were captured by alliances of opposition parties. The economic instability of the period added fuel to the discontent of urban small operators facing first high inflation and then the recession induced by the oil shock. Kakuei Tanaka, then prime minister, is credited with recognizing the need for a much stronger LDP approach to the small business sector as a whole in the face of Minshō activities. The relative decline of agriculture as the foundation of LDP electoral strength was certainly another consideration.

MITI's budget for loans to "very small enterprises" (five employees or fewer in manufacturing and two or fewer in retailing) was expanded dramatically from ¥30 billion to ¥240 billion. The Bureau for Small and Medium Enterprises within MITI was elevated in status to an agency and its budget increased from ¥7.5 billion (1971) to ¥40 billion (1975), and its share of the total MITI budget increased from 16 per cent to 39 per cent.[62] The tax laws were changed to allow the wage deductions noted above.

MITI's role, however, has primarily been indirect. Government loans to very small businesses (funneled through private banks) are largely dependent on the guidance and tacit approval of "small business advisers" operating as employees of local chambers of commerce (who screen and help SFEs prepare loan applications). There was a concomitant increase in the number of such advisers from nearly 16,000 in 1971 to 27,000 in 1975. Half their wages are paid by MITI, making them (at least partly) central government agents to the small business sector. The other half comes from the prefecture and the local chamber of commerce. The result has been a blunting of the influence of Minshō and an increase in LDP visibility in the small business sector. This quasi-governmental loan-adviser system influences a sector of the voting public by channeling special funds to it. It also puts the national chamber of commerce organization in close touch with small businesses across the nation and positions it to represent small business interests to the LDP. Chambers are typically led, however, by executives of larger local firms, who focus on regional development issues, meaning that chambers of commerce are less representatives of the small business sector to the LDP and MITI than means of enrolling SFEs in local campaigns and controlling the small business sector to preclude the formation of opposition activities.

By and large, government economic policymakers apparently see small and medium-size enterprise more as a problem than as a source of economic growth and vitality. The lumping together of "small and medium enterprise" into one category is a convenient misnomer; it combines several different realities, as our discussion of minuscule and small SFEs indicates. It enables the government to channel its resources to relatively larger firms that it considers of greater potential. There is considerable interest, at least at the rhetorical level, in positive programs to modernize and raise the technological level of small and medium-size enterprises, particularly as reflected in publications of MITI's Small and Medium Enterprise Agency. On the whole, nonetheless, MITI's policy approach is defensive.

MITI apparently would prefer to engage in as little protection as possible short of serious economic and social disruption. Its tendency has been to approach problems in depressed industries as "special" and "temporary." With *shingikai* (advisory council) approval, it invokes numerous emergency powers aimed at preventing bankruptcies and encouraging orderly adjustments within the specific industry. The effort is to contain problems without committing itself to long-term protection. The political parties, on the other hand, must regularly appear responsive to the concerns of small and medium business, but each party has constituencies opposed to protective policies. Politicians representing areas of depressed small manufacturing are the most susceptible to pressure, but all politicians seek the small business vote and must be particularly sensitive to complaints of such large groups as retailers or amalgams such as those consisting of various businesses concerned about health inspections.

SFEs are but part of most complex policy issues. Consumer interests (even if politically less unorganized) are a significant factor, as are land use and urban planning, environmental issues, the welfare system, and foreign policy. The large versus small dimension, in other words, is but the most visible conflict requiring a balancing of interests when such matters as the rate of expansion of even small supermarkets or large versus small food producers are the foremost issue. The LDP relies on too broad a spectrum of support to ignore other domestic concerns. MITI, furthermore, is the guardian of economic progress, and it resists protectionist pressures from the standpoint of productivity gains or losses. Finally, Japan's place in the world gives the international dimension at least a very strong potential influence, even though protection against import competition is politically the easiest resolution to small business pressures.

When momentum is great enough (that is, when political pressure is widespread), the interplay of forces, however complex, appears to follow a rather simple pattern. All parties position themselves as sympathetic to the problem, issuing general position statements calling for solutions without specifying a stand that would alienate their other key constituencies. MITI, while adopting a public posture of listening and concern, quietly attempts to delay the production of actual protective legislation in hopes that the momentum will subside. If it does not, MITI authors a compromise bill (largely of its own making) that satisfies the situation politically while pre-empting the generation of legislative bills by the parties and the Diet Legislative Bureau. MITI is thereby responsible. This benefits both the legislators, who do not want to author what is certain to be controversial and (in some quarters) unpopular legislation, and those who want to take credit with their particular constituency. A MITI bill allows all parties to vote for the bill as a "government" resolution, one that has authority (statesmanship) but for which they need not be accountable.

This is precisely the pattern followed in the 1979 strengthening of the basic law on supermarkets, the latest adjustment in a pattern of partial government protection for small retailers that began before World War II. MITI resisted political party pressure for about four years until it became clear that the Diet would introduce legislation on its own. It then prepared its own revised approach aimed at (1) blunting the suburban advance of small supermarkets and (2) shifting some decision making to local committees made up of small retailer and consumer representatives. As with previous laws, the basic effect of this new legislation is to slow but not end the growth of large-scale retailing and to limit the impact of large new stores on a locality by reducing floor space limits and operating hours.

MITI's latitude to respond administratively to circumstances in particular industries is great. Already on the books is a wide set of laws facilitating the provision of aid to medium and small firms suffering serious difficulties.[63] MITI''s emergency powers are notably broad, flexible, and free of legislative encumbrance. Loans, special tax measures, small business cartels in certain industries, insurance, and retraining and reorganizational assistance can be activated at the ministry's discretion (with *shingikai* approval). The total value of the aid available seems never to have been calculated. The organizational channels for these measures are in place since the laws designate industrial associations, chambers of commerce, public financial institutions, loan guarantee programs, and the like as agents for the execution of special relief and restructuring efforts. The response time is thus quite rapid since neither special legislation nor new organizations are required. The result is that precisely targeted, temporary measures based on a multiplicity of financial and other tools can be arranged without political debate. The limitations on this system are the ceilings on resources contained in MITI's budgetary allocations and in the various categories of public loans available.[64] The ministry's continuing effectiveness, therefore, hinges on its conservation and astute allocation of these resources.

In sum, although a great deal of attention and financial support is regularly bestowed on the small business sector, few policies prevent small-scale industries from declining. The family doctor makes many visits and prescribes various medicines, but is not inclined to put patients on life-support systems. Rather, policies have been formulated to ameliorate the pace and therefore the impact of decline, with the intention of facilitating an orderly retreat or basic reorientation. Loans, technical assistance, retraining grants, capacity scrapping programs, and the like are examples. MITI officials essentially seek to balance a strong commitment to encouraging change leading to greater overall economic efficiency with sociopolitical realities (unemployment costs, social dislocation, and political pressures being very real considerations). They find themselves holding out (with considerable success so far) against outright protectionist policies, especially ones that will become chronic. In this the small business sector is fundamentally different from agriculture; the few exceptions, notably leather and leather goods, prove the rule as those products reflect the special Burakumin political problem.

It is also true, however, that the LDP and the government could be pushed in a more protectionist direction by the success of other parties in recruiting small business support. What would permit this to happen? In a major recession, for example, will the political clout of small business increase? They experience hardship early in the business cycle, and this could translate into demands the government cannot effectively meet, causing a shift toward applying pressure through the opposition. Another scenario might begin with national tax reform proposals that unite small businesses against the government. Such a tax package might emerge with the support of a constellation of three pressures: demands by wage earners and consumers to correct the existing inequities in the tax system; Ministry of Finance bureaucrats and politicians anxious to raise taxes to reduce the huge budget deficit; and big business opposition to corporate tax increases. A value-added tax, much less the attempt to close existing loopholes, would meet much small business resistance. A third scenario would have progressives winning governorships on a pro–small business platform and then effecting much greater assistance to small businesses, including local forms of protectionist measures, thereby forcing the LDP to respond accordingly. The latter actually began to happen in the early 1970s.

With the continuing combination of LDP strength and the present mix of government responses to small business issues, there is more reason to work with rather than against the authorities; loans, temporary measures, and partial help are better than rhetorical promises. Small business pragmatism, in other words, reinforces the LDP as long as it proves its electoral dominance and continues to recognize small business interests. It is well worth remembering that the small business sector is rarely presented with viable choices except in highly localized and industry-specific matters, and in most of these instances, it is well within the LDP's capacity to co-opt the issue.

Entrepreneurship

What does all this—factor markets, social networks, educational system, tax treatment, the economic, political, social, and cultural environment—add up to? A great deal of vitality in the small-scale family enterprise sector, for one thing—large numbers of births, deaths, and resurrections. We pull our discussion together by examining the whole set of issues involving entry, profitability, survival, and exit.

In 1979 there were just over 16,000 bankruptcies in Japan. The number of bankruptcies has been steadily increasing over the past decade; almost all involve small companies. Bankruptcies, however, account for only a small part of the total number of enterprises that go out of business each year. From 1978 to 1981, for example, about 217,000 closed their doors, some 70,000 annually. More than 99 per cent of these were small and medium enterprises. The percentage of closings ranged between 3.2 and 4.2 per cent of the total number of establishments between 1966 and 1981. This represents a formidable failure rate, one at the heart of structural adjustment issues in Japan; yet the number of new small businesses forming each year has substantially surpassed the number of closings, resulting in a new increase in business establishments year after year. Again, virtually all of this activity is in the area of small and medium business.

Nothing better illustrates the basic vitality of the small and medium business sector than the above portrait, one that balances the risks of small and medium business with the constant entrepreneurial activity at the lowest organizational levels of stable, growing, and emergent industries. The many new enterprises formed each year attest to the ease of entry in the economy as a whole, though, of course, with immense sector-specific differences. Since many small firms rely extensively on trade credit, one default can cause a chain of bankruptcies. Under Japanese law it is easy to go bankrupt or otherwise exit as an enterprise, reorganize, and be reborn. The net increase in enterprises signifies the basic strength and endurance of SFEs.

There are significant variations in the relationship of openings to closings. Small businesses must respond flexibly to annual as well as longer-term changes. Each industry has its own distinct range of closing and start-up rates. Thus, throughout the 1966–81 period, the rate of openings in the service and wholesale-retail sectors held steady at about 6–7 per cent of total sector enterprises, although in manufacturing the rate plummeted from 6.5 to 3.5 per cent beginning in the mid-1970s. The shift in the economic structure toward the service sector is clearly illustrated by this different response to the oil shock–induced recession and slower growth era, as well as to the evolution of aggregate demand. During that recessionary period, small business opportunities in manufacturing declined sharply, whereas both the retail and service sectors continued to expand. Yet even in manufacturing, the ratio of openings to closings remained narrowly positive, a result probably of a shift toward more, not less, reliance on subcontracting in major manufacturing industries such as machinery and electronics induced by efforts on the part of large firms to control overall labor costs and retain productive flexibility.

This degree of entrepreneurial vitality comes as a surprise, given the stereotype of the Japanese as a cautious, risk-averse people who prefer the security of stable, well-defined relationships.[65] Moreover, the best-educated (and presumably most talented) Japanese are attracted to large firms (and elite government jobs) and rarely leave for any reason. Neither the modern education nor the employment system encourages development of an entrepreneurial spirit or a class of talented people who are recognized and rewarded for their entrepreneurial inclinations. The dominant cultural and social descriptions of postwar Japan do not lead one to expect much in the way of entrepreneurial vitality.[66]

Survey data help us better understand the conditions of entrepreneurship and provide specific evidence bearing on many of the issues raised earlier. The People's Finance Corporation undertakes the most extensive, regular survey.[67] In 1981, of a sample of 1,400 new businesses in all sectors, over half were formed by people in their thirties. Only about 10 per cent of all new businesses were begun by people 45 years old and above. Many older people do find work in small and medium businesses, but they are not founding many of them.

Not surprisingly, the educational level of these entrepreneurs is substantially higher than that of the population as a whole.[68] In 1966, 13 per cent of the sample had university educations, whereas by 1981 35 per cent had four years of post-secondary schooling (higher in urban areas) and another 8 per cent had graduated from junior college or its technical equivalent. Unfortunately, we know little about the quality of the universities involved, but, nevertheless, the general impression is that Japan's new entrepreneurs represent nearly all segments of the population as measured by educational background.

In the same survey, the largest group of entrepreneurs (70 per cent) come from the middle levels of small and medium businesses. Even so, entrepreneurs come from a relatively wide range of firms and levels. Koike found that nearly half of the workers in firms of ten or fewer employees eventually set up their own businesses.[69] In 1982, for example, some 65,000 men established their own (unincorporated) individual proprietorships. Of these, 48 per cent had been employees in SFEs, and 20 per cent had worked in enterprises of 30–299 employees; another 14 per cent had changed the form of their self-employment.[70] This suggests extraordinary mobility and entrepreneurship in the smallest enterprises.

The highly aggregated nature of statistics on small and medium business is vexing because common sense leads one to think there are discrete patterns of entrepreneurship among different types of businesses; for example, between those requiring specialized skills and education (such as business services, high tech, information management, and advertising) and those based primarily on location (such as retailing and restaurants). We can only speculate that younger, better educated people leaving larger firms enter different kinds of business than their less educated peers leaving smaller firms.

The most popular reasons given in the People's Finance Corporation survey for starting one's own company were "to realize technical skills and general ability" (70 per cent), "to be able to work in a manner consistent with my nature" (55 per cent), and "an attraction to managing one's own business" (39 per cent). Improved income was selected by less than one-third, and "dislike of being in another's employ" was chosen by an impressive 30 per cent. An equal proportion complained of being blocked in advancement. The overall impression is one of ambitious, independent people stepping out of employment situations in which they felt limited. Case studies of new small businesses reveal that many start-ups have been planned well in advance, with previous employment being treated as preparatory training. The people involved are not elite managers nor are they big risk takers seeking high returns, but neither are they incompetents forced into small-scale entrepreneurship.

The survey also reveals that various people play a part in encouraging entrepreneurs to start their own businesses. As already noted, new businesses generally begin with a modest plan that relies heavily on existing relationships to reduce risk. In this survey, 45 per cent mentioned a friend, relative, or business client as urging them to set out on their own. The practice of *noren wake* (an employer-guided new business creation) characterized another 9 per cent. In about one-third of the cases (overlapping) customers and/or former employers played a role.

The same survey offers a rather detailed portrait of start-up conditions in terms of capital investment, employees, and so forth. The low level of initial investment is striking—some ¥9.2 million ($36,800) on average—with slightly more for equipment than for working capital. Surprisingly, restaurants were the most capital intensive, both in amount (¥16.4 million, $65,600) and in the share for equipment (80 per cent). The least capital was required in manufacturing and construction.

The average start-up investment of ¥5 million ($20,000) for manufacturers, for example, is so small that it is difficult to grasp the actual cost structure involved. The purchase of used machinery and payment of "key money" on rental space are the two largest items in many cases. The majority of new enterprises in production do one or more of the following: locate in their own homes or in borrowed space; use primarily family labor; acquire leased or used machinery; maintain small inventories; utilize materials supplied by customers; and have low administrative and sales costs. These conditions are best met in subcontracting arrangements, where the new company begins producing for a larger contractor, assembly firm, or trading company. Initial production of one or a few items requiring limited equipment and space is the pattern. If the patron's demand is steady, the new business begins with a level of business that is secure and predictable. In such circumstances, one would expect profits to be squeezed by the knowledge and power of the patron, and this corresponds to the low risks and cost of entry. Unfortunately, the survey does not separate manufacturing start-ups into categories that would further clarify these issues.

According to the People's Finance Corporation, the funds for start-ups come essentially from three sources: owner-operator investment (46 per cent), loans from financial institutions (39 per cent), and personal loans from friends, relatives, and the like (12 per cent). In a separate study of almost 200 incorporated companies in their second year of business, it was found that 38 per cent of assets and working funds originated from business relationships in the form of credits. Owner-operated investment and institutional loans dropped to 30 and 17 per cent, respectively. The one exception to this pattern is restaurants, where business credits accounted for only 5 per cent of total second year funding. The central role of larger, more established firms in setting small businesses in motion by supplying credit is notable since it illustrates the interrelational framework within which small businesses exist. The national pattern is for about six in ten new businesses to be based entirely or primarily in the family, but regional variations are large. Employees are more important than family members in more than half of new businesses in big cities, whereas in rural areas the family is central in 80 per cent of the cases.

The small scale of most start-ups is further shown in anticipated first-year sales. Fewer than 10 per cent of new companies expected monthly sales in their first year to be above ¥10 million ($40,000), and the average was about ¥2 million ($8,000); 10 per cent expected monthly sales of less than ¥500,000 ($2,000).

Since almost all new businesses begin small and rely substantially on the unaccounted assets of land, personal networks, and family labor, barriers to entry are low and center on lack of connection, skills, and family labor. These cannot be purchased on open markets, but are acquired as social and experience assets. Land is often an asset possessed by a household in older industries and neighborhoods. The rental of small spaces is relatively easy in Japan compared to the acquisition of large spaces. This, too, may favor small-scale activity.

We do not have data, however, on other important issues. To what extent, for example, do start-ups of larger firms (with 30 to 100 or more employees) occur? We know these occur regularly as joint ventures or as spin-offs from larger companies. (See the papers by Aoki and by Okimoto and Saxonhouse.) Our hypothesis is that, except for spin-offs, almost all

Japanese new enterprises begin very small and that the current distribution of small and medium enterprises by size is predominantly a consequence of growth. Is this pattern specific to Japan, or is there a similar pattern in Western Europe and the United States?

We also know little about the internal life cycle of small Japanese businesses. If they survive, which kinds continue to grow? A few become medium-size or even large firms. Most reach a plateau while still small. We also note the capacity of owner-operated, family businesses to endure setbacks and cyclical downturns. Labor input and cost elasticities are great since longer hours or less income are tolerated consequences of owning one's own business. In adversity, one or more members of the family can work outside to supplement household income. This flexibility of response to hard times stems from the fact it is the balance between total household income and expenses, not just business income or profitability, that determines the persistence of many marginal enterprises. This capacity for survival helps underwrite the persistence and adaptability of many industries based on small-scale producers. It enhances the industry's tolerance of cycles and buys time to adapt and change when an industry is permanently on a downward trend since neither skills nor location nor connections are lost.

Low costs of entry and risk sharing are thus associated with low expectations about margins and a flexibility in adversity that distinguishes small business in Japan from both larger businesses and small business in countries in which start-up costs are higher, risks are not spread as widely, or family labor and other assets are not pivotal. Any calculation of return on investment and profitability hinges on the value given to family labor, of course, and this is a highly subjective matter from the owner-operator's point of view. Lifestyle and personal satisfactions, other work options for family members, and long-term prospects for success are considerations. So, too, is the fact that success will not be taxed at the same rates as salaried work.

The great number of small businesses is not, however, a testimony to their being an easy or even preferred means of making a living. Working conditions in small factories and other establishments are often among the worst in Japan. Long hours, cramped spaces, lack of safety equipment, poor lighting, noise, and so forth are common; and much of the labor is physical. Although owner-operators have hopes for success, some independence, variety of work, and other modest benefits, their employees experience only the difficulties. They do this because of the absence of other options or because they hope to learn skills and make connections that someday will give them the chance to be independent. Such assets are not cheap viewed in the light of such an apprenticeship.

The Future of Small Business

The many reasons for the continuing existence, expansion, or decline of small family-owned entreprises provide insights into their future prospects. Our overall "best guess" is that small-scale enterprise will continue to be a large, important, and on the whole positive component of the Japanese economy and that any substantial changes in its overall role will come about gradually rather than discontinuously. The essential core of the SFE as an institution—entrepreneurship, family ownership and work effort, special skills, effective social networks, specialized production of goods or services for particular market niches, and above all flexibility and adaptability—provide a strong basis for ongoing economic success.

Of course, the story will differ sector by sector and family by family. There are major unknowns. In general, how rapidly will the political economy and SFEs within it adjust to existing and future inefficiencies in resource allocation as relative prices continue to change? More specifically, what will happen to land prices, and how will land markets change? Will new technologies decrease, or enhance, the competitiveness of SFEs, and in which sectors? What will be the future political role of SFEs? And how will the aging of the population, namely the projected great increase in numbers of old workers, affect the SFE system? We can only speculate briefly on these questions. Before that, however, we provide a general evaluation of small family enterprises in the Japanese economy in terms of allocative efficiency, contracyclical macroeconomic efficiency, and flexibility.

Changes in the absolute and relative role of small enterprises over the long run will be driven predominantly by economic forces: changes in demand, market competition, and market pressures toward efficient allocation of resources, especially the heterogeneous resources of labor and land. New enterprises will seek out new opportunities. On the other hand, the decline of enterprises in increasingly uncompetitive sectors will be mediated and slowed by the time the intergenerational process of change takes. Although their value may be declining, enterprises operated by older persons will persist by living off their specific human capital and the implicit rents of other assets, especially land. Moreover, where small enterprises can maintain or form effective interest groups, they will continue to use the political process to insulate themselves as much and as long as possible against market forces. Inevitably both these processes—political and the time lags of adjustment—create formal and informal barriers to competition, including that from imports.

Certainly some SFEs in some sectors represent a socially inefficient packaging of resources. Capital is overabundant in agriculture, but perhaps still inadequately supplied to some (especially minuscule) SFEs in the secondary and tertiary sectors. Excessive land fragmentation in agriculture and probably in most urban areas results in less than optimal land use. The great heterogeneity of labor accounts for much of the existing wage differentials, but substantial allocative inefficiencies remain, especially in the discriminatory treatment of women, older persons, part-time workers, and minorities. The issue of discrimination against females is more subtle than it appears since it is founded substantially on traditional Japanese conceptions of the "proper role of women." Some may object to our use of the term "discrimination," but the phenomenon is real, whatever the labeling or semantics. At any rate, if these labor market imperfections are taken as givens, SFEs can generally be regarded as effective instruments for reducing such imperfections by taking advantage of them; certainly they do not create them. However, in sectors in which SFEs are on the defensive, notably agriculture and some very small retail establishments, they perpetuate and enhance economic inefficiency. Thus, our overall evaluation of the role of the small enterprise sector in terms of allocative efficiency is mixed; SFEs warrant only moderately good marks.

One of the great costs in macroefficiency of advanced industrial market economies derives from the downswings of the business cycle. The output periodically forgone because of underutilized labor and capital during recessions is huge, far greater than that forgone because of static inefficiencies of resource allocation. Small family enterprise in Japan has been an effective contracyclical as well as secular absorber of labor through a variety of highly flexible mechanisms—from starting one's own business to family labor to newly hired employees. We believe a careful analysis would show that small business plays an important stabilizing role, serving to reduce the overt unemployment that would otherwise occur; this role is subsidized to some extent by the taxpaying employees of larger firms and consumers of protected products. SFEs still earn excellent marks by this criterion.

The small business sector generally provides great flexibility for the Japanese economy, accelerating the process of structural adjustment. Entry is easy. Many enterprises die, either because of their own incompetence (the inevitable price of an active, ambitious, entrepreneurially oriented population) or because of changing market conditions or because of the lack of a successor. Many more are started. Many rapidly transform their product mix and their activities, responding to the pulls and pushes of the marketplace. Offsetting this, however, are the inefficient SFEs able to mobilize political power to retard their own decline; they reduce the overall flexibility. The grade on flexibility is, nonetheless, very good.

The social value placed on small, family-owned and -operated enter-prises—in all sectors—seems quite high. They are regarded not only as natural and inevitable, but as desirable. Japanese consumers and tax-payers have long tolerated high agricultural prices based on economi-cally inefficient production and seem to be willing to tolerate the efforts of small shopkeepers to slow down the entrance of even small super-markets into their neighborhoods. On the other hand, there does not seem to be any great idealization of family farms or small shopkeepers as an essential feature of the Japanese way of life that must be maintained and protected at *all* costs, or indeed much more cost than at present. We believe Japan's new middle mass, or even a healthy new nationalism, are too efficiency oriented, too pragmatic, to suffer permanent or increasing subsidization of notably inefficient SFEs.

The fate of the small enterprise sector is inexorably caught up in the prospects of the Japanese economy and society as a whole. Growing GNP per capita will continue the trend in the composition of demand toward services, many of which are income elastic and are efficiently provided by small-scale enterprises.[71] Within distribution, there will be considerable fighting and jockeying for position among different levels of small enterprises; the smallest (the least efficient as measured by sales per worker) will continue to resist market intrusion by larger, more mod-ern firms. There will be considerable transformation, exemplified by the way in which Itō-Yokado Company has turned traditional mom and pop establishments into 7-Eleven store franchises.[72] As well as their serving as barriers to new (including imported) products, the inefficiency of re-tail services and of distribution in general is likely to be a source of in-creasing political tension.

As Japan progresses toward its current vision of the future as an infor-mation society, small high-tech firms are likely to proliferate—in com-puter software, specific products or components, or related services—since there are few economies of scale and since simple organizational structures encourage creativity, innovation, and quick responsiveness. Many will be in the developing venture capital market. Though efficient, productive, glamorous growth nodes of the future, such high-tech firms will constitute only a tiny share of the SFE sector in numbers, employ-ment, or even direct output.

Real wages will continue to rise and the relative cost of capital to decline. So long as the liberal international economic system remains in order (that is, so long as Japan remains committed to free trade), the trend will be to greater specialization within Japan's manufacturing structure and a substantially higher share of imports of standard labor-intensive manufactured goods. These trends will put increasing market pressure on SFEs in manufacturing, both as producers for final markets and as subcontractors. Perhaps even more important will be the policies of medium and large firms. In a more slowly growing economy, they may seek growth by expanding into domestic markets now dominated by small firms, by vertically integrating, by reducing reliance on subcontractors, or by turning to the cheaper labor of offshore economies for simple components.

Many SFE manufacturers have created effective market niches by specializing in relatively small lot production. Import competition is less a potential problem than the emergence of new, computer-based, flexible production systems that enable large firms to produce small lots competitively would be. Moreover, a few larger firms have recently begun substituting part-time female production workers for full-time (male) workers. If this becomes widespread (not likely in our judgment since large firms prefer a homogeneous, stable labor force), then large firms will bid away one of the advantages of SFEs, given existing labor market imperfections.

We have argued that many of the benefits for SFEs derive from labor and land market imperfections, as well as from the institutional or bureaucratic rigidities of large firms and favorable tax treatment. More perfect financial and capital markets will help SFEs where they have previously been at a disadvantage. On the other hand, more perfect labor and land markets will reduce the opportunities for SFEs to find and take advantage of existing imperfections. Existing disparities between relative wages and productivities may decrease over time, although we suspect they will always persist to some degree since equilibrium is never achieved in practice in a growing economy.

We anticipate that the many barriers to more perfect land markets—institutional, legal, tax, and generational preferences—will remain strong. Even so, underlying conditions affecting land markets are likely to change substantially. In our judgment, the trend of huge increases in the relative price of land between the early 1950s and mid-1970s will not persist in the future. There will not be increases in (relative) prices of agricultural output to be capitalized in higher rural land prices. With some lags, urban land use is becoming more efficient, as witnessed by the increasing average height of buildings. With financial liberalization, financial assets will become more attractive. High inheritance taxes and the inevitability of land transfer through death will force land revaluations, sales, and more efficient use of land. Over time, the lengthy one-shot effect of huge capital gains in land will be adjusted, and high implicit rents will be reduced. However, it is unlikely that the primacy of tenant rights will be seriously eroded: too many vested interests are at stake.

The most problematic area is agriculture, which combines great economic inefficiency and high prices visible at home and abroad, immense political power enhanced beyond mere numbers by gerrymandering and multiple-member voting districts, and a profound incipient generational change. More than a quarter (27.5 per cent) of Japanese farmers are age 60 or older, and almost another third (32.1 per cent) are between 50 and 59. What will happen when they die? Two trends will be at work. Economic efficiency dictates that land should be consolidated into much larger, contiguous production units. But that requires reasonable prices and effective rental and purchase markets for farmland; there are legal and other barriers to both. Land consolidation will proceed at too slow a pace and affect too little land to enable an efficient scale of farm family enterprise to emerge. The second trend will be for (perhaps early) retirees from nonfarm jobs[73] to take over land from their parents or, more likely, to farm as a side occupation. If Japanese-style "gentlemen farmers" contributing little labor and producing simple crops such as rice exercise strong enough political clout to maintain the present system of subsidized farming, a generational transformation may not occur or may be far different from the efficient solution economists hope will come about.

All the evidence indicates that workers in small-scale family enterprises outside agriculture work longer hours, under worse conditions, and for lower pay and fewer fringe benefits than those in larger enterprises or the civil service. Yet there does not seem to be a strong sense of discontent or unfairness or alienation pervading Japanese society. True, opposition parties obtain a majority of the popular vote, but the SFE's vote is little understood.

We can only speculate about sources of the high degree of social and political stability and the role of SFEs in it. Certainly the high rate of employment is important; given wage flexibility, the nonexistence of effective minimum wage legislation, family connections, and the prevalence of family businesses, almost everyone can find some sort of job. Despite ongoing wage differentials, Japanese income distribution is comparatively equal, as Bronfenbrenner and Yasuba's paper documents. Small enterprises offer Japan's minorities economic independence and some opportunity; for Burakumin it is a protected opportunity (beef, leather goods). Most of all, Japanese culture appears to have socialized most Japanese to accept their lot in life, not to rebel against it. Women, both in and outside the labor force, provide the most clear-cut example. For males, a system of economic and social mobility based largely on merit (ability and effort) as screened through the educational system apparently has broad acceptance. For most, the hurdles to get into the elite are accepted as too high. So one plays within the system, taking advantage of it wherever possible—using personal connections, evading taxes, forming narrow-interest pressure groups to influence politicians. Small business is the outlet and opportunity for those who are hopeful and ambitious and either not hired by large employers or not wanting to be.

All this may change—not so much because of worsened circumstances as because of heightened consciousness among the groups constituting the SFE sector (analogous to the increase in agrarian landlord-tenant disputes in the 1920s). Certainly the consciousness of farmers and their capacity to organize effective political pressure are already high and will persist. We think there is a good chance that small business interests, especially in services, will become an even more visible and powerful political force in the coming decade—and we perhaps have not adequately stressed their present effectiveness in protecting their own interests. The postwar eras, first of reconstruction and then of rapid growth, submerged the conflicts of interest between efficiency and income distribution, particularly the protection of income (and wealth) of vested interest groups. It is quite possible that these issues will become more and more pronounced, as other SFEs join with agriculture in pushing their interests, and with increasing effectiveness.

Changes in perceptions and values ("raising of consciousness") will affect the behavior and demands of the two main pools of underutilized labor—women and older workers. Our guess is that the behavior of women will change only very slowly and gradually in terms of Western criteria.[74] A more likely source of social discontent lies in the increasing numbers of older male workers retiring from large institutions not into cushy, minor-league *amakudari* positions (positions obtained by former bureaucrats in the private sector) but into a highly competitive SFE labor market. The question is the degree to which they will have the capacity to organize as an effective interest group on their own or to influence others (their children) on their behalf.

The sharp increase in the number and proportion of older persons in the next two decades and thereafter is likely to have a momentous, wide-ranging impact on the Japanese economy and society (see the paper by Noguchi).[75] One-third (3.1 million) of those over 65 are currently working, and another 640,000 would like jobs, mainly part-time or at home; half say their main reason for working is to increase their income. We anticipate that many in the future aging population will have the desire or need to work. Moreover, this labor market pressure is exacerbated by the relatively early retirement age (not expected to rise above age 60) of large firm and government employees. Retirees and older persons generally will have to seek jobs in SFEs, as owner-operators, family labor, or wage-earning employees. Some will participate in the U-turn phenomenon, returning to their natal home or nearby where landownership will make it possible to have work. The evidence does not indicate that many older people are starting new enterprises. That could change, and more will inherit existing family enterprises—in agriculture, retail, or elsewhere where landownership can be combined with even low-productivity labor input to generate some level of income. Others will be the low-paid, part-time, low-productivity labor force of the future. Some basic questions arise. Which is better for the well-being of old people: being involved in some work or retiring fully? Do they contribute much to value added and GNP? Or do they require, or perpetuate, the inefficient allocation of land and perhaps capital, so that the packaged contribution is negative? Is it efficient or desirable to have a welfare system that encourages, or even virtually requires, old people to work to maintain their accustomed standard of living and way of life?

Daniel I. Okimoto and Gary R. Saxonhouse

Technology and the Future of the Economy

Since the mid-1970s, the relatively sluggish performance of the leading industrial economies of the world has given rise to a growing sense that the industrial world may be facing not just another routine downturn in the normal business cycle, but rather the end of the entire era of postwar economic growth, the most rapid that the world has ever known.

This perception has some substance. The past decade and a half has seen a marked decline in the growth rates of both GNP and productivity in OECD countries (see Tables 1–2). Any explanation of this decline is bound to be controversial.[1] Citing selected evidence of the absence of any relationship between changes in U.S. R&D expenditures and total factor productivity, William Nordhaus argues that scientific opportunities for improving economic well-being on the scale of the early postwar decades may be diminishing.[2]

Support for such a hypothesis can be culled from several indicators. In almost all the 50 countries for which data are available, for example, patents per scientist and engineer as well as per unit of R&D expenditure have declined. This is true in spite of the large absolute increases in R&D resources in most industrialized countries since the mid-1960s. The rate of return from R&D investments measured by the number of patents obtained per scientist and engineer has fallen sharply. The sole exception to this worldwide pattern is Japan (see Table 4 below). Although nationals of major industrial powers like France and West Germany are now receiving only 55 per cent of the number of patents received in the mid-1960s, the number of patents received by Japanese has almost quadrupled between 1967 and 1984 (see Table 3). The Japanese have been so active in overseas patenting that their contributions have offset what would have otherwise been much sharper declines in the patents granted in the other major industrialized economies. If, for instance, patent ap-

TABLE 1
Average Annual Growth Rates of GNP and Productivity in the Advanced Industrial
Economies, 1960-1985

Country	Growth in GNP		Growth in productivity	
	Period	Per cent	Period	Per cent
United	1965-73	3.8%	1960-73	2.9%
States	1974-79	2.8	1974-84	2.3
	1980-85	2.2		
West	1965-73	3.6%	1960-73	5.9%
Germany	1974-79	2.4	1974-84	3.7
	1980-85	1.2		
France	1965-73	4.8%	1960-73	6.4%
	1974-79	3.1	1974-83	4.8
	1980-85	1.2		
Japan	1965-73	8.7%	1960-73	11.0%
	1974-79	3.7	1974-84	6.9
	1980-85	4.4		

SOURCE: Bank of Japan, Kokusai hikaku tōkei, 1985 (International comparative statistics) (Tokyo, 1985).

TABLE 2
Average Annual Rate of Growth of Total Factor
Productivity in the United States and Japan, 1959-1979
(per cent)

Period	United States	Japan
1959-63 and 1964-68	2.25%	1.66%
1964-68 and 1969-73	0.92	2.59
1969-73 and 1974-76	0.39	−0.03
1974-76 and 1977-79	—	1.06

SOURCES: Zvi Griliches and Frank Lichtenberg, "R&D and Productivity Growth at Industry Level," in Z. Griliches, ed., R&D, Patents and Productivity (Chicago: University of Chicago Press, 1984); and Hajime Imamura, "Sources of Quality Changes in Labor Input and Economic Growth in Japan, 1960-1979," Keio Economic Studies, Vol. 19, No. 2 (1982).

provals for Japanese nationals has been excluded from U.S. patent totals, the recorded 0.5 per cent increase in total patents granted between 1967 and 1984 would have turned into a 15 per cent decline.[3]

Moving against worldwide trends, Japan's R&D performance raises a number of important questions. How should patent data be interpreted? Has Japan made as much technological progress as the data indicate? What characteristics distinguish the Japanese R&D system from the U.S. one? What are the advantages and disadvantages of Japan's R&D system?

In this paper, we analyze three important areas in which Japan's R&D system diverges markedly from that of the United States: the role of small companies in technological innovation; the government's role in R&D funding; and the character of advanced training for technical personnel. All three areas are closely intertwined with technology, and national differences in the three have affected the nature of technological change. After discussing Japan's performance, we assess, in the second section, the relationship among firm size, market structure, and the capacity to innovate. How much do small firms spend on R&D? How much have they contributed to technological innovation? Do established, large companies dominate the processes of innovation in Japan?

Contrasts in national approaches to research and development are nowhere more prominent than in the roles of the Japanese and U.S. governments. In the third section, we address such questions as, In what areas, and to what extent, do the Japanese and U.S. governments sponsor R&D? What are their objectives? Does government-sponsored R&D displace or complement private sector R&D? What is the relationship between military R&D and national productivity?

In the fourth section, we deal with the training of technical manpower. How do the Japanese and U.S. systems differ in their approach to technical training? What are the consequences and implications for R&D? What is the relationship between university-based research and industrial R&D? Is the Japanese system, with its emphasis on intrafirm training, at a competitive disadvantage, and if so, in what senses?

By coming to terms with these and other questions, we hope to shed light on the fundamental characteristics of Japan's R&D system, particularly as it compares with what is arguably the world's leading R&D sys-

TABLE 3
Patents Granted in Selected Countries, 1967 and 1984

Country	Patents granted to nationals		Patents granted to foreigners		Patents granted to nationals in foreign countries	
	1967	1984	1967	1984	1967	1984
United States	51,274	38,364	14,378	28,837	73,960	55,201
West Germany	5,126	11,402	8,300	10,356	41,775	35,050
United Kingdom	9,807	4,442	28,983	14,425	17,579	11,868
France	15,246	7,651	31,749	16,015	14,393	15,135
Switzerland	5,388	2,351	16,462	11,626	12,452	9,221
Canada	1,263	1,427	24,573	19,118	2,789	2,358
Japan	13,877	51,690	6,896	10,110	6,843	29,328

SOURCES: World Intellectual Property Organization, *Industrial Property Statistics* (Geneva, 1968, 1985).

TABLE 4
Patents Granted to National Scientists and Engineers (1966 and 1981) and Average Annual Change in R&D Expenditure per National Scientist/Engineer (1966-1981)

Category	1966	1981
United States		
Patents granted national scientists/ engineers	54,634	39,224
No. of national scientists/engineers (000)	521.1	691.4
Patents granted per thousand national scientists/engineers	104.8	56.7
Avg. annual change in R&D expenditure per national scientist/engineer	−1.35%	
United Kingdom		
Patents granted national scientists/ engineers	9,807	6,076
No. of national scientists/engineers (000)	52.8	87.7
Patents granted per thousand national scientists/engineers	185.7	69.3
Avg. annual change in R&D expenditure per national scientist/engineer	−1.41%	
West Germany		
Patents granted national scientists/ engineers	13,095	6,537
No. of national scientists/engineers (000)	61.0	122.0
Patents granted per thousand national scientists/engineers	214.7	53.6
Avg. annual change in R&D expenditure per national scientist/engineer	+1.09%	
France		
Patents granted national scientists/ engineers	14,881	6,855
No. of national scientists/engineers (000)	47.9	72.9
Patents granted per thousand national scientists/engineers	310.7	94.0
Avg. annual change in R&D expenditure per national scientist/engineer	+0.39%	
Japan		
Patents granted national scientists/ engineers	17,373	42,080
No. of national scientists/engineers (000)	128.9	302.6
Patents granted per thousand national scientists/engineers	134.8	139.1
Avg. annual change in R&D expenditure per national scientist/engineer	+1.37%	

SOURCES: National Science Foundation, *Science Indicators* (Washington, D.C., 1982); and Japan, Science and Technology Agency, *Kagaku gijutsu hakusho* (White paper on science and technology) (Tokyo, 1984).

tem, the United States'. In this paper, we do not try to predict which country—the United States or Japan—will win the high-tech sweepstakes. Neither do we try to forecast the specific areas of technology in which Japan is likely to excel (interesting though that question may be).

Instead of crystal gazing, we identify some notable areas in which Japan has already advanced to the frontiers of technology and some areas where it has lagged behind, despite vigorous attempts to catch up. We draw attention to the institutional context within which technological advances have been made. By eschewing technological forecasting and keeping the focus on R&D infrastructure, we hope to provide a conceptual framework within which some of the major strengths and weaknesses of Japan's R&D system can be understood.

Technological Progress in Japan

Although Japan appears to have made great technological progress against the strong currents of worldwide trends, the scope and significance of its technological development is open to some disagreement. How much of Japan's technological progress continues to rest largely on technology transferred from abroad and how much relies uniquely on Japan's R&D activities remains an open issue. Does the decline in the growth rate of Japan's total factor productivity rest entirely on diminished technological transfer? Has the productivity of Japanese R&D activities increased markedly at a time when those of other countries have declined sharply? Answers to these questions depend, to some extent, on the choice of technological indicators.

The enormous rise in Japan's patent productivity can be attributed, in part, to the sustained and steep increases in R&D investment. From 1965 to 1980, real growth rates in Japanese R&D expenditures rose faster than those of any other major industrial state (see Fig. 1). Increases in R&D expenditures may be necessary to raise patent productivity, but they hardly constitute a sufficient explanation. As shown in Fig. 1, other countries have poured larger amounts into their R&D efforts. For example, in terms of increases in real R&D expenditures, West Germany's slope is virtually indistinguishable from Japan's; yet patent applications in West Germany have fallen over time, and the number of patents actually granted has dropped by half. This suggests that investing more R&D money is no guarantee of greater patent productivity.

If patent output is not necessarily correlated with larger inputs of R&D manpower and money, perhaps Japan's extraordinary performance can be attributed to intangible factors at the micro-level, such as superior company incentives; greater research continuity made possible by lifetime employment; closer contact and better communications among

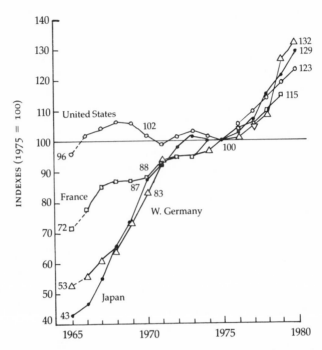

Fig. 1. Rates of growth in real research expenditures in leading nations.
Source: *Japan Science & Technology Outlook*, 1983, p. 131.

divisions engaged in research, production, and marketing; fiercer competition among firms; and greater company prestige derived from patenting. Just how much of the national variation is attributable to such factors is hard to say. For specific companies in specific industries, involved in particular technologies and product markets, the impact might be substantial. In other words, the impact undoubtedly varies across firms, industries, and technologies.

An alternative explanation, which casts Japan's performance in a more realistic light, is that international comparisons of patent data tend to overstate Japanese technological accomplishments significantly. Quantitative indicators reveal little about the quality of patents. Many Japanese companies, including such giants as Hitachi, Matsushita, Fuji Film, Toshiba, and Sony, give their employees special bonuses, both when their inventions result in the filing of a patent application and when the patent application is granted.[4] This may mean that the Japanese have applied for, and registered, more patents than others because the knowledge they seek to protect tends to be less significant technologically.

Larger quantity may reflect lower quality, or at least a greater propensity to seek patents for know-how that others would consider too mundane or short-lived to bother about.

This interpretation is supported by the low rate of success for patent applications in Japan. Nearly half of the applications made by Japanese to their own Patent Office are turned down[5]—compared with less than 20 per cent of foreign applications.[6] In the United States, the ratio of approvals to applications for Japanese nationals is about 75 per cent that of Americans and only 60 per cent that of other foreigners.[7]

Although an unusual zeal to protect run-of-the-mill products and processes may explain the sharp rise in Japanese patent applications, it does not account for the simultaneous decline elsewhere. One explanation may be that patent protection has never been an important feature of the incentive structure underlying R&D investment in the United States and Western Europe. In certain industries, the pace of technological change may be so rapid as to make the lengthy patent approval process an ineffective device for protecting property rights.[8] Moreover, with greater public access to the proprietary information contained in patent applications, U.S. and European companies may feel that patents simply cannot be obtained without disclosing vital information that will help competitors. Also, patenting processes entail increasingly costly legal fees, and the protection provided by patents (assuming applications gain approval) may not be so foolproof as to be worth incurring the up-front costs of the application process.

Of course, the risk of leaking information to competitors is not entirely new. The term "trade secret" long antedates the Industrial Revolution. What is new is the mounting concern in the United States and Western Europe that the advanced state and current orientation of Japanese R&D place Japan in an advantageous position to derive special benefits from the disclosure of proprietary information.[9] Such concerns may make some companies wary about applying for patents—or more hesitant about licensing their know-how as liberally as in the past.

If the rise in the production of patents per unit of R&D effort in Japan and its fall elsewhere truly reflect contrasting changes in the quality of innovative effort, a change in the structural relationship linking R&D effort and the productivity of economic activity more generally might also be expected. Between the mid-1960s and the late 1970s, however, the estimated rate of return on R&D expenditures rose modestly not only in Japan but also in the United States and West Germany (see Table 5). There was no monotonic rise in research productivity. Despite a sharp decline in the number of patents per scientist and engineer in the past 15 years, West Germany—not Japan—continued to record the highest rate of return for R&D expenditures.

TABLE 5

Rates of Return on Net Investments of Capital and R&D for Total Manufacturing in the United States, Japan, and West Germany, 1965-1977

Year	United States		Japan		Germany	
	Capital	R&D	Capital	R&D	Capital	R&D
1965	.09	.08	.09	.07	.14	.13
1966	.10	.10	.08	.07	.12	.14
1967	.09	.10	.08	.08	.07	.12
1969	.10	.13	.09	.09	.15	.16
1970	.08	.12	.10	.09	.16	.18
1971	.07	.11	.13	.10	.12	.17
1972	.11	.13	.15	.10	.10	.16
1973	.14	.16	.15	.10	.13	.20
1974	.12	.13	.13	.12	.11	.18
1975	.08	.11	.10	.11	a	.16
1976	.11	.13	.10	.11	.08	.17
1977	.13	.14	.09	.10	.08	.17

SOURCE: Pierre Mohnen, M. Ishaq Nadiri, and Ingmar R. Prucha, "R&D, Production Structure and Productivity Growth in the U.S., Japanese and German Manufacturing Sectors," *National Bureau of Economic Research Working Paper*, No. 1264 (Aug. 1984).
    a Since Germany disinvested this year, no rate of return figures were calculated.

It is clear that evaluating the significance of comparative patent data is no easy task. Although the weight of the evidence strongly suggests that Japan has made exceptional technological strides over the past two decades, one must be careful not to take the data too literally. They probably exaggerate Japanese accomplishments. To test the validity of patent data, we need to turn to a variety of unobtrusive indicators. Independent indicators should substantiate, modify, or discredit the evidence provided by patent applications and approvals.[10]

Unobtrusive Indicators

Crude confirmation of Japan's technological progress might be gleaned from data on Japan's technological balance of trade. Throughout the entire postwar period, Japan has run a sizable deficit in this balance. Japan has relied heavily on imports of foreign know-how to upgrade its manufacturing capabilities and step up the tempo of industrial output. Although Japan, like West Germany, still runs a large deficit today, the imbalance is shrinking steadily as the value of exported technology rises. In 1971, the ratio of exports to imports stood at 0.12; by 1983, it had risen to 0.30.[11]

Since trade statistics include royalty payments for foreign licenses purchased in the past, such data may understate the pace at which Japanese technology has advanced over the past 15 years. To measure the flow of technological trade at any particular moment, royalty payments for past purchases must be sorted out from new technological transactions. Unfortunately, such data are not available. What is available are data on the overall size of new contracts for technology sales and purchases. According to these data, the ratio of technology exports to imports exceeded 1.00 as long ago as 1972; by 1984 it had risen to 1.76.

As with international patent data, technological trade statistics have to be interpreted carefully. The aggregate figures can inadvertently conceal vital information. The data on new technology trade contracts, for example, fail to provide information about the destination of Japanese technology exports. As of 1984, only about 40 per cent went to advanced industrial states; 60 per cent was sold to developing countries.[12] By contrast, over 85 per cent of U.S. technology exports went to advanced industrial states, with less than 15 per cent being transferred to developing countries. This implies that the bulk of Japanese technology exports may not be state-of-the-art or concentrated in the most sophisticated sectors of high technology. Much of it may fall into the category of incremental improvements in production technology for the heavy manufacturing sectors, especially chemicals, iron and steel, and transportation machinery (Japan's biggest export earners).

Trade data on technology contracts may also be misleading in that a significant portion of technology exports represent intracompany transactions, with overseas subsidiaries' purchasing patents and other knowhow from parent companies based in Japan (presumably for tax or accounting purposes). By contrast, virtually all technologies imported into Japan are arm's-length transactions between foreign and Japanese firms. Moreover, the data on technology contracts include both current and future receipts and expenditures. In a period of Japanese technological progress, this biases Japan's reported balance of trade on new technology upward. This bias is probably exaggerated since the responses by Japanese firms to the questionnaires that constitute the sole basis for this data, tend to magnify the value of technology sold and underplay the cost of technology purchased. This is easily seen. Despite Japan's supposed surplus in the balance of trade in new technology since 1972, the Bank of Japan's data on actual receipts and expenditures on technology transactions continue to show Japan in heavy deficit.[13]

Data on patents and technology sales cast light on applied research and commercial development, the two areas where Japanese government policy has placed overriding emphasis. But is Japan making progress in basic or precommercial research? Or has advancement been retarded by the seemingly low priority assigned to basic research? Since advances in basic research are closely related to at least some of the breakthroughs in applied technology, Japan's capabilities in basic research have a bearing on the nature and scope of its applied R&D, especially in high-technology industries, such as biotechnology and fine ceramics.

Once again, analysis of this question is hampered by the peculiarities of the official statistics. According to these surprising data, Japan has long allocated a disproportionate share of its R&D resources to basic research. As long ago as 1967, Japan was purportedly devoting 28.2 per cent of all its expenditures to basic research. Moreover, the real rate of growth of Japan's R&D expenditure for basic research has almost always exceeded the real growth rate in the United States since that time.[14] Is Japan a basic research paradise? Japan's seeming preoccupation with basic research is an artifact of Japanese definitions of R&D expenditures. By contrast with U.S. and European practice, Japan treats the salaries of all university and college science teaching personnel as if they were full-time researchers. This leads to a substantial overstatement of Japan's overall R&D expenditures, a substantial overstatement of the academic sector's role in Japanese R&D, and, since university research is treated largely as basic research, a substantial overstatement of the role of basic research.

An illustration of how important this statistical convention has been in shaping Japanese R&D data is given in Table 6. By one new estimate of Japanese R&D personnel, the official statistics for 1965 overstate by some 13 times the number of scientists and engineers in Japanese universities and colleges engaged in research and development activities. Over time,

TABLE 6
Scientists and Engineers at Japanese Universities and Colleges Engaged in R&D,
1965-1981
(000)

Year	Official series	Series corrected by sample survey	Year	Official series	Series corrected by sample survey
1965	39.1	2.1	1974	79.2	35.2
1966	43.6	3.3	1975	81.9	36.4
1967	48.5	4.1	1976	88.0	41.4
1968	54.3	7.2	1977	92.8	45.9
1969	52.4	7.6	1978	91.5	45.7
1970	55.2	19.0	1979	96.7	50.2
1971	59.7	18.0	1980	100.7	46.7
1972	60.5	18.7	1981	102.6	44.0
1973	75.2	33.1			

SOURCES AND METHODS: The official series includes all regular research workers in the natural sciences and engineering as reported in Japan, Office of the Prime Minister, *Kagaku gijutsu kenkyū chōsa hōkokusho* (Report on the survey of research and development), various issues. The series was corrected by estimates of full-time faculty and teaching assistants derived from National Science Foundation Sample Survey—a 10 per cent random sample of catalogues and reports of academic institutions stratified by character of government or private control and character of academic institution.

it appears that this overstatement has diminished by a factor of nine. This means that starting from an extremely small base in 1965 there was an extraordinarily rapid increase in the research role of Japanese universities and colleges and an increased role for basic research within Japan's R&D effort. Even today, however, the aggregate Japanese effort in basic research remains modest by U.S. standards.

Everyone knows that Japan is not among the leaders in terms of the number of Nobel prizes won in the natural sciences and engineering. Between 1901 and 1985, Japan won only 4 of the 370 Nobel prizes awarded, compared with 137 by the United States, 63 by England, and 51 by East and West Germany. Countries with populations a fraction the size of Japan's—such as Sweden, the Netherlands, Switzerland, Austria, Denmark, and Belgium—have had more Nobel recipients than Japan. This rank ordering accords with the widespread perception of Japan as a country that has contributed few revolutionary breakthroughs to the world's storehouse of fundamental knowledge.

As a measure of overall progress in basic research, however, the number of Nobel prizes is at best incomplete since it is skewed so heavily toward seminal breakthroughs at the frontiers of theoretical knowledge. Such a measure reveals little about the degree to which aggregate advances, if not quite of Nobel quality, have been made by a growing legion of basic researchers working both inside and outside Japanese universities. Other indicators are needed to round out this incomplete picture.

The number of published research papers, which pass the test of peer review, probably provides a fuller, more representative indicator of a country's overall state of basic knowledge. By this criterion, Japan comes out looking quite respectable. In 1982, it ranked third in terms of research papers published in the world's leading scholarly journals, accounting for 7.3 per cent of the world's total, behind the United States (38.2 per cent) and England (7.9 per cent) but ahead of the Soviet Union (6.4 per cent) and West Germany (5.7 per cent). This research output and ranking is broadly consistent with revised data on what Japan has actually been spending on basic research relative to other advanced industrialized countries.[15]

Over the past 15 years, moreover, Japan has increased basic research not only absolutely but also, as the new Japanese R&D expenditure series implied by Table 6 suggests, relative to what other countries are doing. In chemistry in 1982, for example, Japan accounted for nearly 12 per cent of all scholarly papers published in the world, placing it third behind the United States (21.9 per cent) and the Soviet Union (15.8 per cent) but well ahead of West Germany (6.4 per cent) and England (5.7 per cent). In the telecommunications field between 1981 and 1984, Japan accounted for nearly 10 per cent of the research papers accepted by the

Comité consultatif international telegraphique et telephonique, ranking second behind the United States. In fields such as chemistry, telecommunications, and semiconductors, the Japanese have become major participants in both leading-edge research and in the communication of this research in scientific publications.

Japan's Technological Position

Summary statements about, or measurements of, Japan's technological position are liable to be misleading. Japan's technological position cannot be summarized simply, because there is enormous variation across sectors. According to an authoritative survey of Japanese businessmen done in 1982 and doubtless outdated in some details, Japan has reached state-of-the-art technology in a variety of areas: iron and steel production, agricultural chemicals, new materials, nuclear energy processing (for example, fast breeder reactors), semiconductors (metal oxide semiconductors and gallium arsenide mass memory chips), computer peripherals, office automation, robotics, flexible manufacturing systems, certain areas of telecommunications (power transmission cables and digital switching equipment), pharmaceuticals (artificial blood), biotechnology (fermentation and gamma interferon from synthetic genes), and industrial lasers.[16]

These survey results are interesting because there is a pattern to these areas of excellence. There is a common core of technological and industrial characteristics that appear to fit the particular strengths of Japan's R&D system. Typically, for example, the theoretical parameters surrounding these technologies are well known (for example, solid-state physics). The technological trajectories are predictable, and product advances are made in continuous or incremental steps (for example, random access memory chips). Small adaptations in proprietary designs, such as miniaturization, based on foreign know-how often create vast new commercial opportunities.[17] Similarly, incremental improvements in production technology (such as automated bonding equipment) lower costs and upgrade reliability, making Japanese products more competitive in world markets. Although such technological changes cannot be considered "path breaking," their cumulative impact on the commercial competitiveness of Japanese industry has been substantial. From an economic standpoint, therefore, their significance should not be underestimated.

Progress has been slower in technologies where the theoretical parameters for problem solving are highly complex (jet aircraft design) and technological trajectories are not readily predictable (advanced software). Japanese firms are not as apt to make seminal inventions that lead to the creation of whole new industries, owing in part to the relatively low level of government R&D sponsorship and to the (until recently) narrowly applied nature of much of commercial R&D. Whereas Japanese companies excel at electronic components, they are not as competitive when it comes to complicated systems integration (for example, aerospace), an area U.S. firms have tended to dominate.

Not surprisingly, in the 1982 survey Japan was found to lag far behind the United States in various military technologies: aerospace, jet aircraft, avionics, computer-aided design and computer-aided manufacturing (CAD/CAM), security-related information processing, and so forth. Japan fares well in certain dual-purpose technologies (that is, technologies with both military and civilian applications) where commercial markets are large and the barriers to new entry are not prohibitively high, such as superconductivity components (gallium arsenide), nuclear energy, and supercomputers. Although still behind in lasers and artificial intelligence, Japan is thought to be catching up rapidly, owing to the motivation imparted by the enormous commercial potential of those technologies.

Aerospace is an example of an industry in which Japan—despite industrial targeting—has encountered difficulties in catching up with the technological front-runners. Unlike the United States and Soviet Union, which were motivated by considerations of national security or international prestige, Japan entered space research in order to take advantage of long-term commercial opportunities in communications and broadcasting and for purposes of scientific observation; more recently, its goals have also come to include the construction of space factories for bioengineering and new materials.

Japan takes pride in having been the third country to orbit an artificial satellite in geosynchronous orbit, but the United States and Soviet Union are far ahead of it, accounting for over 95 per cent of the 2,800 satellites launched through 1985. In building its CS Sakura satellite in 1977, Japan relied heavily on U.S. technology and components. Over time, its dependence on foreign know-how has declined; over 60 per cent of the components in the CS-2 communications satellite (1983) were built in Japan. The H-I rocket, once completed, will be capable of launching a satellite weighing around 550 kg into geostationary orbit. Overall progress in Japan, however, has been slower than expected— in spite of the high priority attached to space research. Although the United States holds a seemingly insurmountable lead in space technologies closely related to military security, this is not the case for most commercially significant technologies.

Scale, Market Structure, and Innovative Activity

Japan's capacity to innovate in microelectronics, chemicals, and iron and steel is often attributed to the dominant market positions held by a small number of giant corporations. As Schumpeter noted decades ago, market concentration can enhance innovation because it makes the fruits of R&D more appropriable.[18] Because Japanese industrial organization is said to be dominated by corporate giants, R&D is thought to be heavily concentrated in the big business strata. Indeed, this is assumed to be one of the defining characteristics of Japanese R&D, a central reason for both its achievements and its limitations.

The actual situation is, however, more complicated. Japan is no more dominated by large firms than other countries. For R&D investment, if anything, the opposite may be closer to the truth. In 1981, for example, Japanese firms with under 1,000 employees accounted for 18.5 per cent of all R&D expenditure by private business in Japan.[19] By contrast, no more than 4.1 per cent of the R&D conducted in the United States by private business is undertaken by firms with under 1,000 employees.[20]

Over time, the role of small firms in R&D is becoming less important in both Japan and the United States. Interestingly, this is occurring more rapidly in the United States than in Japan. Between 1975 and 1980, the share of smaller firms in total private business R&D expenditures declined by almost 20 per cent. In Japan during roughly the same time period and starting from a share of total private R&D expenditures almost four times as large, the R&D expenditures of small firms fell by only 10 per cent in relative share.[21]

The relatively large amount invested in R&D by small firms in Japan and the comparatively modest proportion spent by small firms in the United States may seem surprising in view of current policies in both countries. Unlike Japan, the U.S. government has devised policies consciously aimed at allowing small, research-oriented firms to play a critical role in the development of new technology. Accordingly, in the United States, the R&D tax credit can be used to offset 100 per cent of corporate income. The R&D tax credit in Japan, which served as the model for the U.S. credit, allows only 10 per cent of corporate income to be offset. Consequently, small firms in Japan, for whom research is a primary activity, do not benefit greatly from the R&D tax credit. Neither do they enjoy the tax encouragement that their U.S. counterparts receive from limited R&D partnerships, sub–Chapter S corporations, small business investment corporations, pension fund investments in venture capital partnerships, and simplified registration requirements for initial small public offerings of equity. All these U.S. incentives emerged out of legislative and administrative changes since the mid-1970s, causing concern in Japan that the United States may have acquired new, special advantages in the promotion of high technology.[22]

Although small-scale Japanese firms account for a much higher proportion of R&D expenditure than do their U.S. counterparts, the level of research intensity is lower. In 1981, R&D expenditures of small firms with under 1,000 employees in the United States were 1.6 per cent of their total sales. For Japanese firms of this size, R&D expenditures came to only 1.32 per cent of sales. The larger R&D expenditures of small firms in Japan can be explained by their larger overall presence in the Japanese economy. Indeed, the long-term decline of R&D expenditures by small firms in the United States (from 11 per cent of R&D in 1957 to 4.1 per cent in 1985) is only marginally affected by changes in the research intensities for large versus small firms; the main explanation is the smaller number of firms that employ less than 1,000 workers in the U.S. economy. Because the aggregate number of small and medium-size firms in Japan has not shrunk as much as it has in the United States, the R&D expenditures of small Japanese firms have declined only modestly over the past 15 years.

Such data do need to be understood within the context of different corporate environments and organizational structures. Differences in Japanese and U.S. legal, accounting, and tax practices, for example, have made it advantageous for many Japanese firms to eschew the formal vertically integrated structure characteristic of large firms in the United States. Only since 1977 have large Japanese corporations been required to maintain common settlement dates and to consolidate balance sheets and income and earnings statements of their less than wholly owned subsidiaries. This makes it entirely possible that some significant portion of the R&D carried out by small Japanese firms is actually initiated and administered by much larger companies.[23]

It should also be understood that the relative shares of R&D expenditures borne by small versus large firms are not closely correlated with most of the prominent measures of research productivity for both groups. In 1980, small firms accounted for only 4.1 per cent of business R&D expenditures in the United States, but these firms produced 19 per cent of all patents.[24] By contrast, in Japan small firms, which accounted for 18.5 per cent of all business R&D expenditures, produced only 13 per cent of all patents. Given the much lower R&D intensity of small firms in general, the U.S. figures imply a high patent productivity per unit of R&D intensity. Despite major differences in Japanese and U.S. behavior with respect to the filing of patent applications, small U.S. firms produce patents at a higher rate (per unit of input) than either larger U.S. firms or small Japanese firms. Moreover, small U.S. firms of 1,000 employees or less produced more so-called major innovations than larger firms (more than 5,000 employees) between 1953 and 1966 and an equal number between 1967 and 1973 (see Table 7).

The record of Japanese companies with respect to major innovations poses a striking contrast to that of U.S. firms. Although U.S. firms were

TABLE 7
Distribution of Major U.S. Innovations by Size of Company, 1953-1973

No. of employees in company	Percentage (and number) of innovations			
	1953-59	1960-63	1967-73	1953-73
Fewer than 100	23% (23)	27% (29)	20% (20)	23% (72)
100-1,000	26% (27)	23% (25)	23% (23)	24% (75)
1,000-5,000	14% (14)	14% (15)	12% (12)	13% (41)
More than 5,000	37% (38)	36% (38)	46% (46)	39% (122)
TOTAL	100% (102)	100% (107)	100% (101)	100% (310)

SOURCE: Gellman Research Associates, *Indicators of International Trends in Technological Innovation* (Washington, D.C., 1976).

responsible for 310 major technological innovations, Japanese firms accounted for only 34.[25] Of these 34 innovations, 33 were accomplished during the last decade of the 20-year survey period. All but 2 of the 34 innovations were the results of R&D activities by large firms.

Despite spending much less money as a proportion of total R&D expenditures, small U.S. firms play a more pivotal role in stimulating major technological innovations than do their Japanese counterparts. That small Japanese firms have not played as prominent a role in the past or present, however, does not foreclose the possibility of their contributing more in the future. Nor does it mean that there are no institutions in Japan capable of serving as effective substitutes for the role that small, technologically innovative firms play in the United States.[26]

Recently, there has been considerable interest in Japan about the role that small firms might play in the development of high-technology industries. MITI's Office of Venture Business Promotion and Small and Medium Enterprise Agency have devoted much attention to the identification and analysis of small, innovative Japanese firms. Quite apart from their fewer numbers, such Japanese businesses differ markedly from U.S. venture businesses. In particular, few Japanese venture businesses are new firms. In MITI's sample of 850 venture businesses, less than 4 per cent had existed for under three years.[27]

To this point, we have noted basic differences between the United States and Japan with regard to industrial structure, firm size, R&D expenditures, and research productivity. Of these, none is more striking than the role played by small, newly created venture firms. The United States' R&D system fosters the constant formation of small venture firms through favorable labor and capital markets, strict antitrust enforcement, and generous tax provisions on capital gains. In Japan, by contrast, the R&D system is not nearly as supportive. Far fewer venture firms are established, and what they contribute technologically is far less significant.

The marginal contribution of newly created firms to technological innovation can be seen in the experience of Japan's biotechnology and machine tool industries. Although the Japanese government has made biotechnology a national priority, and even though business surveys rank biotechnology as the industry with the most potential for the future, the industry comprises only firms that have entered from established positions in related fields. By contrast, 111 new U.S. firms were formed between 1977 and 1983 with the explicit intention of exploiting the technological and commerical potential of biotechnology. Venture capitalists in the United States have invested $2.0 billion into these biotechnology ventures, not to mention other sources of financing.[28] This is about 13–14 times the entire amount of venture capital available in Japan for all industries.[29]

Newly established firms account for about half the participants in the U.S. biotechnology industry, and their presence is important. The four largest, newly established companies spent as much as 40 per cent of what the four largest existing companies, including such giant firms as Schering-Plough, Eli Lilly, Monsanto, and DuPont, spent on biotechnology R&D in 1985. Moreover, these same four firms are spending more than twice what the four most active, established Japanese companies are spending on biotechnology R&D.[30]

Japan's machine tool industry is often cited as an example of how small, innovative firms can grow suddenly and create an internationally dominant industry. As recently as 1976, for example, Yamazaki Machinery Company, Japan's largest and technologically most innovative machine tool company in the mid-1980s, could not be found among the top five firms in the country's machine tool industry. Yamazaki's rapid rise is not unique. Among the top six machine tool producers in 1970, only two were still among the top six in 1981. The rapid rate of change in market concentration, as reflected in the turnover of top companies, is evidence of the competitive health of Japan's machine tool industry. However, neither Yamazaki Machinery nor any of the other new entrants to the list of the top six producers are in any sense new firms. Each of these four firms has been in existence at least 30 years, with Yamazaki having a history of almost 60 years.[31]

Notwithstanding highly publicized cases, such as in Japan's software industry, the relatively small number of new firms being created to exploit new technological opportunities is directly related to the character of capital and labor markets in Japan. The security offered by permanent employment makes the risks of leaving a job to found a new firm much greater than would be the case in the United States. Japanese labor market conditions make it difficult for new ventures to hire experienced R&D personnel away from existing firms. Of the venture businesses surveyed by MITI in 1984, 75 per cent identified this as a special problem in both their formative and early growth periods.[32]

The problems associated with the absence of a well-functioning market for experienced R&D personnel are compounded by conditions in the capital market. In the United States, 600–700 venture capital companies control $6.0 billion in assets, backed by a regionally diversified and deregulated financial system, which also supplies capital to new companies. In Japan, there are no more than 30 identifiable venture capital companies, whose combined assets totaled no more than $186 million. Japan's over-the-counter equities market is closely regulated by the Securities Bureau of the Ministry of Finance (despite recent changes) and is at most only 1 per cent the size of its U.S. counterpart. It is hardly surprising therefore that only 16 per cent of what MITI defines as venture businesses have ever received venture capital financing and only an additional 11 per cent are currently contemplating such financing for future needs.[33]

Given the corporate sector's slack demand for loans for almost a decade and the financial and analytical resources of the Japanese banking system, it may be surprising that the entry of newly established firms into high technology has been so limited. The competition in Japan's financial sector remains imperfect, despite major steps toward deregulation and efforts at internationalization.[34] To be sure, Japan's banking sector, unlike its U.S. and Western European counterparts, has been more willing to back firms with relatively little capital. But its willingness is contingent on the availability of tangible collateral; in the absence of such collateral, Japanese banks are reluctant to lend money. For small, high-technology firms, where the salaries of R&D personnel may absorb a disproportionate amount of start-up costs, the high collateral requirement is a major stumbling block. Thus, 48.3 per cent of the firms in MITI's venture business sample complained of collateral problems when attempting to secure financing. By contrast, only 23.9 per cent of the firms in MITI's small and medium-size enterprises sample voiced similar complaints.[35]

The limited number of small firms established to exploit technological opportunities does not mean that entry into high-technology sectors is restricted. At least 120 Japanese firms entered the biotechnology industry between 1980 and 1985. But nearly all have entered through "lateral" or "horizontal" routes from established positions in other industries.[36] Japanese corporations in the food-processing, paper and pulp, chemical, pharmaceutical, and textile industries have chosen to undertake R&D

activities in biotechnology, either because (1) their main product lines were structurally depressed; (2) they wanted to hedge against the possibility that products emerging from biotechnology might be competitive with their main product lines; or (3) their existing R&D programs fit in with biotechnology-related R&D endeavors. In almost no case does entry appear to be the result of a strategy to recruit R&D personnel from major universities or government research institutes so as to exploit the commercial potential of basic research they had conducted.

Nor is there much evidence to suggest that established Japanese firms are entering biotechnology research primarily by bidding away R&D personnel from other firms. According to MITI surveys in 1982, only 25 per cent of the established firms starting out in biotechnology research attempted to hire R&D personnel from other firms. The vast majority of firms preferred to reassign and retrain existing research personnel or hire new university graduates. Overall, only 7 per cent of biotechnology R&D personnel in Japan changed jobs in 1982. In the United States, 37 per cent changed jobs at least once.

In the United States, job mobility need not disrupt the R&D agenda of individual researchers (though it can upset corporate R&D programs). Researchers who change jobs find that they can often continue their research or even begin research projects that had not been possible in their old jobs. This transfer of know-how is a positive by-product of a highly mobile labor market and a highly developed capital market for newly created firms. Such an R&D system is apt to be more accommodating of diverse research approaches than Japan's. There may be less structural leeway for research pluralism in Japan because of rigidities in labor and capital markets. On the other hand, there are definite trade-off costs associated with the U.S. system that diminish its luster—such as the propensity of U.S. firms to underinvest in long-term projects that appear likely to be disrupted by the mobility of R&D personnel. Clearly, each R&D system has advantages and drawbacks.

Government Sponsorship of R&D

Japan's R&D system also differs markedly from that in the United States in the role played by the government. Contrary to common misperception, the Japanese government spends much less to underwrite industrial R&D than the U.S. or European governments. The U.S. government funded 32 per cent of all business R&D expenditures in 1982; the Japanese government supplied no more than 1.7 per cent.

Aggregate expenditures are reflected at the sectoral level (see Table 8). Although virtually all U.S. manufacturing sectors receive substantial government funding for R&D, few Japanese industries depend on gov-

TABLE 8
*Government Funding and Research Intensity in the Japanese and
the U.S. Manufacturing Industries, 1971 and 1981*
(per cent of total R&D; R&D as per cent of total sales)

Industry	1971		1981	
	Government funding	Research intensity	Government funding	Research intensity
JAPAN				
Chemicals	0.29%	2.56%	0.82%	3.05%
Petroleum refining and extraction	1.11	0.30	4.48	0.18
Rubber products	0.48	1.41	—	2.32
Ferrous materials	0.46	0.77	4.49	1.44
Nonferrous metals	0.66	1.04	2.82	1.37
Fabricated metal products	1.52	0.64	0.14	1.34
Machinery	15.5	1.64	1.63	2.18
Electrical machinery	1.65	3.21	1.69	4.52
Telecommunications	1.15	3.64	1.63	4.72
Transportation equipment	0.78	1.67	3.88	2.69
Precision instruments	0.92	2.35	0.46	3.73
UNITED STATES				
Chemicals	10.0%	3.91%	7.19%	3.83%
Petroleum refining and extraction	3.36	1.04	7.29	0.72
Rubber products	23.9	2.31	23.8	2.56
Ferrous materials	1.39	0.75	25.0	0.81
Nonferrous metals	3.12	1.06	37.6	1.21
Fabricated metal products	4.54	1.28	12.5	1.40
Machinery	16.9	—	10.9	2.57
Electrical machinery	51.4	7.38	37.9	6.82
Telecommunications	54.1	8.21	33.9	8.90
Transportation equipment	62.8	8.26	59.8	8.37
Precision instruments	22.0	5.71	17.3	8.38

SOURCES: Japan, Prime Minister's Office, *Kagaku gijutsu kenkyū chōsa hōkoku, 1982* (Report on the survey of research and development) (Tokyo, 1983); and National Science Foundation, *Research and Development in Industry, 1981* (Washington, D.C., 1982).

ernment financing for a significant share of their R&D funding. Over time, U.S. government funding has become less concentrated in aircraft, missiles, and telecommunications equipment, but it has risen to 25 per cent in the iron and steel industry and almost 40 per cent in nonferrous metals. By contrast, the Japanese government has reduced its share of R&D funding for the machinery industry from 15.5 per cent in 1971 to 0.81 per cent in 1981. This is significant because the Japanese machinery industry has been the last industry in the early 1970s to receive a substantial share of its R&D funding from the government.

Some Japanese think that they are at a disadvantage in competing with the United States in high-technology industries because their government underwrites so little of the business sector's R&D in comparison to the U.S. government.[37] If what motivates the U.S. government to underwrite a substantial proportion of R&D is a sense that it must compensate for market failures—such as externalities, increasing returns to scale, incomplete information, or even unemployment,[38] then if Japanese firms faced the same market failures but were forced to meet them without government intervention, they would certainly be disadvantaged to the extent that the benefits of government supported R&D could be successfully internalized by the U.S. economy.

Alternatively, suppose that the bulk of government funding for business sector R&D is related to the procurement of public goods, such as defense, having little to do directly with the competitiveness of the U.S. economy. Suppose, further, that the supply of high-quality R&D personnel is fixed, although the total supply of R&D personnel may not be. Under these assumptions, significant government funding of R&D is likely to detract from, rather than contribute to, the production of new technologies that enhance international competitiveness.

Which of these hypothetical cases fit the current Japanese and U.S. situations? Much of the U.S. government's R&D expenditures are related to the provision of public goods (see Table 9). Indeed, in 1980, 44 per cent of all government R&D (equivalent to 0.5 per cent of GNP) went toward improvements in missiles and aircraft. Since 1980, government support of missile and aircraft R&D has risen to 0.75 per cent of GNP. The U.S. pattern contrasts sharply to that of Japan, where about 40 per cent of government support of R&D (equivalent to 0.22 per cent of GNP) is directed toward the promotion of agriculture and industry. Note, however, that roughly two-thirds of this support is directed to the needs of agriculture and has relatively little to do with enhancing the productivity of the Japanese economy.

To identify and highlight the major differences in the role of the two governments in supporting business R&D, we can use an econometric model developed by Richard C. Levin and Peter C. Reiss, which reflects the Schumpeterian insights that market structure both conditions the pace of technological progress and is in turn determined by it.[39] We begin with the assumption that government R&D expenditures are motivated by an interest in (1) promoting technological opportunities, (2) compensating for the inappropriability of R&D returns in particular industries, and (3) facilitating the production of public goods.

TABLE 9

Distribution of Government Support of R&D by National Objective and by Country, 1975 and 1980

Objective	United States 1975	United States 1980	Japan 1975	Japan 1980	West Germany 1975	West Germany 1980	France 1975	France 1980
Defense and aerospace	67.5%	63.7%	19.5%	16.8%	29.4%	24.4%	45.7%	49.3%
Defense	50.8	47.3	4.7	4.9	19.2	15.3	32.8	40.1
Space	14.5	14.5	14.8	12.0	7.4	6.6	6.1	6.8
Civil aeronautics	2.1	1.9	—	—	2.9	2.4	6.8	2.4
Agriculture and industry	2.5	3.0	41.9	25.4	13.2	15.3	13.1	12.2
Agriculture	2.2	2.7	27.7	25.4	3.3	2.9	4.2	4.3
Industrial growth	0.3	0.3	14.2	12.2	9.9	12.4	8.9	7.9
Energy and infra-structure	10.9	14.2	22.9	34.4	25.9	34.1	17.6	16.0
Production of energy	7.2	11.4	16.0	26.2	18.3	20.9	9.4	8.3
Transport and tele-communication	1.2	0.9	3.9	2.9	2.5	3.2	3.3	3.0
Urban and rural planning	0.5	0.4	1.2	2.3	1.9	5.7	1.6	1.5
Earth and atmosphere	2.0	1.6	1.8	2.9	3.1	4.3	3.3	3.3
Health and welfare	14.8	15.2	12.1	11.2	15.9	18.4	6.5	7.5
Environmental protection	0.9	0.8	3.2	3.4	1.7	3.1	0.9	1.2
Health	11.9	12.1	6.3	6.1	5.6	9.3	4.4	4.9
Social development and social services	2.1	2.3	2.5	1.7	8.5	6.0	1.2	1.4
Advancement of knowledge	4.3	3.0	3.0	3.5	15.7	14.2	17.1	15.0
Government R&D as per cent of GNP		1.11		0.56		1.14		1.07

SOURCE: Adapted from OECD, OECD Science and Technology Indicators (Paris, 1982).

In particular, the ratio of government funding of R&D to sales in both Japan and the U.S. is determined by

$$\text{GOVRDS} = h_0 + h_1 \text{ (DEFShR)} + h_2 \text{ (GOVShR)}$$
$$+ h_3 H + \sum_{m=1}^{M} h_{3+m} \text{ OPP}_m + h_{3+m+1} \text{ APP} + \varepsilon$$

where GOVRDS is the ratio of government R&D to industry sales, DEFShR is the share of industry sales going to government for defense purposes, GOVShR is the share of industry sales purchased by the government for other purposes, OPP_m is an element in an N-dimensional vector measuring technological opportunity, and APP is a variable measuring the technological conditions of appropriability. We estimated the equation for 1972, 1976, and 1980 for 20 Japanese manufacturing industries and then compared the results with earlier work done for the United States, using a similar econometric specification. (For the definitions, scalings, and sources of data used in this estimation, see Table 10. For the results of the estimating equation, together with earlier work for the United States, see Table 11.)

As expected, the results indicate that although defense procurement heavily influences the allocation of U.S. government R&D, defense procurement scarcely affects the R&D spending priorities of the Japanese government. The U.S. government supports R&D in those industries in which it is a major customer; the Japanese government appears to use other decision rules. In particular, there is some evidence in Table 11 that relatively speaking, the Japanese government responds more positively to technological opportunities in its allocation of R&D expenditures. Foreseeing the mechatronics revolution, for example, the Japanese government gave special attention in its R&D funding to industries that are electrically or mechanically based. By contrast, the coefficients for these technological opportunity dummies are statistically insignificant in the U.S. equation.

Interestingly enough, the AGE and AGE SQ variables, another measure of technological opportunity, are statistically significant in both the Japan and U.S. equations. Surprisingly, in both equations, the signs are the reverse of what might be expected. Since the AGE profile variables reflecting technological opportunity first fall and then rise, it appears that both governments react to technological opportunity with a substantial time lag. Indeed, the evidence in Table 11 suggests that the Japanese government may respond more slowly than the U.S. government.

The technological dimension in spillovers, indicated by BORROW, appears to have some effect on government R&D. In both Japan and the United States, a higher degree of spillover increases the likelihood of

TABLE 10
Variable Definitions and Data Sources

Variable Definition

GOVRDS: Government-financed R&D expenditures divided by sales (estimated from *KGKCH, KGY, KGH,* and *KTH*)[a]

H: Herfindahl index of concentration (estimated from *KTH* and *KGKCH*)

OPP: Represented by the following variables:
  ELEC: Industry technology base predominantly electrical (scaled 0-1)
  CHEM: Industry technology base predominantly chemical (scaled 0-1)
  BIO: Industry technology base predominantly biological (scaled 0-1)
  MECH: Industry technology base predominantly mechanical (scaled 0-1)
  BASIC: Basic R&D expenditures divided by total R&D (estimated from *KGKCH, KGY, KGH*)
  AGE: Years since first appeared in *KTH* with substantially same definition as today
  AGE SQ: Square of Age

APP: Represented by the following variable:
  BORROW: R&D embodied in inputs divided by total R&D used where latter is the sum of own expenditures on process R&D and R&D embodied in inputs (estimated from *KGKCH*)

DEFShR: Defense-related government purchases divided by industry sales (*KTN*)
GOVShR: Nondefense government purchases divided by industry sales (*KTN*)

Source

KGH: Kagaku gijutsu hakusho.

KGKCH: Kagaku gijutsu kenkyū chōsa hōkokusho.

KGY: Japan, Science and Technology Agency, *Kagaku gijutsu yōran, 1985* (Tokyo, 1984).

KTH: Japan, MITI, *Kōgyō tōkei hyō, 1980* (Tokyo, 1983).

KTN: Bank of Japan, *Keizai tōkei nempō, 1983* (Tokyo, 1984).

[a]R&D data were deflated by an index computed from data available in KGH.

government support. The structural dimension of appropriability, represented by the concentration index, has the expected sign in both the Japanese and U.S. equations, but is not statistically significant.

It is still possible that Japan's knowledge-intensive industries may be handicapped in competition with their U.S. counterparts, even in those industries where the provision of public goods such as national defense dominates U.S. allocation of government R&D funding and compensation for spillovers and incomplete information dominates Japanese funding. The scale and scope of U.S. government and private R&D spending may be so large relative to Japan's and other countries'—with civilian spillovers from defense R&D—to tilt the board to the United States' advantage. It is no coincidence that U.S. competitive strengths have long resided in such industries as aircraft, electrical machinery, telecommunications, and health products, all of which enjoy enormous government support.

On balance, however, Japan's knowledge-intensive industries have probably not been placed at a disadvantage by U.S. government R&D funding over the past 15 years. Already in 1971, if government funding is subtracted from total R&D expenditures, at least four of the U.S. industries listed in Table 8 had become less research-intensive than their Japanese counterparts. Subtracting the full amount of government-funded R&D may distort the comparison, but there is evidence that the private rate of return for U.S. government R&D spending may be very low.[40] The low return may be due to externalities and restrictions on the appropriability of government-funded innovation, but, as we discuss below, the assumption must be that those externalities are no more internal to the U.S. economy than they are to the U.S. firm.

Consideration must also be given to evidence suggesting that rather than being a substitute for private R&D, government funding actually

TABLE 11
Parameter Estimates for Japan and U.S. Government R&D Equation

Variable	Japan		United States	
	(1)	(2)	(3)	(4)
ELEC	0.053**	0.049	0.010	0.009
	(0.037)	(0.035)	(0.016)	(0.014)
CHEM	0.002	0.001	−0.003	−0.003
	(0.008)	(0.007)	(0.010)	(0.010)
BIO	0.007	0.010	0.028	0.033
	(0.006)	(0.012)	(0.034)	(0.031)
MECH	0.039**	0.038**	0.010	0.008
	(0.021)	(0.020)	(0.14)	(0.012)
BASIC	0.005	0.005	0.012	0.015
	(0.012)	(0.013)	(0.159)	(0.141)
AGE/100	0.075†	0.073†	0.224 †	0.220†
	(0.036)	(0.034)	(0.099)	(0.097)
AGE SQ/10	−0.006†	−0.006†	−0.003 †	−0.003†
	(0.002)	(0.002)	(0.001)	(0.001)
H	−0.001	—	−0.038	—
	(0.009)	—	(0.099)	—
BORROW	0.007**	0.007**	0.056**	0.053*
	(0.002)	(0.002)	(0.034)	(0.032)
DEFShR	0.002	0.002	0.066***	0.066***
			(0.006)	(0.006)
GOVShR	0.037	0.034	0.001	0.002
	(0.045)	(0.043)	(0.048)	(0.047)

SOURCE: Adapted from Richard C. Levin and Peter C. Reis, "Tests of a Schumpeterian Model of R&D and Market Structure," *National Bureau of Economic Research Working Paper*, No. 1132 (Apr. 1983).
   NOTE: Asymptotic *t*-ratio indicates significance (*p*) as follows: *p = .10 (one-tailed test), **p = .05 level (one-tailed test), ***p = .01 (one-tailed test), $^\dagger p$ = .05 (two-tailed test).

stimulates additional private R&D spending.[41] Not only is R&D allocation heavily shaped by government funding and directed toward supporting the procurement of public goods in the United States, but publicly funded R&D would also generate additional, privately financed
R&D. To the extent that private sector R&D is directed toward the com-
mercialization of spin-offs from government-financed R&D, the competitiveness of U.S. industry may well be enhanced. On the other hand,
to the extent that private R&D is undertaken in the hopes of improving a
firm's ability to successfully compete with other firms for government
procurements contracts, the opposite may be true.

Japan's low level of defense-related procurements has had important
implications for Japan's R&D system: (1) macroeconomic policies aimed
at expanding aggregate demand have played a greater role than targeted
industrial policy in promoting the growth of high-technology products;
(2) MITI has had to rely predominantly on supply-related incentives, not
demand-pull measures; (3) inefficient resource allocation, waste, and politicization have been kept under relative control; (4) this has prompted
Japanese management to stress applied R&D instead of basic or prototype-
development research; (5) with no assurances of government demand for
new products, Japanese companies have followed a fairly conservative
approach to R&D, emphasizing reasonably high prospects of commercial feasibility; (6) this may be one reason why the Japanese have not
been noted for creating whole new industries or major new product designs; and (7) Japanese engineers and scientists have not been diverted
from commercially oriented R&D to carry on highly specialized research
for military and space applications. Like other characteristics of Japan's
R&D system, the implications here are neither all positive or all negative,
but rather a mixture of the two.

Training and R&D in Japan and the United States

The findings of the preceding section rest heavily on the assumption
that the supply conditions of R&D inputs, particularly research personnel, are relatively similar in Japan and the United States. In fact, as might
be expected, the special characteristics of Japanese labor markets have a
significant impact on the training and supply of Japanese scientific and
engineering personnel and ultimately on the character of Japanese R&D.

From the 1960s through the early 1980s, the total number of scientists
and engineers in Japan's labor force, especially scientists and engineers
engaged in R&D, increased at a rate that surpassed that of every other
major industrialized economy, including the Soviet Union. Indeed, this
rate of increase has been so large that, despite being only half the United
States' size, the Japanese economy added more scientists and engineers

in absolute terms to its R&D labor force between 1969 and the early 1980s than any other advanced industrialized economy including the United States.[42]

Japan's rapidly growing scientific and technological labor force is stirring anxieties in the United States, somewhat reminiscent of old fears concerning the Soviet Union's capacity to turn out large numbers of scientists and engineers. In recent years, careful study of the Soviet Union's higher educational programs in science and technology has added a qualitative dimension to what had been crude, quantitative comparisons. According to the National Science Board,

Soviet graduate training programs are considered to be more narrowly specialized, oriented toward the specific needs of research institutes and geared towards applied science, while U.S. graduates receive a broader based and more flexible theoretical education. Moreover, a third of all non-doctorate U.S. scientists and engineers have increased their skills through further formal training in master's degree programs while the Soviet Union does not have such programs. Therefore, it may be that U.S. specialists, although fewer in number, are better prepared to deal with future problems and goals.[43]

Significantly, there is reason to believe that Japanese government R&D, together with the character of Japanese labor and financial markets, may give rise to science and technology training closer to that of the Soviet Union than to that of the United States.

In order to understand why, we must examine the character and extent of Japanese government support for higher education in science and engineering. Modern industrialized economies face the difficult problem of encouraging a socially optimal accumulation of skills. Until the postwar period, there were few alternatives to self- or family financing for the acquisition of new skills. With worker mobility, firms providing general training implicitly charged their workers for this service. At the same time, because skills are embodied in individuals and no tangible collateral could be confiscated for nonpayment of loans, it was difficult to seek financing for skill accumulation from financial intermediaries. In consequence, in both prewar Japan and the United States, there was probably a persistent underaccumulation of socially beneficial skills, with skill accumulation heavily dependent on personal or family resources.[44]

The growing complexities of industrial life have come to require a more rapid accumulation of industrial skills. Immediately after World War II, a number of extremely significant programs were organized in the United States to subsidize skill accumulation directly or to facilitate the use of financial intermediaries to underwrite advanced training. These programs, including Veterans Educational Benefits, which began with the G.I. Bill of Rights, and Guaranteed Student Loans, required that training be conducted in accredited educational institutions. Thanks to these programs, the demand for, and supply of, vocational undergraduate and graduate education in the United States has expanded enormously.

In Japan, skill accumulation has assumed a different institutional form. No major government programs directly subsidize an individual student's education. The number of public institutions providing education at a heavily subsidized, low rate of tuition has increased to some extent, but the steep rise in the number of Japanese receiving higher education has come about largely through a growth in the number of, and an increase in enrollments at, private universities—which finance themselves to a considerable degree out of tuition fees.[45]

Financial stringency has strapped university-based research. Lacking large government grants, until recently most Japanese universities have been unable to develop and sustain extensive research programs, particularly in the sciences and engineering. They have made little effort to provide specialized graduate programs. The $4.8 billion that the U.S. government provides in support of R&D in universities and colleges is roughly six times what Japanese universities receive in R&D support from their government. Not surprisingly, U.S. academic institutions in 1981 awarded six times as many doctoral degrees in the sciences and engineering as Japanese institutions.[46] In biology the United States graduates 36 times the number of Ph.D.s and in chemistry 10 times the number. Although a third of all U.S. scientists and engineers without doctorates have enhanced their skills through further training in master's degree programs, less than 5 per cent of the same group in Japan have received further training.[47] In Japan, advanced training takes place within the firm.

Although a Ph.D. is practically a prerequisite for participation in a U.S. corporate R&D laboratory, it is not required in otherwise comparable Japanese facilities. More than 1,200 Ph.D.s work in U.S. biogenetic engineering, according to a 1982 survey by the Office of Technology Assessment and the National Academy of Sciences.[48] In contrast, a Keidanren (Federation of Economic Organizations) survey found only 161 scientists and engineers with doctorates doing firm-based R&D work in biotechnology in 1982, including Japanese with Ph.Ds from American universities. A number of subsidized public universities including Tokyo, Kyoto, Osaka, and Kyushu have significant programs in biotechnology, but these programs train only a limited pool of advanced research personnel for Japanese industry. A MITI survey of 104 firms found that about 80 per cent of the research personnel have been trained exclusively in their own firms—a rather surprising figure for a dynamic, high-tech industry like biotechnology.[49] However, over 40 per cent of the biotechnology firms surveyed in 1981 and 1982 indicated some engineering and scientific personnel would be sent abroad for either primary or supplementary training.[50]

Japanese companies have apparently discovered cheaper ways of training than sending large numbers of employees through doctoral programs. Sometimes the right mix of skills and knowledge can be obtained by using foreign consultants on a temporary basis. The in-house training Japanese R&D personnel receive is less general and less theoretical than that which might be received through U.S. graduate schools, but it is more closely coordinated with the Japanese firm's operational needs. Like the Soviet Union but unlike the United States, little emphasis is placed on training well-rounded members of a profession, occupation, or craft.[51] Where well-rounded researchers are needed, the facilities of Japan's relatively few graduate research institutions can be used, or scientists and engineers can be sent abroad for additional training.

The differing locus and character of training in Japan have led, in part, to much lower interfirm mobility of scientific and engineering personnel than in the United States or Western Europe. They have also led to much less of a professional and occupational orientation. The absence of pervasive extra-firm training programs and of an extra-market means of allocating skilled scientific and engineering personnel suggests that by contrast with the United States, large amounts of potentially proprietary scientific information do not readily become public goods in Japan. In the United States, both the prospective employer and the prospective employee may operate under strong incentives to disclose proprietary information as a means of signaling quality. Such disclosure can be done directly or in the context of professional association activities. Strong professional identity makes possible the use of professional associations as a lever for job mobility. In Japan, such motives are much weaker.

In some senses, of course, the small leakage of proprietary information among Japanese firms can be considered desirable. In the United States, the leakage is considerable in spite of extensive legal efforts to protect the proprietary fruits of R&D investments. Such leakage can reduce the rate of return to R&D by diminishing incentives to invest as many resources as might be socially desirable.

On the other hand, there may be some rationale behind the flow of information among firms. In the United States, scientific and engineering personnel and potential employers might disclose information in order to enhance the chances for a labor market transaction at some later date or to receive proprietary information of commensurate value in exchange. Such an exchange could make everyone better off. It could also complement market transactions in information exchange. Often, informal exchanges are a prerequisite to more formal market agreements.

Certain U.S. high-technology industries, such as semiconductors, encourage the sharing of generic information among firm scientific and engineering personnel through regularly sponsored seminars.

To the extent that such information exchanges are useful and facilitated by a large cadre of highly trained, professionally oriented scientific and engineering personnel, the United States may hold a competitive advantage over Japan. Japan's system of in-house training, which once met the needs of catching-up in heavy manufacturing sectors, may not be as well suited to state-of-the-art innovation in high technology, although it offers its own mix of strengths and weaknesses.

Like other aspects of its R&D system, however, Japan's method of in-house training may be changing in response to the changing functional needs of high technology. Since the training of advanced researchers is closely related to the character of advanced research in graduate education, as well as to labor and capital markets, Japan's capacity to adapt its whole approach to training will hinge importantly on the evolution of those institutions.

Summary and Prospects

Japan stands at a historic crossroads. The postwar era of latecomer catch-up in smokestack manufacturing is over. Perhaps the biggest challenge is making the transition from a heavy manufacturing base to an economy capable of adapting to the changing functional requirements of high technology. In this connection, perhaps the two overriding questions are Does Japan need to innovate still more than it has recently in order to maintain its rapid rate of structural transformation, and If still more innovation is required, is it likely to be forthcoming, given the quality of Japan's R&D base? The answers to these questions will be one of the keys to Japan's economic future.

In this paper, we have resisted the temptation to engage in technological forecasting, an intriguing but risky task that others are far better suited to undertake. We have, instead, focused on three major areas in which Japan's R&D system differs sharply from that of the United States: (1) the role of small companies, especially newly established firms, in the R&D process; (2) the role of the government in underwriting R&D and shaping the agenda of private sector R&D; and (3) the nature of advanced training for R&D personnel. The organization of Japanese efforts in all three areas (in conjunction with other important variables) will have a crucial bearing on Japan's capacity to innovate.

Japan's postwar R&D system, which features distinctive institutions in the three areas mentioned, has functioned fairly well in meeting the needs of technological catch-up. Judging from a variety of unobtrusive indicators, Japan has made extraordinary progress over the entire postwar period, most notably during the 20-year period from 1965 to 1985. As noted, by 1985 Japan had already caught up with, or in some instances actually surpassed, the United States in many areas of advanced technology—the most notable exception being the area of highly specialized, military applications. For a country that once trailed as far behind as Japan, the speed and scope of technological catch-up have been impressive.

Rapid progress in applied technology has had the effect of increasing incentives to upgrade the level of basic research—a form of "backward integration," as it were, from applied technology to theoretical knowledge. Instead of achieving technological pre-eminence by building from a strong prior foundation in the basic sciences, Japan has followed the common historical, if not the logical, sequence of backtracking from the forefront of technology to the development of a sturdy scientific base capable of propelling Japan beyond the technological frontiers.

Although Japan's technological progress has been quite remarkable, it should be understood within the context of the backward, early postwar baseline from which progress is measured. Unobtrusive indicators like international patent data exaggerate the inventiveness of Japan's private sector. Patent data convey little or no information about the technological and commercial significance of the innovations registered.

We pointed out that because of different labor and capital market conditions, large corporations account for a much larger share of innovations in Japan than do their counterparts in the United States. Small, newly established firms in the United States appear to generate a steady stream of technological breakthroughs—far beyond their declining share in total R&D expenditures. By contributing disproportionately to technological change, they force big companies to pay greater attention to R&D, step up the intensity of competition, and open up new market niches. With far fewer venture firms in Japan, their impact on technological change is far less significant.

The pattern in Japan is for extant companies—often large corporations—to move aggressively to exploit new technologies, either directly or through the creation of small subsidiaries. Which pattern—the United States' or Japan's—is superior in terms of stimulating innovation is hard to say. Each has advantages and drawbacks. Interestingly, Japan is trying to alter its financial markets in ways that would facilitate the financing of venture firms; but the basic pattern of dominance by big, established firms appears unlikely to change in the foreseeable future.

This is not to say that small-scale firms in Japan fail to make any contribution. Nominally they account for a higher proportion of R&D expenditures than their counterparts in the United States (even though the larger expenditures are not reflected at all in even comparable innovative yields). Although this proportion is declining, it may reverse, if, as Masahiko Aoki points out, large companies continue to set up more and more subsidiaries to which they funnel more R&D funds.[52] Because of their close working relationships with large parent firms, small companies in Japan are well positioned to contribute richly to the improvement of processing and production technologies. If information flows more freely among firms in the United States, it flows more readily up and down vertical networks in Japan (between large parent firms and small subcontractors or subsidiaries). Unlike the small firms in the United States that have played an important role in generating significant innovations, the small Japanese firms likely to be similarly involved are in no sense independent entities.

Although the Japanese government spends far less to support private sector R&D than its U.S. counterpart, Japan as a whole is not placed at a serious disadvantage vis-à-vis the United States. Indeed, because U.S. government funding is so closely tied to the procurement of public goods (specifically military security), large U.S. government R&D expenditures may actually redound to Japan's benefit, if the spillover effects from military to commercial spheres are low or if there are finite supplies of skilled R&D manpower. Of the large industrial states, Japan may be the only one capable of concentrating its finite resources almost exclusively on commercial applications of technology. As is true of other aspects of its R&D system, the relatively low level of government funding for private sector R&D carries both benefits and costs. Over time and on balance, the benefits have come increasingly to outweigh the costs, as Japan competes against the United States on an equal footing.

If the Japanese government spends less, it takes much more initiative than the U.S. government in microindustrial management through the use of industrial policy. Not only does it identify and target key technologies for Japan's economic future, it also coordinates intraindustry efforts at building a binding consensus within industry and between government and industry. Here again, it is hard to say how decisive the government's role has been or, indeed, whether the benefits have outweighed the costs.

The Japanese approach to advanced training of R&D personnel, based on in-house apprenticeship and permanent employment, is not as rigorous academically as that in the United States but may be more cost-effective. Perhaps its most glaring drawback, which intrafirm training can only partially overcome, is the relatively deficient infrastructure for graduate education. Not only is this reflected in the comparatively small output of researchers with advanced degrees, more tellingly, it shows up in the quality of research conducted at Japanese universities. The second-rate quality of university-based research, in turn, diminishes the potential synergism of university-industry interactions. In Japan, university-industry relations are far less extensive and fruitful than is the case in the United States. Aware of the problems, the Japanese government is studying ways of bridging the university-industry gap.

The U.S. approach, based on extra-firm training and a highly mobile labor market, turns out a large cadre of superbly trained researchers. It features the world's finest system of university-based research and university-industrial cooperation. The location of various centers of high technology near major research campuses in the United States—Silicon Valley, the North Carolina triangle, Route 128 near Boston—attests to the vitality of university-industry interactions. The biggest drawback of the U.S. system is the leakage of vast amounts of potential proprietary information, which tends to become public goods for the rest of the world. This aids technological diffusion enormously but may affect both the character and the quantity of research undertaken in the United States.

Although the differences between the Japanese and the U.S. R&D systems are striking, so, too, are some of the similarities (which we have not discussed). Both function within market-based economies; both rely heavily on commercial incentives and interfirm competition to advance technology; and both have managed to satisfy the technological and economic needs of their countries. Both can be considered atypical in that no other R&D system bears much resemblance. Of the two, Japan's may be the most unusual. Few other large industrial states possess Japan's peculiar combination of a "dual industrial structure," extensive vertical networks (between parent firms and subsidiaries or subcontractors), tightly regulated financial markets, low-mobility labor markets, very low military R&D expenditures, and a limited academic infrastructure for advanced training.

As implied throughout this paper, however, Japan's R&D system is undergoing structural change. The impetus comes mainly from two sources: the maturation, deregulation, and internationalization of Japan's economy; and the perceived need to reform certain institutional impediments to the promotion of state-of-the-art innovation. Of the two, the first may impart the strongest impetus for long-term structural change since financial markets and industrial organization are so inextricably intertwined with R&D investments, corporate strategies, government policies, and other factors affecting technological change. The second set of forces (which emerge from conscious design) could also have a substantial impact, especially in areas that are responsive to changes in public policy—such as the reform of higher education and government sponsorship of private sector R&D.

Of course, given the weight of inertia and the strength of vested interests, Japan's R&D system is unlikely to undergo radical transformation overnight. If, however, the impetus for change continues to be strong, aspects of the R&D system could change enough over time, and at the margins, to make a difference in Japan's capacity to innovate. Most Japanese believe that some modification of their postwar R&D system is necessary if Japan is to make the transition from technological catch-up to state-of-the-art innovation.

A tacit assumption underlying this paper is that in order to compete successfully in high technology, Japan will have to devise ways of being more innovative. Is this assumption valid? Why must Japan innovate? Why would it not be possible to do exactly what the Japanese have done so adroitly in the past—namely, be content to follow a conservative, second-to-market strategy and let the United States assume the high costs and risks of pioneering the frontiers of technology? Why not continue concentrating on the unglamorous but commercially critical areas of processing and production technology? Is not the history of technology replete with examples of original inventors being soundly thrashed in commercial markets by technological second-comers?

These and other questions imply that a distinction has to be drawn between technological innovation and market success. It has long been understood that the two are not synonymous. The ability to innovate does not guarantee commercial profits. However, because many high-technology industries have steep learning curves and comparatively short product life cycles, the advantages of being first to market can be worth far more than the costs and risks of early investment. First-comers can find themselves in a favorable position to carve out dominant market shares, gain brand-name recognition, move down the learning curve, and raise barriers to new entry—all of which can push second-comers right out of the market.

The option of relying on foreign technology as an alternative to domestic innovation is available to those countries that wish to exercise it. To the extent that foreign technology is fully appropriable by foreign producers, this strategy can leave companies at the mercy of foreign firms that may or may not be willing to grant patent licenses in return for royalty payments. If foreign patent holders feel they can gain more by withholding patents, second-to-market firms could find themselves closed out of lucrative markets. In this era of high technology, of course, the transfer of technology across national borders is greater than ever, with multiple mechanisms of transfer—licensing, second-sourcing, original equipment manufacturer agreements, and cross-licensing. Nevertheless, most Japanese companies seem to feel that they must possess their own stock of technology in order to obtain foreign know-how. More and more bartering is taking place in international technology transfers because of

mounting costs and risks and the value of innovation. There are therefore immediate or short-term circumstances that require the Japanese to
alter their second-to-market strategy.

We can add to this a mid-to-long-term factor that could offer the most
compelling reason of all: namely, irreversible pressure from below by
newly industrializing countries in Asia moving rapidly up the ladder
of manufacturing value added and forcing Japan to climb ever higher
up the ladder of international comparative advantage or to drop out
and simply resort to protectionism to stave off foreign competition. As
South Korea, Taiwan, and Singapore develop the infrastructure to mass-
produce consumer electronics products, for example, Japanese producers will have no choice—short of protectionism—but to scramble up
the ladder of value added. They will have to move, for example, from
consumer to industrial electronics, from hardware to software, from
components to integrated systems. With "mini-Japans" springing up all
around it, Japan's only sure strategy to stay ahead will be to step up the
pace of innovation.

Part IV

Government and the Economy

George C. Eads and Kozo Yamamura

The Future of Industrial Policy

Although there is little dispute that the Japanese economy has been one of the world's star performers, if not *the* star performer, during the postwar period, there is controversy about what is responsible for Japan's remarkable achievement. In particular, the role of "industrial policy" in the Japanese "economic miracle" has been a subject of considerable dispute. Broadly stated, one school—consisting of many Japanese scholars and some Western analysts—appears to assign to it substantial to overwhelming credit. But another school—of which the most vocal members are neo-classical economists—gives it much less weight, with some members going so far as to assert that its influence has been, on balance, marginal or even detrimental.[1]

In this paper, we do not attempt to resolve this dispute. Indeed, it cannot be resolved objectively by the analytic tools and empirical evidence available today to social scientists.[2] Our goal is to take advantage of the insights offered by the broader political, economic, and social perspective of the first school and by the neo-classical theoretical perspective of the second school.

We first define the scope of industrial policy in a brief discussion of the conceptual issues involved—that is, the conditions required for successful execution of industrial policy. This is followed by a description of a framework for analyzing a possible future structure of Japanese industrial policy and its impact—what objectives it might seek to achieve, what tools it might use, and what results it might produce. We then briefly assess the experience of other industrial countries. Our intent in this short section is to use the implications of other countries' experience to assess the future of Japanese industrial policy.

In the final two sections, we describe the gradual changes in Japanese industrial policy after the mid-1960s[3] and two polar scenarios of the future of the Japanese economy. In the first, the Japanese economy performs quite well, and industrial policy contributes positively to this performance. This does not mean that the Japanese economy resumes the remarkable path achieved during the "high growth period"—the mid-1950s to the first "oil shock" of 1973—when real GNP grew at an average annual rate of 10 per cent. Instead, "doing well" means that Japan outperforms most other industrialized countries in terms of real growth. In our other scenario, Japan's economy performs significantly worse than those of its trading partners, and industrial policy is a major culprit. GNP growth is stagnant or negative, and total per capita output may even decline.

Some Definitional and Conceptual Issues

The Scope of Industrial Policy

In the United States in the past few years, the term "industrial policy" has come to stand for virtually all interaction between government and the industrial sector. As ably summarized in a recent study by the Congressional Budget Office, proposals for a "U.S. industrial policy" have involved everything from "creative tinkering" with existing policy tools, such as the antitrust laws, trade law, and labor market adjustment mechanisms, to the establishment of institutions quite different from any yet seen in the United States—except perhaps in time of war or major economic depression.[4]

Yet for all their variety, these proposals can be distinguished from proposals to improve the macroeconomic climate. Each goes beyond merely addressing the underlying factors that primarily influence the rate of economic growth—factors such as the general level of savings and investment and the pace of technological progress—and places the government in the position of actively and consciously intervening to influence specific firms, industries, or sectors. The former is properly classified as "macroeconomic policy"; the latter, as "industrial policy." Both may affect macroeconomic performance, and both clearly influence the relative health of different industries. But the two categories of policies are fundamentally different.

Analogously, in referring to Japan's industrial policy, we mean policies and methods used primarily to increase the productivity of factor inputs and to influence, directly and indirectly, the investment (and disinvestment) decisions of industries. In Japan as elsewhere, these policies and methods typically relate to areas such as trade, labor markets, competition policy, and tax incentives. The means to carry out the policy goals are also familiar—a broad range of trade protection measures, subsidies in various forms, de jure and de facto exemptions from antitrust statutes, several types of labor market adjustments, a variety of mostly direct and often industry-specific assistance to enhance the pace and range of adoption of new technology, and the like. As we discuss below, informal (nonenforceable in a legal sense) ministerial involvement in the corporate decision-making process—"administrative guidance"—has been a significant element in Japanese industrial policy.

Although the distinction between macro and industrial policy is analytically useful, we argue that, in the Japan of the rapid growth decades, these two policies were more effectively coordinated and overlapped more extensively in practice than in other industrial economies.

Industrial policy: How to measure its success. The issue of the conditions necessary for a successful industrial policy is complicated. The first complication involves the metric used to measure success. Most neo-classical economists feel comfortable measuring "success" by conventional economic criteria—specifically, the intermediate or long-term rate of return on investment. In his critique of the notion that Japanese industrial policy has indeed "picked winners," Paul Krugman considers that the lower rate of return earned by the Japanese steel industry in comparison to Japanese industry in general is strong evidence of the failure of the Japanese policy of "targeting" steel.[5]

Others, including some economists, argue that an industrial policy can be a success if it helps build forward or backward linkages. Thus, Japan's targeting of steel might be considered a success despite the lower than average rate of return because it enabled Japan to develop, among others, the shipbuilding and automobile industries. To the best of our knowledge, no one has attempted a serious and analytically defensible evaluation of the success of Japanese industrial policy on these broader grounds, though such assertions are common.[6]

Still others consider an industrial policy successful if it generates a higher level of employment than would exist in its absence, especially higher value-added employment. Most economists are skeptical of these criteria, and Krugman has provided a convincing argument why they should be.[7] The mere absorption of labor is, by itself, no virtue. Moreover, taken by itself, high value-added employment may merely mean that workers have been given a great deal of physical capital (which itself must be paid a return) to work with.

As we indicated, we think the clearest measure of success would be a demonstration that, but for the industrial policy, the real economic growth of an economy would have been lower.[8] This does not mean that industry by industry comparisons must turn out uniformly favorable. We are less skeptical than Krugman of the existence of linkage effects, although, like him, we would caution that the mere assertion of linkages is not enough to establish their existence. If an industrial policy significantly helped develop important linkage industries that, in turn, contributed to improved productivity and growth throughout the economy, we would be willing to judge it successful. Alternatively, if an industrial policy did nothing more than smooth rough spots in the path of market-dictated industrial adjustment, thereby making the adjustment more acceptable socially and politically, we also would consider it successful.[9] In short, we believe that the important criterion is an economic one, but the assessment of a policy's success need not, and indeed should not, be limited to a narrowly defined economic criterion.

Industrial policy instruments. A second difficulty in defining the conditions necessary for success concerns how broadly we cast our nets in identifying policy instruments and institutions. Again there is disagreement between economists and noneconomists. Just as economists are inclined to consider relatively narrow economic measures (such as the profitability of a targeted industry) in measuring the success of an industrial policy, so, too, are they prone to judge the strength of an industrial policy by the scale on which conventional economic indicators of industrial assistance are used.

Several scholars not only downplay the influence of industrial policy on Japan's postwar economic success (the output side), but also denigrate it as a significant feature of Japanese policymaking (the input side). Philip Trezise, for example, does so because his investigations lead him to the conclusion that the Japanese do not currently employ significant direct subsidies, tariffs, or other customary economic instruments to promote the growth of promising industries. Lacking these proofs of influence, those holding such a view conclude that Japanese industrial policy is nothing but clouds and smoke—a latter-day version of the Wizard of Oz. We believe that this view of Japanese industrial policy is erroneous because it is too narrowly conceived. Moreover, as the evidence presented below demonstrates, it ignores quantitatively significant industry-specific subsidies, tariffs, and other direct economic aid provided to various industries during the 1950s and 1960s.[10] By affecting the productivity and capacity levels of several important industries, along with the market structure of many industries and even the sectoral composition of the economy, direct economic aid unarguably influenced the performance and behavior of Japanese industries. In short, this view can be faulted for ignoring past policy and its continuing effects on the performance of the Japanese economy since the oil crisis.[11]

To many noneconomists and to some Japanese and Western economists as well, the absence of significant direct economic aids does not necessarily mean that the Japanese government lacks an active industrial policy. Indeed, many Japanese and such Western scholars as Chalmers

Johnson and Ezra Vogel consider the institutional setting of Japanese industrial policy as the key to its influence. To Johnson, for example, the Ministry of International Trade and Industry (MITI)—in his phrase, the "economic general staff"—is an absolutely critical element in Japanese industrial policy.[12] This is true not because MITI (and other "economic" ministries) directly controls a significant volume of economic resources but because it coordinates the process of consultation and consensus formulation that these scholars consider the central feature of the Japanese industrial policy.[13]

However, as made clear in our discussion in the next section of the roles played by the administrative guidance of MITI and other ministries, we once again prefer to take a middle ground. We believe that political and social institutions count—and importantly—as elements of industrial policy. But industrial policy is above all essentially economic and is intended to affect economic variables. In the final analysis, the efficacy of a policy must be judged by its visible impact on such economic variables as investment and productivity, not merely by the asserted or presumed influence of the economic ministries. Our position is that if empirically verifiable economic effects cannot be adequately explained without considering the influence of bureaucrats, then we are not reluctant to acknowledge their influence in addition to the influence of the policy tools they used.

A Proposed Analytical Framework

We need an analytical framework broad enough to encompass both the political and social environment and the direct and indirect instruments of economic influence. Fortunately, we need not construct such a framework *de novo*. John Zysman, in his book *Governments, Markets and Growth*,[14] has provided one we can adapt. His framework, which we restate in modified form, gives weight to three broad elements, each of which is necessary, but no one of which is sufficient, to the conduct of a successful industrial policy. These elements are (1) a set of fundamental governmental capabilities to develop and execute policies affecting industry; (2) an appropriate kit of tools to influence industrial behavior; and (3) a prior agreement on the general objectives of the policy.

Two caveats are in order. First, in adapting Zysman's framework, we do not mean to suggest either that we agree with all of his conclusions or that we accept all of his framework. We believe that his framework is deficient because it fails to consider the process of policy formulation and execution, which can affect the character and efficacy of industrial policy no less significantly than the three elements he identified. Second, here we are unable to discuss the international politico-economic conditions that cannot but affect the character and performance of Japanese industrial policy. Our comments on these conditions are limited to a few passing observations.[15]

Governmental capabilities. As many political scientists have stressed, the basic organization of a government is crucial to its ability to design and execute something as politically and economically complex as industrial policy. Three aspects of governmental organization seem particularly important: (1) the source of the upper echelons of the bureaucracy (how rigorous the selection process is, and whether upper-level bureaucrats are recruited from within the civil service or are politically appointed); (2) the extent to which power is centralized; and (3) the degree of autonomy that the executive has from detailed legislative scrutiny. A centralized state, with substantial executive autonomy and a minimum of political appointees, seems likely to be the most capable of conducting an effective industrial policy. At the other extreme are decentralized states, with little executive autonomy and upper ranks staffed primarily by political appointees.

It might seem that the intervening cases would lie on a continuum—the closer a state was to possessing the three desirable attributes, the higher its ability to design and conduct an industrial policy, and vice versa. But this is not the case. Different combinations can lead to sharply different approaches to industrial adjustment. There is no continuum. Although we do not have the space here to describe in full detail the various subcases and their implications,[16] suffice it to say that we find the emphasis on institutional capacity in Zysman's analytic formulation quite congenial. We also find congenial Zysman's recognition that it is only one piece of the puzzle. Unlike others stressing the institutional capabilities of a government in formulating and executing industrial policy, Zysman does not elevate institutional capacity to the central role.

An appropriate kit of policy tools. A capable, highly professional bureaucracy possessing considerable power and the ability to exercise it free of second-guessing by the legislature may be a necessary condition for the ability to design and successfully execute industrial policy. But it is not sufficient. The bureaucrats must have effective and appropriate tools to influence the behavior of target firms, industries, and sectors. Since industrial policy is fundamentally concerned with investment and disinvestment decisions, the effectiveness and appropriateness of such tools are measured by their impact on these decisions.

The most effective and appropriate tools are those that directly influence the supply and cost of investment funds. In countries whose domestic capital markets are subject to extensive political control and are effectively closed to international capital movements, the government can "administer" interest rates and directly allocate investable funds. As domestic capital markets become more autonomous, either because they become more responsive to domestic market forces or because they become open to international influences (or both), the ability of industrial policy authorities to control the pace and direction of investment wanes.

This does not necessarily mean the total loss of the capacity to carry out an industrial policy. But it puts much greater weight on policy instruments whose influence on investment is less direct (and possibly less effective), such as trade policy, subsidies, procurement, competition policy, and regulatory policy. Each clearly can influence profitability differentially by firm, industry, or sector. If appropriately tuned, each can create signals that *should* influence investment in predictable ways. But this influence is subject to attenuation. Trade restrictions that boost an industry's profitability might induce that industry to invest more, but they also might lead to higher wage settlements, slower rates of technological change, or less efficient management practices. The further one moves from direct controls over the price and supply of capital, the more opportunities there are for industrial policies to be subverted.

A consensus on basic goals. The third necessary condition is the existence of some mechanism *outside the conduct of the industrial policy itself* leading to agreement on the policy's basic goals. The mechanism can vary. One is somehow to exclude potentially disruptive actors from the goal-setting process. In some countries, the political power of certain interests is such that they can be ignored. In other cases, more direct means of disenfranchisement might be employed. Another mechanism is to buy off certain interests in ways that do not severely inhibit the conduct of the industrial policy. When an economy is expanding rapidly and the expansion is expected to continue, the prospect of more for everyone may be enough to prevent dissent. When growth is slower or losses for particular groups larger, explicit payoffs may be necessary.

The crucial point is that the process of industrial policy formulation is not the means of developing the basic consensus about such a vital issue as the relative weights a society must place on growth and equity. That consensus, and the means for maintaining it, are developed elsewhere in the political system. If industrial policy formulation becomes the battleground for deciding these core issues, an effective industrial policy becomes impossible.

Indeed, an ineffective industrial policy is not the worst possible outcome. If a country possesses the first two sets of necessary industrial policy elements (governmental capacity and effective instruments to carry an industrial policy out) and if the formulation process becomes a battle over who deserves to win and who must lose, then an industrial policy can become positively perverse—a giant with immense power but no means of effective control.

Japan During the High Growth Period

Although it is not our intention to attempt to settle the debate about the importance of industrial policy in producing Japan's remarkable economic growth, the knowledgeable reader has probably already juxtaposed certain characteristics of the Japanese political and economic systems from the mid-1950s to the 1960s with the framework just presented. Not surprisingly, the fit with the conditions required for a successful industrial policy is remarkably good.

Institutional Capacity

Few familiar with Japan would deny that its central bureaucracy—the ministries in Tokyo manned by rigorously selected elite career officials—enjoys the prestige and power needed to formulate and execute an industrial policy. And, as discussed later, the bureaucracy enjoyed more of both during the rapid growth decades. Much of the prestige was the legacy of post-1868 history and reflected the fact that only graduates of a few of the most prestigious universities have been admitted to the elite core of the bureaucracy.[17] Their power also derived from their position as administrators of a strong, centralized government whose strength was enhanced by the continuity of the policy it pursued under the sustained dominance of the Liberal Democratic Party (LDP). Furthermore, their powers included administrative guidance—the discretionary capacity to suggest, guide, and coerce if necessary—which is discussed below as a principal element in the policy process.

Interpretations of the sources and extent of the effectiveness of Japan's institutional capability and especially that of the bureaucracy differ widely. Some see in the bureaucracy (that is, in the economic ministries) a unique institutional capability to promote economic performance. Johnson, for example, went so far as to characterize MITI as a farsighted "general staff" of a "developmental state."[18] Others credit MITI, the Ministry of Finance (MOF), and other economic ministries with none of these qualities and see them merely as arms of the central bureaucracy with the power to dispense what industries in the rapid growth decade wanted—trade protection, subsidies, exemption from antitrust statutes, and the like. For the reasons summarized at the end of this section, we do not subscribe to either of these views. We are, however, willing to assert that the institutional capability of Japan has been stronger than that of other industrial nations. We believe the validity of this assertion is supported by our description below of the institutional capabilities of the Western industrialized nations.

Access to Tools

During the high growth period, the Japanese bureaucracy enjoyed access to a wide range of policy tools to carry out industrial policy. Laws enacted in 1949 and in the 1950s gave the bureaucracy extensive controls over capital markets (the markets were quite strictly segmented, and interest rates were administered by each segmented market) and effectively insulated domestic capital markets from the international capital market. This control and insulation enabled the goverment to adopt what is often called "the sub-equilibrium interest rate disequilibrium policy." Among other controls, the government could both set long-term loan rates and rates paid on deposits at a level below those that would have resulted had these rates not been administered. The policy encouraged excess demand (for loans at the controlled rate), and this enabled the MOF to ration and guide (the well-known "window guidance") the flow of credit to large firms in industries adopting new technology, thus increasing productivity and exports. In the rapid growth decades when large firms were innovating and competitively expanding capacity, the MOF's power over credit was a potent tool of industrial policy.

Although no one questions the validity of these observations as applied to the 1950s, several specialists debate the significance of some of the specific measures adopted by the MOF and the extent of the effectiveness of the policy in the 1960s.[19] However, most specialists would acknowledge, with varying qualifications, that the fixed deposit rates and the MOF's consistent efforts both to set interest rates in each segment of the capital market and to exercise various forms of administrative guidance provided the ministry with the means to influence, directly and indirectly, the magnitude and destination (recipients) of the scarce credit. Or, to borrow Yasusuke Murakami's words, "If all relevant facts . . . are considered in a comprehensive way, it may be a sound judgment that the interest rate was regulated at an artificially low level in the following sense. The effective interest rates in most financial markets would have been significantly higher, and never lower, if a network of financial regulations had been removed."[20] In discussing the MOF's policy, we should be aware that the ministry controlled a large portion of savings directly (because of its control over the Postal Savings system) and used them in its Fiscal Investment and Loan Program (FILP). As stressed later, this, too, served as a powerful policy tool, especially during the 1950s and the early 1960s.[21]

The Japanese government's arsenal of indirect tools for influencing investment decisions was greatest during the rapid growth period. The major categories of policy tools (to be discussed later) were tariffs (although their influence declined throughout much of the period); import quotas (which had not yet come under especially strong foreign criticism); direct and indirect subsidies (significant for some industries); and an extremely favorable budget situation (which made appropriations for these subsidies and for tax incentives not that much of a problem). Competition policies were not a meaningful hindrance; indeed, just the reverse was true. Industries obtained relatively easily broad exemptions from the Japanese Antimonopoly Law, which had been substantially weakened in 1953.[22]

No less important, since Japan was technologically quite backward relative to other industrialized countries, was the government's ability to assist and influence industry in gaining access to a large stock of foreign technology and making use of it. Because of the Foreign Exchange Law in effect until 1964, MITI had the power to allocate foreign exchange (dollars) selectively, and the ministry effectively used this power both as a carrot and a stick (by withholding allocations) in influencing corporate decisions. Since most Japanese firms required imported raw materials and foreign technology, the ministry exercised this power, for example, to guide firms in their decisions on the rate of capacity increase and to affect the timing, composition, and allocations of the flow of new technology essential to the competitive success of every rapidly innovating Japanese firm.[23]

Strength of the Pro-Growth Political Consensus

Perhaps most important during this period was the strength of the underlying political consensus favoring rapid economic growth over all other goals. The ability of the government to pursue the pro-growth strategy was substantially strengthened by the effective disenfranchisement of the Left.[24] This, together with the policy of "lifetime employment" increasingly practiced by large firms, made labor a supporter rather than an opponent of the rapid growth strategy. If buy-offs were needed (for example, of farmers and the coal industry), the government coffer was able to do so easily. With real incomes increasing so fast, few concerned themselves with the distribution question. In the final analysis, the continued political dominance of the LDP is evidence for the existence of a consensus supporting the pro-growth policies adopted by the LDP.

Policy Formulation and Administrative Guidance

As noted earlier, the effects of Japanese industrial policy cannot be discussed without considering the process of policy formulation and execution. How did, for example, MITI formulate and carry out its policies? And, did the process itself affect the substance and the efficacy of the policies? Referring to other papers in this volume for further observations and insights useful in answering these questions more fully,[25] we present here only abbreviated answers to these questions in an attempt to offer a minimum necessary understanding of the process.

A crucial fact is that policies were and are formulated—perhaps "evolved" is a better word—following intense formal and informal consultation between a ministry and the industry affected by the policy. Although we are unable to provide detailed evidence, we feel justified in asserting that the intensity of this interaction was rarely matched in other industrial democracies. Of course, the shared and easily definable goal of "catching up," and thus the means to achieve it, of the rapid growth period made policy formulation easier,[26] and the ability of the ministries to provide incentives helped to lubricate the process. But, it is naive, in our judgment, to explain the process of Japanese industrial policy during this period and its effects merely in terms of the relative ease of identifying the policy goal and the government's ability to provide incentives.

Rather, this close interaction in policy formulation provided the ministries with sufficient knowledge of the degree and extent of cooperation with the ministry's policy goals that could be expected from the affected industry. To maximize cooperation, the ministry could rely on laws usually enacted at the industry's urging or with its support (because the laws invariably contained provisions for subsidies, tax incentives, antitrust exemptions, and the like). More important, however, the ministries could and did use the power of administrative guidance and adopted policies that were essentially market conforming.

Administrative guidance is non–legally binding guidance issued by ministries mostly in written form but on occasion orally. An important reason for the effectiveness of administrative guidance in increasing or assuring the cooperation of firms is that the relationships between the ministries and firms or industries are long-term and multifaceted. Firms know, like the players of complex and repetitive games, that yielding a little can reap rewards now or later in another aspect of their relationships with the ministries. The reward is rarely a naked quid pro quo, but corresponds more or less to the degree of a firm's cooperation with the ministries. Conversely, uncooperative or recalcitrant firms can expect, immediately or at a later date, indirect retribution from a disappointed or displeased ministry. Any knowledgeable observer would have little difficulty in compiling examples of rewards and retributions, some widely known and others only whispered about among ministry officials and industry executives.

Another important characteristic of administrative guidance is that, as

Murakami stresses, the ministries must deal with each firm in an industry on as equal a basis as possible.[27] This, of course, must be a necessary characteristic of administrative guidance if the ministries wish to obtain maximum and voluntary cooperation from firms. (By definition, however, industrial policy promoting a specific industry or a sector cannot be fair to all industries—a reason, as we shall see, for the increasing problems the bureaucracy faced as the rapid growth period ended.)

Yet another and perhaps the most important characteristic of administrative guidance is that in most cases it is market conforming; that is, the policies pursued through guidance (and also by specific laws) do not defy market signals at the cost of efficiency. Johnson, who also regards the Japanese industrial policy as market conforming, argues that this characteristic helped Japan "avoid the deadening hand of state control and the inevitable inefficiency, loss of incentives, corruption, and bureaucratism that it generates" and cited administrative guidance as "perhaps the most important market-conforming method of intervention."[28] But, for economists, what is meant by a market-conforming industrial policy? Analytically, a fully market-conforming industrial policy can hardly be distinguished from a "visible hand" offering subsidies. In what ways, then, can Japanese industrial policies, especially those of the rapid growth period, be called market conforming?

We offer two observations on the Japanese industrial policy of the rapid growth period as evidence of its market-conforming characteristic. First, unlike the industrial policies of many European states, the touchstone for these policies was competitiveness in international markets. Japan did not seek to build industries that required permanent hothouse protection. Support for protected industries that did not show signs of commercial viability was gradually phased out. (The best example is commercial aircraft—the contrast between the European and Japanese cases is marked.) There were exceptions even in the rapid growth period, and, as noted later, protection became more difficult, for political reasons, to withdraw in the 1970s and 1980s. Nevertheless, we believe that this characteristic was an important feature of Japanese industrial policy.

Second, in developing administrative guidance in the consultative way described above, Japanese officials seemed to be guided generally by considerations of economic efficiency. Their aim was to buffer market swings and to anticipate market developments, not to go against markets. Thus, in electronics, support techniques such as reserving markets for domestic firms have been aimed at enabling such firms to achieve economies of scale and to take maximum advantage of learning curve effects. In short, although market-conforming industrial policies certainly did not slavishly follow every twist and turn of the market, they were generally guided by market signals, unlike the industrial policies sometimes observed in countries such as Britain and France (see the following section).

Perhaps all the foregoing is most effectively summarized by John Haley, who concludes his insightful study of administrative guidance and the character of Japanese industrial policy:

Administrative guidance (*gyōsei shidō*), that ubiquitous process for enforcing administrative policy in Japan, provides one a key to unlock the paradox of industrial policy, of regulation with competition. Although administrative guidance is quite accurately described as the means by which MITI, the Ministry of Finance, and other economic ministries in Japan used to restrict competition and to circumvent Japan's antitrust law, reliance upon guidance rather than formal regulation as a process of governing insured that ultimately the competitive forces of the market place, not bureaucratic aims, determined the course of economic policy in postwar Japan. This does not mean that government intervention had no impact or that all sectors of the economy were effectively governed by market forces or firm rivalry, or that there has been no resort to formal regulation. However . . . there has been a misplaced emphasis on administrative guidance as a means used by the government "to encourage private firms to take actions that [the government] deems useful or necessary." A more accurate description would stress the extent to which government policies reflected the needs and demands of those being "guided."[29]

The discussion and analyses presented in this section demonstrate, we believe, the essential usefulness of Zysman's insights in examining the apparent contributions of Japan's industrial policy in the rapid growth period. We also believe that an understanding of the process of policy formulation, the roles of administrative guidance, and the market-conforming characteristics of Japanese industrial policy provide further justification for the assessment we make of the effects of industrial policy on Japan's economic performance during the 1950s and 1960s.

Implications of European Industrial Policy

Japan was by no means the first country to adopt an industrial policy. (Indeed, as industrial policy proponents in the United States repeatedly point out, it is the absence of a coherent industrial policy in their country that makes it the exception among major industrialized nations.) In Europe, state intervention to aid industry goes back many centuries. Grants of monopoly, high protective tariffs or outright bans on the importation of certain commodities, subsidies, the provision of capital on favorable terms, favoritism in procurement—each of these industrial policy tools has ancient roots. Although occasionally awarded on a purely ad hoc basis, sometimes in return for political or financial favors to the state, in many instances such tools were elements of a conscious strategy of industrial development—that is, a true industrial policy.

Indeed, by the mid-1700s, state assistance to industry had become so widespread that it was instrumental in causing Adam Smith to write *The Wealth of Nations*. It is often forgotten that Smith was describing not a world of laissez-faire capitalism but one of pervasive state intervention—of industrial policy. Smith's central argument—and of others like Ricardo who followed him—was that the state need not assume the primary responsibility for either the day-to-day allocation of resources or longer-term questions such as the development of industry. These could, in most cases, be entrusted to the "invisible hand" of the market.

But Smith's argument went even further. Not only was state intervention to aid industrial development unnecessary; it was likely to be positively harmful. To be sure, both Smith and his neo-classical followers recognized that markets might not always work appropriately—that they might "fail." (The neo-classicists even developed detailed taxonomies of "market failure.") In such cases, however, the proper role for the state was to create the conditions under which this failure might be removed. In other words, the appropriate remedy for market failure was to "perfect" the market. If the activities of private competitors, such as fixing prices or conspiring to create a monopoly, caused a market failure, then actions to prevent such activites were appropriate. If the market itself was flawed because of the presence of a natural monopoly, then either state regulation or state ownership was the prescription. But the touchstone was to try to create conditions that allowed the natural monopoly to mimic a competitive firm.

The development of industry in each nation was to be guided by the principle of comparative advantage. If a country's comparative advantage changed, the industries in which it specialized ought to change also.

This view of the world, coupled with examples illustrating the unfortunate consequences of ignoring it, still forms the heart of neo-classical economists' case against industrial policy. They start with the belief that in most cases government interventions to aid certain industries and disadvantage others are inherently inefficient. They then observe that even the ablest technocrats are bound to guess incorrectly which industries to favor and which to discourage. Finally, they note that these decisions are made not by technocrats interested solely in the good of society but by politicians exposed to extraneous influences. Little wonder that many economists trained in the neo-classical tradition have considered industrial policy a recipe for disaster.

But this view is by no means universally accepted even among economists. A number of different schools of economic thought, though not denying the remarkable organizing properties of markets and admitting the general desirability of relying on them for most decisions, nevertheless consider the neo-classical explanation of industrial growth processes to be excessively narrow and static.

Economists holding such views, such as Schumpeter and Galbraith, consider it appropriate—even essential—for the state to assume a much more active role in guiding the development of industry.[30] Gerschenkron stressed the importance of the state as an agent of development among late developers.[31] Leontief observed that U.S. exports did not appear consistent with that country's apparent factor endowments, which suggests that neo-classical economists might have defined the term "factor of production" much too narrowly.[32] If, as Leontief's work suggested, a country can specialize in technologically advanced goods, there might indeed be a vital role for government in helping to accumulate the necessary skills. Raymond Vernon observed the importance of the product life cycle in trade.[33] Others, extending this work and marrying it to the concept of the "learning" or "experience curve," noted the possibility that significant cost advantages might flow to the country that managed to utilize a technology first. Again, this implied a role for government of a sort not contemplated by neo-classical economic theorists. Moreover, there were those, generally not economists but political scientists, who put great weight on the organizing abilities of the state. To these scholars, markets might be sufficient for minor day-to-day decisions, but were not capable of developing broad-scale integrated strategies and mobilizing the wide support necessary for successful development.

The principal testing ground for most of these theories was Europe. In this section, we present a brief and admittedly broad description of postwar Europe's industrial policy experience and the evaluations of neo-classical economists and others concerning this experience.[34] To this, we add our own observations and our assessment of the relevance this experience holds for future Japanese industrial policy.

Britain

Of all the European examples of industrial policy, the one neo-classical critics of industrial policy are most likely to cite as a model of disaster is Britain.[35] Since the end of World War II, especially during the 1960s and 1970s, Britain engaged in successive rounds of industrial policies, each ostensibly aimed at identifying and encouraging the growth of new industries or helping mature industries reduce their size or otherwise restructure themselves in an orderly manner. At one time or another, the British have employed virtually every industrial policy tool. Almost all of these experiments, however, have been judged failures, and not just by those critical of industrial policy in general.

The most well-documented illustration of the British failure to pick winners is the commercial aircraft industry. During the late 1930s, Britain fell further and further behind the United States in this field. But during the gloomy days of World War II, it became determined to surpass the Americans. The Barbazon Report, completed in the mid-1940s, could serve as the prototype of modern targeting strategy. The report assessed the postwar market for commerical aircraft in detail, identified specific designs that showed promise, and assigned specific firms to produce them.

The result would have made Adam Smith proud. With only one or two exceptions, the designs proved to be unmitigated commercial disasters. Moreover, the only aircraft achieving a technological breakthrough—the Comet—was not included in the plan. De Havilland virtually had to beg the government for allocations of scarce materials—materials assigned to the targeted designs—in order to build the Comet at all.

The initial series of postwar industrial policy failures did not deter the British. Throughout the 1950s and into the 1960s, Britain continued to pour resources into unsuccessful commercial aircraft designs—the Vanguard, the Trident, the VC-10, and, most expensive of all, the Concorde. Gradually the focus of British policy efforts shifted from expansion toward an orderly reduction in industry size. In the mid-1960s, a committee recommended drastic measures to consolidate firms and reduce capacity. Eventually a single nationalized firm—British Aerospace—emerged as the only significant British producer of commercial and military aircraft.[36]

The targeting in the commercial aircraft industry was only the largest and most expensive example of British industrial policy failure in high technology. The National Research and Development Corporation, established in 1949, was specifically designed to aid in commercializing new products, especially products developed by British laboratories. The corporation and its successors enjoyed few successes or even near-successes. Of the latter, the best-known example is probably the hovercraft. Certainly, the aggressive efforts of the British government to promote the development of commercially significant new products and processes in the decades following World War II did not revitalize British industries.

The other major element of Britain's industrial policy was the reduction of capacity in uncompetitive industries. This was accomplished relatively easily in the British aircraft industry—although not entirely without psychic costs and real suffering. The overwhelming dependence of the industry on the government for both military and commercial orders gave the government the tools necessary to force virtually any changes that proved politically palatable. The same cannot be said for the four other British industries—textiles, shipbuilding, steel, and coal—designated as uncompetitive during the postwar period, each of which had occupied a central role in Britain's industrialization.

The British textile industry first came to feel stiff competitive pressures in the interwar period. These pressures intensified after World War II, partly because of the loss of overseas markets. The British government undertook several efforts, first, to help the industry reduce capacity to a more sustainable level, and then, when these efforts proved failures, to maintain employment in the industry as much as possible. Notwithstanding these efforts, the industry has continued to decline.[37]

The actions of the British government also hurt the rationalization of the shipbuilding industry. Here too, market forces eventually became too great. The shipbuilding industry had, for several centuries, enjoyed government support on the grounds of national security. During the 1950s, however, the competitive position of the industry became more and more precarious. Largely because of the regional concentration of employment in shipbuilding, the government sought to aid the ailing firms with numerous loans and subsidies. The futility of these actions came to be recognized, and the decline of this industry was allowed to run its course, with the government acting as a cushion to soften the impact.

Attempts to manage the decline of steel and coal proved even more painful. Because both were state-owned industries, access to subsidies was available for a much longer period than would otherwise have been the case. The delay in the onset of the decline made the blow much stronger. Both industries (and especially coal) have occupied a special role in British social and political history. The British coal miners were the shock troops of the British labor movement and formed the core of the Labour Party. Efforts to halt operations at uncompetitive mines have touched deep nerves. Although the unwillingness of Labour governments to confront this issue is understandable, even Conservative governments were reluctant to act until the early 1980s. The current Conservative government has decided to tackle the problem and is willing to put great strains on the economy to do so, the most extreme example being the recent, humiliating defeat of the unions after a yearlong coal strike.

Although not unmindful of the harsh, human costs involved in the current upheavals in Britain, neo-classical economists would attribute the magnitude of these costs to the failure of successive British governments to accept the inevitable failure of efforts going against the dictates of the market.

Even supporters of industrial policy do not attempt to paint the British picture as successful. They do, however, advance somewhat more complex views regarding the causes for Britain's failure—ones that suggest that the failure of industrial policy is not inevitable.

In Zysman's paradigm, the British failure is entirely predictable.[38] To be sure, Britain has possessed a competent, relatively independent bureaucracy. However, it failed on both the other important counts. Financial markets in Britain have been, both by tradition and explicit policy choice, the most open in the world during most of the postwar era. The government thus had little direct leverage, other than outright financial aid, over the investment decisions of firms. Financial markets have been able to offset efforts to employ direct aids. Thus, except in those cases such as the aircraft industry where the government was the overwhelming purchaser of the industry's output or where the industry is state owned (which carries its own constraints), the British government has little or no effective control over the investment and disinvestment decisions of firms.

More important, British politics became mired in a prolonged confrontation over the issue of income distribution. Industrial policy decisions became an important battleground in this confrontation—especially when the industries in question were state owned. Questions of whether to build up or phase down any particular industry immediately became transformed into issues over how the gain or pain was to be fairly spread. The industrial policy tools employed by successive British governments were used less to advance the competitiveness of British industry and much more to avoid necessary adjustments. The political strength of postwar British governments and the steadily declining economic health of Britain were not sufficient to permit this to continue indefinitely. Britain was able to shield its industries from competition just long enough to allow them to become thoroughly uncompetitive. As it must, this has increased the pain of adjustment.

We would add one more element to this discussion of the failure of Britain's industrial policies: the cost of linking efforts to promote promising industries with efforts to maintain or enhance the military power of a nation. Britain's desire to retain its significance as a military power greatly influenced its efforts to build up the aircraft and electronics industries and to moderate the decline of steel and shipbuilding. The decision to identify specific firms as "champions" in the commercial aircraft and electronics industries was heavily influenced by the desire of British governments to maintain (and even enhance) British capability to build modern weaponry. The fear that these decisions would inevitably have an adverse impact on particular firms' abilities to produce military goods has increased the delays in facing up to the failure of certain commercial products (and hence delayed termination of their support).

In the end, we feel comfortable with the assessment that the failure of

Britain's industrial policy was inevitable. We are, however, less than fully satisfied with the neo-classical assessment of this failure. We are much more comfortable with an assessment that considers institutional and social factors. If these considerations are absent, the British lesson is likely to be misinterpreted.

Germany

If Britain is considered the textbook case of industrial policy failure, Germany (at least for the neo-classical economists) is considered the textbook case of the virtues of the invisible hand.[39] The story one usually hears of Germany is one of a country in which the market was allowed to function relatively freely. Until at least the mid-1960s, protection, subsidies, and other forms of governmental interference were kept to an absolute minimum. Limited tax incentives and the protection of the weakest industries were the only noteworthy policies adopted. Business and labor—with the encouragement of government—worked out arrangements to ease the burden of structural adjustment. This, however, was part of a larger "social contract" and not part of any explicit industrial policy.

What was the result? Living standards in Germany rose steadily in contrast to those in Britain. In 1955, British real per capita GNP was 114 per cent of that of Germany. However, between 1955 and 1973, German real per capita GNP grew by an average of 4.1 per cent per year; the comparable figure for Britain was 2.4 per cent. To be sure, after the oil shock, both of these growth rates fell. Between 1973 and 1979, however, German real per capita GNP still grew at a respectable 2.6 per cent per year. In contrast, real per capita GNP in Britain grew at an anemic 1.0 per cent per year. The result was that the real per capita GNP of Germany surpassed that of Britain by about 1960. By 1979, the latter's real per capita income was only 78 per cent as great as that of the former.[40]

A competing explanation of the German industrial policy experience does not view the German success as solely the result of reliance on markets. Zysman interprets the German case as one in which the necessary elements were in balance, but the balance differed from that in strong industrial policy states such as France (see below).[41] This interpretation does not contend that the Germans owe their success to an explicit industrial policy. It acknowledges that the German adjustment process was negotiated by business and labor, with the government playing only a facilitating role. Under this interpretation, the German bureaucracy was semiautonomous and enjoyed high prestige, but it was also decentralized, thereby limiting its ability to play a significant guiding role. Finally, although not as well-developed as those of Britain, German financial markets, to the extent they were controlled, were controlled by the major banks and not by the government. The banks generally favored adjustments aimed at improving competitiveness and used their considerable leverage to promote these adjustments. The picture that emerges of Germany, therefore, is not one of unbridled laissez-faire capitalism, but of a moderate market, with the primary moderating forces being the agreement between industry and labor on the division of the costs and benefits of adjustment and the important developmental role of the banks. Moreover, the various elements of industrial change and development worked more or less in harmonious balance.

We consider both of these interpretations overdrawn, especially in view of recent German experience. We agree with Zysman that the picture of Germany as the paragon of free markets is significantly oversimplified. However, Zysman's view of a harmonious, bank-led adjustment process is also much too simple.

Since the late 1960s, the German government's intervention into industry has been growing.[42] Its promotion of high-technology industry has become especially important. In the early 1970s, the Germans formed the Ministry for Research and Technology (Bundesministerium für Forschung und Technologie; BMFT) to enhance the technological competitiveness of German industry. The BMFT provides 50 per cent of the industry's financial resources through direct government support for commercial R&D, and in 1982, 78 per cent of BMFT's grants went to firms.[43] Indeed, according to Richard Nelson, in recent years the percentage of government-financed industrial R&D has not been much lower in Germany than in the United States, Britain, or France even though military R&D spending is much lower in Germany than in the other three countries.[44]

The German government has increasingly been forced to involve itself directly in issues of industrial restructuring. Although devoting fewer resources to support declining industrial sectors than do other member-states of the European Community, subsidies to industries such as coal mining and shipbuilding have long been great.[45] Moreover, the highly publicized difficulties of large German firms have resulted in government intervention—albeit reluctantly. To be sure, the most visible role in various restructurings such as at Krupp and Hoesch (both steel firms), Volkswagen (autos), and AEG-Telefunken (electronics and semiconductors) was played by the banks. Nonetheless, the German government has definitely been a major actor.[46]

Finally, the smooth, harmonious labor relations resulting from labor-industry consultations that may have characterized the 1960s and 1970s appear to have changed. As German economic performance has soured along with that of the rest of Europe and pressures to improve competitiveness through industrial restructuring have increased, German workers have become much more confrontational. Strikes to reduce working hours without reductions in pay have become common, especially in the industries under the strongest competitive pressure. Although by no means as bitter as British industrial relations, labor-management relations in Germany can certainly no longer be considered untroubled.

Therefore, Germany neither eschews industrial policy altogether nor executes it through a harmonious balance among industry, the banks, and labor, with government playing only an ancillary role. How then can the German experience best be characterized? Jeffrey Hart's assessment is both provocative and insightful: "German industrial policy is a strange mixture of decentralized control with increasingly ambitious goals. The growth of the capacity of the federal government to intervene in specific regional and industrial crises has been substantial, but the government remains firmly committed to allowing other social actors (especially the banks) to try their hand at resolving crises before it gets involved." Drawing on his case studies of steel, automobiles, and semiconductors, Hart states:

The case of steel highlights the weaknesses of this strategy: 1) the government gets much more involved eventually than it had ever intended, 2) because the banks have incentives to rescue ineptly managed but very large firms, government intervention tends to be very costly when it occurs, and 3) the older and younger workers tend to pay a larger share of adjustment costs than the workers in the mid-range. The case of automobiles shows that the combination of strong firms and avoidance of administrative guidance go hand in hand to produce desirable results—as the rapid adjustment of VW to changed world market conditions attests. The case of semiconductors shows how wrong you can go in pursuing a "national champions" policy when the national champions experience chronic inabilities to catch up to the global leaders. It also shows that the German government learned this lesson well in the 1980s.

Hart characterizes German industrial policy as "very much like U.S. industrial policy" and states that "it would be a big mistake . . . to identify German policy with any extreme on the descriptive continuum." He concludes that "the main lesson of German industrial policy is the need to match public policy to the market conditions and industrial capacities existing in specific industries." [47]

France

France presents the most difficult case both for neo-classical critics of industrial policy and for those more sympathetic to it. Among the major European countries, it has the longest and certainly the strongest tradition of state intervention. Throughout much of the postwar period, France has engaged in explicit efforts to guide industrial development, even going so far as to employ a mild form of centralized economic planning. France has employed large direct subsidies to industry, favoritism in procurement, high tariffs (until the formation of the Common Market), industrial credit allocations, and a variety of informal measures to encourage its industry.[48] It has managed to achieve about the same record of postwar real per capita GNP growth as Germany (4.4 per cent during the 1955–73 period; 2.4 during the 1973–79 period). Whether this has resulted from France's periodic flirtations with the free market or from the success of its industrial policy has been a widely debated subject.

Critics are fond of citing examples of large-scale industrial support projects that degenerated into monuments to national grandeur (as they note, it was the French and not the British who insisted on completing the Concorde) as illustrations that even a highly capable bureaucracy can be led by politics or just plain bad judgment into making unwise industrial policy decisions.

Some supporters of industrial policy credit the French success to that country's willingness to engage in indicative planning. French planning is a loose process, consisting of consultations among the major economic decision makers—the unions, industry, various government departments, and the Planning Commission.[49] Although a formal document stating sectoral targets emerges from this process, its advocates stress the consultative process itself, rather than the document, as the key element.

Over the years, the emphasis of the French plans has changed to reflect the changing needs and priorities of the country. The first three plans (1946–61) stressed postwar reconstruction. They attempted to expand the capacity of war-damaged basic industries and remove bottlenecks to growth. The fourth and fifth plans (1959–70) represent the height of French faith in planning. The fourth was an ambitious analytical effort, containing investment targets and a growth strategy for the entire economy. The fifth began to stress improving the competitiveness of French industry, the restructuring of industry through cartels and mergers, the use of exemptions from regulation to induce firms to engage in certain types of behavior, and the concentration of capital investment in a small number of high-tech breakthrough projects, to be carried out by "national champions."

By the time the sixth (1971–75) and seventh (1976–80) plans were developed, faith in detailed planning was fading in France. Consequently, these documents focused much more on industrial modernization and the promotion of high-tech industry. They called for the continuation of state intervention in a small number of high-tech sectors, including computers, electronics, telecommunications, machinery, and chemicals. Continued support for the Concorde and support for the new Airbus were also elements of these plans. They also included the *Plan calcul,* a scheme to establish an internationally competitive French computer industry, and the *Plan siderurgie,* a scheme to modernize and rationalize the steel industry. Neither of these schemes has been successful, either technologically or commercially.

Ironically, the victory of the Socialists in 1981 appeared to mark a further eclipse of interest in planning. The eighth plan, due to run from 1981 to 1985, was delayed by the results of the 1981 elections. Interim plans were announced in 1982 and 1983, but these merely reinforced previously announced government objectives of modernizing basic industry, increasing competitiveness in processing industries, and promoting new technologies.

Some who consider French industrial policy successful have never placed much weight on formal planning as an element of this success. In Zysman's view, France's good performance is largely the result of the successful marriage of at least two of his three critical industrial policy elements—the administrative environment and the financial environment.[50] France has a long tradition of a strong, capable bureaucracy. But, after the war, it set out to train an even stronger and more capable one—a bureaucracy indoctrinated with the gospel of modernization. This was achieved by utilizing the existing structure of elite education—the *grandes écoles*—and complementing it with a new and even more selective training for public service, the National School of Administration. Particularly after the rise of de Gaulle and the promulgation of the constitution of 1958, this executive elite acquired almost unchallengeable authority to use the power of the state to promote industrial development.

It was aided in this by the relatively underdeveloped state of French financial markets. French firms seeking substantial capital to increase productive capacity or to adopt new technology faced difficulties either in raising such sums domestically or in tapping highly liquid international capital markets. They were forced to rely on industrial banks, which were themselves under a degree of government control.

These conditions helped create the environment for an active government role in promoting industrial restructuring and development. They also created the opportunity for certain French administrations to become sidetracked into projects designed more to promote visions of national grandeur than to raise French competitiveness in international markets. (The Concorde was by no means unique.) The French also suffered, like the British, from a desire to maintain a strong defense capability, in particular, the ability to produce technologically advanced weapons. But unlike the British, they insisted on maintaining a high degree of independence from the United States in their defense policy. This meant that they had to support more or less on their own extremely expensive weapons-related efforts—a broad line of fighter and ground-support air-craft, an intermediate-range ballistic missile, and nuclear-powered, mis-sile-launching submarines. They also maintained an extremely active ci-vilian nuclear power industry, spurred by the lack of indigenous energy resources.

The very features that made effective action by the French government possible in the area of promoting advanced technology helped to shield such action from public scrutiny and accountability. As a consequence, projects that went wrong could go very wrong. The Concorde, *Plan cal-cul*, and *Plan siderurgie* are three examples of those that did. That more did not is a tribute to the skill of French bureaucrats.

Zysman's explanation for French industrial policy success faces an im-portant obstacle in his own theory. The French did not satisfy the third of his necessary conditions for industrial policy success. France did not emerge from World War II with a consensus favoring industrial restruc-turing or the adoption of pro-growth policies involving short-run sacri-fices by some sectors of the economy. Instead, there were strong con-flicts between traditional, politically powerful sectors such as agriculture and retail trade (which favored protection) and potential winners in light and heavy industry. Moreover, even within industry there were sharp conflicts. The Left emerged from the war with high prestige, con-siderable political power, and a constituency concentrated among labor, especially workers in some of the more traditional subsectors of heavy industry such as steel and autos. Questions of who would bear the cost of any restructuring of such subsectors and who had the right to claim the lion's share of any resulting gains thus became national political issues. Such a political environment was not favorable to effective indus-trial policy.

How was this overcome? One possible explanation—an explanation we cannot discount—attributes the French success to a combination of luck and skill, with the former playing a significant role. For a good while, the French managed to do without a pro-growth consensus, rely-ing instead on their ability to generate economic growth rapidly enough to buy off the disaffected sectors. Here a strong element of luck and timing comes in. France achieved its modernization during a period of extremely favorable underlying conditions—the rapid expansion of world trade, the opening of French markets with the founding of the Eu-ropean Economic Community, a relatively high savings rate, and a major rationalization of the agriculture and retail trade sectors, despite their strong opposition. The skill lay in the ability of the French bureaucratic elite to utilize these favorable circumstances to overcome the negative elements.

The luck has now ended. The slowing of French economic growth during the late 1970s set the stage for the Socialist victory of 1981. Through a series of strategic nationalizations (in particular, of the investment banks), the Socialists apparently hoped to bring into the government's hands the elements that would permit a resumption of the modernization of French industry, though with a different emphasis than under the Gaullists, especially the late Gaullists. The Socialists sought to strengthen the tools, especially the financial tools, of industrial policy.

The victory of the Socialists, however, also helped bring into the open the underlying conflicts in French society concerning the costs and benefits of modernization. In a world far less favorable to economic growth than the world of the late 1950s and the 1960s, possessing both the tools with which to influence industrial restructuring and a bureaucracy capable of using them and free to do so has not proved sufficient. French economic performance has sagged, and sagged badly. Since 1981, real French economic growth has fallen somewhat below that of Britain (average annual rate between 1981 and 1984 of 1.0 versus 1.4 per cent),[51] something that must comfort the neo-classical critics of industrial policy.

Lessons for Japan

Both the highly critical neo-classical view of the postwar European industrial policy experience and the relatively more favorable interpretations advanced by others contain important lessons for assessing the possible future of Japanese industrial policy. The most important lesson from neo-classical economists—a lesson that nations forget at their peril—is the danger of ignoring market signals, possibly even in the short run but certainly in the long run. Unlike the strict neo-classicists, we do not believe that the market is always right. But the occasions where its signals can safely be ignored are not nearly as numerous as some might argue. Moreover, although markets clearly fail, so do political institutions. Charles Wolf's parallel taxonomy of "nonmarket failures" is well worth keeping in mind when criticizing the shortcomings of markets.[52]

The danger of ignoring these insights is readily evident in the postwar European industrial policy experience. As already noted, to the extent that Japan's industrial policy has been successful, it was because the policy has been market conforming—that is, government efforts to guide industry did not move far from the discipline of the market. The facile assertions of some extreme enthusiasts of industrial policy that Japan has the ability to create competitive advantage should not be taken seriously. The invalidity of such an assertion is beyond dispute when we examine the record during the past decade of Japan's aluminum industry, several segments of the chemical industry (those using petroleum by-products), and several other industries. These are the industries that, despite aggressive MITI guidance and assistance (through various policy tools), failed to become internationally competitive and have become the objects of MITI's not altogether successful rescue plans.[53]

The lesson to be learned from the studies of those who have a more positive view of the potential benefits of industrial policy (but who are unwilling to attribute miraculous powers to it) is the relatively narrow grounds for its success. An industrial policy cannot substitute for underlying economic conditions favorable to growth and investment. Nor can it be the means of solving fundamental debates within a country over the importance of economic growth and over the distribution of the costs and benefits of it. In Japan, the underlying macroeconomic conditions during the 1950s and 1960s were very favorable to rapid economic growth and to capital accumulation. Moreover, the social consensus favoring economic growth was established before the launching of Japan's industrial policy experiment and continued, as revealed in successive general elections, throughout the rapid growth decades.

The postwar European experience holds other lessons for Japan. It suggests that even if a country establishes conditions favorable to rapid growth and strong international competitiveness—such as Germany and France did during much of the postwar period—these conditions can go sour. The apparent breakdown in recent years of the negotiated bargain between business and labor in Germany plus the lack of a framework for developing policies capable of dealing with the adjustment pressures now facing German industry—especially German industry operating in the context of the European Economic Community—suggests that the favorable political and economic conditions that made the German "economic miracle" possible are disappearing.

An even more sobering example for the Japanese must be the unfortunate stagnation of the French economy in the wake of the Mitterrand victory and the efforts of that administration to use the power of the state to develop French industry. This experience shows how the governmental capabilities and tools that once served to promote the development of international competitiveness can, under the wrong conditions, produce the opposite result—how what was once the source of a country's potential strength can become a source of weakness.

Post-1973 Changes in Japan and Its Industrial Policy

Much of the writing about Japanese industrial policy relates to its contribution during the rapid growth decades. In fact, an examination of the most recent literature reveals that many authors who urge other nations to emulate Japan's industrial policy and its institutions fail to note some significant and subtle changes of the past decade in Japan's industrial policy and its institutional capabilities.[54]

Japan, however, has changed in many ways—in the institutional capabilities of the Japanese government, in the industrial policy tools at its disposal, and in the underlying consensus for a pro-growth policy. There have been numerous and varying degrees of change in all three areas and in the process of policy formulation and execution. If our observations are correct, these changes suggest that since the early 1970s Japan has faced increasing difficulties in maintaining whatever favorable influence industrial policy had in the past.

Changes in Governmental Capabilities

Japan can still be characterized as having, under the LDP, a strong central government administered by elite career bureaucrats enjoying substantial prestige. However, principally because of the decelerated economic growth rate, the increasing politicization of the policymaking process, and changes in the international economy (the flexible exchange rate regime, heightened protectionism, a persisting trade imbalance, and the like), this characterization now requires several important qualifications. Together with their implications, these recent developments suggest a substantial decline in the institutional capabilities of the government to pursue an effective industrial policy.

In the context of this paper, three qualifications are significant. First, the power of the central government has diminished because of its visibly reduced fiscal circumstances. At present, the government relies greatly on deficit financing and has to cope with sharply increased budget rigidity. Unlike the government of the preceding decades, it no longer possesses sufficient wherewithal to influence corporate decisions. This is especially the case vis-à-vis large firms, which are now much less dependent on subsidies. Industrial policy, promoted either by law or administrative guidance, is much less effective when the number of carrots is reduced and when the value of these carrots to their recipients declines.

Second, on matters relating to allocation of fiscal resources, both the cabinet and the bureaucracy face a steadily increasing and more determined political challenge. Individual politicians, especially LDP politicians, today are more eager than before to obtain for their political constituency (an industry or an electoral district) a "fair" share of the budget. Members of the opposition parties are challenging the budgetary decisions of MOF and the LDP. For evidence of this development, one needs only to read the sharply worded and explicit criticism made by the chairman of the LDP's Policy Affairs Research Council in 1984 against "the bureaucracy-led budget-making process"[55] and the determined and seemingly increasingly effective political pressure mounted by the *zoku* ("tribes"), which Seizaburo Sato defined as "groups of veteran members [of both the lower and upper houses] who have served in one or more positions such as political vice-minister (*seimujikan*), chairman of one of the major party councils (*bukaichō*), chairman of one of the Diet committees, or a cabinet minister, and who have become experts in various fields that correspond to those administered by each ministry of agency."[56]

Indeed, because of the increasing intrusion of the *zoku*, the opposition parties, and the more determined, individual Diet members in the budget-making process, the process has become significantly more politicized. Gone are the days when "the decision-making power was almost totally in the hands of the bureaucrats, and politicans could intrude into the decision-making process only partially and in limited ways" or when "politicans played the role of cheerleaders for various ministries and were no more than go-betweens for local interest groups and the Budget Bureau."[57] The increased politicization of the budget-making process, accompanied by fiscal stringency, is more than likely to continue to make formulation and execution of carefully coordinated and coherent industrial policy difficult.

And third, because of the internationalization or liberalization of the Japanese economy forced by Japan's trading partners or undertaken by the Japanese in an effort to reduce trade conflicts, the government and the bureaucracy are today decreasingly able to carry out policies and guidance. The capabilities of the government and ministries, in short, have become considerably more restricted because Japan's trading partners are closely scrutinizing policy formulation and implementation. Japan's policy options have been significantly reduced in comparison with those available during the rapid growth period.[58]

For these and other reasons, the institutional capabilities of the government to carry out industrial policy have undergone significant changes, some qualitative and others quantitative. The LDP, forced to become a catchall party—a party that must please as many voters and interest groups as possible— in order to retain its power but with increasingly limited fiscal resources, is not the same LDP that in the 1960s pursued the National Income-Doubling Plan.[59] Neither can the bureaucracy, which must now cope with much more determined political intrusion in its activities, remain what it was even only a decade ago.

This assessment, however, neglects another crucial development affecting the institutional capability of Japan to execute its industrial policy. Conflicts over policy goals or the means to achieve these goals within and between ministries (and other governmental agencies) play important roles in Japanese industrial policy.

For instance, as well documented by Johnson and many Japanese observers, beginning in the mid-1960s, MITI experienced a serious internal policy conflict between the "nationalists," who wished to continue a basically status quo policy of promoting domestic industries, and the "internationalists," who argued that the Japanese industrial markets should be opened even if it meant serious changes in MITI's policies and practices. This conflict, which ended in a gradual (if less than complete) victory for the internationalists, indicated that even within MITI—the ministry occupying the pre-eminent position in Japan's industrial policy—internal consensus on its policy goals could no longer be taken for granted. As the ministry in the coming decades encounters new and even more complex problems (trade issues, political pressures, internal debates concerning policy priorities, and the like), how well MITI will succeed in maintaining its internal cohesion remains to be seen.[60]

Another, more recent example is the widely publicized internal dissension within the MOF between officials arguing against yielding too rapidly to foreign pressure to liberalize Japanese money markets and others—the "liberalizers"—advocating extensive liberalization as rapidly as possible. This internal dissension reflects, as in the case of MITI, differences in views regarding how best to serve Japan's interest as well as the tendency of many MOF officials to speak on behalf of their respective bureaus, which are responsible for various segments of capital markets that are affected, either favorably or adversely, by liberalization. Like MITI, the MOF will face a new set of increasingly complex (and international) problems. It will constantly be forced to resolve internal conflicts if it is to retain some semblance of the single-minded intraministry cohesiveness regarding policy goals that it possessed when it was pursuing the "sub-equilibrium interest rate" policy in the rapid growth decades.[61]

A much more serious problem is interministry conflicts, which are flaring up more frequently and more openly than in the past. The best known squabbles and confrontations include MITI and the Ministry of Posts and Telecommunications on the so-called VAN (value-added network—various forms of electronic communications) issue; MITI and the Ministry of Education on the copyrighting of computer software; the MOF and MITI on capital market liberalization; MITI and the Ministry of Agriculture, Forestry, and Fisheries on the liberalization of imports of beef, oranges, and other agricultural products still subject to import quotas; and MITI and the Fair Trade Commission on the nature and effects of MITI's administrative guidance that might violate the Antimonopoly Law.[62]

Several facts are evident about these and other recent interministry conflicts. One is that they often involve MITI, especially the "new" MITI that is more "liberal" than other ministries (chiefly because many of the industries under its jurisdiction are export oriented and the ministry as a result is more eager to reduce international trade conflicts).[63] Another is that many of the confrontations are jurisdictional; as new industries are created because of technological changes as in the cases of VAN and computer software, both MITI and the opposing ministry attempt to exert their power over these industries, and jurisdictional clashes result. Most of these confrontations become intense and open to outsiders (the mass media), principally because they are significantly more politicized than those of the past; politicians speaking on behalf of the industries affected and on behalf of the ministry that shares the interest of the politicians tend to become actively involved.

Although much more can be said of these interministry conflicts such as the role of the "vertical administrative structure" (*tatewari gyōsei*) of the ministries,[64] suffice it to observe that these conflicts, too, are developments of the post–oil crisis years characterized by the new problems and issues the Japanese economy and these ministries must now face. The bureaucracy must cope with many more of these interministry conflicts, and as it does so, the collective institutional capability of the Japanese bureaucracy to carry out coordinated and coherent industrial policy will be less than during the rapid growth era.

We are not suggesting that the Japanese government has lost its institutional capability. It is simply that the institutional capability of the Japanese government to formulate and successfully administer its industrial policy has declined since the 1950s and 1960s. The extent of this decline will determine the extent of diminution of whatever effectiveness Japan's industrial policy had before the first oil crisis.

A Reduced Kit of Industrial Policy Tools

Although it is difficult to determine the extent of alterations in the Japanese government's bureaucratic capabilities in the post-1973 period, there can be no dispute that the bureaucrats, whatever their skill, prestige, and discretionary power, had fewer industrial policy tools to work with. The methods of realizing industrial policy—influencing investment and disinvestment decisions at the firm, industry, or sectoral level—can be either direct (as through investment allocation) or indirect (as through the use of tools that alter relative rates of profit and presumably influence investment as a consequence). But altering the pattern of investment from what it otherwise would have been is industrial policy's most essential task.

Few would question that during the high growth period, Japanese officials responsible for industrial policy possessed a remarkably large kit of tools. Since Japanese financial markets were controlled (even if less and less effectively) and insulated from outside influence, direct controls over investment were possible. The range of indirect techniques was also extremely broad. High tariffs and imports quotas were commonplace. De facto exemptions from Japan's relatively weak antitrust laws, which permitted a large number of cartels, were easily obtained. Subsidies in many forms and guises were widely available. Favoritism in government procurement was openly practiced. A long list of nontariff barriers, ranging from rigid and costly methods of inspection to cumbersome and idiosyncratic product standards, were in effect. To be sure, changes in these policies and practices did occur during the second half of the 1960s because of increasing foreign pressure. But, after the oil crisis, the pressure intensified significantly, thus further weakening Japan's industrial policy tools.[65]

Capital market liberalization. The opening of Japan's financial markets has been a protracted struggle. A number of factors, some internal and some external, have created pressure to liberalize. As Japanese firms grew and the rate of investment declined from the frenetic level of the rapid growth decades, many of them could rely less on loans or even finance their own investment needs. This decreased the leverage of control over interest rates and credit availability. The growth of the largest Japanese banks and other financial institutions to world-class status has caused them to bridle increasingly at MOF restrictions. And U.S. pressure to open the capital market has grown stronger.

Furthermore, and no less important, the shift in the Japanese budget to a position of chronic and massive deficit caused the government to become an important competitor for the still-large pool of investable funds. More often than not, MOF efforts to force Japanese financial institutions to digest this huge volume of debt at administered, below-market rates have caused further resentment. By the end of the 1970s, the only way to minimize this resentment was to raise the rates paid on government bonds closer to those prevailing in the market. By the 1980s, the rates differed little from the market rates. An inevitable result has been the MOF's continuing loss of power to administer the rate structure across and even within several segments of the capital market. An important manifestation of this was that savers began to shift their savings in search of the highest yields once banks and other financial institutions were allowed to offer financial instruments competitively.[66]

One should not, however, expect a full liberalization soon. For one thing, despite their dislike of MOF control in many areas of their activities, Japanese banks are fearful of overly rapid financial liberalization. A rapid rise in Japanese interest rates to world levels would cause these banks to suffer massive capital losses on their outstanding portfolios, which contain a substantial amount of long-term government bonds.

Even more important, some MOF controls, especially fixed rates on deposits and limitations imposed on the activities of other financial institutions, still enhance the profitability of the banks. But liberalization is certainly coming. This means that perhaps the most significant industrial policy weapon Japan had during the high growth period will continue to become decreasingly effective. As we saw above in the case of Britain, trying to operate an aggressive industrial policy when financial markets are fully mature and highly internationalized is a difficult undertaking.

A lessened ability to utilize tariffs and quotas. When charged with being protectionist, Japanese government officials are quick to point out that as of mid-1986 Japan imposed quotas on only 27 products (of which 22 are agricultural commodities) and that by 1981 Japan's tariff rate on all imports was 2.5 per cent and only 4.3 per cent on all dutiable imports. What is also true is that these are relatively recent developments.

Import quotas, which covered 466 products in 1962, were gradually reduced during the 1960s under strong pressures from the IMF and GATT, which Japan had joined in 1952 and 1955, respectively. As these restrictions were gradually eliminated, tariffs were imposed on many products as the principal means to protect domestic industries. The average nominal tariff rates in Japan, lower than those of the United States and European nations during the 1950s, rose higher than those of the Western nations during the 1960s and the first half of the 1970s. As late as 1968, the tariff on automobiles in Japan was 40 per cent, and even in 1972, that on computer peripherals stood at 22.5 per cent. And, as two Japanese specialists noted, the Japanese tariff structure of this period was characterized by "tariff escalation" (that is, the rates rose with the degree of fabrication involved); as a result, the effective tariff rates consistently exceeded the nominal rates.[67]

Even with the reduced tariff rates and quotas of the early 1980s, the Japanese economy today is not as open as it could be to all foreign goods. The pattern and amounts of Japanese imports of manufactured products, plus numerous anecdotes by U.S. and other foreign manufacturers recounting the difficulties of selling their wares in Japan, do not permit that conclusion. Stories about industry groups (*keiretsu*), distribution problems, inspection and certification procedures for imports, and many other trade practices are too systematic and numerous to be dismissed. Yet it is absolutely clear that the significance of overt trade restrictions as a tool of Japanese industrial policy has declined. The remaining barriers are much less formal (often deriving their effectiveness as much from custom as from policy) and much less susceptible to political or bureaucratic manipulaton.

A reduced reliance on subsidies. The argument that there is no substance to Japanese industrial policy rests in large part on the observation that the current level and distribution of financial aids is not consistent with a conscious program of targeting promising industries. Trezise, for example, states: "All this can be summed up in the conclusion that in Japan public funds have not been directed in any sizable amounts, relative to total investment requirements, to the private industries or economic sectors with high growth potential. Not only appropriated moneys but also large captive deposits available to the government for investment have gone in overwhelming part either to ailing but politically-important sectors or to purposes normally considered public."[68]

Although Trezise accurately captures the current situation, this picture has not always been true. As we noted earlier, during most of the high growth period and especially during the 1950s and early 1960s, government-supplied funds met a significant portion of the investment needs of certain targeted industries.[69] In the words of Yukio Noguchi, government funds "played a strategic role in the rapid economic growth, especially in the fifties." The Trust Fund of the MOF "provided preferential low-interest funds to heavy industries and export industries through such government affiliated banks as the Japan Development Bank and the Export-Import Bank of Japan." In "the early stage of rapid economic growth, almost 30 per cent of funds supplied to industries" came from the Fiscal Investment and Loan Program administered by the Trust Fund. "In the four basic industries (electric power, shipping, coal, iron and steel) the share was as high as 40 per cent, most of which was loans from the Japan Development Bank."[70]

A number of pressures have reduced the ability of the Japanese government to utilize direct or indirect financial subsidies as a tool of industrial policy. The pressures include increased international criticism of this practice, as represented by the GATT Subsidies Code negotiated in the late 1970s; the altered Japanese budgetary situation; and the recent political developments that no longer permit the LDP to bestow liberal subsidies, as it did in past decades, on selected industries. Thus, subsidies are not likely to increase in importance as a tool for targeting promising industries, although the absolute volume of subsidies might increase should Japan find it politically necessary to support previously targeted industries. That is an eventuality we explore later in this paper.

Decreasing favoritism in government procurement. The lack of a large military sector has limited Japan's ability to use government procurement as a tool of industrial promotion. It is, however, public knowledge that until recently the government had encouraged a "buy Japanese" policy whenever possible. Two recent examples—both relating to high-technology products—are useful in illustrating this policy.

In preparation for the eventual liberalization of the computer market, the cabinet decided in September 1963 to "encourage the use of national products." Although this decision was rescinded in September 1972 and it was agreed during the Tokyo Round of GATT (1980) that all member-nations would discontinue such policies, the effect of the cabinet decision (and other factors that cannot be pursued here) was that IBM's market share in 1982 was only 3.5 per cent of the "public market" (about 18 per cent of the total computer market in Japan), which consists of the governmental agencies and public educational institutions. Each of the four Japanese firms producing computers sold approximately 30 per cent of its respective output in this market. The negative effect of this policy on IBM's market share, which had been 33.1 per cent of the private Japanese market, is difficult to dispute.[71]

Another example is state-owned (until 1985) Nippon Telephone and Telegraph (NTT), often singled out by foreigners as crucial to the success of Japan's microelectronics industry. NTT has been a major (if not the major) market for advanced semiconductors, and, it has been argued, it consciously favored Japanese firms in its procurement in order to help create a market base that aided the later penetration by Japanese firms of export markets.[72] The belief in, if not the reality of, favoritism of this sort helped create the climate that generated the multilateral trade negotiation (MTN) procurement code—an international agreement designed to limit such activities. A major difficulty in the negotiations was whether NTT would be included—it eventually was—and how other countries (principally the United States) would know that NTT was not unfairly favoring Japanese firms in its procurement arrangements. This latter point has been a source of continuing friction between the United States and Japan. Indeed, in the wake of the dismembering of AT&T and the resulting increase in access to the U.S. telecommunications market for foreign suppliers, efforts have begun in Congress to restrict access for any country that does not create equivalent access for U.S. firms to its telecommunications market.

These cases clearly demonstrate the effects of the increasing foreign pressure and scrutiny that Japanese government procurement practices are likely to be subjected to in the future. Prime Minister Nakasone began to encourage government agencies to buy more foreign products in order to reduce the large trade surplus. This will further erode the usefulness of procurement policy as a tool of industrial policy.

Government procurement as a means of industrial policy will be considerably limited by the budgetary difficulties, which are likely to continue in the coming decades. This limitation will probably affect even high-tech industries. During the past few years, for example, the government, eager to trim the rapidly increasing costs of its National Health Insurance programs, did not permit increases (or permitted much less than requested) in the prices of drugs used and charged to the government coffer. Had the generous pricing policy of the past been maintained, it would have provided higher profits to Japanese drug manufacturers and assisted their biotechnological research activities.

International pressure on MITI-initiated joint research ventures. Since the 1950s, the government has assisted the technological progress of large firms capable of taking advantage of such assistance. This assistance included special allocation of foreign exchange (while it was still controlled); industry-specific laws (often providing economic incentives in various ways; exemption from the antimonopoly statutes, and the like); and the supplying of new scientific knowledge (applied and basic) gathered from foreign sources or generated by the research arms of MITI to firms, usually at no cost. It is likely that in many instances, especially before the end of the 1960s, MITI, which actively gathered technological and market information from abroad and maintained close contacts with the most technologically advanced firms, possessed more information than many firms. To the extent this was the case, MITI guidance could have enhanced the ability of the Japanese firms to make technological progress.

Until as recently as the early 1970s, when MITI's Very Large Scale Integration (VLSI) project was initiated (to increase the technological capabilities of six large semiconductor producers), the initiative of MITI and a few other ministries in organizing and carrying out joint research ventures among large, often oligopolistic, firms in various markets elicited little reaction from abroad. Japan's industrial trade partners, especially the United States, had little reason to feel threatened by such governmental assistance to aid technological progress.

But with the success of the VLSI project (which many believe played a significant role in rapidly increasing the export of Japanese 64K RAM chips to the United States and with other evidence of the contributions of government R&D initiatives to high-tech industries, Japan's industrial partners suddenly reacted vociferously to such bureaucratically initiated (and partly subsidized) joint research projects among Japan's large, oligopolistic firms. The targeting of high-tech industries became a major issue in Japan's relations with the United States and the Common Market. The West demanded access to the patents generated by government-sponsored joint research activities and, in time, demanded that Western firms incorporated in Japan be permitted to participate in such joint research projects.[73]

The international conflict over government-sponsored joint research is far from resolved. In the past few years, Japan initiated ten major ten-year projects, all in high-tech industries and all involving only large Japanese firms.[74] Japan, meanwhile, has agreed to make the technological fruits of its joint research activities available to foreign firms (on a royalty basis) and has initiated several governmental programs to undertake international exchange of technology. Although no foreign-owned firms have yet been included in government-sponsored joint research projects, the number of private agreements between Japanese and foreign firms to exchange technology has grown rapidly during the past several years.

Even though the situation remains unresolved and complex, an important change has occurred. MITI and other ministries today can no longer promote joint research projects among large Japanese firms without considering the international reaction. This has already caused some change in the ways such projects are conceived, administered, and funded. The projects today are more oriented toward basic research; fewer subsidies are provided and on terms less favorable to the firms; and large numbers of firms (including smaller firms within an industry, as in the cases of biotechnology projects) are now included in these projects. In short, it is evident that the character of recent joint research projects, now under constant and close foreign scrutiny, differs significantly from that of past projects. The difference need not necessarily imply that these projects have become less effective as a part of Japan's industrial policy, especially in the long run. However, the difference indicates that one of the tools of Japan's industrial policy must now be used much more carefully, even if it means that Japanese firms may benefit from these projects less directly, more slowly, and on a less exclusive and less profitable basis.

Changes in the Pro-Growth Consensus

Possibly the most important factor in the success of an industrial policy is, as we stressed earlier, the development outside the industrial policy process itself of a consensus on the basic aims of industrial policy. Such a consensus permits skilled bureaucrats possessing substantial discretionary power to use their policy tools in coordinated and coherent ways to achieve a clear set of goals. In the absence of such a consensus, the act of designing specific policies becomes inextricably enmeshed with the process of setting broad goals. This has been the curse of the entire postwar British industrial policy experience. It has begun to threaten the previous success of the French. It now appears to threaten Germany's unique industrial policy.

We noted earlier that during the high growth period, Japan was favored with a degree of consensus that was the envy of other governments. The bureaucrats designing and executing industrial policies seldom if ever had to ask what the broad aims of the policies were or to reconcile conflicts among these aims. Indeed, the national goal, supported by a broad consensus, was rapid recovery and rapid growth to catch up with the West.

Since the late 1960s and much more visibly since the oil shock of 1973, cracks have appeared in Japan's pro-growth consensus. Concerns about the social costs of high growth have been raised, taking the forms of, for example, increasing criticism of environmental pollution, urban crowding, and the stress suffered in personal lives. And, the question of how the fruits of growth ought to be distributed has been raised more frequently and more loudly—to the point of nationwide movements of housewives against price fixing, increasingly vocal demands for social welfare programs and better housing, and heightened critical public reaction to many of the subsidies provided to industries and other interest groups. Many, in short, have become openly skeptical of the desirability of rapid growth, which they see being achieved at increasingly higher social and personal costs. Inevitably, these concerns and questions manifested themselves politically in the decline of LDP strength in the Diet and in the composition of the Japanese budget.

Behind these pressures and more directly related to industrial policy was the necessity faced by an increasing number of previously growing industries to stabilize in size or even reduce capacity. Since many of these industries had attained prominence with the assistance of the government, questions have arisen whether, having granted such assistance during their growth phase, the government could now deny it in their decline, and whether governmental assistance could effectively aid these industries in reducing capacity faster than otherwise possible. In the 1970s, the question proved to be moot, given political and economic realities. Because of its past policy, the government had no choice but to involve itself in the declining industries' efforts to reduce capacity. This was the reason for the Structurally Depressed Industries Law of 1978 and its revision, the Industrial Structure Promotion Law of 1983.[75] As could easily be predicted, the government found the task extremely difficult. The process of capacity reduction had to be forced on reluctant industries and local communities where those declining industries were the principal employers.

The government, if at high fiscal and political costs, did achieve some success in reducing capacity in such industries as textiles, shipbuilding, and aluminum. But other candidates who will be even more difficult for the government to deal with—steel, many chemical products, and others—wait in the wings. Already some in these industries have argued that they should be allowed to resort to various "escape clause" techniques to resist adjustment. To date, these arguments have not carried much weight in Japan. However, it remains to be seen how long and how effectively the Japanese government can deflect these arguments as adjustment pressures grow. Japan, too, is about to face a serious test of its political ability to carry out its positive adjustment strategy.[76]

This should not be interpreted as suggesting that the Japanese mood has swung from all-out support of growth to all-out suspicion. Far from it. But in their efforts to promote Japan's economic performance, Japanese bureaucrats must now face a new reality: the distribution issue has been injected into the central arena of Japanese politics, and it will likely demand the increasing attention of all policymakers. Japan, too, must now face politically and economically difficult issues involving declining industries; and Japan, now opened to foreigners' scrutiny and their criticisms of its industrial policy, must at all times remain cognizant of foreign pressures. This reality is likely to have profound effects on the future of Japanese industrial policy.

The Future of Japanese Industrial Policy: Two Polar Scenarios

Japan today is not the Japan of the rapid growth period, and neither is Japanese industrial policy what it was earlier. But what of the future? Will the Japanese economy continue to outperform most of its major trading partners, though probably by not so nearly as wide a margin as it did during the 1950s and 1960s? Or will Japan merely become an average performer, sometimes exceeding and sometimes falling short of the OECD average? Or will Japan reverse its previous position and perform conspicuously worse than average? And what role will Japanese industrial policy play in generating this record?

These questions are inherently unanswerable. At best, we can describe some possible scenarios for the Japanese economy and Japanese industrial policy. Our assessment derives from the framework set out early in this paper and from recent trends in the Japanese economy and in Japanese industrial policy.

Japan Performs Well

One possibility is that for the rest of the century the Japanese economy outperforms its major trading partners and that Japanese industrial policy contributes significantly to this performance. This scenario would not require the Japanese economy to resume the path of the rapid growth period. For a variety of reasons, we consider that impractical. We would consider this scenario fulfilled if the Japanese economy managed to grow, on average, more than a percentage point or two above its nearest major rival and several percentage points above the OECD average.

For such a performance, Japan would have to sustain an extremely high level of capital investment and continue to generate strong productivity performance. A high level of capital investment would help with the latter, but it would not be sufficient. Japan would also have to weather major economic shocks better than its rivals and to generate a superior record of developing competitive high-growth industries and a similar record in phasing out noncompetitive, declining ones.

The role that industrial policy might play in this scenario is clear. It would assist by trying to maintain the strong pro-investment climate that has characterized postwar Japan. But it would also have to speed the reallocation of resources from low-growth industries to high-growth ones. It would have to do so with an increasingly restricted set of policy tools and in a political environment increasingly less committed to economic growth at any price. Given the pressures both within and outside the country to liberalize Japanese capital markets, it is not likely that overt capital allocation will play a major role in Japan's industrial policy during the 1980s and 1990s. Although the ability to exert informal guidance has declined as both Japanese financial institutions and Japanese firms have grown stronger and presumably more independent, as a consensus generator and signaler MITI might still have some role in indicating general investment priorities.

It seems unlikely that the Japanese budgetary difficulties will ease soon. For political and demographic (aging of the population) reasons, pressures for increased domestic social welfare expenditures are certain to grow.[77] So may defense spending, although as a percentage of GNP it probably will remain modest. Funding requirements for the national debt are not likely to decline in the near future and could even rise, unless unanticipated political changes occur in the near future; the same is true for agriculture and other entrenched budget items that stubbornly refuse to decline. Given Japan's undoubtedly correct perception of the importance of high technology in the future, funding for basic and applied research must be increased.

For these and other reasons, the prospects do not seem great that Japan will have the budgetary maneuvering room to permit major fiscal assistance for structural adjustment. This prognosis is strengthened by the increasing international scrutiny of subsidization practices. This does not mean, however, that direct subsidies to promising firms and industries will cease. In this favorable scenario, MITI and other economic ministries are politically able to target their limited subsidy funds primarily toward growth industries and to shield these industries from major antitrust actions. More effectively than in other industrial nations, bureaucratic assistance to declining industries will, on balance, serve to speed up their structural adjustment.

Despite the increased international pressures on the Japanese government's procurement practices, procurement is likely to remain a tool in

Japanese industrial policy during the last years of the twentieth century. The inherent opacity of this tool, plus the difficulty of enforcing sanctions against it, lead us to this conclusion. Furthermore, the particularly promising emerging industries—various new technologies relating to space and deep-sea exploration and those in electronics and biotechnology—seem to lend themselves especially well to the use of the procurement lever. This conclusion would be reinforced if a significant Japanese defense industry were to emerge over the next few decades.

Explicit trade restrictions in the form of tariffs or direct quotas are likely to be less usable in the future. Unless the current world trading system ceases to function—which would damage Japan's economy significantly—pressures from Japanese consumers and from outside Japan are likely to restrict MITI's ability to use a protected domestic market to promote the growth of Japanese industry.

This does not mean, however, that trade policy is likely to be irrelevant to the achievement of this scenario. One of Japan's growing problems will be to deal with political pressures to assist its own industries as they become increasingly vulnerable to imports from countries such as Korea, Taiwan, Brazil, and Singapore. Japan might be able to use the threat of external sanctions in the event it turned protectionist to head off the protectionist pressures that are sure to grow. The role of trade policy will then be to keep domestic industry competitive, even at the cost of increased domestic adjustment.

We referred earlier to the extreme importance of maintaining the pro-growth consensus—even in the face of reduced growth and increasing pressures on the institutions (such as lifetime employment or administrative guidance) that helped to generate and support it earlier. To permit the favorable scenario, Japan will have to begin to develop effective substitutes for certain of these policies. These substitutes can rely on either the private or the public sector. Exactly what forms these substitutes will take to meet the political and economic constraints, both domestic and international, of the coming decades is difficult to anticipate. However, a recent proposal to create a score of "technopolises"—cities with substantial high technology–related activities—throughout the nation and the recent MITI efforts to encourage the development of small and medium-size firms relying on venture capital can be seen as examples of such substitutes. A failure to evolve imaginative and effective substitutes will not only threaten to embroil the conduct of industrial policy in disputes over distribution and fairness (the classic British problem), but also directly jeopardize certain factors that appear to have helped produce Japan's remarkable productivity record (for example, the ability to relocate workers easily to meet structural shifts in demand).

In short, for this favorable scenario to be realized, a great deal has to go right for Japan. The underlying conditions favoring economic growth have to continue despite economic and social conditions that less and less resemble what existed in the rapid growth decades. Shorn of many past tools and facing growing difficulties in maintaining the pro-growth consensus, Japanese industrial policy has to avoid the pitfalls that have kept some industrial policies (such as Britain's) from being a major positive force and that began to hobble others (such as France's) when the premises on which they were based came to be questioned. Clearly this is a tall order.

Japan Performs Poorly

At the other end of the range of scenarios is one in which Japan performs poorly relative to its principal trading partners. In such a case, its rate of growth might be below the OECD average. Indeed, living standards might actually fall. Industrial policy might well be a contributing factor in such a scenario. As we have seen with respect to Europe, the worst outcome of industrial policy is not ineffectiveness. In certain circumstances, industrial policy can be positively perverse. Might such circumstances exist in Japan at some point during the last two decades of the twentieth century?

We noted earlier that perhaps the worst condition for an industrial policy is when both the bureaucratic skills and the tools exist but the formulation and conduct of the policy becomes an arena of massive political dispute. Industrial policy then ceases to be a tool of positive adjustment and instead becomes a tool of "historic preservation"—that is, an economic policy for increased productivity and growth becomes a surrogate for political redistribution.

How, in this scenario, does the institutional capability to conduct an industrial policy continue to decline and the bureaucracy's tool kit suffer further diminutions both in effectiveness and variety? And, how is Japan's industrial policy subverted into a surrogate for political conflict over income distribution?

To answer the first question, readers need only recall the post–oil crisis changes described earlier and make a linear extrapolation, as it were, of the trends of these changes. That is, the LDP's power steadily declines, possibly to the point of requiring increased support from the middle-of-the-road parties. The economy, for various reasons that can easily be speculated, grows only very slowly. Meanwhile, criticism from Japan's trading partners against what they perceive to be "outsider-unfriendly" characteristics of the Japanese economy intensifies.

As a result of these developments continuing into the 1990s, the deficit steadily grows, inducing further politicization of both the budget-making and disbursement processes and limiting the government's wherewithal to pursue its policy goals.[78] And, as the politically weak cabinet grows less decisive and coherent in its policy goals, intra- and interministry rivalries and conflicts continue to increase. Conflicts over goals and jurisdictions deteriorate even more into political struggles.

In addition, each ministry encounters problems of its own. The problems of bureaucrats of the MOF, MITI, and other ministries are intensified versions of developments we described earlier. Industrial policy cannot but become decreasingly effective in the face of a virtually complete liberalization of the capital market, nearly fully opened product and service markets, a further dwindling of the fiscal resources needed to subsidize or procure products from industry, and increased foreign scrutiny that severely limits the ability of the ministries to engage in administrative guidance.

One could perhaps foresee the sharply reduced effectiveness of future administrative guidance in the May 1985 proposal of the Keidanren (Federation of Economic Organizations; the most important body representing the interests of industry) advocating "a fundamental overhaul of the outdated industrial policy, which has now become a hindrance to the industries" and in the strong statement issued in June 1985 by the Japan Bankers' Association demanding that the MOF refrain from taking any action that "could reverse the tide of liberalization."[79]

In this scenario, in which the loss of the once-unquestioned consensus is evident, the combination of all of these factors can turn attempts at industrial policy, now with little coherence and few tools, into uncoordinated and even contradictory efforts by interest groups to increase their own share of a GNP that is no longer increasing or is even declining. This is not to say that Japan within the next two decades will become a "regulatory state," as Johnson characterizes the United States, with its bureaucrats losing all of their tools and discretionary power.[80] Neither is this to say that conflicts between management and labor or between the LDP-dominated cabinet and the Left will suddenly cause the Japanese economy to perform far worse than all of the OECD nations. But in this scenario, Japan will have a far less effective industrial policy than before, and the policy will be capable of being a potent drag on the economy.

Yet Another Scenario: An Average Performance

However useful they may be in analyzing the changing character and effectiveness of Japan's industrial policy, these two scenarios are, we believe, equally unrealistic predictions. Everything will not go right for Japan. But neither will everything turn out wrong.

Instead, Japan is likely to end up somewhere in between. But where?

Much will depend on how favorable the underlying fundamentals are. If Japan maintains a higher than average saving rate, if that higher saving rate translates into a higher than average rate of domestic investment (by no means a certainty in a regime of open capital markets), if Japanese labor remains relatively docile and accepting of structural adjustment, if Japan successfully makes the transition from being principally a borrower of scientific and technological knowledge to being a major generator—then the prospects for Japan's economic growth rate to be at the upper end of the range of industrialized countries will be bright.

Each of these conditions—and others that could possibly be named—are largely independent of what we have labeled "industrial policy." Industrial policy may affect them, but it certainly does not determine them. However, a perverse set of industrial policies can help to offset even a relatively favorable set of underlying fundamentals. Is this likely in the case of Japan?

We believe not, but we admit that our belief is based as much on educated judgment as on evidence. The fundamental factor in our optimism is the recognition that Japan's industrial policy to date, unlike the industrial policies of most advanced European countries, has been market conforming. Japanese economic ministries, especially MITI, have sought to reinforce market signals, not deny them. Moreover, we believe that, in an ironic twist, this market-conforming characteristic of Japanese industrial policy is currently being strengthened, despite stubborn and well-entrenched opposition within Japan, by the continuing strong foreign pressure on Japan to liberalize its markets.

One can cite many examples of policies that were not market conforming. Here, MITI's unsuccessful efforts to create international competitiveness in aluminum and several other industries and Japan's domestic and international policy on agriculture immediately come to mind. There were and are many policies whose market-comforming, as opposed to market-defying, characteristics are debatable. Examples of these policies include the MOF's administering of interest rates and segmentation of the capital market or MITI's guidance in forming cartels and encouraging trade associations to undertake joint research ventures.

But when all the literature is carefully examined in light of the degree of competitiveness prevailing in most Japanese markets since 1945—a competitiveness that is surely not unrelated to the performance of the economy—it is difficult not to conclude that the contribution of Japanese industrial policy to Japan's economic performance has essentially resulted from that policy's market-conforming characteristics. Our view differs from that often advanced by some neo-classical economists who equate superior economic performance with the absence or ineffectiveness of industrial policy. Unlike them, we acknowledge the capacity of an industrial policy to be market conforming, and when it is, it can enhance the performance of an economy.

Moreover, foreign pressure to liberalize the Japanese economy is enabling Japan to abandon industrial policy tools that have outlived their usefulness and to make the remaining tools increasingly more market conforming. Despite the pressures created by such short-run difficulties, Japan can, and is likely to, benefit from this seemingly paradoxical development.

As we have noted, many of the tools of industrial policy were useful principally because Japan was pursuing a catch-up strategy. The efficacy of these tools was rapidly declining by the early 1970s when Japan caught up with the West in most ways, especially in technology. In this sense, the pressure to liberalize—to limit the uses of, or even abandon, many of the tools—came about at the right time.

Limiting or discontinuing the uses of many of these tools would have been significantly more difficult (if not politically next to impossible in some instances) had it not been for foreign pressure. The validity of this observation is evident, for example, when we consider the substantially decreased control over the interest rate structure and other forms of liberalization in the capital market; a visible change in cartel and other policies that had restricted competition in many markets; and changes in policies regarding trade protection, subsidies, promotion of technological innovation, and the like.

It is possible to argue that foreign pressure to liberalize came at an opportune time. We are not unaware that Japan resisted liberalization and, in effect, did its best to choose when and at what speed liberalization was to occur—and even to delay liberalization altogether. But Japan's freedom to delay or limit the scope of liberalization was restricted. Much foreign pressure was determined by Japan's steadily increasing trade surplus (especially with its Western trading partners) and by the performance of the Western economies, which were deteriorating so rapidly relative to that of Japan that protectionism became a prime political concern in most nations.

While the pressure for liberalization was steadily intensifying after the late 1960s, Japan discovered, gradually but increasingly, that some of its policy tools had outlived their usefulness and, more important, that continuation of some policies would be detrimental to its economic performance. To discontinue the policies or to change their character sufficiently to meet the needs of the post-catch-up decades, Japan needed some force sufficiently strong to overcome the opposition of politically powerful interest groups. Such a force would have been extremely difficult to forge within the Japanese body politic—the weakening LDP could ill afford to alienate any major interest group. The force should ideally have come from outside. And, it did.

Two cautions about this largely optimistic conclusion are necessary. First, it is entirely possible that foreign pressure could turn perverse. In the past few years, there has been a decided swing toward protectionism in most of the industrialized Western democracies. Quantitative restrictions, aimed primarily against Japanese goods, have been spreading and now cover a significant proportion of manufactured imports. If other countries, spurred either by their own domestic difficulties or what they perceive as growing Japanese intransigence, abandoned their pressures on Japan to liberalize and instead focused even more on protectionism, Japan's growth prospects could be seriously damaged. For Japan, more than most major industrialized nations, depends on a smoothly functioning world trading system.

Second, as the rest of the world has discovered the Japanese economic miracle, scores of authors, both Western and Japanese, have rushed explanations of it into print. The belief seems to be growing that Japan (and especially Japanese industrial policymakers) can do no wrong—that Japan can create winners whenever and wherever it wishes.[81]

This belief, were it to take deep root in Japan, would pose a great danger to Japan's continuing economic success. Although the attitude expressed by the oft-heard phrase "Japan is a poor nation, bereft of natural resources" is probably overdone in a world where Japan is a leading economic power, it has had the great virtue of reinforcing in the Japanese mind the need for flexibility and adaptability—two characteristics that, we believe, count for much in explaining the essentially market-conforming nature of Japanese industrial policy. If Japan comes to believe the facile assertions that it possesses unique and superior abilities in economic management, there is a real chance that these characteristics will be lost. With them would go not only the possiblility of a successful industrial policy but also some of the important underlying economic fundamentals that have contributed so importantly to the postwar Japanese success.

The fact remains that Japan must continue to struggle against the problems we described in our "Japan does poorly" scenario. If enough of what was described in that scenario occurs, Japan will not be immune to an industrial policy that could become perverse. And even if many of the problems described in that scenario do not progressively grow worse, some of them—a diminution in the number of policy tools, politicization of the budget-making process, interministry conflicts, generally declining political consensus, and others—cannot be avoided. This is what prevents us from predicting that Japan will follow the more favorable scenario.

In concluding, we remind readers that the scope of this essay is limited. We did not examine the changing international political and economic conditions that affect the character and effectiveness of Japan's industrial policy. We were unable to offer more extensive analyses of the political, social, and even some economic aspects that are important to a discussion of Japan's industrial policy. Furthermore, since we were charged to be "forward-looking" in writing this paper, we presented many assertions and speculations. We do not ask readers to accept these. We ask only that they be considered in studying the present and future of one of the largest industrial economies.

Masu Uekusa

Industrial Organization: The 1970s to the Present

$\mathbf{A}$ changing world economic environment transformed the pace and structure of Japanese macroeconomic development in the 1970s. Particularly remarkable was the transformation of the organizational features that had characterized Japanese industry.[1] Cartels and other collusive activities prevalent in the 1960s have declined because of increased import competition, itself a result of trade liberalization since the late 1960s, and the revision of the Antimonopoly Law in 1977. Dependence on foreign technology has given way to domestic R&D activities. Risk sharing or risk spreading has become more important within corporate groupings, the subcontracting system, and other intramarket groups. And administrative control of industry has relaxed. This paper analyzes these changes and considers the future of industrial organization in Japan in light of recent technological innovations.

In the first section, I outline the transformations in the macroeconomy and in public policies toward industry in the 1970s and the early 1980s. Next, I analyze changes in the pricing and investment behavior of Japanese manufacturers and in the industrial market structure. In the third section, I examine the trend in productivity growth and analyze the determinants of the high growth rate of productivity. I then examine government policies intended to assist in structural adjustment and the process of voluntary adjustment at the level of the firm, trade association, or financial grouping. In the fifth and sixth sections, I analyze a recent change in the subcontracting system and describe some features of government regulation of public utilities and other industries as well as the recent moves toward deregulation. Finally, I consider the future of industrial organization.

Changes in the Environment of Industrial Organization

Changes in the Macroeconomy and Industrial Structure

The Japanese economy attained rapid growth and full employment in the 1960s, but several social and economic problems developed in the late 1960s and the early 1970s. Domestically, pollution and environmental destruction, deficiencies in social overhead capital and social public services (roads, ports, public health, public housing, excessive concentration of population and economic power in large cities, and administered prices in highly concentrated industries became more and more serious. These problems reflected the government's overlooking of the failure or incompleteness of the market in its excessive pursuit of rapid economic growth. As these problems became more severe, the comprehensive improvement of social and economic performance replaced the pursuit of rapid growth as the goal of the national consensus.

Internationally, as a result of the increased international competitiveness of Japanese industry, Japan sustained a trade surplus throughout the latter half of the 1960s and expanded it during 1969–72. Consequently, trade frictions arose between the United States and Japan, whose trade imbalance was particularly pronounced. To cope with this friction, the Japanese government reduced tariff rates, decreased the number of import quotas, relaxed other nontariff barriers, and restricted exports of textiles and steel products. As a result of the increased surplus in Japan's current account during 1969–71, Japan agreed at the Smithsonian Conference in 1971 to appreciate the yen substantially. But trade frictions did not disappear. The improvement of domestic social and economic performance and the reduction of trade friction were major policy concerns of the Japanese government in the late 1960s and the early 1970s.

In 1973, three major events had a huge impact on Japan: the final dissolution of the Bretton Woods fixed-exchange rate system, the first oil crisis, and the peak of the global business cycle. The fourfold increase in world oil prices rocked the Japanese economy, with its highly energy-intensive industrial structure and its dependence on imported oil for some two-thirds of its primary energy needs. This contributed to a sharp decline in the economic growth rate, high inflation, and a drastic worsening of the international balance of payments during 1973–75 (see Table 1). As a result of complex changes in the world economic environment and a series of domestic policy failures in the early 1970s,[2] the economic disequilibrium was more severe in Japan than in other major industrialized countries.[3] The Japanese economy was able to adjust to the economic disequilibrium within three years and realized stable economic growth in 1976–78.[4] The second oil crisis upset the economy in 1979–80,

TABLE 1

Trends in Principal Economic Indicators, 1970-1983

Year	Annual growth rate of						Unemploy- ment rate	Current balance of payments ($U.S. million)
	Real GNP	Private final consumption expenditure (real)	Private investment in new plants and equipment (real)	GNP deflator	Wholesale prices	Consumer prices		
1970	9.9	6.9%	17.7%	7.3%	3.6%	7.7%	1.1%	1,970
1971	4.7	5.9	-0.4	5.2	-0.8	6.1	1.2	5,797
1972	9.0	9.5	7.4	5.2	0.8	4.5	1.4	6,624
1973	8.8	9.3	16.0	11.9	15.7	11.7	1.2	-136
1974	-1.2	-0.7	-7.4	20.6	31.6	24.5	1.4	-4,693
1975	2.4	4.1	-3.2	7.8	3.0	11.8	1.9	-682
1976	5.3	3.4	3.1	6.4	5.0	9.3	2.0	3,680
1977	5.3	3.8	2.2	5.7	1.9	8.1	2.0	10,918
1978	5.1	4.7	6.6	4.6	-2.6	3.8	2.2	16,534
1979	5.2	5.9	7.7	2.6	7.3	3.6	2.1	-8,754
1980	4.8	1.3	3.0	2.8	17.8	8.0	2.0	-10,746
1981	3.8	0.8	3.5	2.7	1.4	4.9	2.2	4,770
1982	3.3	4.2	2.5	1.7	1.8	2.7	2.4	6,850
1983	3.0	3.3	0.5		-2.2	1.0	2.7	20,799

SOURCES: Japan, Economic Planning Agency, *Annual Report on National Accounts, 1984* (Tokyo: Government Printing Office, Mar. 1984); and idem, *Japanese Economic Indicators*, monthly.

but the growth rate of real GNP did not decline sharply, and the GNP deflator held constant at the low level of 2 per cent. By 1981, the balance in the current account had recovered from an all-time low and was showing a surplus. There are many reasons for the relatively weak impact of the second oil crisis on the Japanese economy and the economy's comparatively rapid adjustment. One important reason, discussed in the next section of this paper, was the resurgence of the market mechanism.

The changed world economic environment transformed the pace and structure of Japanese macroeconomic development in the decade after the first oil crisis. First, the annual average growth rate of real GNP declined—from around 8 per cent in the early 1970s to 5 per cent in 1976–78 to 3 per cent after the second oil crisis. This seems to have been mainly the result of decreased private investment in new plant and equipment (see Table 1), which was a driving force of the rapid growth in the 1960s. However, although the economic growth rate declined gradually, after the oil crises Japan realized a rate of growth higher than that of other industrialized countries, mainly because of an expansion of exports. It is characteristic of the Japanese economy that exports increase to pull the economy out of recessions, but this "export-drive effect" was especially strong immediately after each of the two oil crises.[5] Consequently, the surplus in the current balance of payments increased remarkably, intensifying trade frictions not only between the United States and Japan but also between the European countries and Japan, and trade frictions once again became a major policy issue in the 1970s and the early 1980s.

Second, Japan's industrial structure changed after the first oil crisis. In such highly energy-dependent basic manufacturing industries as iron and steel, nonmetallic mineral products, and chemicals, the sharp rise in energy costs and the resulting increase in product prices generated a shift in demand to domestic substitutes or related import goods. In addition, the declining trend in macroeconomic growth brought a large decrease in demand for the products of the industries mentioned. On the other hand, in final manufacturing industries,[6] which have a low dependence on energy, the smaller impact of rising energy costs on product prices and rapid improvements in productivity and the quality of products after the first oil crisis (discussed below) expanded domestic and overseas demand. Consequently, the relative importance of basic manufacturing industries within industry as a whole declined, and that of final manufacturing industries increased. This process left many key sectors of the economy in a state of structural depression, requiring industrial adjustment assistance policies.

Japan's industrial structure has been influenced not only by the sharp increase in energy prices but also by waves of technological innovation.

Innovation in microelectronics has resulted in the higher integration, smaller size, and lower prices of integrated circuits, bringing about smaller, faster, and less expensive computers. There have also been dramatic developments in mechatronics: numerical control (NC) machines, machining centers, industrial robots, and computer systems are revolutionizing offices, factories, finance, medicine, and security systems. The revolution in the telecommunications industry is fusing telecommunications with information services through development of optical fibers, satellites, electronic switchboards, value-added networks (VANs), integrated services digital networks (ISDNs), cable television (CATV), data processing, and data-base services. New industrial materials have been developed, such as silicon, gallium arsenide, carbon fibers, titanium, fine ceramics, shape-memory alloys, and other composite materials. Innovation in biotechnology is leading to gene recombination, bioreactors, cell fusion, and other advances. Finally, new power generation systems and batteries are being developed: fast breeder reactors, nuclear fusion, fuel cell generation, solar generation, and solar and biochemical batteries.

Of these high-technology industries, the microelectronic, mechatronic, automation equipment, and telecommunications industries began in the early 1970s and grew rapidly throughout the decade. Since these industries directly or indirectly relate to the storage, processing, conversion, or transmission of information, an information sector embracing most of these industries has developed. In order to locate this new element within a schema of the industrial structure, we can identify four sectors: (1) a basic material sector, which includes the primary sector and basic manufacturing industries in the secondary sector; (2) a processing and assembly sector, comprising final manufacturing industries with the exception of the information-goods and information-equipment industries; (3) an information sector,[7] which provides information goods, equipment, media, and services as well as social services; and (4) a service sector, which consists of the tertiary sector excluding information-related industries. Table 2 shows the changes in the relative importance of each sector in the 1970s. The basic material sector was most important in 1970 but declined throughout the decade. The processing and assembly sector accounted for a larger share by 1980 because of its rapid growth in the late 1970s (particularly in general machinery, electrical machinery, and transport equipment). Most important, the information sector's relative share rose remarkably in the late 1970s. In particular, the growth index for gross output in information equipment (especially in computers and accessories) was the largest of all industries. The indexes for information goods (especially data processing) were also remarkably high. Japan is clearly evolving into an information-oriented society. Should

TABLE 2

Change in Interindustry Gross Output Structure in the 1970s

(gross output as 1975 price = 100)

Sector/industry	Sector[a]	Proportion of gross output			Growth of index of gross output (1970 = 100)	
		1970	1975	1980	1975	1980
Basic material sector	I					
Agriculture		3.6%	2.9%	2.3%	102	99
Forestry and fishery		1.3	1.0	1.0	93	117
Mining		0.7	0.5	0.6	82	137
Textile		3.5	2.8	2.4	102	109
Lumber and wood products		1.9	1.6	1.4	106	111
Pulp and paper products		1.0	0.9	0.9	110	134
Chemicals		3.5	3.2	3.6	116	158
Petroleum and coal products		2.7	2.9	2.4	133	138
Nonmetalic mineral products		1.8	1.5	1.6	101	137
Basic metals		7.3	6.5	6.5	111	138
Metal products		2.2	1.9	2.0	109	143
SUBTOTAL		29.6%	25.8%	24.7%	109	130
Processing and assembly sector	II					
Food		5.7%	5.7%	5.2%	126	141
Leather and rubber goods		0.6	0.5	0.5	104	136
General machinery		3.8	3.9	4.3	127	175
Electric machinery[b]		1.8	1.4	1.9	96	162
Transport equipment		4.5	4.5	5.1	127	179
Other manufacturing products		1.5	1.3	1.4	112	152
Construction		10.3	10.3	9.5	125	143
SUBTOTAL		28.2%	27.6%	28.1%	123	154
Information sector						
Information goods[c]		1.7%	1.2%	1.8%	86	165
Information equipment[d]		2.3	2.3	3.9	123	256
Information media[e]		3.5	3.0	2.8	108	123
Information services[f]		4.3	4.1	4.7	120	172
Social services[g]		4.1	5.3	4.8	162	183
SUBTOTAL		15.9%	15.9%	18.1%	125	175
Service sector	III					
Public utilities		1.9%	2.0%	2.1%	133	170
Wholesale and retail		8.8	9.0	9.0	128	159
Real estate		3.3	4.8	4.2	181	196
Transportation		4.1	5.9	5.8	182	222
Other services		5.9	6.8	6.4	145	167
Miscellaneous		2.3	2.2	1.6	118	108
SUBTOTAL		26.3	30.7	29.1	146	172
TOTAL		100.0%	100.0%	100.0%	125	155

technological innovation in the fields of building materials, biochemicals, and energy progress as it has in microelectronics, mechatronics, and telecommunications, Japan's industrial structure will change even more dramatically.

Changes in Industrial and Antimonopoly Policies

With the transformation of the international and technological environments and the resulting change in macroeconomic structure, economic policy has also changed.

Industrial policy. Over the past decade, the goals, concrete issues, and instruments of industrial policy have changed (see Eads and Yamamura, this volume). The environment of industrial policy had changed by the late 1960s and the early 1970s. First, as already noted, national priorities shifted from maximum economic growth toward the comprehensive improvement of social and economic performance. Second, the relationship between the government and enterprises changed: the principal internationally competitive industries no longer had the same interests as the industrial ministries that had intervened in strategic areas of corporate decision making. A case typical of this change occurred on May 12, 1969, with the announcement that Mitsubishi Heavy Industries had agreed with Chrysler to create a new automobile company (Mitsubishi Automobile Company), despite the disapproval of the Ministry of International Trade and Industry (MITI).[8] Third, since Japan became a major economy and world trader in the late 1960s and trade frictions subsequently arose, Japanese actions have inevitably invited scrutiny and reaction by the United States and other nations.

MITI recognized these changes in the policy environment and promptly decided to change its industrial policy. In May 1971, it published *International Trade and Industry Policy in the 1970s*, which announced: (1) a transformation of policy goals from the pursuit of maximum economic growth to the utilization of economic growth to improve social and economic performance; (2) a change from the vigorous protection and pro-

---

SOURCES FOR TABLE 2: Japan, Administrative Management Agency, *1955-60-65 Link Input-Output Table* (Tokyo, 1980) and *1980 Input-Output Table* (1984).

[a] Sector I is the primary sector, sector II the secondary sector, and sector III the tertiary sector.

[b] Except for items listed in note *d* below.

[c] Includes electronic tubes, integrated circuits, wires and cables, printing ink, paper, and office supplies.

[d] Includes telecommunications equipment, electronic computers and accessories, other electronic equipment, TV, radio and sound appliances, precision machinery, and printing and book-making machinery.

[e] Includes printing and publishing (including newspapers), telecommunications, postal service, broadcasting, and amusement services.

[f] Includes data processing, data-base service, advertising, services to establishments, computer rentals, and finance and insurance.

[g] Includes education, research, health and social insurance, and other public services.

motion of promising industries to limited intervention into firm behavior and "maximum use of the market mechanism"; (3) promotion of a shift from a capital-intensive, energy-intensive, and environmentally destructive industrial structure to a knowledge-intensive, energy-conservative, and environmentally sound one; and (4) promotion of international cooperation.

The policy issues with which MITI and other industrial agencies have to cope have become remarkably pluralistic for several reasons: (1) the need to respond to social and economic problems; (2) the adjustment of economic disequilibria in the two oil crises, including policies dealing with energy conservation and the development of alternative energy sources; (3) the adjustment of international trade frictions; (4) structural adjustment in declining industries; and (5) the promotion of R&D in high-tech industries. As revealed by the frequent use of the word "adjustment," industrial policy in the past decade has become passive and negative, compared with policy in the rapid growth period, which centered on the heavy and chemical industries, the strengthening of international competitiveness, the attainment of a surplus in the international balance of payments, and "catching up with the West."

The pluralism, passivity, and ineffectiveness of the new policy reflects a reduced kit of policy instruments. High tariffs and quantitative restrictions on imports have not been effective since the liberalization of imports was enforced, and as trade friction has intensified, efforts to restrict direct investment by foreign firms and imports have largely subsided. The implementation of fiscal and monetary policies that concentrated the allocation of resources on promising industries has slackened. In particular, direct subsidy payments and tax-exemption measures have become difficult to implement because of reduced fiscal resources and the slower rates of economic growth. Administrative guidance has become ineffective because of the reduced kit of policy instruments and the change in government-enterprise relations. The government's ability to supply industry with information about technological innovation, international relations, and trends in industry has, however, increased in importance. This information is presented to industry in what are called "visions" in Japan. The visions, which are a consensus of opinion formulated in a ministry council by representatives of industry, labor, the media, and certain pressure groups, provide important guidance for the development of business plans by firms and thus might be considered a policy instrument. By publishing a vision, a ministry can induce corporations to behave in ways that it thinks desirable and that many representatives agree to be in accord with future trends.[9]

As stated above, industrial policy in Japan has become pluralistic, passive, and ineffective. To MITI and other administrative agencies, these changes might not seem positive, but from another point of view, they may. First, the so-called targeting policy, which protects and promotes certain industries and expands exports by using various policy instruments, is unfair to nations that do not adopt similar policies. In addition, the Japanese experience shows that a targeting policy accompanied by the promotion of a higher concentration of sellers and vertical integration for the purpose of strengthening international competitiveness increases the market power of oligopolistic firms and thus increases inefficiency in resource allocation (see next section). The decline of a policy with such harmful influences ought to be welcomed. Second, such policies as pollution regulation, structural adjustment of declining industries, adjustment of international trade frictions, and promotion of R&D certainly lead to pluralism and passivity in industrial policy, but such responses to "market failures" contribute to the stability, progressiveness, and development of an economy.[10]

Antimonopoly policy. The deconcentration measures imposed on Japan during the Occupation (1945–51), including the dissolution of the *zaibatsu*, the reorganization (dissolution, division, and divestiture) of big businesses, and the dissolution of cartel organizations, represent the greatest single use of government power in postwar Japan. "The holding companies and their control over their operating companies in major Zaibatsu were almost completely dissolved and the control power of Zaibatsu families was eliminated. Eighteen big corporations received division or divesture measures under the Excessive Economic Power Deconcentration Law and about sixty split themselves into several companies under the Corporate Reconstruction Law. And about one thousand cartel organizations, which were organized in the war time, were dissolved."[11] In addition, the Antimonopoly Law was enacted in 1947 in order to supplement the deconcentration measures; together they encouraged reliance on the market mechanism and competitive conduct by Japanese firms. At the time, the significance of antimonopoly legislation was not necessarily understood by the Japanese public, and in 1953, the law was greatly relaxed.

The Fair Trade Commission (FTC) of Japan did not actively enforce the law in the 1950s because of pressure from business circles and the growing strength of MITI, which sometimes recommended anticompetitive practices. In fact, the annual average number of violations of the Antimonopoly Law prosecuted by the FTC decreased from 27 during the Occupation to 6 between 1952 and 1959. But in the 1960s, a consumer movement angry about price cartels and other collusive agreements and academic circles advocating competitive policies stimulated stricter enforcement of the Antimonopoly Law, and the number of violations prosecuted by the FTC increased sharply, peaking in 1973 (see Table 3).

TABLE 3

Number of Violations of Antimonopoly Law Prosecuted by FTC, by Type of Offense, 1970-1982

Offense	1970	1971	1972	1973	1974	1975	1976
Price-fixing agreement	43	32	16	64	38	18	21
Other collusive agreement[a]	1	4	9	2	3	6	0
Unfair trade practices							
Resale price maintenance	0	0	2	0	2	2	2
Tying arrangements	0	1	0	0	2	1	4
Refusal to deal	0	0	1	0	0	1	0
Other[b]	0	0	0	0	0	2	4
TOTAL	0	1	3	0	4	6	10
Other	1	0	2	0	13	0	0
GRAND TOTAL	45	37	30	66	58	30	31

Offense	1977	1978	1979	1980	1981	1982
Price-fixing agreement	4	2	12	5	8	10
Other collusive agreement[a]	2	0	3	2	0	2
Unfair trade practices						
Resale price maintenance	0	3	0	0	1	4
Tying arrangements	1	1	0	1	1	0
Refusal to deal	2	0	0	3	1	0
Other[b]	1	0	4	0	1	2
TOTAL	4	4	4	4	4	6
Other	0	0	1	5	1	2
GRAND TOTAL	10	6	16[c]	14[c]	11[c]	19[c]

SOURCE: Japan, Fair Trade Commission, *Nenji hōkoku* (Annual report) (Tokyo, 1975-83).
[a] Distribution-channel agreements and quantity restrictions.
[b] Mergers and intercorporate shareholding and other offenses.
[c] Figures do not add to totals shown because some cases fell under more than one heading.

In 1974, the FTC proposed revisions of the Antimonopoly Law. Principal clauses in the revised law stipulated (1) a surcharge on unfair profiteering by cartels; (2) the division of companies with extremely high market shares into smaller units; (3) a detailed investigation by the FTC of parallel price increases in highly concentrated oligopolies; (4) stricter limitations on shareholding by banks and large nonfinancial corporations; and (5) increased fines for illegal behavior. The revised law passed the Diet in 1977. (See the next section for a description of the strong impact of the revised law on the behavior of Japanese enterprises.)

The FTC took action to hinder anticompetitive practices based on MITI's practice of administrative guidance. The FTC prosecuted the petroleum-refining industry before the Tokyo High Court in 1973 for cartel activities, including price fixing and restricted production. The FTC expected the court to punish the cartel members as well as to prohibit further administrative guidance of the kind by which MITI had assisted in the cartel's formation. Although the High Court did not declare MITI guilty, it wrote in its 1980 decision that administrative guidance that conflicted with antimonopoly legislation was not allowed. The Supreme Court confirmed this judgment in 1984, and since then MITI has curbed its use of administrative guidance.

The FTC has severely challenged horizontal mergers since the Yawata and Fuji steel companies merged in 1969, but in 1980 it published formal guidelines for mergers intending to further restrict various types of large mergers. It would challenge mergers when (1) the merging company had a market share of more than 25 per cent; (2) the market share of the merged company would be more than 50 per cent; (3) an oligopoly exists; or (4) the acquiring firm had total assets of over ¥10 billion and the acquired firm of more than ¥1 billion.

Changes in Market Structure and Corporate Behavior

Industrial Organization in the Pre–Oil Crisis Period

Japan prospered in the 1960s, enjoying high economic growth, rapid improvements in productivity, long-term price stability (particularly for wholesale prices), a sustained surplus in its international balance of payments, and low unemployment. But there were several problems in the internal organization of Japanese industry.

First, monopolistic elements were increasing. The decline in the average level of seller concentration in manufacturing sectors following World War II gave way in 1965 to an increase,[12] mainly because of the increase in horizontal mergers among large firms as international trade and capital transfers were liberalized. In addition, oligopolistic firms in the basic manufacturing industries had built large-scale plants in order to pursue economies of scale and had integrated backward to secure a stable supply of raw materials. Large manufacturing firms in final industries controlled their own distribution channels and were eager to differentiate their products through advertising and other sales promotion activities. Such factors reinforced each other, and entry into these oligopolistic markets became more difficult. These conditions came to characterize more and more markets as the period progressed.[13]

Second, cartels and other forms of interfirm coordination became increasingly prevalent in industries where the concentration ratio was high. There is much evidence to support this assertion. In the decade before the first oil crisis, the rate of decrease in wholesale prices at the troughs of the business cycle was less in the highly concentrated oligopolistic markets than in the less concentrated oligopolistic markets and the competitive markets as was the variability of prices, especially in the latter half of the 1960s (see Fig. 1). The existence of administered prices in highly concentrated industries is confirmed in a large number of statistical analyses.[14]

Third, many Japanese studies show that the market power of large firms in highly concentrated industries produced long-run distortions in the allocation of resources in the late 1960s and the early 1970s.[15] In addition, administered inflation occurred during the first oil crisis period.

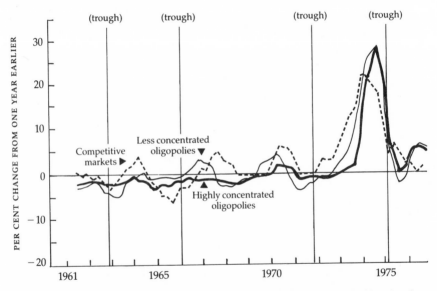

Fig. 1. Movements in wholesale prices by industry group classified by the degree of concentration, 1961 (first quarter) to 1976 (third quarter)—movements measured as percentage change from the same quarter one year earlier. Source: Japan, Economic Planning Agency, *Shūchū keitaibetsu kakaku dōkō* (Analysis of price movements by industry group classified by the degree of concentration) (Tokyo, Mar. 1977). For the classification of industry group by the degree of concentration, see Japan, Fair Trade Commission, *Nihon no sangyō shūchū, 1963–1966* (Industrial concentration in Japan) (Tokyo: Tōyō Keizai Shimpōsha, 1969), p. 34.

The high inflation at that time resulted from the sharp increase in oil prices as well as the failures of economic policy. The excessive supply of money in 1971–73 and the large budget for the Plan for the Remodeling of the Japanese Archipelago in 1973 caused a higher than expected inflation rate. The government enacted two laws—the Law on Appropriation of Demand and Supply of Petroleum and the Law on Emergency Measures for the Stabilization of National Life—in December 1973 to suppress the increase in domestic prices of oil and related products. These laws stimulated cartel-like practices by Japanese enterprises: expecting both governmental price controls and a high inflation rate in the near future, firms organized cartels to raise their product prices. As noted earlier, the number of cartel violations prosecuted by the FTC peaked in 1973 (see Table 3). Yoshi Kusuda and Toshihiro Ike reveal that the high inflation in 1974–75 was caused not only by the sharp increase in the prices of oil and related products, but also by the use of market power in highly concentrated industries.[16] That is, in oligopolistic industries, industrial price levels were inflated by the cartels and other collusive conduct.

It is apparent that the Japanese economy was at a crossroads in the late 1960s and the early 1970s; Japan could take the road toward a less competitive, stagnant economy—the road the United States took in the 1950s and 1960s—or the road toward a competitive, efficient economy like the one that existed in Japan during the 1950s and the early 1960s.

Recovery of Market Function

Decline in cartels. Since the first oil crisis, Japan's market structure has become more competitive, and industrial performance has improved. The most remarkable change in Japanese industrial organization has been the decline in cartel-like practices. One reason for this is that production in the basic industries has stagnated. Imbalances in the growth of production between basic industries and final manufacturing industries after 1976 have resulted in the relative decline of basic industries. If basic industries had engaged in collusive conduct, it would have made them more stagnant since there is little substantial product differentiation and there are strong incentives for collusive conduct. Instead, they have been thrown into a competitive struggle to maintain a certain level of production as demand falls. Moreover, it has been difficult for them to fix prices and otherwise coordinate behavior since they have been exposed to stronger international competition from other advanced and newly industrializing countries (particularly Korea) than they were in earlier periods because the import liberalization measures of the Kennedy Round of GATT (1964–67) and the Tokyo Round (1973–79) were enforced.

Another reason is the revision of the Antimonopoly Law. The number of cartel violations has decreased sharply since the revision of the Antimonopoly Law in 1977 (see Table 3). This reflects enforcement of the clause stipulating a surcharge on unfair profits and a drastic increase in reports of illegal activities from the public to the FTC. In 1978–83, the FTC fined 42 cartels a total of ¥8.6 billion (the average amount per case was about ¥204 million, and the largest amount was the approximately ¥1.2 billion levied against the linerboard cartel). In addition, the annual average number of reports from the public rose from about 1,000 in the three years before the revision of the law to about 5,000 after the revision.[17] Moreover, MITI's self-restraint in the use of administrative guidance after the petroleum-refining cartel case in 1973 seems to have contributed to the decline in cartels and collusive conduct.

The revised law appears to have been effective against such tacit methods of coordination as price leadership and parallel price setting in highly concentrated industries. The revised law allows the FTC to take measures necessary to restore competition (division or divestiture of the largest companies) in those oligopolistic industries where domestic sales exceed ¥50 billion, the share of the largest company or the two largest companies is over 50 per cent or 75 per cent, respectively; the entry of new firms is substantially deterred; and the rate of industrial profit is remarkably high during a "certain period" (which FTC lawyers have often glossed as "three to five years"). The law also allows the FTC to make a detailed investigation of parallel price increases in highly concentrated industries where domestic sales exceed ¥30 billion and the concentration ratio of the top three firms is more than 70 per cent. The FTC may report its findings to the Diet.

Since 1977, the FTC has surveyed 13 industries to which the definition of "monopolistic situation" is applicable. There has been no need to enforce the measures against monopolistic situations, and surveys seem to have been effective in preventing monopolistic behavior in those industries. Moreover, the FTC has continually surveyed price movements in 67 highly concentrated markets that fall under the "parallel price increase" clause. The number of markets in which the commission investigated parallel price increases and reported to the Diet was 2 in 1978, 4 in 1979, 21 in 1980, and 1 in 1981.[18] These figures suggest that the parallel price increase clause has been effective in preventing tacitly coordinated price fixing in highly concentrated industries. Nevertheless, the FTC has been unable to eradicate price fixing completely (note the 21 cases in 1980, during the second oil crisis). Indeed, although the FTC can investigate parallel price increases and present its results to the Diet, it does not have effective means to prohibit them. The clause exerts only moral pressure against tacit coordination. Therefore, it has been impossible to eradicate administered prices and the resulting misallocation of resources in oligopolistic industries. Nonetheless, the revision of the Antimonopoly Law in 1977 was epochal in preventing overt agreements (cartels) among firms.

Competitive and contestable markets. The decline of cartels and collusive behavior in Japanese industry signifies a recovery of the market function. This is also observable in the market structure. Table 4 shows the unweighted and weighted average levels of industrial concentration in the 1970s for 327 commodity-level markets in the manufacturing sector based on a survey published by the FTC.[19] The unweighted average level of concentration, in terms of both the top-three-firm concentration ratio and the Herfindahl Index was almost stable over the decade. The upward trend in the unweighted average concentration in the manufacturing sector in the latter half of the 1960s stabilized in the 1970s. A decline in mergers, particularly horizontal ones, seems to have contributed to this stabilization. The total number of mergers declined from 1,178 in 1971 to 871 in 1979, and horizontal mergers as a percentage of the total number decreased from 28.5 per cent in 1971 to 16.7 per cent in 1980.[20] The declining number of horizontal mergers reflects the strengthening of the merger restriction policy of the FTC.

Another factor contributing to stability is related to the change in industrial structure. The trend in the unweighted average concentration for each two-digit manufacturing industry in the FTC data is toward an

TABLE 4
Trends in Unweighted and Weighted Average Concentrations in 327 Sample Commodity Markets, 1971-1980

Year	Unweighted average Top-three firm concentration ratio	Herfindahl Index[a]	Weighted average Top-three firm concentration ratio	Herfindahl Index[a]
1971	56.14 (100.0)	0.1739 (100.0)	50.82 (100.0)	0.1469 (100.0)
1972	56.02 (99.8)	0.1747 (100.5)	50.55 (99.5)	0.1470 (100.1)
1973	56.09 (99.9)	0.1745 (100.3)	50.24 (98.9)	0.1459 (99.3)
1974	56.04 (99.8)	0.1741 (100.1)	49.53 (97.5)	0.1413 (96.2)
1975	56.07 (99.9)	0.1746 (100.4)	49.62 (97.6)	0.1410 (96.0)
1976	56.11 (99.9)	0.1728 (99.4)	49.28 (97.0)	0.1385 (94.3)
1977	56.16 (100.0)	0.1725 (99.2)	49.71 (97.8)	0.1400 (95.3)
1978	56.25 (100.2)	0.1737 (99.9)	50.89 (100.1)	0.1458 (99.3)
1979	56.21 (100.1)	0.1763 (101.4)	49.94 (98.3)	0.1423 (96.9)
1980	56.31 (100.3)	0.1753 (100.8)	49.34 (97.1)	0.1384 (94.2)

SOURCE: Akira Senō, ed., *Gendai Nihon no sangyō shūchū* (Industrial concentration in contemporary Japan) (Tokyo: Nihon Keizai Shimbunsha, 1983), p. 108.

[a]Herfindahl Index (HI) is the sum of the squared market-share of each firm and is equal to 1 in monopoly and 0 in atomistic competition. Thus, the higher the HI, the higher the degree of seller concentration.

increasing concentration in ten industries (mostly such basic industries as textiles, pulp and paper, chemicals, petroleum and coal products, and clay and stone) and a decreasing concentration in nine industries (usually such final industries as precision machinery, transport machinery, food, and so on). The data also show an increasing concentration in producer goods, which are classified as basic industries, and a decreasing concentration in capital goods and consumer goods, which are final industries. In addition, the FTC points out the correlation between a decline in the growth rate of shipments and an increase in the rate of change in concentration. These facts suggest that in general concentration increased in basic manufacturing industries with stagnant demand and decreased in final manufacturing industries with a higher growth of demand (particularly in the late 1970s). Many economists had predicted that the aggregate level of industrial concentration in the manufacturing sector would increase under a decelerating macroeconomy, but decreasing concentration in the final industries disproved their predictions.

The FTC data do not survey concentration trends in all high-tech industries. There are no systematic data on concentrations for high-tech industries as a whole, though some piecemeal data exist. The number of firms in the office computer industry increased from 8 in 1977 to 20 in 1982, and in the machining-center industry, from 26 in 1976 to 40 in 1982. Major companies in the steel and nonferrous metals industries have entered the titanium-refining industry, formerly dominated by two established firms. About 200 companies appear to have entered the fine ceramics industry. Most major chemical, food, textile, and electrical machinery manufacturers produce biochemical products. Most of the 1,864 establishments in the computer software industry in 1982 are small-scale venture businesses.[21] Thus, the entry of big businesses through diversification and of small ventures into high-tech industries such as electronics, mechatronics, information, new industrial materials, and biochemicals has been so vigorous that the unweighted average level of concentration in all manufacturing sectors, including high-tech industries, has probably been declining since the late 1970s and will probably continue to do so in the near future.

The weighted (by shipments) average level of concentration (WAC) has declined (see Table 4). According to the FTC's analysis, this is because the rate of decline in WAC for 13 (two-digit) industries (most of which are final industries) exceeded the rate of increase in WAC for six other industries (most of which are basic industries).[22] The increase in final industries' relative importance in the total amount of shipments in all manufacturing industries (and the decrease in the relative importance of basic industries) made the WAC decline in manufacturing industries as a whole. Furthermore, the decreasing concentration in final industries and the increasing trend for basic industries contributed to WAC declines for manufacturing industries overall. Therefore, the declining WAC reflects a change toward a more competitive market structure.

One factor reinforcing this trend was the liberalization of international trade and capital transfers in the late 1960s and early 1970s and the relaxation of various nontariff barriers throughout the 1970s in response to growing trade frictions. Although the import ratio (imports as a percentage of domestic demand) in all manufacturing industries is still at a low level, it has increased in food, textiles, pulp and paper, wood products, leather and leather products, clay and stone, petroleum and coal products, nonferrous metals, precision machinery, and miscellaneous products. In addition, the number of foreign companies entering Japanese markets (especially in manufacturing and commerce) has been increasing. This increase in potential and actual competition from abroad has promoted competition within Japanese industry.

Another factor reinforcing competition is related to the characteristics of recently developed high-tech products. In general, products in the fields of electronics, mechatronics, information equipment, new industrial materials, and biochemicals are small and light, have a small scale of production, and are R&D-intensive, high-value products. These product and production features make it impossible to pursue economies of scale, and this reinforces the competitive structure of these particular markets. Moreover, the possibility of developing a new product through R&D activities and the pursuit of economies of scope by established firms make these markets contestable. Competitiveness characterizes not only the product markets but also the service markets (for example, computer software, on-line information services, and data services); it is made possible by the small amounts of capital required for entry and small "sunk costs" (attained through leasing capital equipment). Thus, potential and actual entry by foreign firms and recent technological innovation have exerted pressures in Japan favorable to the development of a more competitive market structure and more competitive behavior. (Many industries with a strong scientific base have also tended to become unconcentrated in the United States, in part because there is no one dominant technology or configuration that can be appropriated by a single company.)

A possible criticism of this argument is that even if an individual market has become more competitive, overall concentration would increase if the majority of entrants are major corporations. The FTC data show, however, that overall concentration, namely the 100 largest nonfinancial corporations' share of total assets in nonfinancial sectors, declined from 25.6 per cent in 1967 to 23.9 per cent in 1975 to 21.4 per cent in 1980. Moreover, the share of the 100 largest manufacturing corporations in the total sales of all manufacturing industries decreased from 29.2 per cent in 1967 to 28.4 per cent in 1975 to 27.3 per cent in 1980.[23] The FTC points to the increase in the total number of firms as the most important factor in the overall trend toward decreased concentration.[24]

A further criticism of this argument might be that Japanese companies have cooperated in R&D and this is essentially monopolistic behavior. Several research and development cooperative associations (RDCA) have been organized in high-tech fields in Japan (for example, the Computer RDCA established in 1962 and the Very Large Scale Integration RDCA in 1976), and there are many cases in which a supplier and a user of a product have cooperated in R&D or invested jointly to improve the product or develop related products. Unless an RDCA induces price fixing or other collusive and predatory behavior, however, it yields social benefits: technological development stimulates innovation in related industries, and the public enjoys cheaper and better products.[25] In point of fact, the FTC's survey shows that the RDCAs and other joint R&D activities have stimulated rather than harmed competition in high-tech fields.[26]

In conclusion, there was a resurgence of the market function in the late 1970s and the early 1980s. Consequently, despite the second oil crisis, Japan's economic performance, symbolized by its stabler price levels (GNP deflator) and higher economic growth, was better than that of other industrialized countries.

Productivity Growth and R&D Activity

Productivity growth declined dramatically in many countries after the first oil crisis, mainly because of remarkable decreases in output and the sharp increase in energy costs. The annual growth rate of productivity in Japan during this time, though much lower than in the pre–oil crisis period, was by far the highest among major industrialized countries.[27]

High Productivity Growth and Its Determinants

Masahiro Kuroda has compared Japanese and U.S. trends in net output at the macro-level and the respective factor contributions (see Fig. 2).[28] Indexing net output (gross value added) in 1960 as 100, he found that net output in both countries grew at a nearly equal pace during 1960–67. During this period, the growth rate of total factor productivity was higher in the United States than in Japan; the equal pace in net output growth depended largely on the rapid growth of capital input in Japan and on a balanced growth of capital input, labor input, and total factor productivity in the United States. A remarkable disparity of net output between the nations developed during 1969–73. This disparity

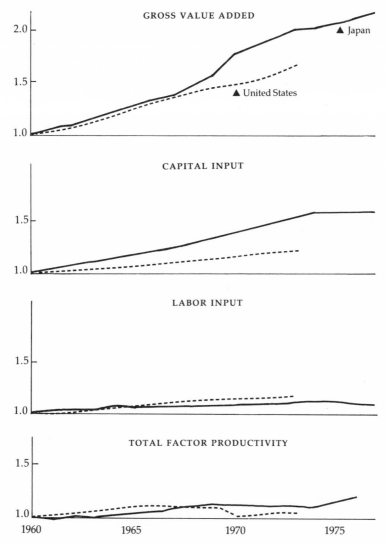

GROSS VALUE ADDED

2.0

1.5

1.0

CAPITAL INPUT

1.5

1.0

LABOR INPUT

1.5

1.0

TOTAL FACTOR PRODUCTIVITY

1.5

1.0

1960   1965   1970   1975

▲ Japan

▲ United States

Fig. 2. Trends in productivity growth in the United States and Japan, and respective factor contributions, 1960–1977 (1960 = 1.0). Source: Masahiro
Kuroda, "Nihon keizai no seisansei suii to shijō performance" (Trend in productivity in the Japanese economy and market performance), *Kikan gendai keizai*, Summer 1981, p. 58.

reflected the continued high growth of capital input and the accelerated growth of total factor productivity in Japan in contrast to a sharp decline in the growth of total factor productivity in the United States.[29] The growth rate of net output in Japan declined during the first oil crisis and then increased to about 50 per cent of the pre–oil crisis level in the late 1970s. The change in this growth rate in Japan was accompanied by a change in the pattern of factor contributions: slowed-down growth of both capital and labor input and accelerated growth of total factor productivity.

What factors explain the high growth of total factor productivity in Japan in the late 1960s and early 1970s and its even higher growth since the first oil crisis? The most important factor before the first oil crisis was the active importing of large-scale production technologies from foreign countries (particularly the United States) and the improvement of these technologies in Japan. In the iron and steel industry, for instance, major companies imported advanced technologies for hot and cold strip mills and oxygen steel-making furnaces, pursued economies of large-scale production and vertical integration, and accumulated know-how to reduce costs and improve product quality. Similar behavior occurred in such basic manufacturing industries as chemicals, synthetic fibers, petrochemicals and nonferrous metals. Major companies in the final manufacturing industries imported innovative technologies relating to new products and processes (for instance, the Taylor system and the Detroit-Ford system) and then improved them. The *kamban* system is an example of a major improvement. This system is a just-on-time supply system of parts from subcontractors to parent companies and results in reduced inventory and production costs.[30] The high growth of productivity in final manufacturing industries (and to a lesser extent in basic industries) was particularly related to experience curves, learning curves, progress functions—that is, average costs diminished exponentially with the cumulative volume of production through a "learning by doing" effect in the processes of labor, scientific work, design, purchasing, inventory control, marketing, and other management practices.[31] In the late 1960s, Japanese managers clearly recognized and actively pursued this learning by doing effect.

The higher growth of total factor productivity after the first oil crisis is undoubtedly related to a revolution in the consciousness of Japanese managers (that is, to *genryō keiei* or streamlined management). Facing the dissolution of the Bretton Woods system and the first oil crisis, managers tried to lower costs and improve product quality as much as possible in order to survive in the domestic and international markets. There was an active effort to introduce energy-conserving and labor-saving technologies: for example, continuous casting facilities in the iron and steel industry; suspension preheater and new suspension preheater kilns in the cement industry; and industrial robots, numerical control machines, and machining centers in many final manufacturing industries. There was also increased pursuit of quality control and the learning by doing effect. For this purpose, most large companies formed quality control circles in each of their workshops (see Koike, this volume). Through this process, it became recognized that improvements in product quality contribute greatly to a reduction in unit costs. Managers increased efforts to reduce input and inventory costs. For this purpose, big businesses asked subcontractors to reduce costs and improve product quality and adopted or refined the *kamban* system. Moreover, management and administrative costs were reduced through the introduction of office automation and computer-aided design systems. Finally, efforts were made to repay money borrowed from banks and other financial institutions in order to lower financial costs.

Another reason for the higher growth of total factor productivity after the first oil crisis was the active introduction of the "order entry system" (OES) and the "flexible manufacturing system" (FMS), mainly in final industries. An important problem in industries in which firms eagerly pursue product differentiation and market segmentation is producing a variety of products at lower unit costs. For instance, one of the biggest Japanese automobile manufacturers sells 20 types of cars, each of which has a large number of variations such as body color, type of transmission, two or four doors, and accessories options. One year the company produced 204,000 cars in 16,400 varieties—an average of only 12 cars with any given combination of variations. The car makers' policy is to produce all of a given type of car within a single plant, but it must produce many variations of each type (and sometimes several types) on a single line. Therefore, it adopted OES and FMS. In the former, a firm's computer center processes orders from dealers and distributes them to the firm's various plants through an information network. The latter is a system of controlling production, inventory, and inspection by computer to allow flexibility and efficiency when many variations of a product are being made in succession. The OES and FMS are now prevalent in final industries. *Genryō* management has also been adopted more extensively in final industries than in basic industries. Consequently, the average annual growth rate of labor productivity during 1974–81 was 10.7 per cent in final manufacturing industries and 4.0 per cent in basic ones.[32]

The Expansion of R&D Expenditure

As noted above, the importing and improving of foreign technology were major sources of productivity growth in Japan at least until the

1960s. The average annual growth rate of payments for imported technology, however, declined from 31 per cent in the 1950s to 21 per cent in the 1960s to 9.8 per cent in the early 1970s to 6.0 per cent in the late 1970s.[33] Japan outgrew its dependence on foreign technology. Domestic R&D expenditure began to increase in the late 1960s and has expanded rapidly since 1975. In 1983 the index (1975 = 100) of R&D expenditure at the national level was 143 in Japan, 133 in West Germany, 132 in France, and 128 in the United States in 1981 (and 152 for Japan in 1982).[34] This rapid expansion has depended not on government funding but on the expenditures of private enterprises. As a percentage of total R&D funds, R&D expenditure funded by the government was about 30 per cent in Japan until the early 1970s (compared with 70 per cent in Western countries) and has been declining since then because of the more rapid expansion of R&D expenditure by private enterprises. The recent rise in expenditure in the private sector reflects increased competition to develop high technology. Intramural expenditure on R&D as a percentage of sales is significantly higher in chemicals (especially in medicines and drugs) and electrical machinery (especially in electronic equipment) than in other industries (see Table 5). Because of the broad industry classifications, the statistics do not show high-intensity R&D for high-tech industries taken as a whole. Some newspapers, however, report that R&D expenditures by major companies that have already entered or are entering high-tech industries have exceeded amounts invested in new plant and equipment. Such R&D activities have generated high-quality integrated circuits, microcomputers, numerical control machines, industrial robots, and new information media, medicines, and industrial materials. Thus, the rapid growth of total factor productivity since the late 1970s is the result of *genryō* management, new order and production controls, and R&D activity in the private sector, especially in high-technology industries.

Structural Adjustment in Declining Industries

Structural adjustment in declining industries has been an important issue in Japan since the first oil crisis forced it to face the prospect of declining competitiveness in many key sectors for the first time in the postwar period.[35] In general, industrial adjustment can be carried out by a governmental adjustment assistance policy as well as by the voluntary actions of private enterprises within declining industries. In Japan, the government has formulated and implemented a positive program of structural adjustment in close cooperation with the private sector, and these policies are believed to have contributed to the successful reorganization and retrenchment of declining industries.[36] It seems to me that

TABLE 5
Intramural Expenditures on R&D as a Percentage of Sales, by Industry, FY 1976-1981

Industry	1976	1977	1978	1979	1980	1981	1982
All industries	1.42%	1.48%	1.57%	1.49%	1.48%	1.62%	1.78%
Agriculture, forestry, and fisheries	0.24	0.31	0.60	0.45	0.17	0.26	0.27
Mining	0.57	0.50	0.54	0.48	0.52	0.46	0.64
Construction	0.48	0.53	0.42	0.40	0.46	0.37	0.43
Manufacturing	1.64	1.70	1.82	1.71	1.73	1.91	2.15
Food	0.49	0.50	0.51	0.51	0.58	0.55	0.63
Textile mill	0.66	0.56	0.77	0.82	0.77	1.09	1.13
Pulp and paper	0.47	0.46	0.49	0.42	0.41	0.43	0.52
Publishing and printing	0.46	0.41	0.36	0.27	0.26	0.21	0.39
Chemical products	2.39	2.62	2.71	2.54	2.55	2.37	3.05
Industrial chemicals	1.69	1.87	1.92	1.71	1.85	2.01	2.17
Oils and paints	2.40	2.71	2.73	2.17	2.48	2.56	2.66
Drugs and medicines	5.05	4.84	5.00	5.53	5.45	5.85	5.56
Other chemical products	2.38	3.12	3.03	2.38	2.19	3.03	3.43
Petroleum and coal products	0.18	0.23	0.27	0.18	0.30	0.18	0.20
Rubber products	2.25	1.96	2.60	2.44	2.10	2.33	2.47
Clay and stones	1.40	1.22	1.29	1.27	1.30	1.39	1.64
Iron and steel	1.02	1.11	1.08	1.04	1.14	1.30	1.50
Nonferrous metals	0.96	1.01	1.00	0.87	1.03	1.36	1.57
Fabricated metals	1.00	1.18	1.08	1.28	1.15	1.22	1.43
General machinery	1.79	2.01	1.93	1.85	1.90	2.10	2.34
Electrical machinery	3.66	3.61	3.74	3.55	3.71	4.06	4.52
Electrical appliances	3.49	3.49	3.59	3.19	3.35	3.80	4.17
Electronic equipment	3.80	3.71	3.89	3.91	3.94	4.21	4.72
Transport machinery	2.08	2.27	2.44	2.37	2.34	2.62	2.69
Motor vehicles	2.20	2.32	2.60	2.51	2.38	2.82	3.02
Others	1.76	2.12	1.90	1.85	2.15	1.94	1.67
Precision machinery	2.37	2.91	3.15	2.96	3.02	3.47	3.97
Other manufacturing	1.24	1.15	1.16	0.91	1.16	1.11	1.30
Transportation, communication, and public utilities	0.27	0.33	0.35	0.40	0.32	0.36	0.32

SOURCE: Japan, Office of the Prime Minister, Bureau of Statistics, *Report on the Survey of Research and Development, 1982* (Tokyo: Nihon Tōkei Kyōkai, 1983), p. 59.

most discussion of Japan's experience in this area has paid too much attention to the government's role and too little attention to voluntary adjustment by private enterprises themselves. Therefore, after outlining the contents and the processes of adjustment assistance policies, I focus on the question of how Japanese enterprises have coped with industrial adjustment problems.

The Industrial Adjustment Assistance Policy

Even after the adjustment of the disequilibrium in the macroeconomy created by the first oil crisis (1973–75), large numbers of industries remained in a state of depression; reducing overcapacity and curtailing employment were urgent concerns. After enacting the Law on Temporary Measures for the Stabilization of Specified Structurally Depressed Industries (the Structurally Depressed Industries Law) in 1978, the government began to enforce a structural adjustment assistance policy toward several depressed industries. Under the law, industries were eligible for assistance if (1) overcapacity in the industry was severe; (2) more than half the firms in the industry had been in dire financial conditions for over three years; (3) more than two-thirds of the firms in the industry signed a petition seeking designation under the law; and (4) a ministerial council agreed on the need to reduce overcapacity to overcome the depression.[37] Although many industries (including the iron and steel industry) had severe overcapacities, the law designated only 14 industries as "structurally depressed," including aluminum refining and synthetic fibers (hurt by high energy costs); shipbuilding (low world demand); electric furnace steel making, ferrosilicon, and linerboard (low domestic demand); and cotton spinning, combed-wool spinning, and chemical fertilizers (hit by the increasing comparative advantages of the newly industrializing countries) (see Table 6).

The Depressed Industries Law called for (1) formation of a basic stabilization plan outlining capacity reduction, employment measures, and other conversion measures, through consultation with industry and union representatives; (2) collective implementation of the capacity reduction plan by all companies in the designated industry; (3) establishment of a joint credit fund to purchase scrapped facilities and guarantee the loans that the relevant firms borrowed from banks for the disposal of facilities; (4) assistance for displaced workers and depressed communities through the National Employment Insurance Law and the laws specific to those workers; and (5) exemptions for the designated industries from antimonopoly legislation (although the FTC can call for alteration if these exemptions have excessively anticompetitive effects).[38]

The law did not introduce such protective measures as import restrictions and direct government subsidies, reflecting concern about foreign

TABLE 6
Plan for Disposal of Facilities in Structurally Depressed Industries, 1978-1988

Industry	Targeted volume of disposal (000 tons)	
	Under the Depressed Industries Law (1978-83)	Under the Structural Reform Law (1983-88)
Steel making by electric furnace	2,850.0 (14%)	3,800.0 (14%)
Aluminum refining	530.0 (32%)	930.0 (57%)
Synthetic fibers and wool		
Nylon fiber	73.4 (20%)	as in 1978-83
Polyacrylonitrile wool	84.9 (17%)	as in 1978-83
Polyester fiber	44.9 (13%)	as in 1978-83
Polyester wool	78.4 (20%)	as in 1978-83
Biscoase wool		44.7 (15%)
Shipbuilding by use of a dock to build ships of over 5,000 GT	3,400.0 (35%)	
Chemical fertilizers		
Ammonium	1,190.0 (26%)	660.0 (20%)
Urea	1,790.0 (45%)	830.0 (36%)
Phosphoric acid by wet process	190.0 (20%)	130.0 (17%)
Phosphoric acid by dry process		240.0 (32%)
Synthetic fertilizer		810.0 (13%)
Spinning mills		
Cotton spinning	67.1 (56%)	as in 1978-83
Combed-wool spinning	18.3 (10%)	as in 1978-83
Ferrosilicon	10.2 (21%)	50.0 (14%)
Paper		
Linerboard	1,150.0 (15%)	as in 1978-83
Western-style paper		950.0 (11%)
Petrochemicals		
Ethylene		2,290.0 (36%)
Polyolefine		900.0 (22%)
Oxidated vinyl resin		490.0 (24%)
Ethylene oxiside		201.0 (27%)
Oxidated vinyl pipe		116.0 (18%)
Sugar refining		1,000.0 (26%)

SOURCES: Japan, MITI, *Kōzōfukyōhō no kaisetsu* (A commentary on the Depressed Industries Law) (Tokyo: Tsūshō Sangyō Chōsakai, 1978), pp. 280-99; and idem, *Kankōhō no kaisetsu* (A commentary on the Structural Reform Law) (Tokyo: Tsūshō Sangyō Chōsakai, 1983), p. 82.
NOTE: Figures in parentheses are targeted volume of disposition as a percentage of total capacity.
ªIncludes 530,000 tons to be disposed under the Depressed Industries Law.

criticism of protective measures and the "positive adjustment policy" encouraged by the OECD Council of Ministers in 1978.[39] The Depressed Industries Law was not an entirely positive adjustment policy, however; MITI and the Ministry of Transportation (MOT—which had taken charge of the industrial adjustment policy toward the shipbuilding industry) assisted in forming production cartels and price-fixing agreements in the electric furnace steel making, chemical fertilizer, and shipbuilding industries and introduced a tariff-quota system for the aluminum-refining industry to provide low-interest financing through tariff credits. Even though a FTC research committee criticized these restrictive measures,[40] by June 1983, when the Depressed Industries Law terminated, some designated industries had nearly achieved the desired levels of capacity reduction. Consequently, those industries not hit by the second oil crisis regained a balance between supply and demand. Particularly in the shipbuilding industry, employment adjustment and the reduction of production facilities appear to have been comparatively successful.[41]

A new law—the Law on Temporary Measures for Structural Reform of Specified Industries (the Structural Reform Law)—was enacted in May 1983 in order to continue industrial adjustment policies toward the aluminum-refining, synthetic fiber, chemical fertilizer, ferrosilicon, and linerboard industries, which were hit by the second oil crisis, and to enforce the policies toward industries that had declined because of the crisis—petrochemicals, sugar refining, and Western-style paper (see Table 6). The law employed the same methods of capacity reduction and employment adjustment as the Depressed Industries Law, but it promoted positive reorganization of these industries through mergers, joint production, production specialization, and development of new processing technology. In short, the 1983 law aimed at both retrenchment and revival of declining industries. The law stipulated that all collective action to dispose of production facilities and reorganize the market structure should be undertaken with the consent of the FTC, that protective measures to restrict imports were prohibited, that policies should be pursued openly and policy contents disclosed publicly, and that there was to be a gradual curtailment of these policies, ending in termination of the law in June 1988. The 1983 law strongly reflects the positive adjustment policy encouraged by the OECD. It is still too soon to evaluate the effects of policies based on the law. If disposal of overcapacity, curtailment of employment, and industrial revival through innovations proceed smoothly, the policy will no doubt receive widespread international attention.

Voluntary Adjustment in the Private Sector

Shipbuilding and aluminum refining are excellent examples of how Japanese enterprises have coped with a difficult situation.

Shipbuilding. The Japanese shipbuilding industry was one of the most developed industries in the rapid growth period, accounting for about 50 per cent of total world production in the late 1960s. Current orders for ships peaked in 1973, but with the first oil crisis late that year, the world tanker market collapsed. The total volume of orders for ships over 2,500 gross tons (GT) declined by over 70 per cent, from 33.8 million GT in

1973 to 9.4 million GT in 1974. By 1978, orders had fallen to 3.2 million GT, a 90 per cent drop from the 1973 peak. Orders climbed to 9.3 million GT in 1980, but this was still less than 30 per cent of the 1973 peak.

In 1974, the Shipping and Shipbuilding Industries Rationalization Council (SSIRC), a MOT advisory group, recommended that each company reduce working hours. The recommendation was not implemented because the Shipbuilders' Association of Japan (SAJ), the trade association for larger shipbuilders, and the Cooperative Association of Japanese Shipbuilders (CAJS), a trade association for smaller shipbuilders, could not agree. With decreasing orders for ships in 1974–78, these trade associations decided to reduce their operation ratio as well as to dispose of productive capacity. In 1978, SAJ president Susumu Shintō (at the time president of Ishikawajima Harima Industry) organized a program of voluntary adjustment and requested a governmental assistance policy for the shipbuilding industry in a report presented to the MOT and Prime Minister Ohira. The MOT designated the industry as structurally depressed under the Depressed Industries Law and in 1978 formulated a stabilization plan for the industry based on a ten-year forecast of demand. The plan called for reduction in the operation ratio, disposal of overcapacity, establishment of a stabilization credit fund, curtailment of employment, and stimulation of domestic demand through the scrapping of old ships and an increase in public orders.

The MOT's capacity reduction plan called for the 61 companies with docks able to build ships over 5,000 GT to dispose of 35 per cent of their total capacity. Because of differences in the disposal ratio, the seven largest companies would dispose of 40 per cent, the 17 larger medium-size companies of 30 per cent, the 16 smaller medium-size companies of 27 per cent, and the other 21 smaller companies of 15 per cent (see Table 7). The companies involved agreed to these ratios and met the proposed

TABLE 7

Capacity Scrapping Plan in the Shipbuilding Industry,
with Results as of February 1982

(10,000 compensated gross registered tonnage)

Size (and number) of companies	(1) Capacity before scrapping	(2) Capacity to be scrapped	(3) (2) ÷ (1) (per cent)	(4) Result (scrapped capacity)	(5) (4) ÷ (2) (per cent)
Largest (7)	569	228	40%	225	99%
Larger medium (17)	289	87	30	103	119
Smaller medium (16)	79	21	27	25	119
Others (21)	40	6	15	5	81
TOTAL (61)	977	342	35%	358	105%

SOURCE: Japan, Ministry of Transportation.

reductions in capacity by February 1982. Most of the companies financed these reductions themselves, but nine did so by selling part of their assets to the Special Shipbuilders Stabilization Credit Fund. The disposal of production facilities and the reduction in operation ratio (to 39 per cent in 1979 and 1980) helped bring supply and demand back into balance.

As for employment curtailment, most of the firms encouraged "voluntary retirement," in part by offering one-year salary premiums in addition to normal retirement allowances. Moreover, most of the larger firms transferred some workers to other companies within their corporate grouping. For instance, some Mitsubishi Heavy Industry workers were transferred to Mitsubishi Automobile Company. Consequently, the total number of workers decreased from 184,000 in 1973 to 116,000 in 1982 (a 37 per cent drop). Subcontractors to the shipbuilding industry were also discharged, and their numbers declined from 90,000 in 1973 to 53,000 in 1982 (more than a 40 per cent drop). After the employment curtailment, most presidents of the larger companies resigned. The figures show that both labor and management in a depressed industry must make painful adjustments at a high cost.

If there were no such risk-sharing systems as trade associations, corporate groupings, and subcontractors, industrial adjustment in the shipbuilding industry would have been much more difficult. Voluntary actions based on these systems, together with government assistance, led to a successful adjustment. By far the most important role was played by the major shipbuilders, who, recognizing severely changed economic conditions, organized a concrete program to carry out the necessary adjustments. Consequently, the industry is now performing well: there were no large-scale bankruptcies; the largest shipbuilders have been diversifying; and the middle-ranking companies have appreciably improved productivity through introducing robots, numerically controlled cutting machines, computer-aided design systems, and so forth.

Aluminum refining. Rapid growth in demand in the 1960s attracted two large companies from major corporate groupings, Mitsubishi Chemical and Mitsui Aluminum, to enter an industry already dominated by three big companies (Nippon Light Metal, Sumitomo Chemical, and Shōwa Aluminum). The industry went into decline in the 1970s. Imports of aluminum ingots had increased gradually in the late 1960s because of liberalized international trade, but they expanded rapidly in the early 1970s because the price of imported ingots declined more than that of domestic ingots after the yen appreciated against the dollar following the Smithsonian Conference in 1971 (see Fig. 3).[42]

The first oil crisis and the destruction of the Bretton Woods system in 1973 forced the Japanese aluminum refining industry into decline. Alu-

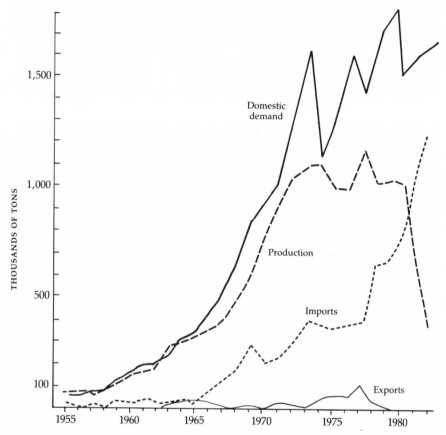

Fig. 3. Trends in demand and production of aluminum ingots, 1955–1982.
Source: Japan Aluminum Federation, *Light Mechanical Statistics in Japan*, annual.

minum refining is so extraordinarily energy intensive that aluminum has been called "congealed electricity," and Japanese aluminum refineries depended on oil-based thermal power generation for 60 per cent of their needs in 1973. The quadrupling of crude oil prices drastically raised their electricity costs and thus the unit cost of their aluminum ingots. In addition, the appreciation of the yen after the shift to the flexible exchange rate system lowered the price of imported ingots. It is estimated that the market price per ton of imported ingots was ¥129,000 but the domestic production cost per ton was ¥170,000-190,000 in late 1973.[43] Hence, imports increased sharply, reflecting the decline in the competitiveness of domestic ingots as well as the excess supply in the world market. After the second oil crisis, the competitiveness of the Japanese aluminum-refining industry declined further. The domestic price per ton had risen to about ¥500,000 by March 1982, but the price of imported U.S. ingots was only about ¥200,000. The rapid expansion of imports paralleled the sharp decline in domestic production (see Fig. 3). The Japanese aluminum-refining industry has declined precipitously and will apparently continue to decline in the near future.

Conditions in the aluminum-refining industry are so severe that structural adjustment is extremely difficult, so much so that it was difficult even to form a stabilization plan under the Depressed Industries Law.[44] The final plan aimed to keep 1.1 million tons of domestic capacity, disposing of 530,000 tons. MITI decided to assist the capacity reduction plan by providing a tariff-quota system and low-interest financing through governmental financial institutions and by arranging governmental purchase of ingots for stockpiling. Although producers asked MITI for an electricity subsidy large enough to allow them to compete with foreign producers, MITI rejected such protectionist measures. Since government assistance was not on a large scale and protectionist measures could not be adopted because of domestic and foreign pressures, producers decided to make bold voluntary adjustments. These were of two types: voluntary actions taken at the company level and assistance arrangements within corporate groupings.

Companies have made three kinds of voluntary responses. First, in order to reduce power costs, the refiners shut down plants using oil-produced electricity and concentrated production in plants using hydro-electricity or coal-produced electricity. Domestic capacity declined from 1.64 million tons in 1977 to 743,000 tons in 1982. Electricity costs, however, were still intolerably high. In cooperation with the government (the Institute of Chemical Technology of the Industrial Science and Technology Agency), the refiners began research on a new refining process in which aluminum ore and coke were melted in the blast furnace and then refined into pure aluminum using electricity generated by carbon monoxide gas produced as a by-product in the blast furnace. If this project is successful, the new process could conserve enough energy for the Japanese aluminum refiners to survive. It is said, however, that the new process will take at least six or seven years to develop.[45]

Second, in order to produce aluminum ingots using lower-cost electricity, Japanese refiners have invested in overseas refining projects since the early 1970s. As of March 1983, nine offshore projects were either already completed, under construction, or in the planning stages. Imports of ingots from those projects are expected to increase sharply in the near future.

Third, although for many years Japanese aluminum refiners did not participate in the fabrication business, they began such forward integration in the late 1970s in order to secure business in fabrication, which is experiencing a fairly high growth of demand (see Fig. 3). The refiners have also endeavored to diversify. For example, Shōwa Aluminum is expanding into the fine ceramics industry by using alumina, which is an important material in that industry.

Moreover, corporate groupings have been involved in the adjustment process. All five refiners are members of a major corporate grouping. These groupings have played an important role in the aluminum industry's adjustment. One component of their involvement is financial assistance from the banks and other financial intermediaries within the corporate groupings, which have provided loans to cover shortfalls in cash and rendered other forms of aid, such as interest reductions.[46] Perhaps far more important is the spreading of financial losses to other members of the group. In March 1976, for example, Mitsubishi Chemical split off its aluminum-refining division and limited its shareholdings in the new Ryōka Light Metal to 21 per cent by obtaining capital investment from 17 Mitsubishi group members and associated user firms.[47] Sumitomo Chemical and Shōwa Aluminum took similar measures in 1976. As Paul Sheard points out,

The splitting off of their deficit aluminum refining divisions in this way had two important effects from the parent firms' point of view. In the absence of established consolidated accounting practices, by removing the operations from the internal structure of the corporation the adverse impact of the losses on the corporation's overall performance could be minimized and rationalizations, particularly sensitive workforce reductions, facilitated. In this context, it is interesting to note that, although one of Japan's most important basic material industries, the only aluminum refining company that was listed directly on the stock exchange after 1976 was Nippon Light Metal. The second effect, reflecting the risk sharing business arrangements of group organization, was to spread the costs of structural adjustment across a wider set of related firms.[48]

This type of risk-sharing or risk-spreading arrangement within a corporate grouping is a distinctive feature of Japanese industrial adjustment. Because of such arrangements, the five aluminum refiners that are members of corporate groups still survive. But one company, Sumikei Aluminum Industry, disappeared from the aluminum refining industry in 1983. One or more of the surviving companies may, however, exit from the industry in the near future because they are in an extremely dire financial condition and are declining in international competitiveness.

Subcontracting System

The subcontracting system is not peculiarly Japanese; it has been utilized widely in the automobile, airplane, electric appliance, machinery, textile, clothing and apparel, and construction industries in many developed and developing countries. The Japanese subcontracting system, however, has several distinctive features: an extremely high level of dependence by larger firms in the industries mentioned above on subcontractors; a significantly high proportion of subcontractors in small and medium-size enterprises; the existence of a cooperative and risk-sharing community consisting of parent companies and their subcontractors; a quick diffusion of technology within this community and consequently high levels of productivity growth and quality control; and distinctive subcontractor control systems developed through long experience with subcontracting, such as the *kamban* system. This section describes these features in detail, supplementing the theoretical analysis of the subcontracting system found in Aoki's paper and the analysis of the role of smaller subcontracting firms in Patrick and Rohlen's paper in this volume.

Subcontracting Relationships

In general, the finished products of assembly industries are composed of a large number of parts, components, and related goods (for example, an automobile consists of about 20,000 items). To "make or buy" those items is a key decision, based on time, quality, and cost considerations, that managers in assembly industries must make.[49] Major Japanese car makers have such essential components or subsystems as engines, bodies, crankshafts, transmissions, and accelerators made within their own establishments or in their subsidiaries. Purchases are made from (1) *kanren sangyō* ("related industries"), when the product is standardized and produced by large-scale established companies, and thus can be bought through pure market transactions (for example, tires, batteries, bearings); (2) independent parts makers, who produce products with no special design specifications from the car makers and sell them to multiple customers in the domestic and international markets (plugs, shock absorbers, some kinds of sheet metals); and (3) subcontractors, who engage in parts production or discrete processing operations under special order, with design, specification, and delivery requirements set by the car makers (engines, parts, electrical systems, bodies, and cast, forged, and electroplated parts).[50]

The *kanren sangyō* companies and independent parts makers supply many of the same goods as subcontractors but are not included in that category. Two important factors define whether an enterprise is a subcontractor. First, a subcontractor's dependence on a subcontractee in regard to a given product is almost total, and the product cannot be sold to several customers. The product is essentially a non-market good, made to special design specifications. (A subcontractor can, however, supply several different products to several different subcontractees.) Second, a subcontractor does not have as much control over product design as the large-scale companies in the *kanren sangyō* or independent parts maker categories.

To give an example, in the automobile industry, each car maker, subsidiary, and independent parts maker has its own subcontractors, and the subcontracting relationship involves primary, secondary, and tertiary subcontractors. A 1980 MITI survey of the relationship between the largest car maker and its subcontractors found that 168 primary subcontractors were large enterprises; 4,700 secondary subcontractors were small and medium-size enterprises; and 31,600 tertiary subcontractors were smaller enterprises.[51] The pyramidal and hierarchical structure found in the automobile industry is a feature of the Japanese subcontracting system as a whole, although the number of subcontractors in each layer is smaller in other assembly industries.

The "buy ratio"—the cost of purchased items as a percentage of total production costs—has been extremely high in the Japanese automobile industry (on average 73 per cent),[52] and almost all purchased items are produced by subcontractors. This illustrates the high degree of dependence of subcontractees on subcontractors. Subcontractors' dependence on a single subcontractee has also been high, particularly for primary subcontractors, although some of them have grown into large independent parts makers and others have contracts with the subsidiaries of major car makers and with other independent parts makers. Major car makers and their primary subcontractors form a cooperative community, which was established in the rapid growth period before the first oil crisis and continues to exist. The members of this community are bound together by a variety of continuing buyer-seller and lender-borrower ties, by shared facilities, technologies, and know-how, and sometimes by interlocking directorates. For instance, a subcontractor's improvement in processing technology might be reported to its parent company, which might reward the subcontractor and then diffuse the improvement among other subcontractors. This type of interdependent relationship becomes even more apparent when we look at the mechanism determining the volume of orders to subcontractors and subcontracting unit prices.

Determination of Subcontracting Prices

As mentioned above, the subcontractee determines design, specification, and delivery requirements. On the other hand, the quantity of orders and unit prices are determined by negotiation. According to Banri Asanuma's analysis, there are two stages in contract negotiations between major car makers and their prime subcontractors.[53] The first stage is carried out over several months before a newly developed car or a new model is produced. Basic contracts are worked out on the quantity of parts to be made by subcontractors and the unit price. Because a full model change generally occurs every four years (minor changes every two years), the basic contracts are effective for four years (or two years). Yet expected demand for the car necessarily changes according to business fluctuations and other factors. Thus, the basic contracts are adjusted in regard to the quantity of production every month and in regard to the unit price every six months. This is the second stage of negotiation. In this stage, contracts are seldom revised within the contract period, partly because this might damage the interdependent relationship and partly because the law prohibits undue revision of subcontracts (see below).

Unit prices are generally determined by the full-cost principle: (unit product cost) × (1 + markup ratio). The markup ratio is fixed and different for every part and component. Subcontractees expect continual cost-reducing productivity growth from their subcontractors. Therefore, major car makers will not approve raises in subcontracting unit prices because of increased labor costs, nor in principle do they approve raises because of increased energy costs, saying that increases in these costs should be compensated for by productivity growth. The car makers are responsible for absorbing the subcontractors' increased production costs when the increases are the result of changes in design by the maker. In addition, car makers reward subcontractors for improving production processes by raising the markup ratio. This mechanism of price determination has brought about a high level of productivity growth among subcontractors. In addition, the continuous growth of productivity in car manufacturing as a result of fierce competition has contributed to the success of the Japanese automobile industry in the international market.

Development of Small and Medium-Size Subcontractors

Although the linkage between the car manufacturers and their primary subcontractors is so tight and cooperative as to approach vertical integration, this is not true of the linkage with the lower layers of subcontractors in the automobile industry or between parent companies and primary subcontractors in other industries.[54] For instance, subcontractors in the electric appliance and electronics industries are mainly small enterprises engaged in the labor-intensive production of switches, wiring, electric coating, cabinets, and so forth; thus, there is not the same need for a high level of technology as in the automobile industry. The subcontractees can easily substitute subcontractors or convert "buy" into "make." Subcontractors often have several parent companies in the same markets. As the size of the subcontractors increases, they contract

with a larger number of parent companies. This is also true in the automobile industry, but the prime contractors there tend to concentrate
their subcontracting work on one subcontractor in order to avoid diffus-
ing technology to competitors.

In 1981, there were 470,000 small and medium-size subcontractors, accounting for 65 per cent of the total number of small and medium-size
enterprises. Most subcontractors are small; 90 per cent of the 470,000
subcontractors had fewer than 20 employees. On the other hand, 82 per
cent of the firms with more than 300 employees had subcontracts with
small and medium-size enterprises.[55] In 1977, the average number of firms
with which the large firms had subcontracts was 68 in all manufacturing
industries, 100 in the electric appliance industry, 130 in the transportation machinery industry, and 170 in the precision machinery industry.[56]

In addition, the number of subcontractors and the ratio of subcontractors to the total number of small and medium-size enterprises have been
increasing in the past decade, mainly reflecting the shift from heavy and
chemical industries to assembly and processing industries. It is reported,
however, that the number of primary subcontractors of larger firms in
major machinery industries has decreased since the first oil crisis,[57]
partly because the parent companies have selected stronger subcontractors with *genryō* management and partly because some subcontractors
have developed into independent parts makers using their specialized
facilities, their own ability to design, and other accumulated management resources. Some subcontractors have gone out of business, but
many subcontractors, including the secondary and tertiary ones, have
grown by securing a variety of subcontracts compatible with their production facilities.

Generally speaking, the Japanese subcontracting system is based on a
technical division of labor in which subcontractors, having their own
special production abilities, can respond flexibly to requests from parent
companies to lower costs, improve quality, or produce new products in
order to meet customers' needs. This Japanese system certainly differs
from that in the United States, where large manufacturers do more subassembly work in-house, and from the system in the newly industrialized countries (particularly Korea), where the number of small and medium-size enterprises is small and thus the dependence of large firms on
subcontractors is significantly lower.

Other Aspects of the Subcontracting System

As the subcontract system has evolved in Japan, the bargaining power
of subcontractors has increased. In particular, subcontractors prefer to
have multiple subcontractees because a subcontractor tied to a single

TABLE 8

Violations of the Act Against Delays in Payment to Subcontractors, 1976-1983

Violation	1976	1977	1978	1979	1980	1981	1982	1983
Undue price cutting								
Number	5	28	25	14	18	77	63	125
Per cent	0.3%	1.3%	1.7%	1.3%	1.4%	5.8%	4.3%	7.5%
Undue delay of payment of subcontracting fee								
Number	358	386	251	172	217	189	196	212
Percent	20.9%	17.8%	16.8%	16.2%	16.4%	14.2%	13.4%	12.7%
Grant of undue long-term billing period								
Number	465	445	287	240	359	297	306	302
Per cent	27.1%	20.6%	19.2%	22.7%	27.2%	22.3%	20.9%	18.1%
Unduly early settlement for materials and equipments lent								
Number	19	24	56	16	40	38	96	77
Per cent	1.1%	1.1%	3.7%	1.5%	3.0%	2.9%	6.6%	4.6%
Contract deficiencies								
Number	869	1,279	876	618	686	730	800	951
Percent	50.6%	59.2%	58.6%	58.3%	52.0%	54.8%	54.8%	57.1%
TOTAL NUMBER	1,716	2,162	1,495	1,060	1,320	1,331	1,461	1,667
TOTAL PER CENT	100.0%	100.0%	100.0%	100.0%	100.0%	100.0%	100.0%	100.0%

SOURCE: Japan, FTC, Nenji hōkoku (Annual report), various issues.

large company is clearly vulnerable to an all-or-nothing offer. In addition, decreasing wage-differentials between large and small firms have weakened the tendency of large firms to utilize the cheap labor of small and medium-size subcontractors. Above all, the enforcement of the Act Against Delays in Payment, etc., to Subcontractors (the Subcontractors' Protection Law), which was enacted in 1956 with the object of regulating the abuse of controlling power by subcontractees over subcontractors, has promoted fair transaction practices. However, what are considered excessively unfair contracts and subcontractees' abuse of controlling power, based on their monopsonistic position,[58] have not necessarily faded away.

The Subcontractors' Protection Law prohibits (1) delays of over 60 days in payment for subcontracted work; (2) payment by long-term notes of over 120 days (90 days in the textile industry); (3) settlement of costs for materials lent to subcontractors before the payment of subcontracting fees; (4) application of reductions in unit prices negotiated in a new contract to goods produced under previous contract(s); (5) refusal to receive subcontractors' products, despite the existence of apparent contracts; and (6) compulsory purchase of materials from subcontractees. In addition, the law establishes that a subcontractee is responsible for drawing up contract papers, giving them to its subcontractors, and preserving them for two years. In this law, "subcontractee" indicates a corporation with paid-in capital of more than ¥100 million; therefore it includes big businesses and occasionally their primary and secondary subcontractors. The FTC and MITI's Small and Medium Enterprise Agency have the power to inquire into unfair practices by subcontractees, and the former enforces the law. The inclusion of such detailed protections for small subcontractors was based on long experience dating to the prewar period and on the relatively weak tradition of contractual thinking in Japan (particularly among small businesses).

According to the FTC data, violations of the Subcontractors' Protection Law have been cyclical: they increased after the first oil crisis, decreased in 1978 and 1979, and increased again after the second oil crisis (see Table 8). About 50 per cent of the violations resulted from deficiencies in contracts. Moreover, although the granting of unduly long-term bills has declined, delays in payment and undue price cutting increased, especially during the recessions following the two oil crises. The FTC points out that about one-third of these violations were by large enterprises listed in the upper class of the Tokyo securities market and that the number of violations has recently been largest in the electronics and general machinery industries, where competition among the parent companies has been especially fierce.[59]

The Japanese subcontracting system has been technically efficient and has promoted development of the assembly and processing industries. But there is still room for improvement. If other countries promote subcontracting (and I think developing and newly developed ones should), laws like the Subcontractors' Protection Law in Japan will be essential because subcontracting systems are open to abuse by subcontractees with monopsonistic power.

Changes in Major Regulated Industries

Thus far my focus has been on recent changes in industrial organization in the manufacturing sector. In this section, I focus on recent changes in market structure and public regulation in such regulated industries as public utilities (electricity, gas, and water supply), transportation (railways, motor carriers, and airlines), communications (postal services, telephone and telegraph, and broadcasting) and industries dominated by a public corporation (tobacco and salt).[60] Relaxation of public regulation and the resulting change in market structure have been proceeding in many of these industries.

The Structure of Regulated Industries

In general, the regulated industries, except for tobacco, salt, and motor carriers, tend (or tended) to be "natural monopolies" or "natural oligopolies" because of economies of scale or a scarcity of natural resources (for example, the limited radio frequency spectrum). It has been legal in Japan for one firm, or at most a few firms, to dominate national or local markets. This is allowed in order to secure the advantages of large-scale production and distribution and the efficient utilization of scarce resources. Many of these firms are public enterprises, which were established to ease the revision of market failures (resulting not only from natural monopolies, but also from externality, publicness, risk, and uncertainty of goods considerations) and to enforce some special policies of the government (for example, securing revenue in the cases of tobacco and salt).[61] These public enterprises exist in three organizational forms: (1) departmental undertakings by a state or local authority; (2) public corporations owned by a state or local authority but administered by outside management; and (3) mixed enterprises in which a state or local authority holds substantial equity but does not administer.

Let us examine the market structure and organizational form of enterprises in the regulated industries at the end of FY 1982. In the communication industry, postal services were monopolized by a departmental undertaking (Postal Services of the Ministry of Posts and Telecommunications), domestic telephone and telegraph services were monopolized by Nihon Telephone and Telegraph Public Corporation (NTT), the international services by a mixed enterprise (International Telegraph and Telephone Company; ITT), and radio and television broadcasting was oligopolized by a public corporation (Nippon Broadcasting Association; NBA) and a few large private (nationwide networks surrounded by a competitive fringe of a small number of local broadcasting companies in each district). In the electric power industry, electricity was generated by nine big privately owned businesses, three mixed enterprises (Electric Power Development Company, Japan Atomic Power Generation Company, and Okinawa Electric Power Company), 19 smaller private companies, and 33 local public undertakings. The supply of electricity was controlled by the nine large companies and Okinawa Electric Power, which held legally sanctioned monopoly power in each of the ten districts of Japan. Gas services were supplied by 175 private enterprises and 73 local public undertakings, each of which was in the position of a local monopoly, although they were exposed to competition from other energy sources. In the railroad industry, a public corporation (Japan National Railways; JNR) and 12 local public enterprises coexisted with 139 private passenger lines. Domestic airlines were oligopolized by a mixed enterprise (Japan Air Lines Company; JAL) and two private enterprises (All Nippon Airways Company and Tōa Domestic Airway Company). Tobacco manufacturing and salt refining were monopolized by Japan Monopoly Public Corporation (JM).

Some Features and Problems of Public Regulation

Public regulation in Japan dates from the Meiji era, but our focus here must for brevity's sake be limited to the major features of public regulation immediately before April 1985, when several public enterprises or industries were deregulated.

Regardless of the organizational form of the enterprise, the primary object of public regulation in Japan is the level and structure of prices, although controls often cover entry and exit, mergers, the quality of services provided, safety rules, and the financial structure and accounting practices of the regulated firms. In the case of public enterprises, regulation extends to such matters as their budget and fixed accounts, investment and financial programs (including new services, issuances of securities and bonds, and borrowing), appointment of top managers, and industrial relations. The higher the degree of public ownership, the wider the range and the stronger the degree of public regulation.

Under the various industry acts, the relevant ministries have formal control over regulated industries. The Ministry of Posts and Telecommunications (MPT) is responsible for the communications industry, the Agency of Natural Resources and Energy in MITI for the electricity and gas industries, the Ministry of Transportation (MOT) for the transportation industry, and the Ministry of Finance (MOF) for the tobacco and salt industries. In addition, the actions and decisions of the public enterprises in these industries are subject to the supervision of the Diet or the local assemblies, whose powers of control vary according to the degree of public ownership.

The relationship between the legal organs' regulatory power (the Diet and local assemblies) and that of relevant ministries varies. In some cases (postal services and local water suppliers), the legal organs control the departmental undertakings and no significant power resides in the ministries. In some cases (NTT, JNR, JM, and NBA), although both the legal organs and the relevant ministries have participated in regulating public corporations, the former have stronger regulatory powers than the latter. Although mixed enterprises like JAL are subject, to a certain degree, to the surveillance of the legal organs, the relevant ministries have had more control. Finally, privately owned companies in the fields of electricity and gas supply, broadcasting, and transportation have been controlled significantly by the relevant ministries.

Regulatory authority also lies outside the legal organs and the relevant ministries. The MOF has participated in the regulation of public enterprises by disbursing large amounts of treasury loans and investments to them through the National Loan Fund. The Economic Planning Agency has taken part in public regulation to combat inflation. The Local Administration Bureau of the Ministry of Home Affairs can involve itself in regulation of local public enterprises through the local assemblies and local governments. Typically, the relevant minister organizes consultative committees, which examine the level and structure of prices proposed by the enterprises and advise reforms in regulation. Obviously one feature of the Japanese public regulation system is its complexity.

Although public regulation is a difficult undertaking in any country, the Japanese regulatory system presents a large number of particular political and economic problems. I cannot describe all of them here.[62] Let us take the cases of NTT, JNR, and JM, which were departmental undertakings before World War II and became public corporations during the Occupation in order to improve managerial efficiency. Initially this organizational change appeared to have been a success, but inefficiency has since become apparent.[63] This results not only from their monopolistic positions (particularly NTT and JM) but also from several other causes. First, strong intervention by the Diet has weakened these corporations' decision-making autonomy and sapped their competency and volition to improve managerial efficiency. Second, excessive or unreasonable Diet requests to corporations (for instance, to construct many local railroads in spite of predicted financial losses) have eliminated cost-reduction incentives and led in JNR's case to huge financial losses. Third, inappropriate prices established through pork barrel politics in the Diet and the lack of specialized understanding in the Diet of the fair return principle, two-part tariff, peakload pricing, cross-subsidization, and so forth has generated managerial and allocative inefficiency. Finally, since many regulatory authorities participate in public regulation, it is difficult to identify where the final regulatory responsibility resides. These problems exist in every form of public enterprise.

In the regulated industries where private enterprises dominate and the relevant ministries have the final responsibility for regulation, regulatory problems have been neither so numerous nor so profound as in the industries dominated by public enterprises. They do, however, have some intrinsic problems. First, the ministries have exercised stronger and wider controlling power than called for by legal statutes. Consequently, established enterprises are often protected excessively, the behavior of innovative firms is restricted, and anticompetitive behavior, illegal under the Antimonopoly Law, is promoted. Second, since Japan's governmental officials have had a high level of regulatory ability and knowledge, they have often bypassed public hearings and consultative committees. Third, because of the close relationship between regulators and regulatees, which is necessarily formed through their negotiations, governmental officials have often bestowed favors on regulated industries and enjoyed in return such benefits as *amakudari* (the appointment of a former government official to a responsible position in a private company). Fourth, governmental officials generally change their post within a ministry every two years. Their experiences in a direct regulation bureau are carried over into an indirect regulation bureau. This has given Japanese industrial policy a flavor of direct regulation. This has been typical, for example, of industrial policy toward the oil-refining industry.

Deregulation

The trend toward deregulation in Japan grew out of the necessity to reduce administrative costs as fiscal circumstances deteriorated after the first oil crisis, although undoubtedly the need to solve the problems discussed above played a role. The trend was also stimulated by the recent wave of technological innovation which has produced a new environment conducive to opening markets previously monopolized by a public or private enterprise, and by the process of internationalizing the Japanese economy, which has involved opening regulated markets to entry by foreign companies.

The most remarkable examples of deregulation are the privatization of NTT and JM and the liberalization of new entry into the telecommunications and tobacco industries. The Administrative Reform Commission (ARC) first proposed deregulation. The ARC was organized to reduce administrative costs by simplifying administrative systems and improving managerial and allocative efficiency through the privatization of public enterprises and the introduction of competition into directly regulated industries. The ARC proposed the transformation of NTT, JM, and JNR from public corporations into joint stock companies partly under public ownership, the division of these corporations into regional companies, and the liberalization of entry into the markets NTT and JM had monopolized. In March 1984, the MPT and MOF proposed bills for the privatization of NTT and JM, respectively, without proposing to break them up. These passed the Diet in December 1984 and went into effect in April 1985.

The Telecommunications Industry Law does not completely remove public regulation and contains many regulatory clauses. The law classifies telecommunication carriers into two types: primary carriers (including NTT and ITT), which own telecommunication transport facilities and can supply not only basic services (telephones) but also enhanced ones (VAN, data processing); and secondary carriers, which borrow facilities from the primary carriers and supply mainly enhanced services. The secondary carriers are further classified into large carriers supplying nationwide or international services and small carriers (the so-called small-size VAN businesses). New entry as a primary carrier requires the permission of the minister of posts and telecommunications, who will not authorize entry by carriers unable to meet the entry requirements. The minister must authorize rates for most services (including the enhanced ones) supplied by the primary carriers. New entry as a large secondary carrier requires registration with the minister and the rates charged by such carriers require notification. New entry by small secondary carriers requires notification. Moreover, the minister has the power to grant permission in technical matters and give orders to carriers. Thus, the MPT has obtained new regulatory powers at the expense of the Diet. The harmful effects of the legal control mentioned above will probably lessen, but problems related to administrative control will undoubtedly arise.

Despite the regulatory clauses, however, five ventures applied to the minister for permission to enter as new primary carriers, six large secondary carriers registered as new entries, and about 100 small ones notified the ministry of new entry at the beginning of May 1985. Managerial efficiency in the new NTT will improve because it is being stimulated by actual and potential competitive pressures and because it is allowed a greater degree of decision-making autonomy than the old NTT had. The new NTT and the new entries will reshape the market structure of the telecommunications industry.

Responding to the ARC's advice, the JNR Supervision Committee (a consultative body under the prime minister) developed a plan to reform the JNR, centering on the huge accumulated financial losses (¥33 trillion) and private regional companies. Responding to another ARC recommendation, the MOT took measures to simplify sanction, registration, and notification procedures in March 1985 and is now exploring concrete measures to relax entry and price regulation in the airline, motor carrier, and railroad industries. These measures took effect in March 1986.

Deregulation is also affecting the electrical power industry. The recent development of cogeneration technology using gas engines, turbines, and fuel cells has made possible the entry of gas and other energy suppliers into the power generation and electricity supply industries. Cogeneration has been utilized in more than a few areas and has continued to grow since MITI decided to permit this type of entry. Although the deregulatory typhoon blows weaker in Japan than in the United States, it is growing in strength.

The Future of Japanese Industry

The future prospects of Japanese industry revolve around industrial structure, industrial organization (particularly market structure), and public policy toward industry.

The Future of Industrial Structure

Japan's industrial structure has changed from a capital- and energy-intensive one centered on heavy and chemical industries to a knowledge-intensive and energy-conserving structure centered on various kinds of machinery and information industries. And it has been shifting further toward becoming a "creative, knowledge-intensive" structure centered on high-tech industries. Above all, the relative importance of the information industry has been rapidly increasing. Information is now an input good with the same magnitude of importance as natural raw materials and energy. Just as the technologies of storing, processing, and transporting natural raw materials and energy generated the industrial revolution and the resulting industrial society, the recent development of information technologies of storage, processing, and conversion (computers) and transportation or transmission (optical fibers, telecommunication satellites, ISDN, CATV, other new media) is bringing about an information society. The relative importance of information media, services, equipment, and goods (the "primary information sector") will certainly continue to increase. It is estimated that between 1980 and 2000 the ratio of value added in the primary information sector to the total value added in all industries will increase from 25.0 per cent to 35.4 per cent and employment in this sector from 25.5 per cent of total employment to 30.3 per cent.[64]

Should these new high technologies blossom, (1) new industrial materials and biotechnology industries will replace a large number of the traditional basic material industries and play a major role in intermediate goods; (2) electronicization and mechatronization will proceed rapidly in the machinery industry; (3) new consumer goods related to the information revolution and biotechnology may be developed; (4) interdependent development among these industries will form a new input-output chain in the manufacturing sector; (5) the energy sector will move toward greater reliance on nuclear, solar, and other sources of power and small-scale, high-quality batteries, which will transform the present system of energy supply; and (6) the financial and transportation sectors will be profoundly influenced by the information revolution and will form a new supply system—perhaps a new network at the international level.

Factors other than technological ones (international environment, industrial policy, change in population structure, growth of real per capita GNP, and the resulting changes in national consumption patterns) have an impact on the changes in industrial structure. The two oil crises certainly had a great impact on Japan's industrial structure. Trade frictions had some effect on the textile, iron and steel, and automobile industries, bringing about export restrictions. If trade frictions intensify and Japan restricts the exports of its major industries more severely, or if the United States and the European Community take measures to restrain imports from Japan, the present structure of Japanese industry will change (though we cannot correctly estimate the degree of the change because we cannot predict changes in the exchange rate). Moreover, growing imports from the newly industrialized countries into Japan (for instance, the rapidly increasing importation of steel products from Korea) will affect Japanese industrial structure.

The Future of Industrial Organization

Technological innovation has been working as a centrifugal force on competition. In particular, several technological features of most high-tech industries have worked to promote competition.[65] First, since small scale and a variety of production technologies rather than mass production characterize the high-tech sectors, firms have pursued economies of scope rather than economies of scale. This factor has lowered the barriers to entry in these sectors. Second, firms in these sectors tend to lease their production facilities because rapid technological innovation in the industries providing the facilities quickly makes these facilities obsolete. This factor has also reduced entry barriers by lowering the capital requirements for entry and the sunk costs of those facilities. Third, the possibility of technological development and of rapidly growing demand in high-tech fields has stimulated the entry of new firms. These new firms include venture businesses and firms created by the diversification of big businesses. Fourth, the fusion of different markets into one through technological innovation (for instance, the fusion of postal services and telecommunications through the development and diffusion of telefax) has intensified the competition in the consolidated markets.

These centrifugal forces will continue. In addition, small and localized technologies such as local area networks (LANs), the cell radiogram, fuel cell generation, small-scale solar generation, and a variety of high-quality batteries have developed rapidly in recent years. The diffusion of these technologies will encourage the decentralization of economic power. Morever, as interfirm competition in R&D, production, and sales of products and services in the high-tech industries unfolds in the international arena, information networks are being connected across national boundaries and data-base services are being used internationally.

However, centripetal forces toward oligopoly and monopoly remain. In the semiconductor industry, which has played a pioneering role in the present wave of technological innovation, mass production has already been introduced, and the pursuit of the learning curve effect plays a key role in strategic decisions. Further, the largest integrated circuit makers now have advantages in production costs over the smaller companies. Therefore, the concentration ratio of the largest companies has increased in the domestic market, and they are gaining stronger positions in the international market. This phenomenon also applies in the personal computer, carbon fiber, and optical fiber industries, where the scale of production has been growing rapidly.[66] If demand for high-tech products or services grows as rapidly as expected in the near future,[67] mass production will be established in these industries, creating a centripetal force toward oligopoly. In addition, as traditional industries like iron and steel, chemical fertilizers, and textiles confront the problem of high-tech substitute products and as they are exposed to stronger import pressure from the newly industrialized and the developing countries, the concentration ratio in these industries may increase. Although we should not underemphasize the possibility of increased intramarket concentration, we have to place more importance on the new type of concentration that is now occurring throughout industry as a consequence of the creation of information networks, technological tie-ups, and joint investment by heterogeneous groups of firms. This type of intermarket grouping will occur not only within manufacturing, financial, distributive, and other sectors but also across these sectors both in the domestic arena and in the international one. Given these tendencies toward the centralization of economic power, we should not overstress the "new era of competition."

The Future of Public Policy Toward Industry

Public policy toward industry includes industrial policy, competition policy, and direct regulation policy. The future of Japanese industrial policy (particularly its effects on the macroeconomy) is analyzed by Eads and Yamamura in this volume; examined here are major issues for industrial policy in the near future and the government's response to these issues. The issues in the decade after the first oil crisis were structural adjustment in the declining industries, settlement of international trade frictions, and promotion of high technologies. These will continue to exist as major policy issues in the near future. Indeed, many industries may decline not only because of the increasing imports from newly industrialized and other nations, but also because of the substitution of high-tech products for traditional products and services. If they do decline, the government must assist the voluntary adjustment of private companies, enforcing a positive adjustment policy that does not conflict with the GATT and OECD policies.

As trade frictions have increased, the Japanese government has implemented voluntary export restrictions, orderly marketing agreements, and export restriction agreements, on the one hand, and measures for opening domestic markets, on the other hand. But as the accumulated manufacturing and quality-control technologies in Japan improve even more in the future, and as the capacity to develop new technology increases through increased R&D expenditures, many high-tech industries will become highly competitive internationally. Therefore, trade friction will not disappear in the near future. The government will have to implement further measures to open domestic markets, promote direct overseas investment by private companies, and stimulate domestic demand.

The Japanese government is concentrating its R&D efforts in the high-tech sectors, judging this to be the most important form of industrial development policy it can implement. MITI and other industrial ministries are providing increased funding for R&D activities in those sectors. Moreover, in order to strengthen basic research in the universities and other research institutions, the Science and Technology Agency and the

Ministry of Education have developed systems to make possible expenditures for creative science of several billion yen per project. One of these projects, the next-generation computer, is expected to bear fruit in the 1990s. Shocked by this prospect, the United States and the European Community have begun similar projects. Although international competition may accelerate R&D and thus stimulate the development of high technologies, contemporary Japanese policy stresses the necessity of international cooperation. To date, a wide variety of cooperative development projects have been carried out at both the private and the governmental levels. Such international cooperation in R&D will be further promoted.

In regard to competition, the most important issue will be coping with monopoly problems generated by the utilization of information networks and the development of new technologies: collusive arrangements utilizing information networks, horizontal and vertical combinations among enterprises connected by information networks, transformation of cooperative R&D systems into price and other cartels, and so forth. Also, more rational business practices must be promoted in the subcontractee-subcontractor relationship, the distribution sector, and other service sectors. The FTC has already begun to address these issues. How they are resolved will have an important impact on the character of the coming "high-tech society."

The deregulatory typhoon is blowing not only through the regulated industries but also through the agriculture, forestry, fishing, mining, and construction industries, all of which have been strongly protected by the government. Japanese agriculture, especially, will be required to open its tightly shut gate.

Michio Muramatsu and Ellis S. Krauss

The Conservative Policy Line and
the Development of Patterned Pluralism

The factors contributing to Japan's postwar economic development and the "economic miracle" of the 1960s have received much attention on both sides of the Pacific. Some have argued that the state has played an important role in that development. For example, Chalmers Johnson argued in his influential book on the Ministry of International Trade and Industry (MITI) that since the Meiji Restoration, Japan has been a "plan rational" or "developmental state," with a government that places greatest priority on "promoting the [industrial] structure that enhances the nation's international competitiveness."[1]

When political factors are seen as causes of Japan's economic development, generally only two are emphasized: the role of the elite, economic bureaucrats (such as those in MITI or the Ministry of Finance [MOF]) in carrying out the rational planning and implementation that brought about rapid growth in the 1950s and 1960s, and the role of the much-vaunted Japanese national "consensus" supporting that growth. Johnson, for example, even sees the primary function of politicians as acting as a "safety valve" for the bureaucracy, insulating it from political and interest group pressures so that it could autonomously carry out the main task of the "developmental state"—economic growth. Many other political scientists have emphasized the power of the bureaucracy in policymaking.[2]

We believe that seeing the political role of the bureaucracy and a national consensus on growth as the exclusive contributions of politics to postwar Japan's economic development is a limited view of political economy. First, it neglects the role of "political" variables (many of which arose from competition and conflict, not consensus) such as political party strategy, political leadership, and relations among politicians, bureaucrats, and interest groups. As important as the bureaucracy's industrial policy may have been in helping to create economic growth, it did not operate in a political vacuum. Politics could not completely insulate the bureaucracy so that it could focus on development; politics also helped determine the nature of development. Second, anyone who assumes an automatic consensus on developmental goals in postwar Japan ignores the many variations and changes in meaning in the goal of development among the Japanese political elite throughout the postwar period in response to changes in domestic and international political pressures.

Finally, Japanese policymaking has changed in the past two decades toward greater influence for politicians, parties, and the Diet, lesser influence for bureaucrats, and stronger and more autonomous interest groups. We do not believe that these were sudden changes from the bureaucracy-dominated system of the earlier postwar period—they emerged and evolved from trends already present in that period.

We emphasize the role of government in economic development. Rather than stressing the role of the bureaucracy and a national consensus, however, we focus on political strategy, political leadership, and political coalitions and competition and show how these were key factors in determining the goal of development and the particular form and timing of that development. Partisan politics and political leadership, in other words, performed more than the safety valve function of insulating the bureaucracy; they helped to create the general framework of goals in the postwar Japanese state and the bureaucrats' role in the political economy.

Specifically, we argue that the institutionalization of a particular "conservative policy line" (*hoshu honryū*) as a political strategy of the ruling Liberal Democratic Party (LDP) in response to the domestic and international environment was a crucial factor in determining the development of postwar Japan's political economy. It was a strategy for coping with the political challenges and dilemmas faced by the conservative political elite and was closely related to the changes in the meaning of development over time. Finally, we demonstrate how the type of development produced by these partisan political considerations led to the emergence of the contemporary policymaking system in Japan, which we call "patterned pluralism."

This paper is not a definitive study of Japan's political economy or the role of the state in postwar development—that task would require several books. We adopt much more limited aims. We deal with the specific issues of (1) the major political problems and dilemmas faced by the conservative party and leadership in different postwar periods; (2) how the conservative policy line, as part of the broader political strategy of the LDP to institutionalize and maintain itself as the dominant party in Japan, evolved in response to those problems and contributed to the major trends in economic development in those periods; and (3) how the strategy and consequences of the conservative policy line eventually produced patterned pluralist policymaking. This is, then, but a partial corrective to previous approaches, which left the "political" out of "political economy."

The Conservative Policy Line (1945 to Late 1960s)

Hoshu Honryū

The term *hoshu honryū* has been used, frequently by journalists and occasionally by scholars,[3] to refer to those conservative factions that could trace their lineage back to the most influential of the early postwar leaders, Nobusuke Kishi and, particularly, Shigeru Yoshida (see Table 1). We use the term, however, primarily to refer to a policy line that may also be traced back to Yoshida. As Shigeru Hori points out, Yoshida wanted to create a political system based on the spirit of the new constitution and a conservatism unlike that of the prewar parties. The conservative principles, or the *hoshu honryū* line, that were to become the "backbone of the Japanese state" were to be built on acceptance of the new constitution and the emergence of a new, independent Japan, but one whose defense was tied to the U.S.-Japan Mutual Security Treaty.[4] Although factionalism is intertwined with the development of this policy line, they are not necessarily coterminous.

We focus on the principles and broad policy line—established by Yoshida in the early postwar period and developed, with some deviations, by later postwar conservative leaders who put more emphasis on economic management—as a political strategy. Within the ruling coalition, a "minority political line" argued for a more independent and nationalistic foreign policy and greater emphasis on political issues such as defense even though such policies might have polarized Japan's political

TABLE 1
Prime Ministers of Postwar Japan

Prime minister	Period	Prime minister	Period
Kijuro Shidehara	10/45–5/46	Hayato Ikeda	7/60–11/64
Shigeru Yoshida	5/46–5/47	Eisaku Sato	11/64–7/72
Tetsu Katayama	5/47–3/48	Kakuei Tanaka	7/72–12/74
Hitoshi Ashida	3/48–10/48	Takeo Miki	12/74–12/76
Shigeru Yoshida	10/48–12/54	Takeo Fukuda	12/76–12/78
Ichiro Hatoyama	12/54–12/56	Masayoshi Ohira	12/78–6/80
Tanzan Ishibashi	12/56–2/57	Zenko Suzuki	7/80–11/82
Nobusuke Kishi	2/57–7/60	Yasuhiro Nakasone	11/82–

culture. The conflict between these two approaches was a salient part of the political debate among conservatives in the earlier postwar period. Once conservative leaders came to emphasize economic issues in the 1960s, however, the *hoshu honyrū* line became institutionalized among them.

Origins of Hoshu Honryū (1945–1954)

Any analysis of the institutionalization of the *hoshu honyrū* line must begin with Shigeru Yoshida's establishment of a conservative identity in postwar Japan. The period from 1945 to the mid-1950s was transitional in the most fundamental aspects of the polity. In the prewar period, the legitimizing myth of carrying out the imperial will had sanctified a strong, bureaucracy-led state. The defeat and the Occupation's separation of sovereignty from the emperor and placement of it in the people had undermined that myth.

In this political vacuum, filled only partially by the democratic principles of the new constitution, the political culture and party system split into two opposing camps. In the immediate postwar period, a broad range of values and ideologies and a rather chaotic multiparty system emerged. No party had a clear electoral mandate. The Japan Socialist Party (JSP), however, became one of the main contenders for power in the early postwar era based on its strength in Marxist labor unions. The Japan Communist Party (JCP) was a growing force, attaining about 10 per cent of the vote in the 1949 election.

The conservatives were fragmented into several parties and were somewhat defensive about the changes wrought by the new constitution and other Occupation reforms. The first major step toward a ruling coalition of conservatives, therefore, could not be accomplished until the Left had been delegitimized as a potential holder of political power. The onset of the cold war, the Korean War, the Communists' militant and violent strategies after 1950, and the Occupation's purge of Communists from political and social organizations all effectively delegitimated the JCP. It was to take another 20 years and a new democratic line before the JCP would become even a partially viable political party again.

The JSP's delegitimation was incomplete since the events that helped confirm it as a viable political party also established its image as a party that should not be trusted with power. The JSP's participation in the Katayama cabinet (1947–48), in which a Socialist was prime minister, and the Ashida cabinet (1948), in which Socialists held cabinet posts, confirmed the party's status as a legitimate contender for political power, but the performance of those two cabinets partially delegitimized it as a party of government. The JSP's failure to implement much of its promised programs—planning programs based on Marxist theory but not desired by the public, such as nationalization of the coal industry—and its enforcement of the Occupation's austerity programs, made it unpopular and seen as being ineffective.

The partial delegitimation of the Left led to a dearth of potential contenders for power, allowing the united conservative party created in 1955 (the LDP) to become a perennially dominant party. The JSP's partial viability meant, however, that the LDP confronted an opposition with considerable public support.

Unlike the dominant parties in other industrialized democracies, such as the Social Democratic Party in Sweden or the Christian Democratic Party in Italy, the LDP lacked a social organization (such as a labor union or a religious organization) to penetrate the society and mobilize support based on a ready-made value system. Without such organizational and programmatic support and because the Occupation's democratization program deprived them of the possibility of reverting to the prewar value system, Japan's conservatives had to create their own organizational and electoral support and define their own identity to give meaning to Japanese conservatism. From this challenge emerged the conservative policy line.

Shigeru Yoshida, Japan's prime minister in the early 1950s, developed a formula to respond to these challenges, with momentous consequences for the subsequent development of Japanese politics. Yoshida understood that countering the ideological challenge of the Marxist Left required the development of a new type of politics that accepted the new democratic framework rather than basing support on an ideological appeal to traditional values. He also understood that the war and the Occupation had thoroughly discredited prewar values and militaristic nationalism. Conservatives would have to develop a new meaning and a new identity for conservatism that broke with the past—namely acceptance of the new democratic constitution and dependence on the security treaty with the United States.

Yoshida added another important element that Hayato Ikeda would assert even more strongly later: economic management for social and political order. Yoshida intended to counter the challenge of the socialist left not only by accepting the postwar framework but also by creating an ideology of economic liberalism to substitute for an ideology of traditional values.[5] One of the primary tasks of the state would be to guide the nation in its economic reconstruction, eventually creating a greater climate of social and political stability.

Finally, Yoshida's adherence to these principles, particularly to economic reconstruction, had another significant implication: an alliance between the conservatives and the bureaucracy. Emerging from the war and the Occupation's reforms more intact than any other institution,[6] the bureaucracy and its resources and expertise formed a natural ally for conservatives attempting to legitimize themselves as a governing party and to penetrate society.

When Yoshida became head of the Liberal Party (one of the LDP's predecessors) in 1946, he recognized the need to build political leadership. He turned to the ranks of higher civil servants, from which he himself had come, to provide leaders for the party and the government, beginning the postwar practice of recruiting elite bureaucrats into conservative politics. In the 1949 general election, such future party leaders and former bureaucrats as Ikeda, Eisaku Sato, and others—a total of 30 in all—ran for election and joined the Liberal Party. These ex-bureaucrats were quickly placed in some of the highest government and party positions and brought the expertise and experience the party needed to make public policy.

Yoshida held firm to these principles even when cold war pressures and the Communist success in China led the United States to try to persuade Japan to rearm. Yoshida had other political and foreign policy goals, such as normalizing relations with China and securing the return of Okinawa, but these took a back seat to the major goal of economic reconstruction. To this day, the definitive characterization of Yoshida is Masataka Kosaka's: a man with a "merchant"-like view of politics.[7] In the context of the immediate postwar period, with the polarization of Japan's political culture over the basic issue of defense[8] and the reaction of many against traditional nationalism based on military might, Yoshida's priorities reflected a pragmatic adaptation to the opposition's sensitivities. The priority given to the "economic line" and a close political relationship with the United States have become the basis for two principles of the conservative policy line and provided the foundation for the ruling coalition's legitimacy.

Interest groups began to play a major role in conservative politics at this time. Many of today's most politically active interest groups were founded between 1946 and 1955 (see Table 2). Business leaders played a major role in pressuring the bickering politicians to counter the reunification of the splintered wings of the Socialist Party in 1955 by forming one conservative party, the Liberal Democratic Party. The new party became increasingly dependent on big business for financing, and the practice of regular meetings between big business leaders and the prime minister became common, reaching a peak in the 1960s.[9] Agriculture, too, became a part of this nascent ruling coalition. The conservatives' reliance on the rural vote and the lack of a grass-roots party organization made many conservative politicians turn increasingly to *nōkyō* (agricultural cooperatives) for support. For their part, the Socialists were backed by labor.

Yoshida's *hoshu honryū* principles gave the conservatives an identity

TABLE 2
Founding Period of Organizations by Type of Organization
(per cent)

Organization	1868-1924	1925-45	1946-55	1956-65	Post-1966	N
Agricultural	4.3%	4.3%	73.9%	13.0%	4.3%	23
Welfare	—	3.3	40.0	33.3	23.3	30
Economic (business and financial)	3.4	4.5	44.3	34.1	13.6	88
Labor	—	3.8	51.9	28.8	15.4	52
Administrative	33.4	6.7	40.0	13.3	6.7	15
Educational	—	8.3	83.3	8.3	—	12
Professional	22.2	—	55.6	22.2	—	9
Citizen/political	—	5.3	26.3	36.8	31.6	19
Other	—	25.0	50.0	25.0	—	4
ALL	4.4%	4.8%	48.8%	28.2%	13.9%	252

SOURCE: Based on a 1978 survey by Michio Muramatsu of 252 of the most influential interest groups.

based on pragmatism, economic priorities, and flexibility, rather than on traditional values or an inflexible symbolic ideology. This was to prove extremely important in building conservative support and in eventually making the LDP into the dominant party. Economic liberalism, the priority given to economic management, and the political necessity of mobilizing conservative support in the countryside marked the beginnings of the close relations among interest groups (in this early period, primarily big business and agriculture), the bureaucracy, and the conservatives. Although this strategy defined conservatism as opposed to the Left's adherence to neutrality and a socialist economy, it partially defused the ideological confrontation with the Left by accepting democracy and eschewing the traditional prewar values and issues considered anathema by the Left. The Left was to be excluded from power, but not from the system.

Consequently, conservatism in Japan rejected both the conservatism based on traditional values developed by, for example, the Christian Democrats in Italy and the independent great-power nationalism of the Gaullists in France. Had the conservatives advocated a revival of traditional values and military power in this period, Japan's ruling coalition and subsequent economic development would have been very different.

Institutionalizing Hoshu Honryū (Late 1950s to Late 1960s)

The consequences of following a more political strategy were shown in the late 1960s when Prime Minister Nobusuke Kishi briefly emphasized issues imbued with ideological conflict. The opposition responded by immediately paralyzing politics and government. When Kishi pushed for

Diet passage of a revised security treaty (in Japan's favor) in 1960, his efforts met with vehement opposition and gave rise to a political crisis of such proportions that Kishi was forced to resign. The treaty crisis gave Yoshida an opportunity to reassert his influence in the party and to ensure that the LDP would remain unified around personnel of the Yoshida "school" and his philosophy.[10]

Kishi's successor was Hayato Ikeda, a follower of Yoshida's policy line. One of the Ikeda cabinet's first actions was to depolarize the government-opposition confrontation by resolving the long-running and bitter Mitsui Miike coal mine strike by informal discussions with both business and labor leaders and by adopting a "low posture" (*teishisei*) toward the opposition in the Diet. More important, Ikeda returned to Yoshida's priorities but with even more emphasis on economic policies.

Among Ikeda's new policies, the most significant was the famous National Income-Doubling Plan. This plan had actually been formulated under Kishi (as a wage-doubling plan) but had been sidetracked by the security treaty crisis. The plan's initial formulation under Kishi had been vague, and the press had received it with hostility, labeling it "clap-trap."[11] But revived with new vigor and specificity by Ikeda, the idea met a different reception. Although many were skeptical that such an optimistic target could be reached in a decade, the plan captured the public's imagination. Politically, it shifted attention to a nonideological issue and provided a vaguely "nationalistic" goal, around which public opinion would rally, that was inoffensive to both Left and Right. Once again, a policy that was at least in part a political strategy undertaken to cope with a challenge to the political order would have significant economic and political consequences.

First, Ikeda created a set of effective, comprehensive economic policies and even got a somewhat hesitant Ministry of Finance to accept the policy. That a political leader would take the initiative in developing such a program and be successful in persuading and utilizing the bureaucracy for such a purpose was almost unprecedented in the postwar period.

Second, there was a subtle but important shift in the emphasis of economic management. The principal goal of economic development in the previous period had been basic production to reconstruct Japan. To this was added concern for the quality of the productive structure and the distribution of the fruits of production. (See Table 2 of Kosai's paper in this volume.) Whereas the 1955 and 1957 plans had concentrated on production facilities and the infrastructure of heavy industry, the Income-Doubling Plan included the policy objectives of improving social overhead capital and the industrial structure and a concern for social stability. The improvement of national living standards and social development continued to play prominent roles in economic plans through the 1960s.

Third, Ikeda's program was the first systematic and comprehensive co-ordination effort conducted by an LDP prime minister. The policy ini-tiatives of Ikeda's immediate predecessors had all been in the area of for-eign policy. Each bureaucracy had had its own policies vis-à-vis the economy; MITI, for example, had industrial policies to develop specific Japanese industries, and the MOF had a monetary policy. Now, on a large scale, these policies were to be coordinated.

Fourth, this government-wide coordination marked the beginning of a new coalition between the governing party and the bureaucracy. Al-though Yoshida had brought ex-bureaucrats into the political world, Ikeda placed them in central LDP positions and used the bureaucracy as an instrument of policy implementation. The bureaucrats-turned-politicians had become the central leadership group within the party. Perhaps more important, they had the training, background, and skills to use the expertise and information contained in the bureaucracy on be-half of their policies.

Ikeda and his successor, Eisaku Sato, who continued these fundamen-tal approaches (with some foreign policy actions), shaped the outlines of Japan's political economy and molded the nature of Japan's ruling coali-tion. For the twelve cumulative years of the Ikeda and Sato cabinets, the LDP government not only emphasized a government active in promot-ing and guiding Japan's rapid economic development, but also stimulated the private sector's activity and autonomy. Nationalism was confined to the economy and defense to the framework of the U.S.-Japan Security Treaty and the constitution. Both Ikeda and Sato, for example, quietly ignored the reports of the LDP's Research Committee for Constitutional Revision calling for repeal of the peace clause. Even when Sato made the return of Okinawa the major foreign policy issue of his last administra-tion, it was to be a return *hondo nami* ("like the mainland"), with the same defense restrictions applying as in the rest of Japan.

In short, the Ikeda and Sato years of the 1960s institutionalized the conservative policy line in the LDP as the dominant approach to the po-litical economy. A program and a set of principles were firmly estab-lished within the party and vis-à-vis society that provided the ruling con-servative coalition with the means to mobilize public support for the LDP and the government. Yet, the political line did not disappear. Al-though each cabinet during the 1960s and 1970s strongly followed the conservative policy line, the political line remained a (progressively less visible) minority viewpoint within the LDP.

The institutionalization of a political strategy of concentrating on eco-nomic growth had myriad consequences for the political economy. With-out Ikeda's and Sato's reassertion and institutionalization of *hoshu hon-ryū*, it is doubtful that the LDP would have been able to establish itself as a dominant party. The creation of the "bureaucrat-politician" helped to develop a new relationship between the LDP and the bureaucracy in which political leaders relied on the bureaucracy, but the bureaucracy served the ends of bureaucratically knowledgeable political leaders. Economic growth widened and institutionalized the relationship between a greater variety of interest groups and the conservative government. These changes opened the system to a greater variety of influences on policymaking. Finally, although the emphasis on rapid economic growth allowed the conservatives to undercut the ideological appeal of the left-wing opposition, it also defused the political polarization manifested in the 1960 treaty crisis and created tacit communication between the government and the opposition.

The conservative policy line shaped by Yoshida, mainly in the foreign policy area, and later defined with more emphasis on economic management by Ikeda and Sato had three basic tenets:

1. The basis of Japan's foreign policy was a close relationship with the United States, a relationship that provided much of Japan's defense.

2. Domestically, one of government's major functions was to guide and develop the economy to produce a stable social and political order.

3. The LDP followed centrist policies designed to dampen the potential Left-Right confrontation inherent in postwar Japan and to establish and maintain a broad political consensus that (particularly after the Ikeda and Sato administrations) incorporated some demands of the opposition.

These three tenets were closely related, and each was predicated on the others. Relying on the United States for defense allowed Japan to concentrate on economic growth and undercut the explosive domestic political issue of rearmament; economic growth required a close relationship with the United States and helped to diminish Left-Right conflict; avoiding confrontation with the opposition provided the political stability necessary to economic growth and Japan's security. In other words, this policy line emphasized the interrelated goals of political, economic, and social stability.

Our description of how these tenets emerged should give pause to those who assume some automatic national consensus in Japan since the 1950s that, by an almost mystical cultural process, created Japan's economic miracle. The *hoshu honryū* tenets developed gradually and in competition with a minority political line even within the LDP. For much of the postwar period, there was not even a consensus among the conservative elite, much less a national consensus. It was not until at least the mid-1960s that the policy line came to be fully developed and institutionalized among the conservative elite and to enjoy widespread public support. As we show in the next section, rather than economic growth being the consequence of an existing consensus, the national consensus that did emerge was probably more the result of the policy line's effectiveness as a political strategy for attaining political stability and economic growth. That consensus was also to be short-lived.

Adapting Hoshu Honryū (Late 1960s to Late 1970s)

Political Pressure from Below: The "New Middle Mass"

The conservative policy line succeeded beyond the expectations of even its staunchest supporters. By the latter half of the 1960s, it was apparent that Ikeda's income-doubling target would be exceeded and that Japan was entering the ranks of affluent nations. Furthermore, through rapid urbanization and the expansion of educational opportunities, Japan was undergoing the transition from industrialized society to a post-industrial society. In Yasusuke Murakami's terms,[12] the 1960s witnessed the emergence of Japan as a "new middle mass" (NMM) society, with strong trends at the mass level toward greater economic equality, an emphasis on political equality but managerial administrative elites based on meritocratic standards, and priority for mass cultural and consummatory (as opposed to instrumental) values. For our purposes, one of the most important aspects of the emergence of the NMM was its widespread acceptance of the *hoshu honryū* principles: the policy line that had primarily functioned as the guiding strategy of a part of the conservative political elite was becoming an element of a national consensus. The conservative policy line harmonized with the "pro-system" interest orientation of the NMM.[13]

For example, the policy line principle of accepting the postwar constitution, in contrast to the political line's desire for revision, became institutionalized at the mass level. In 1958, 40 per cent of the public thought the constitution was appropriate (*fusawashii*) for Japan, compared with 30 per cent who thought it was not. By the late 1960s and early 1970s a majority thought the constitution a good one, and its opponents had declined to a small minority.[14]

Similarly, the policy line's support for a moderate defense policy of maintaining the Self-Defense Forces (SDF) but not indulging in massive rearmament or nuclear weapons received increasing public approval from the late 1960s to the early 1980s. Those opposed to Japan's possessing nuclear weapons rose from 66 per cent of the population in 1968 to 82 per cent in 1981. In addition, as Fig. 1 shows, huge majorities steadily supported the SDF but opposed either their strengthening or their weakening.

In addition, even in regard to the major controversies of the 1970s on which the political parties strongly disagreed, the electorate was often

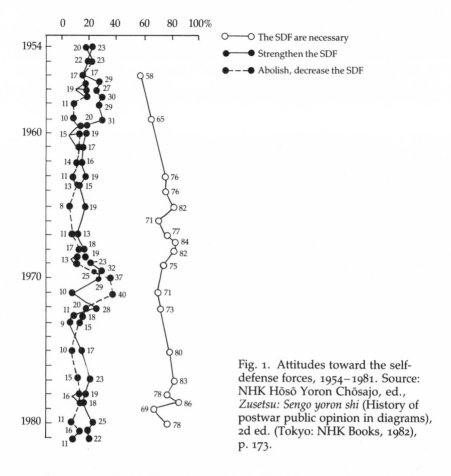

Fig. 1. Attitudes toward the self-defense forces, 1954–1981. Source: NHK Hōsō Yoron Chōsajo, ed., *Zusetsu: Sengo yoron shi* (History of postwar public opinion in diagrams), 2d ed. (Tokyo: NHK Books, 1982), p. 173.

much more moderate than the political elite. Figure 2 shows data from surveys conducted by Michio Muramatsu in the late 1970s of elite and mass attitudes toward national welfare programs, an issue the opposition parties were pushing during this period. The top line records the average scores (a minus indicates negative views of government activity in this area, a plus, positive views) of opposition and LDP Diet members; the bottom line, the average scores of opposition party and LDP supporters among the electorate. The results clearly show that differences at the mass level are moderate compared with the strong disagreement at the political elite level.[15]

These data support the conclusion that at the mass level during this period there was support for the *hoshu honryū* policy line and its anti-ideological approach to politics. When we combine this with data showing a consistent increase in consummatory values and interest orienta-

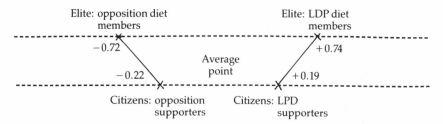

Fig. 2. Difference between elites' and citizens' attitudes toward welfare programs, 1976–1977.

tion and a decline in both instrumental goals and public orientation,[16] the changing attitudes of the Japanese public during this period consistently fit the characterization of the emergence of a NMM society that has adopted the most salient aspects of the *hoshu honryū* line.

Within the LDP, the increasing legitimation of *hoshu honryū* forced the political line more and more into the background. During the 1960s, *hoshu honryū* became less a particular governing strategy of a specific group within the ruling coalition and more the institutionalized legitimizing principle for the LDP-run government as a whole. Almost all ambitious LDP politicians, whatever their personal views or factional lineage, came to conform overtly to the basic principles to legitimize their leadership.

Hoshu Honryū Transformed: Political Strategy Responds

In order for the conservative policy line to be accepted fully, a subtle but important transformation in the meaning of one aspect had to be made. Although the distribution of material wealth through the allocation mechanism would continue to increase in importance because of the NMM interest orientation, interest would not necessarily be defined in industrial society terms of more and more affluence, but rather in more consummatory terms that would include quality of life, social security, and more general lifestyle concerns.

Consequently the NMM, which appeared in the 1960s and 1970s, would challenge the economic growth policies of the conservative ruling coalition over such issues as pollution and the lack of social services and welfare facilities in Japan. The NMM perceived these problems as the failings of the Japanese variant of industrial society created by the very success of the policy line's emphasis on rapid economic growth in the 1950s and 1960s. At the local level, leftist politicians and parties that identified themselves with this anti-industrial orientation reaped the benefits of this transformation in attitudes by capturing power in most major urban areas.

At the national level, too, parties that took a welfare-oriented, anti-pollution line and appealed to the concrete interests of constituents, such as the Kōmeitō (Clean Government Party; CGP) and the Communist Party (JCP) showed the greatest growth during this period. The two parties most identified with the old progressive-conservative dichotomy and the conflicts of industrial society, the LDP and the JSP, suffered the greatest electoral declines.[17] The result was a transformation in the party system, with a decline in the LDP vote to the mid-40 per cent level and in the JSP vote to the low 20 per cent level by the early 1970s but new and important roles for the JCP and CGP. From the "one and a half party system" of the 1950s and 1960s of one predominant majority party (LDP) and one major opposition party half its size (JSP),[18] a party system with a bare majority party and multiparty opposition developed.

One fundamental reason for these changes was the decline in the number of voters tied psychologically or socially to political parties and their networks. The number of independent voters increased in this period, as did the number of more passive party supporters. There was an expansion in the number of NMM voters, particularly in urban areas, who based their vote on the performance of the parties in meeting the problems of post-industrial society, rather than on party identification or the personality of the candidates.[19]

In its protest against the side effects of the economic growth brought about by the ruling coalition's policy line, however, the Japanese public, including the NMM, was not rejecting the system, nor was it rejecting the line itself, as we have seen. This meant that the ruling coalition could adapt and redefine its policy line to appeal to the increasing number of independent and NMM voters; otherwise, it risked losing more of its electoral base.

The great pressure from the mass level during the 1970s, therefore, was to maintain the policy line but to broaden and redefine the meaning of "development" to include NMM concerns. This the ruling coalition was able to do by responding to the demands for environmental protection and increased social and welfare services. In the so-called pollution Diet of 1970, the LDP passed several relatively stringent antipollution laws. Even though watered down somewhat at the behest of the business community, these laws nonetheless represented a flexible response to the active demands to improve the environment.

In retrospect, the administration of Kakuei Tanaka (1972–74) seems an important transition period in the adaptation of *hoshu honryū* to the new domestic political pressures. Tanaka's famous Plan for the Remodeling of the Japanese Archipelago had two basic goals: the redistribution of industry to rural areas to help solve the problems of high land costs for industry and the concentration of industry and population in large metropolitan areas, and the creation of social capital through the development of infrastructure and the improvement of social welfare.[20]

The plan was an ingenious hybrid of rational economic management and political strategy. On the one hand, the involvement of economic bureaucrats in the plan's formulation could clearly be seen in its attention to the major industrial problems of land costs, production location, population imbalances, and inadequate infrastructure. On the other hand, the plan was directed toward the LDP's political problems of an eroding urban base and massive demands for greater environmental quality and social welfare (and the Left's exploitation of these issues to appeal to the NMM and other urban residents) while satisfying the LDP's traditional constituency in rural areas. The rural population would get the industry and local development it had been asking for, and the urban population would get the improvements in the quality of life it wanted.

The 1973 budget directly reflected the goals of the Remodeling the Archipelago Plan. The cabinet increased the general account budget by 25 per cent over the previous year, the highest single-year increase in postwar history. The greatest increases were for social capital and public activities related to the quality of life (sewers, parks, and housing), for large increases in social insurance programs, and for public works infrastructure such as roads and harbor development.[21]

The massive speedup in spending—begun in the late Sato administrations and accelerated by Tanaka and continued by later administrations in the 1970s—to cope with urban and infrastructure problems was premised on the earlier assumption of continued economic growth, but the basis for that growth was to be changed and a new aspect was to be added. Growth was now to be more balanced, and the distortions of the earlier period's industrial development were to be ironed out. In the 1970s, "development" came to mean not only economic production but "social development"—in the sense of concern for the human consequences of development and for social welfare.

These concerns survived the short-lived Tanaka administration and by the mid-late 1970s became established in the conservative policy line. The ruling coalition had co-opted the concept of the welfare state as one of the aims of government. The policy line's principle of emphasizing economic policy for social order and its goal of development to "catch up with the West," now that it had been accomplished in industrial and consumer terms, were extended to include government provision of social services and social welfare. Funding for social welfare expanded at a consistent and proportionately greater pace than any other budget category after 1974. Whereas social welfare occupied an 18–19 per cent share of the budget in the late 1960s and early 1970s, this grew to over 26 per cent in the late 1970s and to 27–28 per cent in the early 1980s. As Noguchi's paper in this volume shows, the largest items in the welfare budget have been medical care and pension plans.

As a political strategy, this adaptation of *hoshu honryū* was eminently successful in maintaining the conservatives in power and overcoming the temporary challenge of the Left at the local level. It is tempting to engage in retrospective determinism and see the inevitable development of the LDP into a party monopolizing power for almost thirty years. We should, however, remind ourselves that when Ikeda's income-doubling plans were formulated, few would have predicted that the LDP would become a perennially dominant party. The party was newly formed, and relations among its factions were still unstable. It had just been the target of the greatest mass protest movement in Japanese history, and electoral trends indicated a perpetual decline in its vote. As we have seen, the credit for the LDP's survival as the dominant party for thirty years rightly belongs to the institutionalization of the conservative policy line and the public's increasing acceptance of it, to the success of its rapid economic growth policies, and, more recently, to the flexible evolution of that line in response to social change.

The Rise of Social Interests and Catchall Parties

Among the profound consequences of the rapid economic growth of the 1960s and the development of the NMM society was the proliferation of interest groups in the welfare and citizen/political areas (the latter including groups such as consumers, housewives, and environmental activists). Influential interest groups continued to be established in other areas after 1966, but at a declining rate (see Table 2). Interest organizations in the welfare and citizen/political areas, however, continue to be founded. The diversity of interest organizations is increasing.

The influence of interest groups on political life has increased. The conservative policy line's emphasis on economic growth through government encouragement of private sector expansion meant enlarging the "pie" of resources in two senses. First, there were more surplus resources for the government to distribute, and the government could continue to play a role in coordinating the distribution of those resources. Consequently, social groups were encouraged to influence policymaking to determine government priorities and the redistribution of those resources. Second, there were more resources available in society. Ikeda's encouragement of the private sector meant that social organizations were among the chief beneficiaries of the new affluence and, therefore, by the late 1960s had more resources to command. Relative to previous eras, the government had to consider social groups more in planning policy in any sector, and social groups had more resources to influence policy-making. In other words, a more pluralistic interest structure with an incentive to influence government policy and a government with an incentive to accommodate interest demands had developed.

Another effect on the ruling coalition was the broadening of its social base. The political challenge faced by the ruling coalition and the expansion of the types and numbers of influential interest groups induced it to broaden its interest group base. From the mid-1960s on, the LDP and the bureaucracy expanded their contacts with social interest groups and attempted to respond favorably to those interests and their demands.

Table 3 shows the widening social interest coalition supporting the LDP. Based on a survey of party support among interest group leaders conducted in 1980 by Muramatsu, the table indicates averages for each category of interest group, ranging from five (the most support) to one (least support). The LDP clearly receives the highest support from all types of interest groups, including welfare groups, with the exception of labor and citizen/political groups.

By the end of the 1970s, the LDP had become a "catch-almost-all" party, much like the Christian Democrats in Italy and other pragmatic centrist parties in Europe, as Murakami points out in his paper in this volume and elsewhere.[22] But so, in one of the major surprises of the survey, had the Japan Socialist Party, despite a decline in voter support. As we might expect, the JSP is the party with the most support from labor and citizen/political groups; it also ranks second or third after the LDP in

TABLE 3
Party Support by Type of Interest Group, 1980

Interest group	LDP	JSP	CGP	JCP	DSP	NLC	SDL
Agricultural	3.69	2.65	2.52	2.30	2.60	2.47	2.17
Welfare	3.33	2.46	2.30	2.03	2.33	2.20	2.03
Business and financial	3.80	2.15	2.15	1.54	2.54	2.23	1.86
Labor	1.50	3.42	2.30	1.96	2.76	1.67	2.00
Administrative	3.93	2.46	2.33	1.86	2.53	2.33	2.20
Educational	3.75	2.83	2.66	2.08	2.83	3.16	2.25
Professional	4.22	2.88	2.77	2.00	3.22	2.55	2.33
Citizen/political	1.89	3.21	2.68	2.52	2.52	2.31	2.52

NOTE: The numbers shown are the average score of each category of interest group based on responses of individual interest groups, placing themselves on a scale of 1 (least support) to 5 (most support).
ABBREVIATIONS: LDP, Liberal Democratic Party; JSP, Japan Socialist Party; CGP, Clean Government Party; JCP, Japan Communist Party; DSP, Democratic Socialist Party; NLC, New Liberal Club; SDL, Social Democratic League.

all categories except business and financial groups. We believe that this unexpected finding is the result of the more interest-oriented political economy described above; even an ideological party like the JSP has had to acknowledge and respond to the stronger social interest pressures in order to compete with the LDP. The explanation for its partial success in doing this lies, we believe, with the role of the opposition in the Diet (see next section).

The enhanced role of interest groups in the ruling coalition is also reflected in the contacts between the bureaucracy and social organizations. In another analysis of interest group influence on policymaking based on the same survey,[23] we found that a significant percentage—ranging from 43 per cent to 100 per cent—of each type of interest group had frequent or regular contact with the middle levels of the bureaucracy (section and division chiefs). All had some contact with the upper levels of the bureaucracy (vice-ministers and ministers) and some, such as administrative, professional, and educational groups, had extensive contact at upper levels as well. Even groups relatively excluded from the LDP's coalition—labor and citizen/political groups—nonetheless had a fair amount of access to the bureaucracy.

The social coalition of the LDP was significantly broadened from the late 1960s through the 1970s to include almost every kind of interest group except labor and citizen/political groups. Even these had established significant contact with government through the bureaucracy. By 1980, the ruling coalition's interest base was a far cry from the narrow big business and agriculture base described by Takeshi Ishida in the late 1950s.[24]

Does support for the LDP or access to the bureaucracy result in greater social interest group influence on government policy? In the 1980 interest group survey, leaders were asked whether their organizations had enjoyed recent success in having policies they desired implemented or having policies they opposed vetoed or revised (see Table 4). This gives us a concrete, behavioral measure of influence and avoids the problem of subjective measures. Educational, professional, and agricultural groups were particularly successful in influencing government. But the most striking result is that between 65 and 91 per cent of each type of interest group claimed a recent success in having a demand on government realized. This is vivid testimony to the extraordinary ability of interest groups to utilize their contacts with the LDP and the bureaucracy to shape policymaking.

The other aspect of the table, the extent of success in preventing implementation or forcing revisions, is also interesting. A fair proportion of all groups has recently been successful in negatively influencing policy. The most successful groups in terms of "veto" influence are profes-

TABLE 4
Lobbying Success by Type of Interest Group
(per cent)

Interest group (N = 248)	Had favorable policy adopted	Had objection-able policy stopped or revised
Agricultural	82.6%	39.1%
Welfare	70.0	23.3
Business and financial	64.8	43.2
Labor	69.2	75.0
Administrative	73.3	46.7
Educational	91.7	41.7
Professional	88.9	77.8
Citizen/political	68.4	78.9
ALL	70.6%	50.8%

sional, labor, and citizen/political organizations. The last two types are least close to the LDP and closest to opposition parties like the JSP. It appears that despite their lack of support for the dominant party, interest groups close to the opposition parties are able to influence policy-making, although they are more successful at vetoing proposals; interest groups closer to the LDP are more successful at having favored policies adopted.

Access and influence are widely distributed among all sectors in the political economy that has developed under the conservative policy line during the past fifteen years. Even groups that primarily support the opposition parties have influence, through their contacts with the bureaucracy, through the opposition parties, or through such channels as advisory councils (*shingikai*) connected to the bureaucracy or cabinet on which experts and representatives of interests, even some from opposition groups, serve.

A New Role for the Opposition

Another major change in the 1970s was a new relationship between the opposition parties and the LDP. The declining LDP vote share in the late 1970s resulted in the era of *hokaku hakuchū*, or nearly equal power between the LDP and the opposition in their share of Diet seats. Prior to the 1970s, the opposition influenced policymaking through its ability to "veto" controversial legislation by paralyzing the Diet with obstructionist tactics and external mobilization of supporters.[25] With *hokaku hakuchū*, the opposition could exert influence more openly and directly through normal Diet channels, especially through Diet committees.[26] Substantial revisions in budgets and changes in the Antimonopoly Law under the Miki administration to encourage more competition are examples of the legislative consequences of the new balance of power. Above, we noted that the opposition parties, especially the JSP, had support from a wide range of interest groups. One reason for this is undoubtedly that the opposition parties do have some influence on policymaking and thus can represent interest groups in the policy process, even if the public does not completely accept their major defense and foreign policy programs.

Hoshu Honryū and the Politics of Expenditure

In the 1970s, the increasing acceptance among the NMM public of *hoshu honryū* principles and the LDP's flexibility in broadening the meaning of that line to incorporate NMM concerns and demands had profound consequences for Japan's political economy. First, these actions maintained the LDP as the dominant party. Second, they resulted in an even wider broadening of the LDP's social coalition and greater integration and institutionalization of LDP, interest group, and ministry ties. Third, by extending its tenure as the dominant party and by deepening and broadening its role vis-à-vis interest groups, the LDP's influence on policymaking relative to that of the bureaucracy expanded. Finally, in the "nearly equal" power age the role of the opposition increased. One of the most interesting trends in recent years, therefore, has been the emergence of a broader policymaking elite in which the bureaucracy, although still retaining a pivotal coordinating role, is only one among many influential actors.

The consequence of these political changes was a public policy of increased expenditure, leading to massive deficits. Deficits have increased tenfold since 1970, from ¥14.973 trillion to ¥56.251 trillion in 1975 to roughly ¥120.000 trillion in 1985. The pluralist interest group sector developed during a time of increased demands for social and welfare services and social interest group allocations and policies, a time when the ruling coalition was attempting to expand the role of the government in these areas for political reasons. The supporting coalition of interest groups was broad, and a fair proportion of each type had influence, with even those groups closer to the opposition parties having some influence. It was difficult for the LDP to discriminate among functional types of interest groups to screen out or prioritize these groups' competing claims on the government. The ruling coalition catered to this diverse, pluralist, and influential social interest base by awarding large-scale allocations to influential groups that contributed to maintaining the dominant party in power and by making "side payments" to co-opt opposition interests.

Changes in the international environment also contributed to the pressures on the Japanese government to spend. American demands on Japan to shoulder a greater part of its own defense burden increased, and the government gradually raised allocations for modernizing the Self-Defense Forces. In the wake of the oil shocks and the consequent worldwide recessions, Japan's economic partners also looked to Japan to become the "engine" of international economic recovery by spending more to stimulate growth.

Therefore, government expenditures increased constantly in response to (1) the new priority given to social services and welfare, as described in Noguchi's paper in this volume; (2) the enormous domestic political pressures from a widened and more diverse and powerful social interest base; (3) the interest intermediation role of the LDP and the growth of entrenched "subgovernments" of party, interest group, and bureaucratic coalitions; and (4) the need to reward a strengthened Diet opposition for parliamentary cooperation and the LDP's need to maintain its interest-oriented base to survive politically. All of these domestic soures for increased spending were reinforced by the new foreign pressure on Japan to shoulder more responsibility for its own defense and for world economic growth.

All administrations from Tanaka's in the early 1970s on continued the expansion of governmental expenditures. Even Takeo Fukuda, noted as a cautious political leader and supporter of an "antispending" policy, had to bow to the combined domestic and international pressures of the late 1970s to continue his predecessor's spending policies. Although Masayoshi Ohira recognized the problem and called for a tax increase to offset high expenditures, the LDP's loss of 30 seats in the 1979 election ostensibly because of this issue, discouraged a search for a solution along the same line.

Once again, political strategy focusing on the conservative policy line had significant consequences for Japan's political and economic development. These changes brought about the emergence of "patterned pluralism," the policymaking system with which Japan confronted the problems of the 1980s.

Japan in the 1980s: Patterned Pluralism

In 1980, the LDP won an overwhelming majority in the Diet. In the general election three years later, this majority was reduced substantially but by the unprecedented device of forming a coalition government with the small New Liberal Club (NLC) of fellow conservatives, the LDP guaranteed itself a solid majority in the Diet. Temporarily and partially freed from the restraints of the equal power age and confronted with a massive public debt, the conservatives now faced the dilemma of balancing the reconstruction of fiscal policy with the political pressures from its domestic and international allies for a continuation of "spending as usual." They also faced the necessity of changing the basic rules of the game of the political economy by accelerating the liberalization of the domestic economy to allow for greater foreign participation and integration into the world economic system.

These problems had to be confronted within a system of policymaking that resulted from the consequences of the conservative policy line described above. To understand how the ruling coalition has been meeting the problems of the 1980s, and the kind of problems it is likely to face in the future, it is necessary to understand this system and its operation.

Patterned Pluralism: An Outline

Most previous models of Japanese policymaking have emphasized the overwhelming power of the government bureaucracy or of a "ruling triad" of the bureaucracy, big business, and the LDP.[27] However, a recent trend has been recognition of the growing number of pluralist elements in Japanese politics and policymaking.[28] We believe that the policymaking system that evolved over the postwar period and emerged in the 1980s contains elements of all these models. Japanese policymaking is characterized by a strong state with its own autonomous interests and an institutionalized accommodation among elites, interacting with pluralist elements. We have called this hybrid state, variations of which we believe exist in several European democracies, "patterned pluralism."[29]

Patterned pluralism is pluralistic in fundamental ways: influence is widely distributed, not concentrated; interest groups have many points of access to the policymaking process; and although interest groups are definitely tied to the government, there are elements of autonomy and conflict in the relationship. We are not dealing here with classical pluralism in which policy was merely the outcome of open-ended, competitive lobbying by pressure groups on a relatively weak government. Rather, the patterned pluralist government is strong, interest groups sometimes have cooperative relations with the government and with each other, and lobbying is not open-ended because interest groups usually are almost constantly allied with the same parties and bureaucratic agencies. Rather, we have in mind a new type of pluralism, as follows:

1. The government and its bureaucracy are strong, but the boundaries between state and society are blurred by the integration of social interest groups with the government and by the intermediation of political parties between social interest groups and the government. The government is not weak, but it is *penetrated* by interest groups and political parties.

2. One of the reasons for this integration between state and society is that one party is perpetually or nearly perpetually in power. This is a

pragmatic, catchall party at least partially responsive to a wide variety of sometimes competing social interests.

3. There is an ideological cleavage in the system with the dominant party and its social allies in a more or less antagonistic relationship with the opposition parties and their interest group allies over important value issues. Unlike the situation under classical pluralism, ideology plays a somewhat greater role, and, consequently, party–interest group alliances are more fixed. However, the opposition has some influence on policy, even if through indirect means.

In patterned pluralism, therefore, there are fairly consistent coalitions of actors with relatively predictable degrees of influence on policymaking. The bureaucracy, the dominant party, and the major social allies of the dominant party are usually involved in most policy issues. Elements of each of these, organized around a common issue or interest, have relatively institutionalized relationships with each other (issue or interest "subgovernments"). On major controversies, however, ideological differences polarize the ruling coalition and the opposition parties and their interest group allies.

The "pluralism" of a system with fairly wide access, a wide variety of competing actors with influence on policy, and a fair degree of responsiveness by the state to social interests, therefore, is "patterned" by relatively fixed and institutionalized party, bureaucratic, and ideological ties. These ties prevent alliances from becoming as fluid, and the autonomy of social groups and competition among them from becoming as advanced or freewheeling, as would be the case under pure pluralism.

In patterned pluralism, there is an integral relationship between the "patterned" and the "pluralist" aspects of the system. One reason the system is so open is that the perennially ruling party has maintained its dominance by giving access to a wide range of social interests. Similarly, the strong state bureaucracy is inclusionary and has close ties to many interest groups, even some of those not affiliated with the dominant party, allowing them to influence policy. An ideological cleavage motivates the dominant party to stay responsive to society to compete with its opposition and maintain its dominance in the face of social change. The institutionalized relationships among segments of the bureaucracy, the dominant party, and social interest groups sharing a common interest (subgovernments) lead to competition and conflict with other subgovernments.

Party, Bureaucracy, and Interest Groups in Patterned Pluralism

In this patterned pluralist system, the relationship between interest groups and the government is characteristic of the mixed nature of the system. There are constant attempts to coordinate and structure the keen intra- and intersectoral competition. The use of *shingikai* to hammer out acceptable policy solutions among competing interests is one such coordinating device.[30]

Another means of interest coordination takes place among social interest groups themselves. Individual organizations and alliances of organizations push their own interests in policymaking, often in competition or conflict with each other. There are, however, circumstances whereby the "peak association" not only attempts to arrange a consensus among competing interests within its sector but also enters the political process as an interest group on behalf of the whole sector.

The business community is a good example of the evolution of interest group sectors in the new political economy of more diverse and influential interest groups. By the 1970s, Keidanren (Federation of Economic Organizations), the most influential promoter of large enterprise, had become an interest group representing business's collective interests and attempting to maintain the basic framework that would advance those interests and preserve political stability.

On all other issues, Keidanren does not intervene to promote the interests of a specific *gyōkai* (industrial sector) or individual companies. Nor is the relationship between peak associations and *gyōkai* always a consensual one. In our interest group survey, we discovered that leaders of peak associations perceived themselves to have more conflict with other organizations than leaders of other types of interest groups do. Peak associations function in a complicated environment that is partly a corporatist division of labor and coordination and partly pluralist competition and conflict.

Bureaucrats and politicians perform perhaps the most significant role in interest group coordination. Here we find the greatest change in influence and roles in recent years. Data from the surveys of interest groups and bureaucrats confirm that politicians and bureaucrats play important roles in mediating interest group demands and that there is a division of labor between politicians and bureaucrats vis-à-vis new versus established policy. All types of interests seek help from both political parties and the bureaucracy; but the more institutionalized interest groups—economic, agricultural, and educational organizations—tend to go more to the bureaucracy and the less institutionalized interest groups with newer policies to promote prefer a political party (see Table 5). In other words, one of the functions of the party system is to promote emerging interests.

The specialized but equal roles of LDP politicians and bureaucrats are shown by other data. Figure 3 displays the average responses of bureaucrats to a survey question of when they have contact with the LDP in the budgetary process. The results indicate that (1) bureaucrats often have contacts with the LDP even at an early stage—namely, at the bureau-decision level; (2) the further along in the budgetary process, the more they need LDP cooperation; and (3) they particularly need the consent of the LDP to introduce new programs.

Our findings strongly imply a major shift in the roles of political elites in the ruling coalition. The bureaucracy is still a major and powerful actor in policymaking, but it now must share the stage with a number of other influential actors. In part, this is a result of the diminishing control of the bureaucracy over social interest groups in an era of financial and international liberalization and the significant weakening of its most influential methods of financial and administrative persuasion and control.[31]

Perhaps more important has been the enhanced influence of party politicians through the performance of new roles. Along with the broadening of the interest base of the coalition has come the strengthening of party ties to interest groups, the growing policy expertise of LDP politicians, and their greater participation in policymaking. The main role of the politician is no longer insulating the bureaucracy from political pressure but intermediating between interest groups and the bureaucracy. The LDP and the opposition parties seem to intermediate most actively on behalf of emerging interests and new policies.

With the LDP's continued political power, its increasing contacts with social interest groups, and its growing openness to their influence, an important development in the part has been the recent growth of *zoku* ("tribes") of Diet members who share an interest and usually some political constituency incentive in a particular area of public policy. Since they contain members of various factions and are organized around a policy area related to a specific ministry, *zoku* have developed as an im-

TABLE 5
Sources of Government Support by Type of Interest Group
(per cent)

Interest Group	Party	Bureaucracy	Other responses and not applicable	N
Agricultural	17.6%	78.3%	4.3%	23
Welfare	53.3	46.7	—	30
Economic	37.5	56.8	5.6	88
Labor	69.2	25.0	5.7	52
Administrative	46.7	46.7	6.7	15
Educational	33.3	66.7	—	12
Professional	55.6	33.3	11.1	9
Citizen/political	47.4	36.8	15.9	19
Others	75.0	—	25.0	4
ALL	46.4%	47.6%	6.0%	252

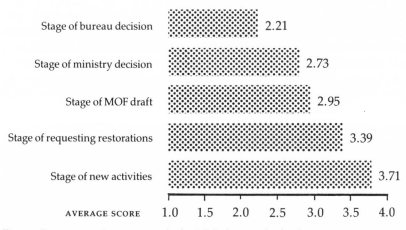

Fig. 3. Bureaucrats' contact with the LDP during the budget process, 1977–1978.

portant horizontal organizational cross-pressure to vertical factional loyalties in the LDP.[32]

Zoku form around interests involving a ministry, a Diet standing committee, and a related section of the Policy Affairs Research Council (PARC), the LDP policymaking organ. Gradually, the process of recruiting *zoku* leaders has become increasingly bureaucratized. After being elected to the Diet four times, an LDP representative becomes eligible to become a political vice-minister. Subsequent to service in this administrative capacity, he returns to the party ranks, usually as the head of a section of PARC relating to the ministry in which he has just served. He then promotes policies advantageous to the major supporting interests in that policy area, together with his predecessors as section chairman who, by this time, have risen to even more influential positions in the party or cabinet.[33] In return for their efforts, social interest organizations support these politicians in election campaigns and financing. *Zoku* have become so important that they are increasingly specialized. Whereas *zoku* used to be rather general, such as those related to "agriculture" or "commerce and industry," today some *zoku* revolve around industries. Forming a new "tribe" can even give a politician a great career boost.[34]

Strengthened relations between interest groups and Diet members have altered relations between politicians and bureaucrats. The recruitment of former bureaucrats into LDP leadership positions, the increasing policy expertise of politicians through their participation in *zoku*, and the strong links established with interest groups have fundamentally changed the relative roles and influence of politicians in policymaking.

In an extended analysis based on survey data of the two elites and their views of their roles in policymaking,[35] we found that the bureaucracy-dominated model of policymaking has long since been supplanted by a more equal but specialized relationship between politicians and bureacrats. All elites saw politicians as having roughly equal influence in policymaking, although they viewed bureaucrats as playing the specialized role of laying the groundwork for political decisions and coordinating social interests.

Nevertheless, the bureaucracy is the pivot around which policymaking alliances are formed on particular issues. For example, the first major stage in the policymaking process is deciding which ministry has prime jurisdiction for a particular policy. Only after this question is settled does the drafting of the law and real discussion of its content begin. Ministries try to establish jurisdiction over policies that they believe will benefit them and to pass off to other units policies they believe will not. Once a particular ministry gets jurisdiction, it must decide which of its sections will be responsible for the policy. The responsible bureaucratic unit is then expected to promote the policy within the rest of the bureaucracy, the appropriate LDP organs, and the relevant *zoku* and their interest group allies. Jurisdictional disputes between ministries often become intense.

In contrast, in the United States's "interest group liberalism" policymaking process, a particular congressional committee often molds a policy conflict from the beginning, with the content of policy being determined to a large extent by the lobbying of coalitions of interest groups. In patterned pluralist policymaking, ministry jurisdiction constrains the range of interest group influence. Interest groups in Japan tend to develop influence with a particular ministry over time and to have limited influence outside the issue area of that ministry.[36]

Consequently, in Japanese patterned pluralism, it is possible to discern recognizable policymaking patterns that depend on the extent of cohesion or competition within the bureaucracy and on what stand the relevant ministry takes on a particular issue. For example, one of the most common patterns is "subgovernmental conflict" with one particular ministry and its interest group allies and sympathetic LDP politicians pitted against another ministry and its allies. A "government versus interests" pattern is seen when the ministry of jurisdiction sides with government against the *zoku* and their interest group allies. Another example is the "ministry stands alone" pattern of the responsible bureaucratic agency having to defend its stand against the key *zoku* and party leaders.

These patterns are complicated by the positions of the opposition parties and other variables. These illustrations of policymaking patterns should, however, suffice to indicate how policymaking conflicts under patterned pluralism are *pluralist* in that many diverse actors whose alliances may shift participate, but *patterned* in that the shifting coalitions occur within the framework of one-party dominance and of a bureaucracy that procedurally structures the types of possible alliances and policymaking patterns.

Recent Cases of Patterned Pluralist Policymaking

Case 1: "Green card."   Several years ago, the Ministry of Finance initiated measures to increase revenue, among them the green card proposal. This proposal would have abolished the tax at the source on interest and dividends—which were taxed separately from other income and therefore of benefit primarily to the wealthy—in favor of a new tax system on total income. To identify depositors and thus interest recipients, the National Tax Authority was to issue green cards to depositors, who would be required by law to use them when making deposits. All bank and Postal Savings system depositors would be identified, effectively eliminating the frequent concealment of interest by small depositors with accounts in false names.

This proposal went through the usual policymaking process, including approval by the Tax Committee of PARC, and easily passed the Diet in March 1980. Soon thereafter, arguments began to be heard that the new system would encourage the outflow of money from banks and postal accounts in Japan to foreign bank accounts where greater returns could be expected. Various groups, including small and medium-size enterprises, opposed the change. A group of concerned LDP Diet members, some of them influential veteran politicians, was organized.

As a result, in 1982 the LDP's Executive Council reconsidered the system and recommended a three-year delay in implementation. The Tax Committee of PARC not only supported this postponement but recommended a five-year delay. Negotiations and discussions continued among the various LDP committees, MOF bureaucrats, and the *zoku* related to tax policy. Finally, in spring 1983 the Diet passed the Special Treatments Law for Taxes, postponing the start of the green card system for three years.

This case, an example of the ministry stands alone pattern, reflects the new power of politicians and the importance of *zoku* in patterned pluralist policymaking.

Case 2: Revision of the banking law.   In February 1981, the MOF sent a proposal to the Joint Committee of the Finance and Budget divisions of PARC to revise the Banking Act (last revised in 1927). Behind the proposal was the MOF's sensitivity to the possible impact of the coming liberalization and internationalization of banking in Japan. One part of the bill reflected the MOF's desire to strengthen its authority to manage this transition. This proposed revision would have strengthened the MOF's legal powers by putting constraints on bank lending and making disclosures obligatory.

The Joint Committee began deliberations, but it soon became apparent that they were not headed in the direction the MOF wanted. MOF officials appearing before the Joint Committee were bombarded with questions by members representing the interests of the banks. The success of lobbying efforts of the banks was apparent at the start of the deliberations when Shintaro Abe, then chairman of PARC and a future contender for the prime ministership, implied that the MOF's proposal for more control went against the natural assumption that this was a time when more private sector initiative was desirable. He also stated that the party would not take action, even if the government proposed a bill based on the MOF proposal.

As a result of PARC participation, the section concerning enhancement of the MOF's control over the banks was deleted and the section concerning disclosure was made only advisory. The MOF had suffered a significant defeat at the hands of the bank lobby and the party. This is another example of ministry stands alone decision making in which party leaders triumphed.

Case 3: Environmental assessment law. This issue involved not only the LDP, bureaucrats, and interest groups, but also the opposition parties and local government leaders. In 1977, the minister of the Environment Agency referred a draft law concerning environmental assessment (similar to U.S. environmental impact procedures) to a subcommittee of the Central Commission for the Environment, a national *shingikai.* The draft bill would have required those engaged in construction work to report on the environmental impact of their projects to relevant government agencies.

Keidanren and the Association of Electric Companies quickly presented negative views on the draft. MITI, and later the Ministry of Construction and Transportation, also opposed the measure. The LDP entered the discussions in 1978 to coordinate the divergent views and interests of the ministries and agencies. Once the PARC Committee for the Environment took up the issue in an attempt to break the impasse, the LDP became increasingly involved. The bureaucratic conflicts were also reflected in conflicts among PARC committees, with, for example, the PARC Committees on Commerce and the Environment on opposite sides.

Finally, after four years, Prime Minister Suzuki, against the opinions of MITI, PARC committees, and business circles, decided to introduce the draft bill in the Diet. In favor of its passage were the Environment

Agency, public opinion, and the opposition parties, although they proposed their own draft bills on the matter. This was the period of nearly equal power between government and opposition in the Diet, and the LDP was under great pressure to be responsive to the public's environmental concerns. Also supporting it were such local LDP leaders as Governor Suzuki of Tokyo, who at one point succeeded in persuading the LDP to reconsider the bill when it had all but died. The PARC Committee on the Environment took a middle stance: it had promoted the submission of the bill to the Diet, but once the bill was introduced, the committee acted to water down substantial parts of the original bill under pressure from MITI and others. The bill, although reintroduced several times into the Diet, has never been passed.

The history of the environmental assessment proposals illustrates how bargaining revolves around bureaucratic agencies and shows the ever-present potential for severe conflict between alliances of LDP groups, bureaucratic agencies, and interest groups and other similar coalitions, sometimes with the opposition involved. Policy immobilism, as in this case, is one possible result of patterned pluralist policymaking.

Case 4: Value-added networks (VANs). VANs transmit data and information through communication lines as a business service, and many government ministries and businesses have become interested in developing such networks as a potentially vital link in the "information revolution" occurring in the Japanese business world. The political issues involved—the extent to which government, particularly the Ministry of Posts and Telecommunications (MPT) under whose purview such communications systems would fall, would continue to regulate and control telecommunications, and how much foreign participation would be allowed in this field—have provoked one of the most intense subgovernmental conflicts in recent years.[37]

The MPT proposed to the 1983–84 Diet two bills concerning VANs and telecommunications whose purpose was to liberalize telecommunications in part by abolishing the government monopoly Nippon Telephone and Telegraph (NTT; Den Den Kōsha). The measures concerning private industry divided procedures into two categories—a "special" procedure for large enterprises and a "general" procedure for smaller-scale enterprise. In the MPT's original draft, a company interested in operating under the special subcategory was required to get a license from the government. Those in the general category were required only to register with the government. The MPT also wanted to see companies with foreign capitalization of over 50 per cent excluded completely from the VAN business.

Despite the myth abroad that MITI is the chief agent of "Japan, Inc.," the ministry has increasingly championed liberalization and deregulation of the Japanese economy. The VAN conflict began when MITI took the position that both subcategories should be completely free from any administrative regulation and that there should be no restrictions on the participation of foreign-owned firms. MITI was backed in this position by intensive U.S. efforts to open the telecommunications industry in Japan to foreign sales and investment. The dispute mobilized business allies on each side—those who feared their inability to compete against such communications giants as IBM and AT&T and those who would gain from unregulated competition.

The conflict began at the section chief level of the two ministries but escalated to the vice-ministerial level, where the chief cabinet secretary attempted to mediate it, and finally up to the ministerial level. Each ministry tried to win allies to its side and bring its influence to bear on the issue: the MPT successfully gained the support of Ryutaro Hashimoto, chairman of the Administration and Finance Division of PARC; MITI mobilized all its former ministers. Unfortunately for MITI, there was a split within the PARC Commerce and Industry Division, undoubtedly reflecting a similar split among business interests, and the usually reliable influence of this fellow member of the MITI subgovernment was not as useful to the ministry as it might have been.

Finally, the dispute reached the top levels of the party, the prime minister/party president and the "big three" party executives (the secretary general, the chairman of the Executive Council, and the chairman of PARC). On April 4, 1984, they resolved this protracted conflict by deciding that both categories should be managed by registration, thus effectively splitting the difference in the positions of the two camps, and that no special restrictions should be imposed on foreign-owned firms. Two days later the cabinet approved these deicisons, and finally so did the Diet.

The VAN issue illustrates the importance of bureaucratic jurisdictions, subgovernmental conflict, and the role of top political leaders in the LDP, as well as the importance of international considerations.

Case 5: Administrative reform. Administrative reform, the key issue of the early 1980s, is an attempt to cope with the large budget deficits caused by the spending policies of the 1970s without resorting to the politically difficult solution of direct tax increases. Prime Minister Suzuki, who succeeded Ohira on the latter's death in 1980, established the Second Provisional Administrative Reform Commission (Daini Rinji Gyōsei Chōsakai, or Daini Rinchō) under the slogan of Financial Reconstruction Without a Tax Increase. The new attempt to solve the dilemma—the pressure for continued high expenditures and the need to cope with deficits perceived to be intolerable—was to be structural. The commission actively mobilized public support by appealing to the public's antitax sentiment through a skillful public relations cammpaign under its chairman, Toshio Doko, a former president of Keidanren. The commission received strong support from cabinet minister Yasuhiro Nakasone, who continued his support after becoming prime minister. The commission was successful in changing the atmosphere from one of growth and distribution to one of low growth and more self-restraint. As a result, the administration succeeded in restraining budget increases.

Once political leadership was provided, it is interesting that the type of policies developed to handle the problem were consonant with the operation of a patterned pluralist system. The commission's major reforms were aimed primarily at reducing the scope of administration by relying to a great extent on "total-scale controls" (uniform guidelines) of cuts in budget, salaries, staff, and bureaucratic organs. As Muramatsu has pointed out elsewhere,[38] this approach relegates to the ministerial level the decisions on the purposes of government and on restraining expenditures by prioritizing government activities. Interestingly enough, although welfare expenditures have been the fastest-growing budget category in the past 15 years, there has been no consistent or intense attempt to make such entitlements the political scapegoat for the financial crisis, as there has been under conservative governments in the United States and Britain.[39] Rather, the size of the bureaucracy (already the smallest per capita among industrialized democracies) and such public corporations as the Japan National Railways have been made the targets of structural reform.

The commission's adoption of the total-scale control approach rather than a selective prioritizing approach and the lack of an attempt to make entitlements the major target of conservative attack are explainable, we believe, by the patterned pluralist system. The ruling coalition may find it impossible to prioritize its goals because it has so many and because they are all connected to the vested interests of its wide political support base. As Allesandro Pizzorno has argued,[40] a fundamental flaw in the classic pluralist model was that such a system would automatically reach an equilibrium and operate to make it efficient, just as competition in markets should. Social groups, however, react to attempts to redistribute benefits not by working harder or consuming less but by threatening to withdraw resources. The only structure that can accomplish redistribution is the government. But what happens when a ruling coalition that has perennially dominated the government is itself penetrated by and dependent on so many social interests that it cannot redistribute without sustaining major political injury?

In the patterned pluralist system, the overall prioritizing of goals, which decides which groups shall receive allocations, is difficult because the ruling party is a catchall party, the bureaucracy is highly active in managing social interests, the party's support base is diverse and national in scope. Consequently, the government must impose restraint equally: because none can be denied a great deal without undermining the ruling coalition, all must be denied a little.

In a system in which the bureaucracy functions as a pivot for policymaking, delegating to each ministry the responsibility to decide on priorities for cuts is rational. Given the long-standing relations between ministries and interest groups and the brokering role played between the two by *zoku*, the bureaucracy can use its extensive coordinating power to forge a consensus on how to meet restrictions and has the persuasive power to implement that consensus. Within these subgovernments, the role of party *zoku* is crucial in creating the consensus, and the *zoku* have a say in how the cuts are to be distributed among related but conflicting interest groups.

Uniform cuts and delegation of decisions about priorities to the bureaucracy are a means of reconciling a strong and autonomous bureaucracy with the political needs of a dominant catchall party and the pressures of pluralist social interest groups, the major elements of the patterned pluralist system.

And finally, the "across-the-board, delegate the problem to the ministries" approach continues another long-standing element of patterned pluralism. Where possible, the ruling party traditionally likes to work through the bureaucracy, an option made possible by the LDP's position as a perennially dominant party.

Present and Future Dilemmas of Patterned Pluralism

The cases presented in the previous section, and others described elsewhere,[41] indicate that trends in the postwar political economy have culminated in a new policymaking system. Indications of the future problems of this system are already beginning to appear, including jurisdictional disputes, the growing internationalization of political economies, the need for new coordination mechanisms, and increasing rural-urban conflict. Will the ruling coalition be able to maintain its power and preserve its policy line under patterned pluralism?

From PATTERNED Pluralism to Patterned PLURALISM

The increasing diversification of social interests in an ever more interdependent and complicated economy inevitably raises complicated policy issues that go beyond the purview of a single ministry. Subgovernmental conflict may become the most prevalent policymaking pattern, and we expect jurisdictional disputes among administrative agencies to become more intense. Such disputes contribute to the trend toward greater LDP involvement in policymaking. For example, whereas the bureaucracy itself (usually the Jimujikan Kaigi, the committee of administrative vice-ministers) used to handle jurisdictional disputes and subgovernmental competition, increasingly such conflicts have come to involve the relevant divisions and committees of PARC or the highest levels of party leadership, as shown in some of our case studies above.

Changes in the LDP's structure can also be expected to mirror such cross-ministry coordinating functions. To give one recent example, the LDP established a special committee to coordinate budgets related to high-tech industries,[42] an area that inevitably spans ministry jurisdictions. The party's increasing involvment in, and its capacity to deal with, cross-jurisdictional policy issues will further enhance the pluralist element in patterned pluralism.

The Internationalization of Subgovernments?

With the integration of advanced industrialized economies and the trade friction between Japan and the West, foreign governments now have an important vested interest in economic policymaking and routinely try to influence it. The textile dispute, the beef and oranges dispute, and the VAN dispute are all examples. Usually this pressure has been exerted directly on the prime minister, but foreign governments and interest groups have increased knowledge of the Japanese policymaking system and a greater appreciation of the importance of the conflict between subgovernments as a key to policymaking. At the same time, subgovernments have learned to appreciate the potential power of foreign pressure for or against one's side in a conflict.

What has become noticeable in recent years has been (1) the increase in the extent to which subgovernment alliances of interest groups, particularly government agencies, and allied elements of the LDP have come to use foreign pressure as leverage in their conflicts with other subgovernments; and (2) the increase in the extent to which foreign governments and interest groups now attempt to manipulate elements of relevant subgovernments to apply pressure on government policymaking. We may be witnessing no less than the inclusion of foreign governments and interests as integral actors in the subgovernmental policy process.

The Need for New Coordination Roles and Mechanisms

The development of policymaking along complex, subgovernmental, patterned pluralist lines creates an enormous problem for decision making: coordination. Policymaking under such conditions is difficult to coordinate because the number and complexity of the actors have increased and their influence has become more equally distributed. But it is difficult for another reason. When the bureaucracy was more powerful, it could be the neutral arbiter of competing interests. In the ruling triad, if it ever existed, coordination could be achieved by the mediation of a small group of top officials from the bureaucracy, the LDP, and major interest groups. When subgovernments are in conflict, it is difficult to find a neutral arbiter; most of the actors are part of the dispute.

Furthermore, the internationalization of subgovernmental conflicts creates problems. As Pizzorno indicates,[43] the realm of pluralist interest decisions and that of international politics are very different. The former tends to be relatively open and negotiated. The latter tends to be secretive and involve few actors. Who can bridge the two levels?

One possibility is that the prime minister or his staff (perhaps an enlarged cabinet secretariat) play the coordination role by remaining detached from too close an identification with any particular side in subgovernmental disputes and act as a broker between the domestic and the international actors. A key issue in administrative reform involves reinforcing the prime minister's managerial power. Another possibility is the increasing management of conflicts by LDP organizations, such as PARC, and the development of more specialized conflict management roles within the party. In the administrative reform case, for example, a special PARC research committee and its chairman played a crucial role in coordinating the demands of LDP interest groups on key legislation. Both these possibilities, however, have inherent limitations. The prime minister's need to form alliances with particular subgovernments to gain power within the party limits his ability after taking power to divorce himself from allies to play the arbiter role. For their part, political parties are ill-equipped at present to perform brokering functions involving international actors.

Increased Urban-Rural Conflict

One particular conflict has the potential to polarize various subgovernments into almost permanent opposition to each other and perhaps split the ruling coalition—the urban-rural conflict. That conflict has remained latent throughout the postwar period, in part because the LDP itself overarched the interests of both with a strong rural voting constituency and alliances with large urban enterprises and, more recently, with welfare and other urban groups. Yet this conflict remains. It remains in the issue of the malapportionment of Diet seats between urban and rural areas; it remains in increasing demands from the business community to rationalize the financially inefficient food and rice control support and subsidy systems that "pay off" the farmers for LDP support; it remains in such issues as the beef and orange trade dispute in which many interests, including business, that must retain good trade relations have come into conflict with powerful farm groups whose interests are directly threatened; and it remains in the special treatment of rural areas in allocations, which once could be justified as a form of redistributive welfare to the undeveloped areas of the country (one study reports that in 1980 the standard of living in rural areas exceeded that in urban areas in such things as welfare, sewage, and housing, not to mention the quality of life in terms of clean air, green areas, and space[44]).

Can the Policy Line and the Ruling Coalition be Maintained?

We have already seen how the conservative policy line has been preserved but greatly modified over the postwar era. It now faces perhaps its greatest challenge, on all three of its principles. The principles of not emphasizing controversial issues and relying on the United States for defense is being challenged by U.S. pressure to rearm. But the policy line is also being challenged by a new domestic consciousness, both at the mass level and at the elite level.

Development and catching up with the West, first industrially, then in terms of living standards, and finally in terms of social services, has been achieved. The Japanese public, including the younger generations, has greater pride and confidence that could manifest themselves as a latent desire to be taken seriously as a political power in international relations. Is catching up with the West *in political influence in the international arena* the next goal? Has Prime Minister Nakasone already made this an overt foreign policy goal?

As Yonosuke Nagai indicated in a recent article,[45] the conflicts over Japanese foreign and defense policies have tended to be fought between the "independence" line of the opposition and the "alliance" line of the conservatives, but both agree on the need to concentrate on distribution of governmental goods, as we have seen. However, a new type of intellectual is appearing, one who stresses alliance *and* defense. Nagai warned that this view may be only a preliminary to a Japanese variant of Gaullism emphasizing independence and defense. If this is the case, then there may be a resurgence of the minority political line of the postwar era.

This situation coincides with the challenges facing the other principles of the conservative policy line. The orientation toward economic management for political and social order, as transformed to greater responsiveness toward the increasing number and diversity of social interest groups, resulted, as we have shown, in a major fiscal crisis and the perceived need to cut back on such policies. Deprived of this pillar of the conservative policy line, how can the ruling coalition maintain its electoral base and mobilize popular suport? It remains to be seen whether the LDP can keep its electoral pluralities intact while it attempts to undermine one of its basic sources of support: the distributive politics of a catchall party. If the JSP modifies its ideology to appeal more to the NMM and combines this with an attempt to expand and appeal more to its already wide social interest base, the ruling coalition may face a serious challenge. Another serious challenge would arise if the opposition parties became more unified. The temptation will be great under these conditions to keep the current ruling coalition and its support base together by using symbolic issues and political themes, possibly nationalist issues.

There are other possible scenarios, however. The fear of alienating its own *passive* conservative supporters with more extreme or traditional appeals,[46] combined with the ever-present need to reach a modus vivendi with the opposition parties to guarantee Diet efficiency, may be more than enough to preserve the moderate, status-quo alliance and defense elements of the conservative policy line. And, it may be possible to find other, non-nationalistic issues or "side payments" to substitute for the lack of expanding resources and for a less rapidly growing social service pie. Issues like tax cuts and greater efficiency in the running of public corporations currently being used by the LDP to mobilize support may be designed with this in mind. Administrative reform may have been designed to appeal to the NMM as a substitute for government expenditures. Attacking the bureaucracy may appeal to the tax-minded NMM voters (and also to former political line conservatives who always felt uneasy over the elite bureaucracy's involvement in the policy line). At the same time, administrative reform holds out the prospect of no tax increases (or even of tax cuts), which appeals to the self-interest-orientation of the NMM.

This point brings up a final question: Is the conservative policy line irrelevant to rational economic management *and* a viable conservative political strategy in the 1980s? For the past 35 years, the conservative policy line has provided the LDP with a political strategy that helped to keep it in power and was generally compatible with rational management of the economy during the different phases of its growth. The dilemmas of the 1908s will not be so easily handled.

Conclusion

We have seen in this paper how the LPD's political strategies, until recently focused on *hoshu honryū*, have been crucial to the development of Japan's postwar political economy. Until the late 1960s, one of the conservative policy line's central tenets, economic management for social and political order, meant development in terms of economic growth. Then, in the 1970s, social development, in terms of welfare and building of infrastructure, was added to the priorities of the government. Finally, in the past few years, coping with the fiscal crisis produced by the lavish expenditures of the 1970s became a high priority of economic management, despite both domestic and international pressures for further spending. There has been, therefore, no simple, single, or consistent meaning to the goal of development in postwar Japan. Rather, the emphasis and content of that term have shifted depending on the one crucial factor that is the theme of this paper—the partisan political strategy of the ruling LDP to ensure its political dominance and political stability in Japan, as represented by the conservative policy line.

The political strategies of the *hoshu honryū* have been quite successful in producing that stability. And, in turn, that stability has been a major factor in Japan's economic success and development. That stability provided the framework for the specific economic policies that produced growth. Johnson argues for a greater appreciation of the role of the state in creating Japan's "miracle"; but it was not just the bureaucrats that constituted the state, the role of political leadership and strategy in building the context for that growth was also crucial.

The LDP's appreciation of its contribution is shown in surveys of Japanese elites conducted in the late 1970s. When asked to name the chief factor in Japan's economic growth, the largest group (which consisted of bureaucrats and opposition party supporters) named the "hard work of the people." But the second largest group—30 per cent (which consisted of LDP politicians) said the "stability of the political party balance" (that is, the long-term rule of the LDP).[47] It is clear, too, that this view is not just hindsight but represents a consistent aspect of the LDP's strategy throughout the postwar period: political stability was one important means toward the goal of economic growth.

But perhaps more important, political stability itself, which the conservatives identified with their own dominance, was a very high priority *goal*, to which economic growth was but the means. As T. J. Pempel has indicated, in discussing economic policy in the first two decades after the war, most conservatives believed that growth policies would not only have economic benefits, but would also ensure longer-term political conditions for continuing the nation's entire political-economic system. If these policies achieved their economic purposes, they "would bring with them political stability and continued conservative dominance."[48]

All governments seek political stability, order, and security, and certainly Japan's political leaders since the "defensive modernization" of the Meiji period have sought political stability and security as some of the most important aims of the state. If Japan is a "developmental state," then that development has been as much a *means* toward political goals as an end in itself. And as the postwar evolution of *hoshu honryū* has shown, development has been variously adapted, modified, and changed toward that goal. Politics has not just been a safety valve allowing for rational economic development; development, variously defined in different periods, has been one of the key strategies to accomplish political goals.

Yutaka Kosai

The Politics of Economic Management

As in all industrial democracies, economic management in Japan involves politics. Numerous political actors and political variables are involved in determining the goals of economic management and the means to realize those goals. The notion that the Japanese economy is managed *apolitically* by its technostructure ("Japan, Inc.") is false. Japan's economic goals are chosen and the means to achieve them are adopted and carried out, as in other democracies, in the political arena. When the inevitable conflicts between sectors or among various interest groups arise, politics is used to resolve or mitigate them. The central intent of this paper is to examine the political involvement in economic management in Japan.

Several models of Japan's political system have been proposed. The best known among them are the "bureaucracy-led" and "ruling triad" models ("triad" refers to the bureaucracy, big business, and the conservative party). These and other models tend to emphasize the roles of the bureaucracy or of business interests, especially those of big business. My intent is not to deny the partial validity of these ideas but to demonstrate that the "patterned pluralism" model, presented by Muramatsu and Krauss in this volume, most accurately captures the Japanese political reality.

On macroeconomic issues, the involvement of business in policy formation is sporadic and limited to those issues that threaten business. That is, a "sense of crisis" drives business into the arena of policy formation, as typified in business leaders' suddenly visible and active support for administrative reform, which is intended to achieve fiscal reconstruction and thus is seen by business as a means to prevent increases in the corporate tax. For its part, the bureaucracy tends to stand by the established rules of economic management. It becomes ineffective when the established rules cease to be applicable, as during the 1971 revaluation of the yen.

The influence of the Liberal Democratic Party (LDP) and its leaders over macroeconomic issues has increased because of the growing experience and skills of party politicians as well as the gradual legitimation of parliamentary democracy in Japan. The LDP has been in power for 30 years, and its dominance appears well established. However, as Japan increasingly becomes a "new middle mass" society, to borrow a phrase from Murakami's paper in this volume, popular support of the LDP may fluctuate over time. In 1974, the electorate forced the government to continue stringent fiscal measures to assure eventual price stability. The LDP's electoral setback in fall 1979 blocked a proposed consumption tax increase and prompted administrative reform.

Japan is known for its extensive use of sectoral economic policies. In general, the bureaucracy and business leaders manage growing sectors; politicians and pressure groups cooperate to defend the interests of lagging sectors through distributive measures. This characterization exaggerates the influence of specific interest groups and disregards programs supported by the general public. Nor is the division of labor among groups stable. Intersectoral conflicts appear to be increasing, inviting LDP politicians and the LDP party machine to become more and more involved as mediators. Distributive measures cannot reduce all social discontent since expenditures must be trimmed to reduce the budget deficit. Indeed, politically thorny intersectoral conflicts may result in protectionist legislation.

To date, however, the management of Japan's economy has been effective. Dilemmas caused by the lag between consensus formation and effective reaction to changed circumstances have been dealt with and have not jeopardized the effectiveness of the management. But, in view of current expectations of rapid social changes, the continuing effectiveness of the political leadership and the machinery for economic management is open to question.

I now turn to a brief discussion of the Japanese political system and then, in subsequent sections, to a description of macroeconomic and sectoral economic management. The concluding section is devoted to a brief analysis of possible trends.

The Political System

In this section the main actors in the politics of Japanese economic management are identified and the principal features of the roles played by each are discussed. To do so, as well as to provide a general background for the discussion in the following section, it is useful to begin with a survey of past studies.

The One, the Three, the Many

Who formulates Japanese economic policy?[1] Political scientists and economists have proposed several analytic models in answer to this question. The most influential among them, in order of appearance, are the bureaucracy-led model, the ruling-triad model, and the patterned pluralism model.[2] The sequence of these models reflects the changes in the structure of policy formation in Japan. The first, the bureaucracy-led model, captures the essential characteristics of the polity of the prewar period and of the years immediately following World War II. The second, the ruling-triad model, describes the policymaking of the 1950s. The last, patterned pluralism, is useful and effective for examining the latest stage of the Japanese political economy, which began around 1960.

The bureaucracy-led model is still considered the orthodox model by many. It derives its strength from three sources. The first is the "continuity" hypothesis of bureaucratic domination, which asserts that the bureaucracy continues to maintain its power. In this view, Japan is still a country of *kanson mimpi* ("revered officials and humble people," that is, a preponderance of official power). The second source, following Max Weber, is the putative trend toward bureaucratization in modern society. The third source, in part derived from the first and the second, is the argument that bureaucracy is the most effective organ in modernizing late developers, such as Japan. Those supporting the bureaucratic model, however, rely on these sources in varying degrees. For example, earlier scholars relied mostly on the first source; recent supporters of the model such as Yukio Noguchi and Eisuke Sakakibara, who offered "the Ministry of Finance–Bank of Japan (MOF-BOJ) dynasty" hypothesis, stress the third source.[3]

The bureaucracy-led model generally assumes that Japan pursues a single, consistent target (for example, modernization) and that a consensus on broad goals exists among elitist bureaucrats. Differences of opinion reflect bureaucratic sectionalism, not the diversity of interests among people. According to this model, each section of government mobilizes the people under its influence to support the shared goal.

In contrast to the bureaucratic model, the ruling-triad model highlights three elite groups: the bureaucracy, big business leaders, and conservative party leaders. In this model, these three groups are the executives of Japan, Inc.—the members of exclusive policymaking forums. This model excludes some social forces from the ruling groups, notably organized labor, and thus conveys an image of a uniquely Japanese-style corporatism.

Among the three groups, differences in interests give rise to differences in outlook and conduct. Nonetheless, this model stresses the cohesion and unity of these power elites and the enduring character of their cooperation. As sources for this cohesion, supporters of this view point to the common social origin of most members of the triad, shared policy objectives (the most important being to make Japan an advanced country), and membership in the "technostructure," where ex-bureaucrats often become either business or political leaders.

The patterned pluralism model tries to present a balanced view of the flexibility and cohesion of the Japanese political economy. This model differs little, in substance, from the analytic view presented in Yasusuke Murakami's "compartmentalized competition" hypothesis, Takashi Inoguchi's "bureaucratic-led mass-inclusionary pluralism" hypothesis, or Seizaburo Sato and Tetsuhisa Matsuzaki's assertion of "canalized pluralism."[4] In contrast to the older models, these hypotheses explicitly recognize the pluralistic character of the Japanese polity.

Patterned pluralism can be described as $(100 - \alpha)$ per cent pluralism, where α represents the element that is "patterned." Interest groups are allowed to form freely, and their voices are heard, but only through such patterned channels as the conservative organs and specific ministries or sections within them. Entry into the pluralist political arena is a privilege accorded to virtually all groups; few groups are totally ignored. In this respect, Japan differs only marginally from a fully pluralist democracy. The marginal difference is the "patterned" element—organized interest groups must observe a more or less formal procedure in presenting their views or making political input through specified channels. Japan's political economy is a type of corporatism in which the membership of the ruling groups is not fixed. It is α per cent corporatism in which $(100 - \alpha)$ per cent represents the competitive element, which lacks, for example, "peak" organizations. When the LDP is called a catchall party, "all" refers to all interest groups, not necessarily all (unorganized) citizens.

Political Leadership in the New Middle Mass Society

In political and economic literature, such concepts as the "public" and the "public interest," together with the agents expected to represent them, have for many years been dismissed as "normative wishing."[5] Recently, however, some authors have been attempting to re-examine and to establish the empirical validity of these classical concepts.[6] Under the Reagan administration, presidential leadership in the United States seems to have regained some of the ground lost to "subsystemic interest group politics."[7] Since the same tendency can be observed elsewhere, the role of political leadership is attracting renewed analytic interest.

Under patterned pluralism, politicians act as arbitrators (instead of relying on impersonal political machinery) in resolving conflicts resulting from the diverse interests of different groups. In a sense, their action is analogous to that performed by a Walrasian "auctioneer" attempting to establish the equilibrium price. When broad policy goals become an issue, political leadership becomes necessary. The more patterned the bureaucratic and party organs become, the greater their role (see below). The general trends today are toward more fragmentation of government and LDP policy machinery, increased conflicts of interest among groups, and greater emphasis on broader and unfamiliar policy issues.

In his paper in this volume, Murakami offers three explanations of these trends: (1) the revival of nationalism hypothesis, (2) the catchall interests hypothesis, and (3) the adjusted expectation hypothesis.[8] His second hypothesis fits extremely well within the framework of patterned pluralism; the first and third hypotheses are concerned with general "mood," not with the satisfaction of specific groups' demands.

What role does political leadership play in Murakami's new middle mass society? Mass democracy gives rise to Caesarist leaders or demagogues who exploit and mobilize mass emotion, as in the exaggerated cases of nazism and fascism.[9] The new middle mass as defined and examined by Murakami, however, differs from these old masses, as well as from the middle class of the nineteenth century. The new mass is not easily moved emotionally; rather, it rationally calculates its own interests. Most members of the new middle mass are well informed and earn high incomes. At the same time, the new middle mass is protected by well-developed social welfare institutions, such as unemployment insurance, public health care, and public pensions, that protect the interests of the entire—or a large part of the—population. Although special interest groups exist and are powerful, it is not these groups but the welfare state that the new middle mass supports and is supported by.

The new middle mass remains a mass because it is unorganized, fluid, and amorphous. Membership in specific groups and political opinions change in volatile and unexpected ways. These facts help explain the importance of political leadership in a new middle mass society, although its importance is not as great as in old mass societies.

For this reason, in discussing economic management in the new middle mass society, we should pay attention to the role of political leaders as coordinators in a situation of patterned pluralism and as representatives of public opinion. This is not to assert that political leadership in Japan has been strong and effective. In fact, political leadership is possible only within the limits imposed by patterned pluralism.

Some Features of Japanese Political Conduct: The Consensus to Adapt

The continuity of broad policy goals, the ability to reach a consensus among those concerned, and an orientation toward adaptive and pragmatic problem-solving are among the oft-mentioned features of Japanese political conduct. It is often asserted that, in Japanese politics, ideological commitment, bold and experimental policy innovations, and drastic changes in policy stances are generally avoided.[10]

If correct, these assertions reflect both the cause and the effect of the LDP's long-standing majority. The uninterrupted rule of the LDP has assured the continuity of policy orientation; people vote for the LDP to ensure that this policy orientation continues. Since circumstances change, the LDP must attempt to accommodate the interests of a large number of groups, including those of newly formed groups. In this context, patterned pluralism is a network used by the LDP to respond to new demands and to reconcile the conflicts of interest among groups, old and new. The LDP, through "creative conservatism,"[11] has managed to avoid the potential trap of upholding the status quo and has attained the consensus necessary to adjust conflicting interests. Tension between a broad consensus and quick adaptations is, however, inevitable. In a changing environment, no one should assume the continuing success of the LDP.

Several theories have attempted to explain the LDP's success in forming the consensus needed to make necessary adaptations. One theory argues that Japan, being a late starter in industrialization, enjoyed a consensus that it had to catch up with the advanced countries. This meant that the LDP had little difficulty in knowing what political and economic adaptations to make: it only had to follow the experience of the advanced countries. Imitation is always easier than innovation. This fact, perhaps, partly explains the prevailing pragmatic, instead of ideologically determined, approach of the LDP government and the greater importance the party attached to the opinions of experienced business leaders and bureaucrats relative to those of academic experts. Another reason for the LDP's success in consensus formation was that the economic growth resulting from positive adaptation helped maintain the domestic consensus. The surpluses resulting from rapid economic growth could be distributed to compensate for the social imbalances resulting from, and the economic sacrifices required by, the promotion of rapid economic growth. However, these conditions no longer exist today—Japan has become one of the most economically advanced nations.

The effect of a wide gap arising between consensus formation and positive adaptation was revealed when Japan experienced "external shocks." In spite of Japan's oft-applauded long-range planning, in recent years lack of foresight and the total absence of preparation for external shock, a consensus on how to cope with it, or quick adjustment based on the consensus, characterize the Japanese response, as was evident in the 1971 revaluation of the yen. For some, such a Japanese reaction appears to be a "slow start" that results in an overreaction. But what they are seeing is the cumbersome process of policy coordination that occurs under necessarily deliberate political leadership within the framework of patterned pluralism. (I discuss this mode of the politics of economic management in later sections.)

The Process of Economic Management

The basic assumption of the models of economic policymaking developed by Tinbergen, Theil, and others is that government chooses the optimal target-instrument mix within the constraints of the prevailing economic structure.[12] These models, in which government is a rational optimizer,[13] must be expanded in several directions to be useful in analyzing the politics of economic management.

First, instead of government as the sole rational optimizer, a multitude of political actors and the interplay among them must be incorporated into the model. Political leaders, party organs, bureaucrats, interest groups, and the general public play their respective role. The problem involved in such an expansion is which of these political agents is the principal agent.

Second, in addition to targets and instrument options, the processes of recognition and evaluation must be examined. That is, the government must somehow recognize the need for policy intervention, and the people through public opinion polls, elections, and the like must evaluate the results of economic management. When government identifies a need for policy intervention, it in a sense anticipates the public's evaluation of a particular situation. The results of such an evaluation necessitate a revision in government policy, thereby initiating a new round of policy actions. Given the number of participants, the feedback processes of recognition and evaluation are neither simple nor automatic. The scope and efficiency of the information network of the bureaucracy and political parties affect these processes. Patterned pluralism presupposes the existence of well-developed information channels centering on a bureaucracy-LDP coalition, but these channels may induce biased outcomes.

Third, not only quantitative, but also "qualitative" policies, such as institutional reform, must be considered. Political factors are important because of their role in determining the rules of the game regulating private and public activities. Because of specific rules imposed by politics, some potential policy instruments may not be employed.

Finally, politics is involved in macroeconomic as well as microeconomic management. Japan is known for its "industrial policy" and for its extensive application of a "formidable set" of sectoral economic management instruments.[14] The government is organized in such a way (*tatewari gyōsei;* "vertically compartmentalized administration") that each of its sections exerts influence over specific sectors of the economy. Politicians, too, have their own respective fields of interests and influence. However, political leaders, the Ministry of Finance, the Bank of Japan, the Economic Planning Agency, and the general policy staff of each ministry are also concerned with macroeconomic management. All these participants somehow coordinate macroeconomic and sectoral management at the various political and bureaucratic levels. How such coordination is achieved requires special attention.

The Politics of Macroeconomic Management

As an Issue of High-Level Politics

In postwar Japan, macroeconomic management has been an important issue of high-level politics. Several cabinets have set various macroeconomic goals as their major policy objective. Well-known examples include full employment by the Ishibashi cabinet (1956–57); doubling the national income by the Ikeda cabinet (1960–64); and price stabilization by the Fukuda cabinet (1976–78).

Of course, prime ministers are not concerned only with economic issues. According to a Japanese saying, "the season of economics alternates with that of politics." Cabinets primarily interested in economic issues were often succeeded by cabinets interested in politics and diplomacy. Nobusuke Kishi (1957–60) concentrated on the revision of the U.S.-Japan Mutual Security Treaty, Eisaku Sato (1964–72) focused on regaining sovereignty over Okinawa, and Yasuhiro Nakasone (1982–   ) has spent a considerable amount of his political energy on administrative reform. To be sure, this is a simplistic view since there can be no clear-cut economically oriented or politically oriented prime ministers as such. Tanaka normalized relations with China, and the Kishi cabinet asked the Economic Council to prepare the National Income-Doubling Plan in 1959. Economic management, even when not the sole concern of politicians, has been important throughout the postwar period.

Expertise in economic management is an implicit requirement for the position of prime minister. Of the ten prime ministers since 1956 (all of whom have simultaneously been president of the Liberal Democratic Party), from Ishibashi to Nakasone, eight had held the post of minister of international trade and industry, and six had been minister of finance.

Four had served as minister of foreign affairs and only one as minister in charge of the Self-Defense Forces (see Table 1). A comparison of these findings with the record for the prewar and the immediate postwar periods reveals that previous experience in diplomatic and military service, as well as in the Ministry of Home Affairs, was more common to the careers of the earlier political leaders. In other words, familiarity with the issues involved in, if not expertise in, economic management has been an implicit requirement for successful political leaders in the past three decades.

The reason why macroeconomic management has been an important issue in postwar politics is not difficult to understand. Economic reconstruction following Japan's defeat in World War II was considered the most urgent of tasks. To catch up with the advanced Western countries and improve the standard of living were widely shared national aspirations. On the other hand, the Japanese shied away from the international struggle for power. The domestic political situation in Japan has been stable since 1955. The LDP has maintained power without interruption, though not without occasional disruption of its plans by the opposition.

Given the situation at home and abroad, economic management appeared "appropriate" as a political issue in postwar Japan. It diverted attention from the political stalemate, as well as from ideological antagonism. Hayato Ikeda tried to soothe the tensions brought about by heated debate and mass mobilization concerning the revision of the U.S.-Japan Mutual Security Treaty by concentrating upon the National Income-Doubling Plan—a typical case of substituting economics for politics.

There is no doubt that many political leaders regarded macroeconomic management as an important political issue. But it is another thing to assert that politics was an important factor in macroeconomic manage-

TABLE 1
Previous Cabinet Positions of Prime Ministers, 1956-1984

Prime minister	Minister of finance	Minister of int'l trade and industry	Minister of foreign affairs	Minister of defense	Party general secretary
Nakasone		X		X	X
Suzuki					
Ohira	X	X	X		X
Fukuda	X		X		X
Miki		X	X		X
Tanaka	X	X			X
Sato	X	X			X
Ikeda	X	X			X
Kishi		X	X		X
Ishibashi	X	X			

ment. It may be that the bureaucracy, not political leaders, formed and executed Japanese economic policy. It may be that macroeconomic policies were not, in fact, effective and that the policy statements of politicians and bureaucrats were ornamental rather than substantive. In order to assess the political aspects of economic management, we must further analyze the process of macroeconomic management.

Goal Setting in Macroeconomic Management

The official Japanese government plans summarize the goals of macroeconomic management in the respective cabinets. The changes in policy emphasis over time can be seen in Table 2. On the domestic front, growth maximization in the National Income-Doubling Plan approved in 1960 by the Ikeda cabinet gave way to stable and balanced growth in succeeding plans. Improving the quality of life has also attracted increasing attention over time. On the international front, general policy objectives shifted from self-support in the 1950s to international cooperation in the 1970s and 1980s.

The procedure behind economic planning has become routine. Each cabinet asks the Economic Council (an advisory organ to the prime minister consisting of leaders of business, finance, trade unions, and other organizations, scholars, and journalists) to suggest the basic themes of the plan and to prepare a draft. The Economic Council sets up subcommittees and special study groups and invites temporary members of the council to participate in its deliberations. The Economic Planning Agency (EPA) serves as secretariat for the council. The initial draft prepared by the EPA is circulated among the ministries concerned with its review and revision; at the same time, it is presented to the subcommittees for discussion. Thus, consensus formation occurs at two levels simultaneously. When the Economic Council presents its draft of the plan to the cabinet, it is usually approved as the official plan without major alteration. Data on the numbers of committees and persons involved in preparing the Outlook and Guidelines for the Economy and Society in 1983 provide an idea on the numbers involved in this process. In this case, there were 27 standing members on the council, 232 temporary members were added, and 14 subcommittees and study groups were established for the 13-month deliberation period.

Economic plans encompass only the general orientation of economic policy. They do not describe in detail how the plans will be implemented or which policy instruments will be utilized. At times, important policy decisions are made without strict adherence to the plan, and in such cases, it is the plan that must be revised. Still, the process of economic planning with its emphasis on reaching a consensus is typical of policy formation in Japan. The process fits well the model of patterned pluralism with its wide scope of participants and deep contacts among the ministries and organizations involved. On the other hand, consensus is often achieved by authorizing the status quo. This approach deprives economic policy of its efficacy in coping with change. This creates a dilemma, and how the dilemma is (or is not) resolved reveals the character of political leadership in macroeconomic management.

Let us examine the case where the objective of maximizing economic growth, advocated by Prime Minister Hayato Ikeda, was replaced by a policy of stable growth. Prime Minister Eisaku Sato, who succeeded Ikeda in 1964, had long been a critic of his rival and predecessor's growth-maximization policy. Sato advocated stable growth (or moderate growth with price stability) and social development. It may well be that these two goals conflict. In a sense, the political rivalry between two of Sato's political disciples, Takeo Fukuda (who stressed price stability) and Kakuei Tanaka (who called for larger public investment and promotion of welfare), centered around this conflict.

The Economic and Social Development Plan (1967), the first economic plan of the Sato cabinet, listed three policy goals: price stability, promotion of efficiency, and social development. Takeo Fukuda, minister of finance at the time, favored moderate growth with price stability. MOF bureaucrats supported his position, as did a group of business leaders, including Kazutaka Kikawada, president of Tokyo Electric Company (the largest firm in Japan) and the standing representative of the Keizai Doyukai (an active business executives' forum), who had been recently appointed chairman of the Economic Council.

Along with price stability, business leaders supported the promotion of efficiency. Their hope was to strengthen the stability of firms by avoiding the excessive competition prevalent during high-growth periods and by promoting mergers, voluntary cooperation, and the coordination of investment programs in order to cope with the impending liberalization of capital transactions. Efficiency promotion was seen as an alternative to the Temporary Law for Promotion of Specified Industries proposed by the Ministry of International Trade and Industry (MITI) but opposed by financial leaders and the MOF on the basis that it was interventionist. Social development was written into the plan, but only in general terms. Thus, the formulation of the plan proceeded as if the support of the ruling triad had been obtained.

Although Japanese economic growth was higher under Sato's moderate growth policy than under the growth-maximization policy of the Ikeda cabinet, Sato's policy was characterized by a relatively stable money supply, a limited dependence on the issuance of national bonds, and a low variability in changes in prices and income. Sato's plan went awry

TABLE 2
Selected Features of Economic Plans in Postwar Japan

Features of plan	Five-Year Plan for Economic Self-Support	New Long-Range Economic Plan	National Income-Doubling Plan	Medium-Term Economic Plan
Date published	Dec. 1955	Dec. 1957	Dec. 1960	Jan. 1965
Cabinet at the time of plan approval	Hatoyama	Kishi	Ikeda	Sato
Plan period (FY)	1956-60	1958-62	1961-70	1964-68
Economic growth rate (FY)				
Performance prior to the plan	1952-55: 8.6%	1953-57: 7.3%	1956-60: 9.1%	1960-64: 11.3%
Projection in the plan	1956-60: 5.0%	1958-62: 6.5%	1961-70: 7.8%	1964-68: 8.1%
Actual performance	1956-60: 8.7%	1958-62: 9.9%	1961-70: 10.7%	1964-68: 10.6%
Method of projection	Colm method (Labor × productivity)	Desirable balance chosen from 3 cases with different growth rates	Growth rate previously decided	Econometric model
Plan objectives	Self-support of the economy; full employment	Maximize growth; improve national life; full employment	Maximize growth; improve national life; full employment	Rectify imbalances
Major policy objectives	Modernize production facilities; promote international trade; reduce dependence on imports; encourage savings	Improve infrastructure; heavy industrialization; promote exports; encourage savings	Improve social overhead capital; improve industrial structure; rectify the dual structure of the economy; improve social stability	Modernize low-productivity sectors; make efficient use of labor force; improve quality of national life

SOURCES: Japan, Economic Planning Agency, Planning Bureau. *Nihon keizai shihyō* (Indicators of the Japanese economy), and idem, *Keizai hakusho*. (White paper on the economy), various issues.

Economic and Social Development Plan	New Economic and Social Development Plan	Basic Economic and Social Plan	Economic Plan for the Second Half of the 1970s	New Economic and Social Development Seven-Year Plan
Mar. 1967	Apr. 1970	Feb. 1973	May 1976	Aug. 1979
Sato	Sato	Tanaka	Miki	Ohira
1967-71	1970-75	1973-77	1976-80	1979-85
1962-66: 10.0%	1965-69: 12.7%	1968-72: 10.4%	1971-75: 5.1%	1974-78: 4.0%
1967-71: 8.2%	1970-75: 10.6%	1973-77: 9.4%	1976-80: a little more than 6%	1979-85: 5.7%
1967-71: 10.9%	1970-75: 5.9%	1973-77: 4.2%	1976-78: 5.7%	—
Econometric model	Econometric model	Econometric model	Econometric model	Econometric model
Attain balanced and steady economic development	Construct an admirable society through balanced economic growth	Promote national welfare, international cooperation	Realize a richer national life and stable development of the country's economy	Shift to a stable growth path; enrich quality of national life; contribute to the development of the international economic community
Stabilize prices; improve economic efficiency; promote social development	Improve economic efficiency from an international viewpoint; stabilize prices; promote social development; maintain adequate economic growth; cultivate foundations of development	Create a comfortable environment; secure a stable and comfortable life; stabilize prices; promote international cooperation	Stabilize prices and secure full employment; stabilize life and create favorable living environment; cooperate with and contribute to the development of the world economy; secure economic security and foster grounds for long-term development	Attain full employment and price stabilization; stabilize and enrich national life; cooperate in and contribute to the development of the world economy and society; ensure economic security and foster the foundations of further development; reconstruct public finance and new monetary responses

when surpluses in the current-account balance occurred toward the end of the 1960s. The tight money policy implemented in 1969 to prevent prices from further rising accelerated the accumulation of foreign exchange. The original policy of moderate growth and price stability was replaced by a new strategy aimed at expanding domestic demand in an effort to restore international equilibrium while promoting welfare. This strategy was adopted in the New Economic and Social Development Plan and further accelerated under the Tanaka cabinet. Some politicians and opinion leaders virtually ignored price stability and advocated "adjustment inflation." MOF and BOJ bureaucrats, traditionally supporters of fiscal orthodoxy and price stabilization, now opportunistically followed this expansive course.

As inflation developed and became substantially worse after the oil shock of 1973, price stability was again pursued, this time under the leadership of Takeo Fukuda, who served as minister of finance, director general of the EPA, and vice–prime minister in the Tanaka and Miki cabinets. Later, as prime minister, Fukuda faced the problem of recovering from stagflation. He expanded public expenditures in response to foreign pressure on Japan to play the role of locomotive in rescuing the world from the post–oil shock recession; still, the importance of attaining price stability as a policy goal was maintained. Fukuda's successor as prime minister, Masayoshi Ohira, also pursued this goal but used a slightly different set of policy instruments to cope with the second oil shock in 1979. Sato's apparent foresight concerning moderate growth and price stability proved correct, but only after repeated inflation in the 1970s.

What political forces pushed the ascendancy of price stability as one of the supreme goals of macroeconomic management? No one favored the kind of inflation Japan experienced in 1973–74, and the Bank of Japan pursued a tight monetary policy with the severity of a penitent. The fact remains, however, that the bureaucracy, including the BOJ, was responsible for pursuing an expansionary policy prior to the first oil shock. The spring wage negotiations of 1974 brought an increase in wage rates of 32.9 per cent compared with a price rise of 26.2 per cent over the previous year. This concession by entrepreneurs strongly suggests that business executives anticipated continued inflation. In fact, the deep recession in 1974–75 can best be explained as a result of the frustrated anticipations of business leaders who had foreseen continued inflation. Unexpected declines in the rate of inflation, increases in income, and changes in other economic indicators brought about an unintended accumulation of inventories, surplus labor, and unutilized production capacities. Many interest groups were opposed to inflation, but the process of disinflation, accompanied by considerable sacrifices, carried greater costs than narrow interest-group politics could bear.

It seems appropriate to look to political leadership and the general public to explain the increasing importance of price stability as a policy goal. Takeo Fukuda became minister of finance after the sudden and unexpected death of his predecessor, Kiichi Aichi. The LDP suffered a serious setback in the 1974 upper-house elections. Whether this poor electoral showing resulted from the problems of inflation, as interpreted by Tanaka himself, or from other reasons is the subject of debate. Business leaders who had been planning to demand the relaxation of stringent measures quickly changed their minds, and in the first cabinet meeting following the election, the government decided to continue these measures. The headlines of the *Nihon keizai shimbun*, in the weeks preceding and following the election on July 7, 1974, show the change in the policy climate attributed to the electoral defeat of the LDP.

In general, the bureaucracy seemed to continue its stand on stringency. The bureaucracy, however, is usually reluctant to change the policy orientation, at least in its public pronouncements, perhaps because it fears that such a change might be interpreted as the failure of the preceding policy, which the bureaucracy had hitherto executed. Furthermore, some flexibility in implementing the stringency measures was suggested before the election, and business and political leaders (except Fukuda) seemed to be eager for relaxation.[15]

The government continued its anti-inflationary policy stance, despite the expectation among businessmen that it would abandon the tight money policy after the election. With their expectations unrealized, many hard-pressed businessmen were forced to make a serious attempt at "rationalization" (cost reduction)—and most succeeded. On the political front, dissatisfaction within the LDP with the Tanaka cabinet mounted after the electoral defeat.

The reorientation of policy priorities is a complicated process. Let me briefly summarize the above observations: (1) bureaucrats tended to change their attitude rather opportunistically according to circumstances; (2) business leaders participated in the process primarily when they felt threatened by a crisis; (3) changes in political leadership usually brought changes in priorities; and (4) drastic changes in policy priorities followed changes in political leadership resulting from the outcome of elections. These observations, I maintain, attest that what was at work was neither narrow interest-group politics nor elitist domination, but majoritarian leadership.[16]

The Rules of Macroeconomic Management

Economic plans remain vague and noncommittal concerning their implementation, partly because of the compartmentalized structure of administrative organization in Japan. Any ministry that controls its own policy instruments does not like to submit to EPA guidance. As for macroeconomic management, two important policy tools, fiscal and monetary policies, are under the control of the Ministry of Finance and the Bank of Japan. These highly respected organs are unwilling to submit to the planning bureau or any other organ.

Historically, the range of choice in available macroeconomic policy instruments depended on rules rather than discretion. Particularly during the period of high growth, a set of fairly strict rules for macroeconomic management existed. These rules became obsolete in the 1970s, causing great confusion and disruption in macroeconomic management. In the 1980s, however, the establishment of a new set of rules is under way. The roles of bureaucrats, interest groups, business leaders, political leaders, and the general public have also changed in response to new circumstances.

Four primary rules applied to macroeconomic management during the period of high economic growth: (1) a fixed exchange rate of 360 yen per dollar, (2) money supply expansion as far as the ceiling of international payments (under fixed exchange rates) allowed, (3) balanced budgets in the central government, and (4) a constant tax burden of around 20 per cent of national income. Some of these rules were formally enacted as law; Article 4 of the Public Finance Law, for example, prohibits the issuance of national bonds except for public construction, an exception the government did not take advantage of until 1966. Others have been officially declared, such as the Government Tax Councils' announcement in its 1960 report to the cabinet that the tax burden should be kept below 20 per cent of national income. The maintenance of a fixed exchange rate was regarded as an obligation under the IMF system.

Adherence to the first two rules brought about a monetary policy aimed at expanding the domestic money supply while keeping international reserves as small as possible and at curtailing the money supply whenever the balance of international payments deteriorated. The working of this system resembled that of the gold standard, in which the balance of international payments determined the domestic money supply.[17] The last two rules established the fiscal orthodoxy of a balanced budget and small government. The rules of macroeconomic management employed during the high-growth period were classical rather than Keynesian.

These guidelines originated from the stabilization policy in effect during 1948 and 1949 under the direction of Joseph Dodge, an adviser to the Occupation forces. A self-made proponent of classical economics, Dodge earnestly persuaded the Japanese to uphold orthodoxy. Dodge's legacy was long-lived, primarily because the devastating postwar inflation left a strong impression on the Japanese.

The application of these rules had several benefits and effects. The knowledge that macroeconomic policy would adhere to these rules greatly facilitated expectation formation in business and the public sector, and minimized political antagonism in the day-to-day exercise of economic management. In addition, although there was experimentation with activist policies, such as large-scale fiscal expansion and tax reduction (Ishibashi cabinet, 1956–57) and lowered interest rates (Ikeda cabinet, 1960–61), policies were changed in accordance with the guidelines regarding the fixed exchange rate and the money supply expansion as soon as the balance of payments deteriorated. As a result of government policies seeking to maintain international competitiveness, the rate of inflation was contained within a reasonable limit. During the high-growth period, consumer prices rose between 5 and 6 per cent annually, and wholesale prices (export prices in particular) remained stable.

These guidelines were abandoned during the latter half of the 1960s and the first half of the 1970s. In the face of mounting current-account surpluses around 1970, adherence to the fixed exchange rate and to policy rules governing the expansion of the money supply became increasingly difficult and counterproductive. In order to prevent inflation at a time of current-account surpluses (a violation of the money supply expansion guideline), the Bank of Japan raised the discount rate in 1969. The BOJ's stringency caused even greater surpluses in the current account. The Japanese government and the Bank of Japan returned to expansive policies (while maintaining the fixed exchange rate) in 1970, in an attempt to promote increased domestic welfare, as well as to balance the current account. These efforts did not attain their declared objectives and merely stimulated domestic inflation. Politicians and bureaucrats were obstinately trying to apply the existing rules to changed circumstances.

The first departure from the principle of a balanced budget occurred in spring 1966, when the Sato government cut expenditures by 10 per cent in order to maintain a balanced budget when tax revenues fell short of expectations. As a result, the recession deepened. By summer, the government had decided to embark on an expansive course, including a national bond issue. On this occasion, the decision was implemented swiftly. Takeo Fukuda, then the minister of finance, played a central role. Fukuda was also responsible for raising the ceiling imposed on the tax burden. The Economic and Social Development Plan called for a gradual increase in the tax burden to 23 per cent of national income.

Fukuda must have believed that as the Japanese economy went into a period of moderate growth and autonomous increases in tax revenue due to rapid growth could no longer be expected, an increase in the tax burden and a new dependence on government bond issues became unavoidable. Since the Japanese were more affluent in the late 1960s than in the preceding decade, a reasonable increase in the tax burden could be tolerated economically and politically.

The abandonment of the balanced budget principle did not signal an era of outright disregard for fiscal discipline. During the latter half of the 1960s, MOF bureaucrats led by Kotaro Murakami, director general of the Budget Bureau and vice-minister of finance, attempted to restrict the expansion of public expenditures under the slogan of reducing fiscal rigidities. The movement was suspended, however, when a policy of domestic expansion was adopted in order to restore the international equilibrium.

The process of establishing new rules and guidelines for monetary policy differed from that for fiscal policy. As already mentioned, the monetary policy rules successful during the 1960s brought about rapid inflation when applied under the changed circumstances of the 1970s. Earlier experience, however, enabled a smooth transformation to new rules. Following the international replacement of fixed exchange rates with floating rates in 1973, the Bank of Japan officially recognized the importance of controlling the growth rate of the money supply.[18] The new monetary policy rules, accompanied with an increased emphasis on price stability as a policy goal, were widely supported.

Immediately following the oil price increase and embargo in 1973, the Diet passed several emergency bills that empowered the government to impose price and quantity controls on petroleum and other important products. Prenotification systems regarding price changes were introduced for 59 important items. These controls, however, were short-lived. Etsusaburo Shiina, vice-president of the LDP and a former Ministry of Commerce and Industry official who had experienced the effects of wartime economic controls, reportedly commented: "Once you begin economic control, you have to fix the price of flowerpots." His pithy remark helped cool the passion for administrative control.

The Japanese government has never formally adopted an incomes policy. Still, some believe that a Japanese-style incomes policy was effective in bringing about wage restraints. Fukuda had publicly promised to reduce the inflation rate to below 15 per cent by the end of FY 1974 and to less than 10 per cent by 1975, while urging labor union leaders to cooperate with the government by restraining wage demands. To what extent the government and labor unions negotiated behind closed doors remains unknown.[19] In any case, it is doubtful that the leaders of national-level labor organizations with contacts in government could exert much influence over the enterprise-level trade unions where the powers to bargain lie. National labor leaders sought to obtain a public commitment from the government concerning price stabilization, in order to save face when forced to retreat from their high wage demands.

Both price controls and the so-called Japanese-style incomes policy (if it ever existed) ceased to be important in dealing with the inflation that resulted from the increase in oil prices in 1979. The price situation before the oil price increases, as well as the personalities and styles of the political leaders, differed from those in 1973: Prime Minister Ohira kept aloof from interventionist measures, and orthodox monetary control prevailed.

In early 1980, Ohira and BOJ president Haruo Maekawa agreed to raise the official discount rate in order to prevent the resurgence of inflation expected to follow the increase in oil prices of the preceding year, although such a measure, at that time, would have an adverse effect on the budgetary debate in the Diet.[20] The authority of the Bank of Japan was increased when the goal of price stability was reached and the new rules of monetary management were established.

In contrast to the relatively smooth transition to new monetary management guidelines, the establishment of new rules for fiscal policy was difficult, although the departure from the old guidelines was complete. The Tanaka cabinet decided to reduce the income tax burden by ¥2 trillion immediately before the oil price hike in 1973, to compensate for the loss of real income caused by inflation, and thereby reduce public discontent. A sharp recession in the succeeding years widened the fiscal deficit, and the government's dependence on bond issues increased. In the mid-1970s, fiscal expansion was urged in order to stimulate domestic demand, to cooperate with international efforts to pull the world out of stagflation, and to mitigate the expected adverse effects of appreciation of the yen. After initial resistance, the Ministry of Finance decided to launch a "final operation" to expand domestic demand. Prime Minister Fukuda advocated stimulative measures; Ohira, as minister of finance, resisted them. Bond revenues accounted for over 30 per cent of the total revenues of the central government in 1977, an upper limit that the Ministry of Finance insisted should be maintained.

At the same time, the Ministry of Finance began to campaign for an increase in tax revenues to restore the fiscal balance. The Economic Council incorporated the same idea in its draft of the New Economic and Social Development Seven-Year Plan, which the Ohira cabinet approved in summer 1979. When the Diet was dissolved in fall 1979, however, rank and file LDP politicians complained that they could not possibly win the election while maintaining such an unpopular policy. The media, which were opposed to the contemplated tax increase, sensationalized the scandals within officialdom, particularly the inappropriate use of official travel expenses. As a result, public opinion became more and more critical of a tax increase. Ohira abandoned his tactics and began to emphasize administrative reform instead of a tax increase, but in vain. The October 1979 elections were a severe setback for the LDP. The introduction of a general consumption tax, at least for the time being, was politically unfeasible. The electoral defeat of the LDP may not be attributable solely to the unpopular tax policy. It may well be that bad weather, for example, was more responsible for its poor showing. In any case, the results were interpreted as a rejection of the proposal to increase the tax on consumer goods.

After Ohira's sudden death, administrative reform, combined with fiscal reconstruction without a tax increase, became the main policy direction of the Suzuki and Nakasone cabinets. The movement toward administrative reform was further accelerated by five factors.

1. Because of an unexpected sharp recession in 1980–81, budget deficits rose sharply. The revenue shortfall approached ¥10 billion yen over the two-year period. Expectations of increased tax revenue and an early business recovery went unrealized. MOF and EPA bureaucrats were widely criticized for their apparent misforecast of expected tax revenues. Reductions in public expenditures were singled out as the principal means of balancing the budget.

2. MOF bureaucrats introduced "zero ceilings" (and negative ceilings)—no increase or a reduction—on public expenditures as a means of reducing expenditures, as well as of implementing administrative reform. "Incrementalism," as the basis of compartmentalized bureaucracy, and "canalized" interest group politics (each group applying political pressure through established channels) was replaced by "decrementalism." The Temporary Administrative Research Council (Rinchō), unable to find more effective ways to reduce the deficits, entered into a de facto coalition with MOF bureaucrats and other supporters of administrative reform.

3. Businessmen felt their position was being seriously threatened by a proposed increase in the corporate tax rate in place of a general consumption tax. They were also alarmed by the mounting fiscal deficit and its possible adverse effect on the economy as a whole. Given its own success in reducing costs in the 1970s, business demanded that the budget be trimmed by cutting wasteful expenditures. Although some business leaders complained of expenditure reductions that affected their businesses directly, the overwhelming call from business was for administrative reform. Toshio Doko, president of Keidanren (Federation of Economic Organizations), agreed to serve as the chairman of the Temporary Administrative Research Council, and Ryuzo Sejima, vice-chairman of the Itoh Chu Shoji Company and a friend of Prime Minister Nakasone's, and others participated as members of the council.

4. Public opinion greatly favored administrative reform over expansive fiscal policy.

5. Prime Minister Zenko Suzuki appointed Yasuhiro Nakasone director general of the Administrative Agency, the agency responsible for administrative reform. Although in a politically risky position, Nakasone succeeded in persuading Doko to become chairman of the Temporary Administrative Research Council, thus securing the support of business circles and setting administrative reform in motion. Under Prime Minister Nakasone, administrative reform can be regarded as the cabinet's central political goal.

The Nakasone cabinet has stated that fiscal balance should be restored by 1990. There is a long way yet to go toward achieving this goal. It is difficult to predict whether fiscal stringency will remain in effect for some years to come. In any case, the process of abandoning the old rules of macroeconomic management and establishing new ones confirms the conclusion reached at the end of the preceding section. As is the case with the goal-setting process, bureaucrats tend to behave rather opportunistically, and business leaders seem to intervene only when they feel their position is threatened. The final decision concerning the guidelines for macroeconomic management depend on the leadership of the prime minister and on public opinion as expressed in elections.

The Politics of Sectoral Economic Management

Policy Formulation

Sectoral economic management is often regarded as a more important factor than macroeconomic management in explaining Japanese economic performance. According to Ryutaro Komiya, the macroeconomic plans of the Japanese government are predictive or indicative at best, but many sectoral plans are effectively implemented.[21] Peter Katzenstein pointed to the use of "a formidable set of policy instruments which directly influence individual industries and firms" as an important feature of Japanese economic policy.[22] Katzenstein apparently assumes that sectoral policy measures are integrated into a set of policies that serves a given macroeconomic purpose. In this section, I discuss who makes sectoral economic policy, how intersectoral conflicts are resolved, and the relationship between the goals of macroeconomic management and sectoral economic management.

The existing models of the Japanese political economy hold up rather well when we examine the formation of sectoral economic policies. The influence of the bureaucracy is certainly strong and visible. The deep-rooted sectionalism and the compartmentalized administration, which make it difficult to accept the bureaucracy-led model as an explanation of macroeconomic management, strengthen that model's explanatory power in regard to sectoral economic management. In several areas, the bureaucracy appears to dominate the formulation and execution of policies.

The bureaucracy-led model, however, does not take into account the activities of interest groups and politicians. This is a serious shortcoming since the importance of the members of the ruling party has generally been increasing relative to that of the bureaucracy. The influence of politicians has increased as parliamentary rule has matured in Japan, and they have acquired the skills necessary for economic management as a result of their experience as members of the long-ruling party. Further explanation of this phenomenon is offered later.

The differences between the ruling-triad model and patterned pluralism diminish as the number of interest groups concerned with the economic activities of specific branches decreases. This is particularly the case when business—one pillar of the ruling triad—is replaced by interest groups. For example, the bureaucracy, politicians, and agricultural cooperatives (nōkyō) form the ruling triad of the agricultural sector, although business interests and consumer organizations are allowed to exert some influence.

More specifically, the roles played by the bureaucracy, interest groups, and politicians differ from sector to sector. Two types of codetermination can readily be observed. In many branches of industry, the collaboration between business and the bureaucracy (MITI) is conspicuous, but the influence of politicians is not so visible. On the other hand, the bureaucracy, interest groups, and politicians compete (among themselves *inside* the policymaking arena) but cooperate with one another (vis-à-vis all others *outside* the arena) in order to promote the interests of a specific sector, as is the case in agriculture. Generally stated, the former circumstance applies more often to growing industries, and the latter applies to declining (or slowly growing) sectors. The contrast may be attributable to an implicit agreement on the division of labor between bureaucrats and politicians. Bureaucrats, in cooperation with business interests, are entrusted with the task of promoting strategic sectors and nurturing the "seeds" of growth; politicians mainly exert their influence over distribution of the "fruits" of economic growth. The allocation of resources can be considered apolitical; income distribution is a political issue over which politicians exert some influence. Based on this implicit understanding, politicians, bureaucrats, and interest groups have formed a coalition; the LDP is therefore able to collect votes from rural areas while depending on big business for monetary support. Murakami's "politics of insulation" theory supports this assessment.[23] This assessment, however, does not help determine the relative roles of the actors in the respective sectors.

The relative importance of each of the actors is dynamic over time. The increasing role of politicians is not confined to the lagging sectors, but is also observable in the management of growing industries. In addition, the rate of growth within a sector is not the sole criterion for political intervention. The correlation may be indirect at best. The influence of politicians is greater when budgetary funds are involved, and, as Yukio Noguchi noted, public funds are used primarily to rectify the imbalances brought about by rapid economic growth, not to promote rapid growth.[24] The greater influence of politicians over the slow-growing sectors is a result of these budgetary policies. In any case, the extent of the politicians' influence varies widely, even among regulated industries such as banking, insurance, electricity, and transportation.

So far in this discussion, the roles of organized interest groups and politicians representing specific interests have been considered. The existing models, however, fail to accommodate or to emphasize sufficiently the role of the general public. This limitation can be overlooked if these models are used primarily in discussing sectoral economic management, but the limitation is a serious one if we are to use these models in discussing specific policies that are adopted even in the absence of strong interest groups, such as policies regarding housing. Real estate businesses, residents' unions, and consumer, labor, and business organizations are all interested in the government's housing policy, and there are politicians who advocate government support in this area.[25] In contrast to agriculture, however, these interest groups are not tightly organized, and political representation is not well formalized. Still, the number of low-interest loans made through the Housing Loan Corporation and subsidized by the general account has increased rather rapidly. An interesting point here is that government housing policy centers around the financing of owner-occupied housing, instead of rent subsidies to low-income families or public housing developments. That is, the government is subsidizing the efforts of unorganized middle-status citizens to build their own homes.[26] This situation can be best explained by hypotheses such as the median voter theorem, rather than by interest group politics.

Even in cases where specific interests are well organized and politically represented, public interests are not entirely disregarded. In spite of the strength of agricultural cooperatives and the widespread support for their demands among LDP politicians, the price of rice paid to producers has been increased only marginally since 1975, when the rice surplus became considerable (see below). Despite the strong opposition of the Japan Medical Association, in 1984 the Diet passed an amendment to the Public Health Insurance Law widely viewed as unfavorable to doctors.[27] Although the Ministry of Finance, one of the strongest sections of the Japanese bureaucracy, actively opposed price increases for rice and strongly supported the amendment to the Public Health Insurance Law in an attempt to keep fiscal outlays under control, these developments suggest that sectoral economic management is not entirely independent of macroeconomic management.

Conflict Resolution

The more powerful the sectoral ruling triads become, the more conflicts among sectors concerning economic management tend to increase, a development seen today. To resolve the conflicts and coordinate sectoral policies will not be easy. Not only are intersectoral conflicts increasing, but these conflicts are becoming increasingly difficult to resolve within the bureaucracy—the ruling party is much more effective in resolving them.

Sectional strife is as old as the bureaucracy itself. Today, however, conflicts tend to arise much more often across ministerial boundaries. Trade friction with another country, for example, induces the Ministry of Foreign Affairs to intervene in the ministry in charge of the industry involved. Greater technical complexities have increased the number of government organs concerned with sectoral policy. The emergence of new technology in telecommunications created serious conflicts between MITI and the Ministry of Posts and Telecommunications (MPT) over deregulation of the telecommunications industry. The long-standing conflict between the MOF and the MPT concerning postal savings took on a new dimension with technological innovations in the finance industry. The rapid scientific progress in the biochemical industry will affect agriculture (Ministry of Agriculture, Forestry, and Fisheries), industry (MITI), and the daily lives of the population (Ministry of Welfare). Furthermore, as Japan's economic growth slows, the struggle for limited fiscal resources will become severe—a situation approximating a "zero-sum game" in which distributional issues dominate.

The resolution of intersectoral conflicts has become an important task for the bureaucracy as a whole, as well as for the LDP. When consensus formation fails, the resulting *immobilisme* must somehow be remedied. The question of which institution, the bureaucracy or the political party, is better qualified to solve conflict cannot be answered with any confidence. As suggested by Masahiko Aoki, bargaining within the bureaucracy can be efficient, in view of their commonly shared code of behavior, language, regard for the national or public interest, and the like.[28] However, the existence of widespread sectionalism, coupled with deep-rooted institutional rigidity, often hampers the bureaucracy in its effort to arrive at an internal consensus. Political parties are more flexible in

organizational adaptability, and political leaders are better equipped to
deal with conflicts.

The political party has been increasingly called on to overcome intersectoral conflicts, and the influence of the LDP over sectoral economic
management, as well as over the resolution of intersectoral conflicts, has
increased. In 1983, the Ezaki Mission to the United States, headed by
Masumi Ezaki (a former minister of international trade and industry and
an influential politician) and consisting of LDP Diet members, provided
an impetus toward liberalization. The mission helped to overcome resistance from protectionist interest groups and some sections of the bureaucracy.[29] LDP leaders were also effective in resolving the conflict
between MITI and MPT concerning the reorganization of the Nippon
Telephone and Telegraph Public Corporation (NTT) in 1984.

There have been several attempts to explain the LDP's increased role.[30]
First, some politicians have acquired experience and influence in sectoral economic management (see the chapters by Muramatsu and Krauss
and by Eads and Yamamura in this volume). Such politicians, or *zoku*
("tribes"), include former bureaucrats, ex-ministers, ex–vice ministers
for political affairs, long-standing members of the LDP Policy Affairs Research Council (PARC), and so on. Bureaucrats can ill afford to ignore the
opinions of LDP members since they are instrumental in pushing policy
through the government and the party by persuading, say, the Ministry
of Finance and fellow LDP members of the Diet to cooperate on policy
matters.

Second, the PARC's authority has increased. It has become customary
for the relevant division and deliberation commission of PARC to review
the important decisions of each ministry before they become the subject
of public debate. An illustrative example is the LDP's Tax Research Council. Its influence surpasses that of the government Tax Research Council
(an advisory organ to the prime minister), once the primary authority on
tax policies and issues. The LDP often sets up special research committees and investigating commissions to cope with new and often cross-
sectional issues as circumstances demand. In other words, the LDP has
shown greater organizational flexibility in comparison with the relatively
rigid structure of the bureaucracy.

Third, a consensus on sectoral economic management can be forged
within the party with little difficulty. Because of intraparty factional
struggles, however, a policy issue involving major points of contention
among the factions often results in a policy *immobilisme*.[31] This is especially the case with diplomatic and macroeconomic policy issues involving
factional differences in ideological orientation. Consensus and compromise within the party are more easily attained on sectoral economic issues. Factional confrontatons can, however, be neutralized significantly

by party organization. Its mediation is effective because of the distribution of party posts among the factions. The chairman of PARC is usually not a member of the faction in power, and the five vice-chairmenships of the party are more or less distributed among the factions. Some factional conflicts can be resolved by a special commission (such as the LDP's Tax Research Council), by consensus among the vice-chairmen, or by a decision of the party executives.

However, conflicts may get out of control, especially when a quick response to changed circumstances is required. Whether the LDP can continue to resolve serious sectoral conflicts and succeed in retaining control in the coming decades remains to be seen.

Macroeconomics and Sectoral Economic Goals

Sectoral conflicts can be mitigated by compromise over the goals of sectoral and macroeconomic policies. The relationship of sectoral policy goals to macroeconomic goals can be classified in four ways: innovative, adaptive, redistributive, and protectionist.

1. Innovative relations can be established when a sector is regarded as pivotal in the pursuit of general economic policy goals. The promotion of growing sectors, for example, is regarded as a policy cornerstone when growth is a macroeconomic goal. Organizational innovation such as the privatization of Japan National Railways, deregulation of the telecommunications industry, or pension reform is regarded as a central concern when administrative reform is the goal. Each sector can attempt to sell itself as an innovative sector in order to obtain the support of the government and a larger share of the promotional measures.

2. Adaptive relations exist when the aim of sectoral economic management is to maintain harmony with macroeconomic management. The sectors in question do not claim to be strategic, but demand support for their efforts to accommodate themselves to the macroeconomic policy goals.

3. Redistributive relations result from a sector's inability or unwillingness to support, or adapt to, the higher-level objectives. When sectoral and overall economic goals conflict, these sectors demand compensation (income redistribution) for their recognition of given macroeconomic objectives. Redistributive measures are often disguised as promotive, as is the case with many of the subsidies to agriculture and small industry. On paper, subsidies are granted to increase productivity, but it is generally recognized that the effects of these measures are primarily distributive.

4. Protectionist relations are also the result of conflicts between sectoral and overall economic policy goals. Instead of adjustment or compen-

TABLE 3
Examples of Types of Sectoral Policy

Type of policy	Agriculture	Industry	Housing
Innovative		R&D support; promotion of growth industry	Japan Housing and Urban Development Corp.
Adaptive	Selective output expansion	Rationalization	Housing Loan Corp. (HLC)
Distributive	Price maintenance; income support	Low-rate loans to small business	Implicit subsidies to interest paid on HLC loans
Protectionist	Trade restriction	Secured sphere of activity for small business; prohibition of new entry by large-scale firms	

sation, the sectors involved attempt to prevent the overall economic policy from interfering with sectoral economic management. Declining, but politically powerful, industries often introduce protectionist measures.

These relations are illustrated in Table 3. The position of each sector depends on current economic conditions, the balance of political power, and the strategies of the agents of both macroeconomic and sectoral economic management.

During the rapid growth period, the promotion of the heavy and chemical industries was an innovative policy, and adaptive or redistributive policies were important with respect to agriculture, small industry, and services. The distinction corresponds to the division of labor among bureaucrats and politicians. The influence of the bureaucracy lies primarily in innovative policy; the influence of politicians is more visible in redistributive relations. The recent fiscal stringency is, however, making it more difficult for politicians to adopt and carry out distributional policies, and increased international integration of the economy has led to friction over protectionist sectoral policies. One of the main tasks of administrative reform today is to reassess the relative positions of sectoral economic policies, vis-à-vis macroeconomic and other policies, in order to better manage the economy in response to these developments.

Policy Instruments

The choice of policy instruments in sectoral economic management has some relation to sectoral goal setting. The instruments for sectoral economic management include special tax treatment, subsidies, allocation of public works, loans from government-affiliated financial organizations, administrative guidance, and regulation.

Special tax treatment. In the 1950s, special tax treatments were liberally granted to promote the modernization of specific industries. An example was the accelerated capital depreciation allowance selectively applied to strategic industries. It was an effective policy instrument of sectoral economic management. As initial objectives were attained, however, many special tax treatments were abolished or limited. Fiscal stringency in recent years has accelerated this tendency. Table 4 shows the size of special tax reductions during FY 1985.

Today, the most important target of special tax treatment is interest income earned by small savers' deposits in financial institutions and the Postal Savings system and by purchasers of national bonds. This measure has come under criticism for violating equity considerations. The total amount of "small" savings now stands at as much as ¥2 trillion; this figure suggests that the preferential treatment of these savings enables the rich to evade taxes. Some argue that appropriate revisions could generate a considerable amount of tax revenue. Making such revisions involves politically sensitive issues and was an important consideration in the budget process in recent years. The existence of strong pressure groups opposed to the revisions, such as the Bank Association and the Local Postmasters Federation, is part of the political difficulties. Furthermore, almost every household would be affected by the revision, as parsimony is still a common and highly valued practice among Japanese families. For these and other reasons, any attempt to make the revisions will encounter substantial political problems.

TABLE 4
Tax Reduction Due to Special Tax Treatments, FY 1985

Reason for reduction	Billion ¥	Per cent
Special treatment of interest and dividend income	568	37.2%
Exclusion of life insurance fees	237	15.5
Special income calculation of social insurance health care rewards	103	6.8
Other personal income tax deductions	211	13.8
Corporate tax deductions (accelerated depreciation, etc.)	406	26.6
TOTAL	1,525	100.0%

SOURCE: Ryūichirō Tachi, ed., *Korekara no zaisei to kokusai hakkō* (Public finance and national bond issues in coming years) (Tokyo: Ōkurazaimu Kyōkai, 1985.)

Another important target of special tax treatment is the formula used to calculate income from social insurance health care benefits. The formula is criticized as being excessively favorable to doctors, although physicians regard it as compensation for the low level of rewards imposed by the government on their profession. The Japan Medical Association, a potent pressure group, is involved in this debate.

Subsidies. Broadly defined, subsidies constitute about 30 per cent of the general account of the central government. They include transfers to local governments and contributions to the social security system, as well as current subsidies in the narrow sense (according to the national account definition) that finance the deficits of (or lower the expenses of) both public and private producers. According to the national accounts, in 1980 current subsidies amounted to some ¥3.5 trillion.

The largest proportion of agricultural subsidies result from the government's support of the producer price of rice.[32] The Foodstuff Control Law dictates that the price of rice paid to producers be determined on the basis of cost in order to maintain farmers' income. The same law requires that the price of rice paid by consumers be based on the household budgets of urban residents. There is no formal requirement on the relationship between the producers' price and the consumers' price. Only political and budgetary considerations can equate outlays and revenues by manipulation of cost calculations and other means. After annual negotiations between the MOF, the Ministry of Agriculture, Forestry, and Fisheries, and the EPA, revisions in the price of rice are proposed. The plan is then deliberated by the Rice Price Council and is finally settled after negotiations between LDP representatives and the ministers involved. Throughout the process, agricultural cooperatives press for a higher price for producers, and a large number of "rice legislators"— LDP Diet members from agricultural constituencies—support their demands. The Ministry of Agriculture, Forestry, and Fisheries is less than wholehearted in supporting the farmers' demands because increases in the subsidy mean that the ministry will have less to spend for other purposes, including agricultural development. The ministry is supported on this issue by the "comprehensive farm policy" faction of the LDP. The main issue in Japanese agriculture today is whether agricultural policy should be distributive-protective or innovative-adaptive. Undeniably, as the rice surplus grew and as fiscal restraints became more and more stringent, the influence of the groups supporting distributive-protective measures declined relative to that of the coalition supporting innovation and adaptation. Although the producer price of rice is five times greater than in other countries, it has remained virtually stable since 1975.

Another large portion of total subsidies goes to the Japan National Railways (JNR). Rationalization and reorganization (and eventual dissolution) of the JNR is now considered a necessary step in administrative reform. The move is supported by some influential LDP Diet members and business leaders, whose representative occupies the chair of the Supervisory Board of the JNR. Opposition to the move comes from trade unions and the Japan Socialist Party.

Public works. The funds for public works undertaken or financed by the central government attract competition among regional interests, as well as among construction firms. Politicians are called on to influence the allocation of the funds by such means as introducing a tax on gasoline to finance road construction. For politicians, the use of political influence is a means of retaining or increasing voter support, as well as a device to raise political funds. Michisada Hirose has presented persuasive evidence showing that the regional allocation of a specific public construction program was proportional to the votes acquired by the politicians, some of them ex-officials, who had the greatest influence over the allocation.[33] Hiromitsu Ishi, Seiritsu Ogura, and others argue that the allocation of public works is not based on efficiency, but is distorted by political influences; public money is apparently exchanged for votes.[34]

Of course, the effects of political influence and exact measurements of the resulting distortion are difficult to determine. On the one hand, the political distortion of the allocation of funds is not compatible with the notion that the Japanese government is a rational optimizer in pursuit of a single national objective. When used inefficiently, the "formidable set of policy instruments" of sectoral economic management may cause a formidable amount of waste. On the other hand, as is the case with the determination of the price of rice, in spite of the widely recognized strength of pressure groups (in construction and related industries) and politicians committed to public works expansion, fixed capital formation by the government remained stable in nominal terms and has declined only slightly in real terms since 1980, when the budget was tightened to decrease deficits. In short, macroeconomic considerations are prevailing over sectoral interests. A balanced and careful judgment is necessary to understand to what extent politicians and pressure groups are influencing the allocation of increasingly scarce public funds.

Government loans. The Fiscal Investment and Loan Program (FILP) is of great importance in Japanese economic management. Using funds generated by the huge accumulations of postal savings, the Japanese government is empowered to allocate funds to public corporations (such as the JNR or NTT) and local governments, as well as to the private sector through government-affiliated financial institutions (for example, the Japan Development Bank, the Small Business Finance Corporation, and the Agriculture, Forestry, and Fisheries Finance Corporation). A trend similar to that seen with special tax treatments is observable with respect to FILP. In the 1950s, the allocation of funds through FILP centered on the growth sector or basic industries. The bureaucracy, particularly the MOF, had complete control over the program at the time. It was not until 1972 that the Diet had to approve the annual plan of FILP. Today, however, FILP supplies financial assistance to a wider range of interests and industries. The share of FILP funds allocated to housing, environment, education, and welfare has increased, and the share for basic industries has continued to decline (see Table 5). FILP, once the innovative engine of growth, has become a distributive device.

Parallel with this change, the influence of politicians concerned with the distributive aspect of FILP seems to be increasing. Furthermore, FILP has become more and more intertwined with budgetary decision making. The Budget Bureau of the MOF tries to substitute FILP funds for general account expenditures, and the institutions connected with FILP demand subsidies to lower the rate of interest on their loans. As money market conditions ease, the merit of FILP, in the eyes of its beneficiaries, lies not in the amount of funds allocated to it, but in the low rate of interest it charges on its loans. Today, the difference between the rates charged by banks and by FILP has narrowed considerably. But to the extent differences still exist, politicians, who once focused on adding subsidies to the budget, are interested in FILP as a source of low-cost funds for their political clients.

TABLE 5

Composition of Fiscal Investment and Loan Program, FY 1970, 1980, and 1985

(per cent)

Program used for:	1970	1980	1985
Housing	19.3%	25.6%	25.4%
Living environment	11.6	13.4	15.7
Welfare institutions	2.8	3.1	2.8
Educational institutions	2.2	3.8	3.6
Small and medium-size firms	15.4	19.0	18.0
Agriculture, forestry, fishing	5.0	4.7	4.3
Land conservation and reconstruction	1.6	1.6	2.3
Roads	8.6	7.6	8.8
Transportation and communication	13.2	9.3	8.4
Regional development	4.0	2.5	2.4
Basic industries	5.7	3.0	2.9
Trade and economic aid	10.6	6.4	5.4
TOTAL	100.0%	100.0%	100.0%
	(¥3.580 trillion)	(¥20.703 trillion)	(¥20.858 trillion)

SOURCE: Japan, Ministry of Finance, *Zaisei kin'yū tōkei geppō* (Financial statistics monthly), various issues.

Administrative guidance and legislation. As a means of government intervention, important differences exist between the effects of fiscal measures and the effects of regulation. Financial intervention may often distort but seldom renders market price mechanisms completely ineffectual. Changes in relative prices, if large enough, do affect resource allocation even under a special tax-subsidy expenditure system. But price distortions, unlike regulation, do not prevent the working of price mechanisms. Regulation amounts to the imposition of prohibitive taxes, the distortive effects of which can be far greater. The difference is analogous to that between export promotion (usually by subsidy) and import substitution (primarily by quota). In theoretical analyses of economic development, the superiority of export promotion strategies over import substitution policies is widely recognized.

Regulation can be achieved through administrative guidance or legislation. Administrative guidance in Japanese sectoral economic management has attracted much attention. It is effective, however, only with the consent of those concerned. Consensus formation must precede administrative guidance if it is to achieve its aim.

There are several types of laws governing sectoral economic management: (1) basic laws, such as the Basic Law of Agriculture[35] or the Basic Laws of Small and Medium-Size Firms, that define broad policy objectives and the general responsibility of the government, without entering into the specific duties of any government agency; (2) public utility laws that determine how public utilities are to be regulated by their respective supervisory organs; (3) rationalization and/or promotion laws for specific industries that define the role of rationalization plans, government support measures, and exemptions from antimonopoly statutes for acts undertaken under these laws; (4) control laws for specific industries, such as the Petroleum Industry Law, that restrict new entry and new equipment investment or define price stabilization measures; (5) coordination of economic activities laws, such as the Export-Import Transaction Law and the Organization of Small and Medium-Size Firms Law,[36] aimed at resolving conflicts between specified private parties and government agencies or between governmental agencies; and (6) other statutes such as antimonopoly laws, environmental protection laws, and labor laws that affect sectoral economic management.

Some examples will illustrate cases of legislation and administrative measures in which political considerations play a major role and in which the market mechanism is impeded.

Agricultural protection. Studies on the levels of agricultural protection in advanced countries (see Table 6) show that the rate of protection is much higher in Japan than in other countries. Japanese agricultural protectionism is symbolized by beef and oranges. Agricultural cooperatives,

TABLE 6
Rate of Protection of Agriculture, Selected Countries,
1955, 1970, and 1980
(per cent)

Country	1955	1970	1980
United States	2	11	0
France	33	47	30
West Germany	35	50	44
United Kingdom	40	27	35
Japan	18	50	44

SOURCES: K. Anderson et al., *The Political Economy of Agricultural Protection: East Asia in International Perspective* (London: George Allen & Unwin, 1986); Yūjirō Hayami, *Nōgyō keizairon* (Agricultural economics) (Tokyo: Iwanami Shoten, 1986), table 6-6.

NOTE: The rate of agricultural protection is agricultural output at domestic prices minus agricultural output at international prices divided by the latter.

consumer unions, and political parties unanimously agree that protection should be continued.

So far, agricultural trade friction between Japan and the United States has been reduced by increasing the Japanese import quota.[37] In order to reach a settlement, the prime minister had to show a firm determination to resolve the friction. The LDP representatives most strongly opposed to liberalization went to the United States to appeal their cause and then persuaded their colleagues and the pressure groups to consider a compromise. The bureaucracy worked toward a compromise but was unable to take the initiative because the various ministries and sections, each backed by pressure groups and politicians who feared a governmental betrayal, failed to agree among themselves.

Protection of small and medium-size businesses. A recent trend is to enact legislation restricting the entry of large-scale firms into areas where small and medium-size firms currently enjoy large market shares. The Large-Scale Store Regulation Law, enacted in 1973, allows the opening of large retail stores (such as department stores and supermarkets) in a neighborhood only with the prior consent of small retailers in the area. Two laws enacted in 1977, the Coordinating Sphere of Activities Law and the Small and Medium-Size Business Cooperatives Law, allow small business cooperatives to appeal to the relevant ministries to restrict the sphere of activities of large-scale businesses or to negotiate directly with large-scale enterprises to reach a mutually satisfactory agreement. These are two typical cases in which political pressure resulted in protectionist legislation. In each case, bureaucrats tried in vain to persuade politicians, pressure groups, and the public to abandon the intended legislation by promising full use of administrative guidance to achieve a similar end. The politicians who distrusted "flexible" administrative guidance chose to enact laws or had the party organs involved adopt resolutions that enforced the exact terms of the regulation.[38]

Emergency controls. Immediately following the oil shock of 1973, the Diet passed several emergency bills that authorized the government to control the prices of petroleum and other important products in order to suppress speculation, and the cabinet requested prior notification of intended changes in the price of important producer goods. In 1979–80, when oil prices again rose sharply, the enactment of emergency measures was an issue for debate, and the opposition attacked the Ohira cabinet for rejecting emergency price controls.

Fiscal measures, combined with administrative guidance, have been utilized more extensively than protectionist legislation in Japanese sectoral economic management. This fact reflects the high level of the consensus on overall economic goals and demonstrates a general preference for innovative, adaptive, and redistributive goal setting in sectoral policies over protectionist ones. As intersectoral conflicts arise more often and as the influence of politicians becomes greater, however, protectionist measures supported by politicians and interest groups may increase further.

Economic Management Under Changing Circumstances

After reaching a peak in economic growth in the 1960s and overcoming the oil shocks of the 1970s, Japan now faces new challenges. Domestic and international circumstances, both political and economic, are changing rapidly.

As noted in the preceding sections, the leadership in economic management, both at the macro- and microeconomic levels, has tended to shift from bureaucrats to politicians. This trend will continue, as can be expected in a parliamentary democracy where legitimacy lies with elected politicians. In addition, politicians have acquired the necessary skills, through experience, for effective economic management.

Although the dominance of the LDP is well established, many observers have detected signs of increasing political instability stemming from increased urbanization and affluence. Although more people support the conservatives today than ever before, probably because of increased affluence, that support is less dependable than in previous decades. Reasons for this include urbanization, which has uprooted traditional community relationships and ties, and the decline in ideological commitment. The majority of LDP politicians may find, from time to time, that retaining their seats in the Diet is far from easy because a large number of their supporters choose not to vote, as was the case in 1980 and

1984. Within the LDP, each faction is becoming more tightly organized, mostly because cabinet positions and the party's leadership posts are allocated among factions according to size. At the same time, some of the opposition parties have abandoned many of their earlier ideological commitments and have become more flexible and pragmatic, creating the possibility that coalitions between LDP factions and some of the opposition parties may be formed. As the opposition parties and possible future coalition partners intervene more effectively in economic management, the inevitable result is likely to be greater politicization of economic management and political instability.

On the other hand, new constraints have emerged, particularly in the form of budget deficits and increased international responsibilities. The deficits of the central government remain large and are expected to increase as the population ages. Because of the deficits, public expenditures have been severely restrained, and a zero or minus ceiling has been imposed on the budget. Bureaucratic incrementalism has now become "decrementalism." More LDP politicians have come to believe that their party, as the "responsible" party, should determine the size and priorities of policy programs and not depend on the bureaucracy to trim the budget. The zero ceiling advocated by the bureaucracy deprives LDP Diet members of the chance to intervene in the budgetary process. Brighter growth prospects and technological innovations may intensify political pressure on the budget. To what extent LDP leaders can take the initiative in formulating budgetary policy remains to be seen.

Japan's position in the world community has changed substantially. Japan is no longer a "small" country and is accumulating a huge current trade surplus. It has been asked to liberalize trade and capital transactions, to adopt a more internationalized institutional framework, and to expand foreign aid and defense expenditures. However unpopular they may be at home, if actions satisfying these international demands are not taken, the existence of effective and efficient leadership will increasingly be questioned.

Simply put, the large budget deficit and the substantial current trade surplus highlight the need to better balance saving and investment at home. The trade-offs involved are complicated. Internationalization of the capital market deprives the monetary authorities of the power, or the will, to manipulate the rate of interest to stimulate domestic private demand. If the domestic saving rate remains high, reducing budget deficits may induce greater capital outflows. In order to balance saving and investment, difficult choices must be made among increased productive investment, expanded public works, large capital exports, and lowered private saving rates. The corresponding political and economic policy instruments, such as the lowering of domestic interest rates, tax-subsidy incentives for investment, issuance of construction bonds, and increased social welfare payments, must be implemented simultaneously.

Increased affluence, accumulating government debts, increased international capital transactions, and technological developments have significantly changed the structure of the Japanese economy. In the financial market, these factors forced the authorities to abandon the regulation of interest rates and institutional segmentation within the capital market. Increasingly affluent investors have become less risk averse, and investors are now more concerned with yields than with liquidity or safety. Instead of indirect financing that tended to rely on credit rationing based on the long-standing relationship between lenders and borrowers, open security markets where interest rate arbitrage occurs freely, even across national borders, are developing (see Table 7).

In the labor market, the participation rate of female workers is rising rapidly, particularly in the form of part-time employees in the service industry. Female workers tend to make "hit-and-run" entry and exit in response to labor market conditions. On the other hand, the ratio of trade union membership to total employment is declining, as the number of employees in large-scale manufacturing industries declines. The labor market has become more important, even in Japan where the labor market within each firm—as discussed fully by Koike in this volume—is well developed (see Table 8).

Increased consumption of mass-produced consumer durables has given way to more sophisticated, individualized consumer goods. The

TABLE 7
Indexes of Changing Financial Markets, 1970 and 1980
(per cent)

Index	1970	1980
Financial assets/annual income (personal sector)[a]	115%	125%
Prospective yield as a determinant of portfolio selection (compared with liquidity and safety)[b]	8.6[c]	24.2
Government bonds/GNP	4.9	30.0
Marketable securities/national financial assets[d]	13.0	26.7

[a]Japan, Office of the Prime Minister, Bureau of Statistics, *Chochiku dōkō chōsa* (Survey on family savings), annual.

[b]Proportion of households who chose "yield" as the most important determinant in portfolio selection compared with liquidity and safety. Chochiku Zōkyō Iinkai (Committee for Savings Promotion), *Chochiku ni kansuru yoron chōsa* (Public opinion surveys on saving), annual.

[c]1971.

[d]Japan, Economic Planning Agency, *National Accounts Yearbook*.

Indexes of Changing Labor Markets, 1970-1980

Index	1970	1975	1980
Female participation rate[a]	49.9%	43.0%	47.6%
Share of service industry employees[a]	46.7%	52.1%	55.4%
Trade union membership rate[b]	35.0%	34.1%	30.5%
Employees of large-scale manufacturing industries (per 10,000 persons)[c]	413	402	365

SOURCES:

[a]Japan, Office of the Prime Minister, Bureau of Statistics, *Rōdōryoku chōsa* (Labor force survey), various issues.

[b]Japan, Ministry of Labor, *Rōdō kumiai kihon chōsa* (Basic survey on trade unions), various issues.

[c]Japan, Ministry of International Trade and Industry, *Kōgyō tōkei hyō* (Census on manufacturers), various issues. "Large-scale industry" refers to establishments employing more than 1,000 persons.

pursuit of economies of scope, rather than of scale, through flexible manufacturing systems, for example, has become more common in industrial production. Firms appear to enter more freely into new fields, taking advantage of developing technological opportunities and competing with each other across sectoral borders. In the electronics industry, the subcontracting system, so efficient in automobile production, is being replaced by more independent, but short-lived, joint ventures.

The concentration rate of industrial production declined during the period of high economic growth as markets expanded rapidly, creating the expectation that the rate would rise in response to slower economic growth. However, as discussed by Uekusa in this volume, a recent study by the Fair Trade Commission shows that the industrial concentration rate continued to decline in the 1970s when the growth rate decelerated in Japan. The Japanese industrial market is more competitive, in spite of more moderate expansion.

Taken together, these changes suggest that the Japanese economy is becoming more market oriented. Contrary to the widely held views concerning the present economic organization of Japan, the relative roles of markets external to the firms will increase vis-à-vis those internal to the firms. Generally stated, in Japan's markets in the future, Walrasian auctioneers will become increasingly more important.

The implications for economic management of becoming more dependent on the clearing mechanism of external (auctioneer-type) markets can only be conjectured. As markets clear themselves, administrative guidance may be less effective as markets are freed of regulation. Tax-subsidy incentives may elicit rapid responses from market participants as adjustment to changes in relative prices becomes more speedy in open markets. Appropriate institutional reforms, combined with a long-run policy stance, may help ensure the effective working of the market mechanism, but ad hoc government intervention may cause large distortions. These changing circumstances imply greater uncertainty in the political and economic environment and more institutional reforms designed to respond to both domestic and international demand for them. The political maturity of representative democracy in Japan is at issue.

Notes

Notes

Murakami: The Japanese Model

This paper is a modified version of Part 2 of a paper presented to the final preparatory conference for the JPERC project (held at the East-West Center, Honolulu, Hawaii, on July 25–29, 1983) entitled "To Leave a Bamboo Thicket" by Shumpei Kumon, Yasusuke Murakami, and Kozo Yamamura. The author owes much to Professors Kumon, Seizaburo Sato, and Yamamura and to all participants in the conference, particularly Professors Masahiko Aoki, Yukio Noguchi, Hugh Patrick, and Henry Rosovsky. He is also indebted to Professor Mary Brinton and Miss Martha Lane for their substantive as well as editorial advice.

1. This idea was first presented in Yasusuke Murakami, Shumpei Kumon, and Seizaburō Satō, *Bummei to shite no ie shakai* (*Ie* society as a pattern of civilization) (Tokyo: Chūō Kōronsha, 1979). For an abridged and modified version, see Y. Murakami, "Ie Society as a Pattern of Civilization," *Journal of Japanese Studies*, Vol. 10, No. 2 (Summer 1984), especially pp. 301f.

2. For the original definition of "stem succession," see Chie Nakane, *Kazoku no kōzō* (Structure of the family) (Tokyo: University of Tokyo Press, 1970), pp. 101–2.

3. For the definition of "kintractship," see F. L. K. Hsu, *Iemoto: The Heart of Japan* (New York: Schenkman, 1975), p. 62. "Kintract" is a portmanteau word formed from "kinship" and "contract."

4. See Murakami, "Ie Society," pp. 308–11.

5. Ibid., p. 357.

6. See Philip Trezise and Yukio Suzuki, "Politics, Government, and Economic Growth in Japan," in H. Patrick and H. Rosovsky, eds., *Asia's New Giant: How the Japanese Economy Works* (Washington, D.C.: Brookings Institution, 1976). See also Patrick and Rosovsky's final chapter in the same volume, pp. 899–903.

7. For summary of past works, see Mitsuo Ezaki, *Nihon keizai no moderu bunseki* (Model analysis of the Japanese economy) (Tokyo: Sōbunsha, 1977), p. 84. Ezaki argues that the unexplained part of Japanese economic growth can be markedly reduced by explicitly introducing a factor of structural change.

8. See Masahiro Tatemoto, "Reontiefu gyakusetsu to Nihon bōeki no kōzō" (The Leontief paradox and the structure of Japanese trade), *Keizai kenkyū*, Vol. 9, No. 1 (Jan. 1958).

9. Kazushi Ohkawa and Henry Rosovsky, *Japanese Economic Growth* (Stanford: Stanford University Press, 1973); and Kazuo Satō, "Nihon no hiichiji keizai no

seichō to gijutsu shimpo, 1930–1967" (Growth and technical progress in Japan's nonprimary economy, 1930–1967), *Economic Studies Quarterly*, Vol. 22, No. 1 (Apr. 1971). See also Ezaki, *Nihon keizai*.

10. See Tadao Kagono et al., *Nichibei kigyō no keiei hikaku* (Japanese and U.S. management in comparative perspective) (Tokyo: Nihon Keizai Shimbun, 1983).

11. In my opinion, one crucial problem in Aoki's approach is to explain why the actors in his game-theoretic formulation are limited to those workers and stockholders who are currently members of the firm in question (managers are arbitrators in Aoki's approach). Other types of actors outside the firm may enter the game and change the picture. We can, for example, at least logically conceive of some institution (private insurance company or public insurance fund) that provides unemployment insurance or insurance for wage reduction. This is likely to reduce the workers' "loyalty" to the firm. By neglecting the actors currently outside the firm, Aoki implicitly presupposes the existence of some group consciousness.

Another crucial problem is why workers accept the hierarchical role structure (for example, wage differentials among jobs) of the firm and are motivated by the long-run promotional prospects in this hierarchy. In the short-term, spot market for labor, the wage is determined for each job in the hierarchy. This cannot be the case with a bargaining process based on a long-run perspective, as Aoki has envisioned. Bargaining about wages requires some agreement about hierarchical structure. Workers' compliance with hierarchy may be attributed, for example, to the *ie* tradition.

12. See Iwao Ozaki, "The Effects of Technological Changes on the Economic Growth of Japan, 1955–1970," in K. R. Polenski and J. V. Skolka, eds., *Advances in Input-Output Analysis* (Cambridge, Mass.: Ballinger, 1976).

13. Rasmussen's "index of the power of dispersion and index of the sensitivity of dispersion" are almost always greater than 1.0 in these industries. See Hideyuki Yamamoto, "Sangyō renkan no kokusai hikaku" (An international comparison of interindustrial relations), in Miyohei Shinohara and Masao Baba, eds., *Gendai sangyō ron 1* (Contemporary industries, 1) (Tokyo: Nihon Keizai Shimbun, 1973), p. 160.

14. See Y. Murakami and K. Yamamura, "A Technical Note on Japanese Firm Behavior and Economic Policy," in K. Yamamura, ed., *Policy and Trade Issues of the Japanese Economy: American and Japanese Perspectives* (Seattle: University of Washington Press, 1982).

15. Y. Murakami, "Toward a Socioinstitutional Explanation of Japan's Economic Performance," in Yamamura, *Policy and Trade Issues*, pp. 3–46.

16. Ken'ichi Imai, *Gendai sangyō soshiki* (Contemporary industrial organization) (Tokyo: Iwanami Shoten, 1976), p. 8.

17. See, for example, Yasushi Kōsai and Yoshitarō Ogino, *Nihon keizai tembō* (The Japanese economy in perspective) (Tokyo: Nihon Hyōronsha, 1980), p. 167.

18. The definition of *keiretsu* is somewhat arbitrary. There can be a weaker definition in which many of the "non-*keiretsu* firms" cited belong to a *keiretsu* weakly defined. See Iwao Nakatani, "The Economic Role of Financial Corporate Grouping," in Masahiko Aoki, ed., *The Economic Analysis of the Japanese Firm* (Amsterdam: North-Holland, 1984), pp. 248–53.

19. For recent contributions, see ibid. and Masahiko Aoki, "Risk-Sharing in the Corporate Group," in Aoki, *Economic Analysis of the Japanese Firm*.

20. Nakatani, "Financial Corporate Grouping," pp. 228f.

21. See Masu Uekusa, *Sangyō soshiki ron* (Industrial organization) (Tokyo: Chikuma Shobō, 1982), pp. 120f and 341f.

22. See ibid., pp. 19–27. For the most recent survey, see Akira Senō, ed., *Gendai Nihon no sangyō shūchū, 1971–1980* (Industrial concentration in contemporary Japan) (Tokyo: Nihon Keizai Shimbunsha, 1983), pp. 106f.

23. Robert A. Dahl, *A Preface to Democratic Theory* (Chicago: University of Chicago Press, 1956), pp. 64f.

24. A good and moderate presentation of the modernization approach may be found in Robert A. Scalapino and Junnosuke Masumi, *Parties and Politics in Contemporary Japan* (Berkeley: University of California Press, 1962). Masao Maruyama and Takashi Ishida were prominent figures in this approach. However, these academic writers tended to be pessimistic, pointing out the barriers against the "modernization" of Japanese politics.

25. Keiichi Matsushita was an early author who pointed out the emergence of mass politics in Japan, though he considered it an aberration; see his *Gendai Nihon no seijiteki kōsei* (Political configuration of contemporary Japan) (Tokyo: University of Tokyo Press, 1962).

26. J. H. Goldthorpe et al., *The Affluent Worker: Industrial Attitudes and Behavior* (Cambridge, Eng.: Cambridge University Press, 1969); Ronald Inglehart, *The Silent Revolution* (Princeton: Princeton University Press, 1979); and Daniel Yankelovich, *New Rules* (New York: Random House, 1981).

27. Yasusuke Murakami, *Sangyō shakai no byōri* (The pathology of industrial society) (Tokyo: Chūō Kōronsha, 1975).

28. Yasusuke Murakami, "The Age of New Middle Mass Politics: The Case of Japan," *Journal of Japanese Studies*, Vol. 8, No. 1 (Winter 1982), pp. 29–72.

29. Otto Kirchheimer, "The Transformation of the Western European Party Systems," in J. LaPalombara and M. Wiener, eds., *Political Parties and Political Development* (Princeton: Princeton University Press, 1966).

30. Recent works by Japanese political scientists tend to stress the pluralistic aspect of the Japanese polity. See Hideo Ōtake, *Gendai Nihon no seiji kenryoku keizai kenryoku* (Political power and economic power in contemporary Japan) (Tokyo: San'ichi Shobō, 1980); Michio Muramatsu, *Sengo Nihon no kanryōsei* (The bureaucracy in postwar Japan) (Tokyo: Tōyō Keizai Shimpōsha, 1981); and Takashi Inoguchi, *Gendai Nihon seiji keizai no kōzu—Seifu to shijō* (Framework of contemporary Japanese political economy: Government and market) (Tokyo: Tōyō Keizai Shimpōsha, 1983).

31. Kirchheimer, "Transformation"; and Suzanne Berger, "Politics and Antipolitics in Western Europe in the Seventies," *Daedalus*, Winter 1979.

32. Nathaniel B. Thayer, *How the Conservatives Rule Japan* (Princeton: Princeton University Press, 1969).

33. Kirchheimer, "Transformation"; and Maurice Duverger, *Les Partis politiques* (Paris: Armond Colin, 1951).

34. Berger, "Politics and Antipolitics."

35. For a similar argument, see Gerald L. Curtis, *Election Campaigning: Japanese Style* (New York: Columbia University Press, 1971).

36. See V. Giscard d'Estaing, *Democratie française* (Paris: Fayard, 1976).

37. NHK Yoron Chōsajo, ed., *Daini Nihonjin no ishiki—NHK yoron chōsa* (The Japanese Consciousness, II—NHK opinion survey) (Tokyo: Shiseidō, 1980), p. 638.

38. For example, see Inoguchi, *Gendai Nihon*, pp. 56f.

39. The Japan Development Bank and the Japan Export and Import Bank are seminationalized institutions, but they do not compete against private banks in ordinary loan markets. In Japan, there were no other nationalized or seminationalized corporations, except for Japan National Railways, Nihon Telephone

and Telegraph (recently privatized), Japan Tobacco Monopoly (also recently privatized), National Forestry, the Postal Service, and a miscellany of corporations (*kōdan* or *jigyōdan*) related mainly with infrastructures.

40. For an argument that emphasizes a corporatist aspect of Japanese polity, see T. J. Pempel and K. Tsunekawa, "Corporatism Without Labor? The Japanese Anomaly," in P. C. Schmitter and G. Lehmbruch, eds., *Trends Toward Corporatist Intermediation* (London: Sage Publications, 1979).

41. Ken'ichi Imai, Hiroyuki Itami, and Kazuo Koike, *Naibu soshiki no keizaigaku* (Economics of internal organization) (Tokyo: Tōyō Keizai Shimpōsha, 1982).

42. See Michio Muramatsu and Ellis Krauss's paper in this volume and Inoguchi, *Gendai Nihon*.

43. Seizaburō Satō and Tetsuhisa Matsuzaki, "Jimintō chōchōki seiken no kaibō (The anatomy of the super-long-term LDP government)," *Chūō kōron*, Nov. 1984, pp. 66–100.

44. Yasusuke Murakami, *Shinchūkan taishū no jidai* (The age of the new middle mass) (Tokyo: Chūō Kōronsha, 1984), part 3.

45. Ibid.

46. Z. Brzezinski, *The Fragile Blossom: Crisis and Change in Japan* (New York: Harper & Row, 1972).

47. Inoguchi, *Gendai Nihon*, pp. 203f.

48. NHK Yoron Chōsajo, *Nihonjin no ishiki*.

49. Hiroshi Akuto, in ibid., chap. 2, sect. 3.

50. Kazuto Kojima, in ibid., chap. 2, sect. 2.

51. See Muramatsu and Krauss's paper in this volume.

52. Robert Gilpin, *War and Change in World Politics* (Cambridge, Eng.: Cambridge University Press, 1981).

53. Theodore J. Lowi, *The End of Liberalism: The Second Republic of the United States* (New York: W. W. Norton, 1979).

Bronfenbrenner and Yasuba: Economic Welfare

1. Yatsuhiro Nakagawa, "Japan, the Welfare Super-Power," *Journal of Japanese Studies*, Vol. 5, No. 1 (Winter 1979), first published in Japanese in *Chūō kōron* (Aug. 1978); and Ezra Vogel, *Japan as Number One: Lessons for America* (Cambridge, Mass.: Harvard University Press, 1979).

2. GNP and GDP differ in their treatment of income received by residents of one country for services performed by themselves or earnings on their capital in another country. This income is part of the GNP of the country where the recipient resides, but of the GDP of the country where the services are performed. For example, the returns to Japanese companies from their investments in Australian iron mines are part of the Australian GDP, but become part of the Japanese GNP on receipt in Japan. It has been suggested that net national income (NNI) or personal income (PI) per capita might be better measures of living standards than GNP or GDP per capita. NNI excludes capital depreciation and indirect business taxes net of business subsidies; PI excludes, in addition, taxes on profits and undistributed corporate income, but adds transfer payments. A difficulty with these measures is the low reliability of the "capital consumption allowances" (depreciation) series.

3. A peculiarity of economic psychology in advanced countries is that only the upper twentieth (approximately) of the population in terms of personal distribution of income considers itself "rich" and only the lower twentieth (almost)

considers itself "poor," leaving nearly 90 per cent in the "middle class." Such estimates imply that income redistribution to the poor must as a practical matter come largely from the middle class and not exclusively from the rich. On this matter, economists of the "basic needs" school of development go much further than ourselves. Their conception of economic welfare (in developing countries, at least) is that the proportion of the population to whom "basic needs" (food, shelter, medical care, education) are available at some minimal level, and nothing else, matters greatly. This philosophy has never dominated public policy in either Japan or the United States, although it has been important in the British Overseas Development Ministry.

4. Japan, Economic Planning Agency, *Keizai hakusho, 1956* (Economic white paper) (Tokyo, 1956), p. 42.

5. Bank of Japan, *Nihon keizai o chūshin to suru kokusai hikaku tōkei, 1983* (Comparative international statistics on the Japanese economy) (Tokyo, 1983), p. 82.

6. The alleged unfairness of the Japanese income tax is summarized in the popular "10-5-3-1" criticism. This asserts that 100 per cent of the wage earner's income is taxed, 50 per cent of the business or professional man's, 30 per cent of the farmer's, and 10 per cent of the politician's (see the paper by Noguchi in this volume for further discussion).

7. Japan, Economic Planning Agency, *Keizai yoran, 1983* (Economic survey) (Tokyo, 1983), pp. 62–67.

8. Vito Tanzi, "The Underground Economy," *Finance and Development*, Vol. 20, No. 4 (Dec. 1983), pp. 12ff. (The wide ranges between low and high estimates reflect the difficulties of data collection in this area.)

9. A pioneering estimate of this type of measure was made by William Nordhaus and James Tobin, "Is Economic Growth Obsolete?" *Economic Growth* (National Bureau of Economic Research), 1972, pp. 4–24 and appendix A. Their version is called Measures of Economic Welfare, or MEW.

10. Hisao Kanamori, "Japanese Economic Growth and Economic Welfare," in Shigeto Tsuru, ed., *Growth and Resource Problems Related to Japan* (Tokyo: Asahi Evening News, 1978).

11. The Harrod formula is $G = s/C$, where G is the growth rate of national income, s is the saving rate, and C the marginal capital–output ratio (the amount of additional capital required to add one unit to the national income). The Domar formula is: $G = \alpha\sigma_i$, where G is the growth rate of net investment, α is the saving ratio, and σ is the productivity of investment.

12. A classic presentation of this issue, including the role of the interest rate, which we omit here, is Oscar Lange, "The Rate of Interest and the Optimum Propensity to Consume," *Economica*, new series, Vol. 5, No. 17 (Feb. 1938).

13. On the other hand, the highest-income families, who had more resources, seem to have hedged against inflation by purchases of automobiles and other durable goods, so that their saving rate was the lowest of the five income classes in 1975. This "rush for the hedges" may also have been irrational.

14. Strictly speaking, the Engel coefficient measures the importance of food expenditures in the entire family budget, including saving or dissaving.

15. National Livelihood Center, *Kokumin seikatsu tōkei nempō, 1982* (Statistical yearbook on national livelihood) (Tokyo: Shiseidō, 1982), p. 81.

16. Alan S. Blinder et al., "The Level and Distribution of Economic Well-being," in Martin Feldstein, ed., *The American Economy in Transition* (Chicago: University of Chicago Press, 1980), p. 428.

17. In 1984, these trends were interrupted, probably temporarily, by a *shōchū* boom (*shōchū* is a traditional Japanese liquor distilled from rice and sweet po-

tatoes). Rather than a change in taste, we see this boom as largely a response to two sharp increases in the controlled price of beer.

18. In Japanese parlance, a "mansion" is a condominium apartment building of concrete construction or an individual apartment in such a building. Many such mansions are both extremely small and extremely shabby.

19. Economic Planning Agency, *Keizai yōran, 1983*, p. 409.

20. National Livelihood Center, *Kokumin seikatsu tōkei nempō, 1982*, p. 134.

21. Bank of Japan, *Nihon keizai, 1983*, p. 158.

22. Japan, Office of the Prime Minister, Bureau of Statistics, *Annual Report on Family Income and Expenditure Survey, 1980* (Tokyo: Nihon Tōkei Kyōkai, 1981), p. 255.

23. Bank of Japan, *Nihon keizai, 1980*, p. 157.

24. For some alternative measures of equality and inequality, see Martin Bronfenbrenner, *Income Distribution Theory* (Chicago: Aldine, 1971), chap. 5.

25. Felix Paukert, "Income Distribution at Different Levels of Development," *International Labor Review*, Vol. 108 (Aug.–Sept. 1973).

26. Malcolm Sawyer, "Income Distribution in OECD Countries," *OECD Economic Outlook*, July 1976, p. 14; and Yasusuke Murakami, "Toward a Socioinstitutional Explanation of Japan's Economic Performance," in Kozo Yamamura, ed., *Policy and Trade Issues of the Japanese Economy: American and Japanese Perspectives* (Seattle: University of Washington Press, 1982), p. 28. Some people suspect that Japan's income distribution is not so equal. For example. Tadao Ishizaki, in his *Nihon no shotoku to tomi no bumpai* (The distribution of income and wealth in Japan) (Tokyo: Tōyō Keizai Shimpōsha, 1983), insists that the property income of the rich is much underreported and that Japan's income distribution as a whole is as unequal as that of the United States. Although he may have a point, Ishizaki does not satisfactorily describe his estimation method, and there is no way of verifying his conclusions. Moreover the distortion he ascribes to the Japanese data applies, albeit to a lesser extent, to data in other countries. Even a casual observation of the lifestyle of the Japanese reveals that personal income distribution is more equal in Japan than in other countries.

27. Yutaka Kosai and Yoshitaro Ogino, *The Contemporary Japanese Economy* (London: Macmillan, 1984), pp. 109ff.

28. Nakagawa, "Japan," pp. 31–33.

29. Japan, Economic Planning Agency, *Kenmin shotoku tōkei nempō* (Yearbook of prefectural income statistics) (Tokyo, various issues).

30. Economic Planning Agency, *Keizai yōran, 1983*, p. 393.

31. Contrary to much Western belief, there are no formal "lifetime," "permanent," or even "long-term" employment contracts in Japan. Such matters are tacit understandings, sometimes called "implicit contracts," even in large firms. The imprecise estimates in the text are those of Kazuo Koike.

32. Japan, Ministry of Labor, *Rōdō tōkei nenkan* (Yearbook of labor statistics) (Tokyo: Rōdō Hōrai Kyōkai, various years).

33. In 1975 in Britain, employed middle-class men and nonemployed middle-class women, age 25–45, spent 120 minutes a day listening to TV and radio. J. I. Gershung, "Changing Use of Time in the United Kingdom: 1937–1975, the Self-Service Era," in *Studies of Broadcasting, 1983* (NHK Radio and TV Culture Institute, 1983).

34. National Livelihood Center, *Kokumin seikatsu tōkei nempō, 1967*, pp. 35ff; NHK, Hōsō Yoron Chōsasho, *Shōwa 55 nendo kokumin seikatsu jikan chōsa, zenkoku-hen* (How people spend their time, 1980, national volume) (Tokyo: NHK Press, 1981), pp. 805–7, 832–34.

35. Japan, Ministry of Labor, *Rōdō tōkei yōran, 1982* (Summary of labor statistics) (Tokyo: Government Printing Bureau, 1982), p. 52.

36. Ministry of Labor, *Rōdō tōkei nenkan*, for 1955, 1970, 1981.

37. *Asahi shimbun*, Dec. 28, 1983.

38. Minamata disease is a form of mercury poisoning caused by eating fish contaminated with mercuric wastes.

39. Remy Prud'homme, "Appraisal of Environmental Policies in Japan," in Tsuru, *Growth and Resource Problems*, p. 194.

40. On contemporary minority problems in Western Europe, see John Nielsen et al., "Rising Racism on the Continent," *Time*, Feb. 6, 1984. Victimized minorities include Indians, Pakistanis, and West Indians in Britain; Africans, particularly North African Arabs, in France; and Eastern Europeans, particularly Turks, in West Germany.

41. These occupations included butchering, tanning, hog raising, and the mortuary trades.

42. United Nations, *Demographic Yearbook, 1981*, pp. 394ff.

43. Prime Minister Yasuhiro Nakasone's private advisory panel or "brain trust" has proposed expansion and formalization of these survey results into a new net national satisfaction index (NNS); *Japan Times*, Oct. 3, 1984.

44. This result is consistent with Kosai and Ogino's finding (*Japanese Economy*, table 7.3, p. 112) that the distribution of savings deposits has grown more equal over time. They also believe, however (p. 220), that the inequality of the wealth distribution may have risen because of the boom in land prices, both urban and rural. This has benefited primarily a small minority of landowners.

45. For the *Kokumin Nenkin*, or "general public," system, 25 years.

46. Kakuei Tanaka, *Building a New Japan* (Tokyo: Simul, 1972). The Japanese version of this work is *Nihon rettō kaizōron* (Tokyo: Nikkan Kōgyō Shimbunsha, 1972).

47. Japan, Ministry of Health and Welfare, *Shōwa 50-nen kōsei hakusho* (Welfare white paper, 1975) (Tokyo: Government Printing Bureau, 1975), pp. 24ff.

48. Sei Fujita, "Nenkin wa dō naruka?" (What will become of pensions?), in Ōsaka Daigaku Hōsō Kōza, *Nihon keizai no mikata, 1983*, p. 84.

49. Noriyuki Takayama, "Kōsei Nenkin ni okeru sedaikan no saibumpai" (Intergenerational redistribution in Employees' Pension Fund), *Gendai keizai*, No. 43 (Summer 1981), p. 117.

50. Fujita, "Nenkin," p. 86.

51. Kosai and Ogino, *Japanese Economy*, p. 122.

52. Japan, Ministry of Health and Welfare, *Kōsei tōkei yōran* (Welfare statistics summary) (Tokyo: Kōsei Tōkei Kyōkai, various years).

53. Ibid., 1982, p. 161.

Sato: Saving and Investment

1. Before World War II, it appears that macroeconomic equilibrium was established through flexible price levels in Japan. See Kazuo Satō, "Senkanki Nihon no makuro keizai kikō" (The macroeconomic mechanism in prewar Japan), *Keizai kenkyū*, Vol. 32, No. 3 (July 1981), pp. 193–201. After World War II, the same degree of price flexibility was not observed except in the inflation of the immediate postwar period (1945–51) and that following the first oil shock (1974–75).

2. The capital–output ratio is found by dividing net domestic investment (gross domestic investment minus fixed capital consumption) by the growth rate of real GNP (see Table 1).

3. Such arguments are common in the media today. For a critical review of this issue, see Nathan Glazer, "Social and Cultural Factors in Japanese Economic Growth," in Hugh Patrick and Henry Rosovsky, eds., *Asia's New Giant: How the Japanese Economy Works* (Washington, D.C.: Brookings Institution, 1976), esp. pp. 856–59.

4. The ratio of gross domestic investment to GDP for 1980–83 was 46.3 per cent in Singapore (with an average annual growth rate of real GDP from 1973 to 1983 of 7.8 per cent), 28.2 per cent in Korea (7.4 per cent), 27.8 per cent in Taiwan (7.3 per cent), and 24.6 per cent in Thailand (6.6 per cent). IMF, *International Financial Statistics Yearbook, 1984* (Washington, D.C., 1985); and Taiwan, Directorate-General of Budget, Accounting, and Statistics, *Statistical Yearbook of the Republic of China, 1984* (Taipei, 1984). As for household saving (as a per cent of household disposable income), in 1979–81 among the OECD countries, Portugal (27.7 per cent) and Italy (20.9 per cent) exhibited even higher saving ratios than Japan (19.0 per cent). OECD, *National Accounts, 1964–1981* (Paris, 1983), vol. 2.

5. Estimates of capital stock are sensitive to depreciation ratios, which must be assumed for their computation. The depreciation ratio of producer capital (obtained by dividing consumption of fixed capital by capital stock), implicit in the estimates underlying Table 2, does not seem to differ markedly among these countries. In 1980, the ratio with respect to private industrial capital stock was 8.3 per cent in Japan, as against 5.5 per cent in Canada, 8.9 per cent in the United States, 8.4 per cent in France, 6.0 per cent in Norway, and 5.3 per cent in the United Kingdom.

6. For an international comparison of housing conditions, see the paper by Bronfenbrenner and Yasuba in this volume.

7. The depreciation ratio implicit in the housing stock estimate is 7.3 per cent for Japan, as against 2.5 per cent for the United States, 1.5 per cent for Norway, and 1.4 per cent for the United Kingdom. Hence, Japan's low level of housing stock is partly the result of its lower durability. This difference does not seem to be a statistical artifact. In terms of the double-declining-balance method, the depreciation ratio implies that the average lifetime of housing in Japan is 30 years, as against 80 years in the United States and some 150 years in Europe. Japanese tax law allows for an economic life of 26 years for wooden buildings and 65 years for reinforced concrete buildings. Even though Japanese houses have improved substantially from the traditional wood and paper house, they are still not as durable as American and European housing built of stones, steel, and concrete. According to Ministry of Construction statistics, the proportion (in floor space) of wooden houses in all housing starts was 82 per cent in 1955; 61 per cent in 1960; 41 per cent in 1970; 47 per cent in 1975; 41 per cent in 1980; and 36 per cent in 1984. Tōyō Keizai Shimpōsha, *Keizai tōkei nenkan* (Yearbook of economic statistics), various issues.

8. Mountains cover 72 per cent of Japan's total area. Thus, inhabitable land makes up less than one-third of the total land area. In Europe, the proportion is closer to 60 per cent.

9. According to the Japan Real Estate Research Institute, the cost of residential land per square meter in 1976 was $118 in Japan, $19 in West Germany, $13 in the United States, and $8 in the United Kingdom. Japan, Ministry of International Trade and Industry, *80 nendai no tsūsan seisaku bijion* (Visions of industrial policy in the 1980s) (Tokyo: Government Printing Office, 1980), p. 306.

10. Noteworthy in this respect is that life insurance is much more popular in Japan. As of 1983, the average face value of life insurance policies was highest in

Japan (¥6.2 million), followed by the United States (¥5.0 million). *Yomiuri shimbun*, July 13, 1985.

11. Japanese household debt consists mainly of housing loans, which accounted for 93 per cent of total household debt in 1984, according to the Family Saving Survey.

12. Another important feature to consider is the distribution of income. The conventional wisdom, employing such inequality measures as the Gini coefficient, maintains that Japan's income distribution is at least as equal as other advanced countries. Tadao Ishizaki, however, asserts that Japan is more unequal than all other OECD countries except for the United States. See his *Nihon no shotoku to tomi no bumpai* (The distribution of income and wealth in Japan) (Tokyo: Tōyō Keizai Shimpōsha, 1983).

13. According to national accounting statistics, in the early 1980s, health expenditure by the government was less than 0.4 per cent of GDP in Japan, as against 6 per cent in Germany, 4 per cent in both Italy and the United Kingdom, and 1 per cent in the United States. This, however, results from treating health insurance premiums paid by the private sector as part of private income and consumption. In 1980, Japan's medical and health expenditure was 5.1 per cent of GDP, of which 0.6 per cent was paid from public funds, 3.9 per cent was paid by insurance, and 0.6 per cent was privately paid. Deliberation Council on the Social Security System, *Shakai hoshō tōkei nempō* (Social security statistical yearbook), as quoted in Tōyō Keizai Shimpōsha, *Keizai tōkei nenkan, 1981*.

14. The effective interest rate adjusted for the compensating balances required by lending institutions is somewhat higher than the nominal interest rate. See Masahiko Aoki, "Shareholders' Non-unanimity on Investment Financing: Banks vs. Individual Investors," in Masahiko Aoki, ed., *The Economic Analysis of the Japanese Firm* (Amsterdam: North-Holland, 1984), pp. 193–224; and Yasuhiro Wakita, "Wagakuni no kashidashi shijō to keiyaku torihiki" (Loan market and contracts in Japan), *Kin'yū kenkyū*, Vol. 2, No. 1 (Mar. 1983), pp. 47–76. However, since the compensating balance has been about 10–20 per cent of total loans, the difference does not seem substantial. Akiyoshi Horiuchi, "Economic Growth and Financial Allocation in Postwar Japan," *Brookings Discussion Papers in International Economics*, No. 18 (Aug. 1984).

15. For the combination of the short-term interest rate (i) and the CPI inflation rate (π), the regression equation is:

$$i = 1.00\pi + 4.4\%, \quad R^2 = .953$$
$$(.10) \quad (.8)$$

Thus, the Fisher theorem holds in this cross-country sample. Deviations from the regression line are Japan, 0.2 per cent; the United States, 1.5 per cent; Canada, −0.1 per cent; France, −0.9 per cent; West Germany, −1.2 per cent; Italy, 0.4 per cent; and the United Kingdom, 0 per cent.

16. According to Keidanren (Federation of Economic Organizations), the effective corporate tax rate in Japan was 51.6 per cent (1984); West Germany, 49.8 per cent (1984); France, 45.7 per cent (1980); United States, 32.3 per cent (1985); and United Kingdom, 18.1 per cent (1982). *Yomiuri Shimbun*, Aug. 17, 1984. For changes in the corporate tax rate over time, see Seiritsu Ogura and Naoyuki Yoshino, "Zeisei to zaisei tōyūshi" (The tax system and the Fiscal Investment and Loan Program), in Ryūtarō Komiya, Masahiro Okuno, and Kotarō Suzumura, eds., *Nihon no sangyō seisaku* (Japanese industrial policy) (Tokyo: University of Tokyo Press, 1984), pp. 105–31.

17. These are the projected figures of the Population Research Committee, "Nihon no shōrai suikei jinkō" (Estimates of future population in Japan), as quoted in Tōyō Keizai Shimpōsha, *Keizai tōkei nenkan, 1985*.

18. The labor force participation ratio of male workers, 65 and older, was 57.1 per cent in 1960, 49.7 per cent in 1970, 41.1 per cent in 1980, and 38.8 per cent in 1982. Japan, Ministry of Labor, *Labor Statistics Yearbook* (Tokyo, various issues).

19. See Noguchi's paper in this volume for a discussion of why the system must be changed. The system was designed such that individuals would receive benefits far in excess of their lifetime contributions. To keep the benefit ratio up for a greater proportion of beneficiaries, the contribution ratio has to be raised very much. As a first step toward reducing the imbalance in the social security system, the law was revised in April 1985 to modify the benefit calculation formula over the next 20 years with a view to keeping benefits at the present level while avoiding anticipated excessive rises in the contribution ratio to some extent.

20. The Bureau of Statistics of the Office of the Prime Minister (since 1984, the Management and Coordination Agency) has conducted a monthly survey of urban family budgets, *Kakei chōsa* (Family Income and Expenditure Survey; FIES), since 1951 with a sample size of about 8,000 households. Household financial assets and liabilities are covered in an annual survey by the same agency, *Chochiku dōkō chōsa* (Family Saving Survey), with a sample size of about 6,000 households, half of which overlap with the FIES sample. A quinquennial survey, *Zenkoku shōhi jittai chōsa* (National Survey of Family Income and Expenditure), began in 1959 and covers the three months from September to November each year; it has a larger sample of about 46,000 households (1974), including single-person households not represented in the first two surveys. Farm households, which are excluded from these surveys, are covered by the *Nōka keizai chōsa* (Farm Household Economy Survey; FHES) conducted by the Ministry of Agriculture, Forestry, and Fisheries (with a sample size of 16,000 farm households in the mid-1970s).

Because of the confidentiality requirement of government surveys, the data on individual households collected for these surveys are not accessible to private researchers not acting in an official capacity. Of the very few available micro-studies, see, for example, Toshiyuki Mizoguchi, *Personal Savings and Consumption in Japan* (Tokyo: Kinokuniya, 1970); Mitsuo Saitō, "Kojin chochiku no keiryō bunseki" (Econometric analysis of personal savings), *Kokumin keizai zasshi*, Vol. 140, No. 4 (Oct. 1979), pp. 1–31; and Albert Ando, "Lifecycle kasetsu ni motozuku shōhi chochiku no kōdō bunseki" (Analysis of consumption-saving behavior based on the life cycle hypothesis), *Keizai bunseki*, No. 101 (Jan. 1986), pp. 25–114.

21. A further revision of the NIPA was released by the Economic Planning Agency in January 1986. The base year was shifted to 1980, and some significant revisions were introduced from 1976 onward. The household saving ratio was lowered by one percentage point for 1983, for example. These changes, which came too late to be incorporated here, do not affect the observations made in this paper in any essential manner.

22. The major difference between the NIPA and the FIES is in the treatment of imputed rent with capital consumption and health insurance premiums. Modifying the NIPA definition to fit the FIES definition, I have found that the saving ratio of 19–20 per cent in 1979–80 in the NIPA definition is equivalent to 29 per cent in the FIES definition. Over the same period, the saving ratio was 22 per cent in the FIES. Hence, the household sector's average saving ratio exceeded

that of worker households by seven percentage points. Another interesting source is the annual survey of savings conducted by the Central Council for Savings Promotion of the Bank of Japan, *Chochiku ni kansuru yoron chōsa* (A survey of public opinion on saving), which started in 1953.

23. The FIES for the 1930s gives the saving ratio at about 11–14 per cent. See Bank of Japan, *Hundred-Year Statistics of the Japanese Economy* (Tokyo, 1966), pp. 356–57.

24. The best study published at that time was Miyohei Shinohara, "The Structure of Savings and the Consumption Function in Postwar Japan," *Journal of Political Economy*, Vol. 67, No. 6 (Dec. 1959), pp. 589–603.

25. This explanation may be related to the permanent income or habit persistence hypothesis. See, for example, Kazushi Ōhkawa, "Chochiku ritsu no chōki hendō: Kojin chochiku o chūshin to suru daiichiji sekkin" (Long-term changes in the saving ratio), *Keizai kenkyū*, Vol. 21, No. 2 (May 1970), pp. 129–36; Kunio Yoshihara, "The Growth Rate as a Determinant of the Saving Ratio," *Hitotsubashi Journal of Economics*, Vol. 12, No. 1 (Feb. 1972), pp. 60–72; and Chikashi Moriguchi, "Makuro keiryō moderu ni miru Nihon keizai no kōzō henka to seisakuteki imi" (Structural changes in the Japanese economy in the recent decades from a macroeconometric viewpoint), *Keizai kenkyū*, Vol. 30, No. 1 (Jan. 1979) pp. 20–29.

26. The effect of inflation on saving has been analyzed in a number of papers. See, for example, Hiroshi Niida; "Changes in Personal Saving Behavior Under the Inflationary Process in Japan," mimeo., Jan. 1983.

27. Real disposable income per capita grew at a rate of 8.0 per cent from 1965 to 1973 and 1.7 per cent from 1973 to 1983.

28. For details of Japan's income tax system in recent years, see Kazuo Sato, "Economic Laws and the Household Economy in Japan: Lags in Policy Response to Economic Changes," in Gary Saxonhouse and Kozo Yamamura, eds., *Law and Trade Issues of the Japanese Economy: American and Japanese Perspectives* (Seattle: University of Washington Press, 1986).

29. An individual (not a household) can claim a tax exemption on interest on deposits up to the combined principal of some $60,000.

30. Bank of Japan statistics show that nearly 60 per cent of all personal financial savings are tax-exempt. Kazuo Sato, "Economic Laws."

31. This rate is 20 per cent if interest income is reported together with other household income; 35 per cent if interest income is taxed separately.

32. Note that employer and employee contributions to social security are excluded from both household income and saving.

33. Kazuo Sato, "Economic Law"; and idem, "Supply-Side Economics: A Comparison of the U.S. and Japan," *Journal of Japanese Studies*, Vol. 11, No. 1 (Winter 1985), pp. 105–28.

34. In the United States, the household saving ratio has been declining steadily. Sometime in the 1970s, s_{3a} crossed over total s. In the framework in the text, the net sum of saving out of labor income and capital income has been slightly negative. Dissaving by the retired must have overwhelmed the positive saving of workers and rentiers.

35. The green card is a small-saver identification card on which an individual is required to register all nontaxable deposits in his or her name. The measure was proposed in an attempt to make abuse of the system more difficult. The green card program was approved by the Diet in early 1980, but was shelved after strenuous lobbying efforts of financial interests. The fate of this program was the topic of discussion through 1984. At the moment, the small-saver tax-

exemption program is still in effect. However, a stricter vigilance over the system was instituted as of January 1986 by requiring depositors to show identification. *Yomiuri Shimbun*, Jan. 5, 1986.

36. There is a burgeoning amount of literature published on the topic of the income tax and saving. For a recent survey, see Lawrence Kotlikoff, "Taxation and Saving: A Neoclassical Perspective," *Journal of Economic Literature*, Vol. 22, No. 4 (Dec. 1984), pp. 1576–629.

37. Using the quintile data of the FIES, Naoyuki Yoshino, "Nihon no chochiku kōzō ni tsuite—maruyū no kōka o megutte" (On the structure of Japanese saving—with special reference to the small-saver tax-exemption program), *Kikan gendai keizai*, No. 58 (Fall 1984), pp. 55–68, finds that the maximum limit of the small-saver tax exemption has a positive effect on financial saving at lower income brackets.

38. On this point, see Martin Feldstein, "Social Security, Induced Retirement, and Aggregate Capital Accumulation," *Journal of Political Economy*, Vol. 82, No. 5 (Sept./Oct. 1974), pp. 905–26. A recent Japanese study notes that the amount of pension benefits is an important determinant in the labor supply decisions of the elderly. See Toshiaki Tachibanaki and Keiko Shimono, "Labor Supply of the Elderly," *Keizai kenkyū*, Vol. 36, No. 3 (July 1985), pp. 239–50.

39. For general discussion, on other countries as well as Japan, see George M. von Furstenberg, ed., *Social Security Versus Private Saving* (Cambridge, Mass.: Ballinger, 1979). Empirical studies in this field in Japan are scarce. See, for example, Yukio Noguchi, "Wagakuni kōteki nenkin no shomondai" (Problems of public pensions in Japan), *Kikan gendai keizai*, No. 50 (Fall 1982), pp. 18–33. For a survey of the literature, see Fumiko Mikami, "Kōreika shakai ni okeru kakei chochiku to shakai hoshō" (Household saving and social security in an aging society), *Kikan gendai keizai*, No. 57 (Spring 1984), pp. 50–61. The evidence is inconclusive.

40. See, for example, Ryutaro Komiya, "The Supply of Personal Savings," in idem, ed., *Postwar Economic Growth in Japan* (Berkeley: University of California Press, 1966), pp. 157–81; Hisao Kanamori, *Nihon keizai o dō miru ka* (How to look at the Japanese economy) (Tokyo: Nihon Keizai Shimbunsha, 1967); Tuvia Blumenthal, *Saving in Postwar Japan*, Harvard East Asian Monograph No. 35 (Cambridge, Mass.: Harvard Asian Research Center, 1970); Andrea Boltho, *Japan: An Economic Survey, 1953–1973* (London: Oxford University Press, 1975); Miyohei Shinohara, "The Determinants of Postwar Savings Behavior in Japan," in F. Modigliani et al., eds., *The Determinants of National Saving and Wealth* (New York: St. Martin's Press, 1983), pp. 201–18; and Yasuhiro Horie, "Kakei chochiku ritsu no dōkō" (Movement of the household saving ratio), *Kin'yū kenkyū*, Vol. 4, No. 3 (Aug. 1985), pp. 45–107.

41. For adaptive expectations, we have $Y^p = (1 - \beta)Y^p_{-1} + \beta Y = \beta Y + \beta(1 - \beta)$ $Y_{-1} + \beta(1 - \beta)^2 Y_{-2} + \cdots$, $1 \geq \beta > 0$. When Y has been growing at the rate of g, we have: $Y^p/Y \doteq 1/(1 + g/\beta)$.

42. Milton Friedman notes that k is dependent on the interest rate, demographic factors, and the proportion of human to nonhuman wealth. See *A Theory of the Consumption Function* (Princeton: Princeton University Press, 1957).

43. Furthermore, adaptive expectations that are backward-looking are not compatible with the permanent income hypothesis because permanent income logically depends on the stream of future incomes. On this critique, see for example, Robert E. Hall, "Stochastic Implication of the Life Cycle–Permanent Income Hypothesis: Theory and Evidence," *Journal of Political Economy*, Vol. 86, No. 6

(Dec. 1978), pp. 1971–87. If adaptive expectations are replaced by rational expectations, the negative relationship between the saving ratio and the growth rate is not observed. The life-cycle saving hypothesis, regarded as equivalent to the permanent income hypothesis, faces the same sort of problems when applied to the aggregate time series.

44. Both this proportion and the saving ratio peaked in 1974. For an illustration of these findings, see Tsuneo Ishikawa and Kazuo Ueda, "The Bonus Payment System and Japanese Personal Savings," in Aoki, *The Japanese Firm*, esp. p. 136.

45. See among others Mizoguchi, *Personal Savings*; Shinohara, "Determinants"; idem, "Chochiku ritsu no nazo" (The puzzle of the saving ratio), *Chochiku jihō*, No. 127 (Mar. 1981), pp. 2–12; and idem, *Keizai taikoku no seisui* (The rise and fall of economic superpowers) (Tokyo: Tōyō Keizai Shimpōsha, 1982), chap. 5. The most recent exercise is offered by Ishikawa and Ueda in "Bonus Payment." Their hypothesis is called the habit–buffer income hypothesis. They argue that "households distinguish bonus earnings from the rest of their income and regard them as a sort of buffer income, capable of being dispensed with discretionarily." They find that workers normally save half of their bonuses (p. 134).

46. The common practice in Japanese households is for a husband to give his paychecks to his wife, who is in charge of household budgeting. It has been suggested that wives save a great deal since they anticipate outliving their husband.

47. For instance, the payment schedule of housing mortgages is geared to the bonus schedule.

48. For a discussion of this view, see Takao Komine, *Nihon keizai tekiōryoku no tankyū* (A study of the adaptability of the Japanese economy) (Tokyo: Tōyō Keizai Shimpōsha, 1980), pp. 96–98.

49. Yutaka Kosai and Yoshitaro Ogino, *The Contemporary Japanese Economy* (London: Macmillan, 1984), pp. 114–15.

50. For a more detailed discussion, see Kazuo Sato, "Wages, Bonuses, and Saving in Japan," mimeo., 1985.

51. This hypothesis is by no means new; for example, see Alan Spiro, "Wealth and the Consumption Function," *Journal of Political Economy*, Vol. 70, No. 4 (Aug. 1962), pp. 339–54; and Michael Evans, "The Importance of Wealth in the Consumption Function," *Journal of Political Economy*, Vol. 75, No. 4 (Aug. 1967), pp. 330–51. Komine also expresses his preference for this hypothesis in the Japanese case but without any factual test in *Nihon keizai*.

52. For the sake of simplicity, Y is taken to be current income. It can be replaced by permanent income.

53. In national accounting statistics, consumption of fixed capital is netted out of changes in both saving and wealth.

54. If the planning horizon is long, w^* may be set at a very high level. In such a case, wealth adjustment is seen to be imperfect, and the speed of adjustment (λ) is low. Such a model is given by $S_t = \lambda(w_t^* Y_t - W_{t-1})$, $1 \geq \lambda > 0$. The first derivative of the above equation is given by $s_t = \lambda w_t^* \Delta Y_t / Y_t + \lambda \Delta w_t^* + (1 - \lambda) s_{t-1}(1 - \Delta Y_t / Y_t)$. In a steady state where income growth is constant, both the saving ratio and the wealth–income ratio converge to their steady-state values, $\bar{s}$ and $\bar{w}$. It is easily seen that $\bar{s}$ responds negatively and $\bar{w}$ responds positively to income growth. Thus, it is possible that movement of s and w in recent years has occurred while w^* has remained unchanged—an important point for future research.

55. This subsection is based on Kazuo Sato, "Japan's Land-Price Determination: A Longitudinal Study," mimeo., 1982.

56. The most important factor in the unequal distribution of wealth in Japan is the appreciation of land values. Noriyuki Takayama and Mitsutaka Togashi, "A Note on Wealth Distribution in Japan," *Philippine Economic Journal*, Vol. 19, No. 1 (July 1980), pp. 163–88.

57. The average floor space per house rose from 60 square meters in 1950 to 80 square meters in 1980, according to the Census of Population. The average lot size per house, however, does not seem to have matched this increase.

58. The most dramatic indicator of qualitative improvements may be the diffusion of flush toilets, which rose from 8.9 per cent of all houses in 1963 to 45.9 per cent in 1978 and 59.1 per cent in 1983, according to the quinquennial National Housing Survey. Increases in other modern facilities like central heating and air conditioning could also be cited.

59. However, average family size continues to decline—from 5.0 persons in 1955 to 3.3 in 1980, thereby raising floor space per resident from 12 square meters to 24 square meters over the same period. Census of Population.

60. For the spread of consumer durables over time, refer to the Economic Planning Agency's annual Survey of Consumer Behavior (*Shōhisha dōkō chōsa*). Smaller consumer appliances and electronic items are well diffused, but furniture is not because of space limitations as well as its high cost.

61. An alternative explanation would be that the rise in w_3 is a result of slow adjustment with no corresponding change in w^* when income growth shifted to a lower level. The slow adjustment arises, among other causes, because of the quasi-fixed nature of a large portion of saving (e.g., repayment of housing loans, life insurance premiums, private annuity subscriptions, and the like). Consequently, wealth has increased at a faster rate than income.

62. For a cross-sectional analysis of life-cycle savings, see Saitō, "Kojin chochiku"; and Ando, "Lifecycle kasetsu."

63. For the importance of saving to purchase housing, see Charles Y. Horioka, "Household Saving in Japan: The Importance of Target Saving for Education and Housing" (Harvard University, Ph.D. diss., May 1985). Horie, "Kakei chohiku," conducts a heroic exercise of breaking down financial savings into various motives on the basis of the Bank of Japan's questionnaire survey.

64. Over 1978–83, land accounted for 42 per cent of the total cost of a new dwelling. Masao Kawakami, "Jinsei 80-nen no shōgai sekkei" (Planning for a 80-year life cycle), *Chochiku to keizai*, No. 143 (Mar. 1985), pp. 31–41.

65. In 1983, the average acquisition price for a new house was five times the average annual household income; 39 per cent of the purchase price was self-financed. Kawakami, "Jinsei 80-nen."

66. In the national accounting convention, households' purchases of new houses and secondhand houses (including house lots) from the business sector are part of household capital formation, whereas purchases from other households are not. When purchased on loans, an increase in w_2 is offset by an equal increase in w_{3d}. When the principal of the loan is paid off, w_{3d} is reduced, thereby increasing the total w. This constitutes a part of household savings. Moreover, interest paid on housing loans is not tax deductible.

67. Elaborating on Kazuo Sato, "Saving of Japan's Worker Households," mimeo., Nov. 1976, Toshimasa Shiba, "The Personal Savings Function of Urban Worker Households in Japan," *Review of Economics and Statistics*, Vol. 61, No. 2 (May 1979), pp. 206–13, considers the urban land price index/CPI as an explanatory variable in the saving function of Japanese worker households.

68. The reason that w^* has continued to rise may be because the income elas-

ticity of demand for wealth has been above unity, especially because of housing demand and an increasing life span after retirement. However, an alternative hypothesis is that w^* was set at a high level to begin with and the realized w has been steadily converging toward it. This hypothesis is currently being investigated by the author.

69. An Economic Planning Agency study by Seinosuke Niwa and Noriki Sasaki, "Kinrōsha no teinen taishoku go no seikei shūshi no suikei" (Estimation of worker household budgets after retirement), *Keizai bunseki*, No. 75 (June 1979), pp. 1–105, speculates that personal savings of worker households fall short of providing self-support for retirement. The life-cycle budget sequence discussed in the text is outlined in detail in Japan, Economic Planning Agency, *Kokumin seikatsu hakusho, 1984* (White paper on people's lives, 1984) (Tokyo: Government Printing Office, 1984). See also Kawakami, "Jinsei 80-nen." The White Paper asserts that a family breaks even after housing cost. There is a puzzling phenomenon of positive saving by old-age households as reported in the FIES. Ando, "Lifecycle kasetsu," points out that this is because their household heads are still working and saving; those who have retired and therefore must be dissaving are merged into their children's households, which maintain positive saving.

70. Severance pay fell from 47.3 times monthly salary equivalents (MSE) in 1969 to 39.1 (MSE) in 1983 for college graduates and from 52.8 (MSE) to 43.0 (MSE) for senior high school graduates. Data based on a survey by the Central Labor Commission, as quoted in Tōyō Keizai Shimpōsha, *Keizai tōkei nenkan*, various issues.

71. The proportion of the older generation living with married children is reported to be 50 per cent in Japan as against 53 per cent in Thailand, 3 per cent in the United States, 2 per cent in the United Kingdom, and 9 per cent in France: Japan, Office of the Prime Minister, *An International Comparative Study of the Life of the Old Generation*, as quoted in *Yomiuri Shimbun*, Sept. 15, 1981.

72. The proportion of nuclear families to all kinship families has increased from 63.4 per cent in 1960 to 75.4 per cent in 1980, according to the Census of Population.

73. Housing advertisements in Japanese newspapers often feature such arrangements for amicable coexistence between the generations. In-law problems are ubiquitous in Japan.

74. The population share of the three metropolitan areas is projected to increase from 47.22 per cent in 1985 to 48.07 per cent in 1995, according to the Population Problem Institute of the Ministry of Welfare (1983 projections as reported in Tōyō Keizai Shimpōsha, *Keizai tōkei nenkan, 1984*, p. 48).

75. The population growth rate fell from a little over 1 per cent per annum in the early 1970s to slightly over 0.6 per cent in 1984. It is projected that it will fall to 0.4 per cent by 2000 and become negative by 2010.

76. Relative to Japan (100), the per capita balance of financial assets is reported to be United States, 150; Germany, 78; and the United Kingdom, 70. *Yomiuri Shimbun*, Jan. 20, 1985.

77. Measures that have been discussed are the elimination of the small-saver tax-exemption program, the expansion of indirect taxes (value-added taxes and the like), and the simplification of the income tax schedule with lower marginal tax rates on high income.

78. The NIPA give a profit breakdown by sector but no data on employee compensations by sector. I have used series on labor cost (wages, salaries, and fringe

benefits) for private nonfinancial corporations as reported in Japan, Ministry of Finance, *Hōjin kigyō tōkei nempō* (Corporate enterprise statistics yearbook). GDP at factor cost is the sum of gross operating surplus and employee compensation. This procedure understates employee compensation and the sector's GDP because of the omission of public enterprises' labor costs.

79. The gross fixed capital stock series is available for nonfinancial corporations from the EPA estimates. In 1975, the gross stock was 22.4 per cent higher than the net stock.

80. Suppose that this aggregate production function is of the constant elasticity of substitution variety; namely, $Y^{-p} = (AK)^{-p} + (BL)^{-p}$, $p = (1 - \sigma)/\sigma$, where Y = output, K = capital, L = labor, σ = elasticity of substitution, and A and B are coefficients that vary over time. The marginal product of capital (MPK) is $\text{MPK} = A^{-p}(K/Y)^{-1/\sigma}$. When capital is paid its marginal product, we have capital's share = $(AK/Y)^{-p}$. Capital's share and the capital–output ratio covary inversely when $p > 0$ or $0 < \sigma < 1$. When this equation is estimated for the secondary sector, it is found that $\sigma = 0.50$ and A was nearly constant. This finding implies that technical change has taken form in steady increases in B, i.e., labor augmentation. The regression equation (1958–82) is:

$$\log \text{(capital's share)} = -.984 \log K/Y - .0014 \, (t - 1976) - .135$$
$$(.052) \qquad\qquad (.0003) \qquad\qquad (.010)$$

(Standard errors are in parentheses.) $R^2 = .9801$, d.w. = 1.64. We thus have $\sigma = .50$ and $\dot{A}/A = .0014$.

81. For a discussion of this policy, see Jūrō Teranishi, *Nihon no keizai hatten to kin'yū* (Money, capital, and banking in Japanese economic development) (Tokyo: Iwanami Shoten, 1982). For a reexamination, see Horiuchi, "Economic Growth."

82. The effectiveness of credit rationing in Japan is a topic popularly discussed in many studies. See Kazumasa Iwata and Kōichi Hamada, *Kin'yū seisaku to ginkō kōdō* (Monetary policy and the behavior of banks) (Tokyo: Tōyō Keizai Shimpōsha, 1980), chap. 6.

83. Young workers moved permanently to cities. Middle-aged farmers either left farms for good or found principal jobs in nearby cities that allowed them to spend time on farms on weekends. During the week, farms were attended by the elderly and housewives.

84. The ratio of job openings to applications reached a peak in 1971 and again in 1974. (The ratio was 6.8 and 6.7 in the respective years for junior high school graduates and 4.0 and 3.9 for senior high school graduates, according to Ministry of Labor data.)

85. My view is that the aggregate production function remained unchanged through the period except for a significant fall in potential growth. The oil shocks, however, may have made the substitution of capital for oil more attractive, but this does not necessarily imply the same for labor. See Jirō Nemoto, "Enerugi to hienerugi seisan yōso no aida no daitai kanōsei ni tsuite—tajū CES gata seisankansū ni yorū keiryō bunseki" (On substitution possibilities between energy and non-energy inputs), *Economic Studies Quarterly*, Vol. 35, No. 2 (Aug. 1984), pp. 139–58. Japan, Economic Planning Agency, *Nihon keizai no genkyō* (The present state of the Japanese economy) (Tokyo, 1984), pp. 225–42, presents the contrary view that the elasticity of capital-labor substitution fell after the first oil shock. J. Sachs and D. Lipton, "The Supply Approach to Oil Shocks and the Slowdown in Japanese Economic Growth," *Shukan Tōyō keizai*, special issue, No. 57 (July 10, 1981), pp. 124–35, argue that the oil shock reduced capital and en-

ergy inputs to such an extent that economic growth slowed. My view is given in Kazuo Sato, "Shifts from High Growth to Low Growth Steady States: Japan's Corporate Sector," mimeo., Mar. 1985.

86. In Japan's conventional national accounting practices, consumption of fixed capital is based on book values rather than replacement values. No valuation adjustment is performed. Thus, the observed fall in the depreciation ratio is spurious. In fact, the net fixed capital stock is estimated on an assumption of a constant depreciation ratio of about 10.5 per cent.

87. The fall would have been further magnified if a capital consumption valuation adjustment had been adopted.

88. For 1970–82, the following regression equation is obtained:

$$CS/GDP = .929\ NP/GDP - .620\ (DV/GDP)_{-1} - .014\ NW/GDP + .026$$
$$(.018) \qquad\qquad (.099) \qquad\qquad (.004) \qquad\qquad (.014)$$

where DV = dividends. $R^2 = .9974$, d.w. = 1.73. In a steady state, $(DV/GDP)_{-1} = (DV/GDP) \equiv (NP/GDP) - (CS/GDP)$.

89. In the United States, Denison's law asserts that personal saving and corporate saving are perfect substitutes so that their sum maintains a stable fraction of GNP. This substitution possibility between the two types of saving requires an examination, although in Japan the sum of the two types of saving has not been a constant fraction of GNP. Also, the fact that only a small fraction of corporate stocks is held by private individuals must be taken into account.

90. The average bank loan rate was 8.5 per cent in 1955–59, 8.0 per cent in 1960–64, 7.5 per cent in 1965–69, 7.7 per cent in 1970–74, 7.5 per cent in 1975–79, and 7.4 per cent in 1980–84. Bank of Japan, *Economic Statistics Annual*, various issues. The implicit interest rate on loans and discounts, as reported in Ministry of Finance, *Hōjin kigyō tōkei nempō*, is about one percentage point higher than the above figures.

91. Even the NIPA rate of return is overstated because of the lack of a valuation adjustment on capital consumption allowances. If properly adjusted on this count, r_2 would be reduced by a little over 1 percentage point.

92. For more detailed computations, see Masahiko Aoki, "Aspects of the Japanese Firm," in idem, *The Japanese Firm*, pp. 3–43.

93. See Takatoshi Nakamura, "Japan's Giant Enterprises—Their Power and Influence," *Japanese Economic Studies*, Vol. 12, No. 4 (Summer 1984), esp. pp. 64–67. According to the Economic Planning Agency, *Nihon keizai*, p. 215, r_1 seems to have been roughly equal in Japan and the United States in recent years.

94. See Dale W. Jorgenson, "Capital Theory and Investment Behavior," *American Economic Review*, Vol. 53, No. 2 (May 1963), pp. 247–59.

95. For simplicity, disregard the existence of nonmonetary financial assets. Then we have total assets (TA) = real assets (K) + monetary assets = liabilities (D) + net worth (NW). The income equation is $(1 - t)(pK - iD - \delta K) = rNW$, where t = tax rate, p = MPK, i = interest rate, and δ = depreciation ratio. As an adequate rate of return, r is determined to be equal to $i - \pi K/NW$, where π = the rate of real asset appreciation. We then have $pK/TA = (K/TA)(\delta - \pi/1 - t) + [i/(1 - t)][1 - t(D/TA)]$. The average rate of return on total assets (left-hand side) is equated to the user cost of capital (right-hand side) in equilibrium. In this equation, K/TA and D/TA should be measured in flows rather than in stocks.

96. Financial institutions derive earnings principally from interest received on their loans to firms and households. Their income, after subtracting operating expenses and interest paid on deposits, is partly distributed as dividends to

stockholders and partly retained as saving. As their capital formation falls far short of their saving, they have positive net lending.

97. The service revolution has received a great deal of fanfare in Japan as a harbinger of the post-industrial society. See for example, Ryuichiro Tachi, "The 'Softization' of the Japanese Economy," *Japanese Economic Studies*, Vol. 13, No. 3 (Spring 1985), pp. 67–104.

98. The ratio of gross fixed capital stock to sectoral GDP (both in 1975 prices) in 1983 was 1.65 for all private industry, 7.19 in the primary sector (agriculture), 1.81 in the secondary sector (mining, manufacturing, construction, utilities), and 1.04 in the tertiary sector (transportation and communications, wholesale and retail trade, finance, real estate, and services). In the secondary sector, its most dynamic industry, heavy manufacturing, has a relatively low capital–output ratio of 1.31, as against 2.10 for light manufacturing.

99. Adjusting items are determined by purchases of land, net, + purchases of intangible assets, not elsewhere classified, net, + statistical discrepancy − capital transfers received, net.

100. These items include purchases of intangible assets from the rest of the world, net, + statistical discrepancy − capital transfers from the rest of the world, net.

101. For a broader discussion of the government sector, see the paper by Noguchi in this volume. For a more detailed discussion of the external sector, see Volume II of this series. For the financial aspects of the macroeconomic balance, see the paper by Horiuchi and Hamada in this volume.

102. The outstanding federal debt held by the public was 36 per cent of GNP in 1984 (*Survey of Current Business*).

103. Suppose that deficits and interest on debt are financed by bond issues, and deficits are kept at a constant fraction of GDP, then, the debt–income ratio converges to a finite value if and only if the interest rate is less than the growth rate of nominal GDP. In the past five years, the latter was 6 per cent and the former was about 8 per cent.

104. This subsection is based on Kazuo Sato and Sheng Yann Lii, "The Yen Exchange Rate, Trade Balance, and Capital Flows: The Case of Japan," paper presented to the Second Conference on U.S.-Asia Economic Relations, New York, Sept. 30–Oct. 2, 1985.

105. See Japan, Economic Planning Agency, *Keizai hakusho* (Annual report on the Japanese economy) (1984), chap. 2; and Japan, Ministry of International Trade and Industry, *Tsūshō hakusho* (Annual report on international trade) (1984), chap. 3.

106. Government economists have based their analyses on a historical pattern of development stages in which a country moves from the position of a net borrower to repaying foreign debt, to a "premature" lender country (capital exports based on a surplus in the trade account), then to a "mature" lender country (capital exports based on investment income). Japan is alleged to have reached the premature lender stage.

107. Economic Planning Agency, *Keizai hakusho*, 1985, speculates that the push for capital exports will weaken as the aging population exerts a downward pressure on excess saving.

108. A good example is the asset-doubling plan (*shisan baizō ron*), proposed in the spring of 1984 by an elder statesman of the Liberal Democratic Party, Kiichi Miyazawa, calling for the doubling of Japan's assets over the next ten years. *Asahi Shimbun*, June 7, 1984; Kiichi Miyazawa, "Watakushi no shisan baizō ron" (My

'asset-doubling plan'), an interview by Masataka Kosaka, *Bungei shunjū*, July 1984, pp. 94–114. The proposal asserts that because major technological break-throughs provide investment opportunities, the country can grow at the rate of 5 to 5.5 per cent annually. The nation should not miss this opportunity to expand its housing and social capital stocks. Increased investment will reduce the de-pendence on external demand. A higher growth rate would expand government revenue, thereby solving the deficit problem as well. The proposal was poorly received and quickly forgotten. The plan itself is internally inconsistent. In addi-tion, the plan does not set a particularly ambitious target, as net fixed assets doubled in the preceding ten years without any such plan.

Noguchi: Public Finance

I am grateful for constructive comments given by JPERC conference participants, especially by Professors Hugh Patrick, Yasukichi Yasuba, Kazuo Sato, Yutaka Kosai, and Akiyoshi Horiuchi. I am also indebted to Professors Charles Horioka (Kyoto University) and David Merriman (University of Texas at Dallas) for their comments on an earlier version of the manuscript.

1. See Gardner Ackley and Hiromitsu Ishi, "Fiscal, Monetary, and Related Policies" and Joseph A. Peckman and Keimei Kaizuka, "Taxation," in Hugh Pat-rick and Henry Rosovsky, eds., *Asia's New Giant: How the Japanese Economy Works* (Washington, D.C.: Brookings Institution, 1976).

2. For further discussion, see Morris Beck, "Public Sector Growth: A Real Per-spective," *Public Finance*, Vol. 34, No. 3 (1979); G. Warren Nutter, *Growth of Gov-ernment in the West: Studies in Economic Policy* (Washington, D.C.: American Enter-prise Institute for Public Policy Research, 1978); OECD, *Public Expenditure Trends: OECD Studies in Resource Allocation* (Paris, 1978); and Sam Peltzman, "The Growth of Government," *Journal of Law and Economics*, Vol. 23, No. 2 (Oct. 1980).

3. Whether the general government's expenditure appropriately represents the "size of government" is an unsettled question. The choice of the denomina-tor (GDP or national income) is also a problem. See George F. Break, "Issues in Measuring the Level of Government Economic Activity," *American Economic Re-view*, Vol. 72, No. 2 (May 1982) for further discussion of this problem.

4. Alan T. Peacock and Jack Wiseman, *The Growth of Public Expenditure in the United Kingdom*, new ed. (London: Allen & Unwin, 1967), proposes the hypothe-sis that significant public sector growth occurs only in wartime because people accept an increase in the tax burden only under an extraordinary circumstance such as war. They reached this conclusion from analyses of U.K. data for the pe-riod 1890–1967. The experience of OECD countries in the past decades refutes this hypothesis, however.

5. Although the growth of the relative size of public expenditures has slowed in recent years, the ratio of tax and social security contributions to national in-come is still rising. The slowdown is superficial for some categories of expen-diture, as discussed below.

6. As mentioned in Appendix C, public corporations are not included in the general government sector of the national account data (they are included in the "corporate sector"). However, subsidies to public corporations such as the Japan National Railways are included in the general government expenditures (and also in the general account expenditures of the national budget).

7. Care must be taken with these figures: in such countries as Sweden and the United Kingdom, medical expenses are included in government consumption

rather than in transfer payments because the government in these countries operates the medical system.

8. Therefore, the nature of public sector growth in Japan is the same as that in other industrialized countries; it has been brought about by a creation of (or at least an attempt to create) a welfare state. This is important because it differs completely from the Marxist thesis that expansion of the state will be brought about by increases in military expenditures and subsidies to monopolistic enterprises.

9. There are two reasons why the ratio of government employees' salaries to GNP rose: (1) the general wage rate rose faster than the GNP deflator, and (2) the pay scale for teachers improved considerably during this period.

10. In this section, the problem of national bonds is discussed from the point of view of fiscal revenues. Another important topic, the impact of bonds on financial markets, is not discussed here.

11. The public sector deficit can be measured either by the saving-investment gap of the general government in the national account statistics or by bond revenues of the general account of the national budget (the relation between the two is explained in Appendix C). In this section I use the latter measure. The former is used in the section below entitled "Public Finance and the Macroeconomy."

12. Short-term bonds were issued. Also, public corporations have issued bonds since FY 1958. The latter was one reason the general account budget was balanced for many years.

13. "Corporation tax" (*hōjin zei*) corresponds to the corporate income tax in the United States. But since "income tax" means only individual income tax in Japan, I use the above term instead of "corporate income tax."

14. It is possible to regard these bonds as financing deficits in "current subaccounts," although no such subaccount distinction is made in the general account.

15. James M. Buchanan and Richard E. Wagner, *Democracy in Deficit: The Political Legacy of Lord Keynes* (New York: Academic Press, 1977).

16. Needless to say, bond revenues of the general account can differ from value of the bonds issued because some of the latter are used to redeem previously issued bonds.

17. Unlike in the United States, social security contributions (*shakai hokenryō*) are not regarded as taxes. They are collected through channels entirely separate from the tax collection system and become revenues of the social security special accounts. See Appendix A.

18. The major items included in direct taxes as defined in the national account statistics are income taxes, corporation taxes, and local income taxes (*jūmin zei*). Property taxes and business taxes (*jigyō zei*) are classified as indirect taxes.

19. Direct taxes in the national tax statistics include income taxes, corporation taxes, and inheritance taxes. All other national taxes are classified as indirect taxes, among which the liquor tax, gasoline tax, and commodity tax are the most important.

20. Contributions to the Employees' Pension Fund are determined in terms of their ratio to "regular earnings," which is wage earnings minus bonuses. In the case of the People's Pension Fund, contributions are set at fixed amounts.

21. Income tax rates are not inflation indexed in Japan.

22. Revisions of the liquor tax and the gasoline tax, whose rates are determined in absolute amounts (so that revisions become necessary in a growing economy to prevent effective tax rates from falling) are also counted as tax increases. Thus, if we confine ourselves to the income tax, the magnitude of the tax reduction was greater: the average ratio of income tax reduction to income tax revenue was 9.1 per cent during the 1960s.

23. Income taxes on business income are imposed on nonincorporated businesses. Incorporated businesses are subject to the corporation tax.

24. These include incomes from business and agriculture.

25. Hiromitsu Ishi, *Zaisei kaikaku no ronri* (Logic of fiscal reforms) (Tokyo: Nihon Keizai Shimbunsha, 1982), chap. 5.

26. Break, "Issues."

27. The Ministry of Finance regards the taxation of entertainment expenses (*kōsai hi*) as a special measure to increase tax revenue. If this is subtracted, the net loss is only ¥0.5 trillion.

28. "Special Analysis G: Tax Expenditures," *Special Analyses, Budget of the United States Government, FY 1985.*

29. See Yukio Noguchi, "Nihon kigyō no zeifutan" (Tax burden on Japanese firms), *Kikan gendai keizai*, Vol. 61 (Spring 1985); and idem, "Tax Structure and Saving-Investment Balance," *Hitotsubashi Journal of Economics*, Vol. 26, No. 1 (June 1985).

30. Note that the budget figures are those of the initial budget, whereas GNP figures are actual figures.

31. Redemption of bonds is carried out through the debt-servicing special account. Debt-servicing costs in the general account are transfers to this special account, which includes, in addition to interest payments, outlays for accumulating the funds for future redemption—the annual amount is set at 1.6 per cent of the outstanding debt. This much is therefore included in the debt-servicing costs of the general account. (However, because of the necessity of reducing expenditures, the transfer for the accumulation of funds has been suspended since FY 1983.) In the income-expenditure account of the SNA data (see Appendix C), only interest payments are included.

32. Primary and secondary schools are run by local governments, to which the national government provides subsidies.

33. The stability of budget shares has been pointed out as one of the major features of the Japanese budget by John C. Campbell, *Contemporary Japanese Budget Politics* (Berkeley: University of California Press, 1977). Note that this does not apply to social security and other expenditures mentioned in the text.

34. This view is seen, for example, in James M. Buchanan, John Burton, and Richard E. Wagner, *The Consequences of Mr. Keynes* (London: Institute of Economic Affairs, 1978).

35. Another important element is the Fiscal Investment and Loan Program (FILP), which is a government-conducted financial program. For a discussion of FILP, see Yukio Noguchi, "The Government-Business Relationship in Japan: The Changing Role of Fiscal Resources," in Kozo Yamamura, ed., *Policy and Trade Issues of the Japanese Economy: American and Japanese Perspectives* (Seattle: University of Washington Press, 1982).

36. Most of the increase was in the number of teachers, fire fighters, and welfare-related personnel. The increases in local government employees were to a large extent caused by the changing needs of the society. But the number of workers in general administrative sections increased as well (from 591,000 in 1967 to 686,000 in 1980).

37. A brief discussion of the social security system in Japan is provided in Appendix B.

38. "Natural increase" is defined as the increase in tax revenues that would be expected if no revision were made to the tax laws. Care must be taken in looking at Fig. 6 since the bond dependency ratio and the growth rate of social security are calculated on the settlement basis, but the natural increase is calculated from

the initial budget. Thus, for example, the natural increase in FY 1975 was not realized.

39. Yukio Noguchi, "A Dynamic Model of Incremental Budgeting," *Hitotsubashi Journal of Economics*, Vol. 20, No. 2 (Feb. 1980).

40. Japan, Ministry of Welfare, Actuarial Division, *Nenkin to zaisei* (Financing public pensions) (Tokyo: Shakai Hoken Hōki Kenkyūkai, 1981), p. 37.

41. Strictly speaking, a high discount rate underestimates the required contribution even in a steady-state economy because it overvalues the funds existing at the time of calculation.

42. This corresponds to "[gross] social security wealth" as defined in Martin Feldstein, "Social Security, Induced Retirement, and Aggregate Capital Accumulation," *Journal of Political Economy*, Vol. 82, No. 5 (Sept./Oct. 1974).

43. It may become necessary to increase bond issues at the supplementary budget stage if tax revenues fall short of estimates, as in FY 1981 and 1982. In FY 1981, a complicated maneuver was used to avoid additional bond issues at the supplementary budget stage. In FY 1982, however, this procedure was not used, and the bond dependency ratio rose from the initial budget level of 21.0 per cent to 30.2 per cent at the supplementary budget stage.

44. Despite a zero or minus ceiling, it is possible for total general expenditures to increase because such items as government employees' salaries are not subject to the ceiling.

45. The nature of this council was significantly different from that of other advisory councils, which are generally said to be controlled by bureaucrats.

46. Needless to say, the drop in the economic growth rate has contributed to the decrease in the expenditure growth rate. The growth rate of general expenditures has, however, been lower than the economic growth rate in recent years.

47. Although the ratio of bond issues to GNP has been reduced, outstanding government debt continues to increase rapidly, even in terms of its ratio to GNP. As a result, debt-servicing costs in the general account are increasing as well.

48. In this section, "private sector" is the sum of the household sector and the nonfinancial corporate sector. Strictly speaking, this definition is wrong. Public corporations are included in the corporate sector in the national account statistics, and I do not include financial corporations and nonprofit private organizations in my definition of the "private sector." For this reason, the sum of "private sector excess saving" and government deficit does not equal current external surplus in Fig. 7.

49. The negative correlation between household and government savings has been pointed out by Yutaka Kosai in "Kojin chochiku to sonota no chochiku tono kankei" (The relationship between personal and other savings), *Chochiku jihō*, Mar. 1981.

50. Here I deal with gross savings. It may be interesting to analyze net savings. It may also be necessary to include expenses for consumer durables in the definition of household saving.

51. Robert J. Barro, "Are Government Bonds Net Wealth?" *Journal of Political Economy*, Vol. 82, No. 6 (Dec. 1974). If people are concerned about government deficit in the current account, Barro's hypothesis implies substitutability between government saving and household saving.

52. Martin Feldstein and G. Fanne, "Taxes, Corporate Dividend Policy and Personal Savings: The British Postwar Experience," *Review of Economics and Statistics*, Vol. 55, No. 4 (Nov. 1973); Paul A. David and John L. Scadding, "Private Savings: Ultrarationality, Aggregation, and 'Denison's Law,'" *Journal of Political Econ-*

omy, Vol. 82, No. 2 (Mar./Apr. 1974); and E. F. Denison, "A Note on Private Saving," *Review of Economics and Statistics*, Vol. 40, No. 2 (Aug. 1958).

The relationship among the various hypotheses can be explained as follows (HS, household saving; CS, corporate saving; GS, government saving [savings are defined in net terms]; NNP, net national product; YD, disposable income; HC, household consumption; T, tax; TR, transfer payments; GC, government consumption). The following identities exist among these variables: $YD + (T - TR) + CS = NNP$; $HS = YD - HC$; and $GS = T - TR - GC$. The proposition that household and corporate savings are perfect substitutes can be written as $HS + CS = a\text{NNP}$, where a is the propensity to save out of NNP. Using the above identities, this can be rewritten as $HC = (1 - a)\text{NNP} - (T - TR)$. David and Scadding interpreted this relationship as reflecting the tendency of households to regard tax-financed government consumption as equivalent to household consumption. Strictly speaking, however, $(T - TR)$ does not necessarily correspond to GC. Substitutability between HC and GC emerges in a more direct way from the Barro hypothesis, which can be written as $HS + CS + GS = b\text{NNP}$, where b is the propensity to save (it is assumed that people are concerned about the government deficit in the current account). This can be rewritten as $HG = (1 - b)\text{NNP} - GC$. For further discussion, see George M. Furstenberg, "Private Saving," *American Economic Review*, Vol. 70, No. 2 (May 1980); and R. Kormendi, "Government Debt, Government Spending, and Private Sector Behavior," *American Economic Review*, Vol. 73, No. 5 (Dec. 1983).

53. Needless to say, this indicator does not capture completely the entire effects of government activities on aggregate demand. For example, we should consider tax variables. It may also be interesting to calculate a full-employment deficit, although the concept of "full employment" becomes ambiguous if one takes the view that recent recessions have been caused by supply-side factors such as the oil price increase rather than insufficient demand.

54. Japan, Economic Planning Agency, *2000 nen no Nihon* (Japan in the year 2000) (Tokyo: Government Printing Bureau, 1982). The basic assumption for estimating future benefits (in the case of employees' pensions) is that the present formula for calculating benefits will remain unchanged. This assumption causes an overestimation bias because the replacement ratio will rise from the present level because of the maturing of the system. The contribution rate is assumed to be the same as the present level as long as the reserve fund remains. After it vanishes around the year 2000, the rate is assumed to be determined on a pay-as-you-go basis.

55. Japan, Ministry of Welfare, *Nenkin seido kaikaku no kaisetsu* (Explanations of pension reform) (Tokyo: Shakai Hōken Kenkyūjo, 1984).

56. This view was developed by Feldstein in "Social Security." For a discussion of the effects of public pensions on savings in Japan, see Yukio Noguchi, "Wagakuni kōteki nenkin no shomondai" (Problems of public pensions in Japan), *Kikan gendai keizai*, Vol. 50 (Autumn 1982).

57. Yukio Noguchi, "Kōteki nenkin ni okeru jukyū, futan no sedaikan kakusa" (Intergenerational differences in the benefits-contributions relation in public pension programs), *Kikan gendai keizai*, Vol. 57 (Spring 1984).

58. For a more detailed description in English of the budget system, see the Ministry of Finance's annual publication, *Budget in Brief* (Tokyo: Government Printing Bureau). The tax system is explained in Peckman and Kaizuka, "Taxation." For a description of the Fiscal Investment and Loan Program (FILP), see Noguchi, "Government-Business Relationship."

59. A more detailed English explanation of the social insurance system can be found in Social Insurance Agency, *Outline of Social Insurance in Japan, 1981* (Tokyo: Yoshida Finance and Social Security Law Institute, 1981).

Hamada and Horiuchi: Political Economy

We highly appreciate valuable comments on early versions of this paper from Masahiko Aoki, Ryutaro Komiya, Hugh Patrick, Kazuo Satō, Kozo Yamamura, Yasukichi Yasuba, and other participants at the JPERC conference.

1. This is pointed out by Eisuke Sakakibara, Robert Feldman, and Yuzo Harada, *The Japanese Financial System in Comparative Perspectives* (Washington, D.C.: U.S. Government Printing Office, 1982), pp. 10–23. The category of "individuals" includes both unincorporated businesses and households. Thus, the figures in Table 1 exaggerate the relative importance of households as borrowers in financial markets.

2. According to estimates based on the Bank of Japan's *Shikinjunkan kanjō* (Flow of funds accounts), during 1954–64, private financial institutions held 80 per cent of newly issued corporate bonds and 36 per cent of newly issued equity stocks. This suggests that private financial institutions were important not only in loan markets, but also in capital markets.

3. For instance, see John Zysman, *Governments, Markets, and Growth: Financial Systems and the Policies of Industrial Change* (Ithaca, N.Y.: Cornell University Press, 1983), pp. 234–51. See also J. Andrew Spindler, *Finance and Foreign Policy in Germany and Japan* (Washington, D.C.: Brookings Institution, 1984), pp. 93–114.

4. The internationalization of Japanese financial markets and foreign pressures on them have been one of the strongest influences on structural changes in the financial system. We discuss them only briefly, however, since they will be discussed more fully in the second volume in this series.

5. For the importance of transaction costs in financial markets, see George J. Benston and Clifford W. Smith, "A Transaction Cost Approach to the Theory of Financial Intermediation," *Journal of Finance*, Vol. 31, No. 2 (May 1976), pp. 215–31.

6. The bond investment trust funds introduced in 1961 would have become strong competition for bank deposits. However, the lack of wide and deep secondary markets for bonds frustrated their development.

7. This situation was called under-liquidity by Ryuichiro Tachi and Ryutaro Komiya, "Under-liquidity and Monetary Policy in Japan," *Economic Review (Keizai kenkyū)*, Vol. 11, No. 3 (July 1960), pp. 288–95. For the influence of public bonds on the financial structure, see Benjamin M. Friedman, "Postwar Changes in the American Financial Markets," in Martin Feldstein, ed., *The American Economy in Transition* (Chicago: University of Chicago Press, 1980), pp. 9–78.

8. Even at present, banks lend at a higher rate than the marginal cost of funds when credit is not tight, but at a lower rate when credit is tight. See Japan, Economic Planning Agency, *The Present State of the Japanese Economy for 1984* (Tokyo: Ministry of Finance Printing Bureau, 1984), table 4-11.

9. See, for instance, William G. Shepherd, *The Treatment of Market Power: Antitrust, Regulation, and Public Enterprise* (New York: Columbia University Press, 1975), pp. 171–82.

10. See Richard E. Caves and Masu Uekusa, "Industrial Organization," in Hugh Patrick and Henry Rosovsky, eds., *Asia's New Giant: How the Japanese Economy Works* (Washington, D.C.: Brookings Institution, 1976), pp. 494–504.

11. According to Iwao Nakatani, "The Economic Role of Financial Corporate

Grouping," in Masahiko Aoki, ed., *The Economic Analysis of the Japanese Firm* (Amsterdam: North-Holland, 1984), pp. 227–58, the *keiretsu* groups did not stimulate economic growth per se but were effective in stabilizing the business performance of their constituents.

12. See Japan, Ministry of Finance, Securities Bureau, *Annual Report on Securities for 1965* (Tokyo: Ministry of Finance Printing Bureau, 1965), p. 113.

13. See Yoshio Suzuki, *Money and Banking in Contemporary Japan* (New Haven: Yale University Press, 1980), pp. 42–45.

14. See Hugh T. Patrick, *Monetary Policy and Central Banking in Contemporary Japan* (Bombay: University of Bombay, 1962), chap. 4.

15. As we argue in the previous section, the establishment of long-term credit banks could be justified to a certain extent as a means of promoting maturity transformation in financial markets.

16. For a well-documented history of the bond issue arrangement, see Securities Exchange Council, Committee on the Working of the Bond and Stock Markets, *Nozomashii kōshasai shijō no arikata* (Report on the desirable bond market for Japan) (Tokyo: Kin'yū Zaisei Jijō Kenkyūkai, 1978), pp. 270–72.

17. Through administrative guidance, the MOF guided banks to refrain from actively providing their customers with commodities instead of higher interest rates.

18. However, according to Saitō and Oga's empirical study, the savings behavior of the Japanese households was independent of real rates of return on bank deposits. See Mitsuo Saitō and Takashi Oga, "Chochiku kōdō no yōin bunseki" (A factor analysis of households' savings), *Keizai bunseki*, Vol. 74 (Jan. 1979), pp. 1–22.

19. See, for instance, Yasuhiro Wakita, "Wagakuni no kashidashi shijō to keiyaku torihiki" (Loan markets and contracts in Japan), *Kin'yū kenkyū*, Vol. 2, No. 1 (Mar. 1983), pp. 47–76.

20. Data on compensating balances from Japan, Ministry of Finance, Banking Bureau, *Nempō* (Annual report), various issues.

21. For the argument that the price mechanism is generally restricted in bank loan markets, see Joseph E. Stiglitz and Andrew Weiss, "Credit Rationing in Markets with Imperfect Information," *American Economic Review*, Vol. 71, No. 3 (June 1981), pp. 393–410. Some empirical studies, such as Kazumasa Iwata and Kōichi Hamada, *Kin'yū seisaku to ginkō kōdō* (Monetary policy and the behavior of banks) (Tokyo: Tōyō Keizai Shimpōsha, 1980), pp. 176–99; and Takatoshi Itō and Kazuo Ueda, "Tests of Equilibrium Hypothesis in Disequilibrium Econometrics: An International Comparison of Credit Rationing," *International Economic Review*, Vol. 22, No. 3 (Oct. 1981), pp. 691–708, suggest the existence of credit rationing in Japanese loan markets.

22. For the working of the Order of Priority in Industrial Loans, see Kaichi Shimura, *Gendai Nihon kōshasai ron* (Studies on bond markets in contemporary Japan) (Tokyo: University of Tokyo Press, 1978), pp. 10–12.

23. For instance, see Akiyoshi Horiuchi, "Economic Growth and Financial Allocation in Postwar Japan," Research Institute for the Japanese Economy, Discussion Paper 84-F-3 (Aug. 1984), pp. 44–47.

24. See, for instance, Gardner Ackley and Hiromitsu Ishi, "Fiscal, Monetary, and Related Policies," in Patrick and Rosovsky, *Asia's New Giant*, pp. 187–95.

25. See Suzuki, *Money and Banking*, pp. 149–224; and Koichi Hamada and Fumio Hayashi, "Monetary Policy in Postwar Japan," in Albert Ando et al., eds., *Monetary Policy in Our Time* (Cambridge, Mass.: MIT Press, 1985), pp. 83–121.

26. See Akiyoshi Horiuchi, *Nihon no kin'yū seisaku* (Monetary policy in Japan) (Tokyo: Tōyō Keizai Shimpōsha, 1980), pp. 137–83.

27. This is a market for conditional sales and purchases of bonds for raising funds on the security of bonds or for investing funds. The *gensaki* market is a free market whose interest rates are not subject to BOJ intervention.

28. Prior to the mid-1960s, the primary method used by securities companies to raise funds was to borrow in the interbank call money market by pledging securities borrowed from owners of the securities. With a crisis developing in the management of securities companies, the urgent danger arose that the securities companies would be unable to return the borrowed securities to their owners. In response to this situation, the monetary authorities prohibited securities companies from borrowing in the interbank money markets.

29. Before March 1981, the short-term prime rate was set at 0.25 per cent above the official discount rate. In March 1981, the difference between these rates was widened to 0.5 per cent.

30. A September 1982 report on industrial finance by MITI's Industrial Structure Council vividly presents the dissatisfaction of nonfinancial firms with the existing domestic financial system. The report recommends re-examination of the traditional requirement of collateral for commercial loans and corporate bonds.

31. During 1982, Japanese corporations and public enterprises raised 7.6 billion Swiss francs by issuing convertible bonds (CBs) in Switzerland. This was twice the amount they raised through CBs in the Swiss market in the previous year. In response, restrictions on CB issuance in the domestic market were relaxed to a certain extent in early 1983.

32. See, for instance, Stuart I. Greenbaum and Bryon Higgins, "Financial Innovation," in George J. Benston, ed., *Financial Services: The Changing Institutions and Government Policy* (Englewood Cliffs, N.J.: Prentice-Hall, 1983), pp. 213–34; and Edward J. Kane, "Accelerating Inflation, Technological Innovation and the Decreasing Effectiveness of Banking Regulation," *Journal of Finance*, Vol. 3, No. 2 (May 1981), pp. 355–67.

33. See Yoshio Suzuki, "Financial Innovation in Japan: Background, Current State, and Prospects," paper prepared for the First International Symposium on Financial Development, Seoul, Dec. 1984.

34. The recent internationalization of the Japanese financial markets is well documented by Eisuke Sakakibara and Akira Kondō, *Study on the Internationalization of Tokyo's Money Markets*, JCIF Policy Study Series, No. 1 (June 1984).

35. See Shōichi Rōyama, *Nihon no kin'yū shisutemu* (The financial system of Japan) (Tokyo: Tōyō Keizai Shimpōsha, 1982), pp. 214–16, for the process undertaken by the Bank of Japan to liberalize Japan's money markets.

36. Japan's monetary authorities have regulated the positions of banks in foreign exchange transactions by several means. The *yen tenkan kisei* was one such regulation. Under this regulation, each bank was obliged to restrict within a limit its short position in spot transactions involving foreign exchanges. The purpose of this regulation was to restrict the inflow of funds into Japan's domestic financial markets.

37. See Kōichi Hamada, *Kokusai kin'yū no seiji keizaigaku* (The political economy of international monetary interdependence) (Tokyo: Sobunsha, 1982); English trans. (Tokyo: MITI Press, 1986).

38. For a discussion of the neglect of consumers' interest in trade issues (including services), see Koichi Hamada and Yoshiro Nakajo, "Trade Issues and

Consumer Interests," in OECD, ed., *Proceedings of the Symposium on Consumer Policy and International Trade* (Paris, forthcoming).

Aoki: The Japanese Firm

1. See Iwao Nakatani, "The Economic Role of Financial Corporate Grouping," in Masahiko Aoki, ed., *The Economic Analysis of the Japanese Firm* (Amsterdam: North-Holland, 1984), pp. 227–58.

2. See Masahiko Aoki, "Innovative Adaptation Through the Quasi-Tree Structure: An Emerging Aspect of Japanese Entrepreneurship," *Zeitschrift für Nationalökonomie*, supplement 4 (1984), pp. 177–98; Banri Asanuma, "The Organization of Parts Purchases," *Japanese Economic Studies*, Summer 1985, pp. 32–53; Japan, MITI, Agency for Small and Medium Size Enterprises, "Survey on Subcontracting Situations" (unpublished report, 1982); and Robert Cole and Taizo Yakushiji, *The Japanese and American Automotive Industry in Transition* (Ann Arbor: University of Michigan Press, 1984), chap. 9.

3. See Japan, Economic Council, Econometric Committee, *Multi-Sector Model for Economic Planning: The Fifth Report of the Econometric Committee* (Tokyo, 1977).

4. This series of works culminated in a book, Masahiko Aoki, *The Cooperative Game Theory of the Firm* (Oxford: Oxford University Press, 1984).

5. For the exact definition, detailed institutional description, and comparative analysis of the efficiency performances of these diverse institutional models, see Aoki, *Cooperative Game Theory*, part 3.

6. Ronald Dore, *British Factory–Japanese Factory: The Origin of National Diversity in Industrial Relations* (Berkeley: University of California Press, 1973), p. 364.

7. See Aoki, *Cooperative Game Theory*, part 2, for detailed discussion.

8. This postulate is called the neo-classical *synthetic* postulate because it is consistent with the neo-classical as well as the Keynesian systems. The former views wage bargaining as conducted individually in the market, whereas the latter views wage bargaining as conducted collectively. But in both systems wages are a given for the firm.

9. See Kazuo Koike, "Skill Formation Systems in the U.S. and Japan: A Comparative Study," in Aoki, *The Japanese Firm*, pp. 47–75; and his paper in this volume.

10. This issue is discussed in detail in Aoki, *Cooperative Game Theory*, chaps. 6–7.

11. Even before the war, the control of *zaibatsu* families was in gradual eclipse. This was particularly the case with the Mitsui family. Under the leadership of Seihin Ikeda, who became a full-time director of Mitsui Gōmei (Mitsui Partners), between 1931 and 1936, all of the family members were made to retire from directorships and executive positions of all Mitsui-related companies except for Mitsui Gōmei, which was the holding company. Also between 1933 and 1934, the stock of important Mitsui member-companies, such as Ohji Pulp, Tōyō Raymon, and Hokkaido Coal Shipping, was made public. Mitsui Gōmei itself was merged into the Mitsui Trading Company in 1940 and made an independent stock company in 1944.

12. Soichiro Honda and Tsuneo Morita may be cited as representative founder-managers. Although active since the prewar period, Konosuke Matsushita is also representative of those who exhibited extraordinary entrepreneurial ability in the turmoil of the postwar period.

13. See Aoki, *Cooperative Game Theory*, chap. 8, for more detail.

14. Direct foreign investment in Japan had been severely restricted by the Law Concerning Foreign Investment (FIL). The FIL was based on the so-called negative principle: all direct foreign investment was prohibited without special validation. However, in 1964, Japan was admitted to the OECD, and admission required the liberalization of foreign investment regulations. Subsequently, the Japanese government approved direct foreign investment almost automatically, except in special sectors such as agriculture, petroleum, leather, and retail trade. However, it did not abandon the negative principle until the repeal of FIL in 1980.

15. According to the 1981 Survey of Corporations by the National Tax Agency, the total amount of expense accounts of all corporations was $3.1 trillion in 1980, equal to 13.3 per cent of total profits and exceeding total dividends payout (9.8 per cent of profits). This suggests that managerial consumption on the job is not negligible. This figure, however, includes the expense accounts of small proprietors, which include de facto profits on which taxes are evaded.

16. Masahiko Aoki, "Shareholders' Non-Unanimity on Investment Financing: Banks vs. Individual Investors," in Aoki, *The Japanese Firm*, pp. 193–224.

17. Yusaku Futatsuki, *Gendai Nihon no kigyō shūdan* (Corporate groupings in contemporary Japan) (Tokyo: Tōyō Keizai Shimpōsha, 1977).

18. According to a recent Bank of Japan estimate, despite the high personal savings rate, the assets of Japanese households are still predominantly in the form of land, houses, and other fixed assets (63.4 per cent of total assets). The relative share of financial assets was only 33.4 per cent at the end of 1982, whereas in the United States 64.1 per cent of individual assets are in the form of financial assets (24.1 per cent in fixed assets). However, the Family Saving Survey of 1983 shows that the relative proportion of shareholdings in individual financial portfolios increases as the income level of the household rises. The average household with an annual income of ¥5 million and financial savings of ¥7 million invests only 3.9 per cent of its assets in stock. But the proportion increases to 12 per cent for households with an annual income of ¥10–15 million and to 17 per cent for households with an annual income of more than ¥15 million.

19. For a detailed description of corporate grouping, see Eleanor Hadley, *Antitrust in Japan* (Princeton: Princeton University Press, 1970); and Masahiko Aoki, "Aspects of the Japanese Firm," in idem, *The Japanese Firm*, pp. 3–43.

20. After his personal misconduct was made public, the former president of Mitsukoshi, the oldest department store in Japan, was dismissed from the position of representative director (chief executive officer) by a resolution passed by the Board of Directors in 1982. The board consisted mostly of inside managers subordinate to him. However, instrumental in this move was the initiative taken by one outside director representing the Mitsui group, who was a former board chairman of Mitsui Bank.

21. Richard Caves and Masu Uekusa, *Industrial Organization in Japan* (Washington, D.C.: Brookings Institution, 1976).

22. Nakatani, "Economic Role."

23. See, for example, Hiroyuki Odagiri, "Kigyō shūdan no riron" (A theory of corporate groups), *Economic Studies Quarterly*, No. 26 (Aug. 1975), pp. 144–54.

24. See Nakatani, "Economic Role"; and Masahiko Aoki, "Risk Sharing in the Corporate Group," in idem, *The Japanese Firm*, pp. 259–64, for this hypothesis.

25. For the sake of simplicity, let us assume that there exist only two firms, A and B. The profitability of investment projects undertaken by the two firms is assumed to be uncertain and dependent on two disjointed events, 1 and 2,

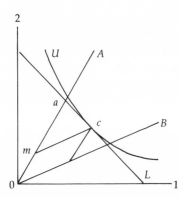 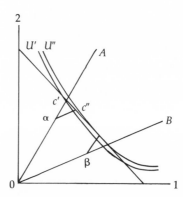

whose occurrences the firms cannot control. The horizontal axes in the accompanying figure represent profit when event 1 occurs, and the vertical axes represent profit when event 2 occurs. Let vectors A and B represent the profit prospects of firm A and firm B, respectively. Suppose that a person owns a certain share a in firm A's stock (left panel of figure) and that the tradability of shares in A for shares in B is represented by the straight line L. If the risk attitude and risk assessment of the individual shareholder is represented by the indifference map U as depicted, his optimal portfolio selection would be point c. In other words, he can ensure himself against uncertain events in the best way by exchanging a proportion am/ao of his shares in firm A for shares in firm B at the market rate. Suppose now that firm B owns α per cent of firm A's stock and firm A owns β per cent of firm B's stock. If the market values of these mutual shareholdings are equal, the opportunities open to the investor do not change (right panel), provided that short sales are possible. So much is obvious since we have assumed unlimited tradability of individual shares in a perfectly competitive market. However, if some no-sales constraint is imposed on individual shareholdings, the role of intercorporate shareholding would change. For instance, let us imagine the situation in which a person cannot sell his shares in firm A on the market for some reason. If the indifference maps for this person are as depicted in the right panel, the utility level under a no-sales constraint without intercorporate shareholding is represented by the curve U' going through c' and obviously inferior to the level U'' achievable at c'' under the same condition but with intercorporate shareholding. Intercorporate shareholding can remedy the inefficiency caused by the absence of salability of individual shares to the extent that they are permissible. (Note incidentally that the complete integration of firms A and B would be able to realize, all things being equal, the optimal risk spreading possible under the perfect capital market. Why then do member-firms of Japanese corporate groups not merge into a single giant firm? I treat this problem in the next section.)

26. Japan Economic Journal, *Ginko no yuutsu* (The melancholy of banks) (Tokyo: Nihon Keizai Shimbunsha, 1978).

27. See Richard Pascale and Thomas Rohlen, "The Mazda Turnaround," *Journal of Japanese Studies*, Vol. 9, No. 2 (Summer 1983), pp. 219–63.

28. Nakatani's econometric studies rely on the classification of corporate grouping established by the Nihon Keizai Chōsakai. According to this classification, Sony and Toyota are members of the Mitsui group, Honda is part of Mitsubishi,

and Matsushita is part of Sumitomo. But as Hadley rightfully pointed out, the validity of this classification is dubious. Eleanor Hadley, "Counterpoint on Business Groupings and Government-Industry Relations in Automobiles," in Aoki, *The Japanese Firm*, pp. 319–27. Sony and Honda may be more appropriately classified as new companies led by founder-managers. Although Toyota and Matsushita have been active since before the war, they are under the strong control of founder-managers. But since those companies are among the most profitable and the fastest growing, an appropriate reclassification of companies would only strengthen Nakatani's findings.

29. See SMEA, *Report of the Basic Survey of the Industrial Situation* (Tokyo: MITI, 1966–81).

30. For greater detail, see Aoki, "Innovative Adaptation."

31. For an excellent field study, see Asanuma, "Organization."

32. Aoki, "Innovative Adaptation."

33. Cole and Yakushiji, *Automotive Industry in Transition*.

34. Aoki, "Innovative Adaptation."

35. As estimated by Shimada, the elasticity of employment to output in 1974–75 shows that the speed of employment adjustment in Japan begins rather slowly, but eventually reaches as high a level as other Western countries, except the United States. The equilibrium elasticity for Japan is estimated at about half the U.S. figure. James Orr, Haruo Shimada, and Atsushi Seike, "U.S.-Japan Comparative Study of Employment Adjustment," a draft final report of the U.S. Department of Labor–Japan Ministry of Labor comparative research project on employment adjustment, mimeo. (1982).

Koike: Human Resource Development

1. Of the many books on this topic, let me cite just one example: OECD, *The Development of Industrial Relations Systems: Some Implications of Japanese Experience* (Paris, 1977).

2. European Community, *Structure of Earnings in Industry, 1972*, Vol. 13 (Brussels, 1975–76).

3. Kazuo Koike, *Nihon no jukuren* (Skill formation in Japan) (Tokyo: Yūhikaku, 1981).

4. Ibid.

5. Yoshiyuki Morikiyo, *Rōdō to ginō* (Work and skill) (Tokyo: Rōdō Kagaku Kenkyūjo, 1981).

6. Japan, Ministry of Labor, *Koyō dōkō chōsa* (Survey of workers' mobility) (Tokyo, 1972).

7. Kazuo Koike, *Shokuba no rōdō kumiai to sanka-rōshi kankei no Nichibei hikaku* (A comparative study of industrial relations on the shop floor in the United States and Japan) (Tokyo: Tōyō Keizai Shimpōsha, 1977). The final chapter of this volume appeared in English as "Japan's Industrial Relations," *Japanese Economic Studies*, Fall 1978, pp. 42–90.

8. Koike, *Shokuba no rōdō kumiai.*

9. Kuramitsu Muramatsu, "Nihon no seizōgyō ni okeru kaiko to sono daitai shudan" (Redundancy and its substitutes in Japanese manufacturing industry), in Kōyō Shokugyō Kenkyūjo, ed., *Gendai no shitsugyō* (Unemployment in contemporary Japan) (Tokyo, 1984).

10. Japan, Ministry of Labor, *Koyō hendō sōgō chōsa* (A survey on employment adjustment) (Tokyo, 1980).

11. Koike, *Shokuba no rōdō kumiai*.
12. Banri Asanuma, "Jidōsha sangyō ni okeru buhin torihiki no kōzō" (Stucture of parts transactions in the automobile industry), *Kikan gendai keizai*, Vol. 58 (Summer 1984).
13. Kazuo Koike, "Kaiko kara mita gendai Nihon no rōshi kankei" (Redundancy in contemporary Japanese industrial relations), in Chikashi Moriguchi et al., eds., *Nihon keizai no kōzō bunseki* (A study on the structure of the Japanese economy) (Tokyo: Sōbunsha, 1983).
14. Ibid.
15. Japan, Ministry of Labor, *Rōdō kumiai kihon chōsa* (Basic survey on labor unions) (Tokyo, 1985).
16. Kazuo Koike, *Japanese Workers Skill* (London: Macmillan, forthcoming), chap. 7.
17. One of the most detailed analyses of this issue is Michio Nitta, "Tekkōgyō ni okeru rōshi kyōgi no seido to jittai" (Joint labor-management conference in the Japanese steel industry), *Shakai kagaku kenkyū*, Vol. 32, Nos. 5–6 (1981).
18. Robert M. Blackburn, *Union Character and Social Class* (London: Batsford, 1967).
19. See Koike, *Shokuba no rōdō kumiai*; and idem, *Japanese Workers Skill*, chap. 8.
20. Kazuo Koike, *Chūshō kigyō no jukuren* (Workers' skill in small and medium-size firms) (Tokyo: Dōbunkan, 1981).
21. Ibid., chaps. 1 and 2.
22. Asanuma's paper (see note 12) has excellent insights on the relationship between large firms and parts suppliers. See also Masahiko Aoki, *The Economic Analysis of the Japanese Firm* (Amsterdam: North-Holland, 1984), pp. 14–15.
23. Koike, *Japanese Workers Skill*, chap. 1.
24. Kazuo Koike, "Rōshi kankei no White-collarization Model" (White-collarization model of industrial relations), *Nihon rōdō kyōkai zasshi* No. 304 (Sept. 1984).
25. Koike, *Shokuba no rōdō kumiai*.

Patrick and Rohlen: Family Enterprises

We have benefited from research assistance especially by Michael Smitka and by Frances McCall, Hilary Hinds, and Noriaki Fukushima and from comments by Kazuo Koike, Kazuo Sato, Ted Bestor, Kent Calder, and Robert Chapman Wood as well as the participants at the JPERC conferences. Aside from correcting many of our errors and misperceptions, they raised many important issues—sufficient to keep us busy the rest of our lives.
1. Japan, Office of the Prime Minister, Bureau of Statistics, *1981 Establishment Census of Japan*, Vol. 3, *Incorporated Enterprises*, table 2. This triennial survey is a basic reference source.
2. Official definitions typically identify "small" enterprises as those with fewer than 100 workers, "small and medium" as those with fewer than 300 workers. The basic labor force survey is Japan, Office of the Prime Minister, *1982 Employment Status Survey—Whole Japan* (Tokyo, May 1984). The annual *White Paper on Small and Medium Enterprises in Japan* (hereafter *SME White Paper*), prepared by the Ministry of International Trade and Industry, Small and Medium Enterprise Agency, is a useful source of data and government policy discussion. Since the 8,950,000 part-time workers are disproportionately employed in small enterprises, the respective employment shares of full-time workers is 64.6 per cent in

small firms, 18.2 per cent in medium ones, and 17.2 per cent in large ones. All ratios are to Japan's private sector labor force, excluding government employees (numbering 5,197,000), unless otherwise stated. The total labor force is 57.9 million; the "mainly working" (full-time workers) number 48.9 million.

3. Direct estimates are not available. This is based on a rough extrapolation of labor force and value-added ratios in manufacturing.

4. A number of Japanese specialists on problems of small-scale enterprise and some American anthropologists have conducted case-study research of Japanese family enterprises. The relevant literature in English includes Hiroshi Wagatsuma and George De Vos, *Heritage of Endurance* (Berkeley: University of California Press, 1983); Barbara Darlington Ito, "Entrepreneurial Women in Urban Japan: The Role of Personal Networks" (Ph.D. diss., University of Iowa, 1983); Jill Kleinberg, "Where Work and Family Are Almost One: The Lives of Folkcraft Potters," in David W. Plath, ed., *Work and Lifecourse in Japan* (Albany: State University of New York Press, 1983); and Dorinne Kay Kondo, "Work, Family and Self: A Cultural Analysis of Japanese Family Enterprise" (Ph.D. diss., Harvard University, 1982).

5. This estimate is based on the conservative assumption that each incorporated SFE with fewer than 30 workers has one family member in addition to the boss on the payroll. Excluding agriculture, where the number of wage-earning employees is minimal, almost one-quarter (24.2 per cent) of the nonagricultural labor force is made up of SFE owners and family members.

6. For such an interpretation in English, see Rob Steven, *Classes in Contemporary Japan* (Cambridge, Eng.: Cambridge University Press, 1983). There is an extensive literature in Japanese.

7. David Harold Stark, "The Yakuza: Japanese Crime Incorporated" (Ph.D. diss., University of Michigan, 1981), chap. 5.

8. David J. Storey, ed., *The Small Firm—An International Survey* (New York: St. Martin's Press, 1983), p. 3.

9. Felix Twaalfhoven and Tomohisa Hattori, *The Supporting Role of Small Japanese Enterprises* (Schiphol, Netherlands: N. V. Indivers Research, 1982), p. 29. Comparative data for Asian developing countries appear in Mathias Bruch and Ulrich Hiemenz, *Small- and Medium-Scale Industries in the ASEAN Countries* (Boulder, Colo.: Westview Press, 1984).

10. William Paul Sterling, "Comparative Studies of American and Japanese Labor Markets" (Ph.D. diss., Harvard University, 1984), table 5-3.

11. Ibid., table 5-37.

12. Robert Chapman Wood, *Small Business: Foundation of Japan's Best Known Successes* (Report prepared for Small Business Administration, revised Aug. 1984), sect. 7. Firms with 1–99 employees employed 40 per cent of U.S. wage earners (1977) and 56 per cent of Japanese wage earners (Wood, table 1, p. 14). In U.S. manufacturing, establishments with 1–99 employees produced 20 per cent of manufacturing value added and provided 25 per cent of employment; in Japan the comparable figures were 41 per cent and 58 per cent (Wood, table 3, p. 18). The exclusion of individual proprietorships and unpaid family workers understates the importance of small-scale activities more for Japan than for the United States.

13. For an appraisal of the SFE growth process, see Tadao Kiyonari, *Chūshō kigyō tokuhon* (Reader on small and medium-size industries) (Tokyo: Tōyō Keizai Shimbunsha, 1980). Useful descriptions in English appear in idem, "The Unsung Mainstays (1): Small Business," in Hyoe Murakami and Johannes Hirschmeier, eds., *Politics and Economics in Contemporary Japan* (Tokyo: Kodansha, 1983),

pp. 157–83; and Douglas Anthony, "Japan," in Storey, *The Small Firm*. A basic reference work is Miyohei Shinohara, "Survey of Japanese Literature on the Small Business—With Selected Bibliography," in Bert F. Hoselitz, ed., *The Role of Small Industry in the Process of Economic Growth* (The Hague: Mouton, 1968).

14. *Japan Statistical Yearbook, 1983*, table 4.9, pp. 134–35.

15. *1982 Unincorporated Enterprise Survey*, reference table 9.

16. *1983 SME White Paper*, p. 95.

17. Effective hourly rates are about half those of part-time female workers and one-third those of full-time regular female employees; Yoko Kawashima, "Wage Differentials Between Women and Men in Japan" (Ph.D. diss., Stanford University, 1983), p. 138.

18. See Ito, "Entrepreneurial Women."

19. M. Anne Hill, "Female Labor Force Participation in Developing and Developed Countries—Consideration of the Informal Sector," *Review of Economics and Statistics*, Vol. 65, No. 3 (August 1983); and idem, "Female Labor Force Participation in Japan: An Aggregate Model," *Journal of Human Resources*, Vol. 19, No. 2 (1984).

20. Table 3 indicates that enterprises with fewer than 100 employees constituted 55.2 per cent of total manufacturing employment in 1982. The 1981 Census of Manufactures indicates that establishments (not enterprises) with 4–99 workers accounted for 55.0 per cent of the labor force in manufacturing, 34.0 per cent of the shipments, and 39.1 per cent of the value added. There are two offsetting differences: manufacturing workers in enterprises with 1–3 workers (mostly unincorporated, self-employed) are excluded, and obviously some multiunit enterprises with more than 100 employees contain establishments (plants) with fewer than 100 employees.

21. Daniel I. Okimoto, Takuo Sugano, and Franklin B. Weinstein, eds., *Competitive Edge: The Semiconductor Industry in the U.S. and Japan* (Stanford: Stanford University Press, 1984), p. 193.

22. For a good comparative analysis of Japanese agricultural costs of products, land and labor inputs, and trade implications, see Emery N. Castle and Kenzo Hemmi, eds., *U.S.-Japanese Agricultural Trade Relations* (Washington, D.C.: Resources for the Future, 1982).

23. *1983 SME White Paper*, p. 6.

24. William V. Rapp, "Firm Size and Japan's Export Structure," in Hugh Patrick, ed., *Japanese Industrialization and Its Social Consequences* (Berkeley: University of California Press, 1976).

25. The information on the Tokyo briefcase industry is derived from Yoshio Satō, ed., *Kyodai toshi no reisai kigyō* (Small business in metropolises) (Tokyo: Nihon Keizai Hyōronsha, 1981), chap. 5. Sato does not discuss the protection of leather goods from import competition. Leather goods are the only manufactures on which import quotas remain because of the social problems and effective political pressures of Japan's outcaste community of some 2 million persons. A case study of pencil manufacture appears in Wagatsuma and De Vos, *Heritage of Endurance*; there are many similarities.

26. "Clustering or community-based industries" (*jiba sangyō*) is a category of analysis in Japan common to government policy as well as academic study. There are over 300 community-based industries recognized by the government and treated according to special laws for this type of industry. See Mitsuru Yamazaki, *Japan's Community-Based Industries: A Case Study of Small Industry* (Tokyo: Asian Productivity Organization, 1980).

27. Ronald Dore (with Koji Taira), *Flexible Rigidities: Industrial Policy and Struc-*

tural Adjustment in the Japanese Economy, 1970–1980, World Employment Programme Research, International Labour Organization, working paper (Geneva, 1983).

28. The most useful overview in English is Yoshio Sato, "The Subcontracting Production (*Shitauke*) System in Japan," *Keio Business Review,* Vol. 21, No. 1 (1983). Much of what follows is based on numerous survey results (including those reported in Sato's article); the ongoing research of Michael Smitka on the automotive industry and Thomas P. Rohlen's research on a plastics subcontractor and his comparison of Mazda and Chrysler; and the summer 1984 issue of *Gendai keizai* (on subcontracting). See also Masu Uekusa, *Sangyō soshiki ron* (Industrial organization) (Tokyo: Chikuma Shobō, 1982).

29. See Richard Pascale and Thomas P. Rohlen, "The Mazda Turnaround," *Journal of Japanese Studies,* Vol. 9, No. 2 (Summer 1983), pp. 219–63.

30. *Kōgyō jittai kihon chōsa, 1976* (Survey of industry) (Tokyo: Tsūsan Tōkei Kyōkai, 1979).

31. The qualities of natural parenting can be observed in this pattern. As the infant matures and gains strength, it also gains independence and shoulders a greater share of the risk. The parent-child metaphor must be understood as implying a growth dynamic similar to the maturation process rather than a static relationship of fixed obligations and dependence. A crucial failing of previous work on Japanese subcontracting has been oversimplification based on a static perspective.

32. *1984 SME White Paper,* p. 97.

33. See Hideto Ishida, "Anticompetitive Prices in the Distribution of Goods and Services in Japan: The Problem of Distribution *Keiretsu,*" *Journal of Japanese Studies,* Vol. 9, No. 2 (Summer 1983), pp. 319–34.

34. Surveys of small retail establishments are numerous. This account is based on Masako Amano, "Reisai kigyō ni okeru shufu no yakuwari kōzō" (The role of housewives in small business), *Kokumin kin'yū koko* (hereafter *KKK*) *chōsa geppō,* No. 264 (1983), pp. 13–27; Chūshō Kigyō Jigyōdan, *Chūshō kourigyō ni okeru atotsugisha no ikusei ni tsuite* (On grooming successors in small and medium-size retailers) (1981); Kokumin Kin'yū Koko Chōsabu, "Kourigyō ni okeru kazoku keiei no jittai" (The reality of family management in the retail sector), *KKK chōsa geppō,* No. 265 (1983), pp. 15–33; Shigehiko Watarai, ed., *Nihon no shōreisai kigyō kazoku keiei no hatsugyō jitsu no chōsa* (Survey of family management in small businesses in Japan) (Tokyo: Kokumin Kin'yu Koko Chōsabu, 1977); and Chūshō Kigyō Jōhō Sentā, *Chūshō kigyō no kigyō kōdō chōsa hōkokusho* (A survey on the origins of business behavior in small and medium-size enterprises) (1979). Since there are sampling issues in every survey, our effort has been to grasp the common pattern revealed in those we have utilized; we have therefore used rounded-off figures.

35. See Ito, "Entrepreneurial Women."

36. Machiko Osawa, "Women's Skill Formation, Labor Force Participation and Fertility in Japan" (Ph.D. diss., Southern Illinois University, 1984). Note also Hill, "Female Labor Force Participation."

37. See Kondo, "Work, Family, and Self"; and Ito, "Entrepreneurial Women," who reports this as an important motivation of her sample of female entrepreneurs.

38. In a careful analysis of a sample of sons who entered upper secondary school in 1964, Bowman finds that sons whose fathers are proprietors or members of an SFE preferred to be independent enterprisers themselves and that working for a large firm was generally not nearly the goal the stereotype would imply; Mary Jean Bowman (with Hideo Ikeda and Yasumasa Tomoda), *Educa-*

tional Choice and Labor Markets in Japan (Chicago: University of Chicago Press, 1981), pp. 208–9.

39. See Thomas P. Rohlen, *Japan's High Schools* (Berkeley: University of California Press, 1983).

40. Shinohara, "Japanese Literature on Small Business," provides an excellent, though now dated, discussion and literature review of dualism in the Japanese economy. A good, recent, empirical description of differences by firm size is Sterling, "American and Japanese labor Markets," chap. 5.

41. Hong Tan, "Wage Differentials in Japanese Manufacturing: Review of Recent Literature," *Economic Record*, May 1982, provides a useful review of the *nenkō* (cultural) versus special and general training (neo-classical) literature and empirical analysis, including results from his dissertation.

42. See Jeremy I. Bulow and Lawrence H. Summers, "A Theory of Dual Labor Markets with Application to Industrial Policy, Discrimination, and Keynesian Unemployment," manuscript, Mar. 1985. Although this model may appear appropriate only to the U.S. system, in which workers are readily fired, large Japanese firms have effective ways of terminating employees and at a far higher opportunity cost to the employee since the only available alternative jobs are at substantially lower wages.

43. *1983 SME White Paper*, p. 32. However, these data apparently exclude the greater differentials in bonus payments and fringe benefits and may be monthly wages unadjusted for the longer hours worked in small enterprises, in which case the differentials remain wider than suggested in this source.

44. See also his following articles in English: "The Formation of Worker Skill in Small Japanese Firms," *Japanese Economic Studies*, Summer 1983, pp. 3–57; and "International Labor Market: Workers in Large Firms," and "Workers in Small Firms and Women in Industry," in Taishiro Shirai, ed., *Contemporary Industrial Relations in Japan* (Madison: University of Wisconsin Press, 1983), chaps. 2 and 4.

45. Osawa, "Women's Skill Formation," p. 93.

46. Cited at ibid.

47. Kawashima, "Wage Differentials," p. 163.

48. Osawa, "Women's Skill Formation," p. 112.

49. *1982 Employment Status Survey*, table 37.

50. Japan, Ministry of Health and Welfare, *Summary of the 1983 Survey on Living Conditions*, cited in Akiko Fuse, "The Japanese Family in Transition, Part II," *Japan Foundation Newsletter*, Vol. 12, No. 4 (Dec. 1984), p. 3.

51. Hugh Patrick, "Japanese Financial Development in Historical Perspective, 1868–1980," in Gustav Ranis et al., eds., *Comparative Development Perspectives* (Boulder, Colo.: Westview Press, 1984), pp. 302–27.

52. The financing of postwar agriculture is a quite different situation. The agricultural sector has generated a surplus of saving over investment and has effectively used agricultural credit cooperatives and other local financial institutions to provide farmers all the credit they demand. Extensive government public works and other programs in agriculture have made the supply of capital in agriculture excessive in opportunity cost terms.

53. Venture capital for new high-tech firms is an important but a special case. Venture capital financing is only nascent in Japan but may well develop rapidly.

54. It may seem strange, but certainly is true in other rent-control situations of rapid rises in the economic value of real estate use, that the real value lies in ownership of the lease of the land, not of the land itself. In Japan leases can be transferred, with a 3–10 per cent payment (*orei*) to the landowner. Local tax

offices on occasion receive land in payment of inheritance taxes; tenants are able to purchase it on favorable terms. See Theodore C. Bestor, "Metropolitan Ethnography: Land, Households, and Mobility in Tokyo," paper presented to the American Anthropological Association (revised Dec. 1984).

55. Much of this section is based largely on interviews with MITI officials, Kyoto city government people, and representatives of the Kyoto Chamber of Commerce, the Central Federation of Small and Medium Business Associations (Chūōkai), and particular industry associations. See also Mike M. Mochizuki, "Japanese Small and Medium Enterprise Policy in the 1970s," paper presented to the annual meeting of the Association for Asian Studies, Apr. 1982; Hidenobu Nakajima, "Sengo ni okeru chūshō kigyō, undō no rekishi to kyōka" (Postwar small and medium-size enterprises: Their history and consolidation) *Chūshō kigyō jānaru* (Aug. 1968), pp. 1–13; Masaru Saitō, "Modernization and the Diffusion Mechanism of Technology," *Keizaigaku ronsan* (Chūō University, Society of Economic Research), No. 5 (1972), pp. 91–103; Japan, MITI, Small and Medium Enterprise Agency, *Outline of Small and Medium-Scale Enterprise Policies of the Japanese Government* (Tokyo, 1984); and Seiji Keizai Kenkyūsho, ed., *Tenkanki no chūshō kigyō mondai* (Small and medium-size enterprises at a turning point) (Tokyo: Shinhyōron, 1976).

56. We do not consider here the formidable political power of the well-organized farm lobby and its interactions with the LDP and opposition parties and with the Ministry of Agriculture, Forestry, and Fisheries since it has been extensively treated elsewhere.

57. Although many exceptions can be cited and comparisons with other countries are not available to prove or disprove a statement such as this, the MITI officials interviewed took this position.

58. This is the case even for companies reporting losses. A Tokyo Regional Taxation Bureau audit of 7,552 small and medium-size enterprises (capitalized at no more than ¥100 million—$250,000) reporting losses for the July–December 1984 period indicated that 85 per cent made false reports understating income, and more than a quarter were actually in the black; *Mainichi Daily News*, May 26, 1985, p. 12.

59. See James Horne, *Japan's Financial Markets: Conflicts and Consensus in Policymaking* (Sydney: George Allen & Unwin, 1985), pp. 137–40.

60. Collected in book form: Nihon Keizai Shimbunsha, *Za-Zeimusho* (The Tax Office) (Tokyo: Nikkei, May 1984).

61. See, for example, the Seiji Keizai Kenkyūsho work cited in note 55. This was confirmed by all persons interviewed.

62. Ibid., p. 343.

63. See Small and Medium Enterprise Agency, *Outline of Policies*, for a lengthy account of the numerous laws, powers, agencies, and procedures involved.

64. See Takashi Yokokura, "Chūshō kigyō" (Small and medium-size enterprises) in Ryūtarō Komiya et al., eds., *Nihon no sangyō seisaku* (Japanese industrial policy) (Tokyo: Universty of Tokyo Press, 1984).

65. For a general consideration of entrepreneurship and Japanese psychology, see Wagatsuma and De Vos, *Heritage of Endurance*. Their study of small-scale pencil making notes the high frequency of openings and closings. See also Hiroshi Wagatsuma and George De Vos, "The Entrepreneurial Mentality of Lower-Class Urban Japanese in Manufacturing Industries," in George De Vos, *Socialization for Achievement* (Berkeley: University of California Press, 1973).

66. Whether the topic is socialization, values, group behavior, or organization, almost no leading studies (in English or Japanese) mention entrepreneurial inclinations, emphasizing instead vertical relationships, dependence, paternalism, and sociocentric orientations.

67. Kokumin Kin'yū Koko Chōsabu, "Shinki kaigyō jittai chōsa" (Survey of new businesses), *KKK chōsa geppo*, Nos. 266, 267, and 268 (1983), reports the most recent data in a periodic survey. This sample is based on loan customers of the People's Finance Corporation and is therefore biased toward more successful, ambitious, and well-grounded start-ups. Very small new operations requiring little capital are certainly underrepresented. As a result, some categories, such as small shops opened by retirees, are likely to be more significant than shown.

68. In 1965, 6.5 per cent of the Japanese population, age 15–64, had some post–high school education; by 1971, this figure had increased to 13.1 per cent. Japan, Ministry of Education, *Waga kuni no kyōiku suijun* (Educational levels in Japan) (Tokyo: Government Printing Bureau, 1975, 1981).

69. Koike, "Workers in Small Firms and Women in Industry," p. 102.

70. *1982 Employment Status Survey*, table 52. Time-series data can be calculated from earlier surveys. We exclude females (their increase in self-employment was 46,000 in 1982) because we cannot determine how many were pieceworkers rather than entrepreneurs.

71. For example, the *1983 SME White Paper* (pp. 76–80) notes rises over the past decade in car parking, funeral services, beauty parlors, automobile rentals, building maintenance services, professional services, and advertising, but absolute declines in dressmaking, movie theaters, and public bathhouses.

72. For a brief description, see Itō-Yokado Company, *Annual Report 1983* (in English), especially pp. 17–20.

73. Of the 20,000 new male farm proprietors in 1982, a quarter previously were in government employment, a quarter were employees in SFEs (1–29 workers), and almost all the rest were spread among larger-size farm categories; *1982 Employment Status Survey*, table 52.

74. Note, however, that the position and role of women has, rather quietly, changed dramatically since World War II, including such areas as mother-in-law relationships, nuclear households, *kyōiku* mamas, my-home-ism, the selection process for husbands, and participants in the labor force as wage-earners.

75. Those 65 and older numbered 10.7 million in 1980 (9.1 per cent of the population) and are projected to number 19.9 million (13.6 per cent) in the year 2000, and 28.0 million (21.8 per cent) in 2020. Comparable figures for those 70 and older are 1980, 6.7 million (5.7 per cent); 2000, 13.0 million (10.2 per cent); and 2020, 20.4 million (15.9 per cent). Japan, Office of the Prime Minister, Bureau of Statistics, *Kojin kigyō keizai chōsa nempō* (Annual survey of the private enterprise sector) (Tokyo, 1983), pp. 3–4.

Okimoto and Saxonhouse: Technology

1. David K. Stout, "The Impact of Technology on Economic Growth in the 1980s," *Daedalus*, Vol. 109, No. 1 (Winter 1980).

2. William D. Nordhaus, "Policy Responses to the Productivity Slowdown," in *The Line of Productivity Growth* (Boston: Federal Reserve Bank of Boston, 1980). See also Martin N. Bailey, "The Productivity Growth Slowdown by Industry," *Brookings Papers in Economic Activity*, No. 2 (1982).

3. U.S. Patent and Trademark Office, *Indicators of Patent Output of U.S. Industry (1963–1981)* (Washington, D.C., 1982).

4. Teruo Doi, "The Role of Intellectual Property Law in Bilateral Licensing Transactions Between Japan and the United States," in Gary Saxonhouse and Kozo Yamamura, eds., *Law and Trade Issues of the Japanese Economy: American and Japanese Perspectives* (Seattle: University of Washington Press, 1985).

5. Japan, Patent Office, *Tokkyochō nempō* (Annual report of the Patent Office) (Tokyo, 1982).

6. Sampson Helfgott, "Statistical Study of the Japanese Patent Office's Handling of Foreign Patent Applications," *Patents and Licensing*, Vol. 5, No. 3 (Spring 1983).

7. U.S. Patent and Trademark Office, *Patent Output.*

8. Christopher T. Taylor and Z. Aubrey Silberston, *The Economic Impact of the Patent System* (Cambridge, Eng.: Cambridge University Press, 1973); Edwin Mansfield, Mark Schwartz, and Samuel Wagner, "Imitation Costs and Patents: An Empirical Study," *Economic Journal*, Vol. 91, No. 364 (Dec. 1981); and Frederic M. Scherer, *The Economic Effects of Compulsory Patent Licensing* (New York: New York University, Graduate School of Business Administration, 1977).

9. See the discussion in Gary Saxonhouse, "Tampering with Comparative Advantage," *Testimony Presented Before the United States International Trade Commission Hearings on Foreign Industrial Targeting*, June 15, 1983.

10. As long ago as the mid-1970s, there were claims that Japan had not only closed its traditional technological gap with the West, but had actually surpassed U.S. levels. The primary evidence for this claim is contained in Dale W. Jorgenson and Mieko Nishimizu, "U.S. and Japanese Economic Growth, 1952–1974: An International Comparison," *Economic Journal*, Vol. 88, No. 352 (Dec. 1978). See also Ezra Vogel, *Japan as Number One: Lessons for America* (Cambridge, Mass.: Harvard University Press, 1979), which cites the Jorgenson-Nishimizu analysis approvingly. The Jorgenson-Nishimizu method, if applied to the period after 1974, implies that by 1979 Japan's technological level was again below the U.S. level. See Hajime Imamura, "Sources of Quality Changes in Labor Input and Economic Growth in Japan, 1960–1979," *Keio Economic Studies*, Vol. 19, No. 2 (1982); and Zvi Griliches and Frank Lichtenberg, "R&D and Productivity Growth at Industry Level," in Z. Griliches, ed., *R&D, Patents and Productivity* (Chicago: University of Chicago Press, 1984). The Jorgenson-Nishimizu findings are very sensitive to their assumptions about the relationship between the average age of the capital stock and the level of technology. The exceptionally high Japanese investment rates of the late 1960s and early 1970s gave Japan a low average age of capital relative to the United States by 1973–74. Since 1973–74, the average age of the Japanese capital stock has risen sharply to once again approach U.S. levels.

11. Bank of Japan, *Kokusai shūshi tōkei geppō*, various issues. This series on Japan's technological balance of trade is the only one based on actual transactions. Japan's Bureau of Statistics has an alternative series based on sample survey data. Unfortunately that series does not present technology trade data on a receipts and expenditure basis, but on the entire value of new and continuing programs, including both current and future contractual receipts and expenditures. In a period of Japanese technological progress, this biases Japan's balance of technology trade upward. For example, not only are the Bureau of Statistics estimates of total technology sales 63 per cent larger than the comparable Bank of Japan figures for 1983, the bureau's estimates of technology purchases are also 41 per cent smaller than the Bank of Japan figures!

12. Japan, Management and Coordination Agency, Bureau of Statistics, *Kagaku gijutsu kenkyū chōsa hōkoku* (Report on the survey of research and development) (Tokyo, 1984), tables 12 and 13.

13. Differences in the pattern of payments between technology sales and purchases may also account for the balance of trade in new technology being in Japan's favor for twelve years without Japan's overall balance of technology moving into surplus. If Japanese sales of technology typically involve lump-sum payments at the time of contract but Japanese purchases rely more heavily on future royalty payments, it is possible that the two series could be reconciled.

14. Japan, Science and Technology Agency, *Kagaku gijutsu hakusho* (Science and technology white paper) (Tokyo, 1984), p. 21.

15. These data have been supplied by the Institute for Scientific Information. Alternative estimates that have put Japanese scientific publication at as much as one-third the U.S. level have been made by Mitsubishi Sōgō Kenkyūshō, *Kagaku gijutsu jōhō no kokusaiteki ryutsu no arikata ni kansuru* (Tokyo, 1984). However, the group of Japanese journals used by the Mitsubishi Sōgō Kenkyūshō does not appear to be comparable in quality to their U.S. data set.

16. Japan, Science and Technolgoy Agency, *Minkan kigyō no kenkyū katsudō ni kansuru chōsa hōkoku* (Survey report on research activities in the private sector) (Tokyo, 1982).

17. For a discussion of technological trajectories and their influence on economic development, see Richard C. Levin et al., "Survey Research on R&D Appropriability and Technological Opportunity, Part 1," working paper, Yale University, July 1984.

18. Joseph Schumpeter, *The Theory of Economic Development* (New York: Oxford University Press, 1961), chaps. 2 and 6.

19. Japan, Office of the Prime Minister, *Kagaku gijutsu kenkyū chōsa hōkoku, 1982* (Report on the survey of research and development) (Tokyo, 1983).

20. National Science Foundation, *Research and Development in Industry, 1980: Detailed Statistical Tables* (Washington, D.C., 1982); and National Science Board, *Science Indicators, 1982* (Washington, D.C., 1983).

21. Between 1976 and 1981, the share in total private business R&D fell from 20.5 per cent to 18.5 per cent. Between 1981 and 1984, however, the share fell to 17.4 per cent. Japan, Office of the Prime Minister, *Kagaku gijutsu kenkyū chōsa hōkoku, 1984* (Report on the survey on research and development) (Tokyo, 1985).

22. The operation of these incentives for U.S. firms is described in more detail in Gary R. Saxonhouse, "Industrial Policy and Factor Markets: Biotechnology in Japan and the United States" in Hugh Patrick, ed., *Japanese High Technology Industries and Industrial Policy* (Seattle: University of Washington Press, forthcoming).

23. For related discussions, see the papers by Aoki and by Patrick and Rohlen in this volume.

24. U.S. Patent and Trademark Office, *Small Business Patenting* (Washington, D.C., 1982).

25. Gellman Research Associates, *Indicators of International Trends in Technological Innovation* (Washington, D.C., 1976).

26. Saxonhouse, "Industrial Policy and Factor Markets."

27. Venture Business Study Group, *Chūkan hōkoku* (Interim report) (Tokyo, 1984).

28. U.S. Congress, Office of Technology Assessment, *Commercial Biotechnology: An International Comparison* (Washington, D.C., 1984).

29. Venture Business Study Group, *Chūkan hōkoku.*

30. For more detail, see Saxonhouse, "Industrial Policy and Factor Markets."

31. Gary R. Saxonhouse, "The National Security Clause of the Trade Expansion Act of 1962: Industry Policy and Japan's Machine Tool Industry," in Saxonhouse and Yamamura, *Law and Trade Issues.*

32. Japan, MITI, Committee to Promote Biotechnology, *Hōkokusho* (Report) (Tokyo, 1984).

33. Ibid.

34. Saxonhouse, "Industrial Policy and Factor Markets."

35. Committee to Promote Biotechnology, *Hōkokusho.*

36. Saxonhouse, "Industrial Policy and Factor Markets."

37. Such arguments figured in the discussions surrounding Japan's celebrated Very Large Scale Integration (VLSI) project. See Daniel Okimoto, Takuo Sugano, and Franklin B. Weinstein, eds., *Competitive Edge: The Semiconductor Industry in the U.S. and Japan* (Stanford: Stanford University Press, 1984).

38. The case for government intervention is described in Robert P. Inman, "Markets, Governments and the 'New' Political Economy," in Alan Auerbach and Martin Feldstein, eds., *Handbook of Public Economics,* vol. 2 (Amsterdam: North-Holland Press, 1985).

39. Richard C. Levin and Peter C. Reiss, "Tests of a Schumpeterian Model of R&D and Market Structure," *National Bureau of Economic Research Working Paper,* No. 1132 (Apr. 1983).

40. Zvi Griliches, "Returns to Research and Development Expenditures in the Private Sector," and Nestor Terleckyj, "Direct and Indirect Effects of Industrial Research and Development on the Growth of Industries," in John W. Kendrick and Beatrice N. Vaccara, eds., *New Developments in Productivity Measurement and Analysis* (Chicago: University of Chicago Press, 1980); and David M. Levy and Nestor Terleckyj, *Government-Financed R&D and Productivity Growth: Macroeconomic Evidence* (Washington, D.C.: National Planning Association, 1981).

41. Edwin Mansfield, "R&D and Innovation: Some Empirical Findings," *National Bureau of Economic Research Working Paper,* No. 1132 (Apr. 1983); and John T. Scott, "Firm Versus Industry Variability in R&D Intensity," *National Bureau of Economic Research Working Paper,* No. 1126 (Apr. 1983).

42. National Science Board, *Science Indicators, 1982.* For more recent, shorter time periods, this is not necessarily the case. In particular, although the number of Japanese scientists and engineers engaged in R&D increased 24.4 per cent between 1975 and 1981, the number of U.S. scientists and engineers increased during the same period by some 29.8 per cent. The rate of increase of Japanese scientists and engineers for this time period is diminished further if the unofficial statistics in Table 6 are used.

43. National Science Board, *Science Indicators, 1980* (Washington, D.C., 1981).

44. To the extent that public subsidy was important in keeping down tuition costs for higher education in Japan and the United States, students were not totally on their own resources. In prewar Japan, as in postwar Japan, such benefits were limited to relatively small groups of individuals. In the prewar United States, publicly subsidized education was much more broadly available, but if the cost of training includes forgone wages plus living expenses and tuition, even this subsidy was relatively small.

45. Akiyoshi Horiuchi, "Daigaku kyōiku no rieki, hiyō oyobi hojokin—Nihon ni tsuite no jisohoteki kentō" (The benefits, costs, and subsidization of higher education: An empirical study on Japan), *Nippon rōdō kyōkai zasshi* (Apr. 1973).

46. National Science Board, *Science Indicators, 1982*; Japan, Office of the Prime Minister, *Kagaku gijutsu kenkyū chōsa hōkokusho*; and Science and Technology Agency, *Kagaku gijutsu yōran* (Handbook on science and technology) (Tokyo).

47. Japan, Ministry of Education, *Gakkō kihon chōsa hōkokusho* (Basic survey report on the schools) (Tokyo); National Center for Educational Statistics, *Digest of Education Statistics, 1982* (Washington, D.C., 1982).

48. U.S. Congress, Office of Technology Assessment, *Commercial Biotechnology: An International Comparison* (Washington, D.C., 1984).

49. Committee to Promote Biotechnology, *Hōkokusho* (Tokyo, 1983).

50. Ibid.

51. Ronald Dore, *British Factory—Japanese Factory* (Berkeley: University of California Press, 1973).

52. Masahiko Aoki, "Innovative Adaptation Through the Quasi-Tree Structure: An Emerging Aspect of Japanese Entrepreneurship," *Zeitschrift für Nationalökonomie*, 1984, Supplement 4, pp. 177–98. In this article, Aoki documents the increasing propensity of Japanese firms to spin off particular firm functions as subsidiaries. Using data from the electric machinery and electronics industry (but without observations on Hitachi and Matsushita), he finds that the more firms spun off subsidiaries, the less R&D they did. From this result, Aoki concludes that firms in this industry were spinning off their R&D activities to smaller firms. Unfortunately, the comprehensive evidence for the electric machinery and electronics industry for 1973–83 available from Office of the Prime Minister, *Kagaku gijutsu kenkyū chōsa hōkokusho*, suggests that, if anything, R&D activities have become more concentrated, not less, in the largest firms. Aoki's statistical work probably just suggests that when firms in financial difficulty begin to spin off some of their activities, they may give up R&D altogether.

Eads and Yamamura: Industrial Policy

1. Among the works on Japanese industrial policy written in English, those that can be classified in the first school include Chalmers Johnson, *MITI and the Japanese Miracle: The Growth of Industrial Policy, 1925–1975* (Stanford: Stanford University Press, 1982); John Zysman and Stephen S. Cohen, "Double or Nothing: Open Trade and Competitive Industry," *Foreign Affairs*, Vol. 61 (Summer 1983), pp. 1113–19; John Zysman and Laura Tyson, *American Industry in International Competition* (Ithaca, N.Y.: Cornell University Press, 1983), chap. 1; John Zysman, *Governments, Markets and Growth: Financial Systems and the Policies of Industrial Change* (Ithaca, N.Y.: Cornell University Press, 1983); Ira C. Magaziner and Thomas M. Hout, *Japanese Industrial Policy* (Berkeley: University of California, Institute of International Studies, 1980); T. J. Pempel, *Policy and Politics in Japan: Creative Conservatism* (Philadelphia: Temple University Press, 1982), pp. 3–68; idem, "Japanese Foreign Economic Policy: The Domestic Bases for International Behavior," in Peter J. Katzenstein, ed., *Between Power and Plenty* (Madison: University of Wisconsin Press, 1978), pp. 139–90; Robert Reich, *The Next American Frontier* (New York: Times Books, 1983), pp. 235–82; idem, "Beyond Free Trade," *Foreign Affairs*, Vol. 61 (Spring 1983), pp. 773–804; idem, "Making Industrial Policy," *Foreign Affairs*, Vol. 60, No. 4 (Spring 1982), pp. 852–81; Ezra Vogel, "Japan's Economic Mobilization: The American Quandary," in *The Japanese Challenge and the American Response: A Symposium* (Berkeley: University of California, Institute of East Asian Studies, 1982), pp. 47–52, and idem, *Japan as Number One: Lessons for America* (New York: Harper & Row, 1979).

Some studies expressing the view of the second school are Philip H. Trezise, "Industrial Policy in Japan," in Margaret E. Dewar, ed., *Industry Vitalization: Toward a National Industrial Policy* (New York: Pergamon Press, 1982), pp. 177–95; idem, "Industrial Policy Is Not the Major Reason for Japan's Success," *Brookings Review* (Spring 1983), pp. 13–18; Paul Krugman, "Targeted Industrial Policies: Theory and Evidence," in Federal Reserve Bank of Kansas City, ed., *Industrial Change and Public Policy* (Kansas City, 1983), pp. 123–56; F. Gerard Adams and Shinichi Ichimura, "Industrial Policy in Japan," in F. G. Adams and Lawrence R. Klein, eds., *Industrial Policies for Growth and Competitiveness: An Economic Perspective* (Lexington, Mass.: D.C. Heath, Lexington Books, 1983), pp. 307–30; Charles L. Schultze, "Industrial Policy: A Dissent," *Brookings Review* (Fall 1983), pp. 3–12; idem, "Industrial Policy: A Solution in Search of a Problem," *California Management Review*, Vol. 25 (Summer 1983), pp. 5–15; Hugh Patrick, "The Future of the Japanese Economy: Output and Labor Productivity," *Journal of Japanese Studies*, Vol. 3, No. 2 (Summer 1977), pp. 219–49; Hugh Patrick and Henry Rosovsky, eds., *Asia's New Giant: How the Japanese Economy Works* (Washington, D.C.: Brookings Institution, 1976); Gary Saxonhouse, "Industrial Restructuring in Japan," *Journal of Japanese Studies*, Vol. 5, No. 2 (Summer 1979), pp. 273–300; and David R. Henderson, "The Myth of MITI," *Fortune*, Aug. 8, 1983, pp. 114–16. See also the testimony and prepared statements of Adams, Patrick, and Trezise in U.S. Congress, Joint Economic Committee, *Industrial Policy, Economic Growth and the Competitiveness of U.S. Industry* (Washington, D.C.: U.S. Government Printing Office, 1983).

These citations are far from exhaustive, and readers interested in further sources that can be classified into one of these schools and others advancing eclectic or variant views are referred to notes 11, 17, 39, and 40 of this essay. The following contain useful bibliographies on the subject: Edward J. Lincoln, *Japan's Industrial Policies* (Washington, D.C.: Japan Economic Institute of America, 1984); John Zysman and Laura Tyson, "U.S. and Japanese Trade and Industrial Policies," a report prepared for the United States–Japan Advisory Commission, Sept. 1984; and Jimmy W. Wheeler, Merit E. Janow, and Thomas Pepper, *Japanese Industrial Development Policies in the 1980s* (Croton-on-Hudson, N.Y.: Hudson Institute, 1982).

Because of space constraints and their limited usefulness to Western readers, we do not discuss the far more numerous works published in Japanese. For Western students of Japanese industrial policy who are able to use Japanese sources, a source deserving special attention is Ryūtarō Komiya et al., eds., *Nihon no sangyō seisaku* (Japanese industrial policy) (Tokyo: University of Tokyo Press, 1984). This conference volume contains 19 essays by Japanese economists and a 17-page bibliography of Japanese and English sources. All the essays belong to the second school; the analyses are based on a neo-classical perspective and define industrial policy "as a means to rectify market failure in allocation of resources" (Komiya, "Introduction," p. 5). The essays are closely reasoned and rich in valuable observations and data and are worthy of careful reading.

2. We cannot enter into a lengthy methodological discussion, but in theory there is no necessary correlation between the contribution of industrial policy and the overall performance of the economy. An industrial policy might be considered successful if it permitted an economy that otherwise might perform dismally to perform less poorly. Similarly, if an economy performed extremely well, but, on balance, industrial policy constitutes a drag on this performance, then the industrial policy clearly cannot be considered successful.

3. For expositional convenience, we use 1973, the year of the first oil crisis, as the turning point of Japanese industrial policy. As noted in the text, however, the character and possible effects of various policy tools changed gradually during the 1960s from those associated with the rapid growth period to those that evolved in the 1970s and 1980s.

4. U.S. Congress, Congressional Budget Office, *The Industrial Policy Debate* (Washington, D.C., Dec. 1983), esp. chaps. 4–5.

5. Krugman, "Targeted Industrial Policies," pp. 144–47.

6. See, for example, Reich, *The Next American Frontier*, pp. 235–82.

7. Krugman, "Targeted Industrial Policies," pp. 126–28.

8. As discussed below in the text, we do not regard economic growth as the only criterion for evaluating the contribution made by industrial policy. Industrial policy can be judged effective if, for example, it minimizes market fluctuation or helps to smooth problems relating to transfer of resources. Note, however, that all these possible contributions enhance, in a broader sense, the performance of an economy, which is, in the final analysis, measured in terms of its growth record.

9. This is Bluestone's argument for his "reindustrialization with a human face," although, in our opinion, his proposals and their consequences go well beyond this. See Barry Bluestone and Bennett Harrison, *The Deindustrialization of America* (New York: Basic Books, 1982), chap. 8.

10. For full descriptions of governmental assistance during the rapid growth period, see Komiya et al., *Nihon no sangyō seisaku*, chaps. 1, 2, 4, and 5.

11. See, for example, Donald F. Barnett and Louise Schorsch, *Steel: Upheaval in a Basic Industry* (Cambridge, Mass.: Ballinger Publishing Co., 1983), pp. 210–13, for a brief account of the magnitude of the economic assistance given by the Japanese government to the steel industry during its period of rapid growth. However, even Barnett and Schorsch conclude that the period of massive direct economic assistance is over: "The Japanese government now plays primarily an advisory role [to the Japanese steel industry], striving to ensure that the plans of individual firms reflect the government-industry consensus and constitute a coherent industry strategy, especially during the periods of weak demand" (p. 213).

12. Johnson, *MITI and the Japanese Miracle*, p. 116; this is the title of chap. 4. See also Vogel, *Japan as Number One*, pp. 65–90.

13. Johnson, *MITI and the Japanese Miracle*, chap. 7, entitled "Administrative Guidance." We elaborate on this point below.

14. See note 1.

15. We cannot include here a bibliography of useful sources on the international (political and economic) conditions and social characteristics of Japan that have affected Japan's industrial policy. Interested readers are referred to the essays to appear in Vols. II and III, which, as described by the general editors in their Preface to this volume, will deal with these conditions and characteristics.

16. Interested readers may consult Zysman, *Governments, Markets and Growth*, chap. 6.

17. An informative English source on the Japanese bureaucracy is Chalmers Johnson, "Japan: Who Governs? An Essay on Official Bureaucracy," *Journal of Japanese Studies*, Vol. 2, No. 1 (Autumn 1975), pp. 1–28.

18. Johnson, *MITI and the Japanese Miracle*, chap. 4.

19. See, for example, the paper by Horiuchi and Hamada in this volume.

20. Yasusuke Murakami, "Toward a Socioinstitutional Explanation of Japan's Economic Performance," in Kozo Yamamura, ed., *Policy and Trade Issues of the*

Japanese Economy: American and Japanese Perspectives (Seattle: University of Washington Press, 1982), p. 14.

21. The best source on the FILP in English is Yukio Noguchi, "The Government-Business Relationship in Japan: The Changing Role of Fiscal Resources," in Yamamura, *Policy and Trade Issues*, pp. 123–42.

22. See ibid.; Komiya, *Nihon no sangyō seisaku*, chaps. 1, 2, 4, and 5; and Kozo Yamamura, "Success That Soured: Administrative Guidance and Cartels in Japan," in Yamamura, *Policy and Trade Issues*, pp. 77–112.

23. For a description of the law and its administration, see Johnson, *MITI and the Japanese Miracle, passim*; and Dan Fenno Henderson, *Foreign Enterprise in Japan: Law and Policies* (Chapel Hill: University of North Carolina Press, 1973). However, for a revealing and firsthand observation of MITI's use of the law to enhance its policy goals, see "Gijutsu dōnyū" (The introduction of technologies), in Ekonomisuto Editorial Bureau, ed., *Shōgen: Kōdo seichōki no Nihon* (Testimonies: Japan in the rapid growth period) (Tokyo: Mainichi Shimbunsha, 1984), 1: 296–310. This chapter contains an interview that the staff of *Ekonomisuto* conducted with a former high-ranking MITI officer directly involved in the administration of the law. The officer's observations provide numerous examples that directly attest the generalized observations contained in the text.

24. For further discussion of this point and other observations offered in this subsection, see the Introduction and the papers by Muramatsu and Krauss and by Kosai in this volume.

25. See the papers by Kosai and by Muramatsu and Krauss in this volume.

26. A thoughtful reflection on this point is offered by Murakami, who in essence notes that *planification* in France and economic planning Japanese-style (*keizai keikaku*), which both made extensive use of administrative guidance, seem to have achieved some success, attesting to the importance of cognitive influence by government on the private sector. Such indicative planning in fact needs a basic consensual understanding of the society's current situation as well as the goals that the society is prepared to pursue. In postwar Japan, there was a strong national consensus for catch-up economic growth; that is, most people shared the belief that the country should and could follow the pattern of industrial development exhibited by advanced nations. This catch-up-growth consensus represents the basic cognitive interaction linking the polity and the economy during the 1950s and 1960s. See Murakami, "Toward a Socioinstitutional Explanation," pp. 16–18.

27. Ibid., pp. 16–17. See also Murakami's paper in this volume.

28. Johnson, *MITI and the Japanese Miracle*, pp. 317–19.

29. John O. Haley, "Administrative Guidance vs. Formal Regulation: Resolving the Paradox of Industrial Policy," in Gary Saxonhouse and Kozo Yamamura, eds., *Law and Trade Issues of the Japanese Economy: American and Japanese Perspectives* (Seattle: University of Washington Press, 1986).

30. Joseph Schumpeter, *Capitalism, Socialism, and Democracy* (New York: Harper & Row, 1950); and John Kenneth Galbraith, *The New Industrial State* (Boston: Houghton Mifflin, 1967).

31. Alexander Gerschenkron, *Economic Backwardness in Historical Perspective* (New York: Praeger, 1962).

32. Wassily Leontief, "Domestic Production and Foreign Trade," in R. Caves and H. Johnson, eds., *Readings in International Economics* (Homewood, Ill.: Irwin, 1968).

33. Raymond Vernon, "International Investment and International Trade in

the Product Cycle," *Quarterly Journal of Economics*, Vol. 80, No. 2 (May 1966), pp. 190–207.

34. This assessment is admittedly "broad," but see *Economic Report of the President*, Feb. 1984, pp. 99–102. The pages that follow are based on a large number of sources, both published and unpublished, and on formal and informal discussions participated in by Eads over a number of years. Eads would particularly like to acknowledge the influence on his thinking of the meetings of the Positive Adjustment Group of the OECD's Economic Policy Group, of which he was a member. The reader seeking formal summaries of European industrial policy experience is invited to review the following: U.S. Congress, Joint Economic Committee, Staff Study, *Monetary Policy, Selective Credit Policy, and Industrial Policy in France, Britain, West Germany, and Sweden*, 97th Cong., 1st Sess., June 26, 1981; W. Kohl, *West Germany: A European and Global Power* (Lexington, Mass.: D.C. Heath, 1980); S. Warnecke and E. Sulerman, *Industrial Policies in Western Europe* (New York: Praeger, 1975); C. Price, *Industrial Policies in the European Community* (London: St. Martin's Press, 1981); Richard R. Nelson, *High Technology Policies: A Five Nation Comparison* (Washington, D.C.: American Enterprise Institute, 1984); U.S. International Trade Commission, *Foreign Industrial Targeting and Its Effects on U.S. Industries—Phase II: The European Community and Member States* (Washington, D.C., Apr. 1984) [hereafter USITC, 1984].

35. USITC, 1984, pp. 94–124, provides a good, up-to-date survey of British industrial policy and targeting practices.

36. For further elaboration, see ibid.

37. See OECD, Directorate for Science, Technology and Industry, "Structural Problems and Policies Relating to the OECD Textile and Clothing Industries" (2nd draft), Nov. 13, 1980, esp. pp. 149–50.

38. Zysman, *Governments, Markets and Growth*, chap. 4.

39. See USITC, 1984, pp. 68–93.

40. These numbers are adopted from Robert J. Gordon, *Macroeconomics*, 2d ed. (Boston: Little, Brown & Co., 1981), table 18-1, p. 546.

41. Zysman, *Government, Markets and Growth*, pp. 251–66.

42. Of course, the neo-classical economists would advance this as the reason for the decline in German economic performance.

43. USITC, 1984, p. 84; see also pp. 84–87, and esp. tables 25 and 26.

44. Nelson, *High Technology Policies*, p. 38.

45. USITC, 1984, pp. 68–69.

46. For a detailed account of these episodes, see Jeffrey A. Hart, "The Politics of Industrial Policy: German Industrial Policy" (draft, 1984; used with permission of the author).

47. Ibid., pp. 32–33.

48. A good summary is provided in USITC, 1984, pp. 44–67.

49. The description that follows is taken largely from ibid., pp. 44–45.

50. Zysman, *Governments, Markets and Growth*, chap. 3.

51. *Economic Report of the President*, Feb. 1985, table B-109, p. 356. Germany's growth over the same period averaged 0.7 per cent; that of the United States, 2.7 per cent; that of Japan, 4.0 per cent.

52. Charles Wolf, Jr., "A Theory of Nonmarket Failure: Framework for Implementation Analysis," *Journal of Law and Economics*, Vol. 22 (Apr. 1979), pp. 107–39.

53. See note 76 below for the case studies.

54. As noted in note 3 above, the subtitle of this section does not mean that Japanese industrial policy underwent a sudden shift in 1973.

55. *Asahi Shimbun*, Nov. 13, 1984, evening ed., p. 1.

56. Seizaburō Satō and Tetsuhisa Matsuzaki, "Jimintō chōchōki seiken no kaibō" (The anatomy of the super-long-term LDP government), *Chūō kōron*, Nov. 1984, p. 90. This article contains excellent, insightful analyses of the changes in the LDP's internal workings and the party's relationship to the bureaucracy. The analyses are valuable in understanding the descriptions relating to the politicization of the processes of policy formulation and administration by the bureaucracy discussed later in this paper.

57. Eisuke Sakakibara and Yukio Noguchi, "Ōkurashō-Nichigin ōchō no bunseki" (An analysis of the Ministry of Finance–Bank of Japan dynasty), *Chūō kōron*, Aug. 1977, p. 129.

58. The extent of the foreign "oversight" of the Japanese policies is evident, for example, in United States–Japan Advisory Commission, "Challenges and Opportunities in United States–Japan Relations," a report submitted to the president of the U.S. and the prime minister of Japan, Sept. 1984. Note also that, as a result of U.S. pressure, beginning in 1984, foreign businessmen have been invited to express their views to MITI's Industrial Structure Council, a council that long occupied a significant place in shaping Japan's industrial policy.

59. Yasusuke Murakami, "The Age of New Middle Mass Politics: The Case of Japan," *Journal of Japanese Studies*, Vol. 8, No. 1 (Winter 1982), pp. 29–72; and Takashi Inoguchi, "Explaining and Predicting Japanese General Elections, 1960–1980," *Journal of Japanese Studies*, Vol. 7, No. 2 (Summer 1981), pp. 285–318; and the minor revision in Vol. 8, No. 2 (Summer 1982), p. 427. See also Satō and Matsuzaki, "Jimintō."

60. For this internal conflict, see Johnson, *MITI and the Japanese Miracle*, pp. 275–304.

61. Of the many mass media descriptions of this intra-MOF debate, a useful source is *Ekonomisuto*, June 21, 1983, a special issue on capital market liberalization.

62. For an example of sharply conflicting views on agricultural trade between MITI and the Ministry of Agriculture, Forestry, and Fisheries (MAFF), see Takashi Shinohara, "Agricultural Protection for National Security," and Naohiro Amaya, "Agricultural Policy Is Rife with Inconsistencies," both in *Economic Eye*, Vol. 5, No. 3 (Sept. 1984), pp. 14–19. The former is a member of the secretariat of MAFF, and the latter is a former high-ranking officer of MITI.

63. See Amaya, "Agricultural Policy."

64. This refers to the fact that the ministries are, from lower to higher levels, divided "vertically," and each vertical segment has virtually exclusive jurisdiction over a specific industry; the close identification between each section and bureau within a ministry with an industry makes a broader coordination of policies difficult. This vertical administrative structure presents little problem when the goal of each vertical segment and that of the ministry (or of the nation) do not differ. However, this structure can and does create problems when the goals diverge, as in recent years.

65. For detailed descriptions of these changes, see the papers by Kosai, Hamada and Horiuchi, and Murakami in this volume and chaps. 3–6 and 10 in Komiya et al., *Nihon no sangyō seisaku*.

66. For further discussion on this development, see the paper by Hamada and Horiuchi in this volume.

67. For a quantitative analysis and an excellent discussion of the changes in the effective tariff rates, see Motoshige Itō and Kazuharu Kiyono, "Bōeki to

chokusetsu tōshi" (International trade and direct investment) in Komiya et al., *Nihon no sangyō seisaku*, pp. 136–39.

68. Trezise, "Japan's Success," p. 16.

69. Barnett and Schorsch (*Steel*, pp. 210–12) contend that immediately after the war, the government provided fully one-half of the Japanese steel industry's funding plus subsidies for its purchase of raw materials. They argue that a significant though decreasing governmental financing role continued until about 1960, after which time Japanese steel was firmly established as a world-class competitor.

70. Noguchi, "Government-Business Relationship," pp. 130–31.

71. Kōji Shinjō, "Computā sangyō" (The computer industry) in Komiya et al., *Nihon no sangyō seisaku*, p. 302.

72. See, e.g., Michael Borrus, James Millstein, and John Zysman, *U.S.-Japanese Competition in the Semiconductor Industry* (Berkeley: University of California Press, 1982), pp. 90–94.

73. Shinjō, "Computā sangyō," pp. 316–23. See also the paper by Okimoto and Saxonhouse in this volume.

74. For these projects and analytic and policy issues concerning these high-tech projects, see, for examples, the paper by Okimoto and Saxonhouse in this volume; and Kozo Yamamura, "Joint Research and Antitrust: Japanese vs. American Strategies," in Hugh T. Patrick, ed., *Japan's High Technology Industries: Lessons and Limitations of Industrial Policy* (Seattle: University of Washington Press, 1986, forthcoming).

75. For further discussion, see Yamamura, "Success That Soured."

76. For further discussion of these adjustments, see chaps. 14–16 on the textile, shipbuilding, and aluminum industries in Komiya et al., *Nihon no sangyō seisaku*; and the papers by Uekusa and Kosai in this volume.

77. See the paper by Noguchi in this volume.

78. See the papers by Noguchi and Kosai in this volume.

79. *Asahi shimbun*, May 15 and June 6, 1985.

80. Johnson, *MITI and the Japanese Miracle*, chap. 1.

81. Zysman, *Governments, Markets and Growth*, pp. 233–51.

Uekusa: Industrial Organization

1. In regard to these organizational features, see Richard E. Caves and Masu Uekusa, *Industrial Organization in Japan* (Washington, D.C.: Brookings Institution, 1976).

2. Although these failures are described in the next section, for details see Toshimasa Tsuruta, *Sengo Nihon no sangyō seisaku* (Industrial policy in postwar Japan) (Nihon Keizai Shimbunsha, 1982), chap. 7.

3. Jimmy W. Wheeler, Merit E. Janow, and Thomas Pepper, *Japanese Industrial Development Policies in the 1980s*, Hudson Institute Research Report HI-3470-RR (Croton-on-Hudson, N.Y., 1982), pp. 31–36.

4. In regard to the adjustment to the oil shock, see Ryūtarō Komiya and Kazuo Yasui, "Japan's Macroeconomic Performance Since the First Oil Crisis: Review and Appraisal," *Carnegie-Rochester Conference Series on Public Policy*, No. 20 (1984), pp. 69–114.

5. Ibid., p. 79.

6. Terms such as "basic manufacturing industry" and "final manufacturing industry" are not academic but journalistic terms. Generally speaking, the former

includes chemicals, clay and stone, iron and steel, and nonmetal products, and the latter includes all kinds of machinery industries.

7. The information sector is almost equal to the primary information sector defined by Marc U. Porat, *The Information Economy* (Washington, D.C.: U.S. Department of Commerce, Office of Telecommunications, 1977).

8. See Chalmers Johnson, *MITI and the Japanese Miracle: The Growth of Industrial Policy, 1925–1975* (Stanford: Stanford University Press, 1982), p. 287.

9. Wheeler et al., *Industrial Development Policies*, p. 7.

10. See also Masu Uekusa, "Sekiyu kiki ikō no sangyō seisaku" (Industrial policy since the first oil crisis), in Ryūtarō Komiya et al., eds., *Nihon no sangyō seisaku* (Japanese industrial policy) (Tokyo: University of Tokyo Press, 1984).

11. Masu Uekusa, "Effects of the Deconcentration Measures in Japan," *Antitrust Bulletin*, Fall 1977; see also Ken'ichi Imai and M. Uekusa, "Industrial Organization and Economic Growth in Japan," in Shigeto Tsuru, ed., *Growth and Resource Problems Related to Japan* (Tokyo: Asahi Evening News, 1978).

12. Caves and Uekusa, *Industrial Organization*, p. 29.

13. Masu Uekusa, *Sangyō soshiki ron* (Industrial organization) (Tokyo: Chikuma Shobō, 1982), pp. 41–44.

14. Ibid., p. 358; and Caves and Uekusa, *Industrial Organization*, pp. 96–98.

15. Caves and Uekusa, *Industrial Organization*, chap. 5.

16. Yoshi Kusuda and Toshihiro Ike, "Seizōgyō no kakaku hendō yōin bunseki" (Analysis of the determinants of price changes in manufacturing industries), *Keizai bunseki* (Economic Planning Agency), Aug. 1979. They analyzed the following equation of price change and revealed the existence of administered inflation.

$$P \quad = 42.22 + 0.715 M(w) + 1.100 W(w) - 0.056 Q + 0.009 CR_4$$

$$(1974–75) \qquad (12.70) \qquad (8.24) \qquad (-1.83) \qquad (2.82)$$

$$(\bar{R}^2 = 0.639, \ N = 147)$$

P is the rate of change in prices, $M(w)$ is the rate of change in material costs weighted by material costs as a percentage of total costs, $W(w)$ is the rate of change in wages weighted by wages as a percentage of total costs, Q is the rate of change in shipments, and CR_4 is the four-firm concentration ratio. $\bar{R}^2$ is the coefficient of determination adjusted by the degree of freedom. The figures in parentheses are t-values.

17. Japan, Fair Trade Commission (hereafter, FTC), *Keizai no henka to dokusen kinshi seisaku* (Changes in the economy and antimonopoly policy) (Tokyo: Government Printing Office, 1984), pp. 346–49.

18. Ibid., pp. 370–74.

19. The true level of seller concentration should be calculated by taking account of the influence of imports and exports on the concentration; see Michael Waterson, *Economic Theory of Industry* (Cambridge, Eng.: Cambridge University Press, 1984), p. 174.

20. FTC, *Nenji hōkoku, 1980* (Annual report) (Tokyo: Government Printing Office, 1981), p. 310.

21. These data are based on Yano Economic Research Institute, *Nihon market share jiten* (Statistics on market share in Japan), annual; Mitsubishi Bank, *Monthly Survey*, June 1983; and Japan, MITI, *Tokutei service sangyō jittai chōsa hōkokusho, 1982* (Survey report on selected service industries) (Tokyo: Government Printing Office, Nov. 1983).

22. Akira Senō, ed., *Gendai Nihon no sangyō shūchū, 1971–1980* (Industrial concentration in contemporary Japan) (Tokyo: Nihon Keizai Shimbunsha, 1983), pp. 123–26, 308–9.

23. Ibid., pp. 29, 230. The figures do not include assets or sales of the affiliations of the largest corporations. The overall concentration ratios, which include the 100 largest corporations and their affiliates, appear to have the same trend as those that do not include them (ibid., p. 44).

24. Ibid., p. 35.

25. Ken'ichi Imai, "Gijutsu kakushin kara mita saikin no sangyō seisaku" (Technological innovation and recent industrial policy), in Komiya et al., *Sangyō seisaku*, chap. 7.

26. FTC, "Minkan kigyō ni okeru kenkyū kaihatsu katsudō no jittai to kyōsō seisaku-jō no kadai" (R&D activity of private enterprises and issues of competition policy) (Sept. 1984).

27. Komiya and Yasui, "Macroeconomic Performance," p. 95.

28. The figures for the United States are from F. M. Gallop and D. W. Jorgenson, "U.S. Economic Growth by Industry, 1947–73," in J. W. Kendrick and B. N. Vaccara, eds., *New Developments in Productivity Measurement and Analysis* (Chicago: University of Chicago Press, 1980).

29. For the decline in productivity in the United States, see E. F. Denison, "Productivity Growth: A Puzzle," *Economic Impact*, Vol. 2 (1981).

30. See Charles J. McMillan, *The Japanese Industrial System* (New York: Walter de Gruyter, 1984), chap. 9.

31. An estimate of production costs of integrated circuits in Japan shows that when the quantity of units manufactured doubles, the unit cost decreases by 27.6 per cent; see Kōji Kobayashi, *C & C to software* (C & C and software) (Tokyo: Simul Press, 1982), p. 21.

32. Japan, Economic Planning Agency, *Keizai hakusho, 1982* (Economic white paper) (Tokyo, 1982), p. 630.

33. Ryūhei Sugiyama, "Sangyō no R&D katsudō to seisaku kainyū" (Industrial R&D activities and government intervention), in Japan Economic Policy Association, ed., *Kagaku gijutsu to keizai seisaku* (Science and technology and economic policy) (Tokyo: Keisō Shobō, 1984).

34. Japan, Science and Technology Agency, *Kagaku gijutsu hakusho, 1983* (White paper on science and technology) (Tokyo, 1983), p. 104.

35. There were industrial adjustment problems before the first oil crisis, but industrial adjustment in large-scale industries was limited to a few (coal and textile) and was comparatively easy because of a smoother transfer of economic resources into other industries in the rapid growth economy.

36. See Wheeler, et al., *Industrial Development Policies*, p. 161; and Hugh Patrick, "Japanese Industrial Policy and Its Relevance for United States Industrial Policy," prepared statement before the Joint Economic Committee, U.S. Congress, July 13, 1983.

37. Japan, MITI, *Kōzōfukyōhō no kaisetsu* (A commentary on the Depressed Industries Law) (Tokyo: Tsūshō Sangyō Chōsakai, 1978), pp. 22–27.

38. Ibid., pp. 60–62.

39. OECD, *The Case for Positive Adjustment Policies* (Paris, June 1979).

40. FTC, Research Committee, *Teiseichō keizaika no sangyō chōsei to kyōsō seisaku* (Industrial adjustment and competition policy in a decelerating economy) (Tokyo, Nov. 1983).

41. For an evaluation of the Depressed Industries Law and the theoretical

background of industrial adjustment assistance policy, see Sueo Sekiguchi and Toshihiro Horiuchi, "Bōeki to chōsei enjo" (International trade and adjustment assistance), in Komiya et al., *Sangyō seisaku*, chap. 13.

42. The appreciation of the yen had the effect of lowering domestic ingot production costs because of a decline in the cost of imported materials. But these reduced costs could not match the falling price of imported ingots because of the small proportion of material input in total costs (about 35 per cent in 1970).

43. Masaki Toshita, "Aluminum seirengyō no kokusai kyōsōryoku to setsubi tōshi" (International competitiveness in the aluminum-refining industry and investment in plant and equipment), *Chōgin chōsa geppō*, No. 146 (Jan. 1976).

44. See Wheeler et al., *Industrial Development Policies*, pp. 179–80.

45. Akira Gotō, "The Aluminum Industry in Japan," discussion paper, Seikei University, Department of Economics, No. 6 (Sept. 1984).

46. Paul Sheard, "Financial Corporate Grouping, Cross-subsidization in the Private Sector and the Industrial Adjustment Process in Japan, Part 2, A Case Study of the Aluminum Refining Industry," discussion paper, Osaka University, Faculty of Economics (Aug. 1984), p. 36.

47. Ibid., p. 27.

48. Ibid., p. 35.

49. J. W. Culliton, *Make or Buy* (Boston: Harvard University, Graduate School of Business Administration, Division of Research, 1942); and Merton J. Peck and Frederic M. Sherer, *The Weapons Acquisition Process* (Boston: Harvard University, Graduate School of Business Administration, Division of Research, 1962), pp. 386–98.

50. Yoshio Satō, ed., *Teiseichōki ni okeru gaichū shitauke kanri* (Management of outside orders and subcontracting in a decelerating economy) (Tokyo: Chūō Keizaisha, 1980), p. 185.

51. Japan, MITI, Small and Medium Enterprise Agency (hereafter, SMEA), *Shitauke kigyō bunya jittai chōsa* (Survey of fields of subcontractors) (Tokyo, Feb. 1980).

52. Ibid.; and Satō, *Shitauke kanri*, pp. 196–97.

53. Banri Asanuma, "Jidōsha sangyō ni okeru buhin torihiki no kōzō" (Structure of parts transactions in the automobile industry), *Kikan gendai keizai*, Vol. 58 (Summer 1984).

54. SMEA, *Shitauke kigyō*; and idem, *Chūshō kigyō hakusho, 1984* (White paper on small enterprises) (Tokyo, 1984), pt. 2, chap. 6.

55. SMEA, *Dairokkai kōgyō jittai kihon chōsa hōkokusho* (The Sixth Fundamental Survey on Manufacturing) (Tokyo: MITI, Research and Statistics Bureau, 1984).

56. SMEA, *Shitauke mondai ni kansuru jittai chōsa* (Survey of subcontracting problems) (Tokyo, Nov. 1977).

57. SMEA, *Hakusho, 1984*.

58. Uekusa, *Sangyō soshiki ron*, pp. 120–26, 335–42.

59. FTC, *Nenji hōkuku, 1984*, p. 253; and Noritami Inuzuka, "Shitauke daikin no sokyū nebiki no kisei to mondai" (Problems and regulation of retroactive price reductions in subcontracting transactions), *Kōsei torihiki*, No. 409 (Nov. 1984), in which it is pointed out that the number of violations of the Subcontractors' Protection Law has recently increased, particularly in the electronics industry.

60. Publicly regulated industries also include banks and insurance, security, and other financial industries. See the papers by Sato and by Hamada and Horiuchi in regard to public regulation in the financial industries. For the position of regulated industries in the Japanese economy, see FTC, *Keizai no henka*, pp. 1–26.

61. Masu Uekusa, "Kōkigyō no sū, keitai to yakuwari" (The numbers, organizational forms, and roles of public enterprises), in Hideyuki Okano and Masu Uekusa, eds., *Nihon no kōkigyō* (Public enterprises in Japan) (Tokyo: University of Tokyo Press, 1983), chap. 1.

62. See Masu Uekusa, "Japan," in Prahlad K. Basu and Alec Nove, eds., *Public Enterprise Policy on Investment, Pricing and Returns* (Kuala Lumpur: Asian and Pacific Development Administration Center, 1979).

63. Okano and Uekusa, *Nihon no kōkigyō*, chaps. 9–10.

64. Research Institution of Telecommunications and Economics, *Wagakuni jōhō sangyō no genjō to hatten dōkō ni kansuru kenkyū* (Research on the present and future of the information industry in Japan) (Tokyo, Mar. 1984), pp. 95, 113.

65. Yutaka Kosai, "Henshitsu suru Nihon no keizai system" (The Japanese economic system is now changing in quality), *Shūkan Tōyō keizai*, Aug. 25, 1984.

66. Long-term Credit Bank of Japan, "Sentan gijutsu sangyō no subete" (Information on high-tech industries) *JETI* (Japan energy and technology intelligence), special issue (June 1984), p. 26.

67. Ibid., p. 18.

Muramatsu and Krauss: Patterned Pluralism

The authors are extremely grateful to T. J. Pempel, Yutaka Kosai, Dan Okimoto, and Kozo Yamamura for their detailed criticisms and suggestions on earlier versions of this paper. We also would like to thank Martha Lane (Japan Program, University of Washington) for her very helpful editing.

1. Chalmers Johnson, *MITI and the Japanese Miracle: The Growth of Industrial Policy, 1925–1975* (Stanford: Stanford University Press, 1982), esp. pp. 19–34. Two other political scientists, T. J. Pempel, in *Policy and Politics in Japan: Creative Conservatism* (Philadelphia: Temple University Press, 1982), and Takashi Inoguchi, in *Gendai Nihon seiji keizai no kōzō* (Contemporary Japanese political economy) (Tokyo: Tōyō Keizai Shimposha, 1983), discuss the role of the state in the development of Japan's postwar political economy (and in their case, with some attention to party factors).

2. Johnson, *MITI*, pp. 315–16; see also Kiyoaki Tsuji, *Nihon kanryōsei no kenkyū* (Study of the Japanese bureaucracy) (Tokyo: University of Tokyo Press, 1969); and Takeshi Ishida, *Gendai soshiki ron* (A theory of contemporary organizations) (Tokyo: Iwanami Shoten, 1961), for less extreme arguments for bureaucratic power.

3. Kenzō Uchida, *Sengo Nihon no hoshu seiji* (Conservative politics in postwar Japan) (Tokyo: Iwanami Shoten, 1969); and Yasushi Yamaguchi, "Nakasone seiken hihan" (Critical comments on the Nakasone administration), *Sekai*, Jan. 1984.

4. Shigeru Hori, *Sengo seiji no oboegaki* (Notes on postwar politics) (Tokyo: Mainichi Shimbunsha, 1975).

5. Hideo Ōtake, "Adenauā to Yoshida Shigeru," *Chūō kōron*, Mar. 1985.

6. Tsuji, *Nihon kanryōsei*; Chalmers Johnson, "Japan: Who Governs? An Essay on Official Bureaucracy," *Journal of Japanese Studies*, Vol. 2, No. 1 (Autumn 1975), pp. 1–28; and T. J. Pempel, "The Bureaucratization of Policymaking in Postwar Japan," *American Journal of Political Science*, Vol. 18, No. 4 (Nov. 1974), pp. 647–64.

7. Masataka Kosaka, *Saishō Yoshida Shigeru* (Prime Minister Yoshida Shigeru) (Tokyo: Chūō Kōronsha, 1968).

8. Joji Watanuki, "Patterns of Politics in Present-Day Japan," in Seymour Martin Lipset and Stein Rokkan, eds., *Party Systems and Voter Alignments: Cross-National Perspectives* (New York: Free Press, 1966).

9. Gerald L. Curtis, "Big Business and Political Influence," in Ezra F. Vogel, ed., *Modern Japanese Organization and Decision-Making* (Berkeley: University of California Press, 1975), pp. 49–50.

10. George R. Packard III, *Protest in Tokyo* (Princeton: Princeton University Press, 1966), e.g., p. 308.

11. Walter Arnold, *The Politics of Planning in Postwar Japan: A Study in Political Economy* (in press), chap. 4.

12. Yasusuke Murakami, "The Age of New Middle Mass Politics: The Case of Japan," *Journal of Japanese Studies*, Vol. 8, No. 1 (Winter 1982), pp. 29–72; see also his *Shinchūkan taishū no jidai* (The age of the new middle mass) (Tokyo: Chūō Koronsha, 1984); and his paper in this volume.

13. Ibid.

14. NHK Hōsō Yoron Chōsajo, ed., *Zusetsu: Sengo yoron shi* (History of postwar public opinion in diagrams), 2d ed. (Tokyo: NHK Books, 1982), p. 123.

15. See also Michio Muramatsu, *Sengo Nihon no kanryōsei* (The bureaucracy in postwar Japan) (Tokyo: Tōyō Keizai Shimpōsha, 1981), pp. 299–305.

16. See, for example, the references in note 12.

17. See Taketsugu Tsurutani, *Political Change in Japan* (New York: David McKay Co., 1977).

18. Robert A. Scalapino and Junnosuke Masumi, *Parties and Politics in Contemporary Japan* (Berkeley: University of Californis Press, 1962), and Yoshitaka Oka, ed., *Gendai Nihon no seiji katei* (The political process in contemporary Japan) (Tokyo: Iwanami Shoten, 1958).

19. Gary D. Allinson, "Japan's Independent Voters: Dilemma or Opportunity?" *Japan Interpreter*, Vol. 11, No. 1 (Spring 1976).

20. Zen'ichirō Tanaka, *Jimintō taisei no seiji shidō* (The political leadership of the LDP system) (Tokyo: Daiippoki, 1981), pp. 347–74.

21. Ibid., pp. 410–18.

22. Murakami, "New Middle Mass Politics," pp. 45–48.

23. Ellis S. Krauss and Michio Muramatsu, "The Structure of Interest Group Influence on Policymaking in Japan," ms., 1983.

24. Ishida, *Gendai soshiki ron*.

25. T. J. Pempel, "The Dilemma of Parliamentary Opposition in Japan," *Polity*, Vol. 8, No. 1 (Fall 1975).

26. See Ellis S. Krauss, "Conflict in the Diet: Toward Conflict Management in Parliamentary Politics," in Ellis S. Krauss, Thomas C. Rohlen, and Patricia G. Steinhoff, eds., *Conflict in Japan* (Honolulu: University of Hawaii Press, 1984); see also Ellis S. Krauss, "Japanese Parties and Parliament: Changing Leadership Roles and Role Conflict," in Terry Edward MacDougall, ed., *Political Leadership in Contemporary Japan* (Ann Arbor: University of Michigan Center for Japanese Studies, 1982).

27. On the bureaucracy-dominant model, see references in note 2 above; on the "ruling triad" and "Japan, Inc.," models, see Chitoshi Yanaga, *Big Business in Japanese Politics* (New Haven: Yale University Press, 1968); and Nathaniel Thayer, *How the Conservatives Rule Japan* (Princeton: Princeton University Press, 1969); on Japan, Inc., see Eugene J. Kaplan, *Japan: The Government-Business Relationship* (Washington, D.C.: U.S. Department of Commerce, 1972), esp. pp. 14–17.

28. For many years, pluralism was the dominant political science model for democratic states. Created by theorists of the U.S. political system, the pluralist approach generally depicted a governmental system open to many social interest groups, competing centers of power that could check any group or interest, and

no permanent coalitions of influential actors—alliances varied depending on the issue. The role of government itself was somewhat limited: policy was the product of a particular combination of "pressures" of social interest groups and parties, in which the state, if taken into account at all, was merely one of the actors involved or, at most, the guarantor of the rules of the pluralist game.

For the past two decades, this model of democratic politics in the West has been the subject of increasing criticism, as analysts argued, for example, that government and interest groups were in much more institutionalized and accommodative, "corporatist" relationships or that the state itself had more power and autonomy than the pluralist model described. In Japan, the trend has been the reverse—from elitist models to more pluralist ones. Recent work on pluralist elements in Japanese policymaking includes Seizaburō Satō and Tetsuhisa Matsuzaki, "Jimintō chōchōki seiken no kaibō" (The anatomy of the super-long-term LDP government), *Chūō kōron*, Nov. 1984, pp. 66–100. Haruhiro Fukui, "Studies in Policymaking: A Review of the Literature," in T. J. Pempel, ed., *Policymaking in Contemporary Japan* (Ithaca: Cornell University Press, 1977); Curtis, "Big Business"; Inoguchi, *Gendai Nihon*; Hideo Ōtake, *Gendai Nihon no seiji kenryoku keizai kenryoku* (Political power and economic power in contemporary Japan) (Tokyo: San'ichi Shobō, 1980); Bradley M. Richardson and Scott C. Flanagan, *Politics in Japan* (Boston: Little, Brown and Co., 1984), pp. 368–77; John C. Campbell, "Policy Conflict and Its Resolution Within the Governmental System," in Krauss et al., *Conflict in Japan*, pp. 294–334; Richard J. Samuels, *The Politics of Regional Policy in Japan—Localities, Incorporated?* (Princeton: Princeton University Press, 1983).

29. Krauss and Muramatsu, "Interest Group Influence." For a related argument that elements of political conflict and negotiated decisions between private interests and government were part of Japan's development even before the recent postwar period, see Richard J. Samuels, *The Business of the Japanese State: Energy Markets in Comparative and Historical Perspective* (Ithaca: Cornell University Press, forthcoming).

30. On *shingikai*, see Pempel, "Bureaucratization of Policymaking," pp. 656–63.

31. Takashi Inoguchi, "Politicians, Bureaucrats, and Interest Groups in the Legislative Process," paper presented at the Workshop on One-Party Dominance, Ithaca, N.Y., Apr. 7–9, 1984, pp. 27–29.

32. Hideo Ōtake, *Nihon no bōei to kokunai seiji* (Domestic politics and Japanese defense) (Tokyo: Asahi Shimbunsha, 1982); and Nihon Keizai Shimbunsha, ed., *Jiyū minshutō seimu chōsakai* (The Policy Affairs Research Council of the LDP) (Tokyo, 1983); also see Sato and Matsuzaki, "Jimintō."

33. Nihon Keizai Shimbunsha, *Jiyū minshutō*.

34. Ibid.

35. Michio Muramatsu and Ellis S. Krauss, "Bureaucrats and Politicians in Policymaking: The Case of Japan," *American Political Science Review*, Vol. 78, No. 1 (Mar. 1984).

36. Ōtake, *Gendai Nihon*.

37. For a recent English-language study of the politics of the liberalization of telecommunications, see Peter E. Fuchs, "Regulatory Reform and Japan's Telecommunications Revolution," in *U.S.-Japan Relations: New Attitudes for a New Era*, 1983–84 Annual Review of the Program on U.S.-Japan Relations (Cambridge, Mass.: Harvard University, Center for International Affairs, 1984), pp. 123–41.

38. Michio Muramatsu, "Administrative Reform in a Pluralist Political System," *Japan Echo*, Vol. 10, No. 3 (Autumn 1983), originally published in Japanese in *Chūō kōron*, June 1983; on administrative reform, also see Shumpei Kumon,

"Japan Faces Its Future: The Political Economics of Administrative Reform," *Journal of Japanese Studies*, Vol. 10, No. 1 (Winter 1984).

39. There have been criticisms of specific welfare programs, and the government did revise laws providing for services that it considered to have become "excessive," such as free medical expenses for the elderly. There has not been, however, an attack on the welfare state as such, and even privatization has been embarked on under the slogan "the welfare society."

40. Allesandro Pizzorno, "Interests and Parties in Pluralism," in Suzanne Berger, ed., *Organizing Interests in Western Europe: Pluralism, Corporatism, and the Transformation of Politics* (Cambridge, Eng.: Cambridge University Press, 1981), pp. 260–61.

41. Inoguchi, "Politicians," also has short case studies on the revision of the Commercial Code, on the Law on Health for the Aged, on the revision of the Public Officials Election Law, and on the Technopolis Law, whose description fits many of our patterns.

42. *Asahi Shimbun*, Sept. 21, 1984.

43. Pizzorno, "Interests and Parties," p. 273.

44. Eiichi Katō, "Toshi no fukushū" (The revenge of the cities), *Chūō kōron*, June 1983. On May 22, 1986, eight urban districts gained one seat each, and seven rural districts each lost a seat. This effort, however, may not satisfy the courts, which have become increasingly concerned with the malapportionment issue during the past decade.

45. Yonosuke Nagai, "Nihon no 'senryakuron' o sotenken suru" (Examining models of military strategies in Japan), *Bungei shunjū*, Apr. 1984.

46. Murakami, "New Middle Mass Politics," pp. 59–71.

47. Muramatsu, *Nihon no kanryōsei*, p. 30.

48. Pempel, *Policy and Politics*, p. 56.

Kosai: Economic Management

1. The subtitle of this section is borrowed from Samuel P. Huntington, *American Politics: The Promise of Disharmony* (Cambridge, Mass.: Harvard University Press, Belknap Press, 1981), p. 5.

2. See Michio Muramatsu and Ellis S. Krauss, "Bureaucrats and Politicians in Policymaking: The Case of Japan," *American Political Science Review*, Vol. 78, No. 1 (Mar. 1984), pp. 128–29, for a survey of, and literature on, the first two models.

3. Yukio Noguchi and Eisuke Sakakibara, "Dissecting the Finance Ministry–Bank of Japan Dynasty," *Japan Echo*, Vol. 4, No. 4 (Winter 1977), pp. 98–123.

4. See Yasusuke Murakami, "Toward a Socioinstitutional Explanation of Japan's Economic Performance," in Kozo Yamamura, ed., *Policy and Trade Issues of the Japanese Economy: American and Japanese Perspectives* (Seattle: University of Washington Press, 1982), esp. pp. 4–5, 16–18, as well as Murakami's paper in this volume; Takashi Inoguchi, *Gendai Nihon seiji keizai no kōzu: Seifu to shijō* (Framework of the contemporary Japanese political economy: Government and market) (Tokyo: Tōyō Keizai Shimpōsha, 1983), pp. 3–29; and Seizaburō Satō and Tetsuhisa Matsuzaki, "Jimintō chōchōki seiken no kaibō" (The anatomy of the supra-long-term LDP government), *Chūō kōron*, Nov. 1984, pp. 66–100.

5. Joseph P. Kalt and Mark A. Zupa, "Capture and Ideology in the Economy Theory of Politics," *American Economic Review*, Vol. 74, No. 3 (June 1984), pp. 279–300.

6. Ibid.

7. For example, see Timothy J. Coulan, "The Politics of Federal Block Grants," *Political Science Quarterly*, Vol. 99, No. 2 (Summer 1984), pp. 247–80.

8. See also Inoguchi, *Gendai Nihon seiji keizai*, pp. 199–245.

9. Max Weber, "Parliament and Government in a Reconstructed Germany," in Guenther Roth and Claus Wittich, eds., *Economy and Society* (Berkeley: University of California Press, 1978), pp. 1451–52.

10. For example, Johannes Hirschmeier commented that "pragmatism rather than principle holds sway." See Hyoe Murakami and Johannes Hirschmeier, eds., *Politics and Economics in Contemporary Japan* (Tokyo: Japan Culture Institute, 1974); in paperback (Tokyo: Kodansha, 1983), p. ix.

11. T. J. Pempel, *Policy and Politics in Japan: Creative Conservatism* (Philadelphia: Temple University Press, 1982).

12. For a summary of the models of quantitative economic policy, see Stephan Turnovsky, *Macroeconomic Analysis and Stabilization Policy* (Cambridge, Eng.: Cambridge University Press, 1977), part 3.

13. This corresponds to Model I outlined in Graham T. Allison, *Essence of Decision: Explaining the Cuban Missile Crisis* (Boston: Little Brown & Co. 1971).

14. Peter J. Katzenstein, "Introduction: Domestic and International Forces and Strategies of Foreign Economic Policy," in idem, ed., *Between Power and Plenty* (Madison: University of Wisconsin Press, 1978), p. 20.

15. The MOF apparently supported stringency in order to curb the large upward revision of the price of rice paid to producers.

16. This conclusion does not contradict the adjusted expectation hypothesis proposed by Murakami and Inoguchi.

17. The difference between this new system and the gold standard system was that international capital transactions were restricted during the high-growth period.

18. Bank of Japan, *Kin'yū hakusho* (White paper on monetary economy), for 1974, published June 29, 1974.

19. Rōdō Jijō Kenkyūkai (Study Group on Labor Economy), *Uneri to sazanami: Hasegawa Rōsei no kiroku* (Large and small waves: A record of Hasegawa's activities as minister of labor) (Tokyo: Kajima Shuppankai, 1976).

20. Kōji Nakagawa (vice-president of the BOJ) tells the inside story of how BOJ executives dealt with political leaders and high government officials in *Takenteki kin'yū seisaku ron: Nichigin no mado kara* (Personal account of monetary policy: Looking through the window of the Bank of Japan) (Tokyo: Nihon Keizai Shimbunsha, 1981).

21. Ryūtarō Komiya, "Nihon no keizai keikaku" (Economic planning in Japan) in his *Gendai Nihon keizai kenkyū* (Studies on the contemporary Japanese economy) (Tokyo: University of Tokyo Press, 1975), pp. 289–330. See also Miyohei Shinohara, Toru Yanagihara, and Kwang Suk Kim, *The Japanese and Korean Experiences in Managing Development*, World Bank Staff Working Papers No. 574 (Washington, D.C.: World Bank, 1983).

22. Katzenstein, "Introduction."

23. See Murakami's "parapolitical nexus hypothesis" in his paper in this volume. See also his *Shinchūkan taishū no jidai* (Age of the new middle mass) (Tokyo: Chūō Kōronsha, 1984).

24. Yukio Noguchi, "The Government-Business Relationship in Japan: The Changing Role of Fiscal Resources," in Yamamura, *Policy and Trade Issues*, pp. 123–42.

25. See "Yosan o kiru: (1) Kōkyō jigyō" (Anatomy of the budget: [1] Public

works), *Common Sense*, Nov. 1984, pp. 76–79, which describes individual politicians' influence on the allocation of the public works budget.

26. Because of high land prices, landowners who plan residential construction must be regarded as relatively wealthy, whatever their reported income. Recently, some measures have been taken to prevent high-income classes from borrowing from the Housing Loan Corporation, and the share of high-income borrowers has declined.

27. According to the amendment, the insured have to pay 10 per cent of medical costs directly to the physician. It is believed that this will decrease the number of patients and doctors' revenues. The Medical Association tried to stir up opposition within the LDP, but failed.

28. Masahiko Aoki, "Keizai keikaku no kinō saikō" (The role of economic planning reconsidered), in Yasusuke Murakami and Kōichi Hamada, eds., *Keizai gaku no atarashii nagare* (New currents in economic thinking) (Tokyo: Tōyō Keizai Shimposha, 1981), pp. 163–91.

29. Nihon Keizai Shimbunsha, ed., *Jiyū minshutō seimu chōsakai* (The Policy Affairs Research Council of the LDP) (Tokyo: Nihon Keizai Shimbunsha, 1983), pp. 40–47.

30. For a discussion of the inner structure of the LDP, see Satō and Matsuzaki, "Jimintō." See also Nathaniel B. Thayer, *How the Conservatives Rule Japan* (Princeton: Princeton University Press, 1969); and Nihon Keizai Shimbunsha, *Jiyū Minshutō*.

31. This was the case in the 1965 Soviet-Japanese Peace Agreement, according to Donald C. Hellmann, "Case Study: Foreign Policy a la LDP," in Murakami and Hirschmeier, eds., *Politics and Economics in Contemporary Japan*; and D. C. Hellmann, *Japanese Domestic Politics and Foreign Policy: The Peace Agreement with the Soviet Union* (Berkeley: University of California Press, 1969).

32. For the politics of rice price determination, see Hemmi Kenzo, "Agriculture and Politics in Japan," in E. N. Castle and K. Hemmi, eds., *U.S.-Japanese Agricultural Trade Relations* (Washington D.C.: Resources for the Future, 1982), pp. 219–68, particularly pp. 235–42.

33. Michisada Hirose, *Hojokin to seikentō* (Subsidies and the party in power) (Tokyo: Asahi Shimbunsha, 1981).

34. Hiromitsu Ishi et al., "Jueki to futan no chiiki kōzō bunseki" (Analysis of the regional structure of benefits and burdens), *Kikan gendai keizai*, No. 45 (Winter 1981), pp. 136–49; and Seiritsu Ogura, "Dōro jigyōhi no chiikikan haibun no koritsusei" (Efficiency of regional allocation of road construction funds), *Kikan gendai keizai*, No. 58 (Summer 1984), pp. 116–26.

35. Fumio Egaitsu, "Japanese Agricultural Policy: Present Problems and Their Historical Background," in Castle and Hemmi, eds., *U.S.-Japanese Agricultural Trade Relations*, pp. 148–81, particularly pp. 157–61.

36. Naoki Kobayashi, "The Small and Medium-Sized Enterprises Organization Law," and idem, "Interest Groups in the Legislative Process," in Hiroshi Itoh, ed., *Japanese Politics: An Inside View* (Ithaca, N.Y.: Cornell University Press, 1973), pp. 49–67 and 68–87.

37. Castle and Hemmi, *U.S.-Japanese Agricultural Trade Relations*; and Atsushi Kusano, *Nichibei orenji kōshō* (Japan-U.S. orange negotiations) (Tokyo: Nihon Keizai Shimbunsha, 1983).

38. MITI, for example, adhered to a resolution of the LDP's Subcommittee on Retail Commerce Problems concerning the regulation of the establishment of new supermarkets in 1982; Nihon Keizai Shimbunsha, *Jiyū Minshutō*, p. 30.

Index of Names

Abe, Shintaro, 544
Ackley, Gardner, 613, 619
Adams, F. Gerard, 636
Aichi, Kiichi, 569
Akuto, Hiroshi, 80f, 598
Allinson, Gary D., 646
Allison, Graham T., 649
Amano, Masako, 628
Amaya, Naohiro, 640
Ando, Albert, 604, 609
Anthony, Douglas, 627
Aoki, Masahiko, 18f, 24, 42, 346, 360, 376, 416, 578, 596, 603, 611–25 *passim*, 633, 635, 650
Araki, Eikichi, 241
Ariyoshi, Sawako, 98, 126
Arnold, Walter, 646
Asanuma, Banri, 501, 621, 625, 644
Ashida, Hitoshi, 518f

Bailey, Martin N., 631
Barnett, Donald F., 637, 641
Barro, Robert J., 213, 616
Beck, Morris, 613
Benston, George J., 618
Berger, Suzanne, 62–66 *passim*, 597
Bestor, Theodore C., 630
Blackburn, Robert M., 625
Blinder, Alan S., 599
Bluestone, Barry, 637
Blumenthal, Tuvia, 606
Boltho, Andrea, 606
Borrus, Michael, 641
Bowman, Mary Jean, 628

Break, George F., 200, 613, 615
Bronfenbrenner, Martin, 12–16 *passim*, 341, 355, 382, 600, 602
Bruch, Mathias, 626
Brzezinski, Zbigniew, 75, 598
Buchanan, James M., 194f, 614f
Bulow, Jeremy I., 629
Burton, John, 615

Campbell, John C., 615, 647
Castle, Emery N., 627, 650
Caves, Richard E., 279–80, 618, 622, 641f
Cohen, Stephen S., 635
Cole, Robert, 284, 621, 624
Coulan, Timothy J., 649
Culliton, J. W., 644
Curtis, Gerald L., 597, 646, 647

Dahl, Robert, 54, 597
David, Paul A., 214, 616f
de Gaulle, Charles, 62, 66, 445
De Vos, George, 626–30 *passim*
Denison, E. F., 617, 643
Dickens, Charles, 127
Dodge, Joseph, 570
Doi, Teruo, 632
Doko, Toshio, 547, 574f
Dore, Ronald, 266, 621, 627, 635
Duverger, Maurice, 63, 597

Eads, George, 23ff, 475, 514, 579, 639
Egaitsu, Fumio, 650
Evans, Michael, 607

New Liberal Club (NLC), 536; voter support for, 57 f, 77, 82
New middle mass: mass affluence and, 60, 526; and party policies, 61, 63, 90, 528–29, 552; and conservatism, 89–90; and "white-collarized" workers, 329; and Yoshida doctrine, 526–27; interest orientation of, 528–29, 552, 559. *See also* Values
NHK (Japan Broadcasting Company), survey by, 77–80, 116
Nihonjinron, 33
Nippon Broadcasting Association (NBA), 507–8
Nippon Light Metal, 496, 499
Nippon Telephone and Telegraph Corporation (NTT), 211, 456, 507–11 *passim*, 545, 579, 584
Nissan, 53
Nonferrous metals industry, 485, 488

One-and-a-half party system, 56, 529

Petrochemicals industry, 40–51 *passim*, 74, 239, 484, 488, 492
Pluralism: and multiparty system, 54–62 *passim*, 61–62, 529, 534; and "compartmentalized competition," 56, 558; "patterned," 71, 537–50, 555–65, 576; "bureaucracy-led mass-inclusionary," 71, 558; "canalized," 71, 558, 574
Policy Affairs Research Council (PARC), 450, 541–50 *passim*, 579 f
Pollution: protests against, 122; legislation against, 122, 136, 529, 544–45
Productivity: marginal product of capital, 167–72 *passim*; and shift of industrial structure, 176, 183; growth of, 386, 486–90; and import of technology, 488–90. *See also* Exports; Small-scale family enterprise
Profit: minimum profit, 42; decline of, 73 f, 169–71, 175; in banking and industry, 238. *See also* Corporate business behavior; *Keiretsu*; Saving
Public debt, 248, 574, 589; structural deficit, 141, 178–79, 183–84, 193–94; balanced-budget principle and, 146, 178, 192, 570, 571–72; and social security, 179, 184, 194, 536; and

bond issues, 179–80, 192–96, 206, 210 f, 247–49, 571, 573; and debt-servicing cost, 179–80, 184, 194–95, 202; ratio to GDP, 179–80, 194, 213–14, 230–31; and fiscal crisis, 215–18 *passim*; and interest group politics, 535–36, 584; and larger international role, 536. *See also* Fiscal reform; Saving-investment balance
Pulp and paper industry, 484 f, 494

R&D, *see* Research and development
Regulation of industries: deregulation, 185, 509–11, 545–46, 578; public enterprises, 506–9
Research and development: and patents, 385–91, 415; expenditure for, 389–91, 489–91; rate of return on, 391–92, 413; in applied technology, 393, 396; in basic research, 393–95; government support for, 396, 403–6, 410, 490, 514–15; in high tech, 396–97, 490; by big business, 398, 415; by small business, 398–404 *passim*, 416; and venture firms, 400–402; personnel for, 402 f; by universities, 412, 416–17; and training in sciences, 412–16; joint, 486; effect on productivity, 490. *See also* Subsidiaries
Retailing, 336–40 *passim*, 350–51; profit in, return to capital in, 351. *See also* Small-scale family enterprise
Ruling triad, 68, 537, 550, 555–58 *passim*, 565, 576, 578
Russia: military threat, 75, 84; national welfare, 128; R&D, 395, 397, 410–11, 413

Saving: ratio to GNP (GDP), 37, 99, 138–41; and economic growth, 40–41, 99–100, 137–42 *passim*, 178; reasons for high savings, 48, 99, 140, 150–51, 153–65; by business, 99, 152–53, 170–78 *passim*, 213–14; by income groups, 101–2; by household, 137, 140, 145, 148–65, 178, 183, 213–15; effects of taxes on, 141, 145, 152–53; by government, 141, 146, 213. *See also* Aging popu-

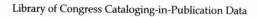

Library of Congress Cataloging-in-Publication Data

The Political economy of Japan.

   Bibliography: v. 1, p.
   Includes index.
   Contents: v. 1. The Domestic transformation / edited
by Kozo Yamamura and Yasukichi Yasuba.
   1. Japan—Economic conditions—1945–   . 2. Japan—
Economic policy—1945–   . I. Yamamura, Kozo.
HC462.9.P57   1987   338.952   86-30037
ISBN 0-8047-1380-4 (alk. paper)
ISBN 0-8047-1381-2 (pbk. : alk. paper)